SQUIRES KITCHEN
INTERNATIONAL SCHOOL

THE ART OF
SUGARCRAFT

SQUIRES KITCHEN

INTERNATIONAL SCHOOL

THE ART OF

SUGARCRAFT

First published in March 2014 by B. Dutton Publishing Limited, The Grange, Hones Business Park, Farnham, Surrey, GU9 8BB.

Reprinted in June 2014 and March 2016.

Copyright: Squires Kitchen International School 2014

ISBN-13: 978-1-905113-49-1

All rights reserved.

Publisher: Beverley Dutton

Group Editor: Jennifer Kelly

Art Director/Designer: Sarah Ryan

Book publishing

Copy Editor: Frankie New

Graphic Designer and Photography Stylist: Louise Pepé

Graphic Designer: Abbie Johnston

Photography: Rob Goves

SKMP Photography: Alister Thorpe

Contributing Photographers: Elio Lischetti, Susanna Righetto, Anna Rosell, Fumihiko Watanabe

Magazine publishing

Editor: Jenny Royle

Copy Editor: Adele Duthie

Senior Graphic Designer: Zena Deakin

PR and Advertising Manager: Natalie Bull

Wallpaper supplied by wallpaperdirect.co.uk

Printed and bound in Slovenia by arrangement with Associated Agencies, Oxford

IMPORTANT INFORMATION

The Author and Publisher have made every effort to ensure that the contents of this book will not cause harm or injury or pose any danger. Please note that some inedible items, such as floral wires, ribbon and cocktail sticks, have been used in the projects in this book. All such inedible items must be removed before the cakes are eaten. Similarly, any non-food-grade equipment and substances must not come into contact with any food that is to be eaten. Neither the Author nor the Publisher can be held responsible for errors or omissions and cannot accept liability for injury, damage or loss to persons or property, however it may arise, as a result of acting upon guidelines and information printed in this book.

WINNER OF THE BEST UK FOOD BOOK FOR PROFESSIONALS IN THE 2014 GOURMAND WORLD COOKBOOK AWARDS

'Dear reader,

'Laid out before you here are some of the exciting secrets of the wonderful world of sugarcraft in the field of celebration cakes of every kind.'

Alex Bransgrove

Acknowledgements

Thanks to Sylvia Guppy for her late father, Alex Bransgrove's, collection of tools; Paddy Dunne, Joan Mooney, Tombi Peck, Mary Ford, Pat Lock and Ken Mulley for their generous gifts of books and donated items to the museum; Peter Brears, Ivan Day at historicfood.com and Robin Weir for their inspiration and exceptional knowledge in the history of sugar and for Peter's kind permission to reproduce his illustrations; and the late Peggy Green who was Squires Kitchen's first senior tutor and whose colour wheel of SFP roses made 20 years ago is still on display at Squires Kitchen.

Thanks also to the amazing B. Dutton Publishing team, especially Sarah, Jenny, Louise, Frankie and Abbie, who have worked so hard to put this book together; to Rob Goves for his beautiful photography; and to the brilliant SK School team, Vanessa, Elina, Natalie and Helen.

Introduction

The idea for this book has been in development for over 25 years, ever since the Squires Kitchen school was founded in 1987 to share our extensive knowledge of cake decorating and sugarcraft. With the help of talented teachers and passionate students, the school has become an internationally recognised seat of learning and a centre of excellence which brings people from around the world to learn with us. I am delighted to be able to bring the work of the school to an even wider audience with this book. Over the following pages you will be able to learn from 20 of the world's top sugarcraft tutors, who all share their amazing skills at Squires Kitchen International School in Farnham, Surrey.

Our philosophy for the school centres around giving you the 'Confidence to Create' in an inspiring and friendly environment and is at the heart of everything we do. Many people have artistic talents which can be transferred to sugarcraft, but to be able to teach these skills in a way that gives students the confidence to be creative themselves is an art in its own right. When new tutors join our team it is, of course, important to us that they are highly motivated and the very best artists in their field. However, the key skill they must possess is to be able to help you, the student, to reach your goals.

Every Squires Kitchen tutor and ambassador has one thing in common that unites them: their love of sugarcraft and the years of practice and dedication that it has taken to become an expert in their particular subject. They are also lovely people who enjoy sharing their knowledge for the benefit of future generations.

I personally wish to thank all of our tutors, past and present, for their support and dedication to Squires Kitchen, with special thanks to our full-time senior tutors, Paddi Clark and Mark Tilling. It is amazing to think that we have over 320 years of combined teaching experience to draw on, all under one roof. At Squires Kitchen International School we also benefit from all the expertise of the wider Squires Group company, from product development and manufacturing to publishing. Members of staff, particularly the design team, can often be found on our courses so that we can continue to develop our skills and be the best at what we do.

The UK has a particularly rich heritage in the use of sugar, and its history is a fascinating one. When you visit Squires Kitchen you can see some of this history on display in our wide-ranging museum collection. Over the years I have collected thousands of items relating to baking, confectionery and the art of sugarcraft. Not all are on display but many of my personal favourites are there, representing over 300 years of sugar art in the UK. You can find images of these special items throughout this book alongside some outstanding work by tutors who have made valuable contributions to securing the future of this art form.

I am extremely proud to continue this wonderful heritage in Squires Kitchen's world-famous school – thank you for being part of it.

Beverley

Beverley Dutton, Founder and
Managing Director of Squires Kitchen

Mark Tilling

Paddi Clark

Eddie Spence MBE

Naomi Yamamoto

Carlos Lischetti

Ann Skipp

Susan Griffiths

Ceri DD Griffiths

Jan Clement-May

Makiko Searle

Kathy Moore

Alan Dunn

Liz Aplin

Linda Garnham

Tessa Whitehouse

Helen Mansey

Claire Fitzsimons

Bea Harling

Geraldine Dahlke

Susanna Righetto

Tutor Biographies

Contents

Learn how to make cakes, fillings and pastries
from scratch. Once you know the basics of
beautiful baking you'll be able to create
recipes to suit your project, introducing new
flavours, fillings and toppings.

BAKING AND PÂTISSERIE

Essential Edibles and Equipment for Baking and Pâtisserie

1   Cake filling/glaze, see recipes on pages 24–30

2   Cake leveller

3   Cake tins and pans, see project list for shapes and sizes

4   Cupcake cases

5   Digital food thermometer

6   Fine sieve

7   Greaseproof paper

8   Large palette knife

9   Measuring spoons

10   Mixing bowls

11   Serrated knife

12   Silicone pastry brush

13   Spatula

14   Stand mixer

15   Weighing scales

16   Wire cooling rack

17   Wooden spoon

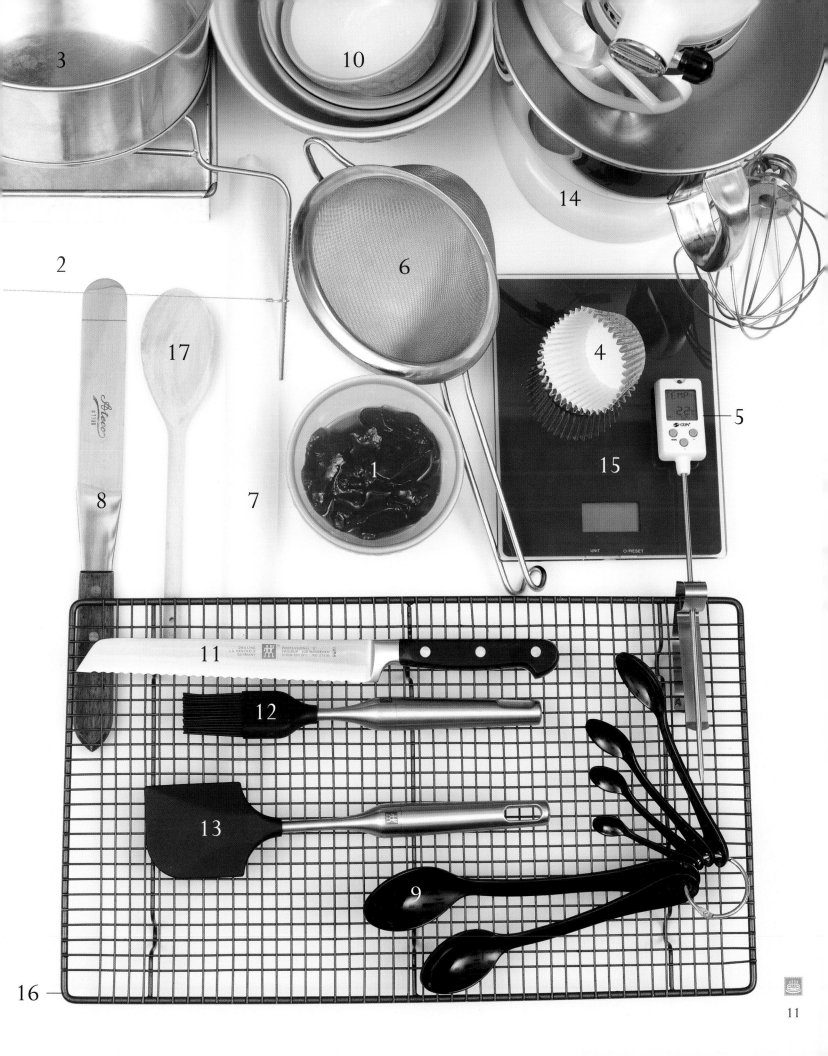

3

10

14

2

6

17

4

5

8

7

1

15

11

12

13

9

16

Cake Recipes

ANN SKIPP

Whether you are baking a simple cake for tea or a multi-tiered wedding cake which will be decorated and served to hundreds of guests, it is important to use tried-and-tested recipes that are reliable and delicious. Recipes for fillings and frostings can be found on pages 24 to 31.

Follow these top tips to achieve the best results when baking:

- Use the best-quality ingredients you can, ensuring that your eggs are very fresh and preferably free range.

- Make sure that all the ingredients are at room temperature and are weighed accurately before you start to mix the cake batter.

- When lining a cake tin, take your time to ensure the greaseproof paper lining is like a close 'skin' inside the tin. A badly-lined tin will lead to a misshapen cake.

- When the recipe states a teaspoon or tablespoon measure, this always means a level spoonful.

- If you need a sponge cake to have greater depth (e.g. for a wedding cake), bake another layer following the same recipe.

- When storing cupcakes, do not place them in an airtight plastic container as this can create condensation which may cause the cases to come away from the cakes. It is best to store them in a tin or cake box instead.

- To work out how to change the recipe for larger or smaller cakes (or different shapes), fill the tin size stated with water to the level the cake mix would normally reach, i.e. approximately ⅔ full. Pour the water into the tin you intend to use and write down how many times the tin has to be filled. This is the number by which you will need to multiply all of the ingredients in the cake mix to achieve the quantity required. Remember to increase the baking time for larger cakes and decrease it for smaller cakes - always test with a skewer to check if it is ready. If you find that you have too much mixture, use it to bake an extra small cake or batch of cupcakes.

- It is best not to open the oven door until the cake is nearing the end of the baking time. When the door is opened, cold air rushes in which causes the cake to sink.

- Ovens do vary so check the manufacturer's instructions.

- Ensure the oven has reached the correct temperature before baking the cake.

- If using a food mixer to make the cake, ensure to use the beater attachment instead of the whisk.

- When using vanilla flavourings, avoid using vanilla essence and use vanilla extract or paste instead.

Peek Frean biscuit and cake tin, circa 1903

Madeira cake

INGREDIENTS

145g (5oz) soft margarine or butter

145g (5oz) golden caster sugar

Zest of 1 unwaxed lemon

3 medium eggs, beaten

175g (6oz) plain flour

Pinch of salt

2tsp cornflour

1½tsp baking powder

EQUIPMENT

20.5cm (8") round cake tin

Makes a 20.5cm (8") round cake

For essential baking edibles and equipment, see pages 10–11

ROUND/SQUARE	20.5cm (8")	25.5cm (10")	30.5cm (12")
Soft margarine or butter	145g (5oz)	285g (10oz)	430g (15oz)
Golden caster sugar	145g (5oz)	285g (10oz)	430g (15oz)
Unwaxed lemon zest	1 lemon	2 lemons	3 lemons
Medium eggs, beaten	3	6	9
Plain flour	175g (6oz)	340g (12oz)	500g (1lb 1¾oz)
Salt	Pinch	Pinch	Pinch
Cornflour	2tsp	3tsp	2tbsp
Baking powder	1½tsp	3tsp	2½tbsp
Baking time	1¼–1½ hours	1½–1¾ hours	2½–3 hours

1 Grease and line a 20.5cm (8") round tin (see page 488). Preheat the oven to 160°C/140°C fan/320°F/gas mark 3.

2 Beat together the margarine, sugar and lemon zest until light and fluffy.

3 Add the eggs to the mixture a little at a time, beating well between each addition.

4 Fold in the flour, salt, cornflour and baking powder using a metal spoon.

5 Pour the mixture into the tin and level with the back of a spoon.

6 Bake for 1¼–1½ hours until the cake is firm to the touch and shrinks from the side of the tin.

7 Allow to cool in the tin and then place on a cooling rack.

Storage

This cake can be wrapped in greaseproof paper and stored in a tin for up to a week.

tutor tip

Please remember that these recipes are guidelines and you can always adjust them to suit your own preferences.

Victoria sponge cake

INGREDIENTS

250g (8¾oz) soft margarine or butter

250g (8¾oz) golden caster sugar

4 medium eggs, beaten

1tsp vanilla extract

250g (8¾oz) self-raising flour, sifted

EQUIPMENT

2 x 20.5cm (8") round sandwich tins

Makes two 20.5cm (8") round sponges

For essential baking edibles and equipment, see pages 10–11

ROUND/SQUARE	20.5cm (8")	25.5cm (10")
Soft margarine or butter	250g (8¾oz)	340g (12oz)
Golden caster sugar	250g (8¾oz)	340g (12oz)
Medium eggs, beaten	4	6
Vanilla extract	1tsp	2tsp
Self-raising flour	250g (8¾oz)	340g (12oz)
Baking time	20–25 minutes	40 minutes

I would not recommend this recipe for larger cakes as the long baking time may make it too dry.

1 Grease and lightly flour two 20.5cm (8") round sandwich tins.

2 Preheat the oven to 180°C/160°C fan/350°C/gas mark 4.

3 Cream the margarine and sugar together until light and fluffy.

4 Gradually add the eggs and vanilla to the mixture, beating well between each addition.

5 Fold in the sifted flour with a metal spoon.

6 Place half of the mixture into each of the tins. Bake for 20–25 minutes or until the cakes are golden in colour and spring back to the touch.

7 Turn the cakes out onto a cooling rack.

Storage

These cakes can be wrapped individually in greaseproof paper and stored in a tin for up to five days.

Variations

Instead of vanilla, other flavourings such as lemon, orange or chocolate can be used. If making a chocolate sponge, replace a tablespoon of flour with the same amount of cocoa powder.

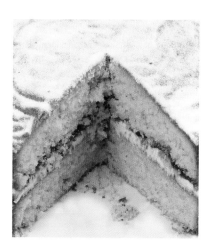

tutor tip

If you are using this recipe to make cupcakes, only make as much mixture as you can bake in the oven at one time. It is not advisable to leave raw mixture waiting to be baked, as the raising agent will start to work before the cakes go into the oven and this will affect the texture of the cakes.

Cake Recipes

15

Rich fruit cake

For best results, prepare the cake mixture the day before baking, especially if it is being scaled up to make a larger cake. This cake needs to be made at least three weeks and up to three months before it is going to be served.

INGREDIENTS

175g (6oz) currants

175g (6oz) sultanas

175g (6oz) raisins

115g (4oz) mixed peel

115g (4oz) glacé cherries, chopped

115g (4oz) ready-to-eat dried apricots, finely chopped

115g (4oz) ready-to-eat dried exotic fruit mix, finely chopped (optional)

Juice of 1 orange

2tbsp brandy

225g (8oz) butter

225g (8oz) dark muscovado sugar

4 large eggs, beaten

225g (8oz) plain flour

1tbsp ground mixed spice

1tbsp black treacle

115g (4oz) flaked almonds

60g (2oz) walnuts, finely chopped (optional)

1 apple, peeled, cored and grated

A little milk (optional)

EQUIPMENT

20.5cm (8") round cake tin

Makes a 20.5cm (8") round cake. See opposite for different quantities of this recipe to make larger round and square cakes.

For essential baking edibles and equipment, see pages 10–11

Victorian queen cake tins, circa 1890s

1 Clean and rinse the currants, sultanas and raisins, removing any small stalks that might have been left on the fruit. Place on a piece of kitchen paper to dry.

2 Place the currants, sultanas and raisins in a large mixing bowl along with the mixed peel, cherries, apricots and exotic fruits. Mix together and add the orange juice and brandy. Mix again, cover and leave for at least an hour.

3 Grease and line a 20.5cm (8") round cake tin (see page 488).

4 Cream the butter and sugar in a bowl until light and fluffy. Add the eggs gradually, beating well between each addition.

5 Fold in the flour, mixed spice and treacle.

6 Add the dried fruit mixture, almonds, walnuts and grated apple. Mix together well and add a little milk if necessary to give the mixture a soft, dropping consistency.

7 Place the mixture into the prepared tin and gently smooth it down with the back of a spoon. Cover and leave in a cool place until the following day.

8 Wrap some brown paper around the outside of the tin and tie with a piece of string.

9 Preheat the oven to 150°C/130°C fan/300°F/gas mark 2.

10 Place the cake in the oven for 30 minutes, then lower the temperature to 140°C/120°C fan/275°F/gas mark 1 and bake for three hours. To check if the cake is cooked through, insert a cake tester, knife or skewer into the cake:

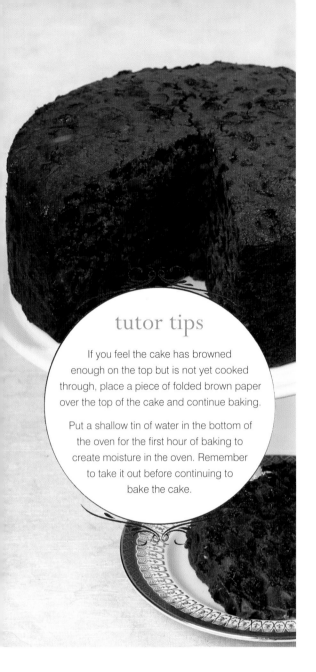

tutor tips

If you feel the cake has browned enough on the top but is not yet cooked through, place a piece of folded brown paper over the top of the cake and continue baking.

Put a shallow tin of water in the bottom of the oven for the first hour of baking to create moisture in the oven. Remember to take it out before continuing to bake the cake.

if it comes out clean the cake is ready. If there are still signs of mixture, return the cake to the oven until baked through.

11 Remove from the oven when baked and leave in the tin to cool.

Storage

Once cool, remove the cake from the tin and double wrap it in greaseproof paper, then wrap in foil. Store in a tin or box and periodically 'feed' with brandy if desired, making sure to wrap it up carefully afterwards.

ROUND/SQUARE	20.5cm (8")	25.5cm (10")	30.5cm (12")
Currants	175g (6oz)	260g (9oz)	340g (12oz)
Sultanas	175g (6oz)	260g (9oz)	340g (12oz)
Raisins	175g (6oz)	260g (9oz)	340g (12oz)
Mixed peel	115g (4oz)	175g (6oz)	225g (8oz)
Glacé cherries, chopped	115g (4oz)	175g (6oz)	225g (8oz)
Ready-to-eat dried apricots, finely chopped	115g (4oz)	175g (6oz)	225g (8oz)
Ready-to-eat dried exotic fruit mix, finely chopped (optional)	115g (4oz)	175g (6oz)	225g (8oz)
Fresh orange juice	1 orange	1½ oranges	2 oranges
Brandy	2tbsp	2½tbsp	3tbsp
Butter	225g (8oz)	340g (12oz)	450g (1lb)
Dark muscovado sugar	225g (8oz)	340g (12oz)	450g (1lb)
Large eggs, beaten	4	6	8
Plain flour	225g (8oz)	340g (12oz)	450g (1lb)
Ground mixed spice	1tbsp	1½tbsp	2tbsp
Black treacle	1tbsp	1½tbsp	2tbsp
Flaked almonds	115g (4oz)	175g (6oz)	225g (8oz)
Walnuts, finely chopped (optional)	60g (2oz)	90g (3oz)	115g (4oz)
Apple, peeled, cored and grated	1	1½	2
Milk (optional)	Enough to make a soft dropping consistency	Enough to make a soft dropping consistency	Enough to make a soft dropping consistency
Baking time	3 hours	5 hours	6–7 hours

Chocolate cake

INGREDIENTS

185g (6½oz) butter

185g (6½oz) dark brown sugar

4 large eggs

115g (4oz) dark chocolate, melted

115ml (4fl oz) pre-boiled, warm water

½tsp salt

200g (7oz) self-raising flour

EQUIPMENT

2 x 20.5cm (8") round sandwich tins

Makes two 20.5cm (8") round sponges. See table for different quantities of this recipe to make larger round and square cakes.

ROUND/SQUARE	20.5cm (8")	25.5cm (10")
Butter	185g (6½oz)	370g (13oz)
Dark brown sugar	185g (6½oz)	370g (13oz)
Large eggs	4	8
Dark chocolate, melted	115g (4oz)	225g (8oz)
Pre-boiled, warm water	115ml (4fl oz)	225ml (8fl oz)
Salt	½tsp	1tsp
Self-raising flour	200g (7oz)	400g (14oz)
Baking time	25–30 minutes or until firm	30–35 minutes or until firm

I would not recommend this recipe for larger cakes as the long baking time may make it too dry.

For essential baking edibles and equipment, see pages 10–11

1 Grease and lightly flour two 20.5cm (8") round sandwich tins, using a little of the weighed flour.

2 Preheat the oven to 180°C/160°C fan/350°F/gas mark 4.

3 Cream the butter and sugar together in a bowl until light and fluffy.

4 Separate the eggs carefully into two bowls, then beat the yolks until light in colour.

5 Melt the chocolate in a bowl over some hot water, then add the pre-boiled, warm water and egg yolks to the mixture.

6 Add the chocolate mixture to the creamed butter and sugar and stir in well. Fold in the remaining flour and salt.

7 Whisk the egg whites until they form soft peaks, then very gently fold the egg whites through the chocolate mixture. Make sure there are no pockets of egg white in the mixture, as these will show up when the cake is cut.

8 Pour the mixture evenly between the two prepared tins and bake for approximately 25 minutes or until firm to the touch.

9 Leave the cakes in the tins to cool for approximately five minutes, before turning them out onto a cooling rack.

Storage

These cakes can be wrapped individually in greaseproof paper and stored in a tin for up to five days.

Doulton Lambeth currant jar (24cm). Firm established in 1815

Carrot cake

INGREDIENTS

300ml (10½fl oz) sunflower oil

4 large eggs

300g (10½oz) soft light brown sugar

200g (7oz) self-raising flour

100g (3½oz) plain wholemeal flour

4tsp mixed spice

4tsp ground cinnamon

2tsp bicarbonate of soda

285g (10oz) grated carrots

80g (2¾oz) sultanas

100g (3½oz) walnuts, chopped

EQUIPMENT

20.5cm (8") round cake tin

Makes a 20.5cm (8") round cake

For essential baking edibles and equipment, see pages 10–11

ROUND/SQUARE	20.5cm (8")	25.5cm (10")	30.5cm (12")
Sunflower oil	300ml (10½fl oz)	450ml (16fl oz)	600ml (1pt 1½fl oz)
Large eggs	4	6	8
Soft light brown sugar	300g (10½oz)	450g (1lb)	600g (1lb 5¼oz)
Self-raising flour	200g (7oz)	300g (10½oz)	400g (14oz)
Plain wholemeal flour	100g (3½oz)	150g (5¼oz)	200g (7oz)
Mixed spice	4tsp	6tsp	2tbsp
Ground cinnamon	4tsp	6tsp	2tbsp
Bicarbonate of soda	2tsp	3tsp	4tsp
Grated carrots	285g (10oz)	430g (15oz)	575g (1lb 4oz)
Sultanas	80g (2¾oz)	120g (4¼oz)	160g (5½oz)
Walnuts, chopped	100g (3½oz)	150g (5¼oz)	200g (7oz)
Baking time	1–1¼ hours	1½–2 hours	2–2½ hours

1 Lightly grease and line a 20.5cm (8") round cake tin (see page 488).

2 Preheat the oven 180°C/160°C fan/350°F/gas mark 4. Whisk the oil and eggs together.

3 Mix the sugar, flours, spices and bicarbonate of soda together in a bowl.

4 Add the carrots, sultanas and walnuts into the dry ingredients and mix together well.

5 Add the oil and eggs and stir together until all the ingredients are combined.

6 Pour the mixture into the prepared tin and bake for 1–1¼ hours. To test when the cake is baked, a skewer inserted into the cake should come out clean. If you can see mixture on the skewer, bake for a little longer.

7 Remove from the oven and leave in the tin until cold.

Storage

This cake can be wrapped in greaseproof paper and stored for at least five days. It can be decorated with a cream cheese frosting, finely chopped walnuts and a sprinkling of mixed spice.

Helen Knight

BIOGRAPHY

My love of baking and cookery started with me watching my mum in the kitchen, especially as she made tea on a Sunday evening. When I was old enough, I was allowed to start making my own fairy cakes; I had to make them all by hand with a wooden spoon, bowl and set of scales, as we didn't have any electrical gadgets. I also had to clean up all my mess afterwards!

I started to help my mum make her own jam with fruits from the garden and hedgerow, then when I had children of my own I would take them fruit-picking in the summer and autumn. As the children grew up, I replaced their grassy play area with canes and bushes to grow my own fruit for jam-making. During the middle of a dreary winter, you can't beat hearing the pop of a jar lid opening and then smelling the fruity scent of summer. And on occasion when a jam doesn't set, I just use it as a sauce and serve it warm over ice cream!

I love baking as I find it a great way to relax. I am happy to try any recipe once and enjoy seeing or hearing my family's reaction to my dishes (whether they are good or bad), but I do

tend to return to tried-and-tested recipes. I do so much baking that I decided to keep chickens in my garden to save me having to buy so many eggs. I started off with three chickens and my flock has now increased to seven, and they are all 'feathered hooligans' who, given the chance, will strip my fruit canes or strawberry plants of all their fruit! One of my favourite things to bake is a Victoria sandwich which I make with the fresh eggs and fill with homemade raspberry jam, having picked the raspberries straight from the garden. I also love to make scones with homemade lemon curd, and again I make the curd using my chickens' eggs.

I started working at Squires Kitchen the week before their 25th anniversary in 2011. I had left my previous job and planned to take a month off, but I was so excited to take on a new challenge that I started immediately and have never looked back. I really enjoy my role as Housekeeper at Squires Kitchen's International School as it is extremely varied. No two days are ever the same, with different tutors and new students coming through the doors. I love to go into the classrooms throughout the day and see how the students work has progressed and it's great to see the end result.

23

Cake Fillings

HELEN KNIGHT

If you are baking a cake at home I always think a homemade filling is the perfect way to finish it off. The recipes here cover the most popular fillings used in all kinds of sponge cakes and fruit cake, so can be used for virtually all of the cake projects in this book. Instructions for filling and preparing cakes for decorating are given on pages 91 to 97.

TECHNIQUES

- Sterilising a jar
- Testing for a jam set

Horner's clotted cream pot.
Firm established in 1846

Apricot jam

INGREDIENTS

500g (1lb 1¾oz) fresh apricots, halved

2–3tbsp water

500g (1lb 1¾oz) granulated sugar

Juice of ½ a lemon

EQUIPMENT

Preserving pan

Long-handled wooden spoon

Makes approximately four 125ml (4½fl oz) Kilner jars

For essential baking edibles and equipment, see pages 10–11

1 Place the apricots and the water in a preserving pan and simmer gently until the fruit becomes soft.

2 Add the sugar and lemon juice, then stir until all the sugar has dissolved.

3 Turn up the heat and bring the mixture to the boil. Boil rapidly for approximately 10 minutes then test for a set. The jam should be a light amber colour and have a nice, thick consistency.

4 Leave to cool slightly in the pan, then pour the jam into warm, sterilised jam jars and seal.

Store the unopened apricot jam in a cool, dark cupboard. If the jar has been sterilised correctly it should keep for up to a year. Once open, keep the jam in the fridge and use within one month. If there is any sign of mould then dispose of the jam.

Apricot glaze

To make an apricot glaze for fruit cakes, first sieve the apricot jam and then boil it to kill any bacteria present. Use a pastry brush or palette knife to spread warm glaze over the fruit cake before covering it with marzipan (see pages 95–96).

Buttercream

INGREDIENTS

50g (1¾oz) softened, unsalted butter

1tbsp milk

½ sachet (1tsp) of vanilla paste

175g (6oz) icing sugar, sifted

Makes enough to fill and crumb-coat a 20.5cm (8") round cake

Boiled/Swiss buttercream

INGREDIENTS

2 large egg whites

100g (3½oz) caster sugar

170g (5¾oz) butter, softened

½ sachet (1tsp) vanilla paste

Makes enough to fill and crumb-coat a 15cm (6") round cake

Chocolate ganache

INGREDIENTS

800g (1lb 12oz) dark chocolate, broken into chunks

220ml (7¾fl oz) whipping cream

50g (1¾oz) glucose

50g (1¾oz) butter

Makes enough to fill and crumb-coat a 15cm (6") and a 20.5cm round (8") cake

For essential baking edibles and equipment, see pages 10–11

---

1 Beat the butter, milk and vanilla paste together in an electric mixer.

2 Add the icing sugar in small amounts until it is all incorporated and the mixture is smooth.

Variation

Fruity buttercream: Beat 250g (8¾oz) of SK Fruit Fondant Icing Mix in your chosen flavour with 125g (4½oz) of softened butter and 3tsp of boiled, hot water until light and fluffy.

Buttercream should be kept in an airtight container in the fridge for up to a week. Remove the buttercream from the fridge an hour before use and re-beat.

---

1 Combine the egg whites and sugar together in a large bowl.

2 Place the bowl over a pan of simmering water, ensuring the bowl does not touch the water.

3 Whisk the mixture over the heat until the temperature of the mixture reaches 60°C (140°F) or is warm to the touch.

4 Pour the mixture into the bowl of an electric mixer and beat at a high speed with the whisk attachment until the mixture is cool to the touch and looks thick and shiny.

5 Add the butter and continue to mix. If the mixture splits, continue to beat the mixture until it is smooth. Add the vanilla paste and mix in well.

Boiled buttercream should be stored in an airtight container in the fridge and used within 2–3 days.

---

1 Place the chocolate in a heatproof bowl and melt slowly in a microwave or over a bain-marie, until the chocolate reaches 45°C (113°F) in temperature and is completely melted.

2 Place the cream and glucose into a pan and bring to the boil. Leave the mixture to cool to 70°C (158°F) before pouring the mixture over the melted chocolate.

3 Add the butter and stir in until completely melted. Continue to stir as gently as possible until the mixture resembles a smooth paste. Allow to cool for two hours.

4 Once cool, whisk the ganache in an electric mixer to make a spreadable filling.

Chocolate ganache can usually be kept in the fridge for up to a week, provided that the cream you use is in date for at least a week. Remove from the fridge a couple of hours before use and allow the ganache to return to room temperature.

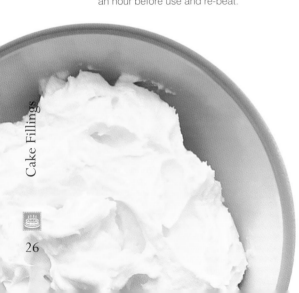

Cake Fillings

Cream cheese frosting

INGREDIENTS

175g (6oz) full-fat cream cheese

75g (2½oz) butter, softened

85g (2¾oz) icing sugar, sifted

Pinch of mixed spice

Makes enough to coat the top of a 1kg (2lb 3¼oz) loaf cake

Lemon curd

INGREDIENTS

4 whole eggs

2 egg yolks

100g (3½oz) unsalted butter

4 unwaxed lemons, juice and zest

200g (7oz) caster or granulated sugar

Makes approximately 750g (1lb 10½oz) or enough to fill approximately three 125ml (4½fl oz) Kilner jars (depending upon the amount of lemon juice)

For essential baking edibles and equipment, see pages 10–11

1 Drain the excess liquid from the cream cheese.

2 Beat the butter, mixed spice and icing sugar together in an electric mixer until light and fluffy.

3 Fold the cream cheese into the mixture.

Cream cheese frosting should be stored in an airtight container in the fridge and used within two days.

1 Whisk the whole eggs and yolks together in a bowl, then sieve.

2 Place the butter, lemon zest, lemon juice and sugar in a bowl, then place the bowl over a saucepan of gently simmering water, ensuring the bowl does not touch the water.

3 Stir occasionally until the butter and sugar have completely melted.

4 Add the sieved eggs and whisk until the mixture thickens.

5 Pour the curd into warm, sterilised jam jars and seal.

Lemon curd should be kept in the refrigerator and used within six weeks.

Variation

Limoncello lemon curd: Replace half the lemon juice with the same quantity of limoncello.

Cake Fillings

Victorian wooden lemon squeezer

Strawberry jam

INGREDIENTS

1kg (2lb 3¼oz) strawberries

500g (1lb 1¾oz) granulated sugar

450g (1lb) pectin sugar

150ml (5¼fl oz) lemon juice

EQUIPMENT

Preserving pan

Long-handled wooden spoon

Makes enough to fill approximately six 125ml (4½fl oz) Kilner jars

For essential baking edibles and equipment, see pages 10–11

1 Place 200g (7oz) of strawberries and 200g (7oz) of granulated sugar in a pan and crush together with a fork or potato masher. Heat gently until the sugar has dissolved, then add the remainder of the strawberries and simmer until the fruit is soft.

2 Add the remaining granulated sugar and all the pectin sugar then gently simmer until all the sugar has dissolved.

3 Add the lemon juice and mix in well.

4 Bring the mixture to the boil, then boil rapidly for 10 minutes. Take the pan off the heat and test to see if the jam has set. The jam should be thicker and have a slight sheen to it. If it has not set, return the mixture to the heat and boil for a few more minutes.

5 Leave the mixture to cool slightly in the pan, and then pour the jam into warm, sterilised jars and seal.

Variation

Strawberry and rhubarb jam: Make in the same way as strawberry jam, but once the first quantity of sugar has dissolved add 250g (8¾oz) of strawberries and 250g (8¾oz) of rhubarb (chopped into small pieces).

Store the unopened jar of strawberry jam in a cool, dark cupboard. If the jar has been sterilised correctly it should keep for up to a year. Once open, keep the jam in the fridge and use within one month. If there is any sign of mould then dispose of the jam.

Cake Fillings

Raspberry jam

INGREDIENTS

1kg (2lb 3¼oz) fresh raspberries

1kg (2lb 3¼oz) granulated sugar

EQUIPMENT

Preserving pan
Long-handled wooden spoon
Fork or potato masher

Makes enough to fill approximately eight 125ml (4½fl oz) Kilner jars

For essential baking edibles and equipment, see pages 10–11

1 Place the raspberries and sugar in a pan and simmer gently until all the sugar has dissolved.

2 Bring the mixture to the boil, then boil rapidly for 10 minutes. Take the pan off the heat and test to see if the jam has set: the bubbles in the jam should be small like the bubbles in sparkling water. If it has not set, return the mixture to the heat and boil for a couple more minutes.

3 Leave the mixture to cool slightly in the pan, then pour the jam into warm, sterilised jars and seal.

Store the unopened jar of raspberry jam in a cool, dark cupboard. If the jar has been sterilised correctly it should keep for up to a year. Once open, keep the jam in the fridge and use within one month. If there is any sign of mould then dispose of the jam.

Seedless raspberry jam

INGREDIENTS

1kg (2lb 3¼oz) fresh raspberries

450g (1lb) sugar per 600ml (1pt) of pulp

Makes enough to fill approximately six 125ml (4½fl oz) Kilner jars

EQUIPMENT

Preserving pan
Fork or potato masher
Long-handled wooden spoon
Ladle
Sieve

For essential baking edibles and equipment, see pages 10–11

1 Place the raspberries in a preserving pan and use a fork or a potato masher to crush them into a pulp. Allow the fruit to simmer gently until all the juices have been released, then pour away the juice.

2 Use a ladle to push the raspberry pulp through a sieve.

3 Discard the pips, then weigh the leftover raspberry purée. Add 450g (1lb) of sugar for every 600ml (1pt) of pulp.

4 Return the purée to the pan, add the appropriate amount of sugar and heat gently until the sugar has completely dissolved.

5 Bring the mixture to the boil, then boil rapidly for 10 minutes. Take the pan off the heat and test to see if the jam has set: the bubbles in the jam should be small like the bubbles in sparkling water. If it has not set, return the mixture to the heat and boil for a couple more minutes.

6 Leave the mixture to cool slightly in the pan, and then pour the jam into warm, sterilised jars and seal.

Store the unopened jar of seedless raspberry jam in a cool, dark cupboard. If the jar has been sterilised correctly it should keep for up to a year. Once open, keep the jam in the fridge and use within one month. If there is any sign of mould then dispose of the jam.

Cake Fillings

How to sterilise a jar

It is important to sterilise jam jars in order to eliminate any bacteria, organisms and yeasts that can cause the jam to spoil once it is in the jar. Check your jam jars before use to make sure that there are no chips or cracks in them: if the jars are damaged they should be thrown away.

1 Preheat the oven to 150°C/300°F/ gas mark 2. While the oven is heating, wash the jar and the rubber seal in hot, soapy water. This soapy water should also help to remove any sticky labels on the jar if it has been used previously. If you cannot remove the sticky label completely, then you may need to use a cleaner for adhesives. Rinse the jars well in hot water.

2 Remove the rubber seal then carefully place the jar upside down in the oven and leave for approximately 10 minutes, or until the jar is completely dry. Turn off the oven and leave to cool (unless the recipe requires the jam to be added to a hot jar), then remove the jar.

3 Place the rubber seals in a pan and fill the pan with enough water to cover the seals. Bring the water to the boil and simmer for 10 minutes. Turn off the heat, place a lid on the pan and leave the seals until needed.

tutor tip

Make sure the jar is the same temperature as the jam when you fill it to prevent the glass from cracking.

How to test for a set

There are three different ways in which to test if a jam has set. For every method, you must always take the jam off the heat before testing for a set.

Cold saucer method: Place two or three saucers or small plates in the freezer before you start to make the jam. When you are ready to test whether the jam has set, remove a saucer from the freezer and place a teaspoon of jam on the cold saucer. Put the saucer in the fridge for a couple of minutes, then take it out and push the jam with your finger. If the jam wrinkles then a set has been reached.

Flake test method: Dip a clean, dry wooden spoon into the jam. Hold the spoon above the pan and allow the jam to cool slightly. A set has been reached if the jam doesn't run off the spoon, but falls off in flakes.

Thermometer method: Take the jam off the heat and stir well. Place a jam thermometer into a bowl of hot water and then place the thermometer in the jam. If a set has been reached, the temperature of the jam should be 105°C (220°F).

Cake Fillings

31

Bea Harling

BIOGRAPHY

I started out as an enthusiastic cook – I trained and worked as a commis chef but quickly realised I preferred my home kitchen. My excitement for food flourished after graduating in Food and Consumer Sciences with a first class BSc degree. I began my career developing recipe dishes and creating new products for Marks and Spencer. As a food selector, my role was to develop concepts from presenting the recipe ideas to styling the food for photography. I was inspired to write and trained with the National Magazine Company to write features for popular magazines. I continued on to the Good Housekeeping Institute where I designed and ran commercial projects for the food and product test centre, GHI.

In the food manufacturing industry, I managed a culinary test kitchen for a major international company, guiding sensory taste panels, developing products and creating recipes. I was appointed the resident 'Food Expert' for a website, contributing regular inspiration and food news streamed to people for weight management. I gained a rich expertise working alongside chefs, nutritionists and respected food professionals.

My enthusiasm for gluten-free and 'free from' diets developed from the challenge to adapt delicious food that everyone could enjoy. Now, I am a regular contributor to recipe books, creating ideas to inspire pleasure in food as well as encouraging people to manage ingredients for healthy and special diets.

Together with my business partner, chef Phil Vickery, we formed Seriously Good!™ Gluten Free Food Ltd. in 2012 to develop and launch a range of gluten-free and dairy-free home baking mixes with Squires Kitchen.

Continuing with my appreciation for baking and desserts, I teach a cookery course for Squires Kitchen, designed to inspire confidence and fun with gluten-free and 'free from' recipes. I find food inspiration while travelling and attending cookery courses along the way. Although I was born in London, my mother was Irish and gave her love of baking to me; I now live and cook close to Lake Geneva in Switzerland as well as in West Sussex, with my family.

Gluten- and Dairy-free Baking

BEA HARLING

Baking for those with food allergies and intolerances can be a daunting task even for the experienced cake maker, but with a basic understanding of special diets and some reliable recipes, it needn't be difficult. The basic recipes given here have been designed as delicious treats for everyone to enjoy and there are plenty of helpful hints and tips about the essentials of 'free from' baking. Once you know how to adapt traditional recipes using alternative ingredients, you will soon find the confidence to bake gluten-free or for other special diets in your home or for your business.

If you are planning to bake for someone else (particularly for business), make sure you understand the impact of the ingredients you choose, special preparation and labelling to avoid any potential pitfalls. This chapter focuses on two of the most commonly requested special diets, gluten-free and dairy-free, however many of the same principles will apply for any 'free from' food.

The difference between a food allergy and a food intolerance

Allergies and intolerances are often confused because they can produce similar symptoms.

The immune system of an allergic person will recognise ordinary proteins in food as a threat, and will produce a specific antibody to attack them. In a person with a dairy allergy, for example, milk proteins in dairy foods will trigger an immune system response. Symptoms of food allergy can range from mild to severe and can be fatal, so it is important to understand which foods can trigger an allergic reaction. There are 14 known allergens, see the links to helpful websites on page 37 for further details.

Food intolerance doesn't involve the same immune system mechanism as a food allergy but refers to difficulty in digesting certain foods. Lactose intolerance, for example, is related to the body's inability to produce an enzyme lactase, which is needed to digest the lactose found in dairy products.

Late 19th-century pressed glass Christmas pudding plate with holly leaf pattern

Gluten intolerance and coeliac disease

Gluten is the name of a type of protein found in cereals like wheat, barley and rye. Oats contain a similar protein which some people are also sensitive to. Oats and any other ingredient can become contaminated with gluten if they are handled in the same area or premises as wheat.

Coeliac disease is not an allergy or an intolerance: it is an auto-immune disease affecting the body and gut, where the body produces antibodies that attack its own tissues. For people with coeliac disease, this attack is triggered by gluten and so they need to avoid all foods containing gluten, including cakes, biscuits and other baked goods containing wheat flour.

note

When buying ingredients for a dairy-free diet, be aware that 'lactose free' does not mean dairy free: check labels on spreads and milk products for milk proteins, as mentioned above, as well as lactose.

Dairy allergy and lactose intolerance

An allergy to dairy and intolerance to lactose are two different things but are often mixed up and people can have one or both. Lactose is milk sugar, a carbohydrate found naturally in the milk of animals. Some people lack the enzyme normally produced in the intestine, called lactase, needed to digest this milk sugar and they are described as being lactose intolerant. In some cases where coeliac disease has affected the gut (and consequently digestion), some coeliacs may also be temporarily lactose intolerant because coeliac disease damages the area where the enzyme is made in the gut.

A dairy allergy relates specifically to milk proteins, which come in many different forms. When baking it is important to recognise the main ones such as casein and whey, and others such as lactalbumin, lactoglobulin, hydrolysates, and caseinates: all are milk proteins widely used in the food industry.

Food labelling

If you are baking for a gluten-free diet, check all ingredient labels carefully to ensure foods are free from gluten-containing cereals. Some foods contain gluten where you would not expect it, for example:

Baking powder, which can contain wheat starch to absorb moisture

Chocolate

Cake decorations

Marzipan

Oats

Barley, in flavours and (cloudy) drinks

Marshmallows

Custard powder, which like many foods may contain flour as a thickener

Meringues

Shortbread

Soft cheese

Dried fruit, where flour is used to help ingredients to flow freely during processing and in the pack

Spices and condiments, including soy sauce, stock cubes, mustard and mayonnaise

Dry roasted nuts

Crisps

Beer.

Gluten- and Dairy-free Baking

Further information and advice

People who are concerned about food sensitivities must be aware of the risk of cross contamination when baking and should always check the label on food ingredients. Just as it is the responsibility of the manufacturer to ensure products are properly labelled, the cake maker is solely responsible for ensuring that their products and premises are safe for those with allergies and intolerances. Further information and guidance can be found on the following websites:

www.nhs.co.uk – NHS Choices, search for coeliac disease

www.food.gov.uk – the Food Standards Agency, for the latest advice on food allergies and intolerances and information on starting a food business

Allergytraining.food.gov.uk – further information from the FSA including online training for food allergies, advice about labelling and making cakes for business

www.coeliac.co.uk – the Coeliac UK website for advice, support and gluten-free recipes.

Troubleshooting tips for success

- When baking with alternative, gluten-free ingredients, it is more important than ever to follow the instructions carefully. Be accurate with measurements and temperatures. Weigh carefully and mix thoroughly. Use the correct tin size because a different tin will affect the cooking time and could adversely affect the texture too.

- Check the date on baking ingredients and flours: out-of-date ingredients can give poor results. Buy gluten-free baking powder in small quantities and replace it every six to nine months.

- For best results, start with all the ingredients at room temperature and have them all ready and prepared in advance. Use a light touch when mixing as overbeating can cause the batter to seize. As a general rule, only add flour into the other ingredients until just combined and no more. For this reason I suggest using an electric handheld mixer in preference to a stand mixer.

- After mixing, gluten-free batters can look a little different to the usual wheat-based flour mixtures and often behave differently compared with conventional baking. Some batters are wetter and thinner than you may be used to; others are thicker.

- Mixtures tend to stiffen when standing and soak up the moisture even more. Be sure to mix and bake straight away, especially if using baking powder or xanthan gum.

- The amount of liquid needed often differs with the ingredients and type of flour you use, or even between batches of the same flour, so learn to judge and adjust to the description in the recipe: too little liquid and the result can be heavy and dry. You will need to increase the liquid if you are introducing gluten-free flour into a normal recipe.

- If you are using a fan oven, please refer to the manufacturer's handbook for the correct oven temperature adjustment (usually 10–20°C lower than a conventional oven). Always preheat the oven to the correct temperature. Get to know your own oven (and microwave) and adjust the cooking time and temperature to suit your individual kitchen; you may find an oven thermometer useful as many ovens differ.

- Don't be tempted to open the oven door to peek until at least three quarters of the way through the baking time.

- Gluten-free cakes can be more crumbly than conventional cakes, although baking with vegetable oil does help to make the crumb softer and moister. Use a knife dipped in boiled water to portion and cut your cakes, wiping it clean between slices.

Adapting baking recipes to make them gluten- and dairy-free: useful ingredients and substitutes

Gluten-free flours

Many people start out using just rice flour but this has a sandy texture and is a poor substitute for wheat flour when used alone. Using a blend of different flours will add personality, texture and flavour to a recipe. Ready-blended, gluten-free flours are readily available or you can make your own by mixing a combination of three or more from the following:

● The heavier base notes, e.g. buckwheat (a relative of rhubarb), millet, maize or cornmeal (polenta), teff, soy, chickpea (or gram) flours and quinoa, flax meal (for added fibre), almond and nut flours, coconut flour (absorbs a great deal of liquid). These contain more protein and fibre, are similar to baking with whole wheat flour and tend to give you a denser, darker and less risen result. Use little and sparingly; although nutritious, they have a strong flavour you may dislike.

● The middle body and lighter notes, e.g. tapioca starch (made from cassava root, it also helps to brown nicely), cornflour, arrowroot, potato starch (not potato flour). These help to give a light, soft structure. I tend not to use white rice flour if I am blending my own flour. Sorghum (jowar) flour, or if this is hard to find, brown rice flour, will lighten the more characterful base notes. Then add some lighter, starchy flours to soften the crumb and help bind the batter or dough.

Mix all combinations of flours together very thoroughly and evenly. If you add xanthan gum (or baking powder) to a recipe, make sure you sift it with the flour a couple of times to mix it well and avoid an uneven rise or texture. Once you start experimenting, you may find you prefer different blends for different recipes, rather than one all-purpose combination.

When substituting gluten-free flours into a standard recipe, you may need to increase the proportion of liquid because they tend to be more absorbent. Expect the baking time, textures and rise to be slightly different and make a note with each recipe so you can adjust it for next time. You may also need to add a small amount of xanthan gum to replace the stretchy 'spring' and structure, see below.

Xanthan gum

Xanthan is a natural gum produced by the fermentation of sugar with 'friendly' bacteria. The bacterium used is Xanthomonas campestris, hence the name xanthan gum. The sugars are removed in processing and so xanthan gum contains no corn protein or sugars and is considered to be corn free.

Add ¼ to ½tsp for every 225g (8oz) of gluten-free flour as a general guide. Note that gluten-free, self-raising flour already contains xanthan gum to improve the texture after baking, making it less crumbly.

Storing flours

Substitute ingredients can be expensive and have a short shelf life, so store in an airtight container in a cool place or in the refrigerator if practical in your kitchen. Make sure there is no risk of cross contamination from other flours in your storage area.

Dairy-free ingredients

Use your favourite choice of unsweetened, dairy-free milk in place of cow's milk. They all have different flavours so try out different alternatives each time you bake to find one you prefer.

● Soya milk has a stronger flavour than cow's milk and is a little denser.

● Rice milk is thinner than cow's milk; use unsweetened in baking.

● Almond milk is rich and creamy.

● Hemp milk has a stronger taste than cow's milk. Check the label for barley enzyme used in vanilla flavouring as this contains gluten.

● Coconut milk beverage is a little lighter and thinner than cow's milk but works well.

Soya and nut milks work well in gluten-free recipes. Shelf-stable cartons are convenient to store; all types settle so shake the container before use. Check the label to make sure dairy-free drinks are also gluten-free, if needed.

Gluten- and Dairy-free Baking

Substitutes for butter all taste different, so try out different brands of dairy-free spread to suit your own taste; some lack flavour and so will benefit from a few drops of vanilla extract to compensate. Others contain milk proteins so check labels to ensure they are dairy free and not just free from lactose.

Vegetable oil instead of spread is very successful for baking cakes in combination with dairy-free milks: use a light vegetable oil, rather than olive oil, as it is too strong in flavour.

Coconut oil is solid at room temperature but liquefies easily for all types of cooking, including baking, fillings and frostings. Coconut oil gives a subtle flavour and a light, silky texture.

Check that any chocolate ingredients you use are dairy-free (or nut-free if necessary for your special diet).

Egg-free, nut-free and other special diets

There are many important elements to consider when baking for special diets, particularly if you are also baking regular cakes in your kitchen. A useful, detailed source of information regarding baking for special diets is *Gluten-, Nut-, Egg- and Dairy-Free Celebration Cakes* by Gemma McFarlane (B. Dutton Publishing), available from bookshops and direct from the publisher at www.squires-shop.com.

One of the main considerations is cross contamination: even the tiniest gluten crumb can trigger a sensitive immune system or make someone seriously ill. Always follow these basic guidelines for special-diet baking:

- Check your ingredients and contact the manufacturer if unsure.

- Organise your kitchen to use a different area for the preparation of special diet recipes. Avoid cross contamination by keeping all 'free from' ingredients, utensils and cooking equipment separate from those used with regular products.

- Store in separate, sealed containers and cupboards.

- Never use shared packs of spreads, oils, jam, etc.

- Keep your work area scrupulously clean. Hand sanitiser and alcohol wipes are useful to clean hands, fridge and cupboard handles, surfaces and shared spaces.

How long does it keep?

Many gluten-free recipes are best eaten fresh and not stored for more than a day or two; dairy-free recipes will keep for up to five days. The recipes given here can be frozen when fresh: defrost to room temperature before decorating/serving. Warming in a microwave oven for a few seconds can give defrosted cakes and cupcakes a just-baked taste (remember to remove metallic paper cases first).

Gluten- and Dairy-free Baking

38

Recipes for Gluten- and Dairy-free Cakes and Fillings

Any basic recipe can be adapted to suit a special diet (see pages 37–38), but here I have given three tried-and-tested recipes which I find particularly good. All are both gluten- and dairy-free.

Gluten- and dairy-free vanilla sponge cake

This is a light and airy sponge that you can easily adapt for different flavours. Using this method and made with oil, the cake is less crumbly than a creamed sponge.

INGREDIENTS

Cake

3 medium eggs

225g (8oz) caster sugar

130ml (4½fl oz) vegetable oil

130ml (4½fl oz) soya or dairy-free milk

1tsp vanilla extract

225g (8oz) gluten-free self-raising flour

Filling

Jam, compote or curd

Buttercream

125g (4½oz) dairy-free spread

250g (8¾oz) icing sugar

Few drops of vanilla extract

For essential baking edibles and equipment, see pages 10–11

EQUIPMENT

Two 20.5cm (8") round x 4cm (1½") deep loose-based metal sponge tins, oiled and bases lined, see page 488

Large jug mixing bowl

Handheld electric whisk

Small palette knife

Makes a 20.5cm (8") round cake

Tin flour sifter, 20th century

1 Preheat the oven to 180°C/160°C fan/350°F/gas mark 4. Weigh all the ingredients carefully and have them ready at room temperature.

2 Mix the eggs and the sugar together in a large jug mixing bowl. Using a handheld electric whisk, beat for about 3 minutes until creamy and the mixture forms a thick trail.

3 Combine the vegetable oil, soya milk and vanilla and then pour gently into the egg mixture, along with the flour. Whisk for just a few seconds until smooth. This batter will be loose rather than thick and the mixing jug bowl allows you to pour it easily.

4 Divide the mixture between two prepared cake tins: I like to weigh the mixture in to get an even result. Level the surface using a spatula if necessary and prick any air bubbles.

5 Bake on the same centre shelf in the oven for about 30–35 minutes. The sponge is baked when the centre springs back if you press lightly with a finger. Usually the cake will have shrunk from the sides slightly too. Alternatively, a knife inserted in the centre should come out clean.

6 Remove the cakes from the oven and allow to cool on a rack. After 10 minutes, loosen gently all round the sides with a small palette knife. Gluten-free cakes are more fragile: if you are using loose-based baking tins, sit them on a small, upturned bowl to loosen the sides and slowly ease downwards. You can then use the base to slide the cake onto a cooling rack.

7 When cold, sandwich the two cakes together with jam. To make buttercream, beat the spread briefly using an electric handheld mixer until light. Sieve the icing sugar and gradually beat this into the spread, slowly at first. Add vanilla extract and a few drops of boiled, cooled water if needed until smooth and creamy. Do not overbeat as, unlike butter, it may split.

8 Dust the whole cake with icing sugar for a simple finish. Alternatively try one of the suggestions below for decorating and filling.

tutor tip

Set a timer when you bake: don't be tempted to open the oven door to peek until the last 5 minutes.

VARIATIONS

Coffee cake

Dissolve 1tbsp of instant coffee granules in 1tbsp of pre-boiled, hot water and add to the mixture with the oil and soya milk. Flavour the buttercream with 1tsp of coffee granules dissolved in 1tsp of hot water instead of vanilla. Use coffee fondant icing to decorate (see below).

Chocolate sponge cake

Substitute 25g (¾oz) of the flour with cocoa powder and add ½tsp of xanthan gum. Add 25g (1oz) of dairy-free grated chocolate along with the flour. Use soft light brown sugar instead of caster sugar. Fill the cake with chocolate ganache (see recipe on page 42), or alternatively make fondant icing using the chocolate fondant mix, or by replacing 20g (¾oz) of sugar with cocoa powder (see below).

Cupcakes

To make 15 large cupcakes, bake in cases in a muffin tin and fill to no more than ¾ full. Do not over-fill the cases otherwise the cakes will blouse over and could sink. Bake for about 20 minutes; the cupcakes should rise to just below the rim of the cases. Leave to cool out of the tin.

Sugar syrup

Dissolve 75ml (3fl oz) of sugar in 100ml (3½fl oz) of water and simmer for a couple of minutes. Infuse with flavouring and cool.

Gluten-free cakes can benefit from a little sugar syrup spooned over after baking. Use 6–8tsp for a moist texture. A contrasting flavour is a good way to boost the flavour of a simple sponge cake: try grated lemon or lime zest or infusing it with lavender.

Fondant icing

1 Sieve 250g (8¾oz) of fondant icing sugar into a large bowl. You can use plain fondant sugar mix or SK flavoured fondant icing mix which is available in different flavours and adds a natural colour to the icing. You could try orange, lemon, blackcurrant, raspberry or strawberry and favourites like coconut, coffee or chocolate.

2 Gradually add 3tbsp of cooled, boiled water, beating well after each addition. If necessary, add extra water until the icing is smooth, soft and easy to spread. It should be firm enough to stay in place but not solid.

3 Place the cake on a serving plate and brush away any loose crumbs. Spoon the icing over the top of the cake and encourage it to spread to the edges using a palette knife. Leave the cake to set, but not in the fridge or it may lose its shine.

Recipes for Gluten- and Dairy-free Cakes and Fillings

40

Gluten- and dairy-free chocolate and almond cake

The almonds lend a firm texture to this chocolate sponge cake. It's moist and fudgy and will keep refrigerated for up to three days (or can be frozen). Serve at room temperature.

For a nut-free chocolate cake as well as gluten- and dairy-free, use the chocolate variation of the vanilla sponge cake recipe on pages 39–40.

INGREDIENTS

Cake

200g (7oz) gluten-free self-raising flour

½ level tsp xanthan gum

50g (1¾oz) cocoa powder

175g (6oz) soft, dairy-free spread

200g (7oz) soft dark brown sugar

4 medium eggs, beaten

1tsp vanilla extract

250ml (8fl oz) almond or soya milk

50g (1¾oz) ground almonds

Filling and topping: dairy-free ganache

200ml (7fl oz) almond or soya milk

300g (10½oz) dairy-free plain chocolate (approximately 55% cocoa solids), chopped

SK Crystallised Natural Rose or Violet Fragments

EQUIPMENT

Two 20.5cm (8") round x 4cm (1½") height loose-based metal sponge tins, oiled and bases lined, see page 488

Handheld electric whisk

Makes a 20.5cm (8") round cake

For essential baking edibles and equipment, see pages 10–11

1 Preheat the oven to 180°C/160°C fan/350°F/gas mark 4. Weigh all the ingredients carefully and have them ready at room temperature.

2 Sieve the flour, xanthan gum and cocoa powder together until evenly mixed.

3 Beat the spread and sugar together in a large bowl until light and fluffy using a handheld electric whisk. Gradually whisk in the vanilla and the eggs, a spoonful at a time. If you do this too quickly, the mixture may curdle; if this happens, add a spoonful of the flour mix and continue.

4 Fold in the cocoa and flour mixture, alternately with tablespoons of the milk, until all is evenly combined. Fold in the ground almonds. Add a little more milk if necessary so that the batter is soft and dropping from the spoon.

5 Divide the mixture between two prepared cake tins: weigh the mixture in to get an even result. Level the surface using a spatula or palette knife.

6 Bake on the same centre shelf in the oven for about 30 minutes. The sponge is done when the centre springs back if you press lightly with a finger. Usually the cake will have shrunk from the sides slightly too. Alternatively, a knife inserted in the centre should come out clean. Don't be tempted to open the oven door too soon, or the centre may sink.

7 Remove the cakes from the oven and allow to cool on a wire rack. After 10 minutes, loosen gently all round the sides with a palette knife. If you are using loose-based baking tins, sit them on a small upturned bowl to loosen the sides and slowly ease downwards. Use the base to slide the cake onto a rack.

8 To make the ganache filling and icing, place the dairy-free milk and the chopped chocolate into a heatproof bowl, set over a pan of barely simmering water and stir until melted. The bowl should not touch the water. Leave to set at room temperature (or overnight) until thick enough to spread.

9 Spread a third of the chocolate icing over the base of one of the chocolate cakes, then carefully top with the other cake. Transfer to a serving plate and spread chocolate icing all over the cake using a palette knife.

10 Decorate the edge of the cake top with crystallised rose or violet fragments. Keep the cake chilled in the refrigerator after icing.

Gluten- and dairy-free carrot cupcakes

This is a great basic recipe that you can tweak with other ingredients. Recipes containing puréed fruit, grated vegetables (carrot, courgette, even beetroot) and yogurt adapt well to gluten free, resulting in a moist texture and binding the crumb together.

INGREDIENTS

Cupcakes

175g (6oz) gluten-free self-raising flour

¼ level tsp xanthan gum

½ level tsp bicarbonate of soda

1 level tsp mixed spice

120g (4¼oz) light muscovado or light brown soft sugar

100ml (3½fl oz) sunflower oil

2 large eggs

175g (6oz) carrots, coarsely grated

1tbsp dairy-free milk, see page 38

Buttercream

200g (7oz) dairy-free spread

450g (1lb) icing sugar

½tsp cinnamon

Sprinkles

Mini assorted sugar flower decorations or edible pink butterflies

EQUIPMENT

12-hole muffin tin

SK Gold, Silver and Bronze Foil Cupcake Cases

Handheld electric whisk

Disposable piping bag

Savoy piping nozzle: star 9

Makes 12 large cupcakes

For essential baking edibles and equipment, see pages 10–11

1 Preheat the oven to 180°C/160°C fan/350°F/gas mark 4. Weigh all the ingredients carefully and have them ready at room temperature.

2 Sift the flour, xanthan gum, bicarbonate of soda and spice together evenly.

3 Place the sugar into a large bowl. Using a handheld electric whisk, add the oil and then the eggs, one at a time. Whisk for about one minute. Stir in the carrots.

4 Fold in the sifted dry ingredients. Add the milk to loosen and soften the mixture.

5 Divide the mixture into 12 cases in the muffin tin to about half full, and smooth the tops.

6 Bake on the centre shelf in the oven for about 20–25 minutes. The cakes are baked when the centre springs back if you press lightly with a finger.

7 Remove the cakes from the oven and allow to cool on a wire rack. Remove them from the tin to cool, otherwise the bases will become wet. Decorate when cold.

8 To make buttercream, beat the spread briefly using an electric handheld mixer until light. Sieve the icing sugar and cinnamon and gradually beat this into the spread, slowly at first, until smooth and creamy. Do not overbeat as, unlike butter, it may split. Chill in the fridge.

9 To decorate the cupcakes, fit a disposable piping bag with a large star nozzle (or simply snip off the end after filling) then ½-fill with buttercream. Starting at the outside edge, pipe round the edge of the cake in a spiral towards the centre. Pull up quickly to finish the swirl. Add some sprinkles to finish then keep the cakes chilled in the fridge after icing.

Gluten-free cupcakes are best eaten fresh or can be frozen: use foil cupcake cases to prevent the cakes separating from the sides.

Cupcakes, Cookies and Cake Pops

ANN SKIPP

Cake pops originated in America and were designed to use up leftover cake. If you have off-cuts from a carved sponge cake, use a food processor to blitz them into crumbs and mix with buttercream for the perfect cake pop mixture. If time is short, shop-bought Madeira cake can be used. The chocolate cake recipe on page 20 is perfect for the favours in this project.

TECHNIQUES

- Making and decorating cupcakes
- Making and decorating biscuits
- Making and decorating cake pops

Cupcake rose bouquet

This cupcake arrangement makes a beautiful centrepiece for a wedding table, with individual portions so guests can pick their own.

EDIBLES

Cakes

Victoria sponge recipe, halved, see page 15

125g (4½oz) SK Sugarpaste: Palm Green

SK Edible Glue

Buttercream

250g (8¾oz) unsalted butter, softened

250g (8¾oz) icing sugar

Vanilla extract

SK Professional Liquid Food Colour: Rose (optional)

EQUIPMENT

10cm (4") diameter round container

10cm (4") diameter dome of dry floral foam

10 SK Soft Grey Rose Cupcake Cases

10 wooden barbecue skewers

Piping nozzle: no. 127 petal

Large Savoy piping bag

Makes a bouquet of 10 cupcakes

For essential baking edibles and equipment, see pages 10–11

Making the cupcakes

1 Preheat the oven 180°C/160°C fan/350°F/gas mark 4.

2 Line a muffin tin with 10 cupcake cases.

3 Make up half the Victoria sponge mixture following the recipe on page 15 and divide the mixture equally between the cases.

4 Bake in the oven for 10–15 minutes until golden in colour and just firm to the touch. When baked, remove from the oven and leave in the tray to cool.

Making the container

5 To prepare the container, roll out the Palm Green sugarpaste until it is large enough to cover the dry foam. Push the dome into the top of the container and brush edible glue over the foam. Cover the dome with sugarpaste and trim to size.

6 Cut the skewers down to approximately 10cm (4") lengths and use the pointed end of a skewer to make a hole into the bottom of each cupcake. Insert the skewers into the covered floral dome and place a cake on each one, ensuring that they are evenly spaced and there are as few gaps as possible.

Cupcakes, Cookies and Cake Pops

Decorating the cupcakes

7 To make the buttercream, cream together the butter and icing sugar until light and fluffy. Add the vanilla extract to taste. Be careful not to make the buttercream too soft or it will be difficult to pipe and won't hold its shape.

8 If you would like to create a two-tone effect, divide the buttercream into two small bowls and colour one half with a little Rose liquid food colour.

9 Spoon the buttercream into a piping bag fitted with a rose petal nozzle. If using two colours, keep the plain buttercream to the side of the bag with the widest part of the nozzle and the pink to the narrow side. Squeeze the bag until the buttercream starts to come through the nozzle.

10 Remove the cupcakes from the skewers and pipe a small cone of buttercream in the centre of each one. Place the cakes in the refrigerator for approximately five minutes so that the cones are firm to the touch. Pipe around each central cone with the widest part of the nozzle touching the top of the cake.

11 Build up each rose by piping concentric circles of petals, with each new petal overlapping the last. Slightly lift the nozzle at the middle of each petal to round the edge. Continue until the top of each cake is covered. Allow the buttercream to firm slightly in the fridge then very gently place the cakes back on the skewers.

tutor tip

If preferred, you can fill any gaps between the cupcakes with non-toxic greenery such as bay leaves or lavender sprigs.

'Mr and Mrs' shortbread biscuits

Present these beautiful, heart-shaped shortbread biscuits in cellophane tied with a matching ribbon for perfect wedding favours that can be personalised easily.

EDIBLES

115g (4oz) unsalted butter

175g (6oz) plain flour

60g (2oz) golden caster sugar

½tsp vanilla paste or extract

500g (1lb 1¾oz) SK Art-ice Cookie Icing Mix

SK Professional Paste Food Colours: Chestnut, Leaf Green

SK Sugar Florist Paste (SFP): Cream, Pale Blue, Pale Pink

Cornflour for dusting

EQUIPMENT

SK Heart Cookie Cutter

Paper piping bags: small and medium

Piping nozzle: no. 2

SK Great Impressions Rose Mould

Small non-stick board

Classic Alphabet Cutter and Embosser (Patchwork Cutters)

Makes 10–12 biscuits

For essential baking edibles and equipment, see pages 10–11

Making the biscuits

1 Preheat the oven to 180°C/160°C fan/350°F/gas mark 4.

2 Place the butter and flour in a mixing bowl and rub together until the mixture resembles breadcrumbs.

3 Add the sugar and vanilla paste or extract and work the mixture into a soft dough.

4 Place on a lightly floured board and roll the dough out to 5mm (¼") thick.

5 Line a baking tray with a non-stick liner, then cut out heart shapes using the cookie cutter and place them on the tray.

6 Bake for 10–12 minutes until they are golden brown in colour and just firm to the touch. Leave on a wire rack to cool.

Decorating the biscuits

7 Make up the cookie icing according to the packet instructions. Colour 4 tablespoons of icing with a tiny amount of Chestnut paste food colour and the same amount of icing with Leaf Green food colour. Cover the icing with a damp cloth to prevent it from drying out.

8 Pipe an outline around the edge of the biscuits using the cream-coloured icing and a no. 2 nozzle. Let down the remaining icing with a little water to run-out consistency and flood inside

the outline. Place under a desk lamp and allow to dry.

9 Make small roses using the centre of the rose mould with Cream, Pale Blue and Pale Pink SFP. Leave to dry.

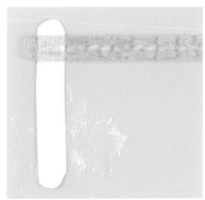

10 Roll out a small amount of Cream SFP on a non-stick board lightly dusted with cornflour until very thin. Use the alphabet cutters to cut out enough letters for the 'Mr' and 'Mrs' biscuits. Allow to dry.

11 When the biscuit covering is completely dry, arrange the roses and letters on the biscuits and stick them in place with a little cream-coloured icing. Pipe a few rose leaves in the space around the roses using green icing and a small piping bag (see page 239).

12 To finish, pipe small dots around the edge of each biscuit with cream-coloured icing in a bag fitted with a no. 2 nozzle.

tutor tip

These biscuits can be made several days in advance and stored in an airtight container. The rose decorations can also be made several days in advance: allow them to dry and store in an airtight container until needed.

Topiary wedding cake pops

These cake pops have been transformed into delicate topiary-style treats that would make fantastic place settings, with two extra-special designs for the happy couple.

EDIBLES

125g (4½oz) chocolate cake crumbs, see recipe on page 20

60g (2oz) unsalted butter

60g (2oz) icing sugar, sifted

30g (1oz) SK Extra Brute Cocoa Powder

300g (10½oz) SK White Couverture Chocolate

500g (1lb 1¾oz) SK Sugarpaste: Palm Green

SK Sugar Florist Paste (SFP): Cream, Pale Blue, Pale Pink

250g (8¾oz) SK Instant Mix Royal Icing

SK Professional Liquid Food Colours: Bluebell, Leaf Green, Rose

SK White Chocolate Vermicelli: Green

For essential baking edibles and equipment, see pages 10–11

EQUIPMENT

SK 19cm (7¾") Lollipop Sticks: Pink, White

4cm (1½") miniature clay terracotta flower pots

3mm (⅛") wide satin ribbon: cream

Makes 12 cake pops

Making the cake pops

1 Beat the butter, sugar and cocoa powder together to make chocolate buttercream. Mix the cake crumbs and buttercream together in a bowl to form a paste. Do not over-handle the mixture or it will become very greasy. The consistency is important: the mixture must not be too soft or crumbly, otherwise you will have trouble getting the cake pops to stay on the sticks.

2 Form the mixture into balls that are approximately the size of a walnut then place them on a tray and leave in the refrigerator to firm.

3 Cut the lollipop sticks to approximately 12cm (5") in length using scissors or a craft knife.

4 Melt a little white chocolate in a small bowl. Push one of the sticks into a cake ball to make a hole, then remove. Dip the end of the stick into the chocolate and push it back into the hole

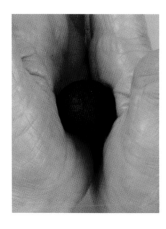

in the cake to secure it in place. Repeat with all the cake pops and leave to set in the fridge.

5 Place the remaining chocolate into a small, microwaveable bowl and temper it following the instructions on pages 104–106.

6 Holding the stick, dip each of the balls into the melted chocolate so that they are completely covered and allow to set.

Decorating the cake pops

7 Fill each of the mini flower pots ¾-full with Palm Green sugarpaste. Once the cake pops have set, insert the

sticks into the sugarpaste in the middle of each pot.

8 For the bride and groom cake pops, make lots of tiny roses using the rose mould and Cream, Pale Pink or Pale Blue SFP (see page 48). Use royal icing to stick the roses as closely together as possible over the whole cake pop. Allow the roses to dry, then pipe small leaves in Leaf Green-coloured royal icing to fill any gaps (see page 250).

9 To decorate cake pops for the guests, pipe little cones of Leaf Green-coloured royal icing over the whole cake pop. Once the green icing has set, pipe tiny blue or pink buds randomly over the cake pops, using Rose-coloured icing for female guests and Bluebell-coloured

icing for male guests. Tie a small bow with cream satin ribbon around the top of each stick.

10 Once you have arranged the cake pops, fill the tops of the flower pots with a sprinkling of green vermicelli to hide the sugarpaste.

tutor tip

The cake pops are decorated with piped royal icing which will dry quite firm. To make them easier to eat, simply break the royal icing away to reveal the cake pop underneath.

   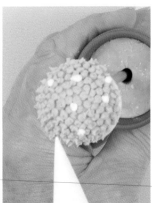

Ann Skipp

BIOGRAPHY

Much to the disappointment of my parents, I proved to be not too strong in my academic studies at school. I had my own ideas as to what I was going to do when I left school, but a strange twist happened that was to change my life. I was taking my mock 'O'-level domestic science exam with an external examiner, and at the end she suggested that I had a natural talent for the culinary arts. I suppose I wasn't too surprised - my mother was not only an excellent cook but also very artistic and creative. She rang the local college there and then and suggested a course that I should take when I left school.

I qualified later in Home Economics at the Bournemouth Municipal College of Education, as it was then. On my course was a mature student who had already qualified in a Baking and Confectionery course and she showed us the art of cake decorating. My first cake decorating attempt was a Christmas cake in my first year: my love for cake decorating was born.

I attended courses at the Mary Ford School of Cake Decorating and before long I had a diary full of cake commissions, ranging from children's birthdays to weddings. After the birth of my two sons I was asked to teach royal icing evening classes at two adult further education centres, which I did for many years, and I was also on the Women's Institute list of demonstrators. All of these activities fitted well into family life until the boys started school.

For ten years I worked as a representative in the food industry and it was through working with one of these companies that that I met Beverley Dutton, the Managing Director of Squires Kitchen. As a result of this meeting, I was asked to run occasional cake decorating demonstrations for their school.

In 1982, I joined Rank Hovis McDougall as a Food Service Advisor and travelled throughout the UK and Ireland and also went to Malta giving cookery demonstrations to chefs. It was whilst I was working for them that they commissioned me to make the commemorative cake for the 25th anniversary of WRVS (now known as the Royal Voluntary Service). I had to make eight large cakes, one of which was taken to Westminster Abbey to be cut by The Queen Mother. The other seven cakes were cut into many pieces, so that every member of the WRVS throughout the country had a portion of cake.

It was during my time with McDougall's that I was asked to make a special cake for the stars of Live Aid. It was a very exciting day; as I drove into London the concert started to blare out of my car radio and I made my way to the nightclub where they were going to meet after the show. My cakes were flat iced in black royal icing with the white Live Aid logo on the top and around the sides. Although I was not at the concert, I still felt a part of it.

In 1989, I was appointed Safeway's Corporate Home Economist which was a very interesting job with many facets including product development, product quality, sensory analysis, food photography, and recipe writing among other duties such as some radio and TV work. I was also responsible for the running of the Safeway Theatre at the Good Food Show in London, where we worked with many celebrity chefs of the time. It was a very demanding job and I had to put my cake decorating on hold.

However after the takeover of Safeway by Morrison's, I found myself sitting in the office of the Managing Director of Squires Kitchen again. Worried that I wouldn't have a purpose after being made redundant, I was immediately asked to take on some projects for them.

So I was back in the world of cake decorating, regularly contributing to *Cakes & Sugarcraft* magazine, teaching sugarcraft at Squires Kitchen International School and demonstrating at their annual exhibition. With my past experience in food styling, I am acknowledged as the Squires Kitchen Food Stylist and produce many of the projects for *Squires Kitchen Bake School* magazine, as well as teaching bakery classes at the school.

When I look back on my varied career, I know that I have helped many home economists get started in their careers, taught many beginners the art of cake decorating, met many very talented people whom I have learnt from, and have also more recently taught my young granddaughters how to cook. Perhaps the most important personal achievement for me is that I found success through my natural creative skill.

Hidden Design Cakes

ANN SKIPP

Once you have mastered the basics of baking, you can get creative with your cakes and make sponge patterns or hidden designs that are revealed once the cake is cut. Making hidden design cakes can be quite time-consuming, but it is worth it once the surprise is revealed.

There are a number of ways to create a hidden design in a cake, but this recipe involves making two cakes and baking one inside the other. This design would be perfect for Valentine's Day but could easily be adapted for all kinds of occasions by changing the cutter shape.

Brass scales, 20th century

Hidden heart loaf cake

EDIBLES

Red sponge cake

175g (6oz) caster sugar

175g (6oz) soft margarine

3 eggs, beaten

175g (6oz) self-raising flour, sieved

SK Quality Food Colour (QFC) Liquid: Red

Plain sponge cake

225g (8oz) caster sugar

225g (8oz) soft margarine

4 eggs, beaten

225g (8oz) self-raising flour, sieved

Vanilla extract

Decoration

25g (1oz) SK Sugar Florist Paste (SFP): Poinsettia

125g (4½oz) unsalted butter, at room temperature

125g (4½oz) icing sugar

Vanilla extract

EQUIPMENT

1kg (2lb 3¼oz) loaf tin

Small heart cutters, from set of 3: 2cm (¾"), 3cm (1⅛") (TT)

Large Savoy piping bag

Medium Savoy rosette piping nozzle

For essential baking edibles and equipment, see pages 10–11

1 Preheat the oven to 180°C/160°C fan/350°F/gas mark 4.

2 Grease and line the loaf tin (see page 488).

3 Using an electric mixer, cream the sugar and margarine together until light and fluffy.

4 Gradually add the beaten eggs to the mixture, then fold in the sieved flour with a metal spoon.

5 Add enough of the red liquid food colour to turn the mixture red. Make sure the colour is distributed evenly throughout the mixture.

6 Spoon the sponge mixture evenly into the loaf tin.

7 Place in the oven to bake for 25–30 minutes, or until well-risen and firm to the touch. Leave in the tin to cool.

8 When cold, cut the cake into slices that are as thick as the depth of the 3cm (1⅛") cutter. Cut out heart shapes from the slices using the 3cm (1⅛") cutter.

9 Allow the sponge hearts to firm a little whilst you make up the mixture for the plain sponge.

10 Follow steps 1–5 to make up the plain sponge mixture in the same way as the red sponge. However, when you get to step 5 do not add red food colouring, but flavour with vanilla extract instead.

11 Grease and line the loaf tin again. Place enough plain mixture into the tin to cover the base with a layer of mixture that is 3cm (1⅛") deep. Try to keep the sponge an even thickness along the bottom of the tin.

tutor tip

All your ingredients should be at room temperature before you start to make the cake batter.

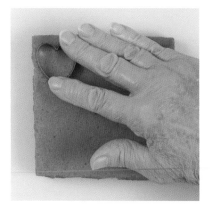

Hidden Design Cakes

55

12 Place the red sponge hearts along the centre of the tin on top of the plain sponge mixture. Pack the hearts tightly together, but avoid pushing them right down into the plain mixture. Leave a 2cm (¾") gap at each end of the tin.

13 Fill the tin with the remainder of the plain cake mixture, carefully covering the row of sponge hearts.

14 Bake for approximately 35–40 minutes, or until the cake is firm to the touch.

15 Once baked, remove from the oven and allow to cool in the tin. Turn out the loaf cake when cool.

16 To decorate, roll out some Poinsettia SFP until very thin and cut out five or six hearts using the 2cm (¾") heart cutter. Allow to dry.

17 To make the buttercream, beat the butter, icing sugar and vanilla extract together in an electric mixer until very light and fluffy.

18 Spread a thin layer of buttercream over the top of the cake, then place the remainder of the buttercream into a large piping bag fitted with a medium-sized rosette nozzle. Pipe rosettes of buttercream across the top of the cake until it is covered. Add a row of SFP hearts along the buttercream.

tutor tip

Crumble up the off-cuts of the coloured sponge cake to make cake pops or leave in larger pieces, soak with sherry and use to make a sherry trifle. The off-cuts can be frozen and used when required.

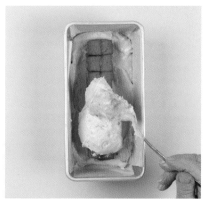

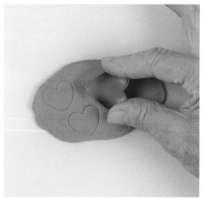

Hidden Design Cakes

note

Please be aware that
only the silicone cups are
ovenproof; the saucers
are for presentation
purposes only.

Hidden heart cupcakes

EDIBLES

Red sponge cake

60g (2oz) caster sugar

60g (2oz) soft margarine

1 egg, beaten

60g (2oz) self-raising flour, sieved

SK Quality Food Colour (QFC) Liquid: Red

Plain sponge cake

115g (4oz) caster sugar

115g (4oz) soft margarine

2 eggs, beaten

115g (4oz) self-raising flour, sieved

Vanilla extract

Decoration

115g (4oz) unsalted butter, at room temperature

115g (4oz) icing sugar

Vanilla extract

15g (½oz) SK Sugar Florist Paste (SFP): Poinsettia

EQUIPMENT

15cm (6") round tin, greased

White silicone cup and saucers, set of 4

Small heart cutters, from set of 3: 2cm (¾"), 3cm (1⅛") (TT)

Large Savoy piping bag

Medium Savoy rosette piping nozzle

Makes 4 cupcakes

For essential baking edibles and equipment, see pages 10–11

1 For the red hearts, make up the sponge mixture following steps 1–5 for the loaf cake (see page 55). Spoon the mixture into a 15cm (6") sponge tin and bake for 12–15 minutes in an oven preheated to 180°C/160°C fan/350°F/gas mark 4.

2 Once cool, cut out four hearts from the red sponge using the 2cm (¾") cutter.

3 Make up the plain sponge mixture following the same method as for the loaf cake (see page 55).

4 Spoon a thin layer of plain sponge mixture into the bottom of each silicone cup and then place a sponge heart on top. To ensure you know which way to cut the cupcake, line the heart up with the handle of the cup. Fill with the remaining plain sponge mixture.

5 Bake for approximately 15 minutes, or until firm to the touch.

6 Decorate each cupcake with a swirl of buttercream (see page 43) and a single SFP heart then present on a saucer.

Hidden Design Cakes

Macaroons

MARK TILLING

Macaroons look fantastic and taste delicious too, making them ideal for everything from a simple afternoon tea to contemporary favours at a wedding. By making a few simple changes to the basic recipe and fillings you can create macaroons with a variety of different flavours, colours and toppings.

TECHNIQUES

- Making macaroons using a packet mix

- Making macaroons using the boiled sugar method

- Adding colour to macaroons

Macaroon packet mix

Macaroons can be tricky to get right if you haven't made them before – even a small mistake can result in a misshaped, cracked or undercooked macaroons. However, using a macaroon mix makes it much easier to create faultless macaroons every time and can also save preparation time.

INGREDIENTS

250g (8¾oz) packet of SK Macaroon Mix

50ml (1¾fl oz) hot, pre-boiled water

SK Dust Food Colour or Liquid Food Colour if required

For essential baking edibles and equipment, see pages 10–11

EQUIPMENT

Plain paper

Pencil

2 baking trays

2.5cm (1") round cutter

Piping bag

1cm (³/₈") round piping nozzle

Parchment paper

Makes 15 macaroons (30 halves)

Tate & Lyle granulated sugar carton, circa 1939

1 Preheat the oven to 130°C/110°C fan/250°F/gas mark ½.

2 Empty the packet into the mixer with the paddle attached. Add dust food colour if required.

3 Pour in the hot, pre-boiled water (with added liquid food colour if required).

4 Turn the machine on and beat for four minutes on a medium speed.

5 Cut the plain paper to the size of the baking trays if needed. Using the cutter and pencil, draw around the cutter several times to make a template, keeping the circles about 1cm (³/₈") apart from each other.

6 Place the plain nozzle into the piping bag and use a spatula to fill the bag with the mix.

7 Place one baking tray on top of the other then place the template and parchment paper on top of this.

8 Using the template as a guide, pipe the mix to the edge of the circles. Remove the template before baking.

9 Bake in a preheated oven for 15–20 minutes. Remove from the tray and leave on a clean work surface to cool. Allow to cool before filling.

There are two ways of adding colour to the packet mix:

1 Colour the hot, pre-boiled water with liquid food colour before adding 50ml (1¾fl oz) of it to the mix.

2 Sprinkle dust food colour to the dry mix before adding the water. Adding dust colour won't change the consistency of the mix so this a good way to achieve a stronger colour.

tutor tips

Do not remove from the parchment paper until the macaroons have cooled down, otherwise they may break apart as you take them off.

If you find the colour is not strong enough when colouring the packet mix using liquid colours, add a little dust colour. This will ensure the mix is not too wet.

Macaroons

Boiled sugar macaroon recipe

INGREDIENTS

150g (5¼oz) icing sugar

150g (5¼oz) ground almonds

150g (5¼oz) caster sugar

50ml (1¾fl oz) water

120g (4¼oz) egg whites

Pinch of salt

SK Dust Food Colour or Liquid Food Colour if required

EQUIPMENT

Food processor

2 baking trays

Silicone baking mat

Piping bag

1cm (³/₈") round piping nozzle

Makes 15 macaroons (30 halves)

For essential baking edibles and equipment, see pages 10–11

1 Preheat the oven to 130°C/110°C fan/250°F/gas mark ½.

2 Mix the icing sugar and ground almonds together, then blitz them in a food processor to make a very fine powder.

3 Sift the almonds and icing sugar through a fine sieve and set to one side.

4 Place the caster sugar and water in a saucepan and gently bring to the boil at 115°C. This is known as 'soft-ball' stage: if you drop a spoonful of the boiled sugar into cold water you should be able to use your fingers to form a soft ball in the water.

5 Meanwhile, place the egg whites and salt in an electric mixer fitted with the whisk attachment and whisk the mixture until it forms soft peaks.

6 Gradually add the boiled sugar to the egg whites until the mixture becomes cool, thick and glossy. At this stage you can add your desired colour and/or flavour.

7 Fold half the almond mix into the egg whites, then fold in the second half until the mixture becomes shiny and has the consistency of a thick paste.

8 Line two baking trays with greaseproof paper or a silicone baking mat. If required, make a template to go underneath the paper (see Macaroon Mix method on page 61).

9 Fit a piping bag with a 1cm (³/₈") round nozzle and spoon the mixture into the piping bag. Pipe dots of mixture in each corner to hold the greaseproof paper in place.

10 Pipe 2cm (¾") circles of the mixture onto the tray, making sure to leave a 2cm (¾") gap between each one. If you have used a template, remove it once all the macaroons are piped. Make sure to tap the tray on the work surface to eliminate any air bubbles and level the mixture.

11 Leave for 15–20 minutes to allow a crust to form, or until the tops of the macaroons are no longer sticky.

12 Bake in the oven for 25–30 minutes or until the tops of the macaroons are firm to the touch and there is no movement at the base of the macaroon.

13 Remove the macaroons from the tray and leave them on the paper or mat to cool before filling.

Macaroons

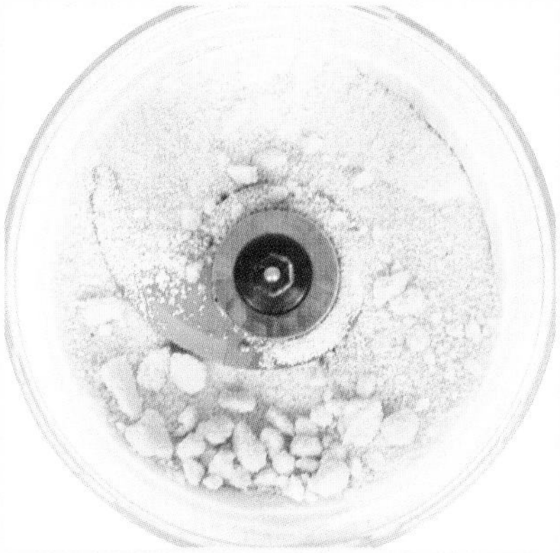
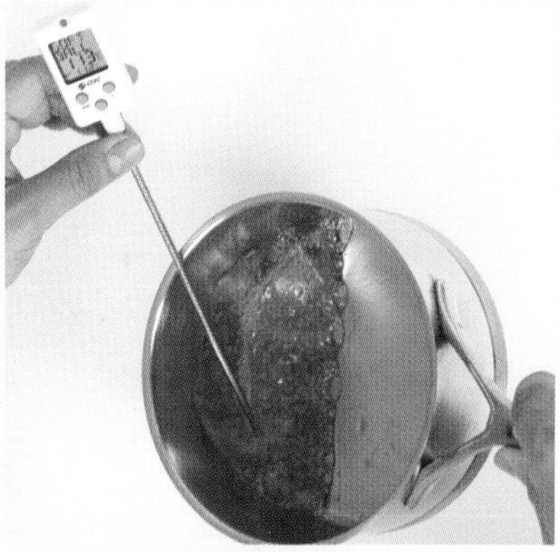
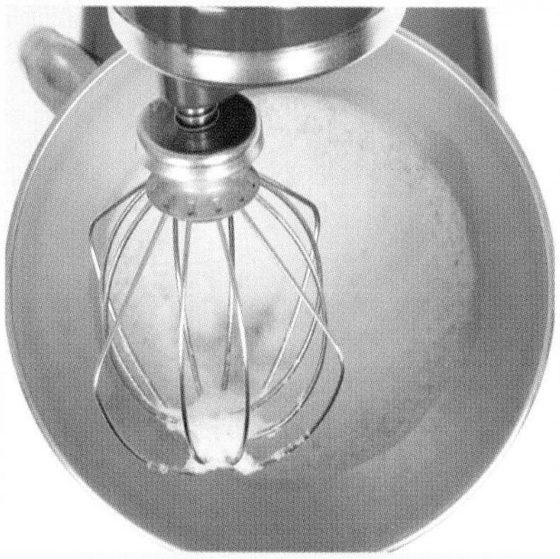
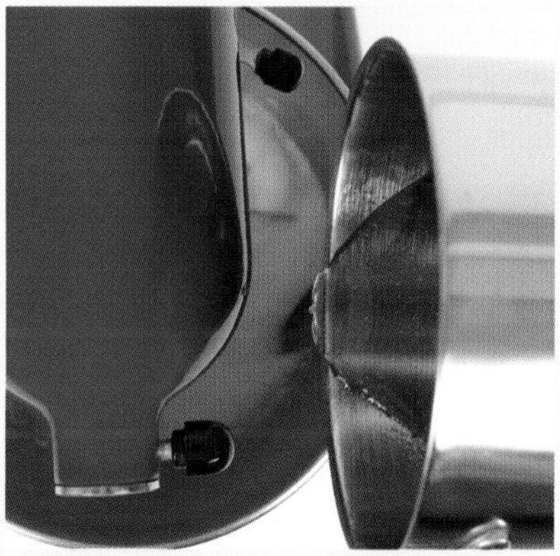
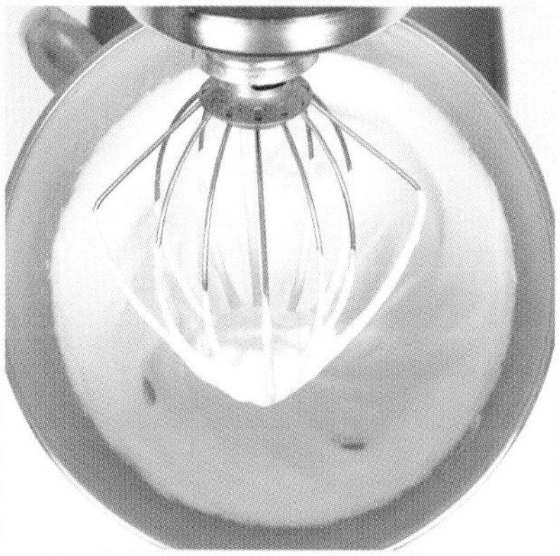
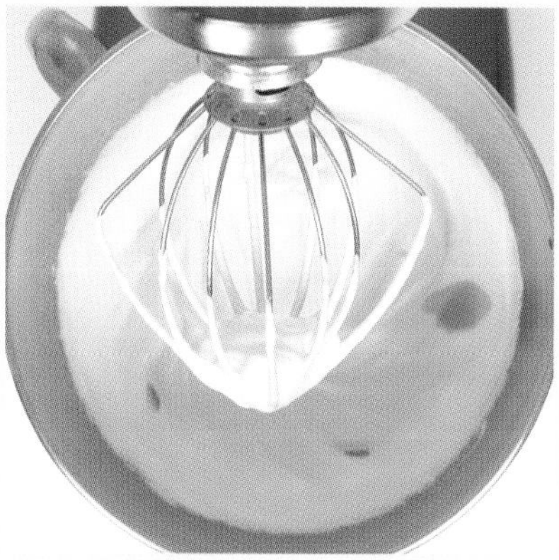
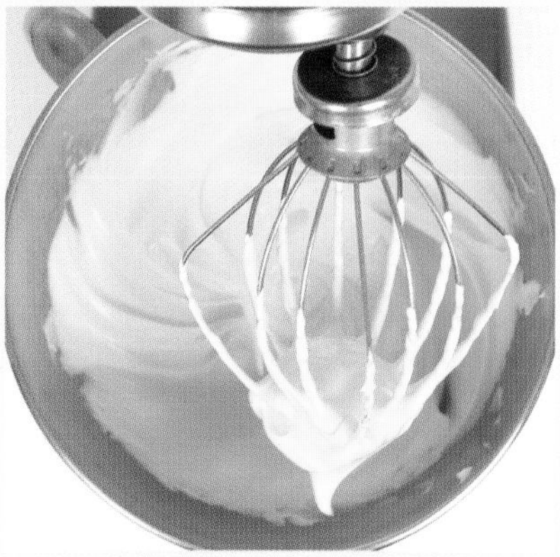
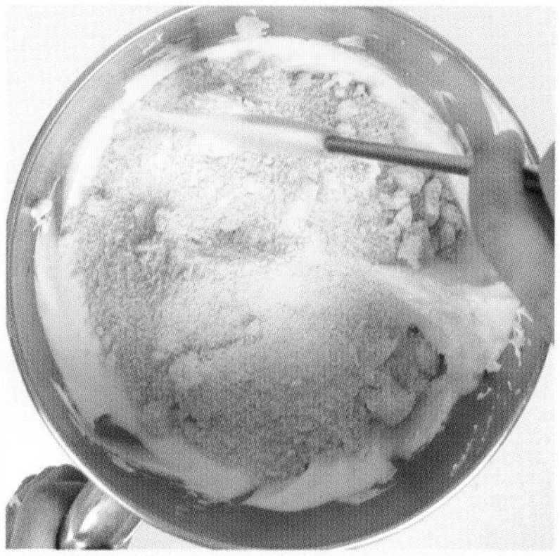
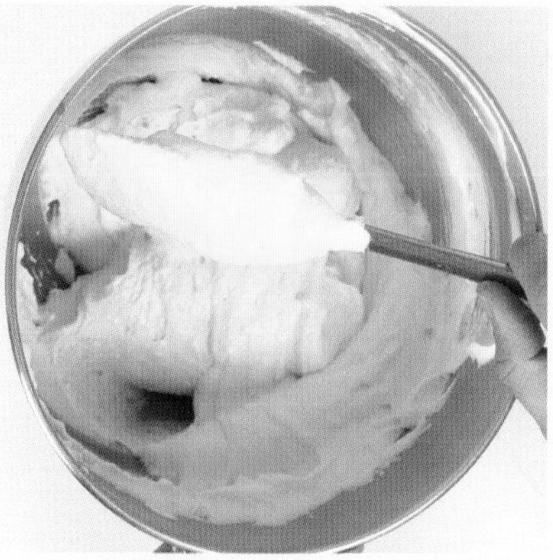
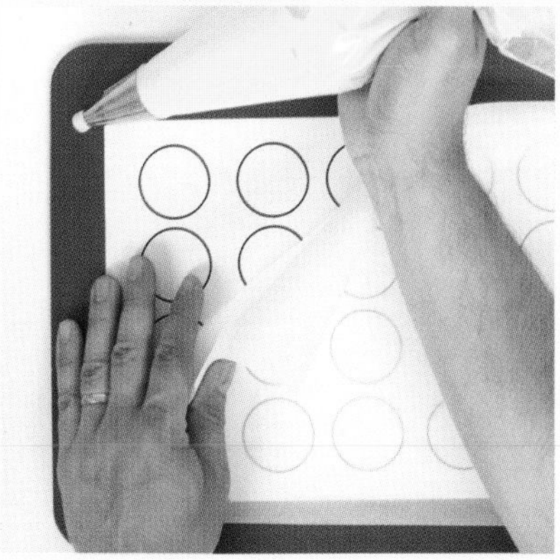
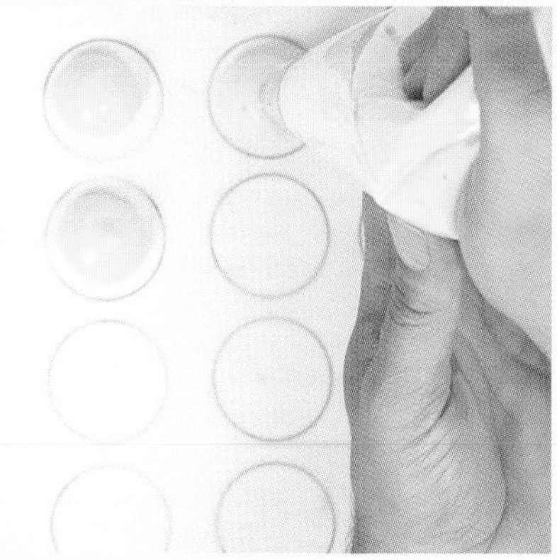
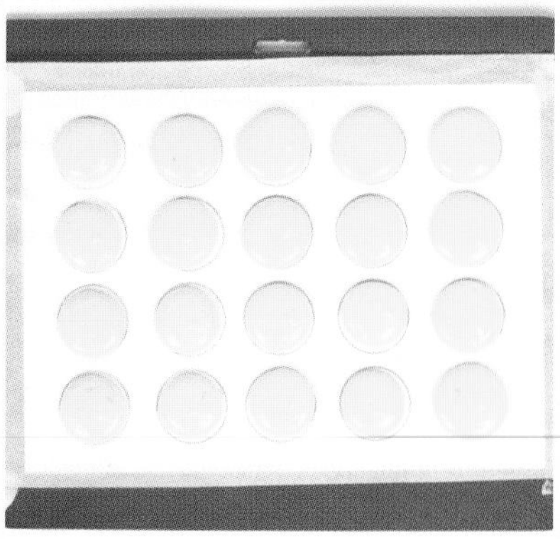

PROJECT

Afternoon Tea Macaroons

Make these delicious lemon curd and cream tea macaroons for an afternoon tea with a twist.

EDIBLES

Macaroon recipe, see pages 60–61

Lemon curd macaroons

SK Lemon Oil

SK Professional Liquid Food Colour: Daffodil (yellow)

Lemon-flavoured buttercream, see page 26

Lemon curd, see page 28

Cream tea macaroons

SK Professional Liquid Food Colour: Teddy Bear Brown

Vanilla buttercream, see page 26

Strawberry jam, see page 29

Icing sugar

EQUIPMENT

Food processor

2 baking trays

Silicone baking mat or greaseproof paper

Piping bag

1cm (³/₈") round piping nozzle

For essential baking edibles and equipment, see pages 10–11

Lemon curd macaroons

1 Make up the macaroon mix following the recipe on pages 60–61, and add a few drops of lemon oil and a little Daffodil (yellow) liquid food colour to the mix as directed in the recipe. Bake the macaroons and leave to cool.

2 To fill the macaroons, pipe a ring of lemon-flavoured buttercream around the outer edge of the bottom half, then fill the hole in the centre with lemon curd. Place the second half on top to finish.

Cream tea macaroons

1 Make up the macaroon mix following the recipe on page 60, and add a couple of drops of Teddy Bear Brown food colour to the mix as directed in the recipe. The macaroons should be an off-white colour. Bake the macaroons and leave to cool.

2 Using a hot teaspoon, scoop a small amount of vanilla buttercream and place it to one side of the bottom half of the macaroon. Pipe a little strawberry jam next to the buttercream and place the other half of the macaroon on top at a slight angle. Dust with icing sugar to finish.

Wooden crate from Tate & Lyle Limited, London, circa 1921–1939

Petits Fours

ANN SKIPP

Petits fours — meaning literally 'small ovens' in French — are very small, sweet cakes that are beautifully decorated with fancy icing or marzipan. These bite-sized sweets are often served at dinner parties or afternoon teas and can be made from sponge, marzipan or chocolate.

TECHNIQUES

- Making fondant fancies
- Making marzipan balls
- Making mini cupcakes
- Making hazelnut and orange marzipan bites

Sulphur marzipan mould, circa 1920s

Fondant fancies

INGREDIENTS

225g (8oz) margarine, soft

225g (8oz) golden caster sugar

4 eggs, beaten

A few drops of SK Vanilla Bean Extract

225g (8oz) self-raising flour, sifted

60g (2oz) icing sugar, sifted

60g (2oz) butter, soft

175g (6oz) SK Marzipan

500g (1lb 1¾oz) SK Fondant Icing Mix

SK Liquid Food Colours (optional)

SK Instant Mix Royal Icing (optional)

EQUIPMENT

Shallow rectangular baking tin approx. 20.5cm x 15cm (8" x 6"), e.g. a Battenberg tin

Chocolate dipping fork

Makes 20 fancies

For essential baking edibles and equipment, see pages 10–11

1 Preheat the oven to 180°C/160°C fan/350°F/gas mark 4. Grease and flour the baking tin, see page 48.

2 Cream the margarine and caster sugar together until light and fluffy.

3 Gradually add the beaten eggs and vanilla extract, beating well between each addition.

4 Fold in the sifted flour with a metal spoon.

5 Place the mixture into the tin and smooth it over with a spoon. Bake for 15–20 minutes, or until the cake is firm to the touch and light golden in colour.

6 Remove the cake from the oven. Leave in the tin for a few minutes, then turn out and place on a wire rack to cool. If the cake has risen above the top of the tin, trim the top with a serrated knife.

7 Beat the butter, vanilla and icing sugar together until light and creamy.

8 Cut the cake lengthways into four strips. Spread the buttercream over the top of the sponges with a palette knife.

9 Roll out the marzipan thinly and place one strip of cake buttercream-side down onto the marzipan. Trim the marzipan to size with a sharp knife.

10 Spread buttercream over the sides of the cake, then place in the refrigerator until firm.

11 Cut the length of sponge into squares, then spread buttercream over the uncovered sides of each piece of cake. Return to the refrigerator until the buttercream is firm.

12 Mix the fondant icing according to the packet instructions, place in a small bowl and colour with liquid food colour if desired.

13 Place each square onto a dipping fork, hold the cake over the bowl and spoon the fondant over the cake until it is covered. Leave to set on a wire rack: the icing should set in approximately 5 minutes.

14 When set, decorate with piped royal icing or small sugar flowers.

Brass funnel for chocolate and fondant work, 20th century

Petits Fours

Chocolate marzipan balls

INGREDIENTS

250g (8¾oz) SK Chocolate Marzipan Mix

300g (10½oz) SK Belgian Couverture Chocolate: Dark

60g (2oz) SK Modelling Cocoform: Dark

SK Designer Metallic Lustre Dust Food Colour: Classic Gold

EQUIPMENT

Chocolate dipping fork

SK Great Impressions Rose Mould

SK Paintbrush: no. 10 (dusting brush)

Makes 8–10 chocolate balls

For essential baking edibles and equipment, see pages 10–11

tutor tip

Try different marzipan fillings, such as Almond and Apricot or Cinnamon and Apple Marzipan Mix.

1 Make up the chocolate marzipan according to the packet instructions. Use your hands to form the marzipan into balls that are approximately the size of a walnut.

2 Place the marzipan balls in the refrigerator to firm.

3 Temper the couverture chocolate (see pages 104–106).

4 Dip the marzipan balls into the melted chocolate using a dipping fork and hold over the bowl until the chocolate has stopped dripping.

5 Place on a non-stick liner or baking parchment and allow to set.

6 Press a small ball of Cocoform into the centre of the rose mould, remove and place onto the top of each chocolate.

7 Allow to firm, then dust the with Classic Gold lustre dust to finish.

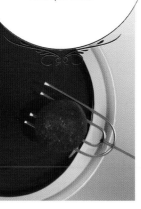
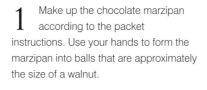
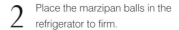

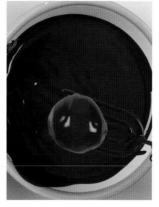

Petits Fours

69

Hazelnut and orange marzipan bites

INGREDIENTS

250g (8¾oz) SK Hazelnut and Orange
Paste Mix

4mm (¼") thick layer of sponge, flavoured
with grated orange rind, see page 15

60g (2oz) buttercream, see page 26

Orange liqueur, e.g. Cointreau (optional)

300g (10½oz) SK Belgian Chocolate:
White

SK Gold Leaf

EQUIPMENT

3cm (1⅛") Silicone Half-Sphere Mould
(Silikomart)

3cm (1⅛") round cutter

Chocolate dipping fork

Tweezers

Makes 24 marzipan bites

*For essential baking
edibles and equipment,
see pages 10–11*

1 Make up the hazelnut and orange marzipan according to the packet instructions.

2 Fill the individual half-sphere moulds with the marzipan: the marzipan should be level with the top of the mould.

3 Leave the marzipan to firm up, then pop the half-spheres out of the silicone mould.

4 Cut out 24 circles from the sponge layer using a 3cm (1⅛") round cutter.

5 Mix a teaspoon of orange liqueur into the buttercream, if desired.

6 Use the buttercream to stick a circle of sponge to the base of each marzipan hemisphere.

7 Temper the white chocolate (see pages 104–106). Place the chocolate in a bowl and use a dipping fork to enrobe the marzipan bites with the chocolate. Hold the marzipan bites over the bowl until they stop dripping.

8 Place on a non-stick liner or baking parchment and leave to set, then use a pair of tweezers to decorate each bite with a small piece of gold leaf.

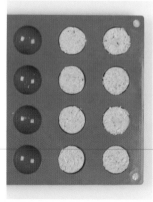

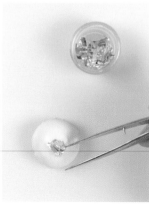

Mini cupcakes

These delightful little cupcakes are baked in mini cupcake cases using half the recipe on page 15. Divide the mixture into approximately 20 mini cases and reduce the baking time to approximately 10 minutes. Decorate with SK Fondant Icing Mix and small moulded sugar roses (see page 48).

Petits Fours

71

Croquembouche

MAKIKO SEARLE

The word 'croquembouche' derives from French, meaning 'crunch in the mouth'. Traditionally decorated with spun sugar, croquembouches have been popular in Italy and France for many years and are now a contemporary choice at weddings in the UK and other countries. The delicate rice paper flowers and silver leaf give this design a modern, opulent feel.

TECHNIQUES

- Making a croquembouche tower
- Making rice paper peonies

EDIBLES

Approximately 150 choux buns, see recipe on page 74

Crème pâtissière filling, see recipe on page 76

2kg (4lb 6½oz) SK Belgian Chocolate: White

SK Silver Leaf

SK Silver Ball Dragées

Approximately 50–60 A4 sheets of rice paper

SK Quality Food Colour (QFC) Dusts: Pink, Yellow

25.5cm (10") round sponge cake base, see page 14 (or dummy cake)

EQUIPMENT

Plastic piping bags, large

Plain piping nozzles: 2mm–3mm (1/8"), 1cm (3/8")

18cm (7") diameter x 40cm (16") height croquembouche cone mould

25.5cm (10") round cake drum (board)

Cake dowels

Soft, food-grade sponge

Chocolate cooler spray (optional)

Peony templates, see page 502

For essential baking edibles and equipment, see pages 10–11

Victorian sugar spoons for sifting and dusting

Choux buns

INGREDIENTS

450ml (16fl oz) water

180g (6¼oz) butter, cut into small pieces

Pinch of sugar

Pinch of salt

270g (9½oz) strong white flour, sifted

7–8 eggs, plus 1 egg wash

Makes 30 mini choux buns

For essential baking edibles and equipment, see pages 10–11

1 Bring the water, butter and pinch of sugar and salt to boil in a medium saucepan. Make sure the butter has melted completely.

2 Take the pan off the stove, add the strong flour and stir well with a spatula. If you are making more than one quantity of the recipe you will find it easier to use a wooden spatula to stir the mixture.

3 Put the pan back on the stove on a gentle heat and beat for approximately one minute until the mix is formed. (This will take longer if you are making more than one quantity.)

4 Put the mixture into a bowl. If you are using a mixer, beat slowly with a paddle attachment. Crack seven eggs into a small bowl and add them slowly. If you are mixing by hand, beat the eggs one-by-one into the mixture.

5 Crack the last egg into a bowl and whisk it roughly. Add half of it into the mixture and beat it slowly. Scoop up some of the mixture with a spatula and tilt it so that it drops back into the mixture: it is ready if it has a smooth, glossy texture which settles back into the mixture slowly (approximately 10 seconds). If it falls off the spatula too quickly it is still too firm, so add the rest of egg little by little until you get the right consistency.

6 Draw a series of 3cm (1⅛") diameter circles on a piece of paper, spacing them a few centimetres apart. Place onto a baking tray and secure a sheet of baking paper over the top using dots of the mixture in the corners.

7 Put the mixture in a plastic piping bag fitted with a 1cm (⅜") plain piping nozzle. Squeeze the bag and pipe 3cm (1⅛") diameter circles onto the baking paper, keeping them as even as possible. Remove the template before baking.

8 Brush egg yolk over the circles with a pastry brush then press the top with a fork to make pretty, round choux buns.

9 Bake the buns at 200°C/180°C fan/400°F/gas mark 6 for 10–15 minutes first. When the choux pastry is nicely puffed up, turn down the oven to 180°C/160°C fan/350°F/gas mark 4 and carry on baking for a further 5–10 minutes. When the choux buns are golden brown, turn down the temperature to 150°C/130°C fan/300°F/gas mark 2 and bake for another 5–10 minutes to dry them out. Do not open the door at any stage during baking.

10 Take out one choux bun at this stage and gently press it. If it is hard, take the buns out of the oven and allow to cool down on a wire rack. If the pastry is still soft, leave them in the oven at the lower temperature to dry out for a few more minutes before checking again.

Croquembouche

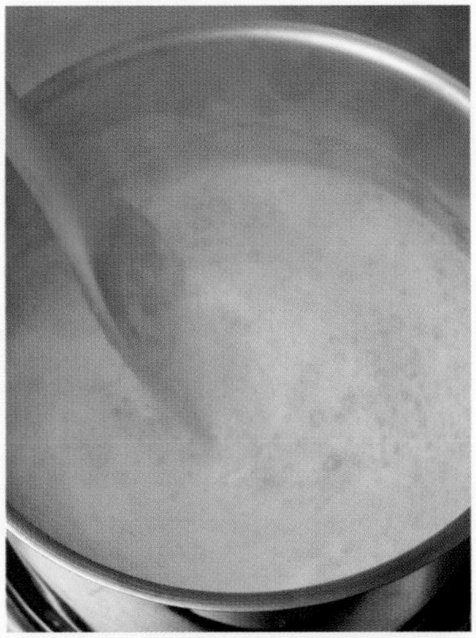

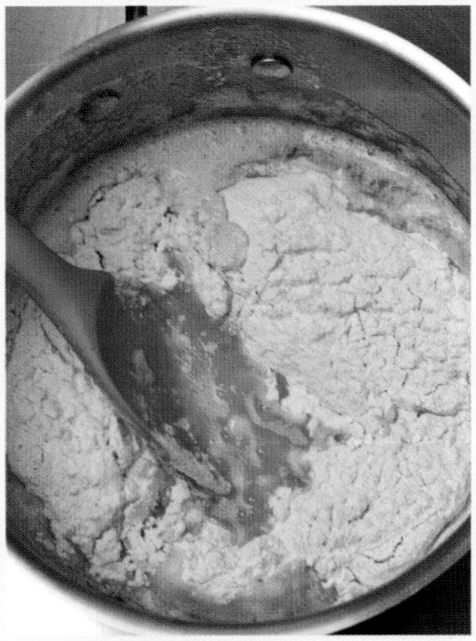

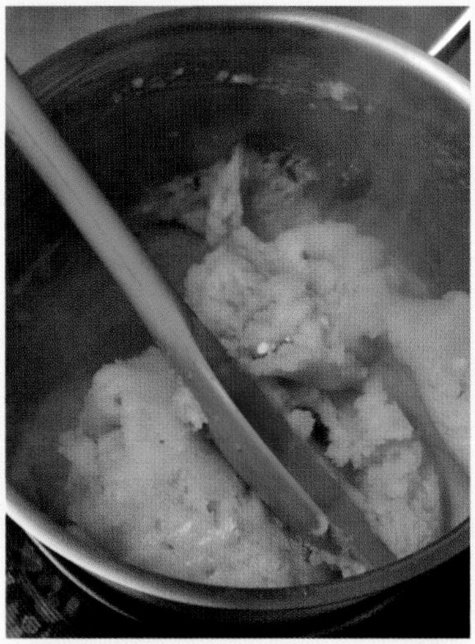

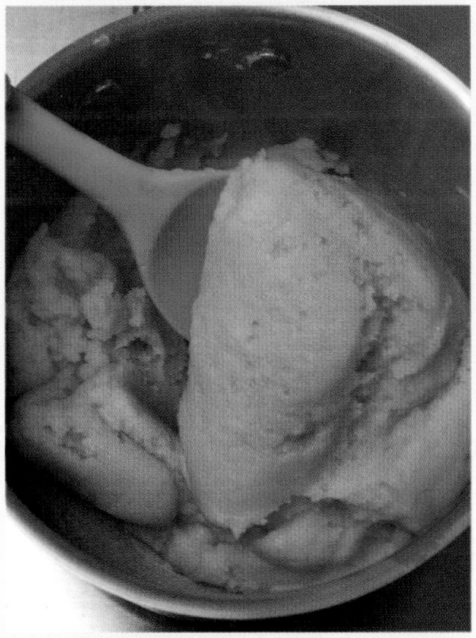

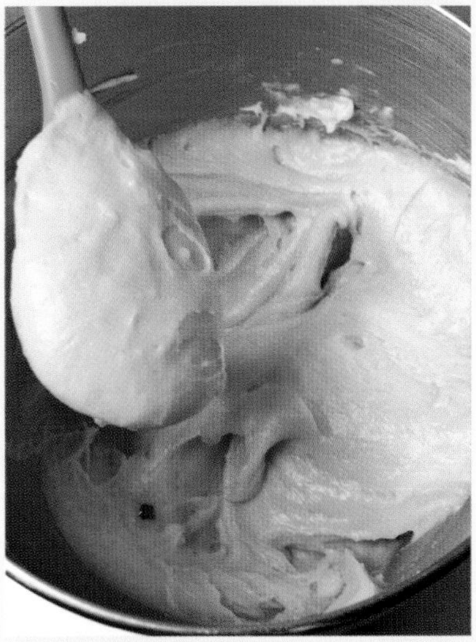

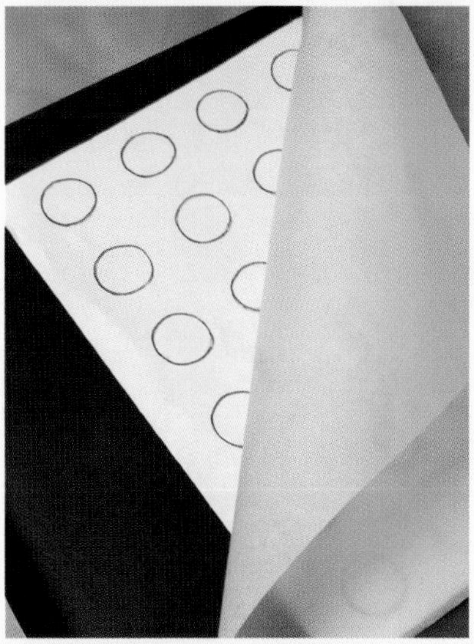

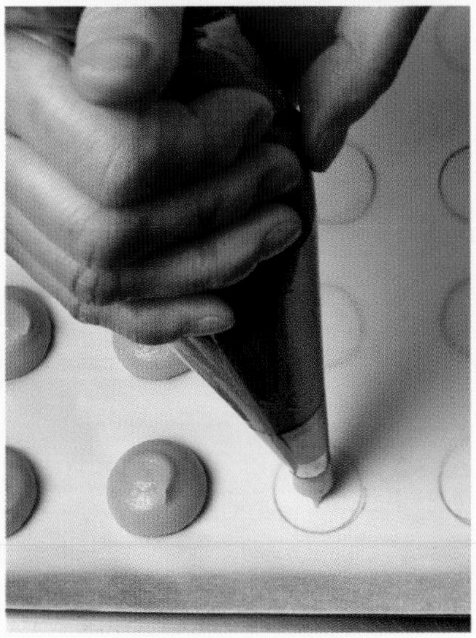

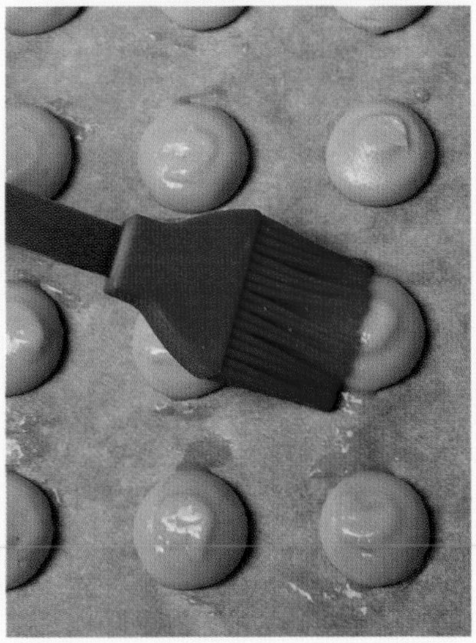

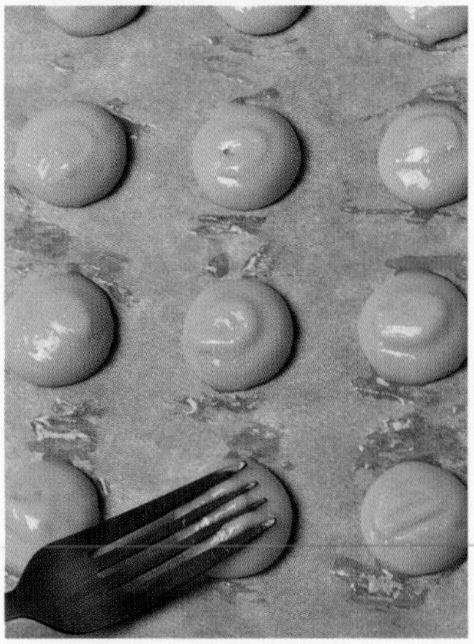

Basic crème pâtissière (pastry cream)

The basic pastry cream recipe can be adapted easily to make different flavours. Simply add your favourite liqueur or fruit purée, or follow one of the variations given below.

INGREDIENTS

80g (2¾oz) egg yolks

125g (4½oz) caster sugar

20g (¾oz) plain flour

20g (¾oz) cornflour

500ml (17½fl oz) milk

30g (1oz) butter

Extra whipped cream (optional)

Makes enough to fill 30 mini choux buns

For essential baking edibles and equipment, see pages 10–11

1 Whisk the egg yolks and caster sugar together in a large mixing bowl until they turn pale in colour. Whisk in the plain flour and cornflour and set aside.

2 Pour the milk into a large saucepan, bring to the boil gently then remove the pan from the heat.

3 Slowly pour half of the hot milk onto the egg and sugar mixture, whisking constantly, then add the remaining milk to the pan. It is important to whisk the mixture as soon as you pour the milk in to prevent the eggs from scrambling.

4 Bring the mixture back to the boil, whisking continuously. It will start thickening but keep whisking until smooth.

5 Remove the pan from the heat then add the butter and whisk into the mixture.

6 Pour the pastry cream into a clean, shallow container and place a piece of cling film over the top to prevent a skin forming. When cool, refrigerate until needed. Use it within two days.

7 For a lighter pastry cream, add approximately one part whipped cream to two parts cold pastry cream (softened) and mix.

Flavour variations

Vanilla

Add the seeds from one vanilla pod to the milk in step 2.

Chocolate

Melt 200g (7oz) of dark chocolate (50%–60% cocoa solids) and add it to the pastry cream at the end. If the mixture is too firm to pipe, soften it by adding some single cream.

Caramel

Make a caramel by boiling 180g (6¼oz) of caster sugar in a pan. Pour 160ml (5½fl oz) of boiled single cream into the pan, mix then allow to cool. Chill in the fridge then mix the caramel into the basic pastry cream.

Coffee

Add 30ml (2tbsp) of coffee extract to the finished basic pastry cream.

Croquembouche

Making a croquembouche tower

Traditionally caramel is used to stick choux buns together to create a croquembouche, but here I have used melted white chocolate. This means that you can keep the tower in the fridge until serving, which will also keep the crème pâtissière fresh.

1 Temper some white chocolate (see pages 104–106). Pour a small amount into the centre of a round cake drum and place the cone on top. Spread the entire outer surface of the cone with melted chocolate.

2 Hold the back of each choux bun and dip the front into the melted chocolate. Leave the chocolate to set. You can do this in advance to save time on the day.

3 Make a small hole in each choux bun with a skewer or similar. Fit a large plastic piping bag with a 2mm–3mm (1/8") plain piping nozzle, half-fill the bag with crème pâtissière and fill all the choux buns through the pre-made hole.

4 Dip the back of each choux bun into a little melted white chocolate and attach the buns to the cone, starting at the bottom and working your way round and up the cone. To speed up the setting process you can use chocolate cooler spray.

5 Dowel the cake (see page 143) then place the croquembouche tower on top of the cake. Attach rice paper peonies around the base cake with royal icing and in any gaps on the choux tower (see page 79). I used approximately 20–25 large flowers and 30–40 small flowers for this project.

6 Brush edible glue or clear alcohol onto some of the choux buns and add the silver leaf using a dry paintbrush.

7 Keep the tower in the fridge until just before serving.

Croquembouche

Making rice paper peonies

1 Copy templates A, B and C onto thick paper and cut them out.

2 Cut three sheets of rice paper into smaller pieces, roughly the same size as each flower template. You will need three flower shapes in each size to make one large peony so you can create two flowers from three sheets of rice paper.

3 Hold three pieces of rice paper together with the template on top and cut out the flower shape. Remove the template and make small, rounded V-shaped cuts between the petals. Gently round off the edges then cut a wavy edge around each petal. If you prefer, you can use zig-zag craft scissors.

4 Colour each flower shape using yellow and pink dust food colours and a large, soft brush.

5 Using a clean pastry brush and cooled, boiled water, lightly moisten the petals to make them slightly sticky. Do not use too much water otherwise the rice paper will disintegrate when you press onto it.

6 Place the flower on a piece of soft sponge and push into the middle of each petal with your thumb or the end of a small rolling pin to cup the petals. Gently lift your thumb/the rolling pin off the paper. You should find that the petals curl a little more when they have dried out.

7 Repeat the same method to shape all the other petals on all the flowers (3 x A, 3 x B and 3 x C) and let them dry on the sponge.

8 Moisten the centre of a large flower (C) and place a second large flower on top at a slightly different angle. Gently make the flower fluffy with your fingers then add the third C flower on top.

9 Repeat with flowers B and A to make a set of flowers in each size.

10 Moisten the centre of flower C and place flower B inside. Moisten the centre again and place flower A inside flower B. Form the shape of the flower using your fingers then let it dry out completely on a piece of dry sponge.

11 To make the smaller flowers, use templates A and B only. You should be able to make two small flowers from one sheet of A4 rice paper.

12 Brush some edible glue around the edge of some of the rice paper flowers. Take a piece of edible silver leaf with a dry paintbrush and place it onto the glue.

13 Stick some silver dragées inside the flowers with edible glue to finish.

Croquembouche

Makiko Searle

I was born in Saitama City in Japan and, as my mother always cared about our health, the food on our table was always homemade and a very important part of family life. Due to my mother's influence, I naturally picked up a skill for cookery. My mother's desserts were mainly Japanese-style desserts, using red beans and sticky rice, so I tried to make European sweets instead from my sister's baking books. I remember that the first cookies I attempted to make were rock hard and my choux buns were squashed as I didn't know anything about the science behind baking.

In the 1980s the Japanese economy was booming, and a lot of information about foreign foods was shared through the media. There were many opportunities to see beautifully presented foods and table decorations in books, and one day I came across a book by Kazuko Horii. Her simple but stylish cookery books gave me a different perspective on how I thought about food. Once I graduated from university and was working in an office, I took evening courses to become a Food Coordinator in Tokyo. These classes made me

realise the importance of practical experience in a kitchen alongside a good knowledge of food.

Once I'd completed the classes, I went on to work and study at the Japanese cookery school, Nezu Club in Tokyo. I learned so many things about Japanese culture such as Ikebana (a Japanese-style of flower arranging), Sadou (the Tea Ceremony) and Shuuji (calligraphy) from my teacher Etsuko Yamada, who is still a great influence for me.

After several years, I changed roles to become a pastry chef in a French pâtisserie in Tokyo, then moved to England to further improve my pastry skills. Most Japanese pastry chefs choose to go to France, but I chose England because I fell in love with the British style of sugarcraft and wedding cake design. I purchased a sugar floristry book by Alan Dunn and contacted the British Sugarcraft Guild to ask for advice on the right place to study. They recommended that I enrol at Brooklands College in Weybridge, Surrey and I was very lucky to learn all kinds of skills from fabulous tutors Chris Jeffcoate, Jane Hatton and Sue Haskell on an

intensive one-year course. The tutors encouraged all the students to enter competitions and I achieved several medals for my work.

After the course I returned to Japan for a few years but came back to the UK to work as a Chef de Partie for my sponsor, the Great Fosters Hotel in Surrey, then moved on to the Mandarin Oriental Hyde Park Hotel. After experiencing the opening of the Mandarin Oriental Hotel in Tokyo, I decided to set up my own cake decorating company called Maki's Cakes, based in Surrey. Since my first book *Cakes to Fall in Love With* (B. Dutton Publishing) was published in 2011, I have been teaching my skills all around the world. I thoroughly enjoy meeting new students, as well as creating individual wedding and special occasion cakes for my clients.

I always feel so lucky and privileged to be one of the tutors at the Squires Kitchen International School. I do not specialise in one particular area, such as royal icing or modelling work, but I love to teach my own unique style of cake design and share my ideas with other cake lovers.

Pâte Décor

MAKIKO SEARLE

The classic French pâtisserie pâte décor technique can be used to make pretty patterned party cakes which don't need any extra decoration. The beauty of this technique is that you can choose your own patterns and colours to suit the occasion.

TECHNIQUES

- Making pâte décor sponges
- Making biscuit Joconde

French sugar carton from the Chalon-sur-Saône
sugar refineries, circa 1894–1944

Basic pâte décor

INGREDIENTS

80g (2¾oz) unsalted butter, softened

80g (2¾oz) icing sugar

60g (2oz) egg white, at room temperature

60g (2oz) soft flour (pastry flour)

SK Liquid Food Colours of your choice

EQUIPMENT

30.5cm (12") square baking tray

7 mixing bowls

7–8 plastic piping bags

Pattern template, see page 503

Textured side scraper

For essential baking edibles and equipment, see pages 10–11

1 Line a 30.5cm (12") square baking tray with a sheet of greaseproof paper.

2 Cream the softened butter and icing sugar together. Add the egg white little by little and finally fold in the flour.

Top tier: flower pattern

3 Divide the mixture equally into six bowls, or as many as required for your chosen pattern. Add some liquid food colour to each bowl to make the colours required for your chosen pattern. The colours used here are yellow, pale pink, dark pink, pale orange, dark orange and red. Spoon a small amount of the yellow mix into another bowl and add a little green food colour. Place each coloured mixture into a plastic piping bag.

4 Place the flower template (or pattern of your choice) under a sheet of greaseproof paper. Snip off the tip from each piping bag and pipe each colour onto the greaseproof paper in turn. Move the template to the other side of the baking tray and repeat. Place the whole tray in the freezer to set for half an hour.

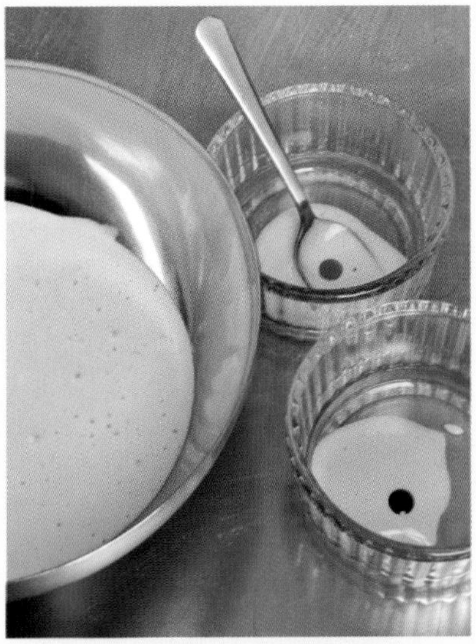

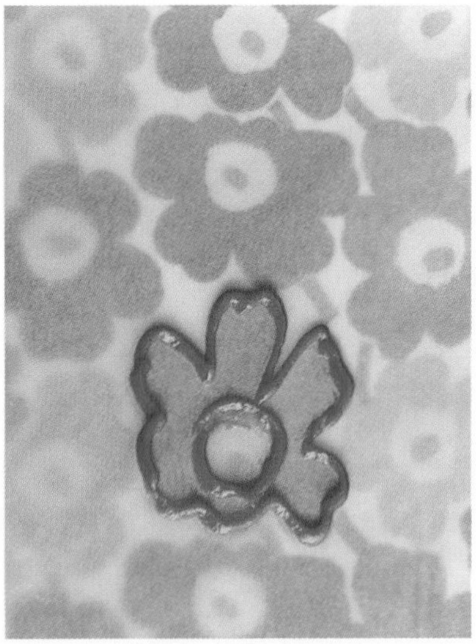

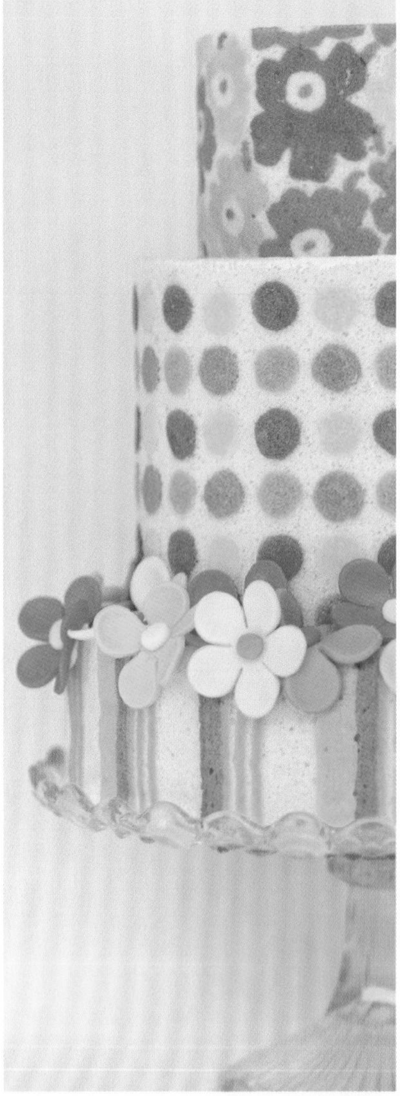

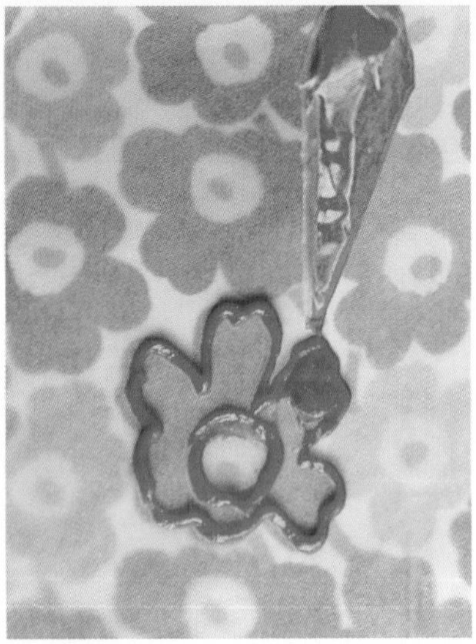

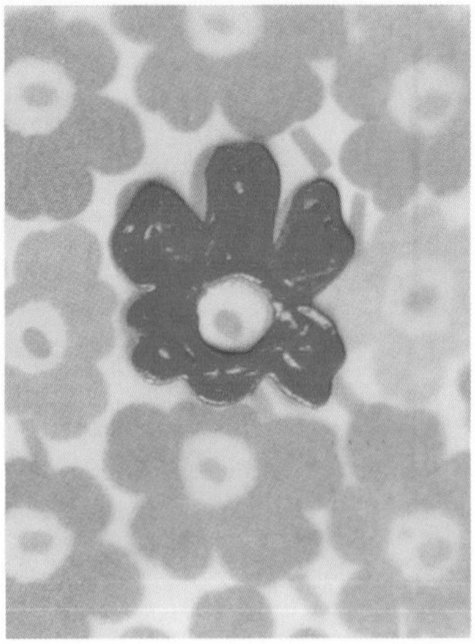

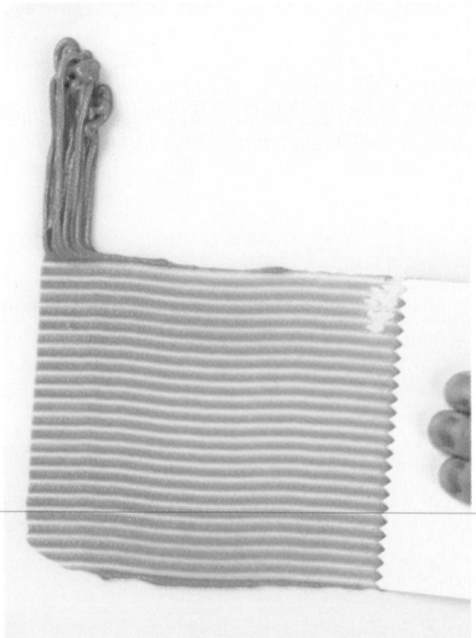

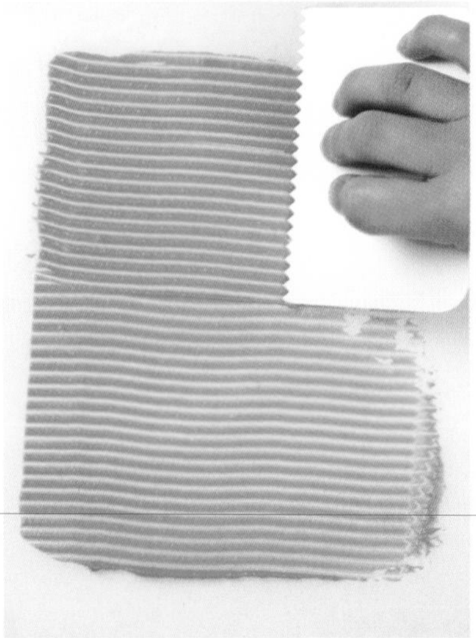

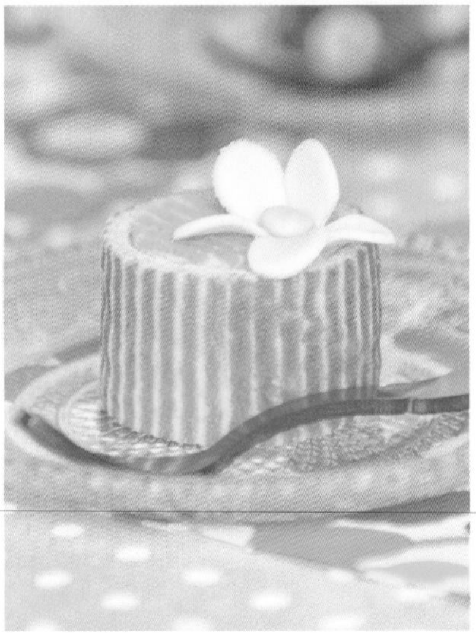

5 Once the pattern has set, remove the baking tray from the freezer and carefully take out the paper template, ready for the biscuit Joconde. Keep the piped pattern in the freezer until the Joconde mix is ready (see right).

Middle tier: polka dots

6 Place the template for the middle tier under a sheet of greaseproof paper and pipe dots with the yellow, pink, red and pale orange pâte décor mix. Move the template to the other side and pipe more dots in the same way. Place the tray in the freezer for half an hour to allow the pattern to set then remove the paper template ready for the biscuit Joconde. Keep the piped pattern in the freezer until the Joconde mix is ready, as before.

Base tier: stripes

7 Check whether you have enough pâte décor at this stage for a third tier; if not, mix up some more colours in the same way as before, in this case yellow, pink and orange. Pipe a thick, straight, horizontal line along one side of the paper. Using the textured side scraper, scrape the mix down the paper to create stripes.

8 Pipe some pink lines randomly alongside the orange lines.

9 Place the tray into the freezer for half an hour to allow the pattern to set before continuing to make the biscuit Joconde recipe. Remove the paper template before proceeding.

Biscuit Joconde

INGREDIENTS

Sponge
2 eggs
65g (2¼oz) icing sugar
65g (2¼oz) ground almonds
15g (½oz) plain flour
15g (½oz) unsalted butter, melted

Meringue
60g (2oz) egg white
15g (½oz) caster sugar

EQUIPMENT

30.5cm (12") square baking tray
Large, cranked palette knife
Hand whisk

Makes 1 x 30.5cm (12") square sponge sheet

For essential baking edibles and equipment, see pages 10–11

1 Preheat the oven to 200°C/180°C fan/400°F/gas mark 6.

2 Whisk the eggs, icing sugar, plain flour and ground almonds together in a mixer with the whisk attachment until the mixture has a fluffy texture.

3 Place the egg whites in a clean bowl and whisk at high speed until soft peaks are formed.

4 Add ⅓ of the caster sugar and continue to whisk at high speed until stiff peaks form. Add the rest of the sugar little by little.

5 Add ⅓ of the meringue mix into the cake batter and carefully mix it through using a hand whisk, taking care not to destroy the meringue.

6 Add half of the leftover meringue into the mix and fold it through using a spatula. Add the rest and the melted butter and fold it through.

7 Check that the pâte décor pattern has set completely, otherwise the pattern may run into the biscuit Joconde mix. Place one pre-made pâte décor sheet on a baking tray and pour the mix on top. Spread the Joconde mix evenly with a large, cranked palette knife.

8 Bake for 10–12 minutes. As soon as the sponge is baked, remove it from the oven and place a clean sheet of baking paper on top. Turn the tray upside down and carefully peel the greaseproof paper off the sponge. Allow to cool on a wire rack.

Pâte Décor

Retro Summer Wedding Cake

This three-tier cake would be perfect for a summer wedding or other special celebration. The bright colour scheme and bold patterns give it a fun, retro feel and the co-ordinating mini cakes make perfect favours for guests.

EDIBLES

10cm (4") diameter x 8cm (3") height round sponge cake

15cm (6") diameter x 12.5cm (5") height round sponge cake

20.5cm (8") diameter x 8cm (3") height round sponge cake

Pre-made Joconde sponges, see page 85

Buttercream for filling and crumb-coating, plus extra for attaching the flowers, see page 26

200g (7oz) SK Modelling Cocoform: White

SK Professional Paste Food Colours: Nasturtium (peach), Rose, Sunflower

EQUIPMENT

10cm, 15cm and 20.5cm (4", 6" and 8") round cake cards

5-petal blossom plunger cutters: set of 4 (PME)

8 cake dowels

25.5cm (10") round cake stand

For essential baking edibles and equipment, see pages 10–11

1 Layer, fill and crumb-coat the cakes following the instructions on page 92. Reserve the remaining buttercream for later. Place each cake on a cake card of the same size and dowel the lower tiers following the instructions on page 143. Carefully stack the three tiers on a cake stand.

2 Cut the pre-made Joconde sponges to 5mm (¼") higher than each cake. Stick the first sponge sheet in position, working from the front of cake. Stick another piece of Joconde sponge beside the first to cover the cake side and overlap the join. Cut through the join neatly with a knife.

3 Add a tiny amount of Sunflower paste colour to half of the White Cocoform. (If preferred you can use sugar modelling paste or marzipan.) Roll out both colours of paste and cut out several five-petal flowers using either the second smallest or second largest cutter in the set. Place each flower in the palm of your hand and press lightly with your finger to round off the petals. Roll some small balls for the flower centres and place to one side.

4 Using the leftover buttercream (or royal icing if preferred), stick the flowers around the bottom tier. Make the flowers in advance and attach them just before serving as they may lose their shape in the fridge.

Mini Pâte Décor Cakes

The patterned exterior of these mini cakes is made using a third of the pâte décor mixture on page 82 and double the biscuit Joconde recipe on page 85. The base and filling are a delicious combination of a chocolate feuilletine biscuit with chocolate and orange mousse.

EDIBLES

Cakes

Stripy Joconde sponges, see page 85

Sugar syrup

Equal quantities of sugar and water, plus flavouring of your choice (e.g. Grand Marnier liqueur)

Chocolate feuilletine biscuits

50g (1¾oz) SK Petit Crunch (Pailleté Feuilletine)

40g (1½oz) milk chocolate

12g (½oz) almond praline or peanut-flavoured buttercream

Dark chocolate mousse

50g (1¾oz) SK Belgian Chocolate Couverture: Dark

150ml (5¼fl oz) double cream (containing 48% milk fat)

Orange mousse

200ml (7fl oz) orange juice

2 egg yolks

40g (1½oz) caster sugar

1 gelatine leaf, soaked in cold water, see page 479

10ml (2tsp) Grand Marnier liqueur

140ml (5fl oz) double cream

EQUIPMENT

Cakes

5.5cm diameter x 3cm height (2⅛" x 1⅛") mousse rings

Chocolate feuilletine biscuits

4cm (1½") round cutter

Orange mousse

Chinoise (fine-mesh, cone-shaped strainer)

Makes 18 mini cakes

For essential baking edibles and equipment, see pages 10–11

Sponge mini cakes

1 Cut several strips of greaseproof paper measuring 19cm x 3.5cm (7½" x 1⅜"). Line the inside of each ring with a strip of paper inside.

2 Prepare the pâte décor mixture for a stripy pattern using the same method as the bottom tier of the main cake: you will only need a third of the quantity given on page 82 to make 18 mini cakes. Pipe a thick, straight, horizontal line along one side of the paper. Using the textured side scraper, scrape the mix down the paper to create stripes. Repeat to make a second sheet then place the trays into the freezer for half an hour to allow the pattern to set.

3 Make a double quantity of the biscuit Joconde recipe, spread it over the stripy pattern once it has set completely and bake according to the instructions on page 85. Allow to cool.

4 Cut a prepared Joconde sponge into 3.5cm x 17cm (1⅜" x 6¾") strips. Insert the sponges into the rings, overlap the join then cut through this with a knife. Using a 4cm (1½") round cutter, make 18 circles from the trimmings and place to one side.

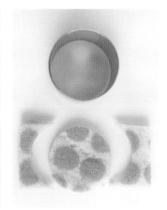

5 To make the sugar syrup, place equal quantities of sugar and water into a pan and bring to the boil. Allow to cool slightly before adding a small amount of your chosen flavouring, if required, such as liqueur or essence. Brush the flavoured sugar syrup inside the sponge ring. If you have any left-over unflavoured sugar syrup, place it in a clean, airtight container and store in the fridge for up to a month.

Biscuit base

6 To make the feuilletine biscuit base for each mini cake, melt the milk chocolate and praline together. Fold in the Petit Crunch.

7 Pour the mixture onto a sheet of greaseproof paper, roll it out thinly using a rolling pin then leave to set in the fridge.

8 Once the mixture is firm, cut out 18 circles using a 4cm (1½") round cutter. If you don't have enough space to cut out all the circles, melt the remaining mix and re-use it in the same way as before.

9 Place the chocolate feuilletine biscuit discs in the bottom of the moulds to line the base of each mini cake.

Mini Pâte Décor Cakes

Chocolate mousse filling

10 To make the chocolate mousse, bring 40ml (1½fl oz) of double cream to the boil, pour it onto the chocolate and stir to make a ganache. Allow it to cool to around 40°C (105°F).

11 Whip 110ml (3¾fl oz) of double cream to form soft peaks. Pour a third of the whipped cream into the ganache and whisk it thoroughly. Fold in the rest of the cream with a spatula.

12 Place the chocolate mousse into a large piping bag, cut off the end and half-fill each mini cake with the mousse. Allow the mousse to set in the fridge for an hour. If you are short of time, place in the freezer for 10 minutes.

Orange mousse filling

13 Heat 200ml (7fl oz) of orange juice in a pan and reduce it by half to 100ml (3½fl oz).

14 Whisk the caster sugar and egg yolks together in a bowl until the mixture is pale yellow and forms ribbons on the surface.

15 Pour the reduced orange juice onto the egg yolk mix, whisking constantly to prevent the eggs from curdling. Pour the mix back into the pan and cook slowly over a low heat, stirring constantly until the mixture thickens enough to coat the back of a spatula (it should be smooth). If you have a thermometer, the temperature should be approximately 80°C (175°F). Add a soaked gelatine leaf and mix well.

16 Pass the mixture through a chinoise strainer and pour into a clean bowl. Place the bowl over a dish of iced water to cool it down and whisk to incorporate cool air. Add the Grand Marnier liqueur and mix.

17 Whip the double cream until semi-soft. Whisk a third of the cream into the cold orange anglaise sauce. Add a third of the remaining cream and mix with a spatula. Add the rest and mix.

18 Spoon the mousse into a large plastic piping bag and pipe it into the mini cakes to 2mm–3mm (⅛") below the top.

To finish

19 Place the remaining Joconde sponge disc on top then decorate with flowers made from Modelling Cocoform (see page 87).

tutor tip

To make mini tiered wedding cakes, follow the method as above with a larger and a smaller size ring and stack them before serving.

Preparing a Cake for Decorating

MARK TILLING

It is important to prepare your cake well before covering to ensure a smooth, professional finish, whether you are coating the cake with royal icing or sugarpaste.

TECHNIQUES

- Layering and filling sponge cakes
- Crumb-coating sponge cakes
- Marzipanning round and square cakes for royal icing
- Marzipanning round and square cakes for sugarpaste

EDIBLES

25.5cm x 7.5cm (10" x 3") square sponge cake, see recipe on page 15

300g (10½oz) jam, curd or filling of your choice, see recipes on pages 24–30

500g (1lb 1¾oz) buttercream, see recipe on page 26

Sugar syrup, see page 40

Apricot glaze, see page 24

SK Marzipan (see table below for correct amounts)

EQUIPMENT

25.5cm and 30.5cm (10" and 12") square cake drums

Turntable

Pastry brush

Cake card

Ruler

Makes a 25.5cm (10") square cake

For essential baking edibles and equipment, see pages 10–11

QUANTITIES OF BUTTERCREAM AND MARZIPAN, SUGARPASTE OR ROYAL ICING REQUIRED FOR COVERING A CAKE

CAKE SIZE		Buttercream for round/ square sponge cakes		Jam for round/square sponge cakes		Marzipan/icing for round		Marzipan/icing for square	
12.5cm	(5")	150g	5¼oz	40g	1½oz	340g	12oz	440g	15½oz
15cm	(6")	300g	10½oz	80g	2¾oz	480g	1lb 1oz	625g	1lb 6oz
17.5cm	(7")	450g	1lb	120g	4¼oz	650g	1lb 7oz	850g	1lb 14oz
20.5cm	(8")	600g	1lb 5¼oz	160g	5½oz	880g	1lb 15oz	1.14kg	2lb 8oz
23cm	(9")	750g	1lb 10½oz	200g	7oz	1.14kg	2lb 8oz	1.42kg	3lb 2oz
25.5cm	(10")	900g	2lb	240g	8½oz	1.42kg	3lb 2oz	1.87kg	4lb 2oz
28cm	(11")	1.05kg	2lb 5oz	280g	9¾oz	1.75kg	3lb 14oz	2.44kg	5lb 6oz
30.5cm	(12")	1.2kg	2lb 10¼oz	320g	11¼oz	2.1kg	4lb 10oz	2.72kg	6lb

Layering, filling and crumb-coating a sponge cake

I have used a square sponge cake here, but you can use the same preparation technique for round cakes and square cakes of different sizes.

tutor tip

When I am preparing sponge cakes for a wedding, I always bake the cakes so they are approximately 2.5cm (1") bigger in size than I need so all the darker crusts can be removed before covering.

1 Place the cake on a 30.5cm (12") cake board, then place the cake and board on a turntable. Use a large, serrated knife to make a shallow cut in the top edge of the cake. Turn the cake on the turntable and continue to trim a thin layer from around the top of the cake. When you return to the start position, continue to cut around the cake once more, but this time position the knife a little closer to the centre. Keep doing this until you have removed both the crusts from the top and bottom of the cake.

For a round cake, trim off the top and bottom crusts in the same way but place a cake board on top of the cake and trim off the sides using the board as a guide.

2 Position the 25.5cm (10") square cake drum centrally on top of the cake. Using the drum as a guide, trim down all four sides of the cake to remove the crusts. Lift off the drum and you should be left with a sponge cake that is 25.5cm (10") square and 7.5cm (3") deep.

3 Make three evenly-spaced horizontal cuts down the side of the cake to divide it into four layers. Following the marks, use a carving knife to cut the cake into four layers in the same way as you removed the crusts. Alternatively, you may find it easier to use a cake leveller and adjust the wire to slice the cake into four even layers.

4 Use a palette knife to spread a little buttercream over the 25.5cm (10") cake drum and place the first layer of the sponge centrally on the drum. Use a pastry brush to spread a little sugar syrup over the cake, but be careful not to use too much or the sponge will go soggy.

5 Spread a thin layer of the filling of your choice (i.e. jam, curd or ganache) over the cake with a palette knife, using only a little more than you would spread on a slice of toast. Smooth a layer of buttercream over the top of the filling so the buttercream is approximately 2mm–3mm (1/8") thick. Place a second layer of sponge on top of the filling and repeat in the same way for the next two layers, and finish by placing the final layer on top.

6 Once the cake is filled, use a palette knife to neaten the outside of the cake and remove any excess jam or buttercream seeping out from between the layers. Leave the filled cake in the fridge to set for approximately 20–30 minutes before crumb-coating it.

7 Remove the cake from the fridge and spread a thin layer of buttercream over the top and sides of the cake with a palette knife. Crumb-coating helps stick the cake crumbs to the cake so they do not affect the cake covering. Use the drum as a guide when you are applying the buttercream so the cake does not become larger than the drum. If you desire, you can use two coats of buttercream but make sure that you refrigerate the cake between coats.

To find out how to cover a sponge cake with sugarpaste, turn to pages 139–140.

tutor tip

When slicing the cake into layers, keep your spare hand on the top of the cake to protect it in case the knife slips.

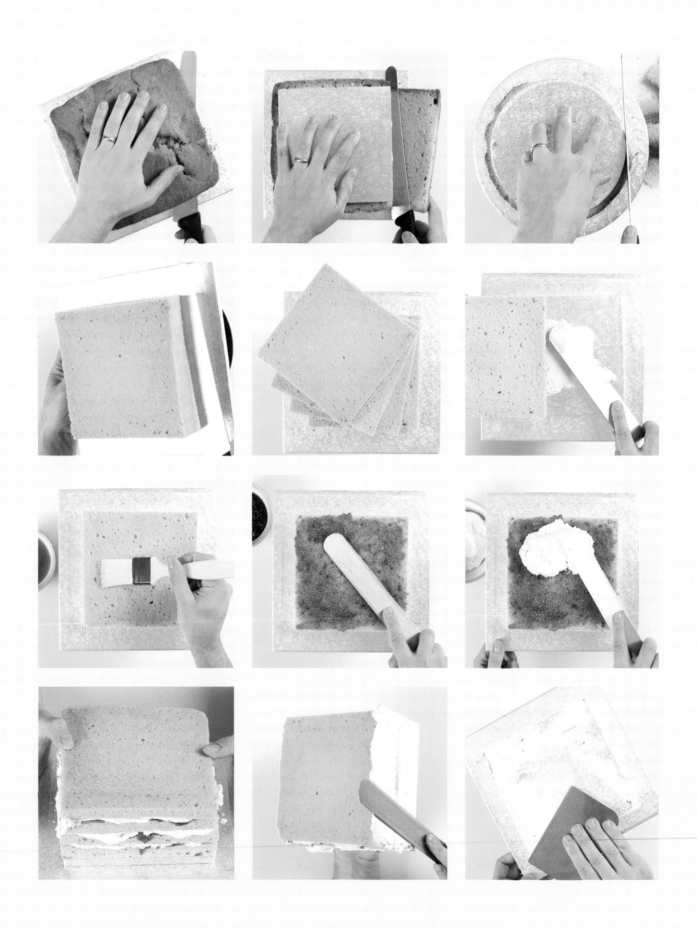

Preparing a fruit cake for royal icing

Fruit cakes are generally used when a royal iced coating is desired as they are denser than sponge cakes and will keep their shape once covered in the firm icing.

1 Make some warm apricot glaze following the instructions on page 24.

2 Use a carving knife to trim off the top of the fruit cake to make it level. Fill in any holes in the fruit cake with pieces of marzipan to help achieve a smooth coating. Brush the top of the cake with the apricot glaze then place the cake to one side.

3 Roll out the marzipan on a work surface dusted with icing sugar until it is approximately 5mm–7mm (¼"– ³⁄₈") thick and slightly larger than the top of the cake. Slide a cake card under the marzipan. Turn the top of the cake over onto the marzipan so that the glaze will stick them together. Use a knife to cut around the edge of the cake to remove the excess marzipan.

4 Brush warm glaze over the top of the cake and place a cake drum on top of it. Using the cake boards to lift it, turn the cake upright then remove the cake card. Brush the sides of the cake with warm glaze and place to one side.

Follow the steps below for marzipanning a round or square cake.

Marzipanning a cake for royal icing

For round cakes

1 Wrap a length of greaseproof paper around the cake and cut to size. Roll out a long sausage of marzipan on a piece of greaseproof paper to the same length as the paper template. Roll out the marzipan to approximately 4mm (¼") thick.

2 Use a sharp knife to cut the bottom of the marzipan strip straight, then loosely roll up the marzipan on the greaseproof paper. Hold the marzipan so the cut side sits on the cake board then unroll the marzipan around the sides of the cake, removing the greaseproof paper as you go.

3 Smooth over the marzipan with your hands and trim the paste neatly at the join and around the top. Use two cake smoothers to smooth over the top and sides of the cake. Allow the marzipan to dry overnight before covering with royal icing. To find out how to cover a round fruit cake with royal icing, turn to page 236.

For square cakes

1 Roll out the marzipan into a long strip that is slightly wider than the height of the cake and allow for 5mm– 7mm (¼"– ³⁄₈") spare at each end of the strip. Repeat to make three more lengths of marzipan in the same way.

2 Place a strip of marzipan along one side of the cake at a time, ensuring the marzipan is flush with the bottom edge of the cake. Use a sharp knife to trim away the excess marzipan from the sides and from the top of the cake, using the top layer of marzipan as a guide. Attach the next length of marzipan to the opposite side.

3 Repeat this around the remaining sides of the cake then use two cake smoothers to smooth over the top and sides. Use a knife to neaten the joins along the top and down the sides of the cake if necessary. Allow the marzipan to dry overnight before covering with royal icing. To find out how to cover a square fruit cake with royal icing, turn to page 238.

tutor tip

Never use cornflour for rolling out marzipan as this can cause bacteria to grow on the cake surface. Always use icing sugar instead.

Preparing a Cake for Decorating

Marzipanning a cake for sugarpaste

For round and square cakes

1 Make some warm apricot glaze following the instructions on page 24.

2 Use a carving knife to trim off the top of the cake to make it level. Fill in any holes in the cake with small pieces of marzipan. Brush the top of the cake with warm apricot glaze, then turn the cake upside down onto a cake drum.

3 Roll out the marzipan to approximately 5mm–7mm (¼"–³/₈") thick, using a little icing sugar to stop the marzipan sticking to the surface. Use a ruler to measure the top and sides of the cake then measure the marzipan to check it is large enough to cover the cake in one go.

4 Lift the marzipan onto a non-stick rolling pin and drape it over the top of the cake, making sure that there is an even amount of marzipan around each side. Use your hands to smooth down the top of the marzipan first then smooth down the sides, making sure not to pleat the marzipan at the base of the cake. If the marzipan does start to pleat, gently lift it away from the side of the cake and smooth down with your hands once more.

5 When you have smoothed the marzipan down to the very bottom of the cake, trim away the excess marzipan from around the base with a sharp knife or pizza wheel. Smooth the top and sides of the cake with a cake smoother in each hand until you achieve a polished finish. To find out how to prepare a cake for a sharp-edged sugarpaste covering, turn to page 298.

Preparing a Cake for Decorating

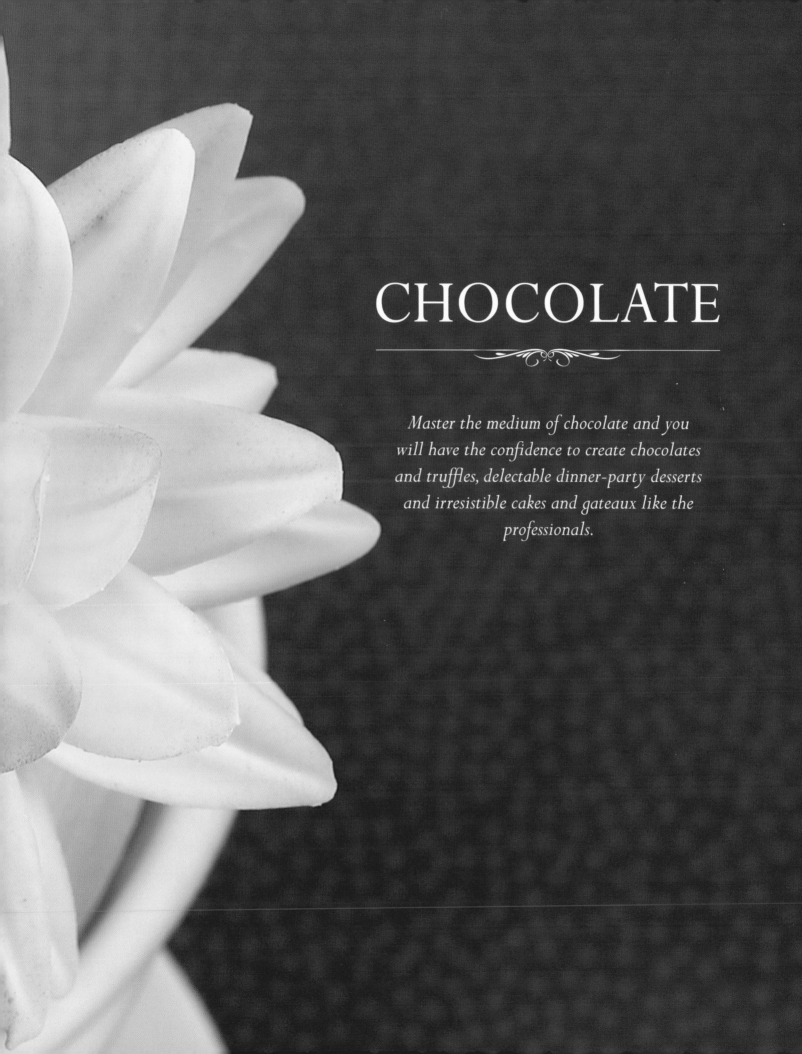

CHOCOLATE

Master the medium of chocolate and you will have the confidence to create chocolates and truffles, delectable dinner-party desserts and irresistible cakes and gateaux like the professionals.

Essential Edibles and Equipment for Chocolate

1 Chocolate scraper

2 Cling film

3 Digital food thermometer

4 Hairdryer/heat gun

5 Marble slab

6 Microwaveable and metal bowls

7 Palette knives, various sizes

8 Polycarbonate chocolate bar mould

9 Polycarbonate chocolate sphere mould

10 Saucepan

11 SK Couverture Chocolate, see project list for quantities

12 Small paring knife

13 Soft, lint-free cloth (not pictured)

14 Spatula

15 Weighing scales

17th-century chocolatière

Mark Tilling

BIOGRAPHY

I have been working for over 25 years as a pâtissier and chocolatier in an industry which I have a great passion for. I remember from a very early age watching both my grandmothers making sweet things, and from as early as that I always knew I wanted to work in this area.

For my first job, I worked at a local hotel at the weekends in the pastry kitchen which I loved. My best memories of working there were the New Year's Eve buffets we made; we could really go to town with them and make all sorts of pastries. I got the job when I was only 16 and this was where I met a very dear man, Martin Nash, who would

have a very big influence on my life and career throughout the years. I would love to dedicate my part of this book to him – I would not be where I am today without him.

Throughout my career, I have worked in many hotels and restaurants including The Lanesborough on Hyde Park Corner in London, Lainston House Hotel in Winchester, Hotel du Vin Group in Winchester and Bristol and the Pave D'Auge in Normandy, France. I have also cooked for several well-known figures including, President George Bush Sr., Cher, Tom Cruise, Nicole Kidman and HRH Prince Edward, The Earl of Wessex to name but a few.

I have received many awards for my chocolate and pâtisserie work over the years: I have earned many gold and silver medals for my desserts and petits fours, as well as double gold for my chocolate showpieces. My highest achievements, however, have been winning the UK Chocolate Masters competition from 2006 to 2008, and coming 12th in 2007 and 7th in 2009 at the finals of the World Chocolate Masters. It was such a great honour to be able to represent the UK.

After these accomplishments, I was made a UK Callebaut Chocolate Ambassador which is a position I have held for the last five years. I now work as a Senior Tutor at the Squires Kitchen International School in Farnham, Surrey. I have a great passion for teaching and enjoy passing on

my skills to all sorts of people. I teach a range of classes from chocolate and pâtisserie, to 5-day chocolate and baking schools and demonstrate every year at the Squires Kitchen Annual Exhibition. In 2010 I accepted the great honour of making the 200th Baddeley Cake for the Theatre Royal in Drury Lane, a tradition that dates back to 1794. The cake was based on the musical *Oliver!* which was running at the time.

I am a regular contributor to *Cakes & Sugarcraft* and *Squires Kitchen Bake School* magazines as well as the author of two books, *Squires Kitchen's Guide to Working with Chocolate* and *Squires Kitchen's Guide to Making Macaroons* (B. Dutton Publishing).

Foundation Chocolate

MARK TILLING

Tempering is one of the most important skills to learn when you start working with chocolate. Once you have learnt to temper, you can move on to create treats such as chocolate bars and truffles.

TECHNIQUES

- Tempering chocolate
- Making chocolate bars
- Making chocolate truffles

20th-century copper bain marie for chocolate work

How to temper chocolate

It is important to temper chocolate before you use it to ensure that it has a good snap and shine when it is ready to eat. Many people are frightened off by the idea of tempering chocolate but with a little practice you will soon get the hang of it: when you do there are endless things you can make.

There are many different ways to temper chocolate but I have explained two different methods here: the microwave method and the bain-marie method.

For essential chocolate edibles and equipment, see pages 100–101

Microwave method

For this method you only need the basic chocolate equipment and a microwave (a domestic microwave is fine). You will also need good-quality couverture chocolate that contains cocoa butter and not vegetable fat.

1 Place two thirds of the amount of the chocolate that you are going to temper into a bowl; the other third will be used later in the tempering process. You will need to use a microwaveable plastic bowl as porcelain will become too hot.

2 Place the bowl into the microwave and heat for 30 seconds on half power. Stir the chocolate and then return it to the microwave for another 30 seconds. Repeat this as many times as required until the chocolate has melted. Don't be tempted to rush this stage of the process as the chocolate may burn if heated for too long.

3 You will notice that the chocolate will start to melt slowly. When the chocolate has melted completely it should be around 45°C (115°F): you can test this with a digital thermometer if you have one.

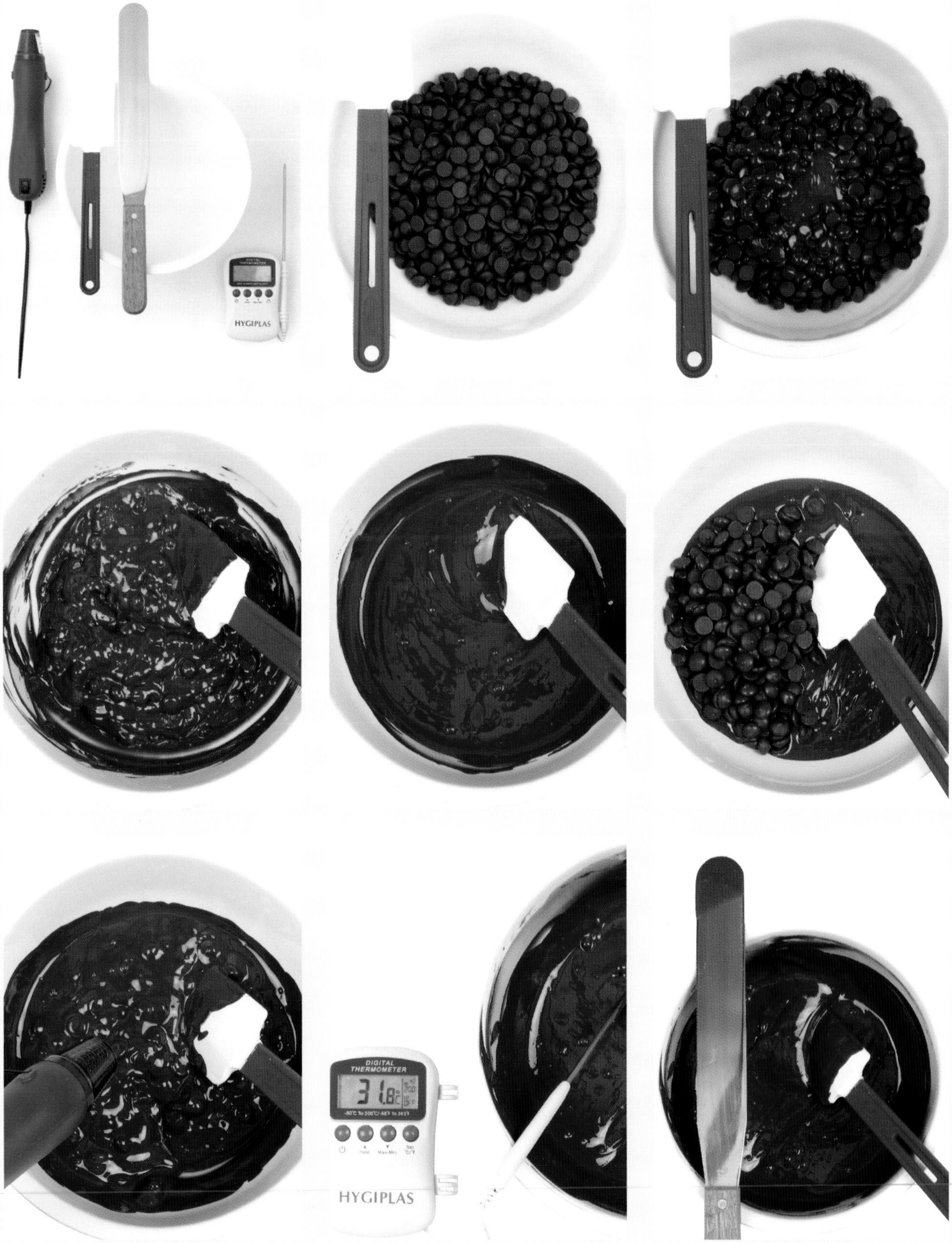
HYGIPLAS
DIGITAL THERMOMETER
HYGIPLAS

4 Add the remaining third of the chocolate to the melted chocolate and stir gently (do not over-stir the chocolate). The cold chocolate will melt into the warm chocolate and will lower the temperature slightly.

5 If the cool chocolate does not melt, use a hairdryer or heat gun to melt the chocolate slowly, stirring at the same time. Take care not to overheat the chocolate. Just before all the chocolate has melted, turn off the heat and let it finish melting by itself (this will prevent it from overheating).

6 Test the temperature of the chocolate to make sure that you have tempered it correctly. If you have a thermometer the temperatures should be as follows:

dark chocolate 31–32°C (87–89°F);

milk chocolate 29–30°C (84–86°F);

white chocolate 27–28°C (80–82°F).

Once the chocolate is at the correct temperature it is ready to use.

7 You can also check that the chocolate is correctly tempered by dipping the end of a palette knife in the chocolate and setting it aside. If it starts to set in around 5 minutes then the chocolate is tempered and ready to use. If the chocolate does not set then it is still too hot.

8 If the chocolate is too hot, gently stir in more cool chocolate until it reaches the required temperature.

9 When you are working with the tempered chocolate it may begin to cool and thicken. Use the hairdryer or heat gun again to heat the chocolate just a little. Check the temperature as before.

Bain-marie method

For this method you need the basic chocolate equipment as well as a metal bowl and a stove top. You will also need good-quality couverture chocolate that contains a high percentage of cocoa butter.

1 Pour a small amount of water into the saucepan and bring to a very gentle simmer.

2 Place the metal bowl on top, ensuring that it does not touch the water. Put two thirds of the amount of chocolate that you are using into the bowl. Stir gently with the spatula as it melts.

3 When the chocolate has melted test it with a thermometer if you have one: it should be around 45–50°C (113–122°F). Remove from the heat and set the bowl to one side.

4 Add the remaining third of the chocolate to the melted chocolate and stir slowly, taking care not to over-stir. This will melt into the chocolate and will also cool the chocolate slightly.

5 Use a hairdryer or heat gun to melt the chocolate, stirring at the same time. You are aiming to melt any remaining chocolate slowly. Take care not to overheat the chocolate.

6 Just before all the chocolate has melted, stop using the hairdryer/ heat gun and let the chocolate melt in its own heat. This will also prevent it from overheating.

7 Test the temperature of the chocolate to make sure that you have tempered it correctly. If you have a thermometer the temperatures should be as follows:

dark chocolate 31–32°C (87–89°F);

milk chocolate 29–30°C (84–86°F);

white chocolate 27–28°C (80–82°F).

Once the chocolate has reached the correct temperature it is ready to use.

8 Follow steps 7–9 for the microwave method to test the chocolate and adjust the temperature, if necessary.

Making chocolate bars

EDIBLES

500g (1lb ¾oz) tempered SK Couverture Chocolate

Mixture of dried nuts and freeze-dried fruit (optional)

EQUIPMENT

Chocolate bar mould

Plastic piping bag

Craft knife

For essential chocolate edibles and equipment, see pages 100–101

1 Place the nuts or freeze-dried fruit into the bottom of the bar mould, if desired.

2 Place some melted, tempered chocolate into a piping bag and cut off the end. Start to pipe the chocolate into the mould. Pipe just to the top: make sure that you don't overfill the mould.

3 Tap the mould on its edge to level out the chocolate. Leave to cool at room temperature until the surface of the chocolate has changed from shiny to matt.

4 Place in the fridge for about 20 minutes until set then turn out the chocolate bar from the mould. If the bar does not come out cleanly from the mould, place back in the fridge for a few more minutes before trying again.

tutor tip

Warm the mould slightly with a heat gun or hairdryer before flooding with chocolate.

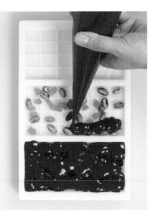

Foundation Chocolate

107

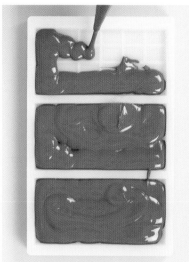

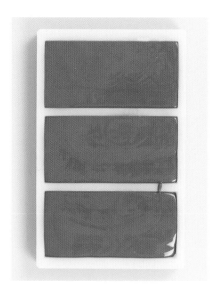

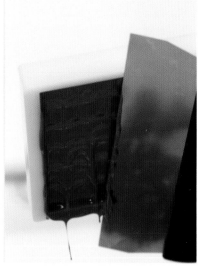

Making filled chocolate bars

EDIBLES

500g (1lb ¾oz) tempered SK Couverture Chocolate

100g (3½oz) of filling e.g. peanut butter, jam or nut paste

EQUIPMENT

Chocolate bar mould

Plastic piping bags

Sheet of greaseproof paper

For essential chocolate edibles and equipment, see pages 100–101

1 Place some melted, tempered chocolate into a piping bag and cut off the end. Start to pipe the chocolate into the mould. Pipe just to the top: make sure that you don't overfill the mould. Give the mould a little tap on the work surface to remove any air bubbles.

2 Place a sheet of greaseproof paper over the work surface. Turn the mould upside down over the greaseproof paper so the chocolate will flood out. Give the mould another tap, then scrape off the excess chocolate with a large scraper. Turn the mould the right way up and leave the remaining chocolate to semi-set for a few minutes.

3 Once the chocolate has semi-set, fill a piping bag with the filling of your choice. Use a heat gun to warm the top of the chocolate then pipe a thin layer of filling over it. Place the mould in the fridge to set for approximately ten minutes.

4 Remove the mould from the fridge. Fill another piping bag with tempered, melted chocolate and fill the mould just to the top. Use the scraper to remove any excess chocolate. Leave to set a room temperature, then place in the fridge again to set completely.

5 Turn out the chocolate bar from the mould. If the bar does not come out cleanly from the mould, place back in the fridge for a few more minutes before trying again.

Dark chocolate with praline

White chocolate with jam

Milk chocolate with peanut butter

Foundation Chocolate

109

Making chocolate truffles

Truffles make impressive gifts but are very simple to make. These delectable chocolates can be decorated with lustre dusts or vermicelli for a special touch.

EDIBLES

250ml (8¾fl oz) whipping cream

1 vanilla pod

250g (8¾oz) SK Belgian Couverture Chocolate: Dark (70–80% cocoa solids)

40g (1½oz) butter

300g (10½oz) SK Belgian Couverture Chocolate: Dark, tempered (for coating)

100g (3½oz) cocoa powder

EQUIPMENT

Airtight container

Melon scoop or teaspoon

Food-grade plastic disposable gloves

For essential chocolate edibles and equipment, see pages 100–101

1 Pour the cream into a saucepan. Cut down the length of the vanilla pod and place the seeds and pod into the cream. Heat the cream and vanilla in a saucepan.

2 Just before the cream boils, remove from the heat and leave to cool to around 80°C or just leave for one minute.

3 Place the chocolate in a large bowl. Remove the pod from the cream and pour over the chocolate. Stir very slowly just to melt the chocolate and make a smooth ganache. Add the butter and stir again.

4 Pour into an airtight container and leave to set overnight at room temperature.

5 Use a melon scoop or a spoon to make small truffle balls from the ganache mixture, then set aside to harden.

6 Using gloves or a spoon, roll or dip the centres into the melted tempered chocolate then into the cocoa powder. When set, roll again to knock off the remaining cocoa powder.

tutor tips

Using a melon scoop will make your truffles more rounded. If you would like to make perfect spheres, pipe the cream and chocolate mix into a truffle shell mould before chilling in the fridge.

To add a metallic finish, roll the truffles in a mixture of cocoa powder and gold lustre dust food colour.

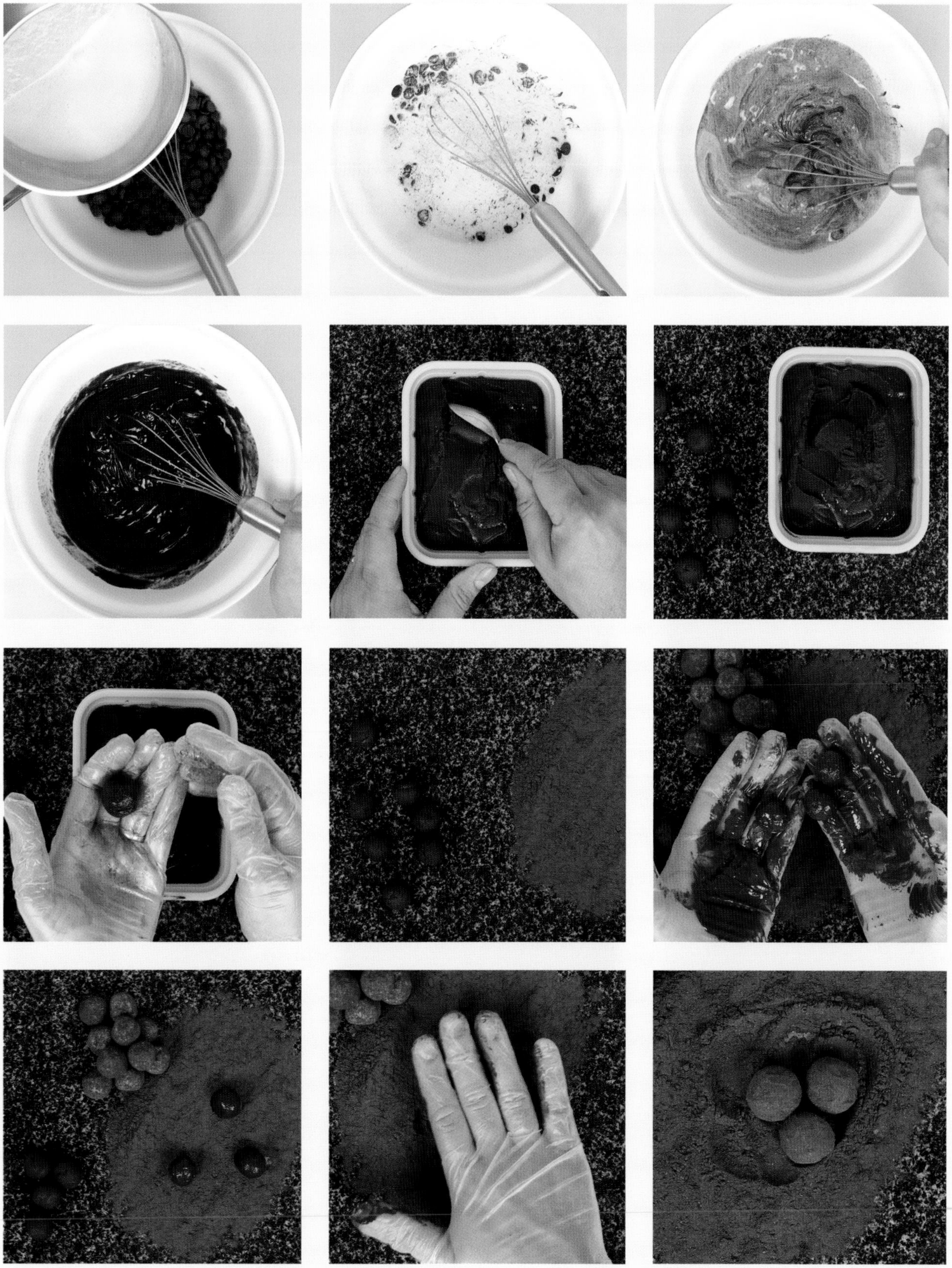

Chocolate Decorations and Desserts

MARK TILLING

Once you've tempered chocolate, you can use it in a variety of ways to add impressive decorative touches to mini cakes, cupcakes, gateaux, desserts and even celebration cakes. The decorative techniques explained below are quick and easy and only require a handful of tools. You can also use readymade modelling chocolate which is ideal for creating simple, modelled decorations in chocolate.

TECHNIQUES

- Making chocolate pots
- Making cigarillos
- Making chocolate fans
- Making Cocoform roses

EDIBLES

Chocolate pots

Transfer sheet for chocolate, in the design of your choice

SK Belgian Couverture Chocolate, tempered

Vegetable oil

Chocolate cigarillos

SK Belgian Couverture Chocolate, tempered

Chocolate fans

SK Belgian Couverture Chocolate, tempered

Chocolate roses

SK Modelling Cocoform: Strawberry

For essential chocolate edibles and equipment, see pages 100–101

EQUIPMENT

Chocolate pots

6 x 5cm (2") SK Round Mini Pans

Cutting mat (or spare cake board/piece of card for cutting on)

Craft knife

Ruler

Clear acetate

Kitchen towel

Chocolate fans

Craft knife

Kitchen towel

Victorian Father Christmas chocolate mould

112

Making chocolate pots

1 Place a transfer sheet onto a cutting mat. Use a ruler and a craft knife to cut off the extra acetate border at one end of the transfer sheet.

2 Measure the height of the mini pans against the trimmed transfer sheet and mark the height on the sheet with a craft knife.

3 Using a ruler and craft knife to achieve a straight edge, cut the transfer sheet at the mark. Repeat to make six strips of the same size.

4 Wrap each strip around a mini pan and trim to the length required, leaving a 2cm (¾") overlap.

5 Cut out six strips of acetate in the same way, making them slightly taller than the transfer sheets. Lightly brush the outside of the mini pans with oil and wrap a strip of acetate around each one.

6 Place one of the transfer sheet strips onto a marble slab, making sure the cocoa butter (patterned) side is facing upwards.

7 Pour some tempered chocolate over the transfer sheet until it is completely covered in a layer of chocolate that is 2mm–3mm (⅛") thick. Use a palette knife to spread the chocolate over the surface, making sure that the chocolate goes up to and over the edges of the sheet.

8 Use a craft knife to lift the transfer sheet, then hang the strip from your fingers and use your other hand to smooth the chocolate down the edges. Place the strip to one side on the slab. Clean the

Chocolate Decorations and Desserts

113

slab with a palette knife or some kitchen towel and start again. Repeat to cover all six strips in chocolate.

9 Once the chocolate on the transfer sheet changes from glossy to matt, lift the sheet up and wrap it around the mini pan with the chocolate facing inwards. Try not to put too much pressure on the sheet.

10 Overlap the ends and apply a little pressure down the seam so that the chocolate sticks together, leaving a small flap on the outside.

11 Repeat with all six transfer sheets then place in the fridge to set for approximately 20 minutes.

12 Remove from the fridge and very carefully push the mini pan and acetate upwards to release the transfer.

13 Pull the flap all the way around the pot to peel the transfer sheet away from the chocolate. Holding the seam down the centre, carefully pull off the excess flap of chocolate: you should be left with a neat seam line. If the seam opens up, smear a little melted chocolate inside the pot to stick the edges back together.

tutor tip

Transfer sheets for chocolate can be used to make decorations in a variety of shapes, such as panels, discs and spirals.

Making chocolate cigarillos

1 Temper some couverture chocolate following the steps on pages 104–106.

2 Use the end of a palette knife to pick up a small amount of melted, tempered chocolate.

3 Scrape the palette knife across the edge of the bowl to take the chocolate off one side. Spread the chocolate from side to side on a granite or marble slab to make a rectangle that is approximately 20cm x 10cm (7¾" x 4") in size. Stop once the chocolate is just starting to set.

4 When the chocolate is touch-dry, place a large chocolate scraper onto the chocolate approximately 6cm (2³/₈") from one end of the rectangle. Using some force, scrape the chocolate off quickly with the scraper almost flat against the marble slab.

5 Move 6cm (2³/₈") along the rectangle of chocolate and repeat to create more cigarillos.

6 Repeat steps 2–5 to make as many cigarillos as required. It is advisable to make extras in case of breakages.

tutor tips

All these steps must be completed very quickly: if the cigarillos crack, the chocolate has been on the slab for too long.

When you are practising, it is best to start with white chocolate as it is the easiest for beginners to use.

Chocolate Decorations and Desserts

Making chocolate fans

1 Place a marble slab in the freezer for a minimum of 3 hours (overnight if possible).

2 Temper some couverture chocolate following the steps on pages 104–106. Use the end of a palette knife to pick up a small amount of melted, tempered chocolate.

3 Spread the chocolate onto the frozen slab and aim to make a rough rectangle shape.

4 Very quickly use a craft knife to cut the down the chocolate lengthways and to cut off the two ends. You should end up with two long rectangular strips, each with a rough edge along one of the longest sides.

5 Using both hands, pick up one of the strips with your fingertips. Hold it with the rough edge towards you and the cut edge facing away from you.

6 Start to concertina the rough edge, making sure you pinch the ends together to create a fan shape.

7 Repeat with the second strip. Set the two fans aside.

8 Wipe the slab clean with some kitchen towel and start again.

9 The slab will start to warm up so you will only get time to make up to 20 fans at a time. When this happens place the slab back in the freezer for about 20 minutes. Once it is cold you can continue to make more fans.

tutor tips

This is a great decoration as it is very quick to make and is an easy way to cover a cake. If you are covering a large cake or decorating a wedding cake you may need to have two marble slabs that you can alternate so you are always working on a cold surface.

Try using two different types of coloured chocolates and marbling them together before spreading onto the frozen slab.

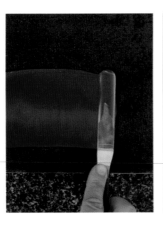

Making chocolate roses

1 Take a piece of Cocoform that is approximately the size of a walnut and roll this into a ball. Model the ball into a cone shape and place the cone on the work surface: this will be the base for the rose.

2 Roll out a large sausage from more Cocoform that is approximately 10cm x 1cm (4" x 3/8") in size. These measurements are just a guide and will depend on the size of the rose you want to make.

3 Cut the sausage into 1cm (3/8") pieces and roll them into balls. Place a ball on a cool work surface such as a marble slab and use your finger to flatten down half of the ball. Make sure you flatten the edge to make each petal nice and thin. Keep moving the ball around each time

you flatten it so it does not stick to the work surface. Repeat with the remaining balls to make several teardrop-shaped petals.

4 Position the first petal halfway up the cone and wrap the thinner edge of the petal tightly around the top of the cone so it is completely hidden. This is very important because if the cone can be seen the rose could end up looking more like a cabbage.

5 Repeat in the same way with the remaining petals, attaching each one around the previous petal. When you get to the outer petals, attach the petals a little further up the cone and pinch the petals downwards to open up the rose.

6 Once all the petals are attached, pinch the base of the rose to neaten

it and open the flower out slightly. Cut off the excess Cocoform with a craft knife to give the rose a clean base.

7 If you wish to dust the rose with a little dust food colour, leave it to firm up slightly for approximately 20 minutes before dusting. Lustre dusts are particularly effective on Dark Cocoform.

tutor tip

If you wish to colour White Modelling Cocoform, knead dust colour into the paste and leave it to rest before working with it.

Chocolate Decorations and Desserts

Chocolate Dessert Pots

Use your chocolate skills to impress guests with these delectable dinner party desserts.

EDIBLES

6 sponge discs, see recipe on page 15

Caramel and chocolate mousse

100ml (3½fl oz) whipping cream, unwhipped

50g (1¾oz) caster sugar

1tbsp glucose

100g (3½oz) SK Belgian Couverture Chocolate: Dark

35g (1¼oz) SK Belgian Couverture Chocolate: Milk

170ml (5¾fl oz) whipping cream, semi-whipped

Decoration

SK Designer Transfer Sheets for Chocolate: Candy Stripe, Pink Roses, White Baroque

SK Belgian Couverture Chocolate: White, Milk and Dark

2 chocolate fans, see page 116

2 chocolate cigarillos, see page 115

2 Cocoform roses, see page 117

Fresh berries

EQUIPMENT

Round cutter: 5cm (2")

Piping bag

Cup, glass or similar

Small whisk

For essential chocolate edibles and equipment, see pages 100–101

Caramel and chocolate mousse

1 Heat the unwhipped cream in the microwave or bring to the boil in a saucepan, then place to one side.

2 Place the sugar in a heavy-bottomed saucepan and cook on a medium heat until it turns a golden caramel colour, stirring from time to time so it does not burn.

3 Once the sugar is the right colour, start adding the hot cream a little at a time, keeping the pan on a low heat until all the cream is incorporated.

4 Remove from the heat, add the glucose and stir in well.

5 Pour the mix onto the chocolate and leave to melt for one minute.

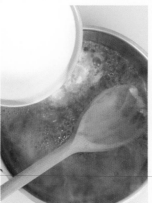

6 Stir the mix with a small whisk or wooden spoon until all the chocolate has melted.

7 Fold a little of the semi-whipped cream into the chocolate, then fold the chocolate back into the rest of the cream mixture.

8 Pour into a cup, glass or similar and refrigerate for 30 minutes to achieve a piping consistency.

Decoration

9 Make six chocolate pots following the instructions on page 113. Make two milk, dark and white chocolate pots using each of the different transfer sheets. Cut out six sponge discs using the round cutter and place one in the base of each chocolate pot.

10 Fill a large piping bag with the chocolate mousse and pipe the mousse into the chocolate pots, making sure to fill them just to the top. Do not overfill the pots.

11 Top the desserts with either a chocolate rose, a chocolate fan or a chocolate cigarillo and some fresh berries.

Chocolate Dessert Pots

Professional Chocolate Skills

MARK TILLING

Once you are proficient in tempering and other basic chocolate skills, you can go on to create impressive show-stopping pieces made entirely from chocolate. This section explains how to create a range of advanced chocolate decorations that can be incorporated into a professional-looking showpiece, including moulding, colouring, and creating stunning chocolate flowers.

EDIBLES

Making chocolate petals

Small bowl of tempered chocolate, see pages 104–106

Making chocolate spheres

Medium bowl of tempered chocolate, see pages 104–106

Making chocolate swirls

200g (7oz) chocolate callets

For essential chocolate edibles and equipment, see pages 100–101

EQUIPMENT

Making chocolate petals

5cm x 30cm (2"x 12") acetate strip

Long, slightly curved former, e.g. a new piece of foam coving

Making hollow and solid chocolate spheres

Soft, lint-free cloth

Large half-sphere mould: 12cm (5")

Small half-sphere mould: 4cm (1½")

Making chocolate swirls

Food processor

Cake smoother

TECHNIQUES

- Making chocolate petals
- Making hollow chocolate spheres
- Making solid chocolate spheres
- Making chocolate swirls and spirals
- Assembling a chocolate showpiece

18th-century chocolatière

Late 17th-century wooden molinet for whipping hot chocolate

Making chocolate petals

1 Place a 5cm x 30cm (2" x 12") strip of acetate along the bottom edge of a non-stick board or granite slab.

2 Fill a small bowl to the top with melted, tempered chocolate.

3 Dip a small paring knife halfway into the bowl of chocolate, then tap the knife on the top of the bowl to remove any excess. Scrape one side of the knife across the top of the bowl to remove the chocolate from that side.

4 Working very quickly, place two fingers approximately 5cm (2") apart on the acetate strip to hold it in place, then lay the tip of the chocolate-covered knife very gently across the width of the acetate strip, until the chocolate just starts to show around the edges.

5 Lift the knife straight up then pull it towards you. This will create the vein down the middle of the petal.

6 Work quickly to repeat steps 3–5, making several petals along one strip of acetate. Once you have finished a row of petals, rest the strip in the coving or other curved former and leave to set. If you find that the petals are setting before you have completed a whole row, cut the acetate into shorter strips so you don't have to create as many petals in one go.

7 When all the petals have set, place them into the fridge and leave them to dry completely fro approximately 20 minutes.

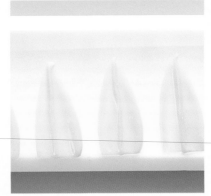

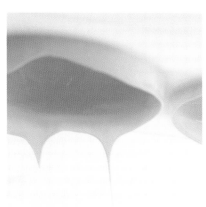

This method could also be used to make hollow Easter eggs.

Making hollow chocolate spheres

1 Make sure that the large half-sphere moulds are scrupulously clean then polish with a soft, lint-free cloth to give the chocolate a shiny surface.

2 Pour the melted, tempered chocolate into both half-sphere moulds and fill to the top with chocolate. Tap the mould on the work surface to remove any air bubbles in the chocolate.

3 Turn the mould upside down over a bowl or baking tray to catch the excess chocolate. Keep the mould straight and give the side of the mould a little tap to release the chocolate: this will make the sphere nice and thin.

4 Once the chocolate has stopped dripping, keep the mould upside down and use a large chocolate scraper to remove all the excess chocolate from around the mould.

5 Turn the mould up the right way and scrape again, then place the mould chocolate-side down onto a piece of greaseproof paper and leave to set at room temperature for approximately 15–20 minutes until the surface has gone from shiny to matt. If you are making a large sphere it is necessary to use two coats of chocolate, so repeat steps 2–5.

6 Once the chocolate in the mould has set, peel away the greaseproof paper and place the mould in the fridge for approximately 30 minutes to set completely.

7 To assemble the sphere, carefully remove the two halves of the sphere from the moulds. Warm a marble or granite slab in the oven on a low heat, then place the two flat sides of the sphere on the slab to soften the chocolate slightly. Stick the two halves together and leave to set at room temperature for five minutes.

Professional Chocolate Skills

Making solid chocolate spheres

1 Make sure that the small half-sphere moulds are scrupulously clean then polish with a soft, lint-free cloth to give the chocolate a shiny surface.

2 Fill a large piping bag with melted, tempered white chocolate and fill the half-sphere moulds to the top with chocolate. Tap the mould on the work surface to remove any air bubbles in the chocolate.

3 Use a chocolate scraper to scrape off the excess chocolate from the top of the mould. You do not need to turn the mould upside down for solid spheres. Leave to dry at room temperature then place in the fridge for approximately 30 minutes to set completely.

4 Assemble the solid sphere in the same way as for the hollow sphere.

Making chocolate spirals and swirls

1 Place the chocolate in a food processor, working with 100g (3½oz) of chocolate at any one time.

2 Blend the chocolate into a fine powder, turn off the machine and place the chocolate into a bowl. Leave the chocolate in the fridge for 20 minutes. This will stop the chocolate from over-heating during tempering.

3 Remove from the fridge and blend again until the chocolate forms a ball of paste. If you find it still has lumps, continue to blend the chocolate but make sure it does not get too hot.

4 Place a small amount of the paste on a marble or granite slab that is at room temperature. Working as quickly as you can, use your hands to roll the paste into a long sausage.

5 Roll the sausage with a cake smoother to give it a smooth finish, then apply a little more pressure at one end of the sausage to taper it into a point. Cut the other end of the sausage straight.

6 Fold the pointed end in on itself to make a spiral, or bend the sausage into a 'S' shape for a swirl then leave to dry for approximately 20 minutes. Once the

swirls or spirals are dry they are ready to be placed onto the showpiece. These steps must be completed swiftly as the paste dries out very quickly. If the chocolate does dry out, blend the chocolate into a paste again in the food processor.

tutor tip

Dark chocolate contains less cocoa butter than other chocolates, which means it dries out more quickly. If you find it too hard, add some more cocoa butter to soften it.

White Chocolate Showpiece

This impressive white chocolate showpiece bursting with delectable truffles would make a stunning centrepiece and would be the talking point at any dinner party.

EDIBLES

1kg (2lb 3¼oz) melted, tempered white chocolate

1 large, hollow white chocolate sphere, see page 123

1 small, hollow white chocolate sphere, see page 123

1 small, solid white chocolate half-sphere, see opposite

6 white chocolate swirls, see opposite

60–70 white chocolate petals, see page 122

50g (1¾oz) cocoa butter

SK Professional Cocol Cocoa Butter Colouring: Red

8–12 chocolate truffles, see recipe on page 110

EQUIPMENT

Greaseproof paper

2 large baking trays

Five pastry rings: four 9cm x 3.5cm deep (3½" x 1³/₈"), one 16cm x 3.5cm deep (6¼" x 1³/₈")

Large piping bag

Round cutter: 3cm (1¹/₈")

Metal ladle

Chocolate cooler spray

Airbrush kit

For essential chocolate edibles and equipment, see pages 100–101

1   Place a piece of greaseproof paper over the top of the baking trays. Position the four smaller pastry rings on one tray and the larger ring on the second tray.

2   Fill a large piping bag with melted, tempered white chocolate then pipe or pour the chocolate into each ring until they are approximately ²/₃ full. Leave the chocolate to set at room temperature until the surface has gone from shiny to matt, then place all the rings in the fridge to set completely for approximately 30–40 minutes.

3   Warm a marble or granite slab in the oven on a low heat. Remove the chocolate discs from the rings once they have completely set. Turn the largest chocolate disc upside down on the warm slab, then move it around for a few seconds to melt the rough surface. Lift the disc off the slab then scrape away the excess chocolate with a large chocolate scraper. You can use a spirit level at this stage to check the chocolate disc is flat. Leave the disc to dry at room temperature. Repeat with the four smaller chocolate discs. Once set, smooth over the discs with your fingers and round off the edges.

4   Choose the best side of the largest disc: this will be the top of the chocolate showpiece base. Warm the centre of the other side of the base with a heat gun and pipe a little chocolate in the middle of the disc. Immediately heat the top of one of the smaller discs, then place this onto the melted chocolate in the centre and use a little cooler spray to set it. Turn the base up the right way so the smaller disc is on the bottom.

5   Repeat for the other discs, heating and sticking each of the discs on top of one another so they are positioned slightly off centre. Smooth over the joins with a little melted chocolate and use the cooling spray to set each layer before you move onto the next one.

White Chocolate Showpiece

6 Using some melted, tempered white chocolate and a firm brush, brush from top to bottom of the large hollow white chocolate sphere to make a swirled pattern in the chocolate. Leave to dry for 5–10 minutes.

7 Heat the bottom of the hollow sphere on the warm slab, then pipe a little white chocolate on top of the uppermost disc. Stick the sphere on top of the disc and use the cooling spray to set in place.

8 For the flower centre, take a small solid white chocolate half-sphere, heat the flat side on a warm metal ladle and attach it to the side of the sphere. Use a little cooler spray to set in place. Heat the base of a small hollow sphere on a warm granite slab until there is a small hole in the bottom, then position the hole over the half-sphere and set them in place with cooler spray.

9 Melt together equal amounts of cocoa butter and white chocolate, then place the mixture in an airbrush and spray over the whole showpiece. Leave the showpiece to dry for approximately 20 minutes, then spray another coat over the top and leave to dry again. Make sure to warm the airbrush with a heat gun so the chocolate mixture doesn't harden.

10 Gently warm the edge of the 3cm (1¹/₈") round cutter with a heat gun, place the cutter on the surface of the sphere then carefully twist the cutter to make a hole. Cut out several holes from the sphere, making sure to leave room for the flower. If the chocolate falls into the sphere, carefully use a knife to pull it out and use your finger to tidy the edges of each hole.

11 Carefully remove the petals from the acetate, pick each petal up by its side and dip into a little melted white chocolate. Position three petals around the very top of the small hollow sphere in a triangle and stick

White Chocolate Showpiece

127

them so they sit very closely together. The bases of the petals can be touching but make sure the petals are separate. Set each petal in place with a little cooler spray. Keep attaching the petals in between the ones before, making sure that you position them closely together so there are no gaps. Work your way down the sphere and slowly bring the petals out until they are almost upside down at the bottom of the sphere. Leave to dry for approximately 10 minutes.

12 Once the flower is dry, place a little melted Red Cocol (coloured cocoa butter) in an airbrush. Spray the cocoa butter lightly over the large sphere and flower to give them a little depth.

13 Attach three chocolate swirls to the front of the large sphere and three more to the back of the sphere with a little tempered white chocolate.

14 To finish, carefully fill the central sphere with chocolate truffles (see page 110).

tutor tip

Do not use too much cooler spray as it may stop other petals from sticking to the sphere.

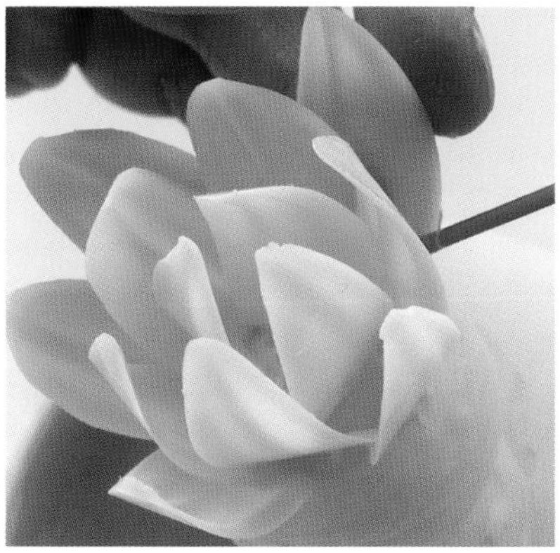
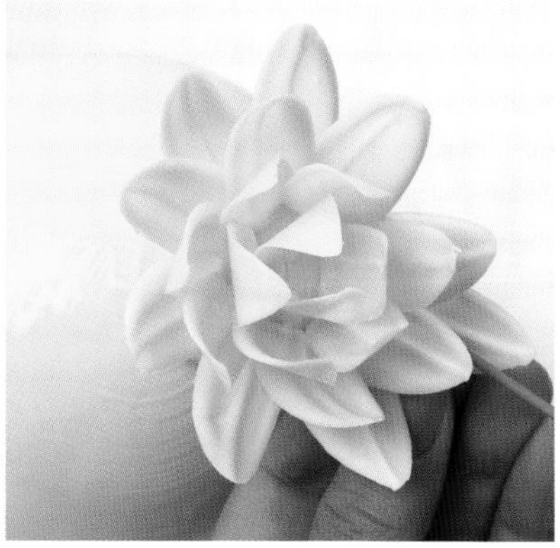
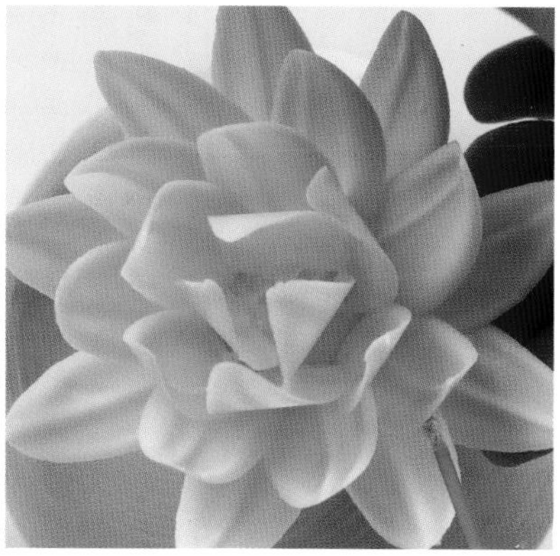
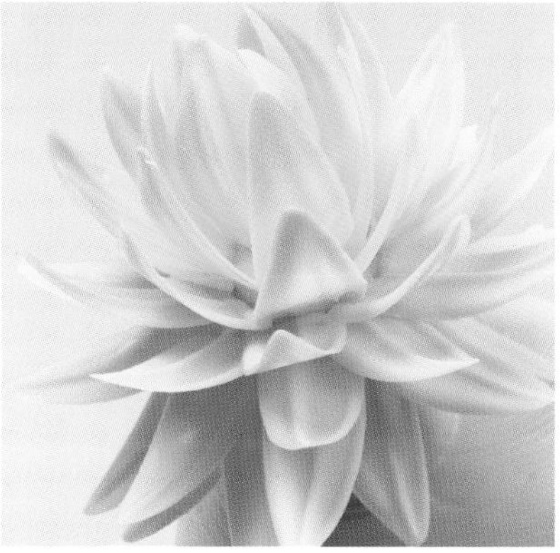
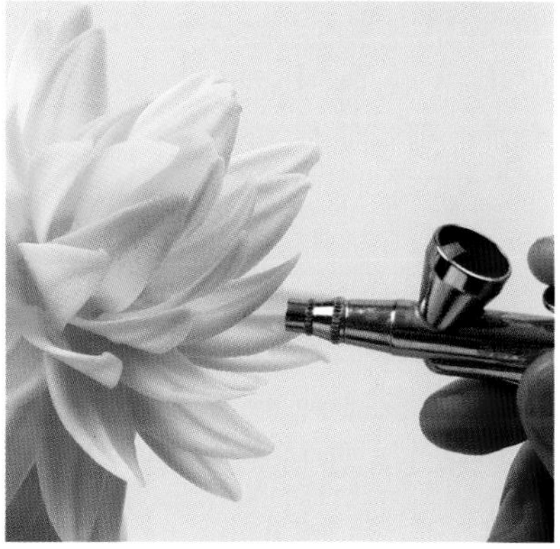
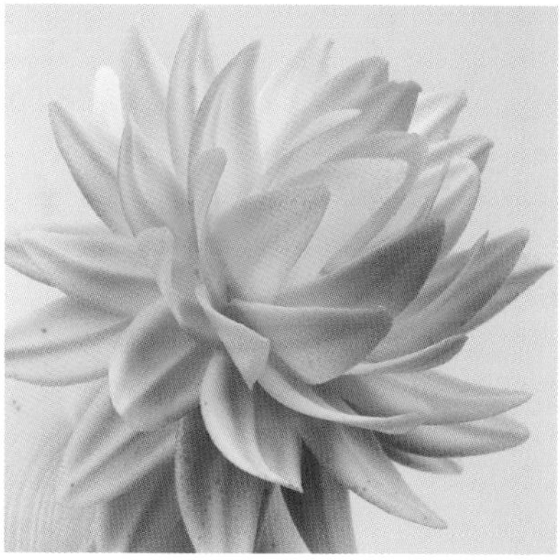
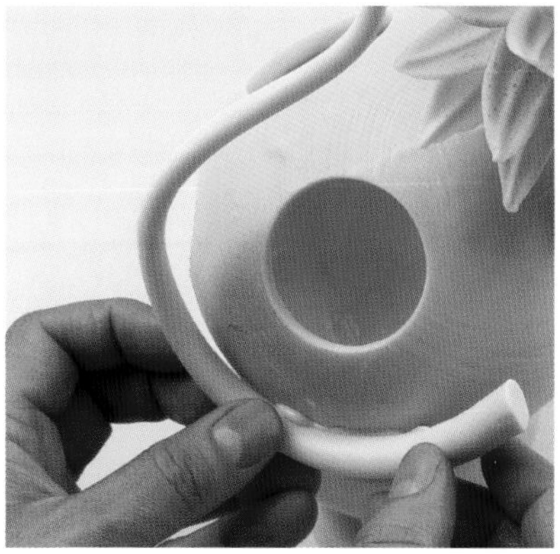
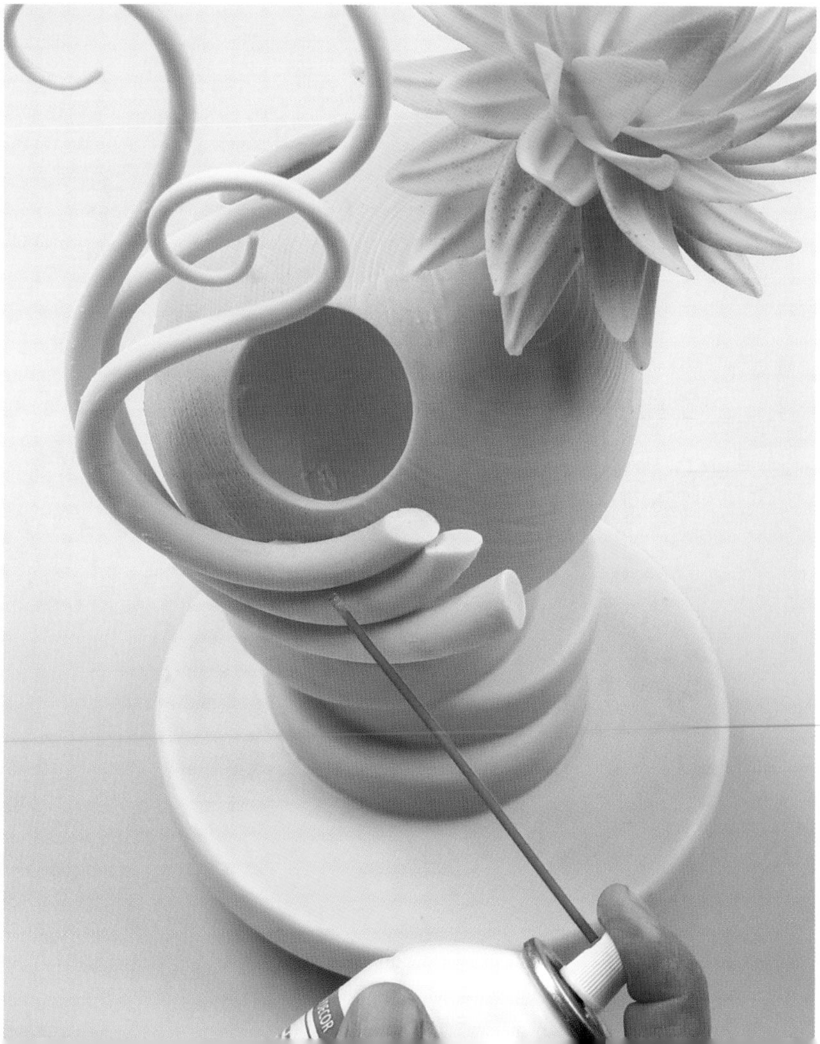
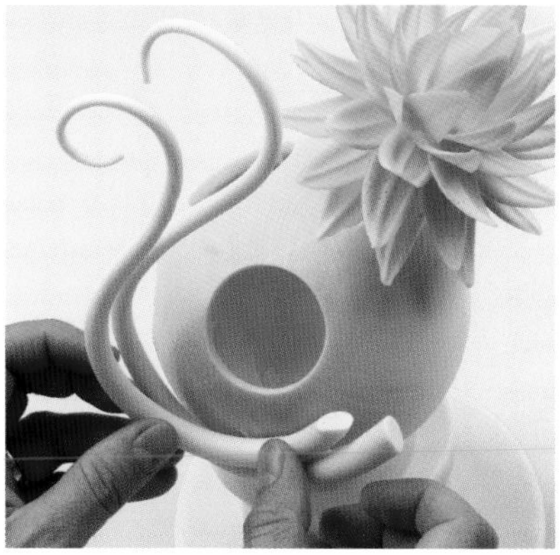

FOUNDATION SUGARCRAFT

*Discover the skills and essential equipment
needed to cover and decorate celebration cakes
using edible mediums such as sugarpaste, royal
icing, modelling paste and flower paste.*

Essential Edibles and Equipment for Sugarpaste

1   Cake drum (board), usually 5cm–7.5cm (2"–3") larger than the cake

2   Clear alcohol, e.g. gin or vodka, or cooled, pre-boiled water

3   Cranked palette knife

4   Food-grade plastic bags

5   Icing (confectioners') sugar in shaker

6   Non-stick board

7   Non-stick rolling pins, large and small

8   Pencil/pen for drawing templates

9   Scissors

10   Small, sharp knife

11   Smoothers

12   Spacers

13   SK Edible Glue

14   SK Paintbrushes, see project list for sizes

15   SK Paste Food Colours, see project list for colours

16   SK Sugarpaste, see project list for colours and quantities

17   Tilting turntable

18   White vegetable fat

SQUIRES KITCHEN'S
Sugarpaste

1

16

14

11

17

7

2

10

15

3

8

4

9

5

18

13

6

12

Linda Garnham

BIOGRAPHY

My interest in sugarcraft began 26 years ago, when I started making cakes for my family after my son was born.

In the beginning I was self-taught and this posed a few problems, but it wasn't until I attempted one particular royal iced cake that I realised I couldn't do it alone. The royal iced coating was so hard that, rather than slicing the cake, it had to be scooped out of the coating. It would have made a better doorstop! So a year after my daughter was born, I enrolled at my local college and soon became hooked on sugarcraft and cake decorating.

Encouraged by my tutors, Katy Ballanger and Anne Bacon, I continued my studies at Barking College in nearby Romford and enrolled on a two-year City and Guilds course with Lesley Herbert. Lesley kept us on our toes at college and we were soon entering competitions. My first competition was at a local agricultural show, then I entered a few British Sugarcraft Guild Regional Exhibitions and was soon entering *Le Salon Culinaire de Londres* held in Earls Court, the Heart of England Culinaire Birmingham and *Le Festival International de la Gastronomie à Malte*. My key skills included royal icing, sugarpaste decorations and sugar floristry, and I gained Gold, Silver and Bronze awards for my work.

I studied Creative Studies: Sugarcraft Skills in my first two years at college, then stayed on for a third year to study the Design and Decoration of Sugar Confectionery. I also gained my Adult Education Teaching and Assessors certificates in that year. I initially taught at Barking College, then in local adult education whilst continuing my studies in sugar floristry. I continue to top up my skills today and have attended courses run by Eddie Spence, Tombi Peck, Alan Dunn, Janet

Carpenter of Coronet Porcelain, Nhora de la Pava and many other talented tutors – you never stop learning!

As a member of the British Sugarcraft Guild for over 20 years, it was after I won a trophy at the International Exhibition in 2004 for a Pastillage Violin Exhibit that I was invited to become a judge. I have been privileged to view some wonderful work judging at many regional and international exhibitions, including Squires Kitchen's Annual Exhibition, Cork Sugarcraft Exhibition in Ireland and at the Excel Exhibition Centre in London. As chairman of my region from 2007–10 I was also involved in the organisation of a Regional Exhibition, and am currently an Accredited Demonstrator, Assessor and Trainer for the Demonstrator Training Committee.

I have demonstrated various sugarcraft skills to branches of the British Sugarcraft Guild and National Sugar Art Association around the UK for over 15 years, and have also taught and demonstrated overseas.

My relationship with Squires Kitchen began when I entered a competition at Squires Kitchen's Annual Exhibition in 2001. I entered a floral piece that included bluebells, primroses and violets for the 'British Wild Flowers' category. We had just experienced a really wet and muddy winter and I wanted to portray life and beauty flourishing from the darkness of the woodlands. I displayed the flowers around the footprint of a wellington boot and incorporated my study of the snails that were persistently crossing my garden that year! My piece looked quite dark as I set it down on the table next to some of the bright and beautiful entries and I went home thinking that I didn't stand a chance. I was thrilled when I found out that I had won first prize.

It wasn't until 2011, however, that I started teaching at Squires Kitchen International School, after responding to an advertisement for new tutors. I currently teach Foundation Floral and Foundation Sugarpaste classes and you may also see me demonstrating, teaching and judging at the Squires Kitchen Annual Exhibitions. I am also a contributor to *Cakes & Sugarcraft* magazine and particularly enjoyed working on the Diamond Jubilee Celebration Cake featured in issue 117 and the Maypoles Celebration Cake for issue 118.

Basic Sugarpaste Skills

LINDA GARNHAM

Sugarpaste (also known as rolled fondant) is a popular ready-to-roll paste that is ideal for covering cakes and can be used for modelling simple decorations, such as blossoms and bows. Sugarpaste allows you to achieve a smooth, high-standard finish on your cakes and allows you to cover cakes quickly and easily. The basic skills covered in this section include colouring sugarpaste, covering round and square cakes and making simple decorative touches.

EDIBLES

Covering a cake and cake drum (board) with sugarpaste

Rich fruit cake pre-coated with marzipan or a crumb-coated sponge cake, see pages 91–97

SK Sugarpaste in a colour of your choice

Dowelling a cake

Cakes, prepared and covered with sugarpaste, placed on a cake card of the same size

Small amount of royal icing

SK Professional Food Colour Pen

For essential sugarpaste edibles and equipment, see pages 132–133

EQUIPMENT

Covering a cake and cake drum (board) with sugarpaste

Cake drum (board), 5cm–7.5cm (2"–3") larger than the cake

Pastry brush

Ribbon

Non-toxic glue stick or double-sided tape

Dowelling a cake

Plastic cake dowels

Dowelling template, see page 504

Craft knife

TECHNIQUES

- Colouring sugarpaste

- Covering a cake with sugarpaste

- Covering a cake board/drum with sugarpaste

- Dowelling a sugarpasted cake

- Simple decorative techniques: embossing, inlaying, appliqué, crimping and marbling

- Basic sugarpaste modelling

Colouring sugarpaste

Sugarpaste is available in a wide range of ready-made colours, including white, ivory, pastel shades and stronger colours. Squires Kitchen have a fantastic range of high-quality ready-to-roll sugarpaste in a wide selection of designer colours. Ready-made colours are extremely useful if you don't have a range of food colourings to hand: they save you time and mean that you are guaranteed a consistent colour throughout the paste.

If you would like to colour your own sugarpaste, paste food colours are recommended. Liquid colours can change the consistency of the paste and dust colours make it difficult to achieve an even colour throughout the paste.

TUTOR TIPS

Always keep any spare paste sealed in food sealing wrap or a food-grade plastic bag to prevent it from drying out.

If you are placing the cake onto a pre-coated drum, the cake should be placed on a thin cake card of the same size before it is coated with marzipan and sugarpaste: this will prevent moisture from the cake affecting the sugarpaste on the board.

Do not use cornflour to dust work surfaces when covering your cakes with marzipan or sugarpaste coatings. The cornflour can react with the marzipan and sugars and start to cause fermentation.

To get rid of any unwanted air bubbles underneath the sugarpaste coating, insert a sterilised, glass-headed pin into the air bubble at a slight angle, then remove the pin and gently ease the air out with your hand or a cake smoother. Make sure you put the pin away safely after use. If you are left with a small hole in the paste, use a dot of royal icing in the same colour as the sugarpaste to hide it or dust over the hole with a little icing sugar if it is white or ivory.

1 To add colour, pick up a little paste food colour on a cocktail stick and transfer it onto a small piece of sugarpaste.

2 Knead the colour into the paste a little at a time until you achieve a shade deeper than the one you require.

3 Mix this piece into the rest of the paste and knead well to fully incorporate the colour. You will need to allow at least a couple of hours for the colour to develop so seal the paste in a food-grade plastic bag to prevent it from drying out. It is a good idea to check the colour of the paste in natural light.

Covering a round cake with sugarpaste

The amount of sugarpaste you need for covering a cake can be found in the table on page 91. If you are covering a rich fruit cake a useful rule of thumb is that the amount of sugarpaste should be approximately half the weight of the cake. For example, if a 15cm (6") round fruit cake weighs 1.15kg (2½lb) then you will need 575g (1lb 4oz) of sugarpaste to coat your cake. Although this is a good way to work out the approximate amount, it is advisable to have extra paste to hand in case it is required.

   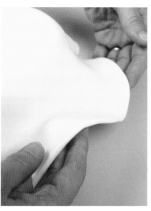

1 Weigh out the amount of sugarpaste required, then knead the paste well on a clean, non-stick board until smooth and pliable. Sugarpaste dries quickly when exposed to air, so wrap any unused paste in a food-grade plastic bag.

2 Lightly dust the work surface with a little icing sugar and begin to roll out the sugarpaste with a non-stick rolling pin, rolling the paste away from you first. Lift the paste and turn it approximately 45° after each roll to ensure the paste doesn't stick and has an even thickness. Roll out the sugarpaste into a rough circle that is approximately 5mm (¼") thick. Rolling out the paste between marzipan spacers will help you achieve the correct thickness easily.

3 To ensure the paste is large enough, use the rolling pin to roughly measure across the top and sides of the cake, then roll out the paste so it is slightly larger than this measurement. Avoid getting icing sugar on the top of the sugarpaste as this will make the icing dry out very quickly and may cause the covering to crack.

4 If the cake is marzipanned, brush a little cooled, boiled water or clear alcohol over the marzipan at this point, ensuring that the entire surface is lightly moistened. If you are using a sponge cake it should be filled and crumb-coated, ready to cover.

5 With the cake to one side, carefully fold the sugarpaste over a rolling pin and lay it over the top of the cake. Use one hand to smooth down the sugarpaste as you cover the cake to eliminate any unwanted air bubbles.

6 If there are any folds in the covering, lift out the sides of the paste, gently smooth them down again with your hands to expel any air and continue smoothing around the whole cake. Do not pull the paste as this will cause it to tear.

7 Use a small, sharp knife to trim away the excess paste from around the base of the cake.

Basic Sugarpaste Skills

139

8 Using an even pressure, polish the paste with cake smoothers until the surface is even, silky-smooth and free from cracks. Gently round off the top edge of the cake with the palms of your hands. For fruit cakes, place a spoonful of royal icing in the centre of a plain or pre-coated drum and stick the cake in place. For sponge cakes, use a little buttercream instead.

tutor tip

Once coated and still fresh, the surface can then be embossed or crimped as required or left to dry ready for further decoration (see pages 144–145).

Covering a square cake with sugarpaste

Follow the same method as for covering a round cake to step 6. As you smooth the covering over a square cake or other shapes with corners, lift out the corners first and smooth these down onto the cake. Once the corners are smooth, gently smooth down the sides.

Covering a cake drum (board) with sugarpaste

Method 1: Covering the whole cake drum (board)

1 Brush the surface of the cake board with a little clear alcohol or cooled, boiled water. The surface should be damp rather than wet. Knead the sugarpaste until smooth and pliable, then lightly dust the work surface with icing sugar. Roll out the paste until it is approximately 4mm (1/8") thick (you can use marzipan spacers to help you achieve the correct thickness) and large enough to cover the board.

2 Fold the sugarpaste over a rolling pin and place onto the board. Rub your hand over the surface to eliminate any air bubbles and stick the sugarpaste to the board. Smooth over the covering with a cake smoother for a polished finish.

3 Trim away the excess paste from around the edge of the board with a sharp knife or palette knife in a downward motion. Alternatively for a chamfered edge, rub a smoother over and along the edge of the board: the smoother will cut away the paste and give a rounded edge. Smooth the edge with the palm of your hand to ensure it is even.

4 To trim the board with ribbon, cut a length of ribbon that is slightly longer than the circumference of the board. Stick the ribbon around the edge of the board with a non-toxic glue stick, taking care to ensure that the glue does not come into contact with the sugarpaste. Alternatively, you can secure the ribbon to the board with double-sided tape. Overlap the ends of the ribbon at the back for a neat finish.

Allow the sugarpaste covering to dry before placing the cake on the coated board. If you are using this method, the cake should be covered on a cake card of the same size before being place on the covered board (see page 139).

Basic Sugarpaste Skills

141

Method 2: Covering the drum (board) using the strip method

This second method is more economical as you only need enough sugarpaste to cover the outer edge of the board.

1 Measure the circumference of the board then secure the cake to the centre. Dust your work surface with a little icing sugar then knead and roll the sugarpaste into a sausage that is approximately $1/2$ to $2/3$ of the length of the circumference.

2 Press the rolling pin along the length of the sugarpaste to flatten it slightly, then roll out the sausage until it is long enough and wide enough to cover the exposed board. Trim one long side of the strip to create a straight edge.

3 Brush the exposed area of the board with a little clear alcohol, or cooled, boiled water, taking care not to splash the cake. Loosely roll up the strip of sugarpaste, then quickly and carefully position the straight edge against the side of the cake and unroll it around the board.

4 Overlap the ends of the paste and cut through both layers with a sharp knife. Remove the excess paste and smooth the join with your fingers and a cake smoother.

5 Carefully rub over the paste with a cake smoother, taking care not to damage the cake. Trim the paste from the board edge using a small palette knife or a smoother (see page 141).

Dowelling a cake

It is important to remember that when you are making a stacked cake with more than one tier, the lower tiers must be dowelled to prevent the cakes above from sinking into them.

note

Make sure you remove the dowels, along with any other inedible items, before the cake is served.

1 Place each cake onto a thin cake card of the same size. Cover with sugarpaste as required and leave to dry overnight (see page 139).

2 Create a dowelling template on a piece of greaseproof paper (see template on page 504) or purchase a ready-made one. Place the template centrally on the cake and mark where the dowels will sit with a scribing needle, modelling tool or similar (see page 490 for more instructions).

3 Immerse the cake dowels in boiling water, or rub them with clear alcohol

to sterilise them before use, then allow them to dry.

4 Insert a dowel into the cake and push it down until it touches the cake board at the bottom. Use an edible food pen to mark each dowel just above the sugarpaste covering. If the height differs between each dowel, cut them all to the tallest mark to ensure the upper tiers remain level.

5 Gently twist and pull the dowels from the cake, taking care not to damage the cake covering. Line up the

dowels, carefully score around the mark with a craft knife, then snap each dowel between your fingers. For thicker dowels, you may need to use a junior hacksaw to cut through them.

6 Tidy up the cut end of the dowel to remove any shards of plastic and sterilise the dowel again before re-inserting into the cake. Carefully secure the next tier on top with a little royal icing or softened sugarpaste. Dowel each of the lower tiers individually before stacking the cake.

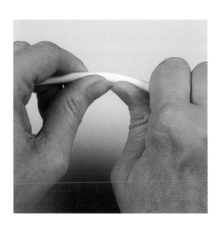

Basic Sugarpaste Skills

Decorative sugarpaste techniques

There are many different decorative techniques to help you embellish your sugarpasted cake designs.

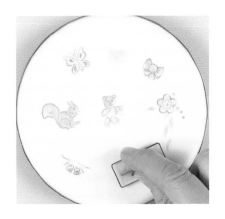

◀ *Embossing*

Embossing is a quick and simple decorative technique for creating patterns in sugar. Whilst the sugarpaste is still fresh and soft, push the embosser into the surface of the paste. Ensure the embosser is clean before use to avoid spoiling the impression. Once the sugarpaste has dried, you can paint over the embossed pattern with diluted paste, liquid or dust food colours to enhance the design.

Inlaying ▶

To create an inlaid design, use a cutter to cut out your chosen shape from the sugarpaste cake or board covering while the paste is still soft. Roll out a different colour of sugarpaste to the same thickness as the covering, then cut out a piece of paste with the same cutter as before. Apply a little edible glue to the gap in the cake covering, then stick the new piece of paste into the gap and smooth over.

▲ *Appliqué*

Appliqué is a decorative technique where you build up a pattern with pieces of sugarpaste. Simply cut out several shapes from thinly rolled paste, layer them on top of one another and secure with edible glue.

▼ *Marbling*

To create a marbled effect in sugarpaste, simply take two different colours of sugarpaste and roll them into long sausages. Place alternate coloured strips together, then twist and roll out the paste to merge the colours.

◀ *Crimping*

Crimping is a quick and effective way to add decorative borders to cake coverings. Crimpers are available in a variety of shapes and can be plain or serrated, depending upon the effect you want to achieve. Press the crimper into fresh paste and gently pinch the paste together to create a raised design effect. Ensure you release the pressure on the crimper as you remove it otherwise you will tear the paste.

Modelling with sugarpaste

Sugarpaste can be used for modelling small and simple decorations such as roses, bows and leaves which can add a finishing touch to a cake design. However, as sugarpaste is quite soft, it is a good idea to mix it with a small amount of SFP (flower paste) in order to make a stronger modelling paste that remains pliable, yet still holds its shape.

Basic blossoms

1 Roll five very small balls of modelling paste, then roll each ball into a small cone shape. Arrange the cones in a flower shape so the pointed ends are in the centre, then stick them together with a little edible glue. Gently push the petals together and press a ball tool into the centre to secure the shape.

2 Roll out a little modelling paste in a different colour and cut out a small blossom using a plunger cutter. Place the blossom on a foam pad and press a ball tool into the centre to cup it. Glue to the top of the first flower. Make a tiny ball of paste, moisten the centre of the flower with a little edible glue and drop the ball in the centre. Press the centre with the small end of a ball tool to secure.

Basic leaves

Roll a small ball of green sugarpaste into a cone shape. Press the flat end of a Dresden tool down the centre of the cone and bend the very tip of the cone to add movement. In order to make larger leaves, you will need to start with a larger ball of paste.

Basic rolled roses

Use the palm of your hand to roll a small ball of sugarpaste into a sausage shape. Roll a small rolling pin over the sausage, then roll one long side of the sausage slightly thinner than the other side. Keeping the thicker edge at the top, roll the paste up from one end into a rose shape. When you are happy with the shape and size, cut off any excess paste and use your fingers to model the back of the rose into a cone.

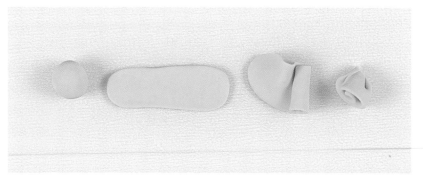

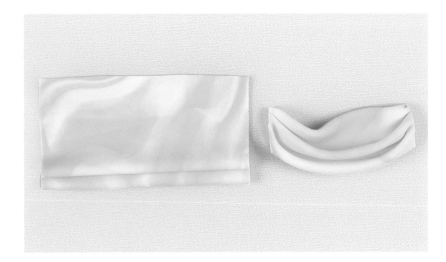

Basic fabric effects

Sugarpaste is often used to create a decorative fabric effect, which can then be draped over or wrapped around a cake. The instructions here describe how to create a simple drape from a single sheet of paste; this can be adapted using more pieces of paste as described in the Bunny Christening Cake project on the following pages.

1 Mix equal quantities of sugarpaste and SFP (flower paste) together to make modelling paste. Produce a template that is the same length and double the height that you require the drape to be.

2 Roll out the paste very thinly, to approximately 1mm–2mm ($^1/_{16}$"). If the paste is too thick you will not be able to form the folds; if it is too thin you may tear the paste as you lift it.

3 Lay your template onto the paste and cut out the shape. Release the paste from the board then dust the work surface with a little icing sugar.

4 Turn the paste over and fold over the top to create a neat edge. Turn the paste back over, slip a barbecue skewer under the paste and use your fingers to create a fold. Continue to lift and layer the folds until all of the paste is pleated.

5 Tuck the bottom edge under the folds for a neat finish. For a swag effect, pinch the two ends together and allow the paste to drape in a curve.

Basic figure modelling

If you want to model larger decorations or basic figures from sugarpaste, add approximately 3g (½tsp) of gum tragacanth to every 250g (8¾oz) of sugarpaste. Knead the gum powder into the paste, then wrap the paste in cling film and keep in an airtight food container overnight to allow the paste to mature. If you model figures from sugarpaste alone, you may find that as the model dries it begins to collapse; by adding gum tragacanth you can strengthen the paste without lightening the colour. Re-knead the paste before you use it.

Most simple figures are made up of a few basic shapes: a ball, oval, cone or sausage. Always knead the sugarpaste well before modelling each shape, then roll the paste firmly between the palms of your hands to make a ball shape. You can model all other basic shapes from a ball. See the Foundation Modelling section starting on page 184 to find out more about modelling basic figures.

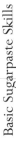

Bunny Christening Cake

This pretty yet simple design with its cute bunny and little rolled roses would be perfect for celebrating a christening, baby shower or a little one's birthday.

EDIBLES

15cm (6") round cake, prepared for covering, see pages 91–97

SK Sugarpaste: 250g (8¾oz) Bridal White, 700g (1lb 8¾oz) Delicate Lemon, 250g (8¾oz) Dove Grey + ½tsp of SK Gum Tragacanth, see opposite

SK Sugar Florist Paste (SFP): 200g (7oz) White

SK Professional Paste Food Colours: Bluebell, Daffodil (yellow), Fuchsia, Leaf Green

SK Professional Dust Food Colour: Rose

SK Gum Tragacanth

For essential sugarpaste edibles and equipment, see pages 132–133

EQUIPMENT

15cm (6") round cake card

23cm (9") round cake drum

Card, approximately 1mm–2mm thick (optional)

Dresden tool

Ball tool

Blossom plunger cutter: medium (PME)

8cm (3¹/₈") round cutter

Square of cellophane

Quilting tool (PME)

Dried spaghetti

SK Paintbrushes: no. 1, no. 10 (dusting brush)

Scribing needle or CelPin

Small foam pad

Non-toxic glue stick

76cm (30") x 15mm (½") wide satin ribbon: lemon yellow

1 Cover both the cake and cake board with Delicate Lemon sugarpaste and allow both to firm overnight (see pages 139–140). Attach the cake to the board with a little royal icing or softened sugarpaste.

2 Cut out two strips from the 1mm–2mm thick card that are 30.5cm long x 4cm wide (12" x 1½") for the spacer and drape templates.

3 Make a greaseproof paper template that is the same height as the cake and long enough to fit around the circumference of the cake. Fold the template into six equal sections, then draw a horizontal line along the length of the template measuring just under 4cm (1½") from the bottom: this will be a guide for the height of the drape. Mark the position of the flowers on the template so that they will sit above this line.

4 Wrap the template around the cake and mark out the position of the flowers with a CelPin or a scribing needle on the sugarpaste. Scribe a faint line around the cake where you will attach the drape.

5 Mix 75g (2½oz) of White SFP with 150g (5¼oz) of Bridal White sugarpaste and knead well. Roll a long sausage of paste that measures about ²/₃ of the circumference of the cake, then flatten with a rolling pin.

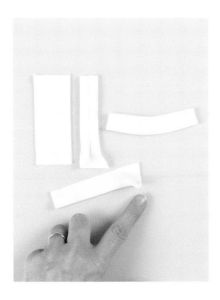

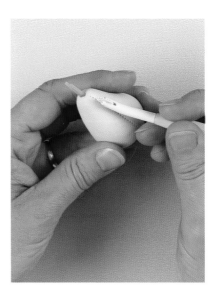

6 Dust the board with a little icing sugar and then roll along the length of the paste. Place the two strips of card either side, then continue to roll out the paste until it is the same thickness as the card spacers and as long as the circumference of the cake. Lay one of the strips of card on the paste and use as a template to cut out a long strip of paste. Trim the ends then fold the paste in half lengthways and stick it down with a little edible glue.

7 Place the cake on a turntable and tilt it into a comfortable working position. Moisten approximately 1cm (³/₈") up from the base of the cake with edible glue, then stick the white strip of paste around the cake. Trim the ends neatly.

8 Make another length of paste, then attach in the same way around the cake so that it overlaps the first layer.

9 For the final layer, make another strip in the same way but instead of folding the length in half, fold over and secure the two edges in the centre of the strip to create a neat edge. Secure this length around the cake in the same way, covering the guideline marked out earlier.

10 Cut out a circle of white modelling paste, fold it in half

then gently pleat the paste. Attach it over the join at the back of the cake and tuck in the sides. The diameter of the cutter should be at least double the height of the drape, possibly even larger depending on the thickness of your drapes. Keep the trimmings to make the bunny's tail later.

11 Trim the cake drum with lemon yellow ribbon (see pages 141–142).

12 Knead together equal amounts of Bridal White sugarpaste and White SFP and divide into four small pieces. Colour each piece of modelling paste to make blue-, green-, pink- and yellow-coloured paste (see page 138).

13 Make six basic blossoms using the blue, pink and yellow modelling paste (see page 145) and attach to the side of the cake with a little edible glue, following the marks made earlier.

14 Make 12 small leaves from the green paste for the side decoration, three small leaves for the bunny's bouquet, three medium leaves for the cake top and five larger leaves for the rolled rose decoration on the board (see page 145). Use edible glue to

attach a small leaf on either side of the blossoms around the cake.

15 Make three small rolled roses for the bunny's bouquet, three medium and three large roses for the cake decoration from the pink-coloured sugarpaste (see page 145). Allow the rolled roses to dry a little, then arrange three small leaves on top of the cake and five larger leaves on the cake board, and secure the roses on top of the leaves with a little edible glue.

16 Roll 27g (1oz) of Dove Grey modelling paste into a soft cone shape and place it on a square of cellophane to prevent the paste from sticking. Draw a seam line around the paste with a quilting wheel. Insert two lengths of dried spaghetti into the top of the cone, pushing them down through the body for extra support. Leave enough spaghetti sticking out to support the head.

17 Roll out a little blue modelling paste very thinly and cut out three small squares for the bunny's patches. Stick two squares to the front and one to the back of the body with edible glue. Mark lines across the squares and body with a cocktail stick or tool.

Bunny Christening Cake

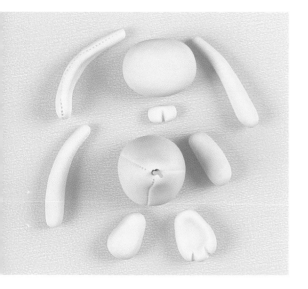

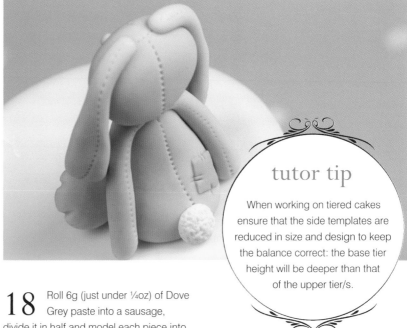

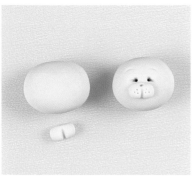

Bunny Christening Cake

18 Roll 6g (just under ¼oz) of Dove Grey paste into a sausage, divide it in half and model each piece into a soft cone for the feet. Holding the thinner end of one cone, use a cocktail stick to mark out the paws on the thicker end and press a ball tool into the centre of the paw. Add a seam line around the edge as before. Repeat for the second paw and secure both to the base of the body with a little edible glue.

19 For the arms, roll 6g (just under ¼oz) of paste into a ball, divide it in half and roll the pieces of paste into long tapered sausages about the same length as the body. Draw a seam line along the length of the arms and secure to the top of the body around the spaghetti.

20 To make the head, roll a 15g (½oz) ball of paste into an oval shape and mark a seam line around the edge. Push the head down onto the spaghetti at the top of the body and secure with edible glue. Ensure that the spaghetti support cannot be seen.

21 For the muzzle, roll a small ball of grey modelling paste into an oval shape. Mark a central line down the oval and attach it to the head. Use a cocktail stick to mark three dots on either side of the line. Roll a tiny ball of pink

tutor tip

When working on tiered cakes ensure that the side templates are reduced in size and design to keep the balance correct: the base tier height will be deeper than that of the upper tier/s.

paste and stick it to the top of the muzzle for the nose.

22 Use a cocktail stick or CelPin to make small holes either side of the nose for the eyes. Angle the stick away from the nose to stretch the holes slightly and create a cute expression.

23 Roll a 6g ball (just under ¼oz) of Dove Grey modelling paste, divide in half and roll each into a long sausage that is slightly thicker in the middle. Push a ball tool along the middle of the paste and mark a seam line around each ear. Attach to the top of the head with edible glue.

24 Roll a ball of white modelling paste for the tail and secure it in place with edible glue.

25 Add a pink blush to the cheeks, paw pads and inner ears with Rose dust food colour and a dusting brush. Allow the paste to firm a little before securing to the top of the cake. Attach a group of small roses and leaves to the top of one paw to finish.

Susan Griffiths

BIOGRAPHY

hilst I was still at school, I started working as a Saturday girl in a little home bakery shop in Hove. They asked me if I would like to work full time, so I left school at 15 to take up my post and that's where my love of cakes began. I was a hard worker even then, running between the bakery at the back of the shop and the till to serve customers at busy times. As part of my role, I was sent on my first cake decorating class to learn how to make a Christmas cake.

After two years it was time to move on to my next love. I had always had a passion for horses, so at 18 I started work at a riding stables. I had a variety of jobs over the next few years then at 30 I had my first daughter, Amy, followed by Abbie two years later, and I started baking again. I had always enjoyed art and the children's birthday cakes became more elaborate over time. Soon my friends were asking me for designer cakes and I moved on to making wedding cakes.

As my interest in cake decorating grew, I joined the local Worthing branch of the British Sugarcraft Guild which had monthly demonstrations. They held exhibitions all over the country and I started to enter pieces into competitions at a novice level. My standard of work improved vastly over the years, and this gave me the confidence to demonstrate myself. I took a City & Guilds course in Art and Design and Sugarcraft and soon became an accredited demonstrator for the British Sugarcraft Guild, travelling all over the country to demonstrate. I was inspired by Nadine Hurst and her sugar collage work and my first demonstrations were on royal icing run-out work. I went on to demonstrate how to model my sugar teddy bears, which turned out to be very popular.

I sent a photo of my sugar teddy bear models to *Cakes & Sugarcraft* magazine in 1996 and they published the picture along with my letter. Having been impressed with my work, they asked if I would like to do a magazine article on sugar teddies and that's how my involvement with Squires Kitchen began. Not long after I began working as the Saturday manager at Squires Kitchen's shop in Farnham, which I still love to this day!

I was invited to demonstrate at Squires Kitchen's Annual Exhibition and in my first demonstrations I showed people how to model with Cocoform (a chocolate modelling paste). Nowadays, I love to work with SK Mexican Modelling Paste (MMP) and I demonstrate how to use sugarcraft moulds and texture mats.

My first book, *Making Sugar Teddy Bears*, was published by B. Dutton Publishing in 2003. Following its success I went on to write a second book, *Making Sugar Cats for Cakes* in 2005. I really enjoyed working on both books and the publishing team helped me all the way.

I now work in the Squires Kitchen shop at the weekends, demonstrating sugarcraft techniques and helping customers. I am so lucky to have a job where I get to interact with different customers and help them with their own cake designs. I will always remember one lovely lady who made a Disney-inspired castle for her sister's wedding, and she came in every week for advice on how to make all the different parts of the cake. When I saw a photo of the finished cake, I was so impressed – it looked amazing!

Teaching at Squires Kitchen International School is a dream job for me. My courses are all Foundation level and I believe I can teach anyone to decorate cakes. My courses include Foundation Sugarpaste, Celebration Miniature Cakes and Couture Cupcakes, all of which are fun and relaxing to teach. It is so lovely at the end of the day to see the variety of designs and colours on the students' cakes and I still pick up new ideas from them, which I can use and pass on to others.

Decorative Mini Cakes

SUSAN GRIFFITHS

Miniature cakes are popular for afternoon teas, weddings and all sorts of other special occasions and can be stacked or placed on stands to make an impressive centrepiece. A contemporary alternative to fairy cakes, mini cakes are just the right size for individual servings and make great gifts. This foundation section explains how to bake and decorate mini cakes using quick and easy sugarpaste techniques with texture mats, cutters and moulds.

EDIBLES

Baking mini cakes

Sponge recipe for 16 mini cakes, equivalent to 25.5cm (10") cake, see page 15

Covering a mini cake and cake card with sugarpaste

20g (¾oz) buttercream per mini cake, see page 26

200g (7oz) sugarpaste per round mini cake with cake card or 225g (8oz) sugarpaste per domed mini cake with cake card

For essential sugarpaste edibles and equipment, see pages 132–133

EQUIPMENT

Baking mini cakes

SK 16-Compartment 6.5cm (2½") Round Mini Pans

SK Re-usable Liners for 6.5cm (2½") Round Mini Pans

Silikomart Half-Sphere Silicone Mould: 6cm (2³/₈") for domed mini cakes

Baking parchment

Large, serrated knife

Covering a mini cake and cake card with sugarpaste

7.5cm (3") round cake cards

3mm (¹/₈") wide ribbon

TECHNIQUES

- Preparing cake cards

- Preparing and covering mini cakes

- Decorative sugarpaste techniques: cutting strips, using templates, rope effect, bow, string of pearls, embossing paste, plunger cutter decorations, simple moulded decorations, multi-coloured moulded decorations, simple rose (unwired), fabric-effect flower, ruffles, pleated paste, frilled drape and flowers

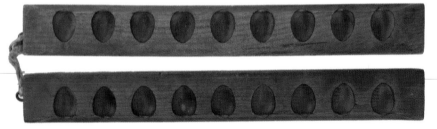

Carved wooden mould for marzipan or sugar eggs

Covering a cake card

tutor tip

Prepare the cake cards a day before you need to mount the cakes on them.

1 Knead a small quantity of sugarpaste in the required colour and roll out on a work surface dusted with icing sugar.

2 Brush the edge of the card with a little cooled, boiled water.

3 Lay the paste over the card and roll over the paste again to make

it thinner. If desired, add texture with a texture mat at this point (see technique on page 161). Trim any excess paste from the edge of the card with a sharp knife.

4 Repeat this process so all the cake cards are prepared in advance. Trim each card with 3mm (1/8") wide ribbon (see page 141).

Baking round mini cakes

1 Preheat the oven to 160°C/140°C fan/325°F/gas mark 3.

2 Line the base of the mini cake pan with baking parchment, then place a re-usable liner in each of the pan rings.

3 Pour the prepared sponge mixture into each of the pan rings to ¾ full.

4 Place the pan on the middle shelf of the oven and bake for approximately 30 minutes: the mixture should rise above the top of the pans.

5 Take the mini cakes out of the oven and leave to cool for a few minutes. Use a serrated knife to trim the top off each cake, making them all the same size.

6 Leave the mini cakes in the pans to cool, then run a small knife around the inside of each ring to release the cakes. Turn all the cakes out onto a wire cooling rack and peel off the liners.

For domed mini cakes: To make the domes you can either make extra cake mix (I use a 7-egg recipe) or bake less mini cakes (approximately 12). Bake the domed part in a half-sphere silicone mould, filling all six moulds almost to the top, for approximately 15 minutes at the same oven temperature as for the mini cakes. Once the cakes are cool, pop the domes out of the mould and stick one on the top of each mini cake with a little buttercream. You will have two spares in case the domes don't all rise to the top.

Decorative Mini Cakes

Covering round mini cakes

1 Once the cakes are cool, use a palette knife to spread a thin layer of buttercream over each mini cake.

2 Knead approximately 200g (7oz) of sugarpaste until pliable, then roll out on a work surface dusted with icing sugar.

3 Fold the paste over a medium rolling pin and lay the paste over the mini cake.

4 Use your palms to smooth the paste across the top and down the sides of the cake.

5 Trim any excess paste from the base of the cake and buff the paste with cake smoothers.

6 Place the cake on a covered cake card and stick down with a little buttercream.

For domed mini cakes: Cover the whole cake with a layer of buttercream, then roll out approximately 225g (8oz) of sugarpaste. Cut out a strip of sugarpaste and wrap it around the main section of the cake. Cover the dome with a separate piece of paste and trim to size. Smooth over the join and trim off any excess paste.

tutor tip

Place the covered mini cakes on a spare cake card or board so that they are easy to pick up and move.

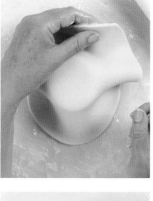

Decorative Mini Cakes

Simple decorative techniques

You can decorate mini cakes in a variety of ways to add a personal touch, but the key is to keep the design simple so the small cake does not look heavy or overloaded. Simple designs can also save you time if you need to create lots of mini cakes for a large event. The basic techniques described here can all be made with sugarpaste and are ideal for decorating mini cakes, as well as for adding finishing touches to larger cakes.

Cutting strips ▼

This technique uses a plastic strip cutter to make straight, even lengths of paste.

1 Roll out a long piece of sugarpaste on a work surface dusted with icing sugar.

2 Rub a little white vegetable fat over the ridged side of the strip cutter, then place the cutter onto the sugarpaste.

3 Press down on the strip cutter so that it cuts through the paste, then lift the cutter away. You can make the strips longer if required by carefully lining up the cutter beside the first set of strips and cutting again.

4 Trim away the excess paste from around the strips, then gently peel the strips of paste apart.

Using templates

If you don't have a cutter for the shape you require, making a template is a useful technique. Keep your templates in a safe place so you can use them again when needed.

1 Draw your chosen template onto a piece of thin card, then cut it out with a pair of scissors.

2 Roll out some sugarpaste on a work surface dusted with icing sugar, then place the template centrally on the paste.

3 Holding the template in place, cut around the shape with a cutting wheel or a small, sharp knife. Remove the excess paste.

Rope effect ▼

1 Roll out a long sausage of sugarpaste and indent a line all the way along the sausage with a blade tool. Turn over and repeat on the opposite side.

2 Twist the length of paste to form a rope and trim to size.

Birdcages

This decorative set of birdcage mini cakes has the same basic design, but they show how this can be further decorated and personalised using simple techniques.

EDIBLES

4 domed mini cakes, prepared for covering, see page 157

SK Sugarpaste: Ballerina Pink, Delicate Lemon, Lullaby Blue, Vintage Ivory

SK Instant Mix Royal Icing (small amount)

SK Quality Food Colour (QFC) Pastes: Black, Green

SK Quality Food Colour (QFC) Dusts: Blue, Brown, Dark Green, Pink, Yellow

EQUIPMENT

4 round cake cards

3mm (1/8") wide ribbon

Piping bags

Piping nozzle: ST50 – leaf (PME)

SK Great Impressions Moulds: Round Boss, Lace Classic Scroll

Strip cutter: no. 1 (3mm, 1/8") (JEM)

Daphne cutter (FMM)

Lace cutter: LA1 from set (OP)

Blade and shell tool (PME)

Templates, see page 505

For essential sugarpaste edibles and equipment, see pages 132–133

1 Cover the cake cards and domed mini cakes with each of the four sugarpaste colours (see page 157). Trim the cards with ribbon (see page 141).

2 Mark where the bars of the cage will be using a template, then cut strips of paste and stick the vertical lines first then the horizontal. Make a handle for the top using the central part of the round boss mould and add a tiny hoop.

3 Yellow mini cake: Place towards the back of the cake card to allow room for the birds. Cut out several Daphne flowers and leave to dry. Make up a bag of green royal icing (see pages 235–236), snip off the tip and pipe trailing leaves onto the birdcages. Stick the flowers in place with the royal icing and pipe a dot in the centre of each flower. Model simple bluebirds from sugarpaste following the step-by-step photo and mark the eyes using a cocktail stick dipped in black paste food colour.

4 Pink mini cake: Make two ropes from a length of sugarpaste and attach to the cake (see page 158). Model tiny rose buds (see page 164), attach in place with the green royal icing then pipe in tiny leaves using a no. 50 leaf nozzle.

5 Blue mini cake: Emboss strips of paste with the Lace Classic Scroll mould and cut out with the lace cutter. Attach around the base and dome. Cut out pink birds using the template (see page 491) then when dry paint with dust colours diluted with clear alcohol.

6 Ivory mini cake: Dilute the dust colours with clear alcohol and use a fine paintbrush to paint the branch and leaf design onto the cake. Add the other details to the birdcage after the paint has dried.

Birdcages

Simple decorative techniques

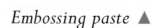
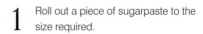

Bow ▲

1 Cut out all the bow templates on page 505 from a piece of thin card or paper. Roll out a piece of SFP, place the templates on the paste and cut around them with a cutting wheel.

2 To make the bow loops, fold the ends of the longest piece of paste into the centre and secure with a little edible glue. Brush a little edible glue between the loops and stick a square of paste over the middle for the knot.

3 Attach the top of the bow tails to the main part of the bow with a little edible glue.

4 Lift up the bow loops with the end of a paintbrush and insert a small piece of kitchen roll to support them as they dry.

String of pearls ▲

1 Take a small ball of SFP and roll it into a long, thin sausage of paste. Rub some white vegetable fat into your palms and roll the paste between your hands.

2 Press the sausage of paste into a bead maker, making sure that it fills all the holes.

3 Use a cranked palette knife to trim off any excess paste from the back of the mould.

4 Carefully release the string of pearls from the mould and cut to the length required.

5 Dust the paste with a little Pearl lustre dust to add a pearlescent sheen.

Embossing paste ▲

1 Roll out a piece of sugarpaste to the size required.

2 Rub a little white vegetable fat over the patterned side of a texture mat to prevent the paste from sticking.

3 Place the patterned side down onto the sugarpaste, and press down on the mat with an even pressure to emboss the paste.

4 Remove the mat and cut the patterned paste to shape with a cutting wheel or a small, sharp knife.

Textured rolling pins can also be used to emboss a pattern into sugarpaste: simply roll over the paste once, pressing firmly to ensure the pattern is transferred effectively.

Pearls and Bows

These delicate designs, featuring vintage brooch decorations and pretty sugar pearls, would be perfect for an anniversary party or would make great girly gifts.

EDIBLES

4 mini cakes, prepared for covering, see page 157

SK Sugarpaste: Antique Lace, Ballerina Pink, Lullaby Blue, Vintage Ivory

SK Sugar Florist Paste (SFP): Cream (small amount)

SK Instant Mix Royal Icing (small amount)

SK Quality Food Colour (QFC) Lustre Dust: Pearl

SK 4mm Ball Dragées: Pearl

EQUIPMENT

4 round cake cards

3mm (1/8") wide ribbon

SK Great Impressions Moulds: Bow, Oval Boss, Rose (Small), Lace Classic Scroll

SK Plain Beads Mould

Piping bag

Lace cutter: LA1 from set (OP)

For essential sugarpaste edibles and equipment, see pages 132–133

1 Cover the boards and cakes with sugarpaste (see page 157), then trim with ribbon.

2 Brooch and pearls mini cake: Make a string of pearls (see page 161) and attach them around the cake with edible glue. Make a bow using the mould, brush with lustre dust and attach at the front. Make a brooch using the oval boss mould, indent it where the pearls will be then use a sugar pearl for the centre and pearl dragées around the outside. Attach the brooch and pearls with a dot of royal icing.

3 Big bow mini cake: Cut out a scalloped piece of sugarpaste and wrap it around the base of the cake. Make tiny bows using the bow mould, brush with lustre dust and position around the scalloped edge. Make a bow from Cream SFP using the template (see page 491) and attach it to the cake, supporting the loops with kitchen roll if required.

4 Rosebuds mini cake: Trim the cake with ribbon, then cut strips of sugarpaste and attach them from the centre of the cake down the sides. Make

several tiny roses using the centre of the rose mould and attach them so that they cover the cake top.

5 Pearl and rose mini cake: Emboss a strip of sugarpaste with the lace mould (see page 161), cut it out with the lace cutter and wrap it around the cake. Make a string of sugar pearls to go around the base then add a moulded rose brushed with lustre dust to finish.

Pearls and Bows

Simple decorative techniques

◀ *Plunger cutter decorations*

This technique is useful for making lots of decorations quickly.

1 Roll out a small piece of sugarpaste on a surface dusted with icing sugar.

2 Push the cutter firmly into the paste. Lift the cutter and press down the plunger to eject the paste.

3 Place the decorations onto a piece of food-grade sponge to dry.

▲ *Simple moulded decorations*

1 Knead enough sugarpaste to fill the mould you are using.

2 Rub your hand with a little white vegetable fat and roll the paste in your hand. Push the paste firmly into the mould.

3 Turn the mould over and tap the back with a small rolling pin to release the decoration.

▼ *Multi-coloured moulded decorations*

1 Choose two or three different colours of sugarpaste and knead a small amount of each.

2 Rub your hand with a little white vegetable fat and roll a small piece of paste in your hand. Push a piece of paste into the bottom of the mould.

3 Repeat with another piece of paste in a different colour, placing the second piece of paste on top of the first.

4 Keep layering the paste as you desire, until the mould is full. Make sure the paste is pushed firmly into the mould.

5 Turn the mould over and tap the back with a small rolling pin to release the decoration.

▲ *Simple rose (unwired)*

1 Mix a small piece of sugarpaste with the same amount of SFP and knead well. Take off a small ball of paste and model a small, pointed cone shape. Squeeze the base into a bulb shape.

2 Roll a sausage of the paste and cut it into 10 pieces. Roll each piece into a small ball then place them into a polythene food bag to stop them drying out.

3 Flatten one of the balls with your finger to make a petal, leaving one edge thicker. Hold the petal with the thinner edge at the top and attach it to the cone with edible glue so it sits slightly above the

point. Wrap the petal around the cone so it is completely covered.

4 Repeat to make another petal and attach it over the join of the first petal at the same height, leaving the edge unstuck. Add another petal, tucking the edge beneath the first.

5 Add further petals around the outside, opening them out gradually. Use fewer petals for a rosebud and more to make a full, open rose.

6 Cut off the base once you have completed the flower.

Roses and Blossoms

*Pretty floral motifs are always popular and you can make impressive decorations
in no time at all with the blossom and rose moulds.*

EDIBLES

4 mini cakes, prepared for covering, see page 157

SK Sugarpaste: Ballerina Pink, Frosted Leaf, Vintage Ivory, Vintage Pink

SK Instant Mix Royal Icing (small amount)

Squires Kitchen Sugar Florist Paste (SFP): Cream (small amount)

SK Quality Food Colour (QFC) Lustre Dust: Pearl

EQUIPMENT

4 round cake cards

3mm (¹/₈") wide ribbon

Piping bags

SK Great Impressions Moulds: Rose (Small), Lace Classic Scroll, Blossom Mould 2

Blossom cutter, small (FMM)

Lace cutter: LA1 from set (OP)

Garrett frill cutter (FMM)

Rose leaf plunger cutter set (PME)

1 Cover the boards and cakes with sugarpaste (see page 157), then trim with ribbon.

2 Add some cooled, boiled water to a small amount of Vintage Pink sugarpaste, place in a heatproof bowl and heat gently in the microwave. This will let the sugarpaste down to a piping consistency. Place it in a piping bag, snip off the tip and pipe a running bead around the base of the ivory and pale pink cakes (see page 242). Repeat to pipe let-down Antique Lace sugarpaste around the base of the blue and pink cakes.

For essential sugarpaste edibles and equipment, see pages 132–133

3 Tiny blossoms mini cake: Make several blossoms using the plunger cutter, allow to dry, then attach them all over the cake with royal icing. Pipe a dot of royal icing in the centre of each one.

4 Big blossoms mini cake: Make three blossoms using the mould, brush with lustre dust and allow to dry in a paint palette or curved former. Position them around the base of the cake when dry.

5 Multi-coloured rose mini cake: Use the four colours of sugarpaste to make roses using the mould (see page 164). Brush with Pearl lustre and leave to dry. Cut out several leaves using a plunger cutter and attach the leaves and roses to the cake with royal icing.

6 Single rose mini cake: Roll out some sugarpaste, emboss it with the scroll mould and cut out a Garrett frill shape. Make pleats from the inner edge and place it on top of the cake. Model a rose (see page 164), brush with lustre dust then secure in place with royal icing.

Roses and Blossoms

Simple decorative techniques

Fabric-effect flower ▶

1 Roll out some sugarpaste thinly and cut out three long strips of sugarpaste, making each strip slightly wider than the last.

2 Fold the top edge of the widest strip of paste into gentle pleats, then flatten the pleats slightly with a small rolling pin and trim the paste back into shape. Fold the paste round into a

circle and join the two ends with a little edible glue.

3 Repeat with the second strip of paste to make a slightly smaller frill.

4 For the third layer, take the thinnest strip and twist the paste in on itself to make a small ruffle.

5 Position the layers on top of each other and glue in place.

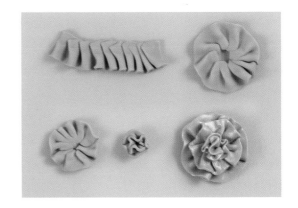

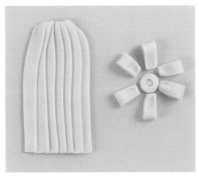

Pleated paste ▲

1 Roll out a thin piece of sugarpaste, then cut out several strips of paste of the same size.

2 Position one strip next to another so that they overlap slightly, then secure with a little edible glue.

3 Continue in the same way with all the strips of paste, gluing them together as you go to make a pleated effect.

4 Pinch the top edge of the paste to make a point.

5 To make a pleated bow, fold strips of paste into loops. Attach six of these in a circle with a flattened ball of paste in the centre. Add a moulded button or ball of paste to finish.

Frilled drape and flowers ▼

1 Thinly roll out some SFP and cut out a long strip. Use a lace cutter to create a serrated edge (see page 169). Attach in position, gently folding along the top edge to give the paste movement.

2 Cut a long thin strip of SFP and place it on a foam pad. Frill along both edges by pressing a cocktail stick onto the paste and rolling it along the edge. Repeat if necessary to accentuate the frill. Attach along the top of the lace piece to neaten the edge and run a stitching wheel along the centre.

3 To make frilled flowers, cut a blossom shape from thinly-rolled SFP and frill the edges on a foam pad as before using a cocktail stick. Add further frilled shapes on top to build up the flower.

Ruffles

1 Roll out a long, thin strip of sugarpaste. Pick up one of the longer edges with a cocktail stick and gather the paste little by little into tight folds.

2 Brush a little edible glue along the un-frilled side and attach to the cake. Make several ruffles and keep layering them around the cake until you achieve the desired effect.

Fabric and Frills

Using simple fabric effects with a touch of lustre dust, you can make elegant mini cakes perfect for a wedding table or individual favours. If you would like to learn how to create more advanced frill and drape effects, see Extended Modelling Skills starting on page 184.

EDIBLES

4 mini cakes, prepared for covering, see page 157

SK Sugarpaste: Delicate Lemon, Lullaby Blue, Vintage Ivory, Vintage Pink

SK Instant Mix Royal Icing (small amount)

SK Sugar Florist Paste (SFP): Cream (small amount)

SK Quality Food Colour (QFC) Lustre Dust: Pearl

SK 4mm Ball Dragées: Pearl

For essential sugarpaste edibles and equipment, see pages 132–133

EQUIPMENT

4 round cake cards

3mm (¹/₈") wide ribbon

Piping bags

SK Great Impressions Mould: Button

Lace cutter: LA1 from set (OP)

Carnation Cutters: 25mm, 35mm (1", 1³/₈") (FMM)

FMM Primrose cutter (FMM)

Quilting tool (PME)

1 Cover the boards and cakes with sugarpaste (see page 157), then trim with ribbon.

2 Pleated mini cake: Make a pleat and pleated bow from sugarpaste (see page 167), then brush with pearl lustre dust. Attach the pleats down the side of the cake and the bow on top. Make a small button using the mould, brush with pearl lustre and leave to dry. Stick it in the centre of the bow with a little royal icing.

3 Fabric flower mini cake: Roll out some sugarpaste and cut a side ribbon to go around the cake. Secure in place and brush with pearl lustre dust. Make a fabric-effect flower for the cake top

(see page 167), dust with pearl lustre and attach in place with royal icing.

4 Frills and flowers mini cake: Make a lace drape and attach it diagonally to the side of the cake with edible glue (see page 167). Make four flowers from Cream SFP using the primrose cutter set, frill the edges and allow to dry. Secure in place with royal icing and finish with a pearl dragée in the centre of each.

5 Ruffle mini cake: Make at least five layers of ruffles (see page 167) and attach them around the sides of the cake. Attach the final layer in a more upright position to hide any joins. Make two sizes of carnation from Cream SFP, frill with a cocktail stick and allow to dry before attaching to the cake. Add a button in the centre of the flower and brush with pearl lustre dust to finish.

tutor tip

Try experimenting with different colour schemes, such as black and white for a dramatic effect, or seasonal colours to suit the occasion.

Fabric and Frills

Painting Techniques

PADDI CLARK

As well as a great way to showcase artistic flair, painted cakes have some practical benefits, too: they are much easier to transport than royal iced or modelled cakes as they aren't as fragile, and you do not need a great deal of equipment to create a stunning design.

To achieve the best effect, however, it is important to use high-quality food colours and paintbrushes. You can use several edible mediums for painting, such as liquid food colours directly from the bottle, dust food colours diluted with confectioners' glaze and clear alcohol, paste food colours mixed with a little water and edible paints. Here, I have shown how to achieve four different types of painting: watercolour painting, brush embroidery, cocoa butter painting and using edible paints.

TECHNIQUES

- Making templates for side designs
- Embossing a design onto sugarpaste
- Watercolour painting
- Brush embroidery
- Cocoa painting
- Using edible paints

Tazza, roundel and chalice made from a recipe for Tudor sugar plate in the late 1980s

EDIBLES

Watercolour painting

SK Professional Liquid Food Colours

Clear alcohol, or cooled, boiled water (optional)

Brush embroidery

SK Instant Mix Royal Icing

Cocoa painting

SK Cocol Cocoa Butter Colouring

Edible paints

SK Designer Edible Paints

SK Confectioners' Glaze

EQUIPMENT

Watercolour painting

SK Paintbrushes: nos. 00, 0, 1, 2

Paint palette

Brush embroidery

Piping nozzles: nos. 1, 1.5 or 2

SK Paintbrush: no. 1 or 2

Small palette knife

Small piping bag

Cocoa painting

Microwave

SK Paintbrushes: nos. 1, 2, 4

Paint palette

Edible paints

SK Paintbrushes: nos. 1, 2, 4

Paint palette

Bowl of water

SK Confectioners' Glaze Cleaner (IPA)

For essential sugarpaste edibles and equipment, see pages 132–133

Making and using templates for side designs

This method would be best for both royal iced and sugarpasted cakes with rounded sides such as circle, oval or blossom shapes.

1 Wrap a length of greaseproof paper around the circumference of the cake. Mark on the height and circumference and unwrap the paper. Draw a rectangle on the paper that is the shape of your cake side(s) and make sure you draw your side design within the parameters of the cake side(s).

2 Carefully place the greaseproof template back around the cake and attach it to the cake with sterilised pins.

3 Mark the design onto the cake using a scribing needle. Mark out the main areas of the design, but do not mark out the whole design as it will be difficult to make out the lines once you remove the template.

4 Remove the template and all the pins, but keep it to hand so you can refer to the design as you are painting.

Embossing a design onto sugarpaste

This method is best for sugarpasted, straight-edged cakes and cake top designs.

1 Prepare a template of the design you wish to emboss on a piece of greaseproof paper as explained in step 1 on the previous page.

2 Wash and sterilise a piece of food-grade acrylic with hot, soapy water and allow to dry thoroughly before use.

3 Place the sheet of acrylic over the template, ensuring that the design is central.

4 Following the template underneath, pipe the outline of the design onto the acrylic sheet with off-peak royal icing and a no. 4 nozzle (see page 235). Remember that the design will be in reverse, so any lettering will appear backwards at this stage.

5 Allow the icing to dry overnight in a warm, dry place or under a desk lamp or similar heat source for at least two hours.

6 Once you have covered the cake with fresh sugarpaste, lightly dust the surface with a little cornflour and polish the paste with the palm of your hand to prevent the embosser from sticking to the paste.

7 Position the embosser centrally over the sugarpaste and press down with light pressure.

tutor tip

When embossing the design onto sugarpaste, make sure you press down gently and do not move the embosser or else the image will be distorted.

If you require a finer imprint from the embosser, use a no. 0 nozzle to pipe the design.

Watercolour painting

The watercolour technique uses edible liquid food colours to paint onto sugar work in the same way as you would with watercolour paints and produces a similar effect.

1 Allow the sugarpaste to firm for approximately 48 hours before painting directly onto it.

2 To make a wash, place a few drops of liquid food colour into a paint palette and add a tiny amount of cooled, boiled water. Use a larger paintbrush to

carefully paint a light-coloured wash over the sugarpaste if desired, and allow to dry.

3 Place another few drops of a different liquid food colour into the palette, but this time do not dilute it. Dip a finer paintbrush into the liquid food colour, being careful not to put too much paint

on the brush or it will flood the area. Paint directly onto the sugarpaste following the marked design. As you start to paint, be aware that the sugarpaste may not be completely dry and can mark easily.

4 Continue to paint all the sections of the design required in the first colour, then allow this to dry before an additional colour is applied. Repeat in the same way until you have completed the design.

5 Once you have finished your painted design, leave to dry for several hours, preferably overnight.

Brush embroidery

Brush embroidery is a simple yet beautiful technique that is usually created with royal icing on cakes coated with royal icing, sugarpaste or pastillage. You can also re-create the technique with melted white and dark chocolate, as well as with softened buttercream on biscuits.

1 Transfer your design onto the cake using either a greaseproof template or an embosser if you are painting onto sugarpaste (see opposite page). Leave the cake to dry for approximately 48 hours if you are painting onto sugarpaste.

2 Make up some off-peak royal icing and colour it with liquid or dust food colours if desired (see page 235–236).

3 Soften the royal icing by rubbing it down (see page 235) and place into a piping bag fitted with a small nozzle, such as a no. 1, 1.5 or 2 nozzle.

4 Start the brush embroidery from the back of the design coming forward; each part of the design should be completed before the next one is piped. It is best to start at the top of the design to prevent your hand smudging the work (so pipe one petal at a time, for example).

Painting Techniques

5 Pipe a thin outline around the first section of the design, then gently catch the inside of the icing with a dampened, round paintbrush and gently stroke the icing in towards the centre. You should still leave a ridge of icing around the edge of the outline.

6 Once you have completed your brush embroidery, leave the icing to dry overnight. Brush edible dust food colours over the design to add highlights to certain areas.

Cocoa painting

Painting with cocoa butter is a traditional technique that uses a mix of melted cocoa butter and cocoa powder. This technique can be used on a variety of mediums including chocolate, sugarpaste, royal icing, pastillage and rice paper. You can colour the cocoa butter mix with dust food colours: if you wish to make an opaque colour then you will need to add white to the mixture as without it the colour is more transparent. Synthetic brushes are ideal for cocoa painting as they are durable and easy to clean.

You can also buy ready-coloured cocoa paints, e.g. Squires Kitchen Cocol, which are more convenient as they just need to be warmed in a microwave before use. Once the mixture has melted it is a good idea to keep it in a palette over a bowl of warm water to keep the paint fluid. Ideally cocoa paints should have the consistency of whipped cream.

When painting with coloured cocoa butter, it is best to start with lighter colours first. Another colour can be painted over it once the paint has set and solidified. Painting a new colour over the first layer while it is still liquid will cause the first layer to smear.

There is no need to change the brushes with every colour, just use natural melted cocoa butter to blot the colour from the paintbrushes on kitchen paper. The brushes can then be washed with warm, soapy water and air-dried once you have finished.

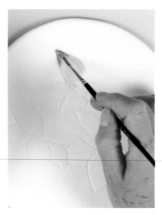

Using edible paints

Edible paints can be used on both royal iced and sugarpasted cakes, leaving the painted design with an attractive gloss finish.

These paints are usually used for folk art (or barge-style) painting as they create a textured finish when used on sugarpasted cakes but it can also be used for general surface painting. However, the cakes need to be left to dry for at least 48 hours before you begin to paint on the surface. Occasionally the paint can separate if the sugarpaste is still soft, so it is a good idea to brush a thin layer over the area using confectioners' glaze. Alternatively, just add a few drops of glaze to the edible paint before use.

Edible paints are also ideal for painting iced biscuits whether as an activity at a children's party or for a sophisticated design which can be used alongside a celebration cake as favours for guests (see ideas on pages 344–345).

tutor tip

If you are using confectioners' glaze, it is advisable when finished to clean the brush with confectioners' glaze cleaner before it dries hard and damages the bristles.

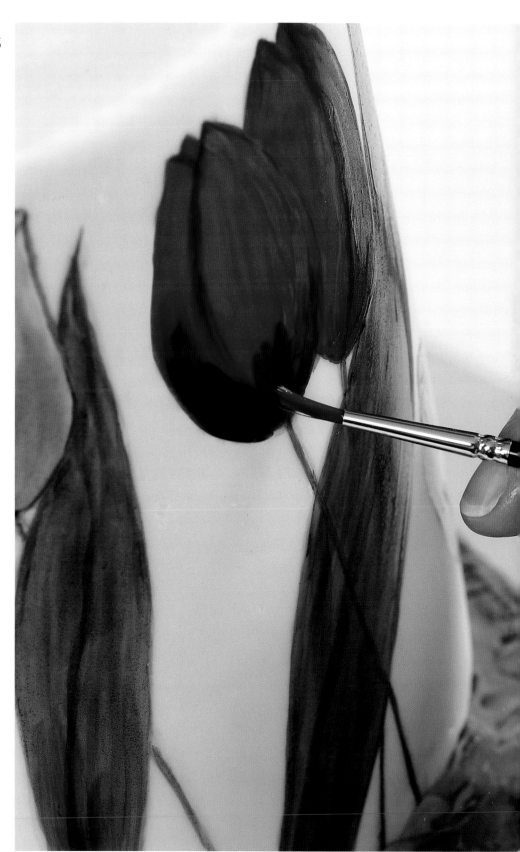

Springtime Tulips

Pretty as a picture, this painted cake with its vibrant floral design would make a great celebration cake for a springtime birthday or intimate wedding ceremony, as well as a lovely gift for Mother's Day.

EDIBLES

2 x 15cm (6") round cakes, prepared for covering, see pages 91–97

2.5kg (5lb 8¼oz) SK Sugarpaste: Lullaby Blue

SK Professional Dust Food Colours: Chestnut, Edelweiss (white), Fuchsia, Holly/Ivy, Poinsettia (Christmas red), Thrift

SK Confectioners' Glaze

Tulip cake-top decoration (optional)

EQUIPMENT

SK Paintbrushes: nos. 0, 1, 2 x 2

Paint palette

Sterilised, coloured round-headed pins

Scribing needle

SK Confectioners' Glaze Cleaner (IPA)

50cm (20") x 15mm (½") wide satin ribbon: burgundy

Template, see page 491

For essential sugarpaste edibles and equipment, see pages 132–133

1 Stack and cover the cakes with Lullaby Blue sugarpaste (see pages 139–140). Leave the sugarpaste to firm for approximately 48 hours.

2 Create a greaseproof paper template following the instructions on page 171 then draw on the tulip design using the template on page 491.

3 Pin the template around the cake using sterilised round-headed pins, and prick out the main details of the design with a scribing needle (see page 171).

4 Place a small amount of Fuchsia and Edelweiss dust colours in the palette and mix with a little clear alcohol or cooled, boiled water to create a light pink wash.

5 Paint a wash over the first tulip with a no. 2 paintbrush. Add shading

to the base of the tulip with Thrift to give depth to the flower. Define the outline of the tulip with a fine no. 0 paintbrush and Fuschia and Edelweiss dust colours mixed with confectioners' glaze. Finish the flower by painting a thin stalk down to the base of the cake, using Holly/Ivy mixed with confectioners' glaze and a no. 1 paintbrush.

6 Paint the red tulips with Poinsettia dust mixed with confectioners' glaze and the dark pink tulips with Fuchsia dust colour mixed with a little alcohol or cooled, boiled water. Paint the leaves using Holly/Ivy dust food colour and confectioners' glaze. Continue painting the other flowers and leaves around the cake until the design is complete.

7 Once completed, the painted design can be coated carefully

with confectioners' glaze to protect it. Make sure there is only a small amount of glaze on the brush each time to prevent it dripping down the cake.

8 Once dry, secure a burgundy ribbon around the base of the cake with a little royal icing.

9 If you would like to create a decoration to go on top of the cake, make a single tulip from SFP to match the design on the cake.

tutor tip

As you become more confident at painting onto cakes, you can use dust colours with confectioners' glaze to paint freehand directly onto the cake.

Springtime Tulips

177

Stencilling Techniques

MARK TILLING

Stencilling is a great way to add professional-looking decoration very quickly and easily. There are several mediums you can use with stencils, from icing sugar to royal icing, and you can decorate everything from a freshly-baked teatime cake to a batch of iced cupcakes to make them look grander. There are many different designs available — make sure you choose stencils which have been approved for contact with food.

TECHNIQUES

- Stencilling with royal icing, dust and liquid food colours, chocolate, cocoa powder and icing sugar

- Embossing using stencils

Royal icing

To decorate the top or sides of a coated cake, place the stencil onto dry sugarpaste or royal icing and hold it in position. Prepare some stiff-peak icing and paddle it on the work surface before use to eliminate any air bubbles (see page 235). Spread the royal icing over the stencil with a palette knife, working the icing into the holes and making sure to keep the stencil straight. Scrape away the excess icing from the template with the palette knife. Remove the stencil carefully and allow the royal icing to dry.

Dust food colours

When stencilling with dust food colour it is best to use SK Gildesol, an edible gilding medium which brings out the true colour of the dust. Roll out some sugarpaste to the required thickness and cut to shape if needed (e.g. a circle of sugarpaste for a cupcake). Brush the surface with a thin layer Gildesol then place the stencil on top. Use a large, flat paintbrush to apply the dust colour onto the stencil, working on small areas at a time. Hold the stencil down firmly to prevent the colour from bleeding underneath the stencil. Remove the stencil carefully.

Liquid food colours and edible paints

Make a flat run-out from royal icing (see page 240) and allow it to dry completely. Squeeze a few drops of liquid food colour or edible paint into a paint palette. Place the stencil on top of the run-out and carefully sponge-paint the surface using a small piece of food-grade foam sponge. Holding the stencil firmly in place, build up the colour in layers, ensuring you don't have too much colour on the sponge at once otherwise the colour may bleed underneath the stencil. Remove the stencil carefully.

 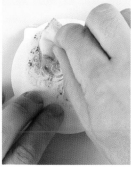 

Stencilling Techniques

179

Chocolate

Temper some dark, milk or white chocolate following the instructions on pages 104–106. Place the stencil onto a sheet of acetate then use a palette knife to spread some of the tempered chocolate over the stencil. Smooth the chocolate over with the palette knife to remove all the excess chocolate then peel off the stencil before the chocolate sets. Leave this to set then spread on some tempered chocolate in a contrasting colour (e.g. white chocolate on dark) to just above the top of the stencilled chocolate. Allow this to semi-dry before wrapping it around a cake or mould as required and place in the fridge to set fully.

Cocoa powder and icing sugar ◄

Place the stencil on the top of a cake, sprinkle icing sugar in a shaker over the top and lift the stencil to reveal the design. You can also create patterns on a cappuccino or hot chocolate using cocoa powder.

Embossing ▶

This is the easiest method if you are not confident at stencilling. Roll out some sugarpaste to the thickness you need and push the stencil onto the surface of the paste straight away to make an imprint. Leave the paste to dry then use a lustre dust colour to bring out the design.

Damask Wedding Cake

This three-tier stacked cake shows how you can use a double-height tier to display a stencilled design, creating the focal point on a simple yet elegant cake.

EDIBLES

10cm (4") round x 7.5cm (3") deep, 15cm (6") round x 12.5cm (5") deep, 20.5cm (8") round x 7.5cm (3") deep sponge cakes, prepared for covering, see page 92

200g (7oz) stiff-peak royal icing, see page 241

SK Quality Food Colour (QFC) Liquid: Red

EQUIPMENT

10cm, 15cm, 20.5cm (4", 6", 8") round, thin cake boards

SK Bellissimo Flexi Smoothers

Cake dowels

SK Art-ice Stencil: Damask

1.5m (3' 11") x 15mm (½") wide satin ribbon: antique lace

Small spray of red roses, see pages 270–276

Essential sugarpaste edibles and equipment, see pages 132–133

1 Place each prepared cake onto a thin cake board of the same size. Cover all three cakes with Antique Lace sugarpaste, giving the top and bottom tiers a sharp top edge (see page 301). The middle tier should have more of a rounded top edge, as per the instructions on pages 139–140.

2 Dowel the middle and lower tiers (see page 143). Allow the middle tier (on which the stencil will be placed) to dry for 24 hours so that the sugarpaste covering is firm before you start working on it.

3 Make up the royal icing to stiff-peak consistency and add a few drops of red liquid food colour to make a reddish-pink shade (see page 236).

4 Hold the stencil at one end and press it against the side of the cake. Before you start stencilling, make sure that the stencil is positioned in the right place and is straight. Some stencils have a wide border around the pattern so you may be able to rest the stencil on the work surface to ensure that it is straight.

5 Take a small amount of the coloured royal icing on a palette knife and paddle it on a clean work surface to remove any air bubbles (see page 235). Spread the icing over the stencil, making sure that all the areas are filled. Scrape down to the surface of the stencil so the icing is not too thick.

6 Remove the stencil very carefully, then wait for the icing to dry before continuing around the cake.

7 When all the stencilling work is dry, stack the cakes and attach ribbon around the base of each one with a little edible glue or royal icing. Place a small spray of sugar roses on top to finish.

tutor tip

Grease the back of the stencil with a little white vegetable fat to help it stay in position whilst you are working. If you have to position the stencil in the middle of the cake side, you may find it easier if someone else holds it in place whilst you work.

Stencilling Techniques

183

Essential Edibles and Equipment for Modelling

1 Ball tool or bone tool
2 Cake cards
3 Cake drums (boards)
4 CelSticks: large and small
5 Cling film and food-grade plastic bags
6 Cocktail sticks
7 Cornflour duster
8 Cranked palette knife
9 Cutting wheel
10 Dresden tool
11 Drinking straws
12 Kitchen paper
13 Modelling paste, such as SK MMP or Sugar Dough, see project list for colours and quantities
14 Non-stick board
15 Non-stick rolling pins, large and small
16 Raw, dried spaghetti
17 Ruler
18 Scribing needle
19 SK Edible Glue
20 SK Food Colour Pens (a variety of colours)
21 SK Instant Mix Pastillage (for pastillage modelling only)
22 SK Paintbrushes: nos. 1, 2, 10
23 Small, sharp knife
24 Smoother
25 Sugar shaper
26 White vegetable fat
27 Wooden barbeque skewers

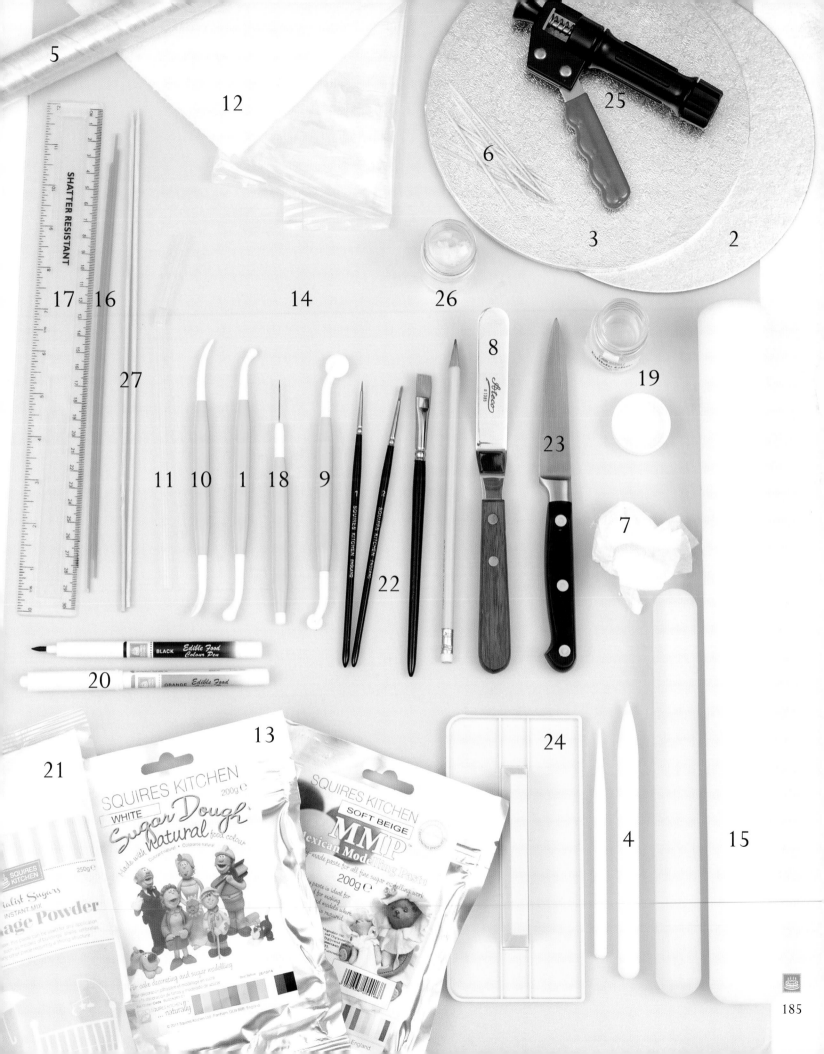

Jan Clement-May

BIOGRAPHY

I started baking cakes from an early age. On a Saturday morning, with my nan's guiding hands, I would try out different recipes on my family who would have them for tea.

I originally trained as a graphic designer/animator at Epsom School of Art and Design and qualified in 1981. Whilst pregnant with my daughter, Emelia, I read a lot of craft books and magazines on knitting, crochet, sewing and cake making and was inspired by the cake designs that were being created from sugarpaste.

I wanted to make a special birthday cake for my daughter's first birthday, but having never used sugarpaste before I followed each step methodically. I had plenty of time to practise and made her favourite toys to decorate the sides of the cake. I was soon hooked! I found I could channel my artistic skills and creative flair into cake decorating and began to make cakes for my children's parties (I also had a son, Christian) as well as for other family and friends.

In 2001, I set up The Too Good To Eat Cake Company from home and shortly afterwards began contributing to *Cakes & Sugarcraft* magazine. Since then, I have become a regular tutor at Squires Kitchen International School and teach students the art of making animals and figures from Sugar Dough. I teach Extended Skills classes, as well as Foundation courses, and it gives me great satisfaction to watch the students grow in confidence throughout the day as they make something they didn't think they could achieve.

After establishing myself as a regular contributor to *Cakes & Sugarcraft* magazine, I went on to write four popular cake decorating books – *Merry Christmas Cakes*, *Bob the Builder™ Celebration Cakes*, *Squires Kitchen's Guide to Making Sugar Animals* and *Squires Kitchen's Guide to Making Sugar Figures* (B. Dutton Publishing).

In January 2012, I was commissioned to make the Baddeley cake for the Drury Lane Theatre which annually celebrates Twelfth Night (6ᵗʰ January) with a cake that is inspired by the show on stage. 'Shrek The Musical' was running at the time and I felt it a huge honour and privilege to have been asked. I was delighted to meet the cast and crew of the production at the special celebration after the show.

That same year I found my wings and travelled to Spain, Italy and Holland to teach and demonstrate. I also demonstrate, by invitation, for the British Sugarcraft Guild in the South region and have attended the Squires Kitchen Annual Exhibition for a number of years.

For the past 15 years I have taught local children between the ages of five and ten how to make sugar animals and figures in the summer holidays at the Tilford Environmental Playscheme. The children are like little sponges, soaking up every part of the day. I see some of them year after year and watch their progress and their creativity flourish, knowing that they might be the sugarcrafters of the future!

Most recently, I've contributed to weekly magazine *Disney Cakes & Sweets* and have made several themed cakes, including Winnie the Pooh, Mickey's Wizard Hat, Pixie Hollow, the Seven Dwarfs, Tangled and Cinderella's Coach.

I'm passionate about modelling as it's a creative edible art which uses the training from my college days. I've learnt a lot along the way and I'm still learning. I enjoy putting smiles on people's faces when they come to pick up their commissioned novelty cakes and the phrase "it's too good to eat" has stuck with me over the years. Sugarcraft and modelling are addictive – once you've mastered the basics you can create almost anything you desire.

Basic Animal Modelling

JAN CLEMENT-MAY

You can make a variety of models using Sugar Dough and just a handful of basic tools. Once you have learnt how to make basic figures, you can personalise your models and display them on celebration cakes, cupcakes, cookies and mini cakes. Sugar Dough is easy to use and is ideal for modelling animals and figures – it holds its shape, has a fantastically smooth finish and tastes good, too.

EDIBLES

SK Sugar Dough (see individual animals for colours and amounts)

SK Professional Food Colour Pen: Black

EQUIPMENT

5.5cm (2¼") long wooden barbecue skewer (for cow, squirrel and rabbit)

For essential modelling edibles and equipment, see pages 184–185

TECHNIQUES

- Working with Sugar Dough
- Modelling basic shapes
- Modelling basic animals

Working with Sugar Dough

Kneading: Rubbing a little white vegetable fat into your hands before kneading Sugar Dough will make the paste more pliable and less likely to crack. It also prevents the stronger colours from sticking to your hands and helps to create an even consistency when adding colour to the paste.

Sticking: Use edible glue to stick pieces together. Using a paintbrush, apply a little glue to the surface of the Sugar Dough before working on the next piece to allow the glue to go tacky. To stick the pieces together, hold them in position and support if necessary until they are secure.

Colouring: Sugar Dough comes in a wide range of colours, but can also be coloured with paste food colours in the same way as sugarpaste (see page 138).

Internal supports: Where you require extra support, such as a head on a figure, you can use a strand of dried spaghetti or a wooden barbeque skewer, depending on the size of the piece. As these internal supports are inedible and cannot be seen it is important to remove them safely before the models are eaten. If the cake is a gift, make sure the recipient is aware that the supports have been used and must be removed.

Basic shapes

There are just a few basic shapes in modelling which can then be made into almost anything.

Ball: Roll the paste in the middle of your hands firmly to prevent cracking.

Sausage: First, roll the paste into a ball then roll backwards and forwards on a work surface to lengthen. Roll just a little to make a short, fat sausage or continue rolling to make a longer, thinner sausage.

Cone: First, roll the paste into a ball. Place onto a work surface then cup your hands around the ball and turn the paste back and forth. The paste will have a flat base from sitting on the surface and the top should come to a point between your hands.

tutor tip

From these shapes you can make teardrops, pear shapes, discs or tapered sausages as needed for your sugar models.

Snake

1 You will need 10g (¼oz) of Red Sugar Dough, 10g (¼oz) of Yellow Sugar Dough and a pinch of Black Sugar Dough to make one snake. Reserve two small balls of Red Sugar Dough for the

eyes. Roll out the Yellow and Red Sugar Dough into long sausages, taper one end of each sausage to a point and round off the other end.

2 Lay one colour on top of the other, then twist the sausages around each other from the head to the tail and gently roll the paste into one. Flatten the head section with your fingers and gently make an incision for the mouth.

3 Roll a pinch of Black Sugar Dough into a thin sausage and flatten it slightly. Make a small cut halfway up the

centre of the sausage with a sharp knife to make the forked tongue. Brush a little edible glue inside the mouth, secure the tongue in place and press the mouth closed again.

4 Glue the eyes to the top of the head with a little edible glue. Push the end of a Black food colour pen into each of the eyes.

Cat

1 Divide 22g (¾oz) of Black Sugar Dough as follows: 4 x 2g for the legs, 6g for the body, 4g for the head, 2 x 1g for the ears, 1g for the tail and 1g for the muzzle. Take 1g of White Sugar Dough and reserve two small balls for the eyes. Mix the remaining White Sugar Dough with a very small pinch of Red Sugar Dough to make a pale pink colour. Reserve the pale pink paste for the inner ears and nose.

2 Shape the body and each of the legs into cone shapes. Place two back legs so that the points are touching and position the end of the body over the top of the back legs. Place two front legs either side of the neck and secure all four in place with edible glue.

3 Roll the head into a ball, flatten the ball slightly between your finger and thumb, then secure to the front of the body and over the front legs with edible glue.

4 Roll the tail into a thin sausage, taper one end to a point and cut the other end at an angle. Secure the flat end to the back of the body so the tail points upwards, then gently bend the tail.

5 To make the toes, roll 20 small balls from the Black Sugar Dough and attach five balls to the end of each leg with edible glue.

6 Roll a smaller ball for the muzzle, then flatten it slightly with your thumb and mark a line down the centre with the back of a small knife. Push the end of a drinking straw at a 45° angle either side of the central line, then push a piece of dried spaghetti into each end to make dimples. Attach the muzzle to the front of the head with edible glue.

7 Brush a little edible glue just above the muzzle, then flatten one of the

reserved white balls for the eye between your fingers and attach to the head. Repeat to make the second eye. Push the tip of a Black food colour pen into each of the eyes.

8 To make the nose take a pinch of pink paste and roll it into a small ball. Rest the ball on your thumb and place your finger against the back of the paste, then pinch the paste with your other finger and thumb to form a pyramid shape. Secure the nose to the top of the muzzle, keeping the flat side at the top of the nose.

9 Divide the remaining pink paste in half and shape into two flattened triangles. Repeat with a pinch of Black Sugar Dough. Rest each pink triangle on top of a black triangle and press them together to form the ears. Cut a straight edge at the base of each ear, then bend the ears around the end of a paintbrush and attach to the top of the head with edible glue.

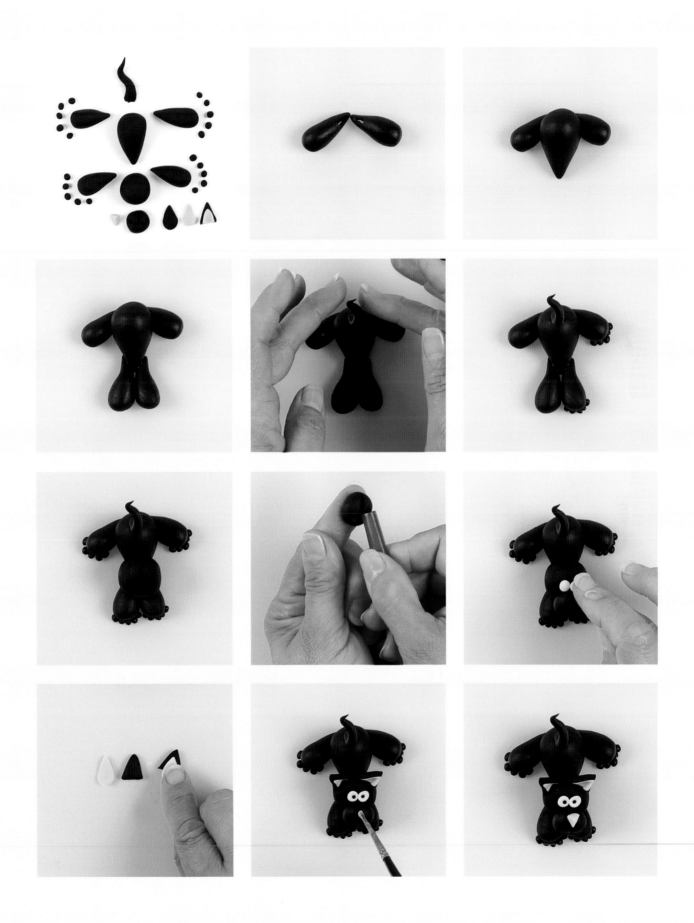

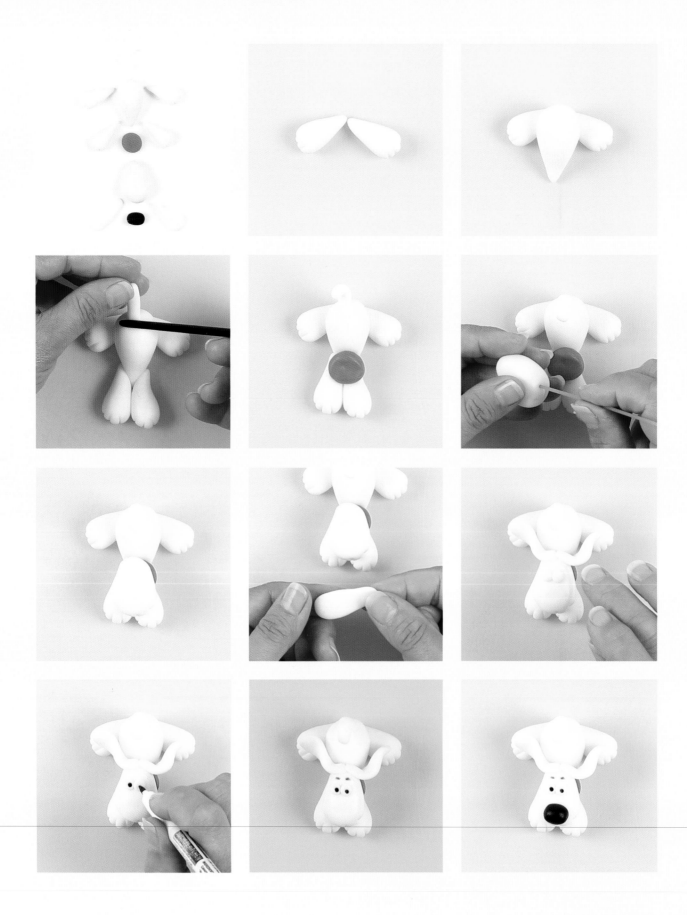

Dog

1 Divide 28g (1oz) of White Sugar Dough as follows: 4 x 3g for the legs, 8g for the head, 5g for the body, 2 x 1g for the ears, 1g for the tail and two tiny eyes.

2 Shape the body and each of the legs into cone shapes. Make three marks down the front of each leg with the back of a small knife for the toes. Place the two back legs with the points together and the toes pointing outwards and secure the body on top with edible glue. Position the two front legs either side of the neck so the paws are together and attach to the body.

3 Roll the tail into a small sausage, then cut one end at an angle and secure to the back of the body with edible glue. Bend the tail slightly so it sits over the dog's back.

4 Roll 1g of Red Sugar Dough into a ball, then flatten the ball between your thumb and finger to form a disc. Attach to the top of the body and over the front legs with edible glue to form a collar.

5 Shape the head into a rounded pear shape and gently flatten the point with your finger. For the mouth, push the end of a drinking straw into the wide end of the head at a 45° angle then push a piece of dried spaghetti into either end to make dimples. Secure the head over the red disc with edible glue.

6 Shape each of the ears into cones and then flatten them down. Attach the ears to the top of the head and rest the ends on top of the back feet, so the ears sit backwards as if they are blowing in the wind.

7 Flatten two tiny balls of White Sugar Dough for the eyes and attach to the head with a little edible glue. Push the tip of a Black food colour pen into each of the eyes, draw on two small eyebrows above the eyes and then draw spots randomly all over the body.

8 For the nose, roll 1g of Black Sugar Dough into an oval and secure to the front of the head with edible glue.

tutor tip

Modelling animals is a great activity for a children's party. Instead of a large birthday cake, bake a batch of cupcakes or cookies and let the children decorate their own edible creations.

Basic Animal Modelling

Pig

1 Knead together 41g (1½oz) of White Sugar Dough and a pinch of Red Sugar Dough to make a pale pink paste. Divide the pink paste as follows: 20g for the body, 4 x 2g for the legs, 10g for the head, 2 x 1g for the ears, 1g for the snout and a pinch for the tail.

2 Shape the body and each of the legs into a cone shape. Mark a line for each trotter with the back of a small knife on the wide end of each leg. Rest one leg underneath the body and another leg alongside the lower body. Attach the two remaining legs over the body.

3 For the tail, roll a pinch of paste into a very small sausage and cut to size if necessary. Secure to the back of the body with a touch of edible glue and curl the end of the paste between your fingers.

4 Roll the head into a smooth ball and stick to the body with a little edible glue. Model the snout into a ball and flatten slightly between your fingers. Push the end of a paintbrush into the upper side of the snout to make two holes for the nostrils and attach to the head.

5 Shape each of the ears into a cone and flatten them down. Stick the ears to the top of the head and position the tips of the ears over each other, so they are just touching the top of the snout.

Sheep

1 Divide 16g (½oz) of Black Sugar Dough as follows: 4 x 2g for the legs, 6g for the head, 1g for the ears and a pinch for the tail. Divide 22g (¾oz) of White Sugar Dough as follows: 10g for the body, two small pinches for the eyes and the remainder will make the woolly coat.

2 Model each of the legs into a long cone shape, mark a line for the hoof at the wider end with the back of a small knife and then bend the two back legs slightly.

3 Roll the head into a pear shape, push the end of a paintbrush into the pointed end to make the nostrils and set aside.

4 Roll the tail into a small cone shape, then arrange the legs and tail so that they are in position for the body to be placed on top. Roll the White Sugar Dough for the body into an oval ball and attach on top of the legs and tail with edible glue. Attach the head to the front of the body.

5 Roll 1g of Green Sugar Dough into a small sausage, then use a knife to cut into the ends of the paste so that it looks like grass. Secure just under the nose with edible glue.

6 Roll the pinches of White Sugar Dough into balls for the eyes. Brush a little edible glue onto the front of the head, then flatten the balls between your fingers and secure to the head. Push the tip of a Black food colour pen into each eye.

7 Brush over the body with edible glue, then roll the remaining White Sugar Dough into different-sized balls and attach them all over the body until it is completely covered. Divide the Black Sugar Dough for the ears in half, then shape each piece into a small cone shape. Flatten both and push the end of a paintbrush along the middle of each ear. Attach the ears to either side of the head with edible glue. To finish, secure more white balls to the very top of the head.

Cow

1 Divide 56g (2oz) of White Sugar Dough as follows: 20g for the body, 18g for the head, 15g for the legs and a pinch each for the tail and eye. Add a small pinch of Red Sugar Dough to the remaining White Sugar Dough, knead together to create a pink-coloured paste then reserve for the daisy.

2 Roll the paste for the legs into a cylinder and mark four lines vertically down the cylinder with the back of a knife to divide it into quarters. For the hooves, mark a horizontal line around the bottom of the cylinder that is approximately 5mm (¼") up from the base.

3 Shape the body into a short, fat sausage and secure to the top of the legs with a little edible glue. Take a pinch of White Sugar Dough and roll it into a thin sausage for the tail. Attach to one end of the body, curling it slightly with your fingers.

4 Model the head into a pear shape, then flatten the thinner end of the pear shapes lightly with your finger for the nose. Push the end of a paintbrush into the flattened end to make the nostrils. Push the end of the skewer into the base of the head and remove. Push the skewer down through the body and legs, then brush a little edible glue over the part of the skewer protruding from the body. Ease the head onto the skewer.

5 Take 6g (just under ¼oz) of Black Sugar Dough for the ears, horns and patches. Shape a pinch of the black paste into a cone to make the tip of the tail. Draw lines down the cone with a Dresden tool to add texture. Secure to the end of the tail with a touch of edible glue.

6 Pinch out a small ball of Black Sugar Dough, flatten the ball into a small disc between your fingers and stick it to the front of the head where the eye will be. Roll the White Sugar Dough for the eye into a ball, flatten into a smaller circle and secure on top of the black patch. Push the tip of a Black food colour pen into the eye and again next to the black patch.

7 Roll a tiny sausage of Black Sugar Dough and cut in half to make two small horns that are 5mm (¼") long. Attach the horns to the very top of the head. Take 1g of Black Sugar Dough for each ear and shape each piece into a cone. Flatten the cone and wrap the ears around the end of a paintbrush to curve them slightly. Attach the ears either side of the horns with edible glue. Pinch out small balls from the remaining Black Sugar Dough, flatten into circles and glue to the body.

8 Roll out the pink-coloured paste and cut out two daisies with a small blossom cutter. Cut each individual petal in half with a small, sharp knife, then glue one blossom on top of the other. Push the end of a paintbrush into the centre of the daisy and attach to the side of the mouth. Gently push a very small ball of yellow paste into the centre of the daisy and texture the surface with a Dresden tool to make a stippled effect.

Basic Animal Modelling

Fox

1 Divide 24g (1oz) of Brown Sugar Dough as follows: 14g for the body, 6g for the head, 2 x 1g for the front paws and 2 x 1g for the ears. Mix a further 10g (¼oz) of Brown Sugar Dough with 12g (½oz) of Red Sugar Dough and knead together well.

2 Shape the Brown Sugar Dough for the body and the front paws into cone shapes. Make three marks on the front of each paw with the back of a small knife, then rest the feet at the pointed end of the body.

3 Reserve 2g of the reddish-brown paste for the tuft of hair, then model the rest of the paste into a long cone shape. Shape the larger end of the cone into a short point for the end of the tail, then draw lines down the paste with a Dresden tool to add texture. Attach one end of the tail to the back of the body, then bring the tail over the front paws and secure it around the other side of the body.

4 Roll the head into a cone shape, position it over the body and tail with the pointed end at the front, then secure in place with edible glue. Shape

the ears into long triangles, then push the end of a paintbrush into the middle of each ear. Cut a straight edge at the base of the ears with a small knife and stick to the top of the head with a little edible glue.

5 Brush a small amount of edible glue between the ears, over the pointed nose and the middle of the face. Take a very small pinch of Black Sugar Dough, roll it into a ball and attach to the tip of the nose. Take a small pinch of White Sugar Dough, roll two soft balls for the eyes, then flatten the balls between your fingers. Stick the eyes in place on the head and push the tip of a Black food colour pen into each of the eyes.

6 Knead the off-cuts of Brown Sugar Dough from the ears and roll into two very small sausages for the eyebrows. Bend the paste into small arches and secure just above the eyes. Shape the reserved reddish-brown paste into two small cones. Add texture with a Dresden tool as for the tail, then attach one on top of the other on the very top of the head and curl the ends around each other.

Mouse

1 Mix 1g of White Sugar Dough with a very small pinch of Red Sugar Dough to make a pale pink paste and reserve this for the ears. Weigh out 10g (¼oz) of Black Sugar Dough and reserve three very small balls from this for the eyes and nose. Mix the remaining Black Sugar Dough with 23g (just over ¾oz) of White Sugar Dough, knead well to make a pale grey paste and divide as follows: 18g for the body, 2 x 4g for the back feet, 2 x 1g for the ears, 2 x 1g for the arms, 1g for the tail and a small ball for the hair.

2 Shape the back feet into long cone shapes, then use the back of a small knife to make four marks on each foot, making sure that each mark finishes at the same point at the front. Roll the tail into a long sausage, taper one end to a point and rest the wider end on the back of the feet. Curl the other end of the tail over one foot and secure in place with edible glue.

3 Model the body into another cone shape and squeeze the middle of the cone a little to indent it slightly. Bend the head slightly then use the back of a small knife to draw an upside down 'Y' at the pointed end of the cone for the mouth. Push the end of a piece of dried spaghetti

Rabbit

into the sides of the mouth to make dimples. Position the body over the back of the feet and secure with edible glue.

4 Push the end of a paintbrush into the top of the head to make the eyes, then brush a small amount of edible glue over the holes and the tip of the nose. Attach a small black ball to the tip of the cone for the nose and push two more black balls into the eye sockets.

5 Roll the arms into small thin sausages, then flatten them slightly between your fingers and mark the paws with a Dresden tool. Bend each arm a little, then mark on the elbows with a Dresden tool approximately 5mm (¼") up from the paw. Secure the arms on either side of the body with edible glue and position them so they are crossed over at the front of the body.

6 Roll the ears into soft balls and flatten them with your finger. Repeat with the reserved pale pink paste. Place the pale pink paste on top of the grey discs and push them together. Wrap each ear around a paintbrush to give movement and secure to either side of the head with edible glue. Roll the paste for the hair into a long point and secure to the head.

1 Divide 31g (1oz) of Golden Bear Brown Sugar Dough as follows: 10g for the body, 8g for the head, 2 x 4g for the back feet, 2 x 1g for the front paws, 2 x 1g for the ears and 1g for the muzzle. Divide 6g (just under ¼oz) of White Sugar Dough as follows: 2g for the tummy, 3g for the tail, 2 x small balls for the eyes and keep the remaining paste for the teeth.

2 Shape the feet into cone shapes, then use the back of a small knife to make three marks at the wide end of each foot, making sure that each mark finishes at the same point at the front. Place the feet so that the points are touching.

3 Roll both the body and tummy into cones. Flatten the tummy cone and attach to the front of the body with edible glue. Position the body over the feet and secure in place with edible glue. Roll the tail into a ball and attach to the base of the body.

4 Model the head into a pear shape, then push the end of a barbecue skewer into the base of the head and remove. Push the skewer all the way down through the middle of the body. Brush a little edible glue over the exposed skewer

and carefully ease the head down onto the skewer to secure it in place. Roll the front paws into small sausages and make three marks at one end of each paw with the back of a small knife. Cut the other end of each paw at an angle and glue to the top of the body, so the paws sit together.

5 Roll the muzzle into a ball, then flatten the ball slightly between your fingers and use the back of a small knife to draw a line halfway down the muzzle. Use the end of a drinking straw to make marks on either side of the central line at a 45° angle. Slide the tip of the knife under the marks and open up the mouth enough to fit the teeth inside. Attach the muzzle to the front of the head with edible glue and add whisker marks with a Dresden tool.

6 Flatten the small balls of White Sugar Dough for the eyes and attach to the head just above the muzzle. Push the tip of a Black food colour pen into each eye, then draw lines above the eyes for the eyebrows. Roll out the remaining White Sugar Dough and cut out a very small square for the teeth. Make a line down the centre of the

square with a knife, stick the teeth inside the mouth with edible glue and close the mouth opening around the teeth if necessary.

7 Roll the ears into sausages that are tapered at both ends, push the end of a paintbrush down the centre of each ear and attach to either side of the head with edible glue. Position the ears so that they are just touching and gently curl over the top of one ear. To finish, take a small pinch of Black Sugar Dough and roll into a ball. Rest the ball on your thumb and place your fore finger against the back of the paste, then pinch the paste with your other finger and thumb to form a pyramid shape. Secure the nose to the top of the muzzle.

---

note

Remember to remove the wooden skewers before the models are eaten.

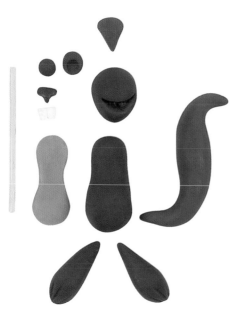

Squirrel

1 Mix 8g of Red Sugar Dough with 10g of Brown Sugar Dough to make a reddish-brown paste and reserve. Mix 2g of White Sugar Dough and 2g of Brown Sugar Dough to make a light brown paste and reserve. Divide 29g (1oz) of Brown Sugar Dough as follows: 12g for the body, 2 x 4g for the back feet, 6g for the head, 2 x 1g for the arms, two small balls for the ears and a pinch for the nose.

2 Shape the back feet into long cone shapes, then use the back of a small knife to make three marks on each foot, making sure that each mark finishes at the same point at the front of the foot. Place the feet so that the points are touching.

3 Roll the body into a sausage shape, making the top half of the body slightly narrower to make a pear shape. Roll the light brown paste into a smaller pear shape, then flatten and glue it to the front of the body. Position the body on top of the heels and secure in place with edible glue.

4 Pinch a small ball from the reddish-brown paste and reserve for the hair. Shape the remaining paste into a long sausage shape bringing both ends to a point. Bend the paste into an 'S' shape, then draw lines down the paste with a Dresden tool to add texture. Attach the tail up the back of the body with edible glue.

5 Roll the head into a ball, then push the end of the wooden skewer into the base of the head and remove. Carefully push the wooden skewer down through the middle of the body. Rest the head in the palm of your hand and draw on the mouth with a Dresden tool. Use the end of the Dresden tool to open up the mouth and push the end of a paintbrush into the corners of the mouth to make dimples. Push the head down onto the skewer and secure in place with edible glue.

6 Draw a line that is approximately 5mm (¼") long up from the middle of the mouth with the back of a small knife. Shape the pinch of Brown Sugar Dough for the nose into an oval, then pinch the centre of the paste between your finger and thumb to create a 'T' shape. Attach the nose over the mark above the mouth with edible glue.

7 Take 4g (just under ¼oz) of White Sugar Dough, pinch out two small balls and flatten each one between your fingers. Brush a little edible glue above the nose and attach the eyes. Push the tip of a Black food colour pen into each eye. Push a bone tool into the centre of the two small balls for the ears and attach to either side of the head with edible glue.

8 For the teeth, roll out the remaining White Sugar Dough and cut out a very small square. Draw a line down the centre of the square with a small knife and attach inside the top of the mouth with edible glue.

9 Shape the remaining reddish-brown paste into a small cone and add texture with a Dresden tool. Make a curl at the pointed end of the cone and attach to the very top of the head with edible glue.

Raining Cats and Dogs

Once you've learnt how to model cute cats and dogs, why not display them on cupcakes for a great party centrepiece? These fun cupcakes also make fantastic gifts for animal lovers of all ages.

EDIBLES

12 vanilla sponge cupcakes, see recipe on page 15

Jam or buttercream

240g (8½oz) SK Sugarpaste: Bridal White

SK Professional Paste Food Colours: Bluegrass, Lilac

30g (1oz) Sugar Dough per dog (see project descriptions for specific colours)

25g (just under 1oz) Sugar Dough per cat (see project descriptions for specific colours)

EQUIPMENT

SK Colour Block Cupcake Cases: Baby Blue, Pure Lavender

5.5cm (2¼") round cutter

For essential modelling edibles and equipment, see pages 184–185

Cupcakes

1 Divide the Bridal White sugarpaste in half, then colour one half with a touch of Bluegrass paste food colour and the other half with Lilac paste food colour (see page 138). Roll out the blue- and lilac-coloured paste to approximately 3mm (1/8") thick and cut out six circles of each colour with a 5.5cm (2¼") round cutter.

2 Level the tops of the cupcakes and spread a little jam or buttercream over the top. Place a circle of sugarpaste onto each cupcake, making sure to match the colour of the sugarpaste to the cupcake case. Smooth each cupcake over with a smoother to seal the cake and create a neat finish.

Dogs

3 *White spotty dog:* Make all the parts of the dog following the instructions on page 193. To assemble, first lay one back leg and one front leg on top of a blue cupcake, then secure the body on top so the dog is laying across the cupcake. Attach the remaining legs to the top of the body. Turn the head on its side and rest it on top of the cupcake. Position the ears so that one sticks up and the other rests on the cupcake.

4 *Light brown dog:* Make the dog using Golden Bear Brown Sugar Dough with Brown Sugar Dough for the nose and assemble on a blue cupcake following the instructions on page 193.

5 *Brown spotty dog:* Following the instructions on page 193, make all the parts of the dog using Golden Bear Brown Sugar Dough with Blue Sugar Dough for the collar. Attach spots of White and Black Sugar Dough randomly over the body and legs. To assemble, lay the legs out across a blue cupcake and position the body on top of the legs so the dog is lying flat.

6 *Dark brown dog:* Make all the parts of the dog using Brown Sugar Dough with Black Sugar Dough for the nose following the instructions on page 193. To assemble, first place the body across a blue cupcake, then attach the back legs so they are sticking up in the air and bend the toes over slightly. Rest the tail and one of the front legs on the top of the cupcake. Position the other front leg over the body and lay the ears on the cupcake so they look like they are flopping backwards.

7 *Black dog:* Following the instructions on page 193, make all the parts of the dog using Black Sugar Dough with Blue Sugar Dough for the collar. Assemble the dog in the same way as for the dark brown dog above, but position the back feet so that they are crossed over. Rest one ear on top of the cupcake and position the other over the edge of the cupcake case.

8 *Dark and light brown dog:* Make the dog with Brown and Golden Bear Brown Sugar Dough following the instructions on page 193, and use Blue Sugar Dough for the collar. Assemble on top of a blue cupcake in the same way as for the white spotty dog.

Cats

9 *Black cat:* Make the cat following the instructions on page 190 and assemble on top of a lilac cupcake.

10 *Grey cat:* Mix White Sugar Dough with a pinch of Black Sugar Dough to make a light grey paste and make all the parts of the cat following the instructions on page 190. To assemble, first lay the body across a lilac cupcake and attach the back legs over the top with the toes pointing outward. Rest one front leg over the body and the other on the cake top. Place the head facing upwards with the ears hanging over the edge of the cupcake case.

11 *White cat:* Following the instructions on page 190, make all the parts of the cat from White Sugar Dough. To assemble, first lay one back leg and one front leg on top of a lilac cupcake, then secure the body on top so the cat is laying across the cupcake. Attach the remaining legs to the top of the body. Turn the head on its side and rest it on top of the cupcake.

12 *Tabby cat:* Lightly knead together Black, Brown, Golden Bear Brown and White Sugar Dough then make the cat following the instructions on page 190, and assemble on top of a lilac cupcake.

13 *Ginger cat:* Following the instructions on page 190, make all of the parts of the cat from Orange Sugar Dough. To assemble, lay the body across the top of a lilac cupcake and attach the back legs so they are sticking up in the air with one leg crossed over the other. Lay one front leg out to the side, then attach the other front leg on top of it. Rest the head on top of the cake so it is facing outwards.

14 *Light brown cat:* Make all of the parts of the cat from Golden Bear Brown Sugar Dough following the instructions on page 190. Assemble in the same way as for the ginger cat above, but position one front leg on the cake top and the other across the body.

Raining Cats and Dogs

Liz Aplin

BIOGRAPHY

had no idea about the world of cake decorating until I took a chance visit to the Squires Kitchen shop in Farnham about ten years ago. I wandered around the shop in complete awe, with no clue as to what most of the equipment and materials were, but fascinated by what the end result could be. I bought some simple equipment (that I still use now!) and a few sugarcraft books and started to experiment.

I initially started out by making cakes for my nephews, Ben and Sam, and for my god-children, Bethan and Brandon, and over the years they have continued to challenge me with their birthday cake requests! I became known as 'that person who makes cakes' and requests kept coming in. Before long, cake making had turned from an occasional hobby to an all-consuming passion.

After experimenting with different styles and techniques, I decided that my great love was to create simple, appealing figures. My style of modelling has developed over time, but my figures generally look like cute children wearing fun fancy dress costumes. I tend to model caricature-style figures and I find that a sweet, smiling figure will distract from anything else on the cake that comes out looking less than perfect. I use the same techniques to model figures but am always surprised to see a unique personality start to emerge as I continue to create the figure.

I am primarily self-taught and I have discovered most of my techniques through trial and error. I have been so lucky to have had huge encouragement from my friends and family, particularly from my mum and dad, my husband Phil and my friend and muse, Mark. I have learned, however, that even if the cake is not quite as perfect as I had hoped, people are still genuinely delighted with the finished

product. I love it when people ask me for unusual and challenging cakes, particularly when I can't initially think of a way for it to work. I spend hours designing cakes in my mind and looking around for inspiration everywhere I go. For me, the greatest satisfaction is seeing the delight that a cake brings to any special occasion.

I am a firm believer that figure modelling is simple enough for anyone to create a masterpiece and I think this is why I love working as a tutor with Squires Kitchen. I regularly teach Foundation Modelling courses and it gives me great satisfaction to work with students who are complete beginners yet still go home with a brilliant, unique model and the confidence to create any other figure they choose. I also contribute projects to *Cakes & Sugarcraft* magazine and continue to enjoy learning from others and hearing about their various cake challenges. I have learned so much from my students and from the other tutors at Squires Kitchen and I love being a part of this cake community.

Caricature Figures

LIZ APLIN

This section introduces you to the basic but effective techniques for modelling caricature figures. Using these techniques you can make your characters look cute and fun, but also make them stable enough to stand up and be transported. To create a caricature figure, I recommend using a polystyrene ball for the head supported by a wooden skewer, then building the body around it.

EDIBLES

SK Mexican Modelling Paste (MMP): 100g (3½oz) Black, 300g (10½oz) Soft Beige, 800g (1lb 12oz) White

SK Professional Paste Food Colours: Bulrush, Chestnut, Edelweiss (white), Hyacinth, Poinsettia (Christmas red), Rose (for female figure only), Teddy Bear Brown

SK Designer Bridal Satin Lustre Dust Food Colour: Bridal Pink (for female figure only)

SK Professional Food Colour Pen: Black

SK Designer Metallic Lustre Dust Food Colour: Classic Gold

Icing sugar or cornflour (optional)

EQUIPMENT

Polystyrene ball: 6cm (2³/₈") diameter

Spare polystyrene cake dummy

Round cutters: 5cm, 10cm (2", 4")

Templates, see page 506

For essential modelling edibles and equipment, see pages 184–185

TECHNIQUES

- Making a caricature-style head, face and body

1920s bisqueware figures for wedding cake decoration

How to make a caricature head

The head for a caricature figure is made by covering a polystyrene ball with MMP. This method means that the head can be large and perfectly shaped which makes the model look cute, but also ensures that the head is not too heavy.

1 Take a ball of Soft Beige MMP (or skin tone of your choice, see page 305) that is about ²/₃ of the size of the polystyrene ball you are using for the head. I have used a 6cm (2³/₈") polystyrene ball for my figure. Knead the paste well to ensure that it is pliable and smooth before you start.

2 Holding the polystyrene ball in one hand, place the ball of MMP on top of the ball and press down. Use the palm of your hand to start gently pushing the paste down and around the ball, being careful not to trap any air underneath the paste. Smooth the MMP roughly halfway down the ball, then roll the whole ball between both hands to smooth the paste down even further.

3 Alternate between pressing the MMP around the ball and rolling

it between your hands, until the paste is almost covering the ball. Press the MMP firmly around the ball to remove any pleats in the covering. If you are making a figure with hair or a hat it is not necessary to cover the ball completely as the gap at the top of the head will be covered.

4 When the ball is sufficiently covered with paste, insert a wooden skewer approximately 3cm (1¹/₈") into the middle of the ball. Hold the skewer and polish the head with the palm of your hand to smooth away any imperfections at this stage.

5 Trim the wooden skewer so about 5cm (2") protrudes from the ball then push the skewer with head into a spare polystyrene dummy ready to create the face.

tutor tip

If necessary, you can dust your hands with icing sugar or cornflour to help you smooth the paste.

Caricature Figures

How to make a caricature face

The basic caricature face is the same for a boy or girl figure, with some very minor additions. The technique is very simple but works well to create a cute and appealing face. You will see that the facial features are grouped in quite a small area on the face, which can look odd until the hair and/or hat are attached. It is important for the face to have the correct proportions so you need to position the nose correctly on the face first, then create the eyes and mouth around the nose.

1 Make a slight dent in the very centre of the ball using the large end of a ball tool. Roll a tiny piece of Soft Beige MMP and then cut it in half with a sharp knife. Take one half and attach it to the dent in the face with a very small amount of edible glue: the flat, cut end should make the base of the snub nose.

2 To create eye sockets, press the small end of a ball tool into the face approximately 1cm (³/₈") from either side of the nose. Try to make the sockets deep enough so that the eyes will sit flush with the face. Roll tiny balls of Black MMP and fit them into the sockets. It is important not to make the eyes too large so try them for size before sticking them down with edible glue. To bring the eyes to life, dot a tiny amount of Edelweiss paste food colour on to each eye with the pointed end of a wooden skewer.

3 Flatten a small ball of Soft Beige MMP between your finger and thumb, then cut the disc in half for the ears. Attach one piece to either side of the head in line with the eyes and nose and push a ball tool into the paste. If you are creating a figure with longer hair, you can omit this step as the hair would cover the ears.

4 For the mouth, hold the head by the skewer and position a 5cm (2") circular cutter over the face, ensuring that you can see the eyes and the nose within the cutter. Gently press the cutter into the lower part of the face to make an indent for the mouth. Create dimples on either side of the mouth with the small end of a ball tool. Use a fine paintbrush to neaten the edges of the cut and then bring the paste out slightly underneath the mouth to widen the smile.

5 *Girl's face:* To make the basic face look more feminine, you can draw a small 'V' shape at the corner of each eye with a black food colour pen to make eyelashes. You can also dust a little Bridal Pink lustre dust over the dimples, around the cheeks and along the mouth line with a dry paintbrush.

 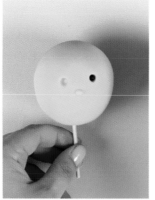   

How to make a caricature figure

Here I explain how to create a cowboy and cowgirl, but you can adapt the techniques to create any other caricature-style figure from your imagination! The figure is modelled on the proportions of a small child with a large, caricature head dressed up in a fun Wild West costume.

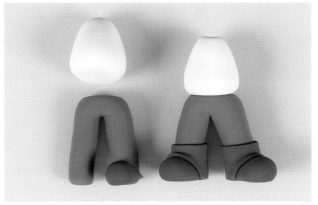  

Legs

1 Take a piece of White MMP that is approximately the same size as the polystyrene ball for the head, then colour it denim blue with Hyacinth paste food colour.

2 Roll the paste into a thick sausage then bend it in half to make a U shape. Flatten down the paste at the bend for the waist. Stand the legs up and leave to dry, supporting them with pieces of foam sponge or polystyrene if necessary.

Boots

3 To make cowboy boots, colour a small amount of White MMP with Teddy Bear Brown paste food colour. Roll the brown paste into two thin strips that are 3cm (1¹/₈") wide then wrap a strip around the ankle on each leg and secure with edible glue.

4 Roll a small amount of brown MMP into an oval then cut the paste in half. Shape each half to fit around the bottom of the legs and attach with edible glue. Roll the remnants of the brown MMP into two thin sausages and attach them over the join between the leg and the boot. Dust the strap with gold lustre dust.

Chaps

5 Roll out some White MMP and cut out a disc that is approximately 10cm (4") in diameter. Stick flat pieces of brown MMP over the white circle to create a cowhide effect. Cut the circle in half and fit each piece around the waist and legs, securing with edible glue.

Upper body

6 Roll some White MMP into a ball, then model the paste into a teardrop shape. Flatten the bottom of the teardrop for the waistline; the pointed end will make the neck.

7 Flatten the paste slightly at the tip of the neck to make a stable base for the head. Insert a wooden skewer about 2cm (¾") down into the top of the body. Remove and leave to dry.

8 Once dry, attach the body to the top of the legs with edible glue. Insert the skewer from the head down into the hole in the body, trimming the wooden skewer if necessary. Secure in place with edible glue.

Cowboy hat

The hat is created in two parts: the crown is attached to the head first and the brim is fitted separately.

9 Take a piece of White MMP that is approximately the same size as the polystyrene ball for the head. Colour the paste with Bulrush paste food colour and cut it in half.

10 To create the crown, roll one piece of paste into a ball and then use a small rolling pin to hollow out one side of the ball. Continue to open up the hole until it is wide enough to fit over the head. Flatten down the top of the crown and create an indent in the middle with your finger. Fit the crown of the hat over the head and secure in place with edible glue.

11 Roll out the remaining piece of paste to 5mm (¼") thick and cut out a circle with a 10cm (4") round cutter. Cut out a hole from the middle of the circle with a 5cm (2") round cutter then cut through the ring with a sharp knife.

12 Attach the brim of the hat around the head with edible glue, folding and flattening the paste at the back of the hat. Bring the front of the brim down slightly over the eyes and bend the brim up at the sides of the hat.

13 Colour a little White MMP with a touch of Poinsettia paste food colour and roll it into a thin strip to create a band for the hat. Secure the band around the hat to cover the join between the crown and the brim. If you prefer, you can colour the MMP with Rose paste food colour to make a pink band for a cowgirl's hat.

Hair

14 *Cowboy:* Cut out several crescent shapes with a 5cm (2") round cutter from MMP in the colour of your choice. Attach the strands of hair randomly around the hairline, fitting them closely under the brim of the hat.

Cowgirl: Roll MMP in the hair colour of your choice into two teardrop shapes. Cut

the wider end straight to create a blunt edge, then attach to either side of the head to make pigtails. Roll pinches of the paste used for the hat band into two very thin sausages. Fit the sausages around the join between the head and the pigtail to make hairbands.

Arms

15 Roll a piece of Soft Beige MMP into a thin sausage and cut it in half to make two arms. Flatten the rounded end of each piece to create the hands. Make a very small cut at the elbow of each arm and bend slightly. Wrap a very small piece of White MMP around the top of each arm to create the sleeve of the T-shirt. Secure the arms to either side of the body and stick the hands flat on the hips for stability.

Accessories

16 Colour some more White MMP with Bulrush paste food colour. Roll out a thin sausage of brown paste and flatten it between your fingers. Secure around the waist as a belt. Flatten a tiny ball of brown paste into a disc, stick it to the front of the belt to create the buckle and dust with Classic Gold lustre dust.

17 Roll out the remaining brown MMP thinly and cut out the waistcoat shapes following the template on page 506. Make tiny cuts into the bottom edge to create tassels, then secure the pieces around the body with edible glue, fit it carefully around the hands. Make a very small disc of brown MMP for a badge and dust with Gold lustre dust.

18 Colour a small piece of MMP with Poinsettia paste food colour and cut out the bandana shapes following the template on page 506. Attach the bandana around the neck.

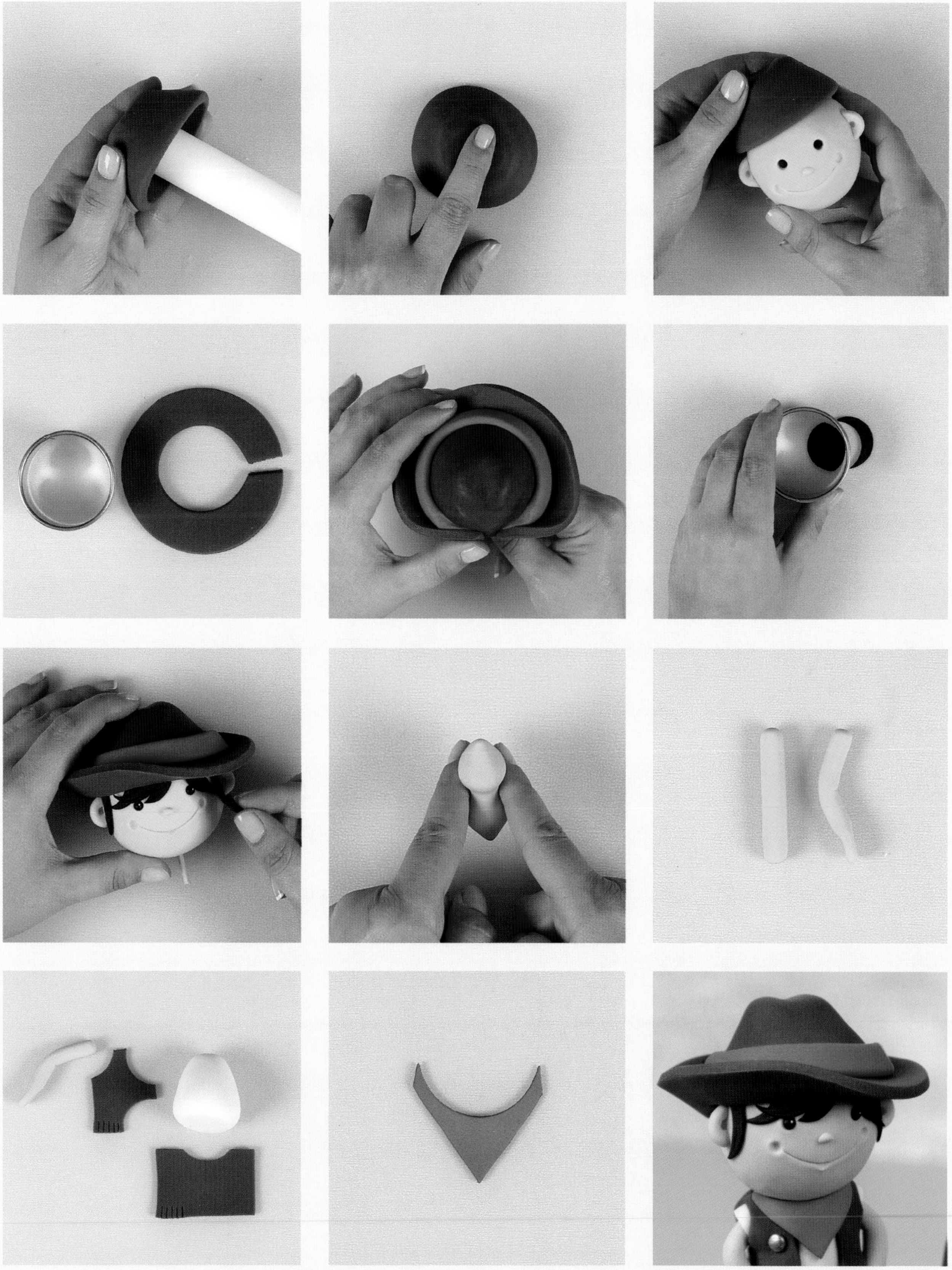

Wild West Party Cake

Cowboys and cowgirls are always a popular theme for children's birthday parties and this cake uses very simple techniques to create a wonderful Wild West centrepiece that everyone will love. Remember that you can always enhance the theme of a novelty cake by modelling small decorations to go around the base.

EDIBLES

20.5cm (8") round cake

875g (2lb) SK Sugarpaste: Bridal White

SK Mexican Modelling Paste (MMP): 140g (5oz) Black, 300g (10½oz) White

SK Professional Paste Food Colours: Bulrush, Chestnut, Vine

SK Designer Metallic Lustre Dust Food Colour: Classic Gold

Cowboy figure, see pages 204–209

EQUIPMENT

25.5cm (10") round cake drum

81cm (2'8") x 10mm (³/₈") wide ribbon: red

For essential modelling edibles and equipment, see pages 184–185

1 Colour 875g (2lb) of Bridal White sugarpaste with Chestnut paste food colour to make it look like the colour of sand. Cover both the cake and drum in the Chestnut-coloured sugarpaste (see pages 139–142.

2 Secure the cowboy to the top of the cake with softened sugarpaste ensuring you leave room for the toy horse.

3 Colour some White MMP with Bulrush paste food colour and roll a small amount of the brown paste into a ball. Draw lines lengthways around the barrel with a sharp knife to create a wood effect. Roll out two thin strips of brown paste and attach them around the top and bottom of the barrel. Dust with Classic Gold lustre dust then repeat to make a second barrel. Secure the barrels to the cake drum with edible glue.

4 Roll some White MMP into a long thin sausage, loosely twist the sausage into a lasso shape and place it on top of the cake in front of the cowboy.

5 Create grey MMP by mixing a little Black MMP with White MMP. Roll into several balls of different sizes and secure these pebbles in clusters around the cake drum.

6 Colour some White MMP with Vine paste food colour for the cacti. Set aside a small amount of paste for the spines then roll the remaining paste into a wide sausage. Insert a wooden skewer through the base of the cactus to make it more stable, then draw several lines down the paste with the handle of a paintbrush. Roll the rest of the green MMP into three teardrop shapes and cut the wider end straight to create a flat edge. Stick to

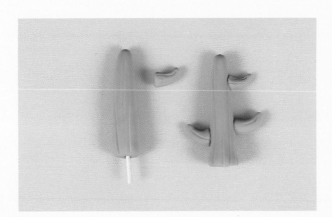
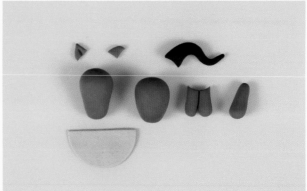

the body of the cactus with edible glue and leave the cactus to dry flat. Once dry, secure to the top of the cake behind the cowboy. Use the remaining green paste to make other smaller, ball-shaped cacti to go on the board around the base of the cake.

7 For the toy horse, divide 140g (5oz) of White MMP into two pieces: a larger piece for the body and a smaller piece for the muzzle. Colour the larger piece of paste with Bulrush and the smaller piece with Chestnut paste food colour. Divide the Bulrush-coloured paste into three pieces, then roll two of the pieces into thick ovals for the body and head. Flatten the body slightly at the neck end to create a base for the head.

8 Roll out the Chestnut-coloured MMP into a thin disc, cut it in half and stick this around the end of the head to make the muzzle. Attach the head to the body with edible glue and use the small end of a ball tool to make nostrils. Cut out the mouth and make dimples and eyes in the same way as for the basic caricature face (see page 206).

9 Roll a sausage from the remaining Bulrush-coloured MMP and cut into four equal sections for the legs. Position the legs around the body so the front legs are tucked under the head as if the horse is lying down. Make two tiny triangles from the same paste for the ears, indent in each ear with a ball tool and stick them to the top of the head.

10 Make a long, thick teardrop shape from Black MMP, shape it into a wavy tail and secure it to the end of the body. Make approximately 12 small teardrops from Black MMP for the mane and attach them between the ears and down the horse's back.

11 Trim the cake board with red satin ribbon to finish (see page 141).

Cake Carving

JAN CLEMENT-MAY

Carving cake shapes can seem quite daunting, but making templates before cutting the cake makes it much simpler. Laying the templates over the sponge cake first maximises the amount of cake that can be used for any design with the least wastage.

EDIBLES

Tray bake sponge cakes, see recipe on page 15

Buttercream, see recipe on page 26

Jam, see recipes on pages 20–30 (optional)

SK Sugarpaste in your chosen colour

Crisped rice cereal mix

50g (1¾oz) butter

200g (7oz) marshmallows

150g (5¼oz) crisped rice cereal

EQUIPMENT

Serrated carving knife

Small, sharp knife

Greaseproof paper

Pencil

Scissors

Templates

For essential modelling edibles and equipment, see pages 184–185

Preparing sponge cakes for carving

1 Make the templates for your cake design from greaseproof or parchment paper before baking the cakes.

2 Arrange the templates onto the baking trays in which the cakes will be baked: this will allow you to calculate how many cakes you need to bake. The instructions given here can be used with most sponge recipes (or would work with a fruit cake) and are based on a 4cm (1½") deep cake.

3 Line the baking trays with greaseproof or parchment paper before baking the cakes and allow to cool thoroughly before carving.

TECHNIQUES

- Preparing sponge cakes for carving
- Carving a sponge cake into a ball
- Carving a sponge cake into a cone
- Carving a sponge cake using templates
- Modelling with crisped rice cereal mix
- Covering an unusually shaped cake with sugarpaste

Carving using templates

1 Make one or more templates for the cake, depending on the shape. If necessary, enlarge the template to the size required using a photocopier or scanner.

2 Trace the shape onto a piece of greaseproof paper or thin food-grade card and cut out with a pair of scissors.

3 Position the template on the cake, making sure that it does not overhang at the edges. If you are using more than one template, try to position them in such a way that allows you to use up as much cake as possible.

4 Carefully carve the cake with a small, serrated knife following the template.

5 Remove the template and use the knife to round off the edges of the cake.

TUTOR TIPS

Keep the designs simple to start with using a basic shape, carving into the cake to shape and sculpt your design. Work slowly to prevent mistakes until you create the shape you require.

Small mistakes can be rectified and patched up with either small pieces of sponge cake and buttercream where necessary. Small amounts of sugarpaste can be used to fill in difficult areas after covering the whole cake with a layer of buttercream and before covering with sugarpaste.

Carving a ball

1 Draw two circles the same size as the ball you want to make onto greaseproof paper and cut out. Make another two circular templates approximately 2.5cm–4cm (1"–1½") smaller than the first two.

2 Lay the templates over the top of the cake to maximise the amount of cake used and cut around the templates with a small, serrated knife. Layer the cakes with buttercream and jam filling on a cake drum (see page 92). Start with a small sponge circle at the base, two larger circles in the middle and finish off with the other small sponge on top.

3 Use the serrated knife to gradually trim away the cake from the top and down the sides of the top two layers all the way around the cake to form a dome, supporting the top with your other hand.

4 Turn the cake over and repeat step 3 to form a ball.

5 Cover the whole cake with a thin layer of buttercream and refrigerate for an hour before covering with sugarpaste.

Carving a cone

1 Cut the templates for your cake from greaseproof paper: start by making the base circle to the size you require and then make subsequent circles 2.5cm (1") smaller than the one before until you finish off at the top with a 4cm (1½") diameter circle.

2 Lay the templates onto the sponge cakes to maximise the use of cake and minimise wastage. Layer the cakes on a cake drum with buttercream and jam filling between them (see page 92).

3 Shape the sides of the cakes with a small serrated knife, working from top to bottom at a slight angle. Work all around the cake to form a cone with a point at the top.

4 Cover the whole cake with a thin layer of buttercream and refrigerate for an hour before covering with sugarpaste.

Modelling with crisped rice cereal mix

Lighter than sponge and easy to mould into shape when warm, crisped rice cereal mix is great for making large, bulky shapes, particularly when you want to create a cake design that is top heavy. For example, in the Little Lion Cake project starting on page 218 I have used crisped rice cereal mix to make the lion's head: this makes the cake much lighter as a whole and means there is less risk of the cake collapsing. Make the mix following the simple recipe and model into shape before it cools down and hardens.

1 Place the butter and marshmallows in a pan and allow them to melt.

2 Add the crisped rice cereal and stir in until fully incorporated.

3 Leave to cool slightly so that you can handle it, then mould into shape whilst it is still warm. Gently re-heat the mixture if it cools down and hardens too quickly.

Cake Carving

Covering an unusually shaped cake

1 Carve the sponge cake into the desired shape and assemble on a cake drum/board.

2 Sandwich the layers of the cake together then crumb-coat the whole shape with a thin layer of buttercream. Place in the fridge for around one hour to allow the buttercream to firm.

3 Roll out the sugarpaste into a rough circle on a work surface dusted with icing sugar. The sugarpaste needs to be large enough to cover the cake all in one go.

4 Use a rolling pin to lift the sugarpaste, then drape it over the top of the cake. Gently smooth down the paste with your hands, working from the top of the cake then down the sides. Ease the paste into the carved areas of the cake using your fingers.

5 Trim off any excess paste where necessary with a sharp knife, then run a cake smoother over the larger surface areas.

6 Cut away the excess paste around the base of the cake, knead together and reserve for later.

Victorian blancmange mould

Cake Carving

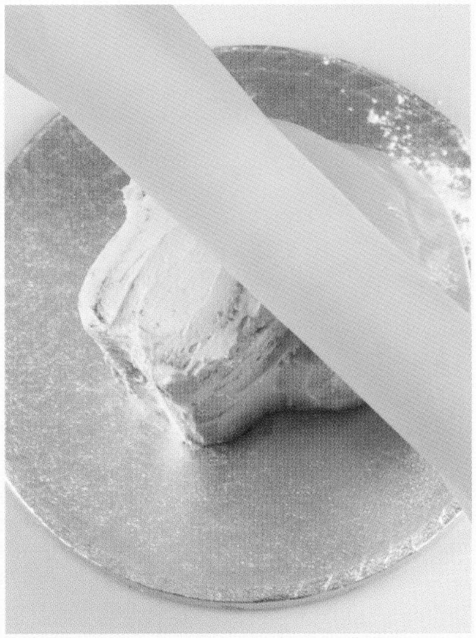
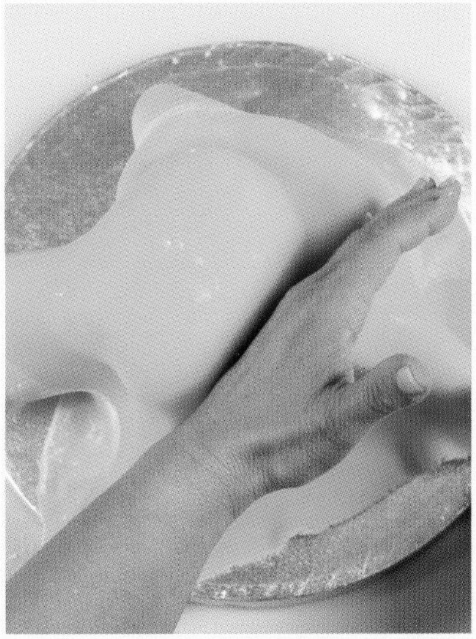
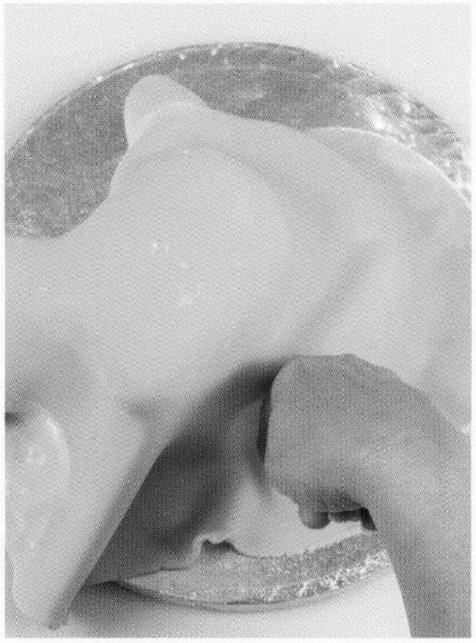
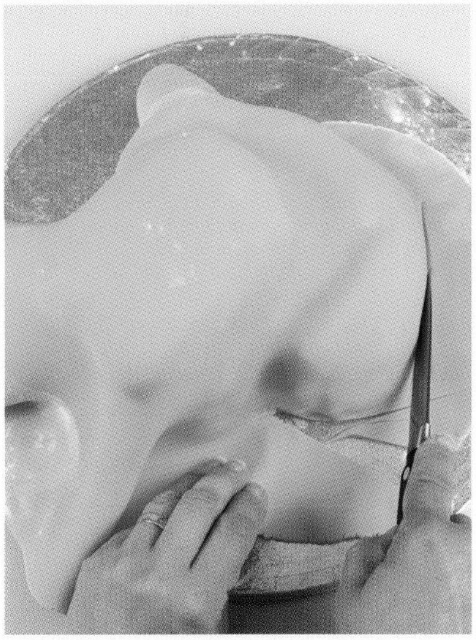
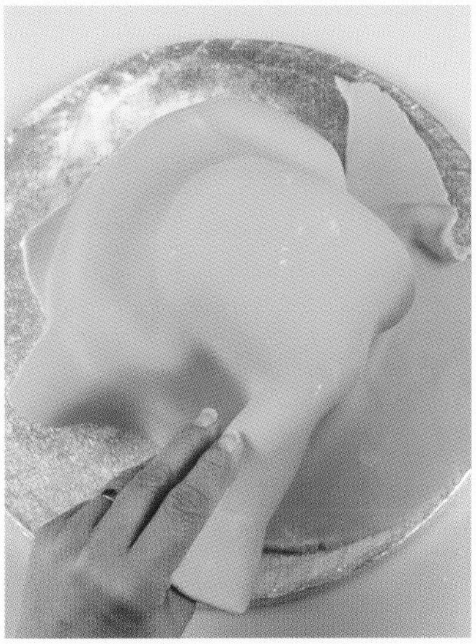
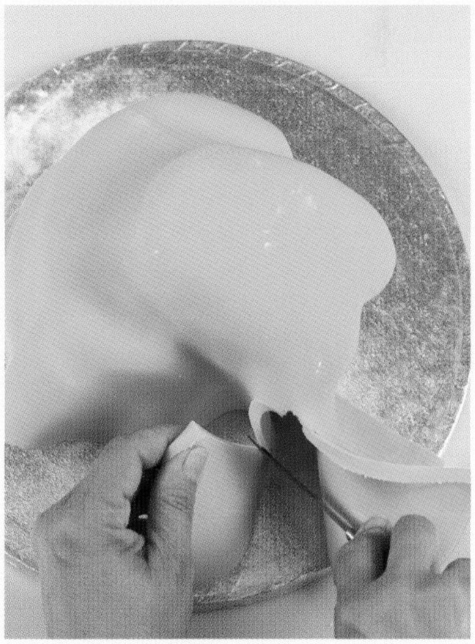
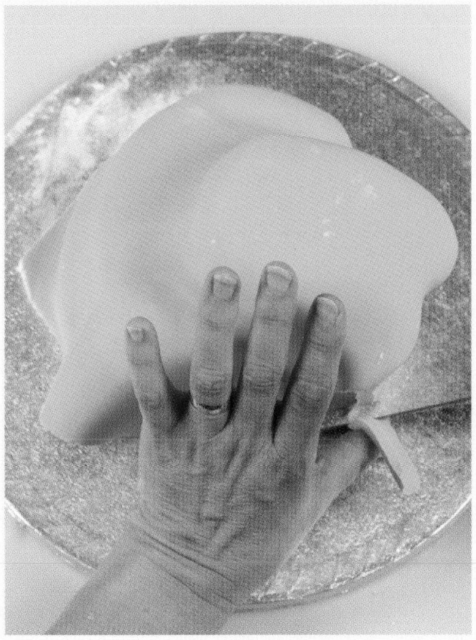
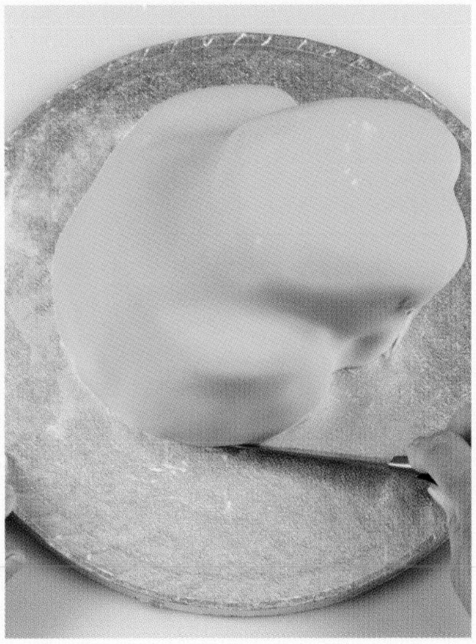
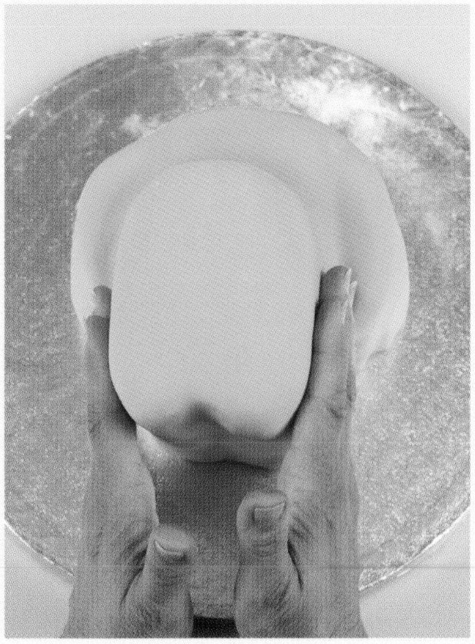

Little Lion Cake

This novelty lion cake with its bright colours and cute expression is perfect for a child's birthday party. You can adapt the carved design to make other animals too, such as a cat, a dog, or even a pig!

EDIBLES

23cm x 30.5cm (9" x 12") tray bake sponge cake

450g (1lb) buttercream, see recipe on page 26

Jam, see recipe on pages 29–30 (optional)

Crisped rice cereal mix, see recipe on page 215

SK Sugarpaste: 8g (¼oz) Bridal White, 160g (5½oz) Coco Brown, 250g (8¾oz) Palm Green, 1g (a pinch) Tuxedo Black, 2.25kg (5lb) Zesty Orange

For essential modelling edibles and equipment, see pages 184–185

EQUIPMENT

30.5cm (12") cake drum

1m (40") x 15mm (½") wide satin ribbon: brown

Dowelling rod

Small round cutters: 1cm (³⁄₈"), 1.5cm (½")

Piping nozzle (any size)

Templates, see page 507

1 Make up 400g (14oz) of the crisped rice cereal mix, following the recipe on page 215. While the mix is still warm, model a ball for the head that is approximately 12.5cm (5") in diameter. Slightly flatten the bottom of the ball and leave to one side to cool completely. Push the end of a dowelling rod approximately 6.5cm (2½") into the flattened base of the head, then remove.

2 Cut out the templates on page 507 from greaseproof paper, then position the templates so they all fit on top of the cake (see picture on page 214) and cut around them with a carving knife. Stack the layers on top of each other on the cake drum, starting with the largest

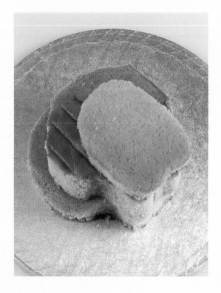

cake at the bottom. Position each layer so the smaller ends line up at the front of the cake.

3 Use a serrated knife to carve down the sides of the middle and bottom tiers to make the body more rounded. To bring out the back legs, carve a 'V' shape that is approximately 1.5cm (½") deep on either side of the top tier. Carve down the back of the legs to make them slightly rounded and trim down the sides of the top layer as indicated on the template. Sandwich the layers together with jam, if desired, and buttercream, then crumb-coat the whole cake and place it in the refrigerator to chill for approximately one hour.

4 Roll out 750g (1lb 10½oz) of Zesty Orange sugarpaste and cover the whole cake following the steps on page 216. Push a dowelling rod down into the top of the lion's body until it touches the cake drum. Mark on the dowel approximately 6.5cm (2½") above the covered cake, remove the dowel, cut at the mark and replace back in the body.

5 Cover the exposed cake drum around the cake with 160g (5½oz)

of Palm Green sugarpaste (see page 142) and push a bone tool randomly into the paste to add texture. Trim the cake drum with brown ribbon (see page 141).

6 Knead 300g (10½oz) of Zesty Orange sugarpaste and divide as follows: 2 x 100g (3½oz) for the back feet and 2 x 50g (1¾oz) for the front feet. Shape each piece of sugarpaste into a smooth ball, then flatten down on the work surface to make a paw. Use the back of a small knife to mark three lines down the front of each foot for the toes. Attach to the base of each leg with edible glue. Push the end of a paintbrush into each of the toe sections to make four holes in each foot. Make 16 x 1g balls of Coco Brown sugarpaste for the claws, then shape each ball into a long cone at one end and a point at the other end. Push the cone end of each claw into the holes in the feet then bend the pointed tip downwards.

7 For the tail, roll 50g (1¾oz) of Zesty Orange sugarpaste into a long, thick sausage. Cut one end of the sausage at an angle and attach to the back of the lion's body with edible glue. Curl the tail up over the side of

the body and rest it on the covered cake drum. Model 50g (1¾oz) of Coco Brown sugarpaste into a cone shape and bend the tip over slightly. Draw lines down the cone with a Dresden tool to add texture then position it at the end of the tail and secure it to the cake drum with edible glue.

8 Cover the crisped rice cereal head with a layer of buttercream, then roll out 400g (14oz) of Zesty Orange sugarpaste into a large circle and cover the head. Cut away any excess paste and smooth down the paste with a cake smoother. Make an incision at the hole in the base of the head and gently ease the head over the exposed dowel at the top of the body and secure with edible glue.

9 Work 30g (1oz) of Zesty Orange sugarpaste into a smooth ball and flatten slightly. Draw a line ¾ of the way down the centre with the back of a small knife, then push the wide end of a metal piping nozzle either side of the line to form the mouth. Push the end of a paintbrush into the paste either end of the mouth to make dimples. Use a Dresden tool to mark five small circles either side of the central line for the whiskers. Attach the muzzle ⅔ of the way down the face with edible glue.

Little Lion Cake

219

10 Divide 6g (just under ¼oz) of Bridal White sugarpaste in half, then shape each piece into a long triangle with rounded corners for the eyes. Secure the eyes approximately 5mm (¼") up from the muzzle. Using the round cutters, cut two 1.5cm (½") circles of Coco Brown sugarpaste and two 1cm (³/₈") circles of Tuxedo Black sugarpaste. Secure the black circles in the centre of the brown circles, then secure them onto the white triangles. Push the end of a paintbrush into the pupil, brush a little edible glue in each hole and push a tiny ball of White sugarpaste into the holes. Divide 6g (just under ¼oz) of Zesty Orange sugarpaste in half, then roll each section into a sausage and taper both ends to a point. Bend the sausages into arches and secure over the eyes as eyebrows.

11 For the nose, shape 6g (just under ¼oz) of Coco Brown sugarpaste into a sausage. Pinch the paste halfway down the nose to make a triangle and secure to the top of the muzzle with edible glue. Divide 30g (1oz) of Zesty Orange sugarpaste in half and shape into two smooth balls for the ears. Push the end of a small rolling pin into each of the ears and secure to either side of the head.

12 To make the mane, brush edible glue around the area in front of the ears and shape 40g (1½oz) of Coco Brown sugarpaste into several small cones. Flatten each cone slightly and texture with a Dresden tool as for the tail. Attach to the glued area, use the Dresden tool to blend the joins and secure the piece in place then bend the tip of each cone slightly. Use 650g (1lb 7oz) of Zesty Orange sugarpaste to make the rest of the cones for the mane. Work on small sections around the face first, then fill in the areas in front of the ears and around the neck before building up the beard using the remaining 40g (1½oz) of Coco Brown sugarpaste. Make sure the head is completely covered, then make the fringe at the top of the head from Orange sugarpaste.

Little Lion Cake

Pastillage Techniques

LINDA GARNHAM

Although pastillage is made of sugar it dries very hard so it isn't easy to eat. However this strength means that pastillage is an extremely useful medium for modelling. It can be used to create boxes, cradles, pillars, models of buildings and any other piece that requires a strong structure.

EDIBLES

Making pastillage

250g (8¾oz) pack of SK Instant Mix Pastillage

25ml (¾oz) cooled, boiled water

Colouring pastillage

SK Paste Food Colours

SK Liquid or Dust Food Colours

Clear alcohol, e.g. gin or vodka

Shaping and assembly

SK Instant Mix Royal Icing

For essential modelling edibles and equipment, see pages 184–185

EQUIPMENT

Making pastillage

Measuring jug

Mixing bowl

Sieve

Airtight food container

Large palette knife or spatula

Colouring pastillage

Paint palette

Shaping and assembly

Cutter or template

Shaped former, e.g. polystyrene ball or plastic pipe

TECHNIQUES

- Making pastillage
- Colouring pastillage
- Working with pastillage
- Shaping pastillage
- Assembling pastillage pieces

French 19th-century pastillage figurines, Dutton collection

Making pastillage

Pastillage can be made from icing sugar, gum tragacanth and egg albumen and is also available as an instant mix powder. I use SK Instant Mix Pastillage as it is quick and simple to make and gives consistent results.

1 Sift between ½ and ⅔ of the pastillage powder into a clean mixing bowl.

2 Add 25ml (¾fl oz) of cooled, boiled water and stir with a palette knife or spatula until the mixture starts to come together.

3 Turn the mixture out onto a clean work surface and continue to knead in the remainder of the powder until it is fully incorporated and the paste is smooth.

4 Once made, smear the surface of the paste with a little white vegetable fat to prevent a crust forming on the surface, then double wrap the paste in cling film. Place the pastillage in a sealable food-grade plastic bag, then place the bag into an airtight container. Leave the paste to rest for several hours, overnight if possible.

Colouring pastillage

Pastillage can be coloured using paste food colours in the same way as sugarpaste and other modelling pastes. If you require the pastillage to be a very deep shade, you can also surface-paint it with liquid or dust food colours once it is dry.

1 To add colour, pick up a little paste food colour on a cocktail stick or mini palette knife and transfer it onto a small piece of pastillage. Knead the colour into the paste a little at a time until you achieve a shade deeper than the one you require.

2 Gradually knead this darker paste with the remaining pastillage until you are happy with the colour. Pastillage lightens as it dries, so you will need to add extra colour if you want to create a deeper shade. However, avoid adding too much colour, as this may compromise the strength, appearance and quality of the paste; you can always surface-paint the pastillage once dry.

3 Colour the pastillage to a base shade as described above, then model, cut or shape the pastillage as required and leave to dry.

4 Mix your chosen paste, liquid or dust food colour with a little clear alcohol or cooled, boiled water in a paint palette. Load a wide, flat paintbrush with the colour and remove any excess moisture on a piece of kitchen paper. Paint the mixture directly onto the dry pastillage, brushing over the surface with long, sweeping strokes.

5 Allow the first layer of paint to dry before adding another layer of colour. Keep building up the layers until you are happy with the colour and the coverage. For a more intense colour, dissolve a little more food colour in the mixture before you apply subsequent layers.

If the paste becomes too moist, or if you work on the same area for too long you will find that the sugars will start to absorb the moisture and begin to dissolve. You should also take care not to splash your dried pieces with liquid as this can also dissolve the sugar and leave unsightly marks. It is a good idea to make spare pieces to allow for mistakes and breakages.

Working with pastillage

Pastillage dries very quickly once exposed to the air, so it is essential to have any tools, templates and cutters ready so that you can model the pastillage before it dries out. If you find that the paste becomes dry during use, add a couple of drops of cooled, boiled water to the paste to replace any lost moisture.

1 Unwrap the paste and knead on a clean, dry work surface: this makes the paste more pliable and easier to model. Take off the amount of pastillage required, then re-wrap any paste that you aren't working with.

2 Lightly dust a work surface with cornflour and roll out just enough paste for the piece you are making. You can use card or marzipan spacers to help you achieve an even thickness (see page 225).

3 Release the paste from the board using a small palette knife then dust the work surface with a little more cornflour. If you want to emboss the paste, do so at this stage before you cut out the shape required.

4 Use a cutter to cut out the shape required, or place a template onto the paste and cut around it with a small, sharp knife or cutting wheel. Being careful not to distort the shape,

lift it and place it on a flat surface, e.g. a flat foam pad or a chopping board dusted with cornflour. Leave to dry.

5 After a couple of hours, turn over any smaller pieces to allow them to dry evenly on both sides. Larger pieces should be left overnight before turning, as they will take longer to dry and will break if moved too soon. Drying times will depend on the size and thickness of the pieces and the climate you are working in. The paste will dry quicker if the climate is hot and dry; it will take longer to dry out if it is cold, wet or humid. Allow the pieces to dry for at least 24 hours and up to three days before assembly.

Shaping pastillage

Pastillage can be shaped and formed whilst it is still soft and pliable to produce a variety of structural pieces.

Curved bowl (e.g. an umbrella or basket) ▶

Roll out the paste as described above and cut out a circle of paste with a round cutter or template. For a parasol or similar, dust a polystyrene ball former with a little cornflour, immediately place the paste over the ball and allow it to dry. Attach a length of dried pastillage to the centre of the circle to make a handle. For a basket shape or similar, dry a circle of paste over a large rolling pin dusted with cornflour. When dry it can be filled with sugar flowers for a pretty cake-top decoration.

Tube (e.g. a pillar or other cylinder)

Use a piece of plastic pipe or a cardboard tube from a kitchen roll to make a former. Cover the tube with a piece of acetate or food sealing wrap, secure with a little masking tape and dust lightly with cornflour. Make a template for the required shape that is slightly longer than the circumference of the tube. Cut a strip of pastillage following the template, then lay the paste over the tube. Overlap the ends of the pastillage and use a sharp knife to cut through the excess paste. Moisten one edge of the paste with a little edible glue and join the two ends together around the tube. Once the outside is dry, carefully remove the tube from the centre and allow the inner part to dry. ◀

Assembling structural pieces

It is best to stick freshly-rolled pieces of pastillage together with edible glue; royal icing is recommended for assembling dried pieces as it is strong and quick to dry.

If you need to attach a piece of soft pastillage to a dry piece you should use a little edible glue, but you may need to give the pieces extra time to set firmly before continuing to work on them.

TUTOR TIPS

Icing sugar absorbs moisture at different rates and sometimes you may find it hard to knead in all of the pastillage powder. If this occurs, simply add one small droplet of cooled, boiled water at a time and continue kneading until all the powder has been incorporated and the paste becomes smooth. Do not add too much extra water as this will alter the consistency of the paste and make it too soft to work with.

When cutting pastillage, chop downwards through the paste rather than slicing along it as this will keep the edges neat and smooth.

Knead any excess pieces of soft pastillage together and return to the sealed bag with the other paste so that they can be re-used.

Pastillage Techniques

Christmas Gift Boxes

Handmade and filled with a selection of sweets or chocolates, these little gift boxes are the perfect addition to any Christmas table.

EDIBLES

500g (1lb 1¾oz) SK Instant Mix Pastillage

SK Sugar Florist Paste (SFP): White

SK Quality Food Colour (QFC) Pastes: Black, Red

SK Professional Paste Food Colour: Rose

SK Professional Dust Food Colour: Poinsettia (Christmas red)

SK Confectioners' Glaze

SK Instant Mix Royal Icing (small amount)

Clear alcohol e.g. gin or vodka (optional)

Cooled, boiled water

EQUIPMENT

Pieces of card: 2mm (¹/₁₆") and 3mm (¹/₈") thick

Paintbrushes: no. 2, 15mm (½") flat

9cm (3½") fluted round cutter

5cm (2") round cutter

6cm (2³/₈") diameter tube former, covered with acetate

Piping nozzles: nos. 1, 2, 3, 4

Piping bags

Holly/poinsettia micro cutter (Coronet Porcelain)

Teardrop micro plunger cutter

10mm (³/₈") circle cutter: 1845B (Fine Cut)

Holly leaf cutter: HL1 (FMM)

Star plunger cutters, set of 3 (PME)

10mm (³/₈") heart shape plunger cutter (PME)

Modelling quilting tool (PME)

SK Confectioners' Glaze Cleaner (IPA)

Templates, see page 506

For essential modelling edibles and equipment, see pages 184–185

Boxes

1 Make two sets of spacers from the card. For the first set of spacers, cut two strips from the 2mm (¹/₁₆") thick card measuring 23cm long x 4cm wide (9" x 1½"). For the second set of spacers, cut two strips of the same size from 3mm (¹/₈") thick card.

2 Make a template for the side of the box from greaseproof paper measuring the same as the card spacers and fold into six equal sections. Mark out the position of the side design on the template. You can also make a template for the lid decoration, if desired.

3 Cut out the bird template from a piece of thick card, or if you prefer you can use a leaf cutter of a similar size and shape for the wing. Prepare the tube former (see page 224).

4 Mix up the bag of pastillage (see page 222): this will be enough to make six boxes plus spares to allow for breakages. Seal as recommended on page 222 and leave to rest overnight.

5 For the red boxes, colour 300g (10½oz) of pastillage with a little Rose and Red paste food colours (see pages 222–223), then allow the paste to rest. Leave the remaining pastillage for the white boxes uncoloured.

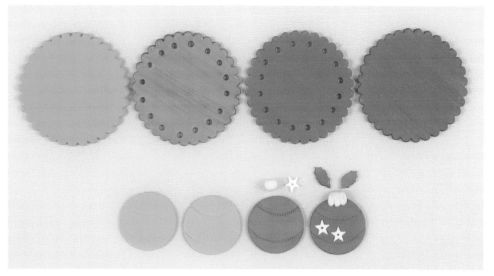

6 Dust the work surface with a little cornflour, knead the paste and roll out a length of pastillage to a thickness of 2mm (¹/₁₆") using the first set of spacers. Place one of the spacers on the paste and cut around it with a small, sharp knife. Wrap the pastillage around the former and trim neatly at the join (see page 224).

7 Carefully remove the pastillage strip from the former, lay it out flat and place the side template onto the paste. Mark the layout of the design on the pastillage with a scribing tool. Wrap the paste around the tube again and secure at the join with edible glue (see page 225). Place the tube on a flat foam pad or board and leave to dry. Remove the tube after approximately two hours to allow the inner paste to dry.

8 Roll out some more pastillage to a thickness of 3mm (¹/₈"). Cut out a lid and base with the fluted cutter and lay on a flat foam pad. If you have a template, mark out the lid design at this stage. Cut out a circle with the plain-edged round cutter, then allow all the pieces to dry overnight on a flat surface. Turn the pieces after a couple of hours to allow them to dry evenly.

9 For the red boxes, dilute some Red paste food colour in some clear alcohol or cooled, boiled water and apply a thin base coat over the box (see page 223). Using sweeping movements, paint across the lid and the base pieces until fully coated. When dry, turn the pieces over and paint the other side. Allow to dry once more. Paint the sides of the box from join to join in the same way and allow to dry.

10 Dilute some Poinsettia dust colour and apply another coat over the box. You can strengthen the colour by adding a little more dust to the paint.

11 Once all the pieces are painted and dry, apply a layer of confectioners' glaze in the same way: this will help to set the colours and give the box a soft sheen. Do not overload your brush with the glaze as it will run as it dries and allow the coating to dry before assembly. Wash the brush with glaze cleaner after use (see page 175).

12 Make up some soft-peak royal icing and colour with a touch of Red paste food colour to match the colour

of the box. Place the icing in a small piping bag and cut a hole in the tip of the bag. Pipe a line of icing around the bottom of the side piece, position centrally onto the base and press down gently to secure. Clean up the join with a paintbrush and leave to dry.

13 Attach the smaller circle to the bottom of the lid with a little royal icing: this piece will help keep the lid in place.

Bauble design

14 Colour a little White SFP with Red paste colour so it is the same shade as the box. Cut out a small circle of paste and draw two curved lines across the bauble with a quilting tool. Paint the circle in the same way as the red box to ensure the colours match and leave to dry. Cut two holly leaves from the red paste with a plunger cutter, colour red and leave to dry in the same way.

15 Roll out a little White SFP thinly and cut out three small star shapes with a plunger cutter. Make a hole in the middle of each star with the tip of a

no. 3 nozzle and attach to the bauble with edible glue. Stick the bauble to the lid with a little royal icing. Colour a small amount of SFP grey with a touch of Black paste colour, then model into the top piece of the bauble. Secure the top of the bauble and the holly leaves in place.

16 Cut out six small circles and 12 small holly leaves from the red SFP. Leave them on the side of the tube former to dry so that they will lay flat against the curved sides of the box. Paint in the same way as before and leave to dry. Cut out six small stars from White SFP and make a hole in the centre of each with a no. 2 nozzle. Attach a star to each small red circle.

17 Add a touch of Black paste colour to a little royal icing and place into a piping bag fitted with a no. 1 nozzle. Pipe a line of light grey icing between each of the marks in the paste you made earlier, then pipe a dot of royal icing and attach the baubles and the holly leaves to complete the design.

Bird design

18 Roll out a little White SFP and cut out several small circles with a no. 4 nozzle. Attach these circles evenly

around the top of the lid, using the fluted edge as a guide.

19 Roll out a thicker piece of White SFP and cut out the bird and wing using the templates. Use the plunger cutter to cut out a heart shape from the body and then cut out the eye with a no. 3 nozzle. Run the quilting tool around the edge of the bird and wing, then secure them to the lid of the box with a little edible glue. Glue the circle from the eye in the centre of the heart.

20 Use the plunger cutters to cut out several hearts, circles and teardrops, then secure them over the marks you made earlier around the side of the box.

Snowflake design

21 Roll out a little White SFP and cut out several small circles with a no. 4 piping nozzle. Attach these following the marks you made earlier on the side of the box.

22 Roll a thicker piece of White SFP and cut out three snowflakes with the plunger cutter. Attach these to the lid of the box with a little edible glue.

TUTOR TIPS

As with any design, templates are essential if you want to ensure that the patterns on your work are even. Templates can be made from greaseproof paper or food-grade card and kept for future projects.

Make sure the ends of the pastillage around the former do not overlap, otherwise they will form an uneven shape when dry.

Placing pastillage pieces to dry on a flat foam pad or piece of sponge allows the air to circulate underneath the paste, helping the paste to dry quicker.

After using confectioners' glaze, always clean your brush in glaze cleaner (IPA) to protect the bristles of the brush.

If you have trouble getting small pieces to stick to the acetate around the former, simply smear a little white vegetable fat on the surface and the fresh paste will stick to the fat.

Roll out pastillage on a work surface that is lightly dusted with icing sugar or cornflour to prevent it from sticking to the surface.

Christmas Gift Boxes

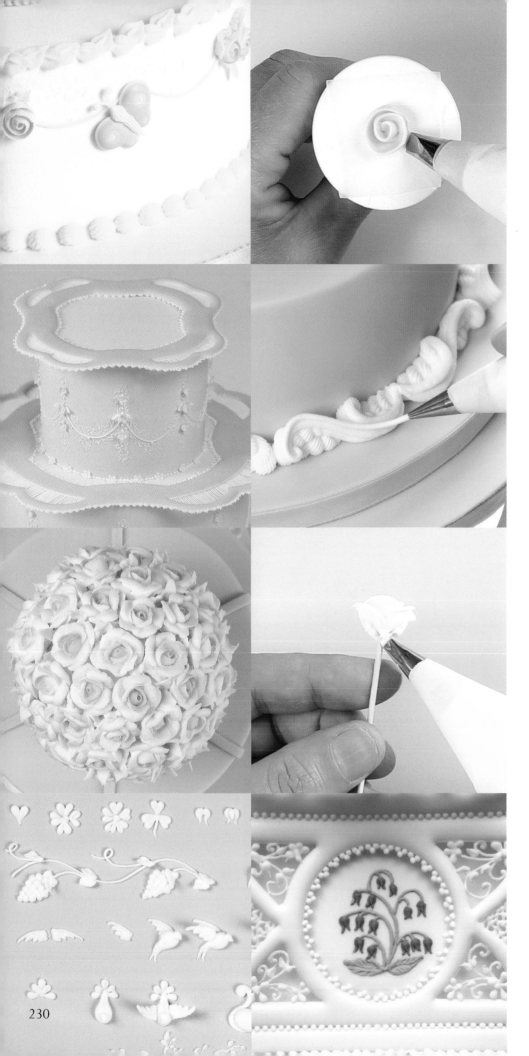

Essential Edibles and Equipment for Royal Icing

1   Acetate/cellophane

2   Angled lamp with 40W bulb

3   Bowls, various sizes

4   Cake drums and boards, for drying work and displaying cakes

5   Cling film

6   Cranked palette knife

7   Food-grade sponge or pastry brush (for stippling)

8   Greaseproof paper

9   Icing (flower) nail

10 Icing ruler/straight edge

11 Kitchen cloths, new

12 Masking tape

13 Non-stick board

14 Paper and pencil for templates

15 Piping bags, small and medium

16 Piping nozzles, see project list for sizes

17 Ruler, clear plastic

18 Scissors

19 Side scraper

20 Sharp knife

21 SK Glycerine

22 SK Instant Mix Royal Icing, see project list for quantity

23 SK Paintbrush: no. 1

24 SK Professional Dust Food Colours, see project list

25 SK Professional Liquid Food Colours, see project list

26 Stand mixer with flat beater attachment

27 Tilting turntable

28 Wax paper squares

29 White vegetable fat

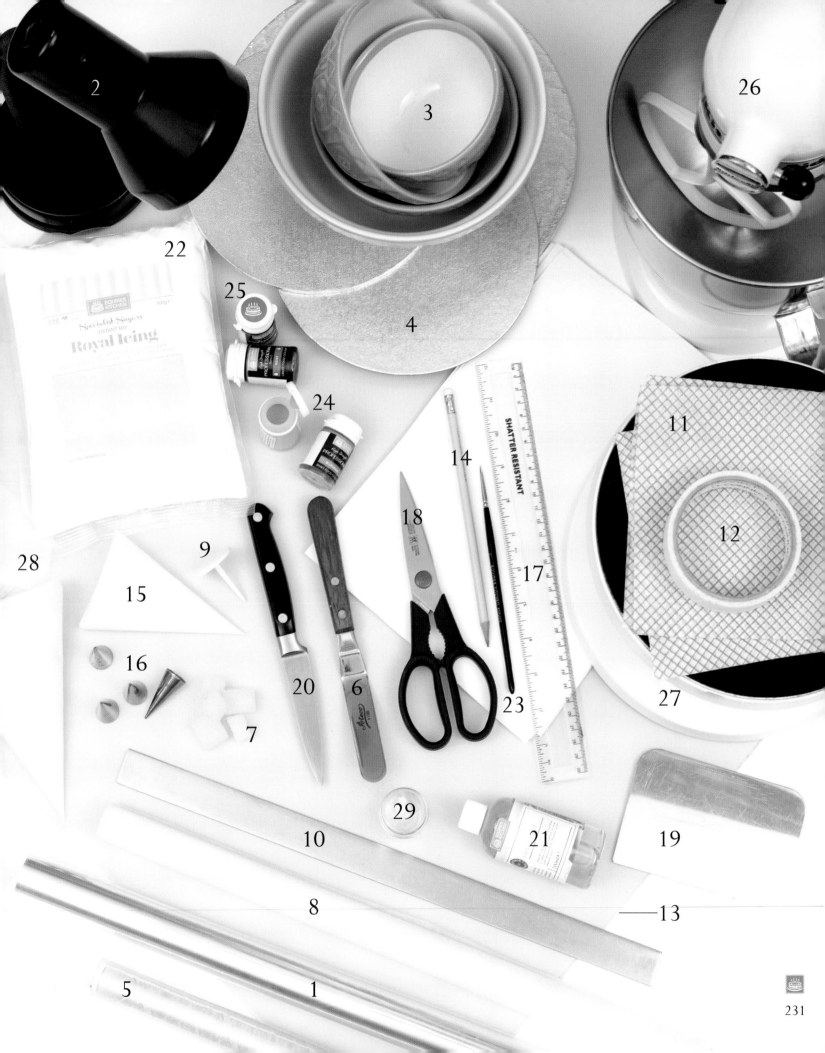

Tessa Whitehouse

BIOGRAPHY

I have enjoyed decorating cakes since I was very young and I can't really remember a time when I wasn't 'helping' in the kitchen. Both my mum and grandmother were great cooks and encouraged me to participate – the first cakes I remember decorating were Christmas cakes which I helped my grandmother to ice. I started to learn about sugarcraft from books and was never one to shirk a challenge, even making sugar flowers for the first time for my own wedding cake just three days before the big day!

I gained a BSc Honours Degree in Home Economics and went on to have a career in market research. My degree has led me to have a rigorous approach to any project that I

undertake, and my previous career nurtured my love for working with people. I took several courses at Squires Kitchen International School to further improve my cake decorating skills and developed my chocolate skills at the Callebaut Academy.

While I enjoy all aspects of sugarcraft, I developed my lifelong love of royal icing by attending classes with Eddie Spence MBE for five years. I simply love what can be achieved with a simple mix of icing sugar and egg white and I am driven by a constant desire to improve. It was with the encouragement of Eddie Spence that I took my first steps as a sugarcraft professional and undertook private commissions for celebration cakes.

My professional association with Squires Kitchen started when I became a regular demonstrator in the Farnham shop, a role that I still enjoy today. My royal icing designs can be seen regularly in *Cakes & Sugarcraft* magazine, which gives me

the opportunity to share my knowledge with thousands of readers. In 2013 I accepted the honour of making the annual Baddeley Cake – a long-standing tradition that celebrates Twelfth Night at the Theatre Royal Drury Lane – currently undertaken by a Squires Kitchen representative each year. I took up the challenge to combine the traditional techniques and styles of royal icing with the theme of Shrek and the design incorporated a hidden surprise.

In 2012, I became a tutor at Squires Kitchen International School, specialising in royal icing. I teach royal icing at Foundation level, as well as Extended Skills classes such as oriental string work and brush embroidery and am always thinking of ways to make royal icing more accessible. Inspired in particular by Eddie Spence's skill and passion for royal icing, I hope to encourage others in a similar way and help bring back the popularity of royal icing.

Basic Royal Icing Skills

TESSA WHITEHOUSE

Royal icing is a mix of icing sugar and egg white beaten together to create a thick, creamy consistency which dries to a firm finish. Manipulating the consistency of royal icing means that it can be used for a wide variety of decorative effects. The skills covered here will introduce you to the basics of royal icing including coating a cake, simple run-outs, piped borders and flowers.

EDIBLES

SK Instant Mix Royal Icing

SK Ouality Food Colour (QFC) Liquids of your choice

EQUIPMENT

Templates for run-outs, see page 506

Piping nozzles: plain, rope, leaf and petal (nos. 1.5, 43, 51 and 57) (PME)

TECHNIQUES

- Making royal icing
- Colouring royal icing
- Coating a cake and cake board with royal icing
- Filling a piping bag
- Pressure piping: drop line, shell, running bead, leaf and ribbon rose
- Preparing run-out icing and making off-pieces
- Making a decorative stippled finish

For essential royal icing edibles and equipment, see pages 230–231

Making royal icing

Egg white for royal icing comes in various forms: dried pure albumen, dried fortified albumen, pasteurized egg white and pre-mixed into icing sugar. For health and safety reasons the use of raw, fresh egg white in royal icing is not recommended; I have used SK Instant Mix Royal Icing because it is easy to use and produces consistent results, making it ideal for those who are new to royal icing. If you prefer to make your own, recipes are given in the Extended Royal Icing chapter on page 358.

1 Shake the bag of Instant Mix Royal Icing before opening to distribute the ingredients evenly. Empty into the clean bowl of a stand mixer and add 75ml (2½fl oz) of cooled, boiled water. Attach the flat beater and beat at a slow speed until the icing looks white, thick and slightly glossy. To test when the icing has reached off-peak consistency, press a clean palette knife gently onto the icing, lift out and turn over; there should be an upright peak of icing which bends slightly when the knife is turned on its side. This consistency of icing is also known as soft-peak and normal consistency. If the peak flops over the icing needs to be beaten more. If you do not have a stand mixer royal icing can be made by hand, which takes 20 minutes of beating. Some handheld mixers can be used but they are often not sufficiently strong to make royal icing.

2 Once made it is important to keep royal icing covered with a damp, lint-free cloth to prevent it crusting over. To store it for longer periods of time, place it in a clean, grease-free container with an airtight lid or covered with two layers of cling film. Ensure the sides, top edge and lid of the container are completely clean and free of any icing. Royal icing does not need to be kept in the fridge in temperate climates such as the UK. However, in hot climates it is advisable to store royal icing in the fridge. Always allow it to return to room temperature and re-beat before using. Icing can be stored and used for up to a week.

Consistencies of royal icing

Flat icing/cake covering

A slightly softer consistency than normal, off-peak icing is required: this is achieved by paddling or 'rubbing down' freshly-beaten, off-peak icing on a non-stick board in small amounts using a palette knife.

Piping

Off-peak consistency is required, as described above. Some piped decorations, such as ribbon roses, require stiff-peak icing which still has flow but holds its shape.

Run-outs

Off-peak, piping consistency icing (as described above) is required for the outlines. A more fluid, creamy consistency is required for filling the outline, also known as 'flooding'.

Basic Royal Icing Skills

235

Coating a round cake with royal icing

The amount of royal icing you need for covering a cake can be found in the table on page 91. If you are covering a rich fruit cake a useful rule of thumb is that the amount of royal icing should be approximately half the weight of the cake. For example, if a 15cm (6") round fruit cake weighs 1.15kg (2½lb) then you will need 575g (1lb 4oz) of royal icing to coat your cake.

Colouring royal icing

1 Make up the royal icing following the instructions on page 235, then weigh out the amount of icing that you need in a separate, clean bowl: it is always best to colour too much rather than not enough.

2 Use a dropper to add liquid food colour to the icing. Count how many drops you add then make a note for reference, in case you need to make the same colour again.

3 Mix the colour into the icing using a palette knife. If the colour isn't strong enough, add some dust food colour in the same shade and mix in: the combination of liquid and dust will prevent the consistency of the icing from changing.

1 Cover the cake with marzipan as described on page 95. A royal iced coating is built up in several thin layers, each layer drying before the next one is applied, with the top and sides of the cake coated separately.

2 Mix the SK Instant Mix Royal Icing according to the directions above. Reserve two tablespoons of royal icing in an airtight container to coat the board later, then add glycerine to the remainder and stir well. Without glycerine the icing will become too hard to cut. You will need approximately 5ml (1tsp) of glycerine per 500g (1lb 1¾oz) of royal icing.

3 Place the cake on a turntable to coat the top of the cake. Use a palette knife to put one to two tablespoons of royal icing onto a clean and grease-free board and paddle the icing: keeping the knife in contact with the icing, spread the icing backwards and forwards until it looks smooth and shiny. This action removes large air bubbles and makes the icing more fluid. Gather the icing up on the knife and put it in the centre of the cake. Spread the icing across the top by paddling again: keep the end of the palette knife in the centre and use small paddling motions. Move the turntable at the same time until the icing is spread evenly across the top of the cake to the edge.

4 Wipe an icing ruler with a clean, damp cloth and rest one flat side gently on the far edge of the cake at an acute angle (i.e. tipped towards you). Using even pressure pull the ruler towards you, swivel the top of the ruler on the front edge of the cake and push away from you; if the icing doesn't have a smooth finish pull the ruler back towards you once more, continuing off the cake to finish.

5 Use a clean palette knife to trim away any excess icing from the edge by cutting straight down away from the wet icing. Put the cake aside to dry and clean all tools.

Tala icing set from the 1920s, Dutton collection

6 Put the cake back on the turntable to cover the sides. Paddle some royal icing and spread over the side of the cake. Hold the palette knife in a vertical position against the cake and paddle the icing to spread and smooth it over the sides of the cake.

7 Wipe the side scraper with a clean, damp cloth. If you are right-handed, place your left arm and hand over the cake and take hold of the cake drum on the right-hand side (at the three o'clock position as though the drum was a clock face). Hold the scraper in your right hand and place it against the cake at an acute angle by your left hand. Keep your right hand still and apply even pressure whilst rotating the cake drum anti-clockwise with your left hand. Turn the cake in one smooth movement until the scraper is at the start point and then gently pull the scraper towards you and off the cake. If you are left-handed, hold the scraper in your left hand and use your right hand to rotate the cake clockwise. Trim away the excess icing from the top by cutting away from the wet icing with a palette knife. Clean up the icing from the cake drum. Set aside to dry.

8 When dry, remove any lumps gently with a sharp knife before repeating steps 3 to 7 to give the cake a second coat. Allow to dry.

9 Repeat again to apply a third coating.

10 To coat the board, add cooled, boiled water drop by drop into the reserved glycerine-free icing to make it thinner. It is the correct consistency when a clean knife drawn across the icing leaves a line which disappears on the count of 16–18 seconds. If it takes longer add more water, if less stir in more royal icing powder or icing sugar. Cover with a clean, damp cloth and leave to stand for 30 minutes.

11 Disperse any surface bubbles by gently stirring the icing. Using a palette knife thickly spread the icing onto the outer edge of the drum, all the way around the cake. Spread the icing onto the drum, leaving a narrow gap between the icing and the cake side. Rest the edge of the side scraper on the icing and against the side of the cake, apply light pressure and turn the cake 360° as for step 7 above. Clean the edge and leave to dry completely before decorating.

Coating a square cake with royal icing

Follow the same technique as for the round cake to coat the cake top. When dry, coat two opposite sides of the cake, allow to dry then coat the other two opposite sides. Repeat to give the cake three full coats then cover the board as for the round cake.

Filling a piping bag

Ready-made paper piping bags are quick and easy to use. However, if you would like to make your own piping bags from greaseproof paper, see instructions on page 359.

1 Make a small cut in the top of the piping bag and fold one side flat to form a V-shape. This will hold the bag firmly in place and prevent it from unwrapping.

2 If you are using a nozzle, cut a hole in the end of the piping bag large enough for about half of the nozzle to come through and drop the nozzle into the bag. If you are using a piping bag with run-out icing omit this step as you won't need a nozzle.

3 Use a small palette knife to half-fill the bag with icing. Fold the top two corners into the middle and then roll down towards the nozzle to form a neat and plump bag.

4 For run-out icing (no nozzle), snip off the very tip of the bag with scissors when you are ready to pipe.

TUTOR TIPS

In very dry climates it may be necessary to add up to 10ml (2tsp) of glycerine per 500g (1lb 1¾oz) of royal icing for coating. In very humid climates you will need less than 5ml (1tsp) per 500g (1lb 1¾oz).

Run-out pieces are fragile so always make extras in case of breakages. Store in a cardboard box between layers of kitchen paper.

To prevent nozzles becoming blocked with dried royal icing when not in use, keep bags of royal icing in a plastic bag or with the tip tucked under a clean, damp cloth.

Adapt the designs shown here by changing the number on the plaque or making an arrangement of ribbon roses and/or butterflies for the cake.

Basic Royal Icing Skills

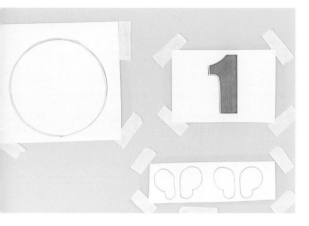

Simple run-outs

1 Make up a bag of Instant Mix Royal Icing as described on page 235. Divide into bowls and colour the icing as required using liquid food colours.

2 Make paper templates for all of your run-outs and trim so they fit well within the size of the drying board. Cut a piece of cellophane slightly larger than the template but smaller than the drying board, place over the template and secure to the board using masking tape at the corners.

3 Very lightly grease the cellophane with white vegetable fat so that the run-outs can be removed easily when dry.

4 Prepare the run-out icing by putting about a tablespoon of each colour into a clean bowl. Thin each colour by adding a little cooled, boiled water: the correct consistency for run-out

icing is when a line cut into the icing disappears after the count of nine to ten seconds. Cover with a clean cloth and leave to stand for approximately half an hour to allow any air bubbles to rise to the surface. Once you can see the bubbles, stir gently to eliminate any air.

5 To pipe the outlines, snip off the tip of a small paper piping bag and drop a nozzle into the bag, usually a no. 1 or 1.5. Half-fill the piping bag with off-peak icing. Squeeze the bag gently and apply an even pressure to outline the shapes.

6 If you want to pipe outlines in different colours, repeat step 5 using off-peak royal icing in the colour required and the same size nozzle.

7 Half-fill piping bags with the run-out colours.

8 Cut a very small hole in a bag of run-out icing and fill the shape: working in sections, pipe icing up to the outline and then fill the centre.

9 To make run-outs in more colours, fill in the outlines as before using one colour at a time.

10 Dry all the finished run-outs under a small desk lamp fitted with a 40 watt bulb (or similar) for at least half an hour for small pieces, or longer if possible. This is particularly important in humid climates otherwise the icing will not dry fully.

11 Allow all run-outs to dry for 24 hours in a warm, dry place.

12 Slide a small palette knife under the run-outs when dry to release them from the cellophane.

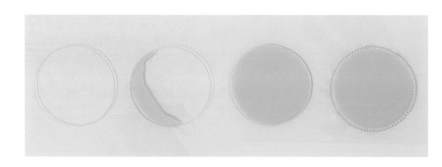

Ribbon roses

1 Add one teaspoon of sifted icing sugar to a small bowl of icing in the colour of your choice and stir until fully combined. The icing should stand in a stiff peak.

2 Cut several 2.5cm (1") squares from cellophane or wax paper.

3 Fit a medium-sized piping bag with a no. 57 petal nozzle and ½-fill with the stiff icing. Put a small dot of icing onto a flower nail and stick a cellophane square on top. Holding the flower nail in your left hand (or in your right hand if you are left-handed) rest the wide end of the nozzle in the centre of the flower nail in a vertical position. Turn the flower nail anti-clockwise (clockwise if you are left-handed) while at the same time gently squeezing the piping bag to form a small cone in the centre. Without breaking the ribbon of icing continue squeezing and turning until you have the required size of rose. Release the pressure and gently pull down and away to finish.

4 Remove the square from the nail and put aside to dry. When dry, carefully remove from the cellophane.

Stippled scallops and drop-line technique

1 Make a template for the coloured scallops by cutting a piece of greaseproof paper the same circumference as the cake and approximately 2.5cm (1") less than the depth. Fold into 12 equal sections.

2 Draw and cut out a scallop shape. Unfold the template, wrap it around the cake and hold the two ends together using masking tape, ensuring the tape does not come into contact with the cake.

3 Put a teaspoon of royal icing in your chosen colour onto a clean surface, add a drop of cooled, boiled water and

Basic Royal Icing Skills

mix. Dip either a clean pastry brush or piece of food-grade sponge into the softened icing and dab it onto the exposed side of the cake. To create a two-tone effect, repeat with a second colour of icing. Remove the paper template.

4 To add the scalloped line underneath, fit a small piping bag with a no. 1.5 nozzle and ½-fill with off-peak royal icing in your chosen colour. Using the stippled areas as a guide, drop lines around the cake: starting at the point of each scallop attach the icing by squeezing gently, move the nozzle slightly away from the cake whilst applying even pressure, then move in a straight line to the next point allowing the icing to fall into shape. This is called the drop-line technique.

Simple piped borders

Shell border ▼

Put a no. 43 nozzle into a medium piping bag and ½-fill with off-peak icing of your chosen colour. Pipe the border using the same technique as described for the running bead.

Vary the size of the nozzle to pipe a shell border in a different size.

◀ Running bead

This simple border works well as a decorative edge for a plaque (either a run-out or a shape cut out from sugarpaste). Place a no. 1.5 nozzle into a small piping bag and ½-fill with off-peak royal icing in your chosen colour. Point the nozzle slightly into the edge of the plaque, keep it still and squeeze out a small bead, then release the pressure and slide the nozzle away to leave a small gap. Increase the pressure again until the next bead fills the gap. Continue all around the plaque, moving it as you work so you always pipe towards yourself.

Use a larger plain nozzle to pipe a running bead around a cake, cupcake or cookie.

◀ Leaf border

Stir one teaspoon of sifted icing sugar into a small bowl of off-peak icing. Half-fill a medium piping bag fitted with a no. 51 nozzle. To pipe the herringbone leaf pattern place the nozzle on the edge of the cake, squeeze to attach and, while reducing pressure, move the nozzle towards the centre. Tuck the nozzle under the leaf just piped, attach and move the nozzle away from the centre of the cake while reducing the pressure.

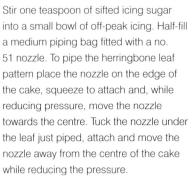

First Birthday Cake

EDIBLES

20.5cm (8") round fruit cake

800g (1lb 12oz) SK Marzipan

1kg (2lb 3¼oz) SK Instant Mix Royal Icing

SK Quality Food Colour (QFC) Liquids:
Blue, Green, Pink, Yellow

For essential royal icing
edibles and equipment, see pages 230–231

EQUIPMENT

30.5cm (12") round cake drum (board)

Piping bags: small, medium

Piping nozzles: nos. 1.5, 43, 51, 57 (PME)

1m (39") x 15mm (½") wide ribbon: pale blue

Food-grade sponge or pastry brush

Templates, see page 506

1 Prepare the cake for royal icing by covering it with marzipan (see page 95). Place centrally on the cake drum.

2 Make up one 500g (1lb 1¾oz) bag of SK Instant Mix Royal Icing following the instructions on page 235. Coat the cake with royal icing then coat the drum. Allow to dry.

3 Make up the second bag of Instant Mix Royal Icing. Take four bowls and colour the icing using liquid food colours as follows: colour approximately half yellow, then divide the remainder equally into three and colour pink, blue and green.

4 Copy the run-out templates onto paper and trim so they fit well within the size of the drying board. Cut a piece of cellophane slightly larger than the templates but smaller than the drying board, place over the template and secure to the board using masking tape at the corners.

5 Very lightly grease the cellophane with white vegetable fat so that the run-outs can be removed easily when dry.

6 Prepare the run-out icing by putting about a tablespoon of each colour into a clean bowl. Thin each colour by adding a little cooled, boiled water so that when a line is cut into the icing it disappears after the count of 9–10 seconds (see page 235). Cover with a clean cloth and leave to stand for around half an hour.

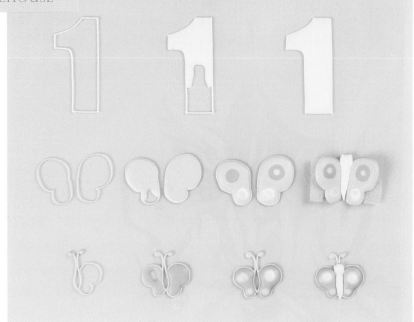

7 Meanwhile, snip off the tip of a small paper piping bag and drop a no. 1.5 nozzle into the bag. Half-fill the piping bag with blue off-peak icing. Squeeze the bag gently and apply an even pressure to outline the circle, one pair of large butterfly wings and three pairs of small butterfly wings.

8 Half-fill a small piping bag fitted with a no. 1.5 nozzle with yellow off-peak icing and outline the number 1 and three small butterfly wings.

9 Half-fill piping bags with each of the four run-out colours.

10 Cut a very small hole in the bag of blue run-out icing and fill the circle: working in sections, pipe icing up to the outline and then fill the centre.

11 Cut a very small hole in the bag of yellow icing and fill in the number 1.

12 Cut a very small hole at the tip of the bags of pink and green run-out icing. Flood the first butterfly wing with the pink icing and then immediately drop a blue spot onto the upper part of the wing, then drop a yellow spot onto the blue spot. Create a pattern on the lower part of the wing in a similar way. Complete all other butterfly wings.

13 Dry all the finished run-outs under a small desk lamp for at least 30 minutes, then allow all run-outs to dry completely for 24 hours.

14 Pipe six ribbon roses and six buds using stiff-peak pink royal icing (see page 241) and allow to dry for 24 hours.

15 Make a template for the sides of the cake to create the scalloped pattern, then stipple blue and pink royal icing above the scallop (see page 241). Allow to dry.

16 Finish off the cake sides by piping a drop-line of off-peak green royal icing along the scalloped edges (see pages 241–242) and allow to dry.

17 Pipe a blue running bead around the edge of the run-out circle with a no. 1.5 nozzle (see page 242). Pipe a leaf border around the top of the cake using a no. 51 nozzle and a shell border around the base using a no. 43 nozzle in yellow off-peak icing.

18 Slide a small palette knife under the circle to release the run-out from the cellophane. Paddle a small amount of icing and spread this onto the

centre of the cake. Gently place the plaque on top and wiggle it onto the icing to settle it into position. Attach the number 1 onto the plaque in the same way.

19 To finish off the butterflies, prepare a bag of yellow off-peak royal icing in a piping bag with a no. 43 nozzle and pipe a short line of icing where the butterfly is to be positioned. Push each wing into the icing, leaving a gap between the two, and support the wings in an upright position with a small piece of food-grade foam sponge or kitchen paper. Pipe in the body and head using the same bag of icing. To create small antennae on the head, gently push the nozzle into the front of the head and pull away to form a small peak. Finish the butterflies for the side of the cake on a piece of cellophane in the same way.

20 Fix a ribbon rose and bud to every other scallop point by piping three leaves in green off-peak royal icing with a no. 51 nozzle and pushing the roses into the wet icing.

21 Fix a small butterfly to every other point with a small dot of icing.

22 Attach a length of ribbon to the edge of the cake drum with non-toxic glue (see page 139).

First Birthday Cake

Borders, Blossoms and Run-outs

CERI DD GRIFFITHS

Once you have learnt the basic royal icing skills you can develop them to create a wider variety of decorations. All of the skills shown in this chapter will familiarise you with the various consistencies of royal icing and how each of them can be used.

EDIBLES

Round fruit cake, marzipanned and coated with royal icing on a round cake drum/board coated with royal icing (see pages 236–238)

SK Instant Mix Royal Icing

SK Instant Mix Run-Out Royal Icing

SK Professional Liquid Food Colours of your choice

SK Professional Food Colour Pen (any colour)

EQUIPMENT

Square cake card or acrylic board

Piping nozzles: plain, star, leaf and petal (nos. 1.5, 13, 51, 56 – left- or right-handed petal nozzle as required) (PME)

Long, narrow roll of food-grade paper, e.g. greaseproof paper

Templates, see page 506

TECHNIQUES

- Side detailing (scratch work)
- Piping borders
- Making run-outs
- Piping blossoms and leaves

For essential royal icing edibles and equipment, see pages 230–231

Side detailing (scratch work)

Scratch piping has been used for many years to give the appearance of a lacy texture. This technique is particularly useful for decorating cake sides as it can be done straight onto the cake. To best achieve a neat, crisp band of scratch work around the side of a cake you will need to create a simple template. Strips of paper can be used, but make sure it is suitable for food contact.

1 Firstly measure the height of your cake, then decide on the width of the scratch-piped design. You will need to make long templates to mask off the top and bottom sections of the cake: the cake shown here measures 7.5cm (3") tall with a 2.5cm (1") band of piping around the middle, therefore each band of paper measures 2.5cm (1") wide, one each for the top and bottom edges of the cake. Adjust the measurements accordingly, keeping the piping area centralised around the cake side.

2 Wrap a length of paper around the circumference of your cake, cut it to size and place it on a flat surface. Fold it in half lengthways to create a narrow, double-layered strip. Using a pencil and ruler mark a line to the width required, in this case 2.5cm (1") from the folded edge, and cut the strip to size.

3 Unfold the paper roll and cut down the folded central line to give you two strips of equal width.

4 Wrap the lower template around the base edge of your cake and secure

it to itself with a small piece of masking tape: the tape must not touch the surface of the cake. Attach the top template in the same way. Using a clear plastic ruler check that the exposed area is equal all the way around the cake: if not, slide the top template up or down to ensure it is straight.

5 Fit a piping bag with a plain nozzle (I have used a no. 1.5 here) then fill the bag 2/3 full with off-peak royal icing (see page 235). If you find that the icing is too firm to pipe, soften it with a few drops of cooled, boiled water and make up a new bag.

6 The technique of scratch piping onto a cake is simple: keep the tip of the piping nozzle in contact with the cake surface, apply gentle, even pressure and pipe onto the cake. To make filigree, pipe wavy lines in random patterns, making sure you do not pipe over the edges of your paper template.

7 Once the scratch work is complete, leave it to dry for a few minutes before taking the upper and lower templates away from the cake.

Tala piping nozzles.
Taylor Law was
established in 1899

Borders, Blossoms and Run-outs

Piped shell borders

When piping borders, a right-handed piper would naturally pipe from the left to the right; if you are left-handed you would usually reverse this to pipe from right to left, making shells that appear mirrored to the ones shown here.

1 Fit a piping bag with a star nozzle: the one shown here is a no. 13. Fill the bag ²/₃ full with off-peak royal icing.

2 To pipe a border along the top edge of a cake, hold the piping bag at a 45° angle and pipe evenly spaced shells on the outer edge of the top surface so that they protrude from the cake edge.

When you have finished piping the last shell use a slightly damp paintbrush to tuck its tail underneath the first shell if necessary.

3 For a shell border at the base of a cake, pipe the shells into the 90° angle where the cake side touches the cake drum (board).

Piped blossoms

1 Fit a piping bag with a petal nozzle (right or left-handed as appropriate): the nozzle used here is a no. 56. Colour some firm-peak royal icing using the liquid colour of your choice and fill the bag ²/₃ full.

2 Attach a square of wax paper to the top of a flower nail using a small touch of royal icing. Check that your piping nozzle is the correct way up: if you look at the petal nozzle it should appear as a small teardrop, with the widest part of the nozzle at the base of the petal.

3 Hold the flower nail between your thumb and index finger and slowly roll the nail in an anticlockwise direction as you pipe, or clockwise if you are left-handed. At the same time pipe a

small arch with the petal nozzle to create an individual petal. Ensure that you start and finish at the centre of the nail and that there is no gap in the centre of your petal.

4 Continue to pipe petals one at a time from and to the central point. It is important to stop piping between each petal as this will give the final blossom more definition. When you pipe the fifth and final petal, finish it by lifting the piping nozzle directly upward, then use a damp paintbrush to bring the edge of the last petal against the first.

5 Whilst the blossom is still wet, tidy up its centre if necessary with a damp paintbrush. Once it is finished, lift the square of wax paper off the flower nail and set it aside to dry.

6 Repeat steps 2 to 5 to make as many blossoms as required. It is always a good idea to pipe spares as they can be kept for future projects.

7 To finish the blossoms, colour a small amount of off-peak royal icing with liquid food colour. Fit a small piping bag with a no. 1.5 nozzle and fill it ²/₃ full with the coloured royal icing. Pipe a small bulb in the centre of the blossom where the petals meet to make the flower centre. Touch the centre down with a damp paintbrush if the nozzle leaves a peak of icing. Leave the blossom to dry completely (approximately three hours depending on the climate).

8 Remove the blossom from the wax paper before use.

Piped leaves

1 Fit a piping bag with a leaf nozzle: I have used a no. 51 here. Colour some off-peak royal icing with a small amount of Leaf Green liquid food colour to make a pale green. Fill the bag ⅔ full with the pale green icing.

2 Rest the tip of the leaf nozzle on the cake where you wish the leaf to be placed and apply pressure to the piping bag. When the leaf has reached the correct width, stop the pressure and gently pull the nozzle away from the end of the leaf to give a sharp point. If the icing is too stiff it will not form a point, so add a little more cooled, boiled water to the mixture.

Run-out design: flowerpot and bows

1 Using the templates on page 506, draw the flowerpot and bow onto a piece of paper then secure this to a flat surface such as a square cake card or acrylic board. Place a sheet of clear cellophane over the entire template and secure it in place using masking tape. Lightly smear the cellophane with white vegetable fat.

2 Mix the run-out icing following the instructions on the packet. Alternatively you can use royal icing let down to run-out consistency (see page 235). Divide the run-out icing into two bowls and colour one half terracotta using Berberis and Chestnut liquid food colours for the pot and the other half peach using Nasturtium for the bow. It is always advisable to make run-out icing approximately one hour in advance to reduce the number of air bubbles in your final piece (see page 240). Once mixed always make sure you keep the run-out icing covered with a clean, damp cloth to prevent it from crusting over. Stir the run-out icing just before use (do not beat it as this will incorporate air bubbles).

3 For the flowerpot outline fit a piping bag with a no. 1.5 nozzle and fill the bag ²/₃ full with the Terracotta-coloured off-peak royal icing. Carefully pipe an outline of icing onto the cellophane following the lines drawn on the paper. Using a small, damp paintbrush make sure all joins are neat and level with each other.

4 For the bow outlines fit a piping bag with a no. 1.5 nozzle and fill the bag ²/₃ full with the peach-coloured icing. Carefully pipe the outline onto the cellophane following the template. Using a small, damp paintbrush, make sure all joins are neat and level with each other.

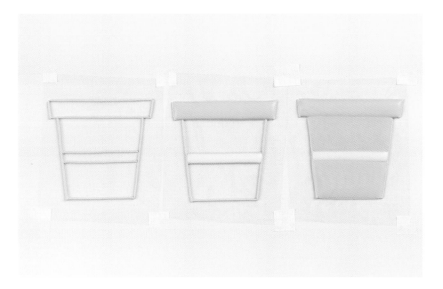

5 When the outlines are complete, use a small piping bag half-filled with coloured run-out royal icing to flood in the outlines; you can either snip the tip of the bag off or use a no. 1.5 piping nozzle. When making run-outs it is advisable to avoid flooding adjacent sections at the same time otherwise they may run into each other. If possible flood non-adjacent areas and then place the part-flooded piece to one side for around half an hour under a desk lamp. This will allow the icing to skin over before flooding in the remaining exposed areas. Be careful not to overfill any areas of the run-out as they could flood into each other, losing the definition created by the piped outline.

6 When the outline is completely flooded in use a small, damp paintbrush to remove any air bubbles and ensure that the run-out icing meets the entire outline. Place this under a desk lamp to retain the sheen of the run-out and prevent it from collapsing in the centre. The lamp only needs to be on the run-out for approximately one hour, after which the icing should be left in a warm, dry place for at least 24 hours. You will need to extend the drying time in particularly cold or humid atmospheres or if the run-out is large in size.

Borders, Blossoms and Run-cuts

Mother's Day Celebration Cake

This pretty flowerpot design with its colourful piped blossoms would make a lovely gift for Mother's Day.

EDIBLES

20.5cm (8") round fruit cake, coated with marzipan in preparation for royal icing, see page 95

500g (1lb 1¾oz) SK Instant Mix Royal Icing (this quantity will allow extra to practice with)

150g (5¼oz) SK Instant Mix Run-Out Icing (or royal icing let down to run-out consistency, see page 235)

SK Professional Liquid Food Colours: Berberis, Bluebell (navy blue), Chestnut (soft beige), Daffodil (yellow), Leaf Green, Lilac, Nasturtium (peach), Rose, Sunflower

White vegetable fat

EQUIPMENT

30.5cm (12") round cake drum (board)

20.5cm (8") square cake card or acrylic board

Piping nozzles: nos. 1.5, 13, 51, 56 (left- or right-handed petal nozzle as required)

Long strip of food-grade paper

SK Professional Food Colour Pen (any colour)

1m (39") x 15mm (½") wide satin ribbon: delicate lemon

Double-sided tape

Templates, see page 506

For essential royal icing edibles and equipment, see pages 230–231

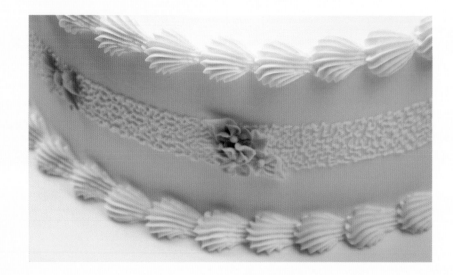

1 Prepare the cake for royal icing by covering it with marzipan (see page 95). Place the cake centrally on the cake drum and coat the cake and the board with royal icing (see pages 236–237).

2 Trim the cake drum with delicate lemon ribbon and secure at the back with double-sided tape.

3 Make two templates for the cake side from a long strip of food-grade paper and scratch-pipe around the middle of the cake using white royal icing and a no. 1.5 nozzle (see page 241). Save one of the templates for the assembly later.

4 Place some off-peak royal icing into a piping bag with a no. 13 nozzle and pipe a shell border around the top edge of the cake. Repeat around the base of the cake (see page 248).

5 Prepare several bowls of coloured icing for the blossoms: you will need to use Bluebell, Nasturtium, Rose, Sunflower and Lilac. Make up a bag in each colour with a no. 56 petal nozzle and pipe each blossom onto a flower nail (see page 247). You will need approximately 22 coloured blossoms; spares can be piped and kept for future projects in a dust-free, damp-free place.

6 Draw the flowerpot and bow templates onto a 20.5cm (8") square piece of paper: make five copies of the bow template on the same page.

Secure the paper template to a 20.5cm (8") square cake card or acrylic board, tape a sheet of clear cellophane over the top and lightly smear the cellophane with white vegetable fat. Mix up the soft beige and peach required for the run-outs and pipe one flowerpot and five bows for the cake (see pages 250–251). Allow to dry completely.

7 Divide one of the paper templates from the scratch work into eight equal sections and wrap it around the cake just above the line of your scratch work band. (You may need to fold the paper band lengthways to allow it to lay smoothly against the side of the cake.) Adjust the template so that one of the marks on the paper band is at the front

of the cake and lightly tape the template to itself (not to the cake). Mark tiny dots at each of the eight points using a food colour pen then remove the paper template.

8 When they are completely dry, carefully peel away the cellophane from the back of all of the run-out pieces. They can be fragile so handle them gently.

9 Decide if you would like either the bow or the cluster of blossoms to be the front feature, then attach them alternately around the cake. The three blossoms are attached with small, pale green piped leaves (see page 250), whilst the bows are attached with a small bulb of white off-peak royal icing.

10 Attach the flowerpot to the top of the cake with a few bulbs of royal icing, ensuring that it sits in the lower half of the cake top. Do not press the flowerpot down on to the cake surface as this could break the run-out. What's more, having a little gap between the cake and the flowerpot will give the illusion of depth. Attach the bow to the flowerpot in the same way as for the side bows.

11 Fit a piping bag with a no. 1.5 nozzle then fill the bag two-thirds full with pale green off-peak royal icing. Pipe a number of stems coming out of the top of the flowerpot and attach the piped blossoms to the stems. Once the blossoms are in place pipe leaves where you feel they would naturally grow.

Mother's Day Celebration Cake

253

Essential Edibles and Equipment for Sugar Flowers

1   Ball tool or bone tool
2   Cake cards/boards for drying
3   CelStick, small
4   Cocktail sticks
5   Cornflour duster
6   Craft knife
7   Cranked palette knife
8   Double foam pad (PME)
9   Dresden tool
10 Floral tape (various colours, see project list)
11 Floral wires (various colours and thicknesses, see project list)
12 Flower drying stand or similar
13 Food-grade plastic bags

14 Kitchen paper
15 Non-stick board
16 Non-stick board with vein grooves
17 Non-stick rolling pin, small
18 Paint palette
19 Petal and leaf cutters, see project list
20 Plain-edge cutting wheel
21 Posy picks
22 Ruler
23 Scissors
24 Scribing needle
25 Silk veining tool
26 SK Confectioners' Glaze
27 SK Confectioners' Glaze Cleaner (IPA)

28 SK Edible Glue
29 SK Great Impressions leaf and petal veiners (various, see project list)
30 SK Paintbrushes: nos. 1, 2, 10
31 SK Pollen-style Dust Food Colours, see project list
32 SK Professional Dust Food Colours, see project list
33 SK Sugar Florist Paste/SFP/ flower paste, see project list for colours and quantities
34 Stamens (if applicable), see project list
35 Tape shredder (not pictured)
36 Tweezers
37 White vegetable fat
38 Wire cutters

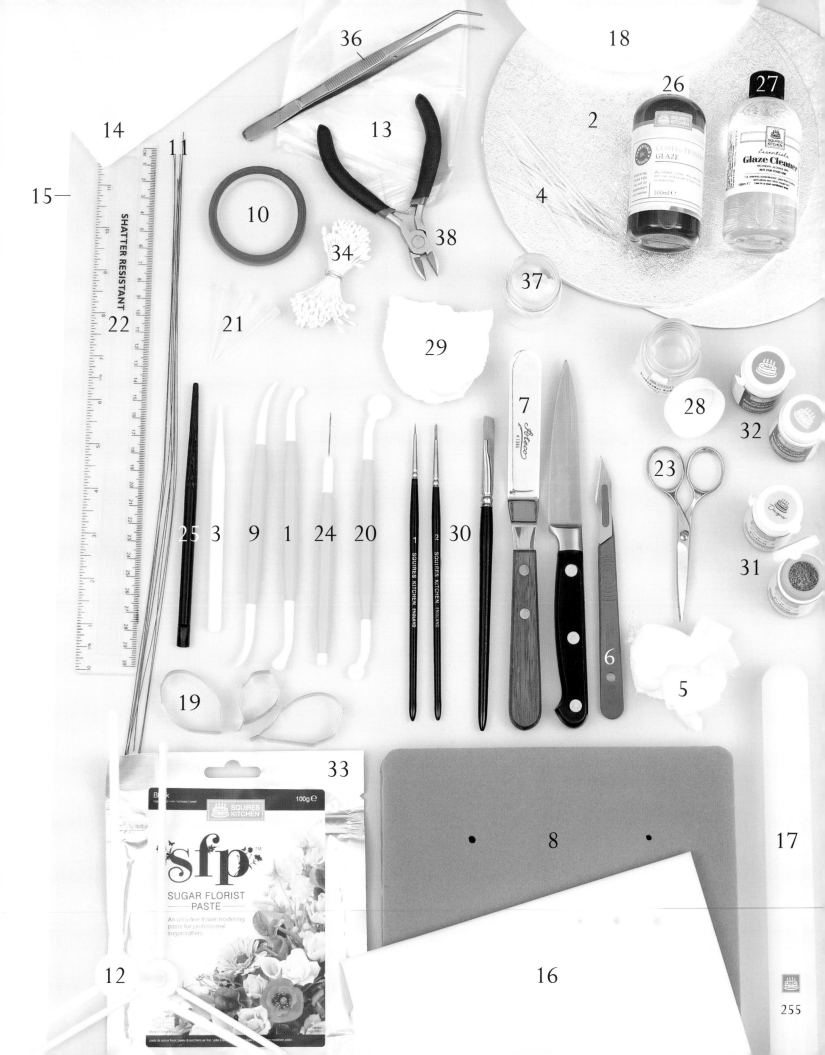

36

18

26

27

14

11

13

2

15

4

10

38

34

21

37

29

25 3 9 1 24 20

7

28 32

23

30

31

19

6

5

22

33

8

17

12

16

SHATTER RESISTANT

SUGAR FLORIST PASTE

sfp™

SUGAR FLORIST PASTE

An ultra-fine flower modelling paste for professional sugarcrafters

Claire Fitzsimons

BIOGRAPHY

When I was growing up, food always took centre-stage for my Yorkshire family. My Nana in particular, was a very forward-thinking and experimental cook and decided to collect a new monthly publication called the *Cordon Bleu Cookery Course.* From that point on, the meals in our home subtly changed. Amongst the usual dishes came chicken Veronique, pavlova, strawberry millefeuille and a host of other French delights. By the time I came to take my O- and A-levels in cookery, the magazines had been reprinted into a set of 20 books; Nana kindly bought me the set and these became my complete recipe reference guide.

From a very young age I had always wanted to teach so, on leaving school in 1979, I moved to London to train as a primary school teacher where my studies combined education with Art and Graphic Design. I continued to cook and bake throughout college and shared meals with like-minded friends.

I began teaching full time in 1982 and, during my career, I taught all ages at primary school level as well as taking on management responsibilities for Art and display. I used my design skills to create the school logo, which is still used by the school today on signs and school jumpers. I also acted as an art adviser for my London borough, providing workshops and co-writing an art handbook for teachers.

Cooking was my main hobby during this time, but I also enjoyed other creative pastimes such as sugarcraft and making stained glass windows. My mum has been a keen sugarcrafter and a major influence on my work. She would make the most beautiful sugar flowers for celebration cakes. During the weekends and school holidays I attended various sugar floristry courses with the wonderful Paddi Clark at Squires Kitchen. I remember Paddi saying to me, 'Be careful Claire, this is very addictive!'

After 25 years of full-time teaching and having helped nurture so many others to fulfil their potential, I wanted a change of direction that meant I could focus on my own creativity and ambitions. Sitting in the kitchen one evening with my husband, my eyes wandered up to the shelf of Cordon Bleu books and I heard myself say, 'I think I'd like to go there.' Before I had time to change my mind, I gave up teaching and enrolled on a nine month Diploma Course in Cuisine at Le Cordon Bleu in London. The course was very exciting, challenging and physically exhausting (I was twice the age of my fellow students!), but in September 2007 I qualified as a Chef de Cuisine.

Having worked as a supply teacher and private caterer for a short spell, I decided to develop my sugarcraft skills and enrolled at Brooklands College in Weybridge. My tutors, Sue Haskell and Jane Hatton, were both very encouraging and

inspirational and I trained in sugarcraft and wired flowers to an advanced level. I gained distinctions for my work, as well as winning a medal in the Wedding Cake category at the annual Salon Culinaire competition for two successive years.

Although I loved the creative side of cake decorating, I missed teaching as it was the career I had trained for originally. Whilst staying with my mum for a few days, I came upon an advert for a new tutor and demonstrator role at Squires Kitchen. I applied and was thrilled to be able to join this talented team. I now demonstrate in the shop every week and teach both Foundation Sugarpaste and Foundation Floral courses. I feel very privileged to be working for Squires Kitchen as this is where my love of sugarcraft began. Now my passion for teaching and obsession with sugarcraft have finally been brought together in one place.

Basic Floral Skills

CLAIRE FITZSIMONS

All sugar flowers are constructed differently, although many use similar methods. The flowers described here are suitable for a beginner to make and use three different techniques: hand pulling, using petal and leaf cutters, and using a mould.

TECHNIQUES

- Using flower paste
- Shaping petals and leaves
- Using floral wire
- Taping flowers
- Colouring petals and leaves
- Simple pulled flower (jasmine)
- Simple flower using veiners (hydrangea)
- Simple cutter flower (sweet pea)
- Simple wired leaves

EDIBLES

Jasmine

SK Sugar Florist Paste (SFP): White

SK Professional Dust Food Colour: Fern

Hydrangea

SK Sugar Florist Paste (SFP): Eucalyptus, Pale Blue, Pale Green, White

SK Professional Dust Food Colour: Fern

Sweet pea

SK Sugar Florist Paste (SFP): Daffodil, Nasturtium, Pale Green, Pale Pink, Pale Yellow, Soft Lilac, Soft Peach, White

SK Professional Dust Food Colours: Daffodil, Leaf Green, Nasturtium, Violet

SK Quality Food Colour (QFC) Dusts: Extra White, Pink

Leaves

SK Sugar Florist Paste (SFP): Pale Green

SK Professional Dust Food Colour: Leaf Green

For essential floral edibles and equipment, see pages 254–255

EQUIPMENT

SK Paintbrushes: nos. 2, 10 (dusting brush)

CelStick: medium

Jasmine

Tapered star cone tool

28-gauge floral wire: white

Floral tape (½-width): white

Hydrangea

28-gauge floral wire: white

Floral tape (½-width): Nile green

SK Great Impressions Hydrangea Veiner

SK Hydrangea Cutter

Sweet pea

28-gauge floral wire: white

Floral tape: Nile green (full width and ½-width), white (½-width)

Small rose cutter (FMM)

Sweet pea cutter: large 2.5cm–3.5cm (1"–1³/₈") (TT)

Calyx cutter: R13a (OP)

Leaves

28-gauge floral wire: white

Floral tape: Nile green (full-width and ½-width), white (½-width)

Leaf cutter: large, 4.5cm–6cm (1¾"–2³/₈") (TT)

SK Great Impressions Tea Rose Leaf Veiner: extra large, 9cm (3½")

Basic techniques for flower making

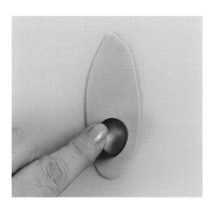

Using flower paste ▲

You can make your own flower paste or you can use a manufactured paste, such as Squires Kitchen's Sugar Florist Paste (SFP). Flower pastes are designed specifically for making sugar flowers and should be consistent in texture. SFP is very pliable but dries hard, meaning that it can be rolled paper-thin. You will need to roll the paste very finely in order to create professional-looking flowers.

SFP dries quickly, so work with small amounts at a time and ensure the rest is covered (e.g. in an airtight, food-grade bag). Make sure that the paste is well-kneaded before you start to roll it out or make your flower to prevent it from cracking at the edges.

Shaping petals and leaves

To soften the edges of a leaf or petal, place it onto a foam flower pad and press along the edges with a ball or bone tool, keeping the tool half on the paste and half on the pad. The harder you press the frillier the finished result will be.

You can also use a ball tool to cup petals: place the flower on a foam pad and move the ball tool around the centre of the petals in a circular motion. ▼

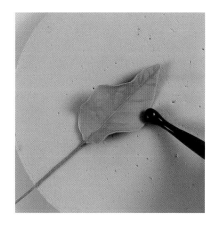

Using wires

Covered floral wires give petals and leaves extra support and allow floral arrangements to be assembled together. Always use covered wires, not bare ones. Note, however, that although the flowers and leaves are made of sugar they are inedible if wires are used.

There are a number of different gauges (widths) available; the higher the gauge number, the thinner the wire. The gauge of wire you need will depend on the size of the petal or leaf being made and the level of support it needs.

Colouring petals and leaves ▲

Dust food colours are ideal for enhancing your flowers and leaves and giving greater depth (for example, colouring the centre of a flower a darker colour). They should always be used sparingly. Dip a dusting brush into your chosen colour, remove the excess by rubbing on a piece of kitchen roll and brush gently over the petals or leaves. Colours can be mixed together or brushed on in layers to give greater depth.

Paste food colour will not alter the consistency of SFP as liquid colour can. Sugar Florist Paste can be coloured with paste food colours to create the colour you want.

Taping

Floral tape is used to cover the wires and to enable you to attach flowers and leaves together into an arrangement or spray. To release the glue from floral tape, stretch it before taping a wire. Remember that you can cut it into narrower strips if it is too wide, depending upon the width of the stem you are making.

Tape as far down the wire as necessary; you may not need to tape the whole wire. If you are wiring an arrangement, too much tape will make the stems bulky. In this case, tape down to just below where the next leaf or flower will be attached.

Basic Floral Skills

Jasmine flowers and buds

Pulled flowers are made from a single piece of paste. The petals are usually cut and shaped before a wire is inserted into the centre and pulled downwards through the base until it is embedded in the paste. These flowers are simple and quick to make so are ideal for beginners.

TIPS FOR MAKING SUGAR FLOWERS

Always knead flower paste in your hands before use to make it soft and supple.

Seal any paste that you are not using in a food-grade polythene bag to prevent it from drying out.

To prevent flower paste from sticking to the board when rolling out, lightly grease the board with white vegetable fat. This also helps to keep the paste pliable.

Use a cornflour duster to prevent the paste from sticking when the paste is slightly firmer but still pliable.

1   Begin by softening a small piece of White SFP with your fingers. Roll a pea-sized ball. Model it into a cone shape, then insert the pointed end of a CelStick to hollow the centre.

2   Insert the five-pointed end of the star cone tool into the ball to mark five grooves. Carefully cut along the grooves using small, sharp scissors. Open up the petals by pressing your finger gently into the centre.

3   Take each petal one by one and squeeze the cut edges inwards, then place your thumb on the top and index finger underneath and squash the petal flat, flick your thumb upwards to finish and release the petal.

4   Using pliers, cut a 28-gauge wire into three or four pieces and bend a tiny hook into one end of each wire. Dip the hooked end of each length of wire into edible glue and wipe off the excess. Push the straight end of the wire down through the centre of the flower and pull it down until the hook is embedded in the thickest part of the flower base. Gently roll the paste at the base of the flower onto the wire to secure it and give a more tapered look. Allow to dry.

5   Dust the centre with Daffodil dust colour using a no. 2 paintbrush.

6   Tape each stem using ½-width white floral tape. To finish, lightly dust the stem and base of each flower with Fern dust.

7   To make the buds, roll a ball of White SFP into a narrow cone. Cut and hook a 28-gauge wire and glue the hooked end, as before. Push the hook into the narrow end of the cone then roll the paste gently onto the wire to elongate it and secure it to the wire. The bud should be approximately the same size as the finished flower. Allow to dry then tape and dust as before.

VEINER FLOWER

Hydrangea bracts

There are many different flower and leaf veiners available, making it easy to create lifelike replicas in sugar. The basic method for using silicone veiners is the same for any flower, petal or leaf: simply roll out some SFP thinly, cut out the shape required then press it between the veiners and wire as needed. The hydrangea is a good flower to start with because the bracts can be cut out in one piece rather than individually.

1 Begin by making the centres. Cut a 26-gauge wire into three. Soften and roll a tiny amount of Eucalyptus SFP into a ball. Dip one end of the wire into edible glue and wipe off the excess. Push the ball of paste onto the wire and taper the paste down onto the wire to make a 'T' shape. Use a scalpel or sharp knife to mark a cross on the top. Allow to dry.

2 Rub a tiny amount of white vegetable fat onto a non-stick board to prevent the paste from sticking. Soften a small amount of Pale Blue SFP in your fingers and roll it out into a thin sheet using a small rolling pin. Cut out the flower shape using a metal hydrangea cutter. Place the cut-out flower on a foam pad and soften the edges of the petal with a bone tool: position the tool half on the paste and half on the pad, then push down and work around the edge of the flower to thin the paste.

3 Sandwich the flower between the two-part veiner, making sure the two halves of the mould are lined up correctly. Press down and then remove the petal from the veiner.

4 Use a scribing tool to make a tiny hole in the centre. Leave the petal to dry in either a curved, shaped palette or curved foam pad. This will give the petal a natural cupped shape.

5 When dry, apply a tiny dot of edible glue to the centre of the petal and thread the green centre through. Allow to dry before taping each stem and dusting with Fern dust colour.

6 To finish, dust the centre and edges of the petal with Fern dust colour. To set the colour on any dusted flower or leaf it can be steamed. To do this, boil a kettle of water and, as the kettle begins to boil, hold the flowers in the trail of steam for two or three seconds only, otherwise the sugar will begin to dissolve. Take great care to avoid scalding yourself. This step gives a slightly better finish but is not strictly necessary so can be omitted if preferred.

7 Tape the wire with ½-width Nile green floral tape.

tutor tip

When cutting out several petals at a time ensure to cover the petals you have made with a Stay Fresh mat to prevent them from drying out.

Basic Floral Skills

SIMPLE CUTTER FLOWER

Sweet Peas

The third basic technique for making wired flowers is to use the cutter technique. Cutters created for each specific flower allow you to make the exact petal or leaf shape without having to cut it out freehand. This means that the flowers should be the same shape and you can cut out several petals at a time quickly and easily.

1 Begin by cutting some white 26-gauge floral wire into three. Make a tiny hook at the end of each wire.

2 Soften and roll a small ball of SFP in your chosen colour. In the centres of the flowers I used Daffodil SFP for the yellow sweet peas, Nasturtium mixed with a little White for the peach sweet peas, and Soft Lilac and Pale Pink.

3 Dip the hooked end of each wire in edible glue. Push the ball of paste onto the hook and gently roll it down on to the wire to secure. Use the rose petal cutter as a size guide: the centre should be shorter than the length of the rose petal.

4 Grease a non-stick board with a little white vegetable fat and roll out your chosen colour of SFP. Cut out several rose petal shapes with the cutter then transfer the petals to a foam pad and soften the edges with a bone tool, as before. Apply some glue over half the petal, place the wired centre in the middle of the rose petal and pinch both sides together to form a mini Cornish pasty shape. Gently push the top of the 'pasty' back. Allow to dry.

5 Next, make the central petals of the flower in your chosen colour of SFP (I used the original colours for this part of the flower). Roll out the paste as before

then cut out several petals using the 'wing'-shaped sweet pea cutter. Soften each petal edge with a bone tool on the foam pad. Dust the non-stick board with a little cornflour and place the petal back on the board. Using a veining tool, work around the petal with a gentle, back-and-forth motion to gently frill the petal.

6 Brush edible glue along the central line of the petal before placing the dried flower centre in the middle. Allow to dry.

7 For the final, third petal I added some White SFP to the original colour to give the flower a graduated effect. Cut out the final petal shape from the lightened paste then frill and vein the petal just as before. Glue the central line and add it to the back of the flower to complete. Allow to dry.

8 Dust the edges and centre of the petal with your choice of dusts. I used Nasturtium for the peach flowers, Daffodil for the yellow, Pink for the pink flowers and a mix of Violet and Extra White for the lilac flowers. At this point you may want to steam the flowers as described previously to set the colour.

9 To make the calyx I have used the 'Mexican hat' method which can also be used to create some other

flowers. Grease around the smallest hole on a grooved board then thinly roll out some Pale Green SFP over the hole. A small 'pimple' in the paste will indicate where the hole is. Place the calyx cutter centrally over the hole and press down. To achieve a neat cut, hold the cutter down whilst pulling away the excess paste from around the edge. Remove the calyx using the end of the veining tool or CelStick. Soften the edges if necessary with a bone tool on the foam pad. Add a tiny dot of edible glue to the centre then thread the wire down through the calyx and push it up the wire to sit at the base of the flower. Allow to dry.

10 Tape the wire as described earlier using ½-width Nile green floral tape. To make the tendrils, twist a short piece of ½-width tape almost to the end. Wrap around the end of either a CelStick or paintbrush and slide off. Attach the untwisted end to the flower stem.

11 To make the pea pod, roll four or five tiny balls of green SFP and push onto a glued wire. Allow to dry. Cut out the pod using the rose petal cutter. Soften the edges as before and brush with edible glue. Wrap the 'pod' around the peas. Allow to dry, before adding the calyx as described before. Bend the pod downwards, using angled tweezers to help you. Dust with Leaf Green to finish.

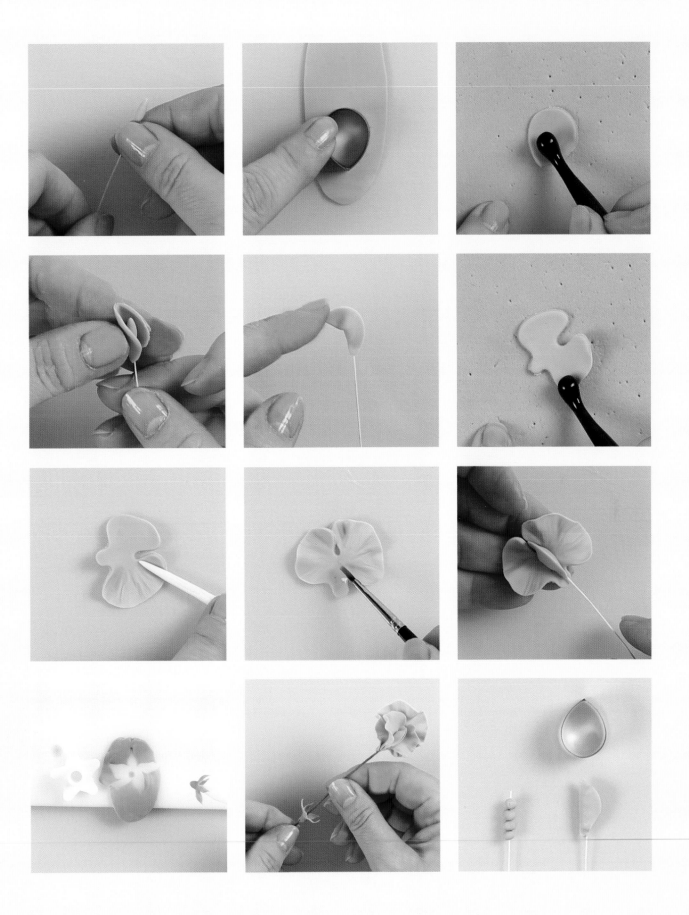

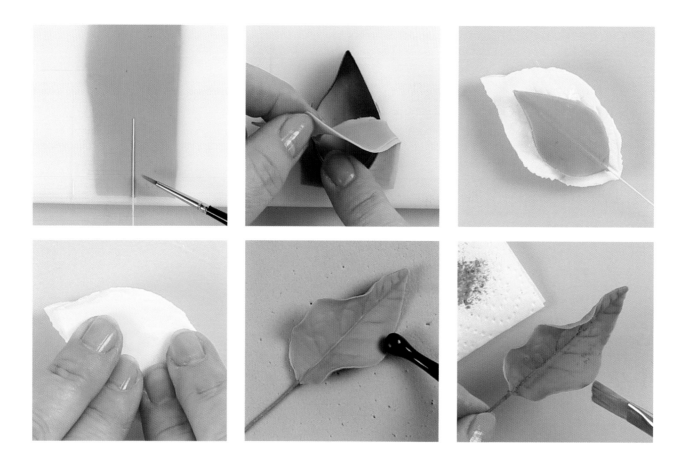

Simple Wired Leaves

This technique uses a grooved board which allows you to create a 'groove' of paste within which to insert the floral wire. Other popular methods for wiring leaves include inserting a wire into a sausage of paste and rolling the paste out around it, and making a very thin sausage of paste on a wire and securing this to the leaf.

1 Cut a 26-gauge wire into thirds. Roll out some Pale Green SFP very thinly onto a greased, grooved board, twice as long as the leaf cutter. Dip the wire into edible glue, wipe off the excess and place the wire into the centre of the groove. Use the leaf cutter as a size guide. The wire needs to take up ¾ of the length of the leaf. Fold the top of the paste down over the wire and roll to press both sides of the paste together.

Cut out the leaf. To get a clean cut, hold the cutter down firmly, whilst pulling the excess paste away with the other hand.

2 Soften the edges with a bone tool on a foam pad as described before then place the leaf into the double-sided rose leaf veiner. Use a ball tool to soften the edges as before to give some movement to the leaf. Leave to dry.

3 Dust with Leaf Green dust food colour and then steam the leaves, as described before, to set the colour and give a natural shine.

4 Tape the wire with ½-width Nile green floral tape.

Silver Wedding Anniversary Corsage

This is a delicate spray of pastel-coloured flowers, which could be used as a simple cake topper or as a small table decoration.

EDIBLES

5 sweet peas with one pod, see page 266

3 hydrangea bracts, see page 265

5 Jasmine flowers, 2 buds and 5 leaves, see page 262

For essential floral edibles and equipment, see pages 254–255

EQUIPMENT

Floral tape (½-width): Nile green

Silver boutonnière (buttonhole holder) approx. 5cm (2") long (available from florist suppliers)

1   To make the corsage you will need five sweet peas with one pod, three hydrangea bracts, five Jasmine flowers, two buds and five leaves. Prepare the flowers following the instructions.

2   Place all the flowers and leaves onto a foam pad and loosely arrange them. Once you are happy with the position of the flowers you can tape them into a spray. Begin by taping the centre flower to a leaf and build outwards either side of the spray. Carefully tape together using ½-width Nile green tape. Use pliers to cut away unnecessary stems to avoid the central stem becoming too thick.

3   When the corsage is assembled, carefully place it inside the buttonhole holder.

Wired Roses

PADDI CLARK

Roses are one of the most popular flowers among gardeners. The range of colours and species is vast, making them a versatile flower for sprays and arrangements and popular with those new to sugar floristry. They can look beautiful as part of a floral sugar arrangement or presented singly.

There are many methods for making sugar roses – the one described here is called the 'all-in-one method' using a blossom cutter. By changing the size of the blossom cutter, you can use this method to make roses of various sizes.

TECHNIQUES

- Making a wired rose bud, half rose and full rose
- Simple sugar flower arrangements

EDIBLES

SK Sugar Florist Paste (SFP): Holly/Ivy, Pale Green, Pale Pink, White

SK Professional Dust Food Colours: Fuchsia, Holly/Ivy, Leaf Green, Vine

SK Professional Paste Food Colour: Fuchsia

For essential floral edibles and equipment, see pages 254–255

EQUIPMENT

Five-petal blossom cutter: F6C (OP)

Rose calyx cutter: large (7cm/2¾") (FMM)

Rose leaf cutters: set of 3 (FMM)

SK Great Impressions Tea Rose Leaf Veiner: Large

22- and 28-gauge floral wires: white, green

Floral tape: dark green

Apple tray or foil former

Rose wire (optional)

Making a wired rose

I have described below how to make hot pink roses and buds, although roses are available in a wide variety of colours.

Centre

1 Cut a 22-gauge white floral wire into three pieces using wire cutters. Make a small hook in the end of a piece of wire with a small pair of pliers.

2 Roll a small ball of White SFP or the same colour as the rose petals into a cone shape. Apply edible glue to the hooked end of the wire, then push the hook into the base of the cone and secure the cone firmly to the wire. Allow the cone to dry.

Petals

3 Grease a section of a non-stick board with white vegetable fat to prevent sticking then roll out some SFP quite thinly. To achieve the bright pink colour of the petals, I have mixed Pale Pink SFP with Fuchsia paste food colour. Turn the paste over onto an ungreased part of the board and cut out a set of petals using the five-petal blossom cutter. Place the blossom onto a foam flower pad and soften the edges of each petal by pressing a ball tool half on the paste and half on the pad.

4 Brush a little edible glue over the base of the cone. Place the centre of the blossom over a hole in the foam pad, then push the wired cone into the centre of the blossom and down through the hole in the foam pad. Balance the foam pad on a tall glass or container: this frees both hands to work on the rose.

5 Apply a little edible glue onto the cone and halfway up the length of one petal. Wrap one side of the petal around the cone, then wrap the other side around it to cover it. Make sure that the cone is not visible. Miss out the next petal and repeat the process with the third, folding it gently around the first petal and over the join.

6 Brush edible glue onto the left-hand side of the remaining three petals. Stick the first of these petals to the bud at the same level, leaving the right-hand side free and unstuck. Interlock the next petal so that it is tucked under the previous one and repeat this with the final petal to create a spiral effect. Gently ease the petals downwards as you stick them in place, keeping the top of the petals at the same level as the others. To make a rose bud, add a calyx at this stage (see steps 14–16).

7 To make a half-open rose, cut out another set of petals for the next layer with the blossom cutter. Cut away two petals opposite each other then place on the foam pad and stretch the sides of the remaining three petals with a ball tool (do not lengthen the petals when you stretch them). Soften the edges of each petal with the ball tool, then roll the ball tool in the middle of each petal to cup them.

8 Turn the petals over and use a cocktail stick to curl the edges of each petal from the central point at the top to the middle point on each side at a diagonal angle. Turn the petals back over so that the edges curl outwards and place the petals in a flower former, e.g. an apple tray or foil former. Leave them to semi-dry so that they hold their shape.

9 Apply edible glue to the base of the opening bud and feed the prepared petals up the wire. Position the petals so that they stand away from the bud slightly. If you want to make a half-open rose, attach a calyx at this stage (see steps 14–16).

10 To make a fuller rose, cut out another set of the petals using the same blossom cutter. Stretch the petals both lengthways slightly and widthways to make them larger. Cup each petal in the centre with a ball tool on a foam pad then turn the blossom shape over and curl the edges of each petal to the centre point with a cocktail stick, as before. Leave the petals in a former to semi-dry so that they hold their shape. Check that the petals are the right size to sit level as the previous set of petals once they are added to the flower.

11 Apply edible glue to the base of the half-open rose then thread the end of the wire into the centre of the last set of petals. Turn the flower upside down and gently arrange the outer layer of petals so that they rest over the edges of the second layer, overlapping this set of petals but not completely covering them. Gently press the base of the outer petals to secure them in place but ensure they stand away slightly from the previous layer.

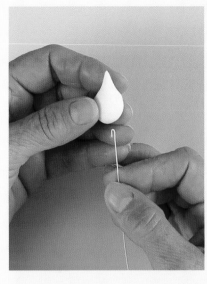

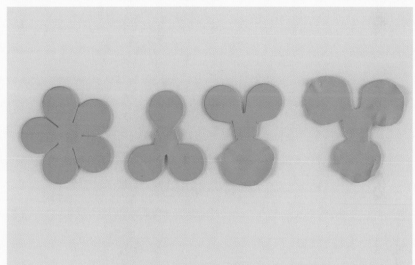

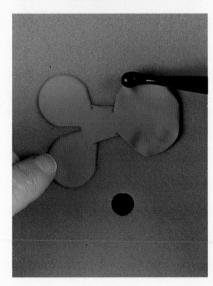

Wired Roses

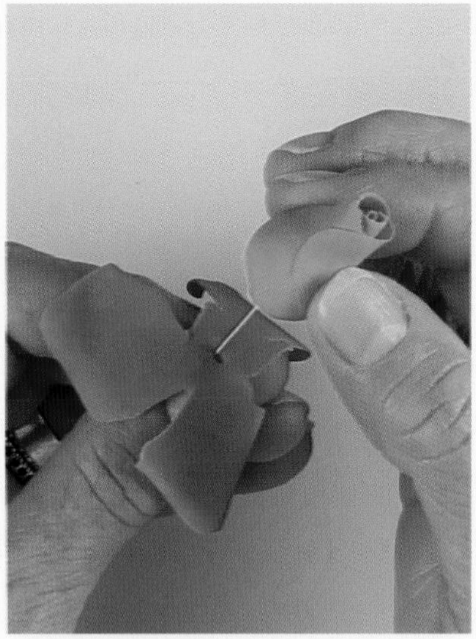
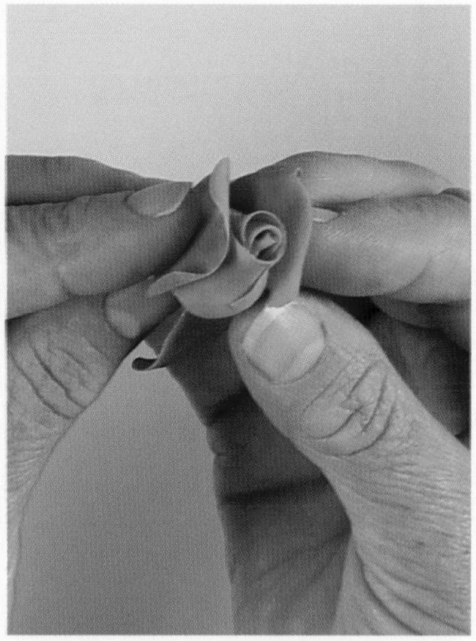
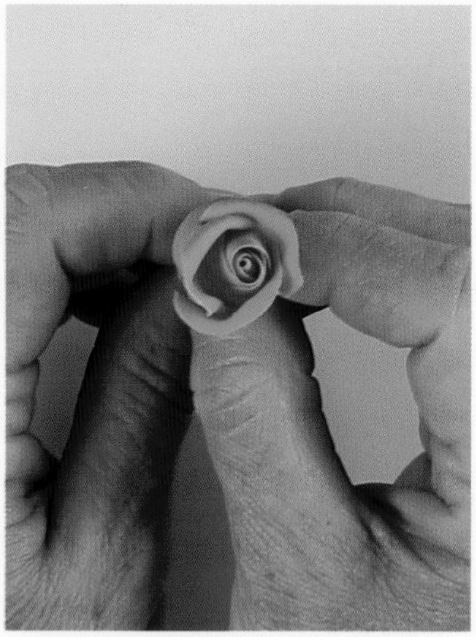
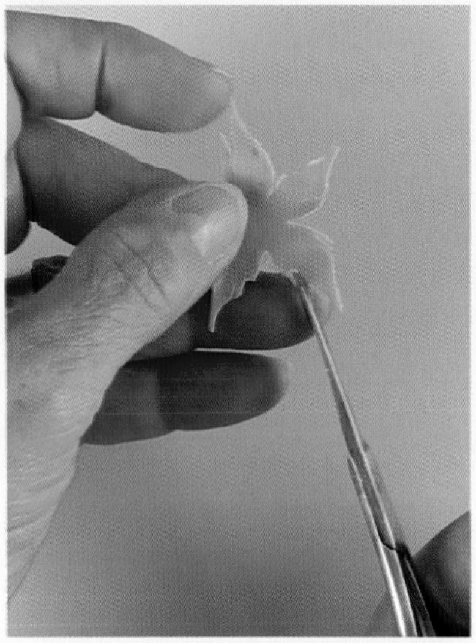
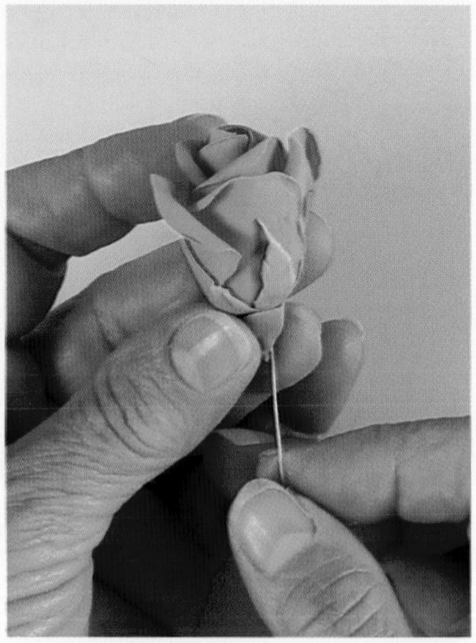
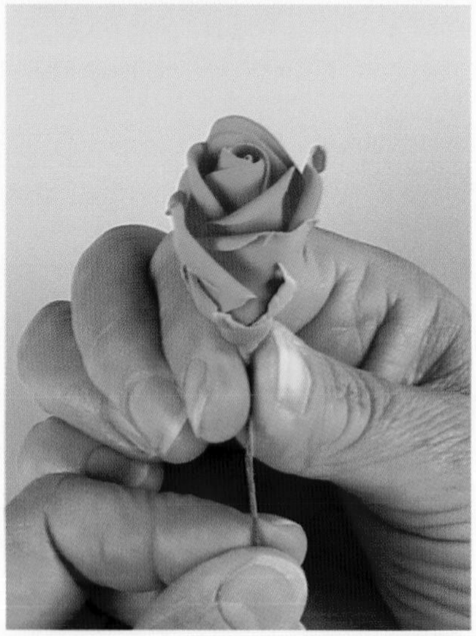
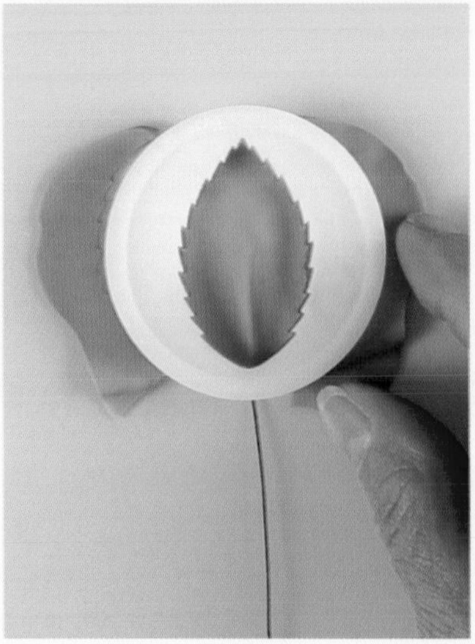
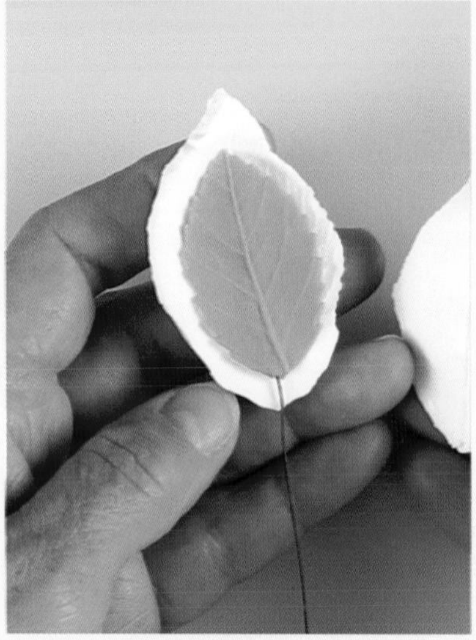
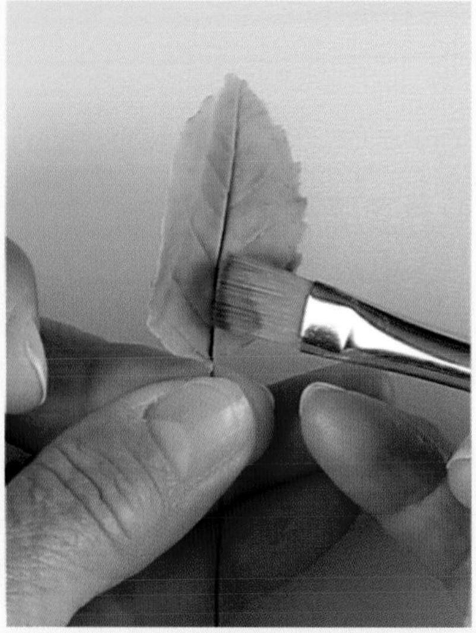

Add another layer of petals if you require an even fuller rose.

12 Dust the centre of the rose with Fuchsia dust colour or, for a lighter rose, dust with Edelweiss dust colour.

Calyx

13 Shape some Holly/Ivy SFP into a cone, then flatten and pinch out the base of the large end. Place the cone onto a non-stick board and thin the edges of the large end using a CelStick to make a Mexican hat shape (see page 266). Place the largest calyx cutter over the bump and press out the calyx from the paste. Turn the calyx over and use the pointed end of a CelStick to open the centre, then widen the indentation with the rounded end.

14 Make two or three tiny cuts in the sides of the sepals (pointed ends) using fine, pointed scissors, then brush edible glue in the centre of the calyx. Thread the calyx up the wire and stick it onto the back of the rose. Arrange the sepals so that they curl away from the base of the rose slightly.

15 Brush some confectioners' glaze over the calyx to create a natural sheen. When you have finished, immediately clean the paintbrush with glaze cleaner (IPA).

Leaves: sausage method

16 Cut a 28-gauge green floral wire into three pieces, then roll a sausage of Holly/Ivy or Pale Green SFP and gently insert a piece of wire through the middle in a twisting motion.

17 Grease the non-stick board with a little white vegetable fat, place the wired paste onto the board and gently roll over it with a small rolling pin.

18 When the wire is just visible, roll the paste with a CelStick outwards from the centre to the edges on both sides of the wire. Roll over the tip of the leaf away from the top of the wire, leaving a ridge in the centre.

19 Cut out the leaf shape using the Tea Rose leaf cutter. Place the leaf onto a foam pad and gently soften the edges of the leaf with a ball tool. Use the ball tool to stretch the edges at the top.

20 Vein the leaf by pressing it into the Tea Rose leaf veiner: the veins on the top of the leaf should press inward and the back of the leaf (with the ridge) should stand out from the surface. Soften the edges once more with the ball tool. Repeat the process again to make leaves in varying sizes.

21 Dust the leaves with Holly/Ivy and Vine dust food colours and add touches of Cyclamen dust on the edges. Steam the leaves and allow to dry (see page 265).

22 Dip each leaf into ¼-strength confectioners' glaze to create a sheen then allow to dry. To make this solution, mix one part glaze with three parts glaze cleaner or clear alcohol in a small jar.

23 A stem of rose leaves has one large leaf at the top, two medium leaves below this and then two small leaves. Tape down each of the leaves for about 2.5cm (1") with green floral tape, then tape them close to the central wire. Start with the largest leaf, then tape the medium-sized leaves opposite each other, followed by the smallest leaves further down the stem. (Further instructions for taping can be found on page 261.)

Wired Roses

275

Simple arrangements

Before you assemble an arrangement, make sure you have completed all the required flowers and leaves plus a few extra pieces in case of breakages.

Posy ▶

A posy is a circular arrangement where the spray is assembled around a central flower or bud. Most arrangements start with the basic posy shape which you add to in order to change the shape.

1 Start by holding the central rose between your thumb and forefinger, just below the base of the flower head. Position a rose bud with leaves underneath the rose and attach with floral tape to the central flower's stem at the point of your thumb and forefinger. This will now be the attachment point for the other roses and leaves.

2 Repeat the step above, adding and taping in one flower, bud or leaf at a time around the central rose to the same point underneath it.

3 Gradually increase the length of the stem from the attachment point as you introduce each rose, bud or leaf. Each

new flower should reach the edge of the previous one to maintain the shape of a gentle arc.

4 Once the posy is completed, tape down the length of the wires, cutting off a few as you go to remove the bulk.

5 If the posy needs strengthening, wind a length of rose wire around the attachment point to secure the flowers and leaves and stop them slipping and turning around.

Crescent ▲

The crescent or semi-crescent spray is made in the same way as for the posy but using 'return ends' (a floristry term) to create the curved appearance.

1 First make the posy as described, then tape together two small identical sprays of roses, buds and leaves. Bend the stem and tape these either side of the central posy to create the curved ends of the arrangement.

2 Once the crescent is complete, trim the excess wire from under the spray at intervals down its length to remove the bulk of wire and form a tapered effect.

3 Tape down the wire with floral tape to finish.

Hogarth curve or 'S' shape

This is a long arrangement with a collection of flowers in the centre and trailing ends at the top and bottom, curving in opposite directions to create a gentle 'S' shape. Again, this type of spray can be created using the posy method. Once the central posy is complete, make two long, curved sprays and attach them either side of the posy.

Romantic Rose Anniversary Cake

Roses are always a popular choice for romantic occasions and this beautiful crescent-shaped arrangement would be perfect atop any anniversary, engagement or wedding cake. The mixture of hot pink with pale pink and white roses gives this pretty floral display a contemporary twist. You can save the rose bouquet and keep it as a souvenir of the special occasion.

EDIBLES

20.5cm (8") round sponge cake, prepared for covering, see page 92

SK Sugarpaste: 880g (1lb 15oz) Bridal White

28 wired roses in bright pink, white and pale pink, see pages 272–275

6 sets of leaves, see page 275

For essential floral edibles and equipment, see pages 254–255

EQUIPMENT

25.5cm (10") cake drum (board)

Small rose embosser, from flower set of 4 (FMM)

1.5m (59") x 15mm (½") wide satin ribbon: pale pink

1 Place the cake centrally onto a 25.5cm (10") cake drum and cover the cake and drum with Bridal White sugarpaste (see page 139).

2 Trim the base of the cake and the cake board with pale pink ribbon.

3 Use the rose embosser to emboss four small roses around the sides of the cake for extra detail whilst the sugarpaste is still soft.

4 For the crescent arrangement you will need 28 roses, including a mixture of full roses, half roses and buds in white, pale pink and bright pink SFP, following the instructions on pages 272–275. Make six sets of leaves following the instructions on page 275.

5 Place all the roses and leaves on a foam pad and arrange them loosely. Once you are happy with the arrangement, start taping the flowers together into a posy following the instructions opposite. Tape together two small, identical sprays of roses, buds and leaves and attach these either side of the central posy to make a crescent arrangement.

6 Place the arrangement into a posy pick filled with white sugarpaste and then insert the pick into the cake covering. Position the arrangement diagonally across the cake.

EXTENDED
SUGARCRAFT SKILLS

Extended skills projects demonstrate how to take the techniques learnt at foundation level to the next stage, giving you the confidence to create beautiful cakes, models and flowers for every special occasion.

Geraldine Dahlke

BIOGRAPHY

*I*n my early years I had no idea I would become so passionately involved with sugarcraft, as at first I specialised in fabrics and woven textiles at teacher training college. I chose Coventry as it had a strong art and craft department and a swimming pool. I think I only swam in the pool twice, but spent the major part of my time in the art department. What joy! Forget lengths of cloth, woven structures were my passion, from huge, hanging structures to small, richly coloured freestanding tapestries, and the freedom to invent techniques to make them with.

Leaving with an honours degree from Warwick University I had to earn a living, so weaving became a hobby, although I still managed to exhibit woven structures using new techniques in Leamington and Edinburgh. I went on to take my M.Ed at Sheffield University and became a Deputy Head in London's East End.

There was no time for hobbies, although I joined a gliding club, learnt to fly and found a husband there, followed by supply teaching, two children, and time to make them birthday cakes. "Oooh," said the mothers of all the other little children at the parties, "can you make me one too?" This grew into a business carving novelty cakes: cats, violins, squirrels, teddies and more, then gradually moving onto cakes for grown-up parties followed by many wedding cakes. Did I take on an assistant to help me? No, my children came first so the business had to go and I started learning sugarcraft and design at Brooklands College. It seems the wrong way round, but that's how it happened!

I was so lucky to have Chris Jeffcoate as a lecturer as she provided not only excellent tuition, but the freedom to experiment and try out new ideas again. She helped me develop my own style: cakes with a definite leaning towards sculpture and fabrics, and many experiments with sugarcraft techniques.

During this time I won Gold at *Le Salon Culinaire International de Londres*, Gold and the Cup for Creative Sugarcraft at Bournemouth, the City and Guild Silver Medal for Excellence, and mixed with some very enthusiastic sugarcrafters who were also passionate about this emerging art form.

Once leaving the college, I invited all those with a similar passion for art and sugar to form what became the Taste of Art group, exhibiting three times over six years in art galleries in Guildford. With members from as far as New Zealand and Canada, many of the artists became very well known later including Lindy Smith, Gary Chapman and Paddi Clark. We wowed the public not only with sugar flowers and cakes but with sugar sculptures and pictures, colour, texture, and artistry, long before sugar became accepted by the general art world and cake making became so commercialised. Recognition came at last: we were invited to take the first exhibition to the Birmingham NEC for display at the International Sugarcraft Exhibition and the whole of the 2002 Taste of Art 3 for exhibition at The Bowes Museum in County Durham.

After co-ordinating the group for six years, it was time to branch out again and exhibited my sugar art twice at The Fountain Gallery in Hampton Court, and also had work accepted in the Eat Art exhibition at The Riverside Gallery in Walton-upon-Thames; finally, sugar in a fine art exhibition! A career best!

During this time I had already become interested in developing ways of creating woven-pattern effects in sugarpaste. Frustrated by all the painting, dusting, or meticulous stencilling required, I wanted a quicker, simpler, and more colourful approach. Enter skills from other crafts like polymer clay, glass blowing and sweet making, and after many trials and experiments I came to understand how to use these ideas

with various sugar pastes and develop a range of patterns suitable for sugarcraft. Squires Kitchen became interested in the techniques and in 2006 I published a small book called *The Book of Patterned Pastes* (B. Dutton Publishing), then went on to submit many articles to *Cakes & Sugarcraft* magazine, and hold workshops at Squires Kitchen International School.

Meanwhile, I had been invited to teach part-time at Brooklands College working with Jane Hatton and Sue Haskell, and some incredibly talented students. It was a wonderful time, learning a great deal from everyone there and having the pleasure of passing this knowledge onto a new set of students every year. Sadly after six years it was time to move on and now I have much more time to spend with my family, while teaching privately, demonstrating patterned pastes around the UK and abroad, and judging at international exhibitions.

Patterned Pastes

GERALDINE DAHLKE

Patterned paste techniques can be used to create many different patterns such as swirls, dots, lines, checks, and combinations of all these, allowing you to create great decorative effects without the need for airbrushing, painting, stencilling, or petal dusting. You can use the following techniques to create a patterned cake covering, patterned petals for sugar flowers or even finishing touches such as bows and drapes.

EDIBLES

SK Sugarpaste: Tuxedo Black, Vintage Ivory (or any other two colours of your choice)

SK Sugar Florist Paste (SFP): Black, Ivory (or any other two colours of your choice)

Icing sugar in a shaker

EQUIPMENT

Cutting mat

Dampening cloth (see tip)

Long, plain-bladed, sharp knife

Food-grade plastic bags

For essential modelling edibles and equipment, see pages 184–185

TECHNIQUES

- Making a rose pattern
- Making a checked pattern
- Making triangular and thin stripes
- Making striped leaves

Follow these top tips to achieve the best results when making patterned pastes:

• Use a high-quality sugarpaste (also known as luxury pastes) which, unlike cheaper pastes, roll out using very little icing sugar and yet stick together without any extra moisture.

• Knead the pastes well before you start so they are soft and malleable. Take care not to overwork the paste or it will become difficult to form a pattern.

• Do not cut the paste to size, instead always roll out the correct weight of paste to the size given.

• Try starting with a cube, rather than a ball of paste, when rolling sugarpaste into a square or rectangular shape.

• Luxury sugarpastes may not require dampening especially if you work quickly, but always have a damp, sterile cloth to hand just in case the surface of the paste does dry out. Use a sterile, damp cloth rather than a paintbrush to dampen the paste, as a cloth spreads moisture more evenly and is less likely to apply excess liquid.

• To make a dampening cloth, fold a small cloth into a pad and soak it with a solution of 60% clear alcohol to 40% cooled, boiled water. Squeeze out the excess liquid until the cloth feels lightly damp. Store in a small, airtight container to prevent it from drying out too quickly. Keep a bottle of spare, sterile liquid handy to moisten the cloth again. Always wash out the sugar and any colouring frequently from the cloth and dry before dampening once more.

• Use a sharp, long, plain-bladed knife in a light, sawing motion to cut slices cleanly from a block of patterned paste. Too much

pressure will drag the layers together and smudge the pattern. If you find the patterned block distorts and flattens as you cut slices from it, turn the block over and cut from a different side each time.

• When slicing patterned blocks of flower paste, slightly chill the paste first to firm it up a little.

• You may prefer to slice the patterns on a cutting mat or spare cake board, but if you are using a non-stick board then take care to avoid damaging the board with the sharp knife.

• Always butt the pastes together as quickly as possible when making a pattern, so they stick without having to be dampened. Cutting a few at a time hardly ever works unless you are able to work very quickly.

• When using double-sided paste, make sure the paste is an even depth all over before you start.

• If the pattern starts to distort as you are rolling out, check you are applying an even pressure on the rolling pin: too much pressure will widen the work, and too little pressure will prevent it expanding. It is this pressure that will control the final pattern, so use it to your advantage.

• Once assembled, the patterned blocks can keep fresh and useable for some hours provided they are wrapped tightly in a few layers of food-grade plastic (not cling film as it is slightly porous).

I have used black and ivory sugarpaste to clearly demonstrate the techniques below, but feel free to use any paste colours you prefer.

Making a rose pattern

1 Roll 30g (1oz) of Tuxedo Black sugarpaste into a 10cm (4") long sausage.

2 Roll out 60g (2oz) of Vintage Ivory sugarpaste into a 10cm x 8cm (4" x 3¹/₈") rectangle and dampen with the cloth. Wrap the ivory paste around the black paste to make a sausage with a black centre.

3 Roll the paste into a tapered sausage that is 20cm (8") long, 1cm (³/₈") wide at one end and 2.5cm (1") wide at the other. Mark out six equal sections on the paste. Cut off one section from the narrower end and wrap it tightly in food-grade plastic and reserve.

4 Pinch a small ridge down the length of the tapered sausage to one side of the central line. Use a non-stick rolling pin to flatten it into a wedge shape that is 2.5cm (1") wide at the narrow end and 5cm (2") wide x 8cm (³/₈") high at the other end. Turn the paste over and dampen the underside with the cloth. Cut the paste into five equal sections.

5 To form the rose pattern, use the reserved piece of paste as the central point. Starting with the smallest piece, wrap the wedges of paste anti-clockwise around the centre so they overlap. Make sure each 'petal' is the same way around throughout. Roll the completed rose into a 6cm (2½") long sausage to neaten.

6 Take 70g (2½oz) of Vintage Ivory paste and roll it into a rectangle 6cm x 13cm (3" x 5") in size. Dampen the paste then roll it around the rose pattern to form an ivory coating.

7 Slice narrow pieces from the sausage and arrange them as required to make a rose pattern.

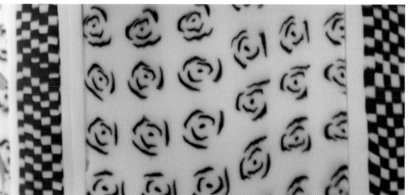

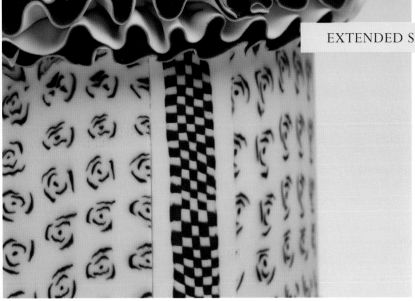

Making a checked pattern

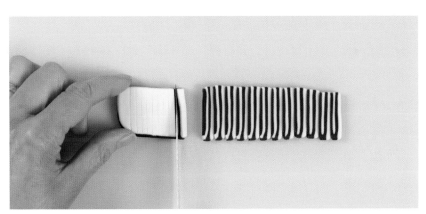

1 Roll out 20g (¾oz) of Tuxedo Black sugarpaste and 20g (¾oz) of Vintage Ivory sugarpaste into 7cm (2¾") squares. Place the black square on top of the ivory square, then cut in half. Stack one half on top of the other, with the ivory side on the black side.

2 Cut a 3mm (⅛") slice from the end of the pastes and let it fall flat. Cut a second slice in the same way, then butt the second slice up against the first, making sure the stripes are alternating. Continue adding more slices until you have a long line of narrow stripes all stuck together.

3 Very gently roll down the stripes (not across them) just enough to flatten the surface of the paste. Try not to roll the paste any thinner. Carefully turn the paste around by 90° so the stripes are all arranged horizontally in front of you. Trim one long side to create a straight edge.

4 Cut off a 3mm (⅛") wide strip from the longer side of the striped paste to create a line of tiny black and ivory squares. Push aside a little and straighten it up with the side of a palette knife. Slide the long palette knife under the edge of the strips so you can line up the tiny squares, sticking the black squares against the ivory and vice versa. Slide the paste off the knife, but as the paste will stretch a little you may have to adjust the position of the squares as you work. Butt the slices together as soon as you can and use the knife to straighten.

5 Make a straight cut 3mm (⅛") in from the first row of squares to create the second row of squares. Slide the palette knife under the stripes and slide them off once more, positioning them ready for a third row. Continue as before to create a checked pattern.

Patterned Pastes

285

6 Very gently roll across the squares to smooth them out, taking care not to distort the pattern or thin the paste. Straighten the rows of squares again and trim the edges if necessary. Check the underside of the checked paste as this may be neater than the top.

Making triangular stripes

1 Roll out 30g (1oz) of Vintage Ivory sugarpaste and 6g (just under ¼oz) of Tuxedo Black sugarpaste into 8cm x 6cm (3" x 2¼") rectangles. Lift the black paste onto a rolling pin and carefully lower it onto the ivory paste, making sure there aren't any air bubbles.

2 Roll out both pastes together into a rectangle that is 14cm x 8cm (5½" x 3⅛") in size and lay it in front of you lengthwise. Make sure it can still move freely on the board and trim away any rough edges.

3 Use a sharp knife to cut a narrow triangle down one side that is approximately 1.3cm (½") wide at the base and as long as the length of paste. Flip the triangle over to reveal the ivory side and use a smoother to quickly butt it up against the double-sided sheet of sugarpaste so it sticks in place.

4 Cut out an inverted triangle of the same size next to the first one. Turn the sheet of sugarpaste over to reveal the ivory side again, butt the paste together and cut out a third triangle. Keep repeating the process until you have used the whole sheet of sugarpaste, ensuring the shapes are all joined together as you work.

5 Roll over the paste carefully to bond the pattern together and hide all the cut marks. Only when you are sure the pattern has firmly stuck together, slide a long palette knife under the paste to release it and sprinkle extra icing sugar underneath.

tutor tip

This pattern is made with thin, narrow triangles of contrasting colours rather than with regular stripes to provide interest and movement for fabric effects.

Very often the triangular patterns will become distorted, but you can avoid this by turning the sheet of sugarpaste around and cutting from another side, or cut a triangle with the base next to the base of the previous one. Any slight variation in the pattern only adds additional interest.

Making thin stripes

1 Roll out 60g (2oz) of Vintage Ivory sugarpaste and 10g (¼oz) of Tuxedo Black sugarpaste into 6cm x 7cm (2³⁄₈" x 2¾") rectangles. Place one rectangle on top of the other, making sure there are no trapped air bubbles.

2 Roll out the paste again into a 15cm x 8cm (6"x 3¹⁄₈") rectangle and cut this into 15cm x 5cm (2"x 6") long strips. Lightly moisten the top of all the strips using the cloth. Stack one strip on top of the other (black on ivory) to form a block of pattern.

3 Cut a slice from the 15cm (6") long patterned side that is 2mm (¹⁄₈") wide. Allow the slice to fall away as you cut to avoid smudging the pattern. Lay the strip flat on the board and use the side of a smoother to pat it back into straight, vertical stripes.

4 Dampen the top of the block and cut four more slices, making sure to butt each one up against the last one and straighten them with a smoother. Check all the slices are sticking to each other, then gently roll along the stripes to smooth out all the joins. Slide a large palette knife under the paste to release it and sprinkle some icing sugar underneath.

tutor tip

To make the paste longer roll along the stripes, but to make it wider roll diagonally across the pattern as this helps to keep the paste smooth and helps prevent the stripes from distorting.

Making striped leaves

1 Roll out 10g (¼oz) of SFP in each colour into 12cm x 3cm (5" x 1¹⁄₈") rectangles. Place one on top of the other, moistening each layer with a damp cloth.

2 Cut the paste into four equal lengths and stack one on top of the other, alternating the colours. Moisten the top surface again, then cut this block in half and stack once more to create a block of 16 stripes that is approximately 2.5cm (1") high.

3 Lay the block on its side so the stripes are uppermost, then cut diagonally across the block with a sharp knife to create two triangular pieces. Turn one triangle over, and then push the two pieces together again.

4 The leaves are made from slices cut from this block, so carefully press the ends of the block together to form a leaf shape. Cut off very thin slices of the striped pattern to create rose leaves that are approximately 4cm (1½") long.

tutor tip

If you find the block of paste squashes out of shape, turn it over and cut from the other side. Sometimes the paste can become very sticky and soft, so wrap it in food-grade plastic and chill it for a while to help it firm up. Always clean and dry the knife before cutting another slice.

Patterned Pastes

Monochrome Wedding Cake

A visit to an exhibition celebrating post-1950s British glamour at the V&A Museum in London inspired me to make a cake echoing the sumptuous use of material and accessories found on many of the costumes, especially a design by Victor Edelstein which featured a huge, striped bow. I then added some patterned paste techniques to create a cake with a luxurious and contemporary feel. Although this is a four-tier cake, each tier can be made separately or in combination with one or more of the others.

EDIBLES

7 round, deep fruit cakes:

    4 x 20.5cm (8")

    2 x 15cm (6")

    1 x 10cm (4")

SK Sugarpaste: 2kg (4lb 6½oz) Vintage Ivory, 100g (3½oz) Tuxedo Black mixed with 100g (3½oz) Vintage Ivory

SK Gum Tragacanth

SK Sugar Florist Paste (SFP): Black, Ivory

For essential modelling edibles and equipment, see pages 184–185

EQUIPMENT

15cm and 10cm (6" and 4") round cake boards

25.5cm and 2 x 23cm (10" and 2 x 9") round cake drums

20.5cm (8") wax paper square

Waxed card, e.g. cake box card

Sterilised round-headed pin

Ribbon cutter

Greaseproof paper for templates

81cm (32") x 15mm (½") wide satin ribbon: black

1.05m (41") x 15mm (½") wide satin ribbon: ivory

Templates, see page 507

Flowers

20-, 26- and 28-gauge wires: white

Small black seed-head stamens

Floral tape (5mm width): ivory

Preparing the cakes

1 Cover the 25.5cm (10") cake drum with black sugarpaste, and the remaining cake drums and cake boards with Vintage Ivory sugarpaste (see page 141). Leave to dry overnight.

2 For the first tier, stack and dowel two 20.5cm (8") cakes and round off the edges at the top and base of the cake (see page 143). As the cake will be covered with panels, cover with marzipan or a thin layer of sugarpaste (see page 96).

3 For the second tier, prepare two 20.5cm (8") cakes in the same way as for the first tier, but cover with Vintage Ivory sugarpaste (see pages 139–140).

4 For the third tier, prepare two 15cm (6") cakes in the same way as for the first tier.

5 Round off the top edge of the 10cm (4") cake and cover with Vintage Ivory sugarpaste. Place the cake on the 10cm (4") cake board and secure an ivory ribbon around the base of the cake.

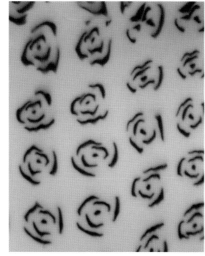

Base tier

6 To make a template for a rose pattern panel, measure ¹/₅ of the cake's circumference, then subtract 3.5cm (1³/₈") to allow a gap between them for the checked panels. This will be the width. The height of the rectangle will be the height of the cake. Extend the top of the template to meet at the central point on top of the cake. Mark out the equally spaced sections on the cake top and sides with a scriber.

7 Roll out 120g (4¼oz) of Vintage Ivory sugarpaste to ²/₃ of the size of the rose panel template (approximately 8cm x 22cm (3" x 8½") for the cake pictured here). Smear a very thin layer of white vegetable fat over the paste to keep it moist. Lightly cover with food-grade plastic while working on the rose pattern.

8 Make a sausage of rose-patterned paste following the instructions on page 284. Roll out to approximately 60cm (24") long, dampen and cut into 12 equal lengths. Lay these side-by-side on the board and stick them together as you go. Roll 20g (³/₄oz) of Vintage Ivory sugarpaste to 22cm (8½") long, dampen the paste and cut it into 5cm (2")

lengths and lay along the hollows between each length. This helps to keep the sausages round when placed together on the backing paste.

9 Trim one long side of the pattern to neaten the edge, then dampen the top of the paste and cut one 3mm (¹/₈") slice from the cut edge. Lay the strip vertically on one side of the backing paste. Cut five more slices and arrange them next to the first side-by-side, butting them up closely together and making sure the rose patterns line up. Carefully push out any gaps from between the roses, dampening between them if necessary.

10 Roll out the pattern on some icing sugar to fit the size of the template, taking care not to distort the pattern. Dampen the cake and place the first panel on the side of the cake, trimming the sides to fit. Repeat to make four more panels and attach them around the cake.

11 Create a template for the five checked panels that are each approximately 3.5cm (1³/₈") wide to fit between the rose-patterned panels. Make five checked strips with Vintage Ivory and

black sugarpaste following the instructions on page 285.

12 Roll out a length of Vintage Ivory sugarpaste to the same length and thickness as the squares. Cut a straight line down the centre of the ivory strip and insert the squares between the two halves, quickly pushing the ivory against the squares. Dampen the edges with the cloth if necessary. Trim the piece to fit the template and secure it into place, moistening the cake first. Repeat to fill all four of the gaps and leave to firm a little.

13 Secure a 23cm (9") ivory-coated drum in the centre of the 25.5cm (10") black drum, and attach the first tier to the ivory board.

14 To make the frills, add ½tsp of gum tragacanth to 530g (1lb 3oz) of Vintage Ivory sugarpaste and a pinch of gum tragacanth to 50g (1³/₄oz) of black paste and leave to rest.

15 Secure a ribbon around the second 23cm (9") ivory cake drum and place centrally on top of the first tier. This will be your guide for attaching the frills.

Monochrome Wedding Cake

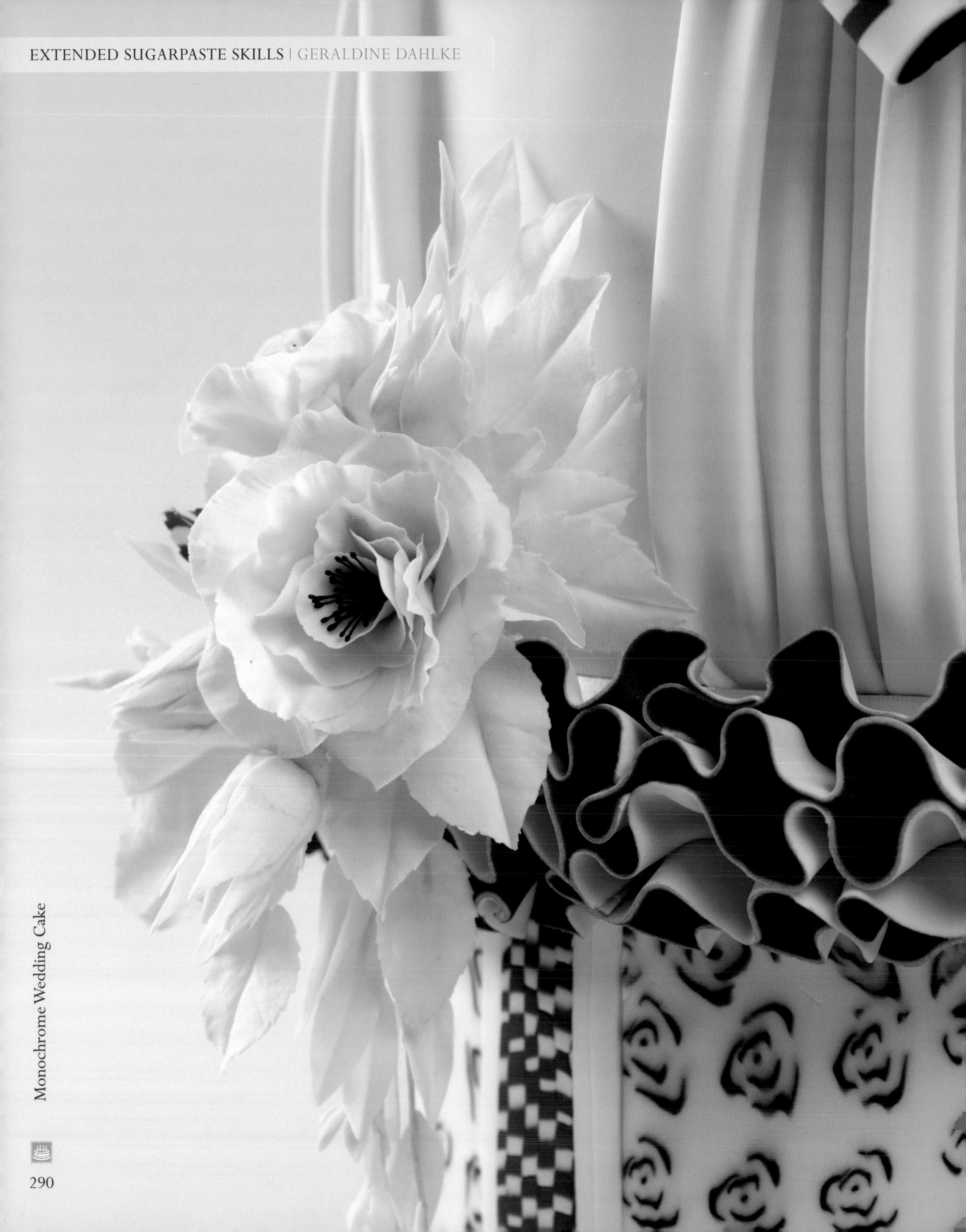

16 Soften some Vintage Ivory sugarpaste with hot, pre-boiled water and place in a piping bag. Pipe a thin line of the softened sugarpaste around the cake, 1.5cm (½") below the drum. Roll a long, narrow sausage that is 7mm (¼") thick from 30g (1oz) of Vintage Ivory sugarpaste and secure it to the line of softened sugarpaste. Leave to dry completely.

17 Roll 125g (4½oz) of Vintage Ivory sugarpaste and 12g (½oz) of black sugarpaste into rectangles that are 2cm x 6cm (¾" x 2½") in size. Lift the black paste onto the rolling pin and lower onto the ivory paste. Pierce any air bubbles with a sterilised pin before rolling both layers together into an 11cm x 26cm (4½" x 10½") rectangle. Set the ribbon cutter to 3cm (1¹⁄₈") wide and cut into long strips.

18 For the first layer of frills, pipe zigzags of softened sugarpaste between the band of sugarpaste and the board above. Carefully press one end of a strip into the softened paste, with the black side uppermost. Continue to attach the strip around the cake whilst folding pleats

in the paste that are 5mm (¼") wide and 2cm (¾") apart. Repeat around the cake, rolling out more double-sided paste as necessary.

19 Secure a second row of frills just above the first, this time with the ivory side uppermost. Arrange the pleats between those below to define each layer. Support with tissue paper until firm. Continue in the same way for the third and fourth rows, alternating between the ivory and black sides.

Second tier

20 Mix 1½tsp of gum tragacanth into 500g (1lb 1¾oz) of Vintage Ivory sugarpaste and leave to rest wrapped in food-grade plastic.

21 Divide the circumference of the second tier into five sections as before, and mark on the position of the 8cm (3¹⁄₈") wide pleated drapes. Place the 15cm (6") ivory-covered board on the top of the cake and weigh it down slightly so it does not move.

22 Fold some waxed card into 1cm (³⁄₈") deep concertinas, scoring the folds with a craft knife. Place the sheet of wax paper on top of the folded card.

23 Roll out 100g (3½oz) of strengthened ivory sugarpaste into a 20cm (8") paper-thin square and lift onto the wax paper. Gently pull the paper away until the edge of the paste falls into the first slot in the folded card. Lay a dowel or barbecue skewer on top of the paste to ease it into the slot. Continue forming all the pleats in the same way.

24 Carefully lift the pleats from the card and lay on a non-stick board, tucking under the sides to hide the cut edges. Dampen the top and sides of the cake where you want to attach the drape. Pinch together the top of the pleats and lower the folds onto the top of the cake, placing the drape between the scribed lines. Let the rest of the folds fall into place down the side of the cake and tuck them under with a Dresden tool, trimming away any excess. Try to avoid touching the folds as it may flatten them. Leave to dry.

Monochrome Wedding Cake

Third tier

25 Divide the circumference of the cake into five equal sections and make a template for the striped panels, allowing room for five, checked panels that are three squares wide. Use the template and a scribing needle to mark out the sections on the cake.

26 Make five striped panels following the instructions on page 287. Dampen the cake with the sterile cloth and attach each panel, trimming the sides to fit within the scribed lines. Repeat with the four remaining panels.

27 Create and attach five checked panels in the same way as for the base tier but the panels should only be three squares wide.

28 Once the paste has firmed, secure the cake onto the 15cm (6") ivory-covered board.

Striped bow

29 Mix ¾tsp of gum tragacanth into 400g (14oz) of Vintage Ivory sugarpaste and a pinch of gum tragacanth into 80g (2¾oz) of black sugarpaste then leave to rest, tightly wrapped in food-grade plastic.

30 Make paste with thick, triangular black and white stripes following the instructions on page 286. Cut out two tails using the bow template.

31 Mix a little cooled, boiled water with some Vintage Ivory sugarpaste to make a sticky glue. Spread a little of the glue on the cake where the bow will sit and dampen the tops of each tail. Gather the tops and press them into place so they overlap each other slightly.

32 For the largest set of bow loops, roll out 60g (2oz) of Vintage Ivory sugarpaste and 12g (½oz) of black sugarpaste into rectangles that are 9cm x 7cm (3½" x 2¾") in size. Layer the black onto the ivory as before. Roll the paste into a 23cm x 12cm (9" x 4¾") rectangle and create another sheet of thick stripes. Cut the paste in half, fold it into two wide loops

and gather in the ends. Stick the bow loops to the top of the tails and along the top of the first tier cake. Support the loops with tissue paper and leave to dry.

33 Make the smaller loops in the same way as for the larger set, using the smaller template. Attach on top of the dried bow and leave to dry completely.

34 Use 40g (1½oz) of Vintage Ivory sugarpaste and 8g (¼oz) of black sugarpaste to make another sheet of stripes that is 7cm x 5cm (2¾" x 2½") in size. Fold in the long edges then wrap the paste around the centre of the bow to hide the gathered ends. Leave to dry.

Finishing touches

35 Create two teardrop-shaped sprays incorporating ivory roses (see pages 270–275), ivory and striped rose leaves (see page 275) and ivory jasmine (see page 262).

36 Carefully assemble the four tiers. Place the sprays into posy picks and insert them into the first and third tiers.

Helen Mansey

BIOGRAPHY

I decided to train to be a professional chef after leaving school, having first studied fashion design at art college before changing my career direction. It was whilst taking a break from my career to raise my young family that I discovered my passion for cake decorating.

In order to raise money one Christmas whilst having three young children to look after, I decided to bake and decorate Christmas cakes to sell at local markets. I got an overwhelming response from happy customers and this gave me the confidence to establish my own wedding cake-making business, Bellissimo Cakes.

I am greatly inspired by the clean lines and sharp edges of Australian cake design, and these elements have now become part of my signature style. In order to achieve these sharp edges easily on a sugarpasted cake, I developed the Bellissimo Flexi Smoothers with Squires Kitchen.

Hand piping is another one of my specialities, a skill I have been taught by fellow Squires Kitchen tutor, Eddie Spence MBE. Using the skills Eddie taught me, I like to use brush embroidery or pressure piping techniques to create lace designs and I often try to replicate lace details from a bride's wedding dress on her cake. I also enjoy making individual lace pieces using the run-out technique and attaching these to the base of a cake to give the illusion of lace, an idea I have developed from traditional royal-iced collars. I am also self-taught in the art of sugar floristry and clients often mistake my flowers for real or silk flowers due to their delicate appearance.

In 2011 I was awarded gold for my entry at the Squires Kitchen 25th Wedding Anniversary Cake competition. I have also exhibited my cake creations at the Squires Kitchen Annual Exhibition and the Cake and Bake Show in London. As well as exhibiting, I have demonstrated how to create sharp edges and pipe lace pieces at the shows and have taught my students how to achieve sharp edges on ganache-covered cakes on my course at Squires Kitchen's International School.

As well as regularly contributing to *Wedding Cakes - A Design Source*, *Cakes & Sugarcraft*, and *Squires Kitchen Bake School* magazines, my work is often featured in bridal publications and bridal blogs and in 2012 I was shortlisted in the Hitched Breakthrough Awards for Best New Wedding Cake Designer.

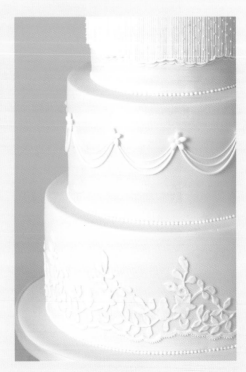

Pastillage Collars

HELEN MANSEY

Pastillage is a good alternative to royal icing for collar work as it can be rolled and cut out and is not as fragile, making it a great medium for beginners. Here I also explain how to create a slanted cake that is ideal for displaying a cake-top collar design, as well as the technique for creating sharp edges on a sugarpasted cake which gives the cake a clean, defined edge on which to present the collar.

TECHNIQUES

- Making a slanted cake for cake-top collar designs
- Creating a sharp-edged sugarpaste cake covering
- Making pastillage collars for sugarpasted cakes
- Making pastillage tree decorations

EDIBLES

Slanted cake

23cm and 25.5cm (9" and 10") round cakes, chilled in the refrigerator overnight

Firm chocolate ganache

Sugar syrup

Sharp-edged sugarpaste cake covering

Slanted cake as above, layered, filled and crumb-coated with ganache (see page 298)

SK Sugarpaste: 1.25kg (2lb 12oz), in the colour of your choice

Pastillage collars

SK Pastillage: 750g (1lb 10½oz)

SK Instant Mix Royal Icing: 500g (1lb 1¾oz)

Edible pearl lustre spray (PME)

For essential modelling edibles and equipment, see pages 184–185

1920s Father Christmas bisqueware figures

EQUIPMENT

Slanted cake

Cake leveller

Food-grade flexible plastic or thin card

Compass

Pastry brush

20.5cm, 23cm and 25.5cm (8", 9" and 10") round cake boards

Spare round cake boards

Large, serrated knife

Tilting turntable

Stainless steel metal rule, or large palette knife

Side scraper

Sharp-edged sugarpaste cake covering

Non-slip mat

SK Bellissimo Flexi Smoothers

Sterilised needle

Pastillage collars

Food-grade flexible plastic or thin card for templates

2 x 35.5cm (14") square cake drums (boards)

Acetate

Piping bags

Piping nozzles: nos. 1, 1.5, 3

Templates, see page 508

How to make a slanted cake for cake-top collar designs

The following steps explain how to make a slanted cake that measures 23cm (9") around the top and 20.5cm (8") around the base. You can, of course, vary the size to cater for more or less guests.

1 Trim the browned bottom off each cake. Set a cake leveller to 2.5cm (1") and cut two layers from each sponge.

2 On food-grade flexible plastic or thin card, use a compass to draw five circles with the following diameters: 22.2cm, 21.7cm, 21cm, 20.4cm and 19.7cm (8¾", 8½", 8¼", 8" and 7¾") and cut out to use as templates.

3 Place one of the 25.5cm (10") cake layers on a spare cake board, then lay the 22.2cm (8¾") template on top and trim around it with a sharp knife. Repeat using the 21.7cm (8½") template with the remaining 25.5cm (10") layer of cake; the 21cm (8¼") template with the first 23cm (9") cake layer; and the 20.4cm (8") template with the remaining 23cm (9") cake layer. Stack the layers on top of each other with the largest at the bottom and smallest at the top.

4 Place the 19.7cm (7¾") template on top of the assembled cake and use this as a guide to trim the edge of the cake so that it slants down at an angle from the template to the bottom layer.

5 Smear a dab of firm ganache in the centre of the 25.5cm (10") cake board, place the 20.5cm (8") board on top and press down to secure.

6 Heat the chocolate ganache in a microwave at half-power in short, 10-second bursts, until the ganache reaches the consistency of peanut butter.

7 Smear some ganache in the centre of a 20.5cm (8") cake board and place the smallest cake layer onto it, so it is facing cut-side up. Brush lightly with sugar syrup, then spread a 4mm (³/₈") thick layer of ganache over the first layer of cake. Repeat in the same way for the next two layers.

8 For the final layer, start at the top of one side of the cake and slice down diagonally to the bottom on the opposite side to make the slanted cake top. Brush the cut tops with sugar syrup and spread one with a thin layer of ganache. To accentuate the slant, place one half on top of the other with the thickest ends together. Spread the top of the cake with a thin layer of ganache and place the slanted layer on top of the cake, slightly overhanging the thick edge. Trim this edge slightly so that it follows the line of the slant.

9 Transfer the cake onto a turntable and place a 23cm (9") cake board on top of the cake. Hold a metal rule or large palette knife so that it touches the top and the bottom boards and run the rule around the whole circumference of the cake. You should have a 4mm (¹/₈") gap between the edge of the rule and the cake. Trim the cake down to size if necessary.

10 Remove the board from the top of the cake, crumb-coat the cake with ganache and leave to set for 15 minutes.

11 Spread a 4mm (¹/₈") layer of ganache over the slanted top.

Smooth with a palette knife and leave to set for another 15 minutes or until it is no longer tacky.

12 Take the 23cm (9") cake board and brush it with clear alcohol or cooled, boiled water. Place the board with the foil-side down on top of the cake. Use a palette knife to liberally apply more ganache over the sides of the cake. The aim is to fill in the gap between the side of the cake and the edge of the boards.

13 Take a side scraper and pull it around the sides of the cake to remove any excess ganache; where the cake is at its deepest you may need to use the metal rule to scrape off the ganache evenly. If you notice a few gaps in the ganache covering, fill these in with more ganache and scrape again until the sides are perfectly smooth. It may help to chill the cake for five minutes between each application. Leave the cake to set at room temperature for approximately two or three hours, depending upon the temperature of your kitchen.

14 Run a paring knife around the top edge of the cake board and, if necessary, use the cake leveller to help lift the cake board from the cake. If you find there are any air pockets on top of the cake, warm some ganache again and use it to fill in the gaps. Use a palette knife to smooth the top of the cake. If you have a slight overhang of ganache at the edges, leave it to set overnight then remove with a paring knife the next day.

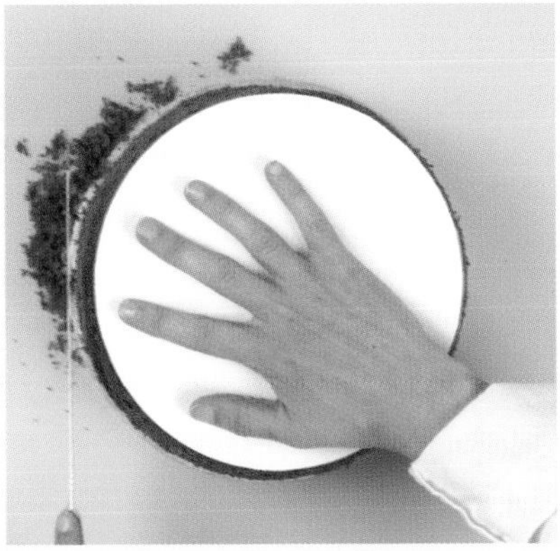
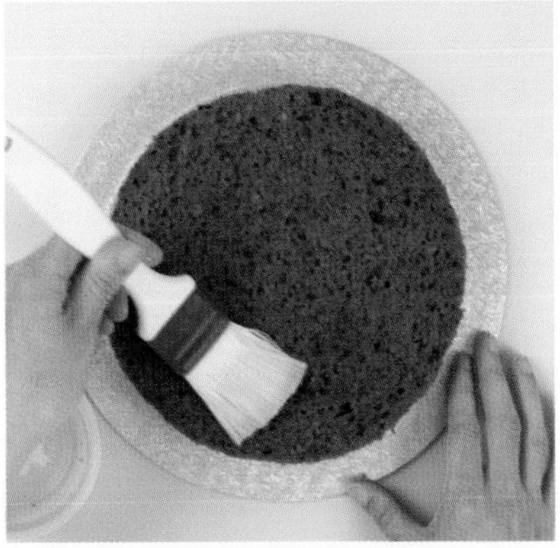
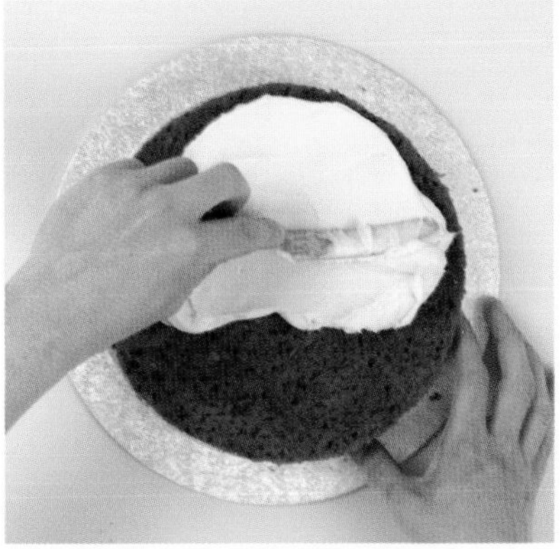
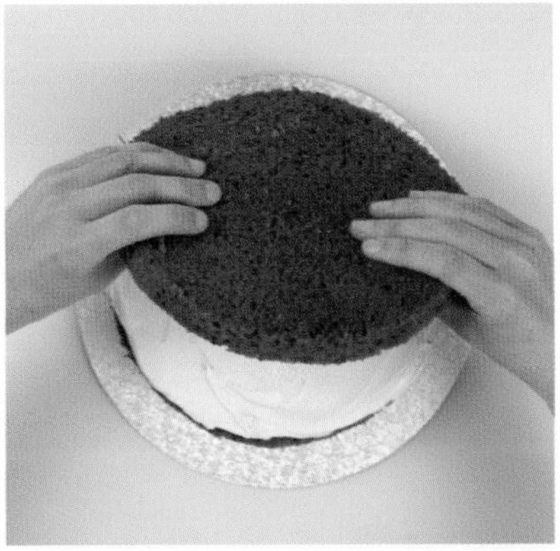
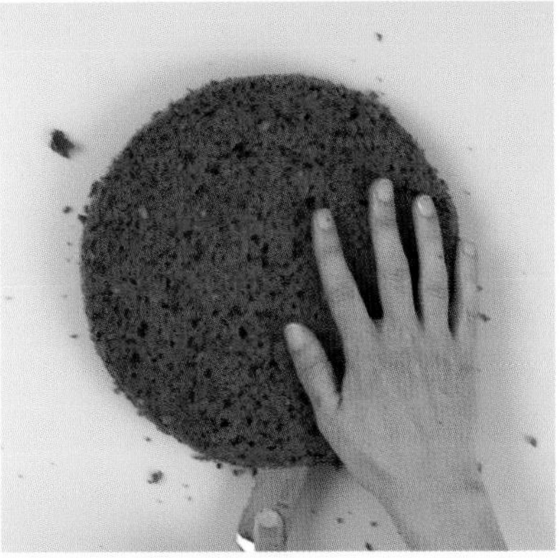
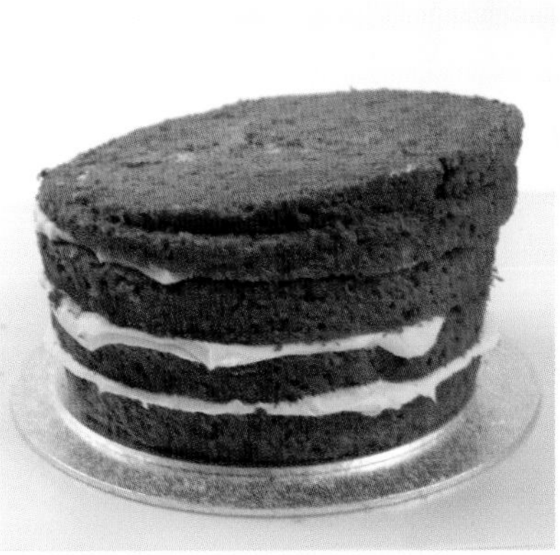
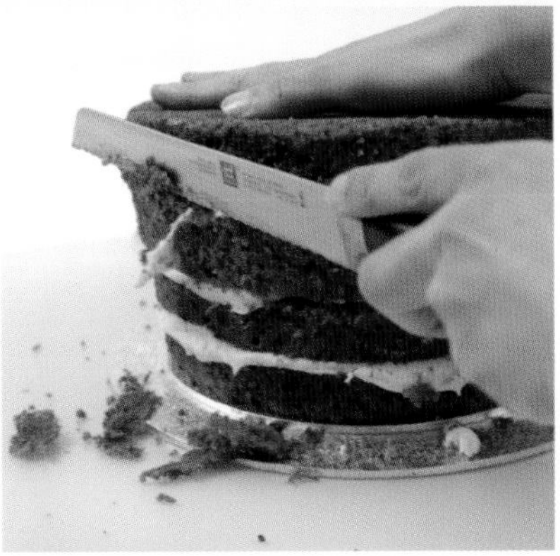
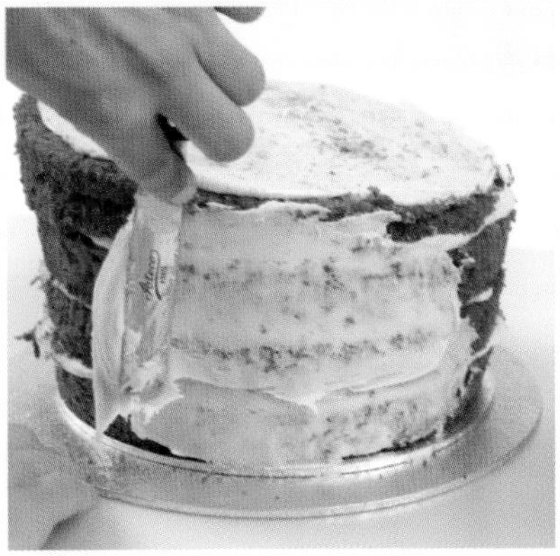
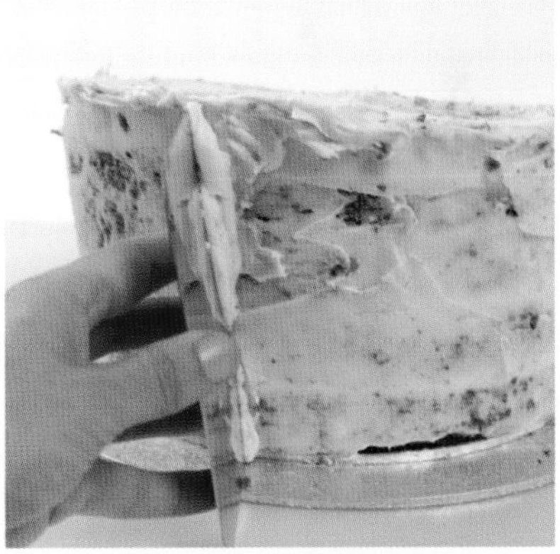
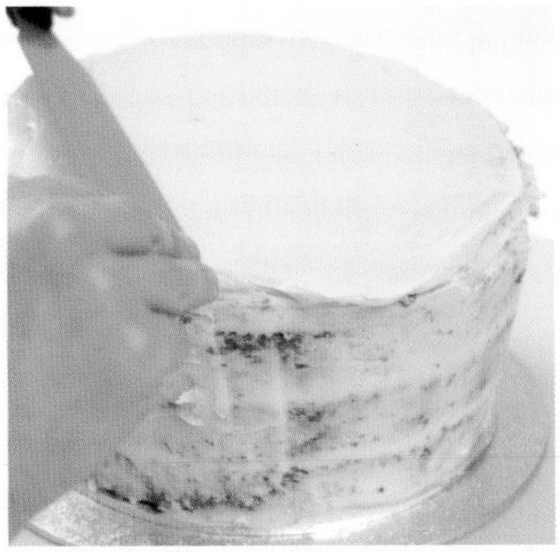
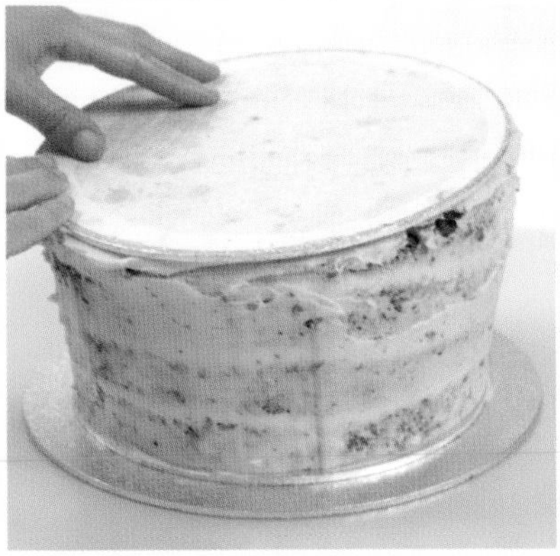
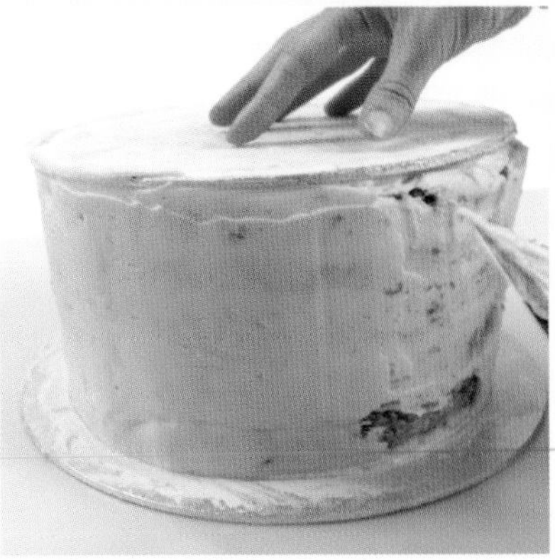

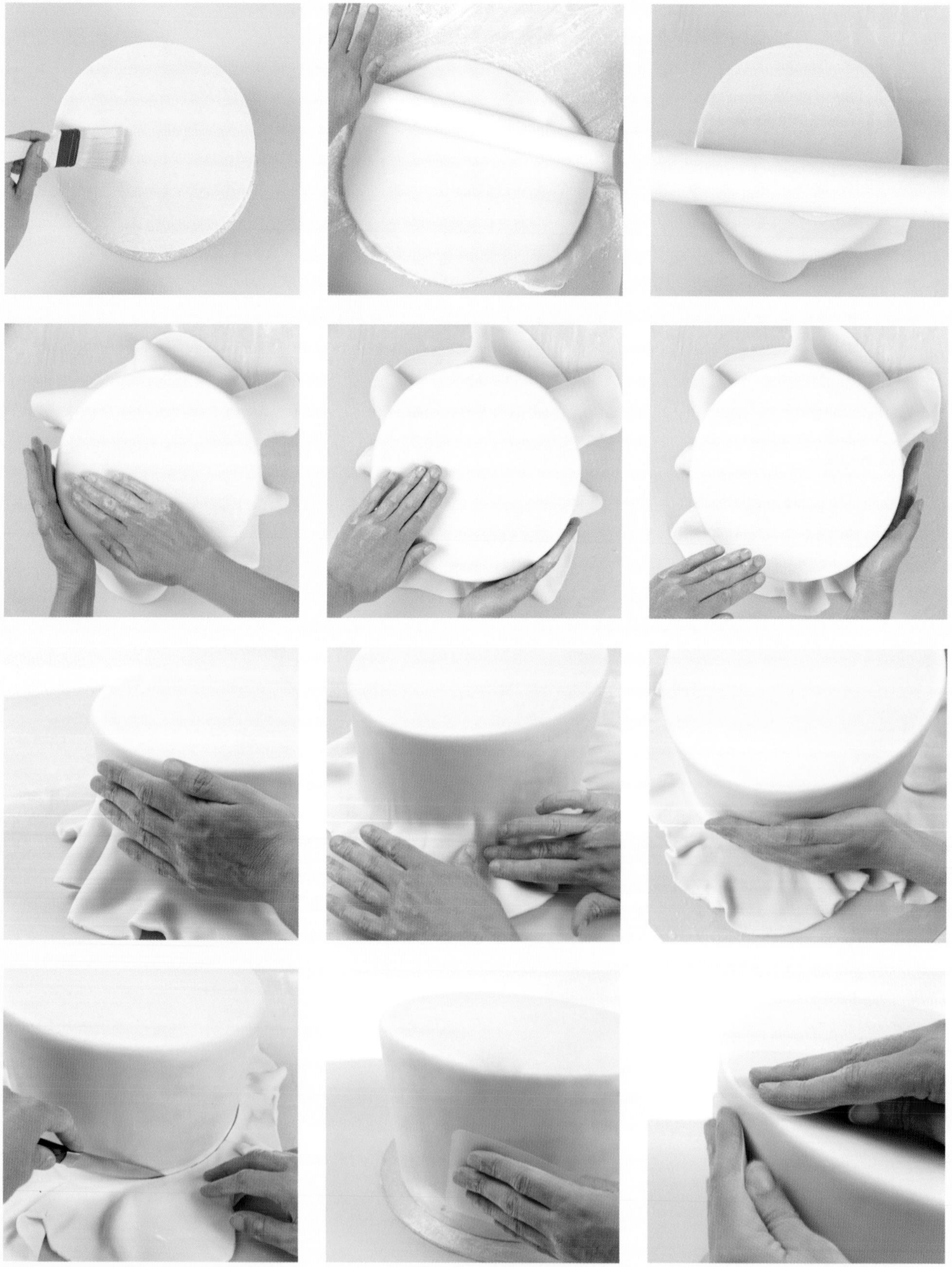

How to create a sharp-edged sugarpaste covering

1 Brush a ganache-covered cake (see page 298) with either clear alcohol or cooled, boiled water.

2 Dust a non-stick board lightly with icing sugar, then knead the sugarpaste well and roll it out to a 4mm (1/8") thickness.

3 Drape the sugarpaste over a rolling pin and lay it over the cake. Working quickly, smooth over the top and secure the paste at the edges of the cake. The sharp edges can cause the sugarpaste to stretch and tear if you do not fix the sugarpaste to the edges immediately.

4 Fan out the sugarpaste as you work down the sides. Smooth upwards with your hands in order avoid stretching the sugarpaste. Using a sharp knife or pizza wheel, remove the excess paste from the base.

5 Place a non-slip mat under the cake board. Smooth the cake with a smoother and prick any air bubbles with a fine, sterilised glass-headed pin. Ensure you store the pin safely away from the cake after use.

6 To achieve a sharp edge in the covering, hold the straight-edged smoother against the side of the cake and the round-edged smoother on top. Applying medium pressure, run the two smoothers together around the top edge of the cake: you should notice a crisp edge appearing. Continue around the whole cake until you are happy with the finish. Remove any indentations on the top of the cake with a smoother.

tutor tip

Fix the edges straight away to prevent stretching or tearing the paste along the sharp edge.

How to make a pastillage collar for a sugarpasted cake

The following steps explain how to make a snowflake-shaped collar for the slanted cake described above, but these basic steps can be adapted to make any shape you wish. If you are making your own collars, it is best to create a template for them first.

1 Cut out the templates for the snowflake from thin card or food-grade flexible plastic.

2 Cover two 35.5cm (14") square cake drums with acetate and tape them securely at the edges so the acetate is pulled taught. Lightly grease the acetate with white vegetable fat.

3 Make up the pastillage according to the instructions on the packet. Roll out a small amount of pastillage to a 3mm (1/8") thickness on a work surface dusted with icing sugar, then transfer the paste to a non-stick board.

4 Lightly grease a template with white vegetable fat and place it on top of the pastillage. Keep the remaining pastillage covered with cling film to prevent it from hardening. Following the template, use a craft knife to cut out the shape from the pastillage. Remove any excess and place it in a small, food-grade plastic bag to re-use.

5 Transfer the shape back onto the acetate with the template still attached. Once the pastillage is flat on the board, carefully peel off the template. You will need six large snowflake pieces, six small pieces, one circle, six small

strips and six longer strips. It is advisable to make a few extra of each to allow for breakages. Allow the shapes to dry overnight.

6 Make up the royal icing according to the instructions on the packet, then paddle (rub down) a small amount of icing on a work surface (see page 235). Fit a piping bag with a no. 1.5 nozzle and ½-fill with the icing. Use a scribing needle to score a line down the centre of each collar piece, starting 8mm (just over ¼") from the top and finishing 2.75cm (1") from the bottom of each piece. Pipe the design onto each piece of the collar, following the scribed line and using the templates as a guide.

7 Fit a piping bag with a no. 1 nozzle and ½-fill with paddled icing. To give the snowflake a delicate look, pipe a row

of dots along the top edge of each piece, then another row of dots in between the first row. Allow to dry, then spray lightly with edible pearl lustre spray.

8 Mark the centre of the cake and the centre of the pastillage circle with a scribing needle. Fit a piping bag with a no. 1.5 nozzle and ½-fill with off-peak consistency royal icing (see page 235). Pipe some icing onto the back of the pastillage circle and attach in the centre of the cake.

9 Pipe a wiggly line of icing onto one of the long strips and attach it to the back of a large snowflake piece, approximately 3cm (1⅛") along from the pointed end. This back piece will raise the collar a little from the top of the cake, adding more depth to the design. Pipe another wiggly line of icing onto the back

of the strip and the pointed end, then attach to the cake. The point of the collar piece should meet the centre of the circle. Repeat with a smaller snowflake piece and attach immediately next to the larger piece. Continue alternating the pieces until they are all attached.

tutor tip

It is important to keep the template attached to the snowflake until you have transferred it to the food-grade flexible plastic to prevent distorting the shape.

Seasonal Snowflake Cake with Snowflake Tree Decorations

If you are looking for a contemporary take on the traditional Christmas cake, this pretty pastel design uses pastillage collars to create a seasonal snowflake motif. As pastillage dries very hard, it is also great for making tree decorations, so I have shown how to make twinkling snowflake decorations that coordinate beautifully with the cake.

EDIBLES

23cm and 25.5cm (9" and 10") round cakes, layered, filled and crumb-coated with ganache, see page 298

SK Sugarpaste: 1kg (2lb 3¼oz) Bridal White mixed with 250g (8¾oz) Frosted Leaf

750g (1lb 10½oz) SK Instant Mix Pastillage

SK Instant Mix Professional Royal Icing

Edible pearl lustre spray (PME)

For essential modelling edibles and equipment, see pages 184–185

EQUIPMENT

Equipment for making a slanted-top cake, see page 294

Equipment for creating a sharp-edged sugarpaste covering, see page 294

Equipment for making a pastillage collar, see page 294

35.5cm (14") round cake drum

SK Winter Snowflake Cutter

2m (6' 6¾") x 15mm (³/₈") wide satin ribbon: frosted leaf

3m (9' 10") x 3mm (¹/₈") wide satin ribbon: frosted leaf

Templates, see page 508

Cake

1 Prepare a slanted-top cake for covering with sugarpaste, following the steps on page 298.

2 Knead together 1kg (2lb 3¼oz) of Bridal White sugarpaste and 250g (8¾oz) of Frosted Leaf sugarpaste to make a duck-egg-blue-coloured paste. Cover the cake with the sugarpaste, creating a sharp edge around the cake (see page 301).

3 Create and attach the snowflake pastillage collar, following the steps on pages 301–302.

4 Cover the 35.5cm (14") cake drum with the duck-egg-blue-coloured sugarpaste (see page 141). Place the cake on the cake drum and secure in place with a dab of royal icing.

5 Trim the cake drum with the wider ribbon and secure at the back with a non-toxic glue stick. Attach another length of the same ribbon around the base of the cake and secure with a dab of royal icing.

Tree decorations

6 Roll out some pastillage to 3mm (1/8") thick and cut out several shapes using a snowflake cutter. Cover a spare cake drum with a piece of acetate, then place the pastillage shapes on the drum and leave to dry.

7 Use a no. 3 piping nozzle to cut out a hole for the ribbon, approximately 1.5cm (1/2") from the top of each shape and allow to dry overnight.

8 Draw a six-pointed snowflake shape in the centre of the large snowflake with a scribing needle. Start each point of the scribed snowflake approximately 2cm (3/4") from a point on the larger snowflake.

9 Make up some royal icing and rub it down on a work surface. Fit a piping bag with a no. 1.5 nozzle and 1/2-fill the piping bag with the paddled icing. Following the scribed design and using the template as your guide, pipe the pattern onto each snowflake.

10 Fit a piping bag with a no.1 nozzle and 1/2-fill with paddled icing. Pipe a row of small dots around the outside of the snowflake, then another row of dots in between the first row. Allow to dry, then spray lightly with edible pearl lustre spray.

11 Once dry, carefully release the shapes from the acetate. Cut a small length of 3mm (1/8") wide frosted leaf ribbon, thread it through the hole in each shape and tie into a loop ready to hang from a tree.

note

Although it is made of sugar, pastillage dries very hard and is difficult to eat so it is advisable to remove the pastillage collar before serving the cake.

1920s bisqueware snow babies

Wedding Party

JAN CLEMENT-MAY

Modelling bespoke figures for a single project, such as the bridal party on a wedding cake, is a great way to personalise a design. The different ages, genders and skin tones of the characters can be made to resemble real-life people and their facial expressions and poses can add a fun and amusing element to the design. The different techniques explained here should help you to create your own unique and personalised sugar figures for any celebration cake.

TECHNIQUES

- How to create different skin tones

- Making a basic head

- How to model different facial expressions

- How to model different hairstyles

- Modelling the bride and groom

- Arranging modelled figures on a sugarpasted cake

Skin tone

To give your sugar figures different skin tones, use these examples as a guide to the colours you will need. Remember that you can mix any of these colours in different proportions to make a wide range of different skin tones.

Pale skin: Soft Beige Sugar Dough

Olive, mid-tone skin: Golden Bear Brown Sugar Dough with a small pinch of Brown Sugar Dough

Dark skin: Brown Sugar Dough

How to make a basic head

I have explained here how to make a basic head shape with simple facial features and a smiling expression. I have used this basic method for all of the figures in this section and it can be developed to create more complex facial expressions. You will need approximately 10g (¼oz) of Sugar Dough in the colour of your choice (see page 305) and a Black SK Professional Food Colour Pen.

1 Take 10g (¼oz) of Sugar Dough in your chosen skin colour, pinch out a small ball for the nose and two slightly larger balls for the ears and set aside.

2 Knead the remaining paste, roll into a ball then gently shape into an oval. Push the end of a spare barbecue skewer into the base of the head and rest it in the palm of your hand.

3 Push the end of a drinking straw into the paste at a 45° angle to make a mouth. Push the end of a piece of raw spaghetti into both ends of the mouth for dimples.

4 Attach the smallest ball of reserved paste above the mouth with a little edible glue for the nose.

5 Brush edible glue on either side of the head, level with the nose. Take the two remaining balls of paste and push the smallest end of a bone tool into one side of each ball. Secure to the side of the head, smoothing the paste with the bone tool towards the front of the head.

6 For the eyes, push the end of a Black food colour pen into the paste twice above the nose.

7 Once the head is complete, remove the barbecue skewer from the base and attach it to the body, securing with edible glue.

| Smiley face | Surprised face | Sleeping/Sad face | Cheerful face | Toddler | Young girl | Woman |

All of the facial expressions above use the same basic methods, but you can use them in different ways to make any type of character you wish. Make sure you have all the basic modelling equipment to hand before you start.

Facial expressions

▼ *Open-mouthed smile*

1 Mark a line for the mouth with a Dresden tool. Use the tip of the Dresden tool to open the top lip first. Turn the Dresden tool downwards and bring out the bottom lip in the same way. Smooth down the inside of the mouth with a bone tool.

2 Run the bone tool under the bottom lip and smooth over any grooves with your finger. Push the end of a Dresden tool into each corner of the mouth to make the cheeks.

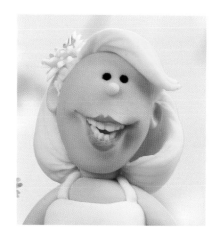

▲ *Smile with teeth*

1 Create an open-mouthed smile as explained above. Roll a pinch of White Sugar Dough out flat, then use a sharp knife to cut a straight line horizontally through the middle of the paste for the top and bottom rows of teeth. Cut a curved smile shape from the paste.

2 Mark out the individual teeth with a sharp knife then push the tip of the knife into the edge of each mark to define the teeth.

3 Pick up the bottom teeth with the tip of a Dresden tool and carefully secure them inside the bottom lip. Arrange the teeth so they are upright and look like they are disappearing into the back of the mouth. Repeat with the top set of teeth, making sure that the two front teeth are central.

4 For a woman's mouth, colour the lips with a Red food colour pen and brush the colour to the back of the lips with a damp paintbrush for a natural look.

▼ *Sideways smile*

1 Use a small, sharp knife to make an incision in the face at an angle, then curve the mouth up a little at one end.

2 Push a piece of dried spaghetti into the side of the mouth and run a bone tool under the mouth to define the bottom lip. Smooth over any ridge left by the tool with your finger.

▼ *Pout*

1 Run a bone tool around the mouth area. Flatten a tiny ball of paste and cut out a pair of lips with a small, sharp knife.

2 Secure the lips in the centre of the mouth area and carefully colour them with a Red food colour pen.

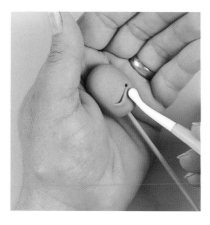
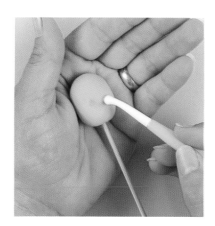

Wedding Party

Hairstyles for male figures

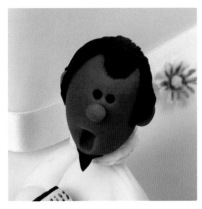

▲ Singing

Push the handle of a paintbrush into the lower half of the head and pull the paste down to open up the mouth.

Closed eyes

Use a Black food colour pen to draw two arches for the closed eyes.

Wrinkled forehead

1 Use a Dresden tool to mark one straight line across the top of the forehead, then mark two slightly slanted lines underneath the first. Mark an upside down 'V' between the previous two lines.

2 Draw two eyebrows above the ridge in the forehead with a Black food colour pen.

Short hair

1 You will need approximately 8g (¼oz) of Sugar Dough in your chosen colour for a short hairstyle. Before you start working on the hair, brush edible glue over the head and in front of the ears.

2 Roll 4g (⅛oz) of the Sugar Dough into a ball, flatten it out so that it fits over the back of the head between the ears and mark on the hair with a Dresden tool. Attach to the back of the head and use a Dresden tool to smooth over the edges.

3 Pinch out two small balls of Black Sugar Dough for the sideburns and shape each into a triangle. Secure in front of the ears then use a Dresden tool to texture the paste and blend it into the back piece of hair.

4 Shape the remaining paste into a cone, slightly flatten it towards the thinner end and mark with a Dresden tool. Attach to the top of the head and blend the paste backwards to join the hair at the back of the head.

Longer hair

1 You will need approximately 10g (¼oz) of Sugar Dough in your chosen colour for a longer hairstyle. Before you start working on the hair, brush edible glue over the head where the hair will be attached.

2 Roll 4g (⅛oz) of Brown Sugar Dough into a ball, flatten it out so that it fits over the back of the head between the ears and mark on the hair with a Dresden tool. Attach to the back of the head and use a Dresden tool to smooth over the edges.

3 Pinch out two small balls of Brown Sugar Dough and shape each into a triangle. Mark as before and attach just in front of the ears for the sideburns. Smooth over the join with a Dresden tool to blend the sideburns with the rest of the hair.

4 Divide the remaining paste into different-sized pieces for the strands of hair and shape each into a long cone. Mark on the hair with a Dresden tool, secure around the head in different directions and gently curl up the ends.

Curly hair

1 You will need approximately 10g (¼oz) of Sugar Dough in your chosen colour for a curly hairstyle. Before you start working on the hair, brush edible glue over the head where the hair will be attached.

2 Take several small balls of Sugar Dough and roll each one into a short sausage that is pointed at one end. Curl the paste (do not twist the curl or it will break) and attach it to the back of the neck with a Dresden tool.

3 Continue to make and attach more curls, working towards both ears for the first layer. Make another two layers above the first, then add curls in front of the ears and around the forehead.

4 Attach more curls to fill in any gaps at the back of the head, then finish with a final layer just above the forehead.

Quiff

1 You will need approximately 10g (¼oz) of Sugar Dough in your chosen colour for a quiff hairstyle. Before you start working on the hair, brush edible glue over the head where the hair will be attached.

2 Roll 4g (just under ¼oz) of Sugar Dough into a ball, flatten it out so that it fits over the back of the head between the ears and mark on the hair with a Dresden tool. Attach to the back of the head and use a Dresden tool to smooth over the edges.

3 Pinch out two small balls of Sugar Dough and shape each into a triangle, mark as before and attach just in front of the ears for the sideburns. Smooth over the join with a Dresden tool to blend the sideburns into the rest of the hair.

4 Roll a ball of Sugar Dough, pinch one side between your finger and thumb and mark across the wide end with a Dresden tool. Secure the paste to the top of the head with the wider end at the front.

5 Smooth over any joins with a Dresden tool to blend the paste then press the tip of a Dresden tool across the top of the quiff to create a spiky effect.

Goatee beard

Roll a pinch of Sugar Dough into a tiny ball. Shape the ball into a small cone, mark on the hair texture with a Dresden tool and secure under the chin with edible glue. Smooth the paste onto the face with a Dresden tool.

Hairstyles for female figures

Bob with side parting

1 Before you start working on the hair, brush edible glue over the head where the hair will be attached.

2 Divide 12g (just under ½oz) of Sugar Dough in your chosen colour into five parts as follows: 4g for the back of the head, 2g for each side of the head, 2g for the top of the head and 2g for the fringe.

3 Flatten the back section into a rounded triangular shape and mark on the hair with a Dresden tool. Gently curl the base of the hair under to make a long bob and attach to the back of the head. Smooth the hair onto the head with a Dresden tool to secure it in place.

4 Shape the two side sections of hair into long, flattened cones and mark on the hair as before. Curl under and attach to the sides of the head. Bring the hair in front of the ear on one side and smooth over any joins with a Dresden tool.

5 Roll the top piece of hair into a ball and pinch the sides down to flatten them slightly. Mark with a Dresden tool as before, attach to the top of the head and smooth down.

6 Shape and texture the fringe as for the side sections of hair, then make a slight kink at the base of the fringe.

Bob with fringe

1 Before you start working on the hair, brush edible glue over the head where the hair will be attached.

2 Divide 9g (¼oz) of Sugar Dough in your chosen colour into four parts: 4g for the back of the head, 2g for the longer side, a pinch for the side piece to go behind the ear and 2g for the fringe.

3 Shape the back section into an oval and flatten it down. Mark on hair with a Dresden tool and curl the bottom under. Attach to the back of the head and smooth the paste down with a Dresden tool.

4 Shape each of the side sections into cones and flatten them down slightly. Mark as before and attach to

the sides of the head: the smaller piece should go behind the left ear. Smooth over any joins with a Dresden tool.

5 Shape the fringe into a triangle, mark on hair with a Dresden tool then make some incisions with a small, sharp knife across the base of the fringe. Attach to the front of the hair and smooth down with a Dresden tool.

Half-up with curls

1 Before you start working on the hair, brush edible glue over the head where the hair will be attached.

2 Divide 10g (¼oz) of Sugar Dough into five parts as follows: 4g for the back of the head, 1g for each of the side

Modelling a bride and groom

Modelling the bride and groom for the top of a wedding cake is the perfect way to add a personalised, finishing touch. The figurines can also be given as a gift for the happy couple to keep. The colours, hairstyles and expressions can, of course, be changed to suit the couple.

sections, 3g for the top section and the remainder will be used to make the curls.

3 Shape the back section into a flattened sausage and mark on hair with a Dresden tool. Curl the base under, attach to the back of the head and smooth down the paste with a Dresden tool.

4 Shape and mark each of the side sections in the same way as for the back section. Attach the side sections at the front of the hairline, bring them around to meet at the back and secure in place with edible glue.

5 Roll the top section of hair into a small sausage, pinch one side between your finger and thumb then mark on hair as before. Secure to the top of the head and smooth over the joins as before.

6 Brush edible glue over the hair where you want to attach the curls. Shape small pieces of paste into teardrop shapes, curl and attach around the hairline and at the join at the back.

EDIBLES

Bride

115g (4oz) Cream Celebration SK Mexican Modelling Paste (MMP)

SK Sugar Dough: 5g (just under ¼oz) Maroon, 25g (just over ¾oz) Soft Beige, pinch of White, 12g (just over ¼oz) Yellow

SK Professional Food Colour Pens: Black, Red

Groom

SK Sugar Dough: 19g (¾oz) Black, 11g (just over ¼oz) Brown, 20g (¾oz) Golden Bear Brown, 95g (3¼oz) White

SK Designer Metallic Lustre Dust Food Colour: Silver

SK Professional Food Colour Pen: Black

EQUIPMENT

2 x 19cm (7½") long wooden barbecue skewers

Jacket template, see page 507

For essential modelling edibles and equipment, see pages 184–185

BRIDE

Shoes

1 Divide 3g (⅛oz) of Cream Celebration MMP into two balls. Shape the balls into cones and flatten down slightly with your fingers. Leave to one side.

Dress

2 Knead 100g (3½oz) of Cream Celebration MMP until soft then roll into a wide sausage that is slightly narrower at one end. Push your thumb into the wider end and pinch the paste downwards to form the wavy hem of the skirt. Push and twist a 19cm (7½") long wooden barbecue skewer into the top of the skirt all the way down and out of the base. Secure the shoes under the base of the skirt so that the tips of the shoes are just showing. Mark fold lines over the base of the skirt with a Dresden tool.

3 Shape 10g (¼oz) of Cream Celebration MMP into a short cylinder and gently press your fingers into the ends to make an oval shape for the bodice. Pinch in the paste at the base of the bodice to make it the same width as the top of the skirt. The wider end of the paste will form the bust. Push your thumb

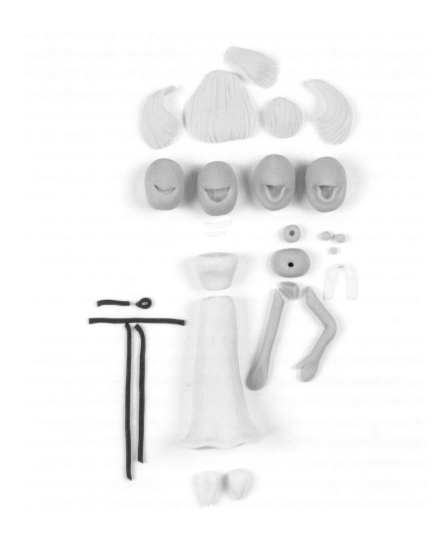

Shoulders and neck

6 Roll a pinch of Soft Beige Sugar Dough into an oval shape that will fit inside the top of the bodice. Push a spare skewer through the middle of the oval to make a hole then remove. Push the paste down onto the skewer sticking out of the dress and secure in place with edible glue.

7 Roll a small ball of Soft Beige Sugar Dough for the neck, make a hole through the paste as before and secure to the shoulders.

Arms

8 Roll 12g (just over ¼oz) of Soft Beige Sugar Dough into a long sausage, then pinch each end between your finger and thumb to form paddle shapes for the hands. Use a small, sharp knife to make a small incision on one side of each hand to bring out the thumbs, then smooth over the cut edges with your finger. Make two diagonal cuts in the centre of the sausage to separate the arms. Mark on the crease of the elbows with a Dresden tool and slightly bend each arm. Secure the arms to the shoulders with a little edible glue and position the hands at the front of the dress.

Strap

9 To make the halterneck strap, roll out a small piece of Cream Celebration MMP and cut out a strip of paste measuring 3mm (¹⁄₈") wide. Attach the strap to one side of the bodice, bring it around the neck, secure to the other side and trim to size if necessary.

Head

10 Make a basic head from Soft Beige Sugar Dough (see page 306). Give the bride an open-mouthed smile with teeth and colour the lips with

into the top of the paste and pinch the paste upwards to make a slight hollow for the shoulders. Make a hole through the centre of the bodice with a spare barbecue skewer then remove. Push the bodice down onto the skewer protruding from the skirt and secure to the top of the skirt with edible glue.

Sash

4 Roll 5g (just under ¼oz) of Maroon Sugar Dough into a long, thin sausage and flatten with a small rolling pin. Cut the paste into 3mm (¹⁄₈") wide strips with a sharp knife. Brush edible glue over the join between the top and skirt

then attach a strip around the waist to make a sash. Trim the ribbon to size and stick the ends down neatly at the back of the bodice. Cut two strips of Maroon Sugar Dough to 9cm and 7.5cm (3½" and 3") long, then brush a little edible glue over the join in the sash and down the back of the skirt. Secure the ends of the sash side-by-side down the back of the dress.

5 For the bow, cut two 1.5cm (½") long pieces from the strips of Sugar Dough. Bring the ends together and secure with a little edible glue to make a bow loop. Attach the bow loops above the ends of the sash and press the end of a Dresden tool into each loop to secure the bow in place.

a Red food colour pen (see page 307). Following the steps on page 310, use Yellow Sugar Dough to make a bob with a side parting and ease the head onto the skewer sticking out of the body. Attach a daisy to the side of the head with edible glue if desired (see instructions for making daisies on pages 315–316).

GROOM

1 Mix together 3g (¹/₈oz) of Black and 80g (2¾oz) of White Sugar Dough to make a light grey colour. Divide the grey paste as follows: 30g (1oz) for the trousers, 3g (¹/₈oz) for the cummerbund, 1g (small pinch) for the bow tie, 12g (½oz) for the jacket and 12g (½oz) for the sleeves.

2 Mix together 20g (¾oz) of Golden Bear Brown Sugar Dough and a small pinch of Brown Sugar Dough to make an olive skin tone. Divide the paste as follows: 2 x 2g (¹/₈oz) for the hands, 1g (small pinch) for the neck, 14g (½oz) for the head, two small balls for the ears and an even smaller ball for the nose.

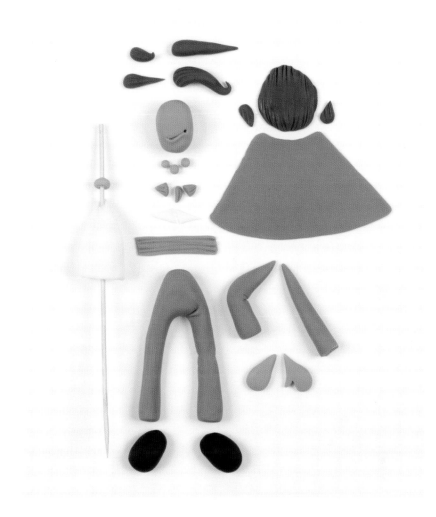

Shoes

3 Divide 8g (¼oz) of Black Sugar Dough in half and shape each piece into an oval for the shoes.

Trousers

4 Roll the trousers into a sausage which is slightly wider in the middle. Bend the paste in half and bring the ends together to make the legs. Cut to the required length with a sharp knife. Carefully push and twist a 19cm (7½") long barbecue skewer through the top of the trousers, down the leg and into one shoe. Attach the second shoe to the bottom of the other trouser leg with edible glue. Pinch the top of the trousers around the skewer to secure and leave to dry.

Shirt

5 Shape 15g (½oz) of White Sugar Dough into a cone for the shirt. Push your thumb into the underside of the wider end and pinch the paste downwards around the edges so it will cover the join of the trousers. Push a spare barbecue skewer through the centre of the shirt to make a hole. Ease the shirt down over the skewer in the trousers and secure in place with edible glue. Mark a line up the centre of the shirt with the back of a knife.

6 Roll the cummerbund into a sausage, flatten the paste down with a small rolling pin and make creases along the paste with a Dresden tool. Cut the sides of the paste straight and make the cummerbund approximately 1cm (³/₈") wide. Brush Silver lustre dust over the cummerbund, then place a little edible glue around the join between the shirt and trousers and secure in place.

7 Roll the paste for the neck into a smooth ball, slightly flatten it between your fingers and make a hole through the centre with a spare skewer. Attach to the top of the shirt with edible glue. To make the collar, roll out a pinch of White Sugar Dough and cut out two small triangles. Attach to the top of the shirt and over the neck.

to make two arms of equal length. Use a Dresden tool to mark creases halfway along the arms for the elbows. Push the end of a paintbrush into the wider end of each arm to fit the hands inside. Bend the right arm at the elbow and attach it to the top of the jacket with edible glue. Position the arm across the jacket so the paste gathers under the arm and rests over the cummerbund. Press the top of the shoulder with a Dresden tool to secure the sleeve to the jacket. Attach the other arm to the shoulder as before but this time rest the arm across the back of the bride.

Hands

11 Shape each piece of paste for the hands into a cone and flatten the paste slightly between your fingers. Use a small, sharp knife to make an incision on one side of the paste, ease it out a little to form the thumb and smooth over the cut edge with your finger. Secure the hands inside each of the cuffs with edible glue. Position the right hand over the cummerbund and the left behind the bride's back.

Head

12 Make a basic head from 14g (½oz) of olive skin-tone paste (see page 305). Give the groom a sideways smile (see page 307) and use Brown Sugar Dough to make longer hair (see page 308). Ease the head over the skewer sticking out of the body and secure with edible glue.

13 Attach a daisy to the lapel with a dot of royal icing if desired (see instructions for making daisies on pages 315–316).

8 Take the grey paste for the bow tie and pinch out a very small ball for the centre. Divide the remaining paste in half and shape each piece into a triangle. Use a Dresden tool to mark two creases from one corner of each triangle, then attach the triangles close together at the base of the groom's neck. Flatten the small ball for the centre between your fingers, mark a few creases across the paste with a Dresden tool, then secure this onto the middle of the bow. Cut the centre to size and fold the ends to the back of the tie.

Jacket

9 Roll out 12g (½oz) of grey paste thinly and cut out the jacket following the template on page 507. Brush edible glue across the back and sides of the shirt and wrap the jacket around the body. Fold the front of the jacket back on itself and turn out the lapels.

10 Roll the grey paste for the sleeves into a sausage and bring both ends to a rounded point. Cut the sausage in half with a small, sharp knife

Three-tier Wedding Party Cake

As well as the traditional bride and groom on top of the cake, the offset design allows plenty of room for the rest of the bridal party. Bridesmaids, pageboys and choristers all make an appearance on this contemporary design, but you could add a vicar, parents of the bride and groom, or perhaps a tipsy best man!

EDIBLES

15cm, 20.5cm and 25.5cm (6", 8" and 10") square sponge cakes, filled and crumb-coated, see page 92

3kg (6lb 9¾oz) SK Sugarpaste: Vintage Ivory

SK Instant Mix Royal Icing

SK Designer Metallic Lustre Dust Food Colour: Silver

SK Professional Paste Food Colours: Cyclamen, Fuchsia

SK Professional Food Colour Pens: Black, Red

Bride, see instructions on pages 311–313

Groom, see instructions on pages 313–314

Standing bridesmaid

SK Sugar Dough: 5g (just under ¼oz) Maroon, 20g (¾oz) Soft Beige, 62g (2¼oz) White, 10g (¼oz) Yellow

Sitting bridesmaid

SK Sugar Dough: 9g (¼oz) Brown, 20g (¾oz) Golden Bear Brown, 5g (just under ¼oz) Maroon, 42g (1½oz) White

Gospel choir

SK Sugar Dough: 53g (2oz) Black, 32g (1oz) Brown, 51g (1¾oz) Maroon, 170g (5¾oz) White

Standing pageboy

SK Sugar Dough: 15g (½oz) Black, 10g (¼oz) Soft Beige, 60g (2oz) White, 8g (¼oz) Yellow

Lying pageboy

SK Sugar Dough: 12g (½oz) Brown, 15g (½oz) Black, 10g (¼oz) Golden Bear Brown, 60g (2oz) White

Blossoms

SK Sugar Dough: 1g (small pinch) Green, 90g (3oz) White, 10g (¼oz) Yellow

EQUIPMENT

35.5cm and 40.5cm (14" and 16") square cake drums (boards)

15cm and 20.5cm (6" and 8") square cake boards

Cake dowels

Several barbecue skewers

2.2m (90") x 15mm (½") wide satin ribbon: light pink

3.3m (132") x 15mm (½") wide satin ribbon: silver

5-in-1 blossom cutter: F2M (OP)

Piping bag

Piping nozzle: no.1

5cm (2") long piece of raw spaghetti

Cake and board

1 Cover both of the cake drums with Vintage Ivory sugarpaste (see page 141). Trim the 40.5cm (16") cake drum with silver ribbon and the 35.5cm (14") cake drum with light pink ribbon. Position the smaller cake drum centrally on top of the larger drum and secure in place with royal icing.

2 Cover all of the cakes with Vintage Ivory sugarpaste (see pages 139-140). Place the 25.5cm (10") cake on the 35.5cm (14") cake drum at a 45° angle and secure in place with a little royal icing or softened sugarpaste. Dowel the base tier then secure the 20.5cm (8") cake on top at a different angle (see page 143). Dowel the second tier in the same way and secure the third tier on top. Trim the base and top tiers with silver ribbon and the second tier with light pink ribbon.

3 Position the bride and groom in the centre of the top tier and insert the skewers sticking out of the bottom of the figures into the sugarpaste.

Daisies

4 Roll out a small amount of White Sugar Dough at a time and cut out several blossoms with a small blossom cutter. Cut each petal in half lengthways with a small, sharp knife and secure one

For essential modelling edibles and equipment, see pages 184–185

blossom on top of another: you will need 200 blossoms to make 100 daisies for this cake. Push the end of a paintbrush into the centre of each flower and leave to dry.

5   Dilute a small amount of Fuchsia paste food colour with a little cooled, boiled water and paint 50 daisies with the mixture. Dilute some Cyclamen paste food colour in the same way, paint 50 more blossoms and leave to dry. Roll out a tiny ball of Yellow Sugar Dough for each daisy, push the paste into the centre and mark with the end of a Dresden tool. Reserve 18 daisies for the lapels and bouquets then secure the remaining flowers around the cake and board with royal icing.

6   To make a bouquet, mix 7g (¼oz) of White Sugar Dough with a pinch of Green Sugar Dough to make a pale green colour. Divide the paste into three equal parts, then divide each piece in half again. Roll a piece of green paste into a sausage shape for the handle of the bouquet and mark with a Dresden tool. Roll the remaining paste into a ball, secure on top of the handle and leave to dry. Once dry, attach 4–5 daisies around the green paste with a little royal icing: you will need three bouquets for this cake once they are secured to the bride, bridesmaid and cake top.

Standing bridesmaid

7   Colour 62g (2¼oz) of White Sugar Dough with a small amount of Fuchsia paste food colour to make it pale pink. Divide the pink paste as follows: 5g (just under ¼oz) for the shoes, 50g (1¾oz) for the skirt and 7g (¼oz) for the top of the dress.

8   Make the skirt, shoes and sash in the same way as for the bride, using a 10.5cm (4¼") long skewer (see pages 311–312). Only push the skewer down as far as the shoe, then secure the figure to the cake drum with edible glue.

9   Shape the pink paste for the top of the dress into an oval, then push the larger end of a bone tool into the top to make room for the neck. Make a hole through the middle with a spare barbecue skewer, then push it down the skewer sticking out of the skirt and secure in place with edible glue. Attach the sash around the waist (see page 312).

10   Divide 1g (small pinch) of Soft Beige Sugar Dough into two: one piece should be slightly larger than the other. Roll each piece into a ball then make a hole through the centre of each piece with a spare barbecue skewer.

Brush a little edible glue over the top of the dress and secure the slightly larger ball in place first, then attach the smaller piece on top for the neck.

11   Make the arms and hands in the same way as for the bride on page 312. Secure one arm across the front of the dress and rest the other over the side of the base tier.

12   Make a basic head from 10g (¼oz) of Soft Beige Sugar Dough (see page 306). Give the bridesmaid a pouting mouth (see page 307) and secure below the nose. Use Yellow Sugar Dough to make a half-up hairstyle with curls, following the instructions on pages 310–311. Attach a bouquet in the bridesmaid's right hand with edible glue.

Sitting bridesmaid

13   Reserve 5g (just under ¼oz) of White Sugar Dough for the petticoat then colour the remainder with a little Fuchsia paste food colour to match the other bridesmaid's dress. Divide the pale pink paste as follows: 3g (⅛oz) for the shoes, 30g (1oz) for the skirt and 4g (just under ¼oz) for the top of the dress.

14 Mix the paste for an olive skin tone (see page 305) and divide the paste as follows: 2g (pinch) for the legs, 1g (small pinch) for the neck, 8g (¼oz) for the arms and 10g (just over ¼oz) for the head.

15 Take the paste for the shoes and pinch out a tiny ball of pale pink paste for the straps. Roll the remaining paste for the shoes into two equal balls, then push the small end of a bone tool into one side of each shoe. Divide the legs into two equal pieces and shape each piece into a cone. Secure the rounded end of the legs into each shoe then brush a little edible glue on either side of the shoe. Roll the tiny ball of paste for the straps into a sausage, cut it in half and attach a strip across each shoe.

16 Make the skirt in the same way as for the bride (see page 311), but bend it slightly in the middle so it looks like she is sitting down. Sit the skirt on top of the first tier and secure with edible glue. Roll some White Sugar Dough into a sausage, flatten it down and mark folds across the paste with the end of a paintbrush. Attach inside the base of the skirt as a petticoat. Secure the legs to the underside of the petticoat and over the side of the cake with edible

glue. Push a 10cm (4") long skewer in through the top of the skirt and into the cake to secure.

17 Make the top of the dress, sash, neck and arms in the same way as for the standing bridesmaid and attach (see opposite). Secure the hands to the front of the dress and attach a daisy between the hands with a little royal icing.

18 Make a basic head with a smile from 10g (just over ¼oz) of olive skin tone paste (see page 306). Make a bob with a fringe from Brown Sugar Dough (see page 310) then ease the head over the skewer sticking out of the body and secure to the neck.

Gospel choir

First chorister

19 Divide 8g (¼oz) of Black Sugar Dough in half and shape each piece into ovals for the shoes. Position on the cake drum and secure with edible glue.

20 For the cassock, roll 15g (½oz) of Maroon Sugar Dough into a

small cone and shape in the same way as for the skirt of the bride's dress (see page 311). Model 35g (1¼oz) of White Sugar Dough into a larger cone and shape as for the cassock. Fit the surplice over the top of the cassock and secure with edible glue. Push and twist an 11.5cm (4½") long barbecue skewer into the body, mark a line up the front of the surplice with the back of a small knife then use a Dresden tool to mark folds around the base.

21 Divide 18g (just over ½oz) of White Sugar Dough in half, shape each piece into long triangles and bend slightly to make the sleeves. Push a Dresden tool into the wider end of the sleeve and pinch the end of the sleeves into a point. Press the end of a paintbrush into the top of the wider end to fit the hands inside. Attach the sleeves to the top of the body and bring them around to the front. Roll two small balls of Maroon Sugar Dough, push the end of a paintbrush into each ball and secure inside the sleeves as cuffs.

22 Make each of the hands from 1g (small pinch) of Black Sugar Dough in the same way as for the groom's hands (see page 314). Secure the hands inside each sleeve, position them upwards and rest the second hand over the first.

23 For the hymn book, roll out 1g (small pinch) of White Sugar Dough to 3mm (1/8") thick and cut out a rectangle that is 2cm x 1.4cm (¾" x ½") in size. Mark down the middle of each rectangle with the back of a small knife. Roll out 1g of Black Sugar Dough and cut out a slightly larger rectangle for the book cover. Secure the white rectangle on top of the black cover with edible glue and bend the sides upwards. To finish, draw wiggly lines over the pages with a Black food colour pen. Secure the hymn book on top of the hands with edible glue.

24 Roll 1g (small pinch) of Maroon Sugar Dough into a small ball and make a hole through the centre with a spare barbecue skewer. Push the collar down the skewer sticking out of the body and secure to the surplice with edible glue. Divide 2g (pinch) of White Sugar Dough into three equal balls, then flatten them into discs between your finger and thumb. Mark lines around each disc with a Dresden tool and make a hole in the centre of each with a spare skewer. Secure the three discs on top of each other over the neck.

25 Make a basic head from 9g (¼oz) of Brown Sugar Dough in the same way as for the bride. Open up the mouth as if singing (see page 308) and draw on the closed eyes (see page 306). Using Black Sugar Dough, follow the instructions for making short hair and a goatee beard on page 309. Ease the head down onto the neck ruff and secure with edible glue.

Second chorister

26 To make the second chorister, follow the steps for the first chorister (see overleaf). Make the basic head using 12g (½oz) of Brown Sugar Dough (see page 306) then make a slight indent in either side of the face with a bone tool to bring out the cheeks and open the mouth as if singing (see page 308). Make short hair as for the first chorister but use 8g (¼oz) of Black Sugar Dough and make the sideburns longer and the top section much bigger (see page 308).

Third chorister

27 To make the third chorister, follow the steps for the first chorister (see overleaf). As the third chorister's cassock is being lifted by a stick, make sure to lift one side up a little by the side of the shoe. Make the basic head using 10g (½oz) of Brown Sugar Dough (see page 306) and use Black Sugar Dough to make curly hair following the instructions on page 309.

Standing pageboy

28 Make the pageboy in the same way as for the groom but using Soft Beige Sugar Dough for the skin colour and a 12.5cm (5") long barbecue skewer (see pages 313–314). Secure the pageboy into the third tier with the left leg slightly behind the right, rest the back foot up on its toe and mark the heel of the shoe with the blunt edge of a small knife. Bring one arm around to the front of the jacket and position the other resting on the corner of the third tier. Give the pageboy an open-mouthed smile without teeth (see page 307) and use Yellow Sugar Dough to create a short hairstyle with a quiff following the instructions on page 309.

Lying pageboy

29 Make the pageboy in the same way as for the groom using the olive skin tone paste (see pages 313–314) but position the pageboy so he is lying down. Do not skewer the legs but rest them over the two cake drums then twist a 6.5cm (2½") long skewer down through the shirt into the trousers and continue to construct in the same way as the groom. Position one arm against the side of the cake and the other along the top of the cake drums. Mark the heels of both shoes with the back of a small knife. Make the basic head and smile (see page 306) then ease the head onto the skewer and position so that he is looking towards the gospel choir.

30 Make two small balls and one slightly larger ball of Brown Sugar Dough for the stick. Roll a pinch of Brown Sugar Dough into a small sausage and insert a piece of glued, raw spaghetti along the paste. Roll the small balls into thin sausages and attach to the top of the stick. Roll the remaining ball into a small sausage, make a 5mm (¼") cut along the centre and attach to the stick. Once dry, attach the stick inside the pageboy's hand and secure the other end under the chorister's cassock. Support with a little kitchen paper whilst drying.

Naomi Yamamoto

BIOGRAPHY

My sugarcraft career is a result of two important aspects: my passion inherited from my mother, and some lucky encounters in my life.

My mother was a passionate painter; she was especially good at portraits with a touch of Degas. When I was a little girl, the house was full of her paintings and artistic works such as elaborate embroidery and knitting designs. I was her little daughter who loved flowers. I have always liked decorating with flowers and so it is no wonder that cake decorating attracts me so much.

I made my first decorated cake soon after my marriage, when my daughter was still little. My favourite hobby was to bake cakes for celebrations and I was always curious about how to decorate cakes beautifully to make them look really special. At that time in Japan, there were no decorated cakes or cake decorating lessons, so when my family moved to the US for three years, it was a delightful chance for me to learn how to decorate cakes. When my daughter had her second birthday party, I made a tall two-tier birthday cake decorated in pink with an elephant on top – it was a lovely moment.

After our return to Japan, people who were interested in sugarcraft came to my home to have private lessons. Meanwhile, I returned to the US and travelled to England to learn sugarcraft professionally. My students and I held exhibitions in Japan and sugarcraft started to appear in the media.

One of the most important encounters in my career happened in 1985, when Meiji Kinenkan, the prestigious wedding ceremony company, phoned me. Known for being the wedding company for the Japanese royal family, they had a new sugarcraft school project. At that time, the royal wedding of Prince Charles and Lady Diana in England was big news in Japan, and their beautifully decorated wedding cake caught the attention of Japanese people. It was the start of a busy career as an executive instructor at the Genteel Academy of Meiji Kinenkan in Tokyo, where I taught sugarcraft for 13 years. The relationship between Brooklands College in the UK and the Genteel Academy was very enriching – we learned so much from instructors from the college who came to Japan every year to give sugarcraft lessons to the students, and little by little sugarcraft came to be well-known throughout Japan.

Another significant connection for me was with Beverley Dutton, Managing Director of Squires Kitchen. When Squires Kitchen first published *Wedding Cakes – A Design Source* in 1999, I submitted photos of my work to the magazine. Beverley kindly included them in the following issues and my work was featured on three front covers.

Beverley and her husband Robert welcome me very warmly every time I visit Farnham for the annual Squires Kitchen Exhibition. It has a unique and special atmosphere, which makes me always look forward to coming back although it is far from Japan. I wish sugarcraft could be integrated into Japanese confectionery culture, as much as bakery and chocolate.

My own creations started to appear in Japanese media, including TV, as well as internationally at the Squires Kitchen Exhibition and the BSG's International Exhibition in 2004. Since then, I have been teaching sugarcraft at Squires Kitchen International School and at the Japan Confectionery School in Tokyo. I also teach sugarcraft in Korea and students from overseas come to my atelier in Tokyo to have private lessons. I would like to send my sincere thanks to all the motivated international students whom I have met at both schools. It makes me happy to think of so many young, passionate students actively working on sugarcraft in their home countries around the world, including South East Asia.

My first book, *Delicate Sugarcraft from Japan*, was published by Shibata Shoten in August 2007. It was a big project which I started at the same time as teaching at the Genteel Academy. Although it is in Japanese, I am delighted to hear that people abroad are interested in the rich quality of the photos and explanations in my book. In March 2013, *Wedding Cakes: The Couture Collection* was published by B. Dutton Publishing. It was truly an honour for me to write this book and I am deeply appreciative to everyone involved.

Making Frill Decorations

NAOMI YAMAMOTO

Delicate-looking ruffles and frills make beautiful decorations for wedding cakes. There are various ways to incorporate frills into a cake design — here I have shown how to make simple frills, layered frills, frilled flowers and lacy frills, as well as pleated sashes and pearl decorations to complement the design.

EDIBLES

Horizontal pleated sash

120g (4¼oz) SK Sugar Florist Paste (SFP) in the colour of your choice

Vertical pleated sash

120g (4¼oz) SK Sugar Florist Paste (SFP) mixed with 30g (1oz) SK Sugarpaste in the colours of your choice

Layered and single frills

SK Sugar Florist Paste (SFP) in the colour of your choice

Frilled flowers

Modelling paste (3 parts SK Sugarpaste + 1 part SK Sugar Florist Paste (SFP)) in the colour of your choice

Lace frills

SK Flexi-Ice

EQUIPMENT

Pasta machine (optional)

Large palette knife

Round cutters: 2.5cm, 5cm, 6cm, 7.5cm, 8cm, 9cm, 10cm and 11cm (1", 2", 2³/₈", 3", 3¹/₈", 3½", 4" and 4¼")

Bead makers: 4mm and 8mm (¹/₈" and ¼")

Aluminium foil

5-petal blossom cutters: F6 (6cm, 2³/₈"), F6B (9cm, 3½") (OP)

Silicone lace mat: leaves

For essential modelling edibles and equipment, see pages 184–185

TECHNIQUES

- Making pleated sashes
- Making frill decorations
- Making frilled fantasy flowers
- Making lace frills

tutor tip

When you are making frills you will need to use a mixture of SFP and sugarpaste. If you find the paste is too firm then add some sugarpaste to the mixture to soften it; if the paste is too soft, add some SFP to make it firmer.

Horizontal pleated sash

The following steps explain how to make a sash that is long enough to wrap around a 20.5cm (8") round cake.

1 Roll out 120g (4¼oz) of SFP in the colour of your choice very thinly. It is easiest to do this with a pasta machine: roll out the paste lightly with a rolling pin first, adjust the pasta machine so that it is on the first or second setting then feed the paste through the machine. Change the pasta machine to a higher setting and repeat to make thinner and longer strips of paste. Alternatively, use a rolling pin to roll the paste thinly into a long rectangle.

2 Cut out one long strip of paste that is approximately 12cm (4¾") wide x 35cm (14") long and a second strip that is 12cm (4¾") wide x 37cm (14½") long. Fold back the edges of the longest sides

a little to make them neater, then use a large palette knife to fold the length of the paste over by 2cm (¾"). Fold the paste back over again by 1cm (³/₈") to make a pleat in the paste. Repeat this three times to make darts that are 1cm (³/₈") apart and a sash that is 5cm (2") wide. Do the same with the 37cm (14½") long strip of paste. Dust with lustre dust if desired.

3 Secure the 35cm (14") long sash around the side of a cake with edible glue. Fold back both ends of the 37cm (14½") long sash a little and, starting from the end of the first sash, attach the second sash around the remainder of the cake.

Vertical pleated sash

The following steps explain how to make a vertical sash that is 15cm (6") long.

1 Mix together 30g (1oz) of sugarpaste and 120g (4¼oz) of SFP in the colours of your choice. Roll the modelling paste out thinly and cut out a strip that is 10cm (4") wide x 15cm (6") long.

2 Fold back the edges of the longest side a little to make them neater, then use a large palette knife to fold the length of the paste over by 1cm (³/₈"). Fold the paste back over itself again by 5mm (¼"). Repeat this again to make a second 5mm (¼") pleat. Repeat on the opposite side of the paste to make a sash that is 4cm (1½") wide. Brush with lustre dust if desired.

3 Attach the sash vertically down the side of the cake with edible glue.

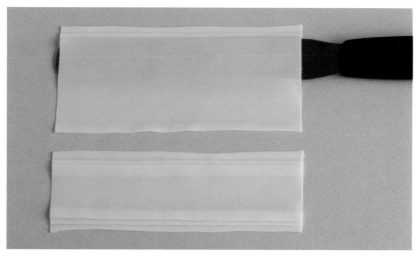

Making Frill Decorations

323

Frill decorations

Layered frill

1 Roll out some SFP in the colour of your choice very thinly and cut out several circles from the paste using 9cm, 10cm and 11cm (3½", 4" and 4¼") round cutters. Flare the paste around the edge of each circle with a ball tool.

2 Layer three different-sized circles on top of each other, starting with the largest first and making sure each circle is central within the previous layer. Position a 2.5cm (1'') round cutter in the middle of the paste and cut out a circle from the centre to make a ring. Dust with White Satin lustre dust, if desired.

3 Make a single cut in the ring of paste from the edge to the central hole and open out the ring on a non-stick board. Hold one end of the ring and fold the paste loosely from side to side to make a ruffled vertical band. Adjust the overlapping paste to make the ruffles sit neatly.

Single frill

1 Roll out some SFP very thinly and cut out several circles with 6cm (2³/₈") and 5cm (2") round cutters to make different-sized frills. Flare the edges of each circle with a ball tool and brush with lustre dust if desired.

2 Fold each circle in half, leaving a 5mm (¼") gap between the edges. Loosely overlap the sides of the semicircle to make a vertical band. This frill is ideal for filling in gaps between larger frills or frilled flowers.

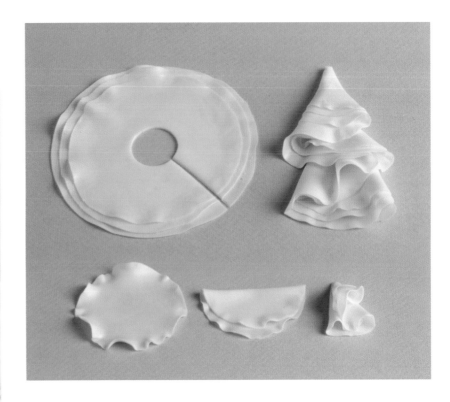

Frilled fantasy flowers

Round frilled flower

1 Make one large pearl with some White SFP and an 8mm (¼") bead maker then leave it to dry. Make a string of pearls using White SFP and the 4mm (⅛") bead maker (see page 328). Secure the string of pearls around the larger pearl and leave it to dry.

2 Make up approximately 35g (1¼oz) of modelling paste (3 parts sugarpaste + 1 part SFP) in the colour of your choice for one flower. Roll out the modelling paste thinly and cut out 10cm (4"), 9cm (3½"), 8cm (3⅛"), 7.5cm (3") and 6cm (2³/₈") circles with each of the round cutters. Flare the edge of the paste around the circle with a ball tool. Starting with the largest, layer the circles on top of each other in descending size order, making sure they sit centrally within the previous circle. Dust with lustre dust if desired.

3 Cut out a 12cm (4¾") square of aluminium foil, then make a single cut from the corner to the centre. Overlap the cut edges and fold out the two corners to make a cupped former. Place the layered paste into the cup, pinch the bottom of the foil and press a ball tool into the centre of the paste to make a pleated, cupped shape.

4 Shape the edge of the paste with your fingers to make five or six waves around the flower. Make a small ball of White sugarpaste and secure it in the centre of the flower. Make a space in the centre of the flower with a ball tool and secure the pearl decoration onto the ball. Leave it to half-dry inside the foil.

Blossom-shaped frilled flower

1 Make up approximately 40g (1½oz) of modelling paste (3 parts sugarpaste + 1 part SFP) in the colour of your choice for one flower. Roll the paste out thinly and cut out a circle with the 11cm (4¼") and 10cm (4") round cutters. Flare the edge of the circles with a ball tool.

2 Cut out two blossoms from the modelling paste with the 9cm (3½") 5-petal cutter, and one blossom with the second smaller 6cm (2³/₈") 5-petal cutter. Make gathers in the paste with a bamboo skewer and flare with a ball tool. Dust all the pieces with lustre dust if desired.

3 Starting with the largest, lay the circles on top of each other then layer the blossoms on top. Follow steps 3 and 4 for the round frilled flower to shape.

Lace frills

1 Make up the mixture following the instructions on the packet. The mixture should be a creamy consistency.

2 Spread the mixture over the silicone lace mould, ensuring the mould is completely covered. Leave the mixture to set between half a day and a day, depending on the humidity. You can check whether it has set by gently touching the surface of the mix. If it is dry, lift the edge of the lace a little to see whether you can easily remove it from the mould. If it does not come away easily, then leave it to set further. Do not force the paste out of the mould or it will tear.

3 Carefully peel back the mould to release the lace. While the paste is still soft, cut the lace into 5cm (2") wide strips and gather the bottom of each section with your fingers to create a fan shape. Attach it to the cake immediately with edible glue.

tutor tip

Be aware that lace mixes are quite sensitive to humidity: you need to be careful when the humidity is higher than 50% as the paste will take a long time to dry and won't hold its shape as well. If there is low humidity the paste will dry very quickly, so you need to work fast while the lace is still soft.

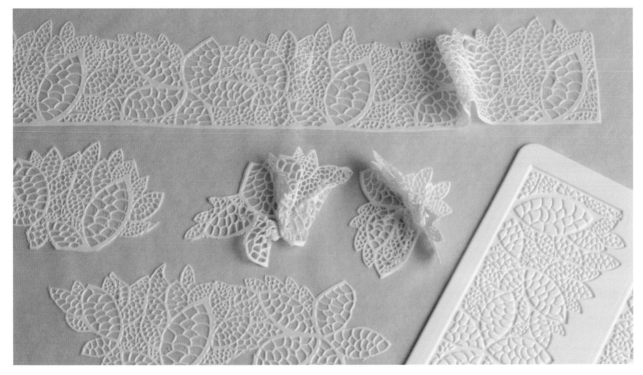

Making Frill Decorations

Cascading Frills Wedding Cake

Ruffles, frills and delicate lace pieces make this cake the perfect romantic centrepiece for a couple's special day. This pretty design demonstrates how frilled decorations can be used in a contemporary way to make a cake that is both beautiful and refined.

EDIBLES

3 x round cakes:

    2 x 20.5cm (8") x 9cm (3½") deep

    12.5cm (5") x 10cm (4") deep

2.2kg (5lb) SK Marzipan (optional)

SK Sugarpaste: 2.22kg (5lb) Antique Lace, 110g (3¾oz) Bridal White

SK Sugar Florist Paste (SFP): 1.17kg (3lb) Cream, 720g (1lb 9½oz) White

300g (10½oz) SK Flexi-Ice

SK Instant Mix Royal Icing

SK Designer Bridal Satin Lustre Dust Food Colours: Light Silver, White Satin

SK Edible Glue

Clear alcohol or cooled, boiled water

EQUIPMENT

20.5cm (8") round cake board

12.5cm, 15cm and 20.5cm (5", 6" and 8") round cake cards

Cake dowels

Bead makers: 4mm and 8mm (1/8" and ¼")

Round cutters: 2.5cm, 5cm, 6cm, 7.5cm, 8cm, 9cm, 10cm and 11cm (1", 2", 2³/8", 3", 3¹/8", 3½", 4" and 4½")

5-petal blossom cutters: F6 (6cm, 2³/8"), F6B (9cm, 3½") (OP)

Bamboo skewer

Aluminium foil

Silicone lace mat: leaves

For essential modelling edibles and equipment, see pages 184–185

Cakes

1 Secure the first 20.5cm (8'') cake onto the cake board of the same size and cover with marzipan if desired (see page 96). Dowel the cake with five dowels: place one dowel in the centre of the cake and evenly space the others 5cm (2") from the central dowel (see page 143).

2 Place a 15cm (6'') cake card centrally on top of the second 20.5cm (8'') cake. Insert cocktail sticks at approximately 6cm (2³/8") intervals around the sides and 3cm (1¹/8") down from the top of the cake. Use a sharp, serrated knife to cut away the cake between the cocktail sticks and the cake card to make the cake dome shaped. When you are happy with the shape, remove the cake card and the cocktail sticks. Secure the cake onto a 20.5cm (8'') cake card and cover with 800g (1lb 12oz) of marzipan if desired. Dowel the cake with four dowels, inserting them 4cm (1½") out from the centre of the cake (see page 143).

3 Secure the second cake on top of the first, with a small amount of royal icing. Cover both cakes all in one go with 1.7kg (3lb 12oz) of Antique Lace sugarpaste (see pages 139–140). Leave the cake to dry overnight.

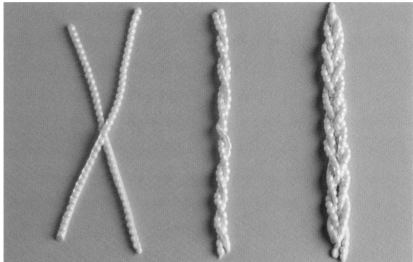

4 Mark six evenly-spaced points around the top of the cake with a scribing needle as a guide for attaching the frill decorations later.

5 Trim the top edge off the 12.5cm (5") cake with a sharp, serrated knife to make the top of the cake rounded. Cover the cake with 500g (1lb 1¾oz) of marzipan if desired (see page 96), then cover with 500g (1lb 1¾oz) of Antique Lace sugarpaste (see pages 139–140) and leave to dry overnight. Secure the cake on top of the base tier with a little royal icing.

6 Mark six evenly-spaced points around the top and bottom of the cake with a scribing needle, making sure to line them up with the marks on the tier below.

Sashes

7 Mix together 90g (3oz) of Cream SFP with 30g (1oz) of White SFP and make a horizontal pleated sash following the steps on page 323. Dust the sash with White Satin lustre dust and secure around the base of the cake with edible glue.

8 Mix together 30g (1oz) of Antique Lace sugarpaste and 120g (4¼oz) of White SFP and make a vertical pleated sash following the steps on page 323. Dust with White Satin lustre dust and attach vertically between the points on the top and bottom of the second tier. Repeat to make five more sashes in the same way then secure them vertically between the points marked out around the cake.

Pearl decorations

9 Knead 300g (10½oz) of White SFP well, then roll some of it out into a long, thin sausage. Dust the 4mm (¹/₈") bead maker with Light Silver lustre dust and place the paste in the mould to make a string of pearls (see page 161). Make two lengths and twist them together to make one plaited pearl chain. Secure with edible glue whilst the paste is still soft. Make 11 more plaited pearl chains from the remaining paste and secure them immediately onto the sash around the base of the cake. You should have enough to make a double layer of pearls.

10 Make six more plaited pearl chains as before and secure one down the centre of each vertical sash on the top tier with edible glue.

Frills

11 Mix 750g (1lb 10½oz) of Cream SFP and 250g (8¾oz) of White SFP together and make five sets of layered frills following the steps on page 324. At one of the marks you made earlier, measure 2cm (¾") up from the base of the bottom tier, brush a little edible glue over the back of the frill and attach it up the side of the cake.

12 Starting from the top of the first set of frills, secure the second and third sets either side of the previous set. Secure the fourth and fifth sets in the same way above the previous frills, so the frill decoration finishes at the top of the bottom tier. Adjust the frills with your fingers so that they hide any joins. Make and secure another five sets of frills around the cake at each of the five remaining marks you made earlier.

Frilled flowers

13 Mix 50g (1¾oz) of Bridal White sugarpaste with 150g (5¼oz) of Cream SFP and make six round frilled flowers (see page 325). Secure one flower to the top of each frill decoration around the bottom tier with edible glue.

14 Mix together 60g (2oz) of Bridal White sugarpaste and 180g (6¼oz) of Cream SFP and make six blossom-shaped frilled flowers (see page 325). Position five frilled flowers on the top tier in a wreath shape and secure with edible glue. Adjust the frills with your fingers so that the flowers look like they are merging together.

15 Make a small ball of Antique Lace sugarpaste, secure it in the centre of the wreath and attach the final flower onto the paste: the ball of paste allows the central flower to sit a little higher than the other flowers. Adjust the flowers again to make the arrangement look more dome shaped. Make six pearls with the 8mm (¼") bead maker (see page 161) and glue one into the centre of each flower.

Finishing touches

16 Make a few strings of pearls and secure them into any gaps between the frilled flowers. Make several single frills (see opposite) and secure them between any remaining gaps in the flowers to fill out the arrangement.

17 To finish, make six lace frills (see page 326) and secure them behind each frilled flower on the bottom tier.

Animated Animals

CARLOS LISCHETTI

Once you've practised the basic skills you need for modelling figures, the next step is to bring your characters to life and personalise them with different expressions, poses and clothing. Although the male and female cats explained here are both modelled from the same basic shapes, this project demonstrates how you can create unique, expressive characters by combining different proportions, textures and colours. By giving animals human characteristics you can create cute figures that almost have a life of their own.

TECHNIQUES

- Proportions of animated characters
- Facial features
- Transporting sugar figurines
- Modelling animated cats

EDIBLES

SK Mexican Modelling Paste (MMP): 50g (1¾oz) Black, 300g (10½oz) White, 10g (¼oz) White coloured with Cyclamen and a touch of Poppy Paste Food Colours, 50g (1¾oz) White coloured with a touch of Marigold (tangerine) Paste Food Colour, 10g (¼oz) White coloured with Poppy Paste Food Colour, 300g (10½oz) White coloured with a touch of Wisteria Paste Food Colour, 10g (¼oz) White coloured with a touch of Rose Paste Food Colour

SK Sugar Florist Paste (SFP): 150g (5¼oz) White, 50g (1¾oz) White coloured with Wisteria Paste Food Colour, 10g (¼oz) Soft Lilac

50g (1¾oz) SK Instant Mix Royal Icing

SK Professional Paste Food Colours: Cyclamen, Daffodil, Poppy, Wisteria

SK Professional Dust Food Colours: Cyclamen, Fuchsia, Violet

SK Quality Food Colour (QFC) Dust: Black

SK Designer Pastel Dust Food Colour: Pale Peach

SK Professional Food Colour Pen: Black

SK CMC Gum

EQUIPMENT

Spare cake dummy or polystyrene block

Bulbous cone tool

Pliers

Stephanotis petal cutter, set of 3 (TT)

Rose petal cutters, set of 3 (TT)

Paintbrushes: nos. 00, 3, 10

Small scissors

White stamens

Paper piping bags

Plastic dowels

Templates, see pages 508

For essential modelling edibles and equipment, see pages 184–185

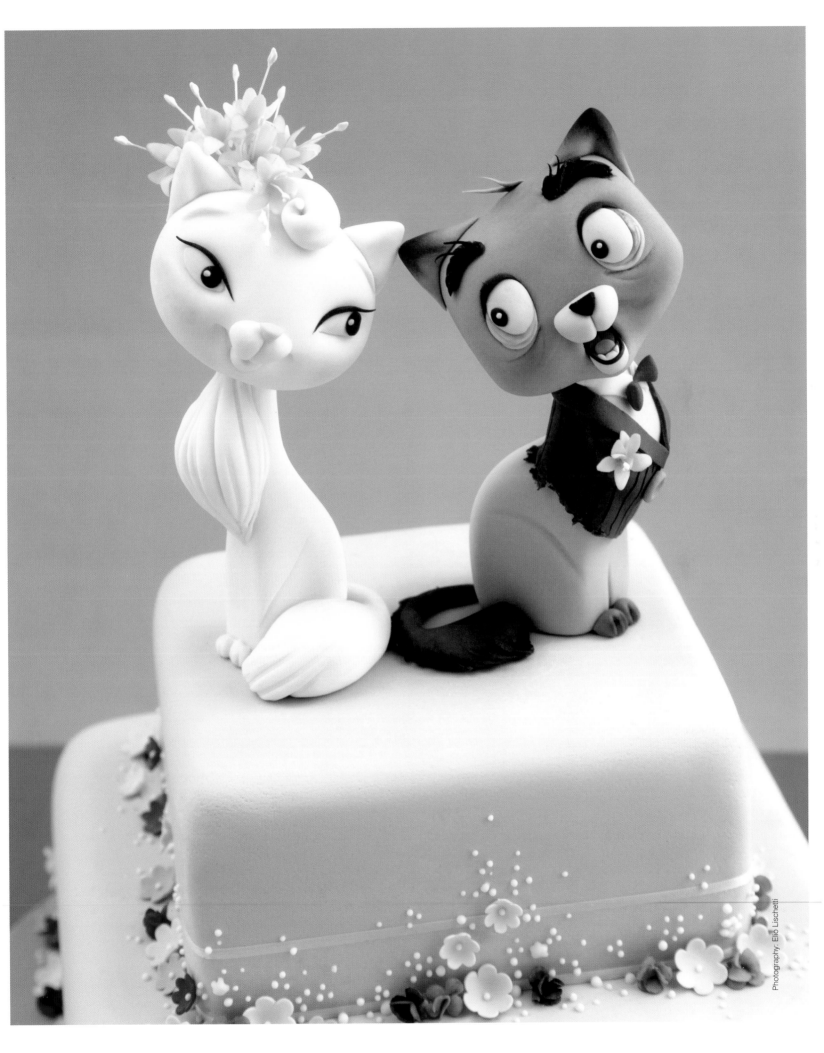

Proportions of animated characters

When modelling animated characters the proportions of the figurines affect whether they look cute (larger head) or more realistic (smaller head). If you make the head roughly the same size as the torso you will end up with a cute-looking character. You can vary this head:torso ratio if you want to create a specific type of figure, but the volume of both the head and torso should be roughly the same if you want to create cute human or animal characters.

As well as experimenting with different head:torso ratios you can make the legs, arms, or neck longer to stylize the character.

Facial features

You can portray different ages simply by moving the eyes. Once you have made the head, draw an imaginary line across the middle of the face. To make a young person or animal place the eyes below this line; for an older character place the eyes on or above the line.

As a rule, the lower the eyes are from the middle line, the younger the character looks; the higher they are above the line the older the character looks.

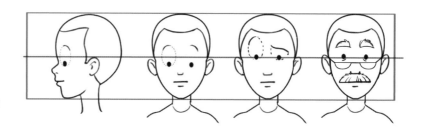

Transporting sugar figurines

Once you have made your sugar models you need to make sure you transport them safely to the venue where the cake will be served. These tips should help you avoid damaging your work in transit, especially when you are travelling long distances. If you don't have to take the cake anywhere or if you are making more robust figurines you may not have to take any precautions, simply place them onto the cake when they are finished.

1 Place the figurine, which must be fully dry, in a cake box which has a piece of polystyrene in the bottom. Stick several cocktail sticks into the polystyrene around the figurine to stop it rolling around. When transporting a slender figurine, place it lying down on the polystyrene as shown in the picture to prevent it from wobbling about on the cake.

2 Depending on the type of figure you are transporting you can also fill in the spaces between the polystyrene base and the figure itself with soft material such as pieces of polystyrene or foam sponge. This should reduce the risk of breakages, especially of more fragile pieces such as necks and arms. Look at the shape and dimensions of the figurine to see how you can support the whole structure.

Animated Animals

3 Once you have arrived at your destination, secure the figurine(s) to the cake, pastillage base or dummy cake support with a dot of ready-made royal icing. If the figurine is slim and tall do not remove the skewer that supports the whole structure. Make sure that the recipient is aware of any skewers, dried spaghetti or other inedible items you have used to support your figures so that they can be removed safely before the cake is served.

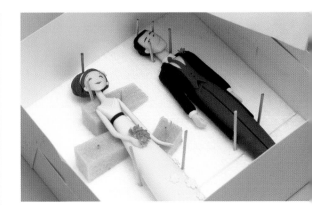

tutor tip

Always make spares of any pieces that you think are likely to get damaged, such as little flowers or other small, fragile objects, and take them with you. I usually take spare pieces of paste just in case I have to fix something to the piece upon arrival.

Male cat

Body

1 Colour a small amount of White MMP with a little Wisteria paste colour to make a light purple shade. Shape a piece of this light Wisteria-coloured paste into a rounded bottle shape following the template as a guide for the size (see page 508). Lay the bottle shape on its side and flatten it slightly against the work surface. Press the sides in with your fingers to square off the edges, then cut the base of the body straight with a sharp knife.

2 Use a Dresden tool to mark a curved line halfway up either side of the body for the hind legs and a straight line halfway up the front of the body for the front legs. Insert a wooden barbecue skewer into the neck and down through the body and leave to firm.

3 Model some light Wisteria-coloured MMP into a soft pyramid shape for the fur on the chest. Skewer the body into a spare cake dummy or polystyrene block then attach the fur to the front of the body with a little edible glue. By standing the model in a piece of polystyrene, you can avoid flattening the rounded shape of the back.

4 To make the shirt, roll out some White SFP very thinly on a lightly greased non-stick board and cut out a teardrop shape with the cutter. Use the pointed tip of the teardrop cutter to cut a small 'V' shape out of the rounded end of the paste to make the collar. Stick the White SFP over the chest and mark a line down the front of the shirt with a Dresden tool.

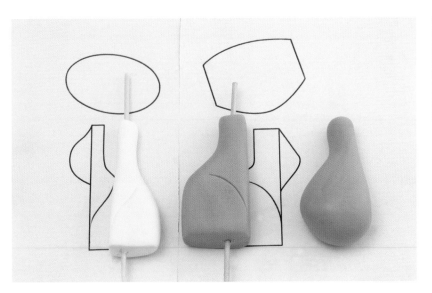

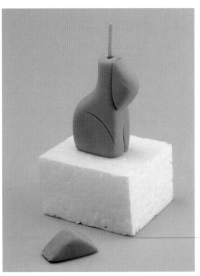

Animated Animals

5 For the jacket, colour some White SFP with Wisteria paste food colour to achieve a much darker shade than the body. Roll out some dark Wisteria-coloured SFP very thinly and cut out a rectangle that is just large enough to fit around the upper body. Press the rounded end of a Dresden tool along one of the longer sides to create the effect of ripped material. Wrap the shape around the upper body so that the ends are at the front of the chest and secure in place. Trim away the excess paste at the front of the body neatly with a pair of scissors. Once the paste has firmed up, draw pinstripes down the jacket with a Black food colour pen.

6 To make the shirt collar, cut a strip of White SFP and attach it around the neck so the ends meet at the front of the shirt. Roll out a thin strip of dark Wisteria-coloured SFP and cut it so that one side is slightly curved and tapers towards the ends. Attach the strip around the collar and along the top edge of the jacket.

7 Roll a small ball of Soft Lilac SFP and flatten it between your fingers. Attach it to the front of the jacket with edible glue and press a ball tool in the middle to make the shape of a button. Use the tip of a cocktail stick to make two holes in the middle of the button.

8 Colour some White MMP with Cyclamen and a touch of Poppy paste food colours. Shape two small teardrops from the paste and flatten each teardrop slightly between your fingers. Square off the ends to make the loops of the bow tie. Position the two teardrops so that the pointed ends are facing inwards and stick to the front of the shirt collar.

Head

9 Roll some light Wisteria-coloured MMP into an oval shape and flatten

it slightly. Press the shape against a non-stick board or use cake smoothers to square off the sides of the head. Open up the mouth in the lower half of the face using the tip of a bulbous cone tool, then push a ball tool into the face to make two large eye sockets.

10 To bring out the cheeks and dimples, press and roll the side of a bulbous cone tool from the top of the mouth out towards the sides of the face. Draw a curved line under each eye socket with the sharp edge of a Dresden tool to add wrinkles.

11 Mix a very small piece of light Wisteria-coloured MMP with some White MMP to make an even paler shade. Shape the paste into two ovals and fill each eye socket: this paste is to highlight the eyes and create the bags under them. Colour some White MMP with a touch of Daffodil paste food colour for the eyeballs and make two smaller ovals from the paste. Stick each oval toward the upper left-hand side of each eye. Draw soft, curved lines in the paste under the eyeballs with the sharp end of a Dresden tool to add detail to the bags under the eyes.

12 To make the muzzle, roll a small piece of MMP from the same paste as for the bags under the eyes. Mould the paste into a small oval, attach it above the mouth with a little edible glue and gently push down on the top of the muzzle to square it off. Press the blade of a small knife down the front of the muzzle and make a small indent in the top with the tip of the knife: this will be where the nose is attached later on.

13 Roll two very small pieces of Black MMP into ovals for the pupils and stick them onto the lower left-hand side of the eyeballs. Flatten the pupils to make them the same level as the eyeballs. To make the eyelashes, roll a tiny piece of Black MMP into two thin,

tapered sausages and stick them over the top of each eye.

14 Roll a small teardrop of Black MMP for the nose, stick it to the indent in the top of the muzzle and pinch it into shape.

15 For the lower lip, roll a small piece of very pale Wisteria-coloured MMP into a thick sausage with pointed ends and glue the paste under the mouth. Push the rounded end of a Dresden tool into the paste to bring out the bottom lip. To give the mouth depth, roll a very small piece of MMP coloured with Cyclamen and a touch of Poppy paste food colours into an oval and push it into the bottom of the mouth with a Dresden tool.

16 Roll a tiny piece of pale Poppy-coloured MMP into an oval for the tongue, stick it into the bottom of the mouth and press it down with a Dresden tool. To make the teeth, roll a thin, tapered sausage of White MMP and attach it in the mouth between the tongue and the lower lip. Make two marks on the teeth and fold the pointed ends up to create pointed canines. Roll a very thin sausage of Black MMP and stick it around the top of the lower lip to finish the mouth.

17 For the eyebrows, roll small pieces of Black MMP into tapered sausages and stick them above each eye with a little edible glue. Press the edge of a Dresden tool along them to add texture. Roll a few more thin sausages of Black MMP to make strands of hair and stick them to the eyebrows and to the top of the head, positioning them so they stand on end.

Tail

18 Colour a piece of White MMP with Wisteria paste food colour so it is a much darker colour than the body. Roll the paste into a long teardrop for the tail and bend the wider end round slightly to

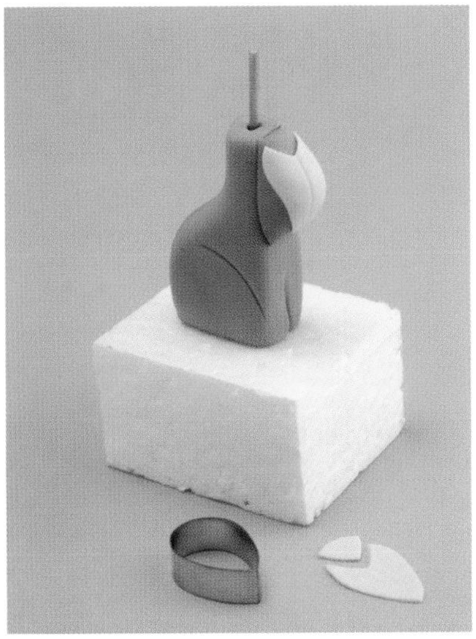
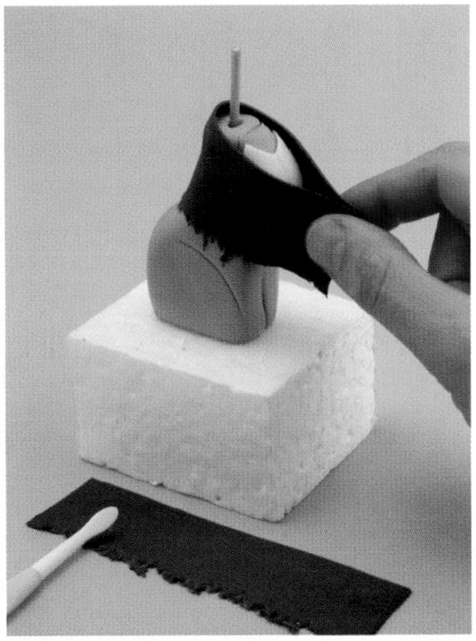
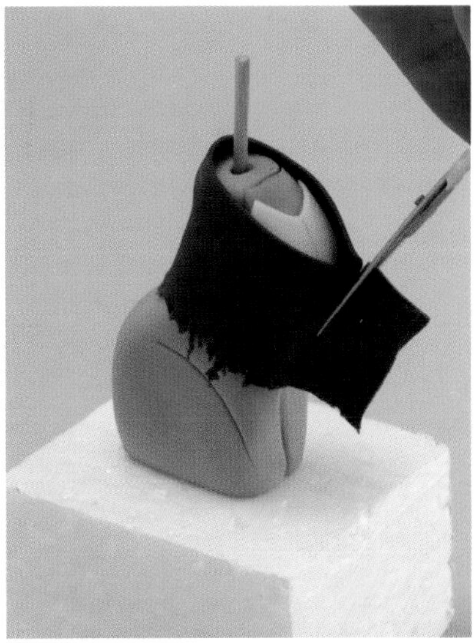
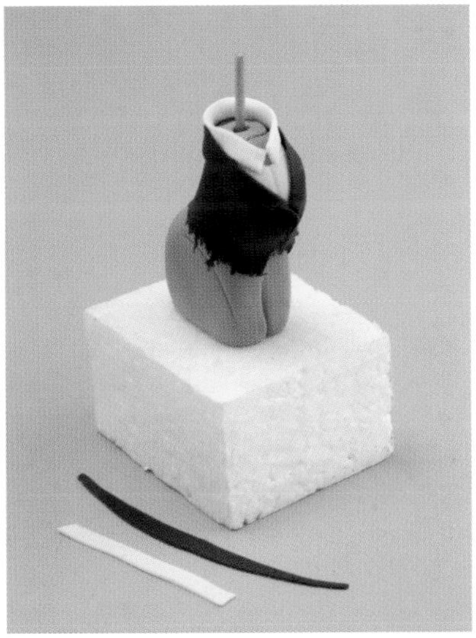
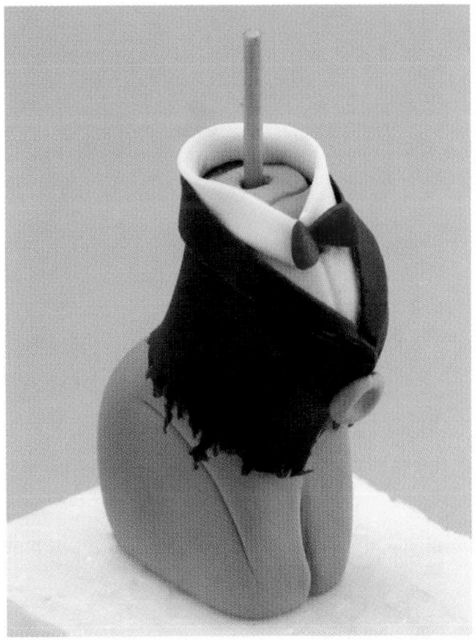
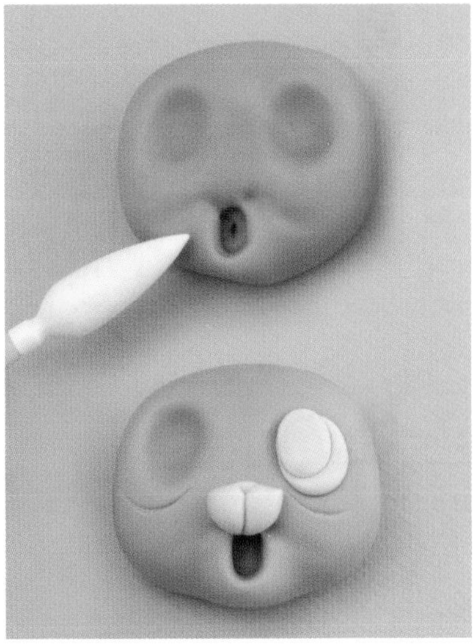
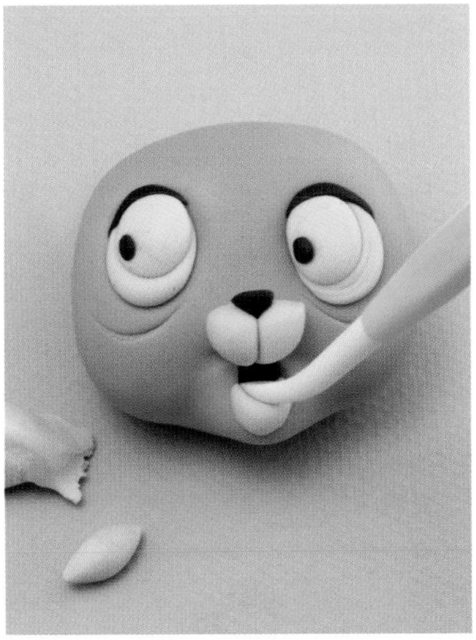
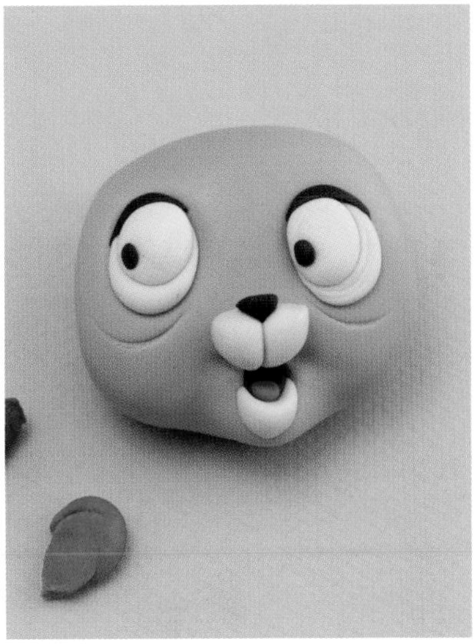
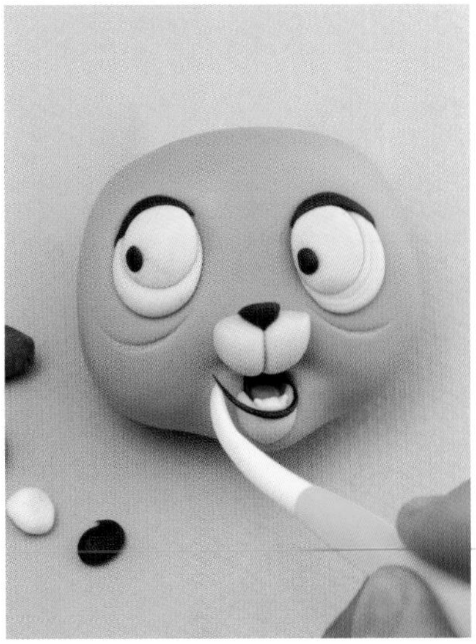

give shape. Press the sharper end of a Dresden tool all the way along the outside of the tail to create a fur effect. Place the smaller end of the tail at the base of the back: the tail should be sitting flat on the work surface. Do not attach the tail with edible glue as it is heavy and may break once you remove the figure from the polystyrene. Position the tail on the cake once the figure is in place.

Finishing touches

19 Roll a very small piece of the lighter Wisteria-coloured MMP into an oval for the front paws. Attach the paws to the front of the legs, use a small knife to mark a line down the middle of the oval, then make small indents across the front of each paw for the claws.

20 Roll some of the light Wisteria-coloured MMP into teardrops and cut off the rounded bases to create a straight edge. Press a bulbous cone tool into the middle of each ear then attach the ears to either side of the head with a little

edible glue. Highlight the pupils with tiny circles of White MMP.

21 Using a little Black dust food colour and a soft brush, dust the tips of the ears, the tip of the tail and the front paws. Mix a small amount of Fuchsia dust with a little cornflour to soften the colour, then brush the mixture over the cheeks to create a blush. Once the head has dried slightly, gently push it down onto the skewer sticking out of the top of the body and tilt the head to one side.

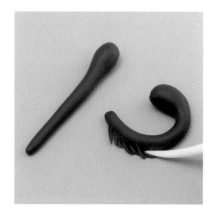

A wheel made of walnut tree that is 2" thick and 18" diameter used for engraving figures in wood.

'The author has constructed a wheel, which he has used with great success; it is pierced in the centre and it turns on a spindle, fixed to the table; the board to be engraved is fixed in the middle to this wheel with four screws and nuts, according to the size of the wood wheel being full of small holes to receive different sizes. [...] You must have tools from the size of a needle to that used by carvers in wood: the wood fittest for engraving is pear-tree, or box, and it must be chosen very dry.'

Extracted from *The Italian Confectioner* by Jarrin, 1820

Animated Animals

Female cat

Body

1 Take some White MMP and shape the body in a similar way as for the male cat following the template on page 508. Roll a piece of White MMP into a wide sausage with pointed ends and stick it to the chest with a little edible glue. Use a Dresden tool to mark fine lines down the chest, mark on the legs and insert a skewer down the body. Stand the model in a piece of polystyrene and leave to firm up while you work on the head.

Head

2 Add a pinch of CMC gum to some White MMP and roll it into an oval shape, using the template for reference. Push the rounded end of a small rose petal cutter into the lower half of the face to create the smile, then press the rounded end of a Dresden tool into either end of the smile to make dimples. Use the same end to open the mouth slightly and bring out the lower lip.

3 Push the side of a bulbous cone tool into the face just above the smile and pointing down towards the middle of the face to make the eye sockets. At this stage, push the head down onto the skewer and position it so her head is slightly tilted to the side as if she is looking towards her partner.

4 Roll a small piece of White MMP into an oval shape for the muzzle and attach it just above the smile and between the dimples. Make a vertical mark down the centre of the muzzle with the blade of a knife. Roll a very small piece of MMP coloured pale pink with Rose paste colour into a teardrop, fix it to the very top of the muzzle and pinch it to achieve a sharp edge. Roll a small sausage with pointed ends and attach underneath the muzzle to make the lower lip.

5 Use White MMP to make the ears following the instructions for the male cat on pages 333–334.

6 Roll small pieces of pale yellow MMP into almond shapes for the eyes and stick them into the eye sockets. Gently press the paste into the sockets to fill them and flatten the eyes, then push a small ball tool into the far right-hand side of each eye to mark out the position of the pupils. Roll two very small balls of Black MMP and fix them into the marks with a touch of edible glue.

7 Model two thin sausages of Black MMP, taper the ends into points and attach them over the top of each eye so that the ends flick upwards. For the eyebrows, model two pieces of White MMP into thin tapered sausages and attach them to the head above each eye.

8 Mix a small amount of Pale Peach dust food colour with a little cornflour to soften the colour, then dust over the cheeks to create a blush.

9 To make the fringe, roll a little White MMP into a long teardrop and texture the paste as for the chest. Curl the paste up and fix it to the head with edible glue. Highlight the pupils with tiny circles of White MMP.

Tail

10 Roll some White MMP into a long bottle shape with a pointed end and add texture with a Dresden tool as for the chest, then bend to give shape. Place the smaller end of the tail at the base of the back and position the tail around the legs. Allow to dry.

Fascinator

11 To make the fascinator, roll out some White SFP thinly on a non-stick board and cut out several flowers with a stephanotis cutter. Soften the edges of each petal with a ball tool, then fold the petals inwards and pinch the base to give shape. Cut a stamen in half, insert through the centre of the flower and secure in place with edible glue. Repeat to make approximately 8–10 flowers and leave to dry.

12 Dust the centre of the flowers with a mix of Pale Peach dust food colour and cornflour as for the cheeks. Once the flowers are dry glue them onto her head with dots of white royal icing.

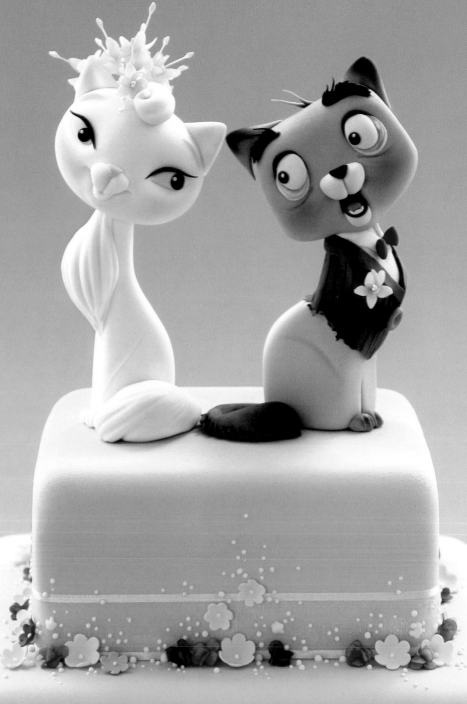

tutor tip

Mexican modelling paste (MMP) is non-sticky and ideal for all models where a smooth, strong finish is required. However, if you find that the modelling paste is too soft then mix it 50:50 with SFP to strengthen it.

Purrfect Day Wedding Cake

EDIBLES

12cm square x 6cm deep (5" x 2³/₈") and 20.5cm square x 6cm deep (8" x 2³/₈") cakes, filled and crumb-coated, see page 92

SK Sugarpaste: 2.5kg (5lb 8¼oz) Bridal White coloured with a touch of Cyclamen and Lilac paste food colours

SK Professional Dust Food Colours: Cyclamen, Fuchsia, Violet

EQUIPMENT

30.5cm (12") round cake drum (board)

12.5cm and 20.5cm (5" and 8") square cake cards

Lily of the Valley petal cutters, set of 2 (TT)

1m (3' 3½") x 15mm (⅝") wide satin ribbon: white

1.35m (4' 5") x 20mm (¾") wide sheer ribbon: white

For essential modelling edibles and equipment, see pages 184–185

tutor tip

If you want to transport the figurines on the cake, then it is a good idea to remove the heads and replace them on arrival.

1 Thinly roll out some White SFP on a non-stick board and cut out several flowers using different-sized lily of the valley cutters. Soften the edges of the petals with a ball tool and pinch the back of some of the blossoms to fold the petals inwards. You will need approximately 150 flowers for the whole cake. Once the flowers have firmed up, dust some of them with Cyclamen, Violet and Fuchsia dust colours.

2 Colour some Bridal White sugarpaste with a little Lilac and Cyclamen paste food colours and cover the cakes with sugarpaste (see pages 139–140). Add a touch more Cyclamen to the sugarpaste and cover the cake drum (see page 141). Dowel the bottom tier then secure it to the centre of the cake drum with royal icing or softened sugarpaste (see page 143). Secure the second tier centrally on top of the first. Trim the cake drum with white satin ribbon then attach the sheer white ribbon around the bottom of each cake and secure with a little royal icing.

3 Model the bride and groom cats following the instructions on pages 333–338.

4 Position the cats on top of the second tier so that their heads are tilted towards each other but their bodies are facing outwards. Push the skewer protruding from the bodies into the top of the cake and secure in place with royal icing or softened sugarpaste. Attach a little buttonhole flower to the male cat's jacket.

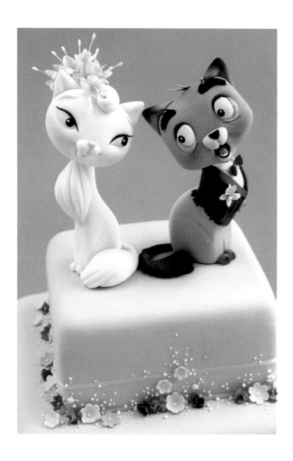

5 Secure the blossoms around the bottom of each tier with dots of royal icing to create a pattern using the various colours and sizes. Fill a paper piping bag with white royal icing and finish the design with dots of icing.

Important note: Where you have used inedible supports such as wooden barbecue skewers in models, make sure to inform the recipient that the models should be safely removed from the cake before it is served.

Royal Icing Collar Work

PADDI CLARK

Run-out royal iced collars frame the top of a cake beautifully and can be used to impressive effect on single and multi-tiered cakes alike. Once you have a good grasp of basic royal icing techniques, you can try experimenting with different designs and colours but always ensure that the collar is smaller than the cake on the inside circumference and bigger on the outer circumference.

EDIBLES

SK Instant Mix Professional Royal Icing

SK Professional Liquid Food Colour: Chestnut

EQUIPMENT

Paper piping bags: medium and small

Piping nozzles: nos. 0, 1

Templates, see page 509

For essential royal icing edibles and equipment, see pages 230–231

TECHNIQUES

- Making and attaching royal iced collars

How to make royal icing collars

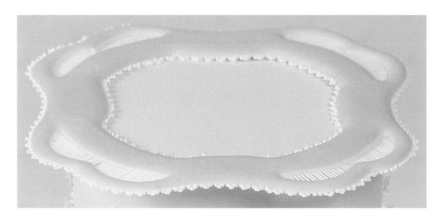

1 Use a photocopier to enlarge or shrink the collar design template to fit the size of your iced cake exactly. The template provided on page 509 is the appropriate size for a 15cm (6") round cake, although remember that each cake will vary slightly once it has been iced.

2 Place the template on a flat board and secure it in place with small pieces of masking tape in the corners, making sure that the template is flat. Cut out a piece of acetate slightly larger than the template, place it over the template and stick it to the board, again ensuring that it is flat.

3 Smear a small amount of white vegetable fat over the acetate around the collar design. Using a sharp knife, cut a small cross in the middle of the acetate to allow for shrinkage as the royal icing dries.

4 Make up some royal icing according to the instructions on the packet. Colour the royal icing with liquid food colour at this point if desired.

5 Add a few drops of cold, pre-boiled water to the icing to let it down to a run-out consistency (see page 235). After pulling a palette knife through the icing, it should flow back together between 9 and 10 seconds. You can also paddle (rub down) the icing down on a board to achieve the same consistency and remove any air bubbles. Half-fill two medium-sized paper piping bags with the icing, but do not snip the tips off the bags at this point.

6 Fit a small piping bag with a no. 0 nozzle and half-fill it with white icing that is just a little softer than firm-peak. Pipe the fine vertical lines in the arches of the collar design, making sure to extend the lines over the outline of the arch.

7 Fit another small piping bag with a no. 1 nozzle and half-fill with the firmer icing. Continue to pipe the remaining outline for the design.

8 Cut off the tips of the prepared bags of run-out icing to approximately the size of a no. 1 nozzle and start to flood in the collar (see page 240). Use gentle pressure on the bag to flood an area approximately 4cm (1½") wide within the outline of the collar. Flood another small area to one side of this,

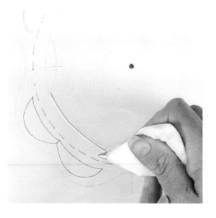

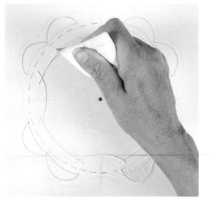

Royal Icing Collar Work

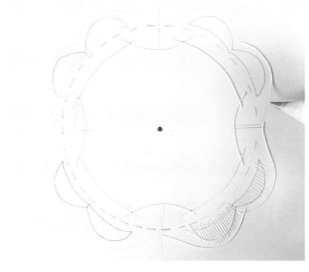
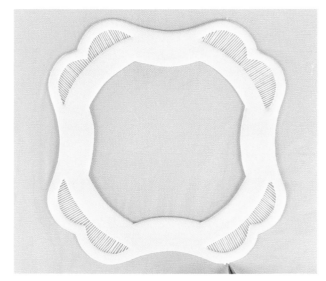
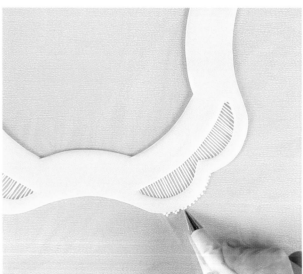

then continue to switch between one side and the other, filling in small areas on either side at a time until they join up at the bottom. Working in this way means that the icing won't have time to dry so there won't be any joins in the collar. (If you start at the beginning and work round in a circle, the icing at the beginning will dry out and you will be left with a visible join.) Once you have finished, place the collar under an angled lamp or a similar heat source and leave to dry.

9 Before removing the collar from the acetate, paddle some royal icing to soften it slightly, then place in a small piping bag with a no. 1 nozzle. Pipe a few tiny dots at a time around the edge of the collar, leaving a very small space between them. To make a picot dot design, pipe another dot above and between two dots to join them together and form a triangle shape. Continue in this way around the outside of the collar. Pipe a single line of small dots around the inside edge of the collar and leave to dry for at least an hour (depending on the temperature of your work room).

10 Once the collar is dry, carefully remove it from the acetate. To avoid breaking the icing, place the collar on its board on the edge of the work surface, gently remove the tape from the acetate and slide it so that the collar and acetate overhang the edge. Carefully pull the acetate downwards to release the edge of the collar, then gently slide a cranked palette knife underneath it or lift it with your hand. Pipe a thick line of icing around the top of the cake where you wish to attach the collar and carefully secure the collar in place. Leave to dry.

Cookies and Cream Royal Iced Anniversary Cake

Combining delicate royal iced details with a neutral colour scheme and elegant collar work, this cake design is both subtle and sophisticated. The cookies make great favours and can be personalised with initials or numerals to suit the occasion.

EDIBLES

10cm and 15cm (4" and 6") round cakes

3kg (6lb 9¾oz) SK Instant Mix Professional Royal Icing

700g (1lb 8¾oz) SK Marzipan

SK Sugar Florist Paste (SFP): White

Biscuit recipe, see page 47

SK Professional Dust or Liquid Food Colours: Bulrush, Chestnut, Cyclamen, Daffodil (yellow), Holly/Ivy, Leaf Green, Rose, Violet

EQUIPMENT

23cm (9") round cake drum

10cm (4") round cake board

Paper piping bags: medium and small

Small blossom plunger cutter (FMM)

Cookie cutters: circle, heart, oval, fluted circle, fluted oval

SK Paintbrush: no. 1

Piping nozzles: nos. 0, 1, 1.5

Templates, see page 509

For essential royal icing edibles and equipment, see pages 230–231

Cake

1 Cover the cakes with marzipan and leave them to firm up for 48 hours (see page 95). Make up 2kg (4lb 6½oz) of royal icing and colour with a few drops of Chestnut liquid food colour to make a cream colour (see page 236).

2 Place the 15cm (6") cake on a 23cm (9") cake drum and the 10cm (4") cake on a cake board of the same size. Coat the cakes and the drum with the cream-coloured icing and leave to dry (see pages 236–238).

3 Following the steps on pages 341–342, make the collars for the first and second tiers using run-out icing coloured with a touch of Chestnut liquid food colour to make it slightly darker than the cake covering. Leave to dry under a heat source.

4 Using the dotted line on the template as a guide, follow the instructions for making collars on pages 341–342 to create four collar sections that fit around the base of the cake. Instead of piping a continuous outline around the whole collar, divide it into four separate pieces and leave to dry.

5 Make a template for both cakes to create a scalloped side design and transfer the design onto the cakes with a scribing needle (see page 171). Fit a piping bag with a no. 1 nozzle, ½-fill with off-peak white icing and use the drop-line technique to pipe between the marks (see page 240). Pipe a column of small dots above and below the joins between scallops and pipe a small bead in the centre of each dropped line.

6 Roll out some White SFP very thinly and cut out approximately 60 flowers with the blossom cutter. Attach a flower at the join between each scallop, then secure flowers above and below the first flower. Pipe a small dot in the centre of each flower, then pipe two small leaves behind each of the central flowers. Fit a piping bag with a no. 0 nozzle and white off-peak icing then scratch pipe around the side design (see page 247).

7 Secure the larger cake to the centre of the covered cake drum then position the collar sections around the base of the cake and secure in place with softened royal icing. Attach white flowers between each of the sections.

Pipe a thick line of royal icing around the top edge of the bottom tier and carefully secure the larger collar in place.

8 Secure the smaller cake centrally on top of the bottom tier, being careful not to touch the collar on the lower tier. Pipe a small bead border around the base of the top tier with white off-peak icing and a no. 1.5 nozzle (see page 242). Secure small flowers at approximately 2cm (¾") intervals around the border. Attach the small collar to the top tier in the same way.

Biscuits

9 Make up the biscuit dough using the recipe on page 47, roll out and cut out several shapes from the dough using different cookie cutters. In order to make the biscuits stand up like a frame, you will need small trapezium-shaped biscuits to secure to the back (see template on page 509). Bake according to the recipe and allow to cool.

10 Make up some icing to off-peak consistency and colour with Chestnut liquid food colour to match the

cake. Half-fill a piping bag fitted with a no. 1 nozzle and pipe a continuous line around the edge of the biscuit. Let down the icing with a little cooled, boiled water and flood the cookie with cream-coloured royal icing. For the white cookies, repeat the same method but leave the icing uncoloured. Allow to dry.

11 Paint your own design onto the icing using either liquid food colours or dust food colours mixed with clear alcohol or cooled, boiled water (see pages 172–173). Take care not to make the mixture too wet otherwise the royal icing may dissolve. Leave to dry.

12 To finish, pipe a decorative border around the edge of each cookie using white off-peak royal icing and a no. 1 nozzle.

13 Secure the stand cookies to the back of the larger cookies with a little royal icing to create a picture frame effect. Stand your favourite biscuit on top of the cake and position the others around the base, or use them as name places or favours for your guests.

Ceri DD Griffiths

BIOGRAPHY

I was born in Cardiff in 1960 and, after leaving school at 17, I found myself in the catering industry. I first worked as a cook, then as a grill chef in a restaurant and eventually worked in a five-star hotel assisting the pastry chef. It was clear that I had a flair for desserts, so my head chef encouraged me to enrol on a bakery and confectionery course. Three years later I graduated as a Master Baker and Confectioner, with bakery awards and distinctions in cake decoration and design from Cardiff College of Food Technology and Science. My first employer was my former cake decorating teacher, who took me on as a confectioner and cake decorating assistant in her family-run bakery. A couple of years later the family bakery sadly closed, and I soon found myself working for big scratch bakeries and supermarket bakery departments.

Whilst working in the bigger, open-plan bakeries, I developed a lung condition (pneumoconiosis) brought on by flour dust, which meant I had to leave the career I loved as a baker and confectioner. To regain my lung capacity I had to become physically fit so, as I had always enjoyed theatre productions during my school years, I enrolled in dance classes. I was soon auditioning for the top three dance colleges in London and after being awarded a place, I moved to London for a whole new career. During my time at dance college, I continued to decorate cakes in order to support myself financially. I worked in a decorating room in Oxford Street where the flour dust wouldn't affect me, and I wore a mask over my nose and mouth to prevent any further problems; my increased fitness meant that my lungs coped better with the working conditions.

Before I had even finished my dance training, I was already travelling around the world as a professional dancer in musical theatre. I loved the theatrical world with its bright colours and lavish settings – you can see this theatrical influence in some of my cake designs. I was still decorating cakes for show openings, birthdays and farewell events but I found it could be quite a challenge trying to find the ingredients to make and decorate a cake in an unfamiliar country. I think that is where I learnt the ability to adapt and make do with what was available. Along the way I met some great cake decorators and they generously shared advice and expertise, giving me an education in cake artistry that I would otherwise never have known. Over the years, living and working in various countries has strongly influenced my style of design: my cake designs now range from minimalist to theatrically ornate.

Several years ago I retired from the world of dance and returned to my first love, cake artistry. The bakery industry had changed a lot in my absence and it is now a world where I no longer have to work in a large bakery producing bread, confectionery and decorated items. Nowadays, I can be an independent cake decorator and the world is beginning to appreciate that cake decorators are artists who work with the medium of sugar. I truly believe that everything happens for a purpose and that everything I have been through in my life was to one end. I would not be the cake artist I am today without all those different elements of my life; my individual style is influenced by everything from theatre to travel.

Four years ago I took some classes at Squires Kitchen International School with expert sugar florist, Alan Dunn. We became friends and when

Alan discovered that I was a royal icing decorator he suggested that I send some pictures of my cakes to Beverley and Robert Dutton at Squires Kitchen. Alan mentioned that they were always looking for new, talented cake decorators to contribute to the magazines or become tutors at the school, so the very next day I sent them my images. Within the week I had met both Beverley and Robert, had been commissioned for my first magazine article and had been asked to teach at the school.

As a result of my passion for royal icing I am now an international judge, demonstrator, teacher and author of several books, including *Squires Kitchen's Guide to Making Iced Flowers,* and the follow-up *More Iced Flowers* (B. Dutton Publishing). My personal aim is to give royal icing a makeover and show the world that this versatile medium very much has its place in the world of contemporary cake design.

Piped Roses and Scroll Borders

CERI DD GRIFFITHS

Adding the wow factor to your cake creations is easy once you have mastered the art of scroll borders. Built-up — or stacked — line work can be used on borders to make the cake look grander and to give the impression of a larger cake. I have also covered piped roses here as they are the most popular flower for celebration cakes, particularly wedding cakes.

EDIBLES

Round or square cakes coated with sugarpaste or royal icing on covered cake boards, see pages 236–238

SK Instant Mix Royal Icing

SK Professional Liquid Food Colours of your choice

SK Professional Dust Food Colour of your choice

SK Designer Bridal Satin Lustre Dust Food Colour of your choice (optional)

SK Sugar Florist Paste (SFP): 50g (1¾oz) White

EQUIPMENT

Piping nozzles: nos. 1, 2, 3, 44, 51, 56 (left- or right-handed petal nozzles as required) (PME)

Cocktail sticks

Small dusting brush

Small polystyrene block

For essential royal icing edibles and equipment, see pages 230–231

TECHNIQUES

- Piped roses
- Scroll borders
- Built-up/stacked line work

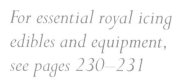

Squires Kitchen shop in pastillage by Ceri DD Griffiths, 2012

348

Piped roses

Miniature roses

1 Smear a little white vegetable fat onto the top section of a cocktail stick then wipe off the excess. Fit a small piping bag with a no. 56 petal nozzle then fill the bag two-thirds full with off-peak royal icing (see page 235). The ivory-coloured roses shown here are made using royal icing coloured with a touch of Chestnut and Sunflower liquid food colours.

2 Line up the piping nozzle with the tip of the cocktail stick and apply pressure to the icing bag until the royal icing attaches to the cocktail stick. With the end of the royal icing attached to the cocktail stick, continue piping to create a ribbon of icing whilst turning the cocktail stick in an anticlockwise direction, or clockwise if you are left-handed. The icing will wrap around the cocktail stick to form a bud.

3 When you have created a rose bud, stop piping and bring the end of the royal icing ribbon down to the cocktail stick beneath the bud, wiping the nozzle against the cocktail stick to finish.

4 Using an arching motion pipe three overlapping petals around the bud. Start and end each petal beneath the bud, piping towards you.

5 Using an arching motion as before, pipe five overlapping petals around the outside. Start and end these ones beneath the first three petals and this time pipe away from you.

6 Repeat step 5 to add seven further petals around the five. Once the rose is complete, insert the cocktail stick into a block of polystyrene to dry for 24 hours. When dry the rose should come off the cocktail stick quite easily if it has been greased with white vegetable fat. If your royal icing is a little soft, push the cocktail

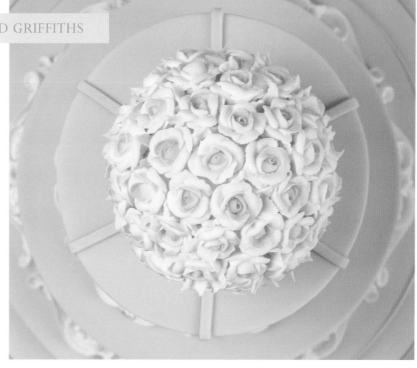

stick through a square of wax paper and leave to dry with the rose attached to the paper. Make as many roses as required.

7 When dry, use a soft paintbrush to dust the very centre of each rose to give it depth then brush with lustre dust to create a light sheen. The roses shown here are dusted with Marigold in the centre and Double Cream lustre dust to finish.

Medium roses

1 If you wish to remove the rose from the cocktail stick when dry, grease the tip with a little white vegetable fat. (The medium roses used to make the ball on page 356 are left on the sticks so do not need to be greased.) Model a small teardrop of White SFP and push it onto the tip of a cocktail stick (see opposite).

2 Fit a piping bag with a no. 51 petal nozzle (R for right-handed pipers and L for left-handed) then ²/₃ fill the bag with royal icing coloured as required. The roses shown here are made in ivory to match the miniature roses.

3 Line up the piping nozzle with the tip of the SFP teardrop and apply pressure to the piping bag until the royal

icing attaches to the teardrop. With the royal icing still attached, continue piping to create a ribbon of icing and turn the cocktail stick in an anticlockwise direction if you are right-handed, or clockwise if you are left-handed. This will wrap the icing around the SFP cone, creating a bud.

4 When you have created a rose bud, stop piping and bring the end of the royal icing ribbon down to the cocktail stick beneath the bud, wiping the nozzle against the cocktail stick to finish.

5 Add a further three petals then five following steps 4 and 5 for the miniature roses. Allow to dry for 24 hours in a block of polystyrene.

6 Dust the roses as required. The roses shown here are dusted as for step 7 of the miniature roses.

7 Remove the roses from the cocktail sticks or wax paper when you are ready to use them. Alternatively, if you are using them to make a ball topper, leave the roses on their cocktail sticks (see page 356).

8 Using Leaf Green-coloured royal icing and a no. 51 nozzle, pipe five small leaves on the back of the rose for the calyx.

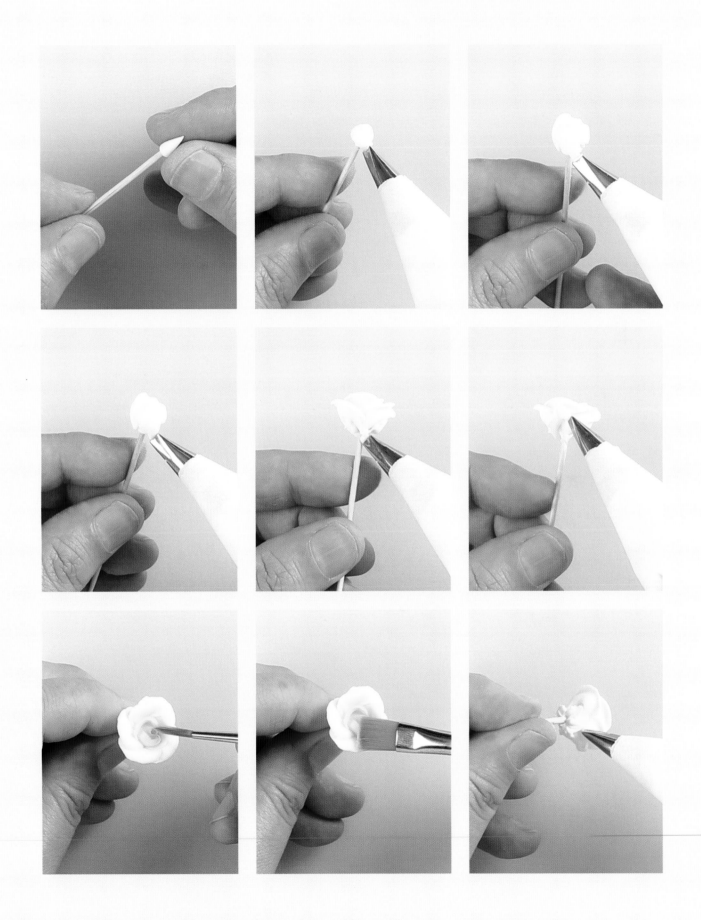

tutor tip

Scroll borders can be given a finishing touch by adding a miniature piped flower. Instructions for attaching the mini roses made on page 350 are given in the Rose Ball Wedding Cake project on the following pages.

Scroll borders

Barrels ▼

1 Divide the cake into equal sections for the border, ensuring that you have an even number. To re-create the design shown here the sections must be divisible by four. The easiest way to do this is to make a paper template to go around the circumference of the cake, fold it into quarters, eighths and so on, then mark these on the cake covering (see page 247).

2 Fit a piping bag with a star nozzle: the one used here is a no. 44. Fill the bag two-thirds full with off-peak royal icing. The scrolls shown here are coloured ivory using a touch of Chestnut and Sunflower liquid food colours. To pipe a barrel scroll, hold the bag at an angle of 45° or less to the cake surface and rotate the nozzle as you pipe, known as a rope action. To make the tapered barrel shape, squeeze and rotate the nozzle, increasing the pressure towards the centre of the barrel and decreasing it towards the end. Pipe evenly spaced barrels around the cake, following the marks made earlier.

Mirrored S and C scrolls ▲

3 To add the next layer to the border you can add S and C scrolls on top of the barrels using the same nozzle. Starting at the end of one of the barrels, pipe using a rope action in a gentle upward curve over the length of one barrel. Stop the rotations but continue the S shape downward and across the next barrel. Stop at the end of the second barrel.

4 Pipe a C scroll with a rope action so that it sits on top of the second barrel and the latter half of the S scroll. Stop at the end of the second barrel and S scroll.

5 For this design, every other set of scrolls needs to be piped in the reverse direction to achieve the mirrored S and C scrolls on this cake. Starting two barrels along, pipe a reverse S and C scroll and finish at the same point as before.

Built-up line work ▼

6 Over-pipe the S and C scrolls using a no. 44 nozzle staying in contact with the scrolls beneath; this will establish a base for your line work. If possible have the tails of the scrolls joining as a support for the piped rose when attached.

7 Fit three separate piping bags with nozzle nos. 3, 2 and 1, and then fill the bags ²/₃-full using the same coloured royal icing as before.

8 Pipe line work on top of the S and C scrolls (and reverse scrolls) using the no. 3 plain nozzle. Once you have piped round the whole border, repeat with the no. 2 nozzle then the no. 1, stacking the lines on top of each other. Use a slightly damp paintbrush to adjust any wayward lines and help you achieve clean, sweeping line work.

Rose Ball Wedding Cake

Although a traditional technique spanning centuries, decorative royal icing has found a home amongst multi-medium cakes in contemporary cake artistry. This versatile medium is particularly useful for creating fully edible decorations and exquisitely piped work, particularly on more elaborate projects such as wedding cakes.

EDIBLES

2 x 15cm (6") round fruit cakes

23cm (9") round fruit cake

1.5kg (3lb 5oz) SK Marzipan

Apricot glaze

SK Sugarpaste: 150g (5¼oz) Ballerina Pink, 1.5kg (3lb 5oz) Iced Mint, 50g (1¾oz) Vintage Ivory

500g (1lb 1¾oz) SK Instant Mix Royal Icing

SK Professional Liquid Food Colours: Chestnut (soft beige), Leaf Green, Sunflower

SK Bridal Satin Lustre Dust Food Colour: Double Cream

SK Sugar Florist Paste (SFP): 50g (1¾oz) White

SK Professional Dust Food Colour: Marigold (tangerine)

For essential royal icing edibles and equipment, see pages 230–231

EQUIPMENT

2 x 15cm (6") round cake cards

30.5cm and 35.5cm (12" and 14") round cake drums (boards)

9 plastic cake dowels

Silicone pastry brush

Marzipan spacers (optional)

SK Bellissimo Flexi Smoothers

Double-sided tape or non-toxic glue stick

15mm (½") wide satin ribbon: 1m (40") ballerina pink, 1.2m (48") hot pink

Piping bags (parchment or plastic)

Piping nozzles: nos. 1, 2, 3, 42, 44, 50, 51, 56, 58 (left- or right-handed petal nozzles as required) (PME)

Cocktail sticks

7.5cm (3") polystyrene ball

4cm (1½") round cutter

SK Paintbrush: no. 4

Small dusting brush

Craft knife or pizza wheel

Scribing tool

Small polystyrene block

Pointed tweezers (optional)

Top tier

Note that the top tier is double the height of a normal single tier and made from two separate 7.5cm (3") high fruit cakes.

1 Brush the top of both 15cm (6") round cakes with warm, boiled apricot glaze and cover the top of each cake with marzipan, ensuring that the edges are flush with the sides of the cake (see page 95). Place each of the cakes onto its own thin 15cm (6") cake card.

2 Choose which of the cakes will be the base of the top tier and then dowel this cake with four dowels (see page 143). Stack the other cake on top of the dowelled cake to make the double-height top tier.

3 To cover the side of the top tier, brush the cake with warm, boiled apricot glaze and cover the cake side following the method for royal iced cakes (see page 95). Ensure that the covering has a crisp top edge and straight sides.

4 Coat the 23cm (9") round base tier with marzipan following the instructions on page 95.

Coating the cakes and drums

5 Coat both tiers using Iced Mint sugarpaste and use Bellissimo Flexi Smoothers to obtain a sharp top edge on each tier, as described on page 301. Cover the 30.5cm (12") and 35.5cm (14") round cake drums using the remaining Iced Mint sugarpaste.

6 Centralise and attach the 30.5cm (12") round cake drum onto the 35.5cm (14") round cake drum using a small amount of royal icing to hold it in place. Mount the 23cm (9") round base tier onto the 30.5cm (12") round cake drum using royal icing and then dowel this tier using four cake dowels (see page 143). Finally, stack the top tier onto the base tier, securing it with royal icing.

Vertical stripes

7 Accuracy is the secret to success when it comes to stripes: make a greaseproof paper template to fit precisely around the circumference of the top tier and fold it into six equal sections.

Decide on the width you would like your stripes to be then measure the distance between the stripes. On the cake shown the stripes are 5mm (¼") wide with a 7.5cm (3") space between them. Mark all of the stripes onto your template using a pencil and ruler for accuracy. Wrap the paper template around the top tier with the pencil on the outside and mark the top and bottom edges of the sugarpaste with either a cocktail stick or a scribing tool. Remove the template.

8 Dust a work surface with a little icing sugar and roll out the Ballerina Pink sugarpaste to a depth of approximately 2mm (⅛"). Cut out the stripes using a pizza wheel or craft knife and ruler. Be as accurate as you can and trim the edges neatly.

9 Whilst the sugarpaste stripes are still soft attach them to the sides of the top tier using a little edible glue. Take care to place the stripes on the markings to ensure they are perfectly vertical. Bend the stripes over the top edge of the cake until they reach the centre then cut them to size. Note that the central area will eventually be hidden by the rose ball.

Rose Ball Wedding Cake

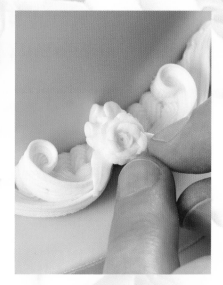

Piped roses

10 Make seven miniature roses (plus spares) for the base tier and side decoration in ivory royal icing following the instructions on page 350.

11 Make approximately 65–75 medium ivory roses (plus spares) for the rose ball following the instructions on page 350. Do not remove the roses from their cocktail sticks as you will need these to hold the roses in place on the ball.

Piped borders

12 Mark the bottom edge of the base tier in line with the stripes on the top tier. Follow the step-by-step instructions on page 353 to pipe four evenly-spaced barrels between each mark, then pipe the S and C scroll border with over piping around the base of the bottom tier in ivory royal icing. Allow to dry.

13 Repeat the same method to pipe the border for the base of the top tier but this time using a no. 42 nozzle. Allow to dry.

14 Gently remove all of the miniature roses from their cocktail sticks and select six that are most similar in size and shape. Colour a small amount of off-peak royal icing with Leaf Green liquid food colour and place in a piping bag with a no. 51 leaf nozzle. Rest the tip of the leaf nozzle onto the join of the border where you wish the leaf to be placed and apply pressure to the piping bag. When the leaf has reached the correct width, gently pump the tip of the nozzle in and out whilst elongating the leaf. To finish, stop the pressure and gently pull the nozzle away from the end of the leaf to give a sharp point. Pipe a second leaf then carefully set a miniature rose into the centre of the leaves and leave them to dry. Note there are no miniature roses at the base of the top tier.

Rose ball

Note that the cake top decoration is purely for decoration and is not intended to be edible, so must be removed safely before the cake is cut.

15 Take each medium rose on the cocktail stick and pipe five small leaves on the back to represent the calyx.

Use the same pale green royal icing as for the leaves and a no. 50 leaf nozzle and start each one at the base of the rose where the cocktail stick enters it.

16 Insert the last remaining cake dowel into the base of the 7.5cm (3") polystyrene ball then trim it so that there is approximately 7.5cm (3") protruding. This will eventually be inserted into the top tier to hold the ball in place.

17 Depending on the diameter of the polystyrene ball it may be necessary to cut the cocktail sticks shorter with wire cutters or kitchen scissors: this will enable you to insert the cocktail sticks deep into the ball without them coming into contact with each other. Using pointed tweezers to hold each cocktail stick, push the roses into the polystyrene ball, spacing them evenly over the surface. Make sure you leave a space around the dowel where the ball will rest on the surface of the cake.

18 Once the ball is covered with roses, insert the dowel into a block of polystyrene as this will make piping the leaves easier. Using the same nozzle (no. 51) and royal icing that you used for piping the leaves, pipe more

leaves between the roses to fill any gaps. Once complete, leave for 24 hours to dry fully before inserting into the top tier of your cake. If you are planning to travel with this cake it is best to insert the rose ball topper at the venue to avoid damaging it.

Side decoration

19 Dust the work surface with icing sugar and roll out the ivory sugarpaste to a depth of approximately 2mm (⅛"). Cut out a disc using a 4cm (1½") round cutter. Measure and mark the central point between the two front stripes, midway up the side of the cake. Attach the disc of paste using a little edible glue.

20 Pipe two small, green leaves and attach one of the miniature roses; you may have to hold it in place gently for a few seconds to allow the royal icing to set.

21 Using double-sided sticky tape attach ballerina pink ribbon around the cake drum and hot pink ribbon around the 35.5cm (14") round cake drum to finish.

Rose Ball Wedding Cake

Pressure-piped Decorations

EDDIE SPENCE MBE

Pressure piping is a great technique to learn because it is beautiful and delicate and is a quick way to personalise a cake. Practice the skills shown here on spare boards or plaques before piping them directly onto a cake.

EDIBLES

Royal icing, either using SK Instant Mix Royal Icing or following the recipe given here

For essential royal icing edibles and equipment, see pages 230–231

TECHNIQUES

- Recipes for royal icing
- Making a piping bag
- Pressure piping basic shapes and flowers
- Pressure piping wedding motifs
- Pressure piping christening motifs
- Scratch piping
- Piping basic letters and numerals
- Pressure piping on plaques

Recipes for royal icing

EDIBLES

Recipe 1: using dried albumen

15g (½oz) dried albumen (fortified or pure*), sieved

85ml (3fl oz) pre-boiled, lukewarm water

455g (1lb) icing sugar, sifted

Recipe 2: using fresh eggs

90g (3oz) free-range egg white from Lion Mark eggs (equivalent to 3 medium eggs)

455g (1lb) icing sugar, sifted

5–7 drops lemon juice or 4–5 drops white vinegar

*If you are making the icing for run-outs or off-pieces, use pure dried albumen (or fresh eggs, see recipe 2) as this is more stable than fortified albumen.

For essential royal icing edibles and equipment, see pages 230–231

1 If you are using dried albumen, reconstitute it in the lukewarm water, following the instructions on the packet. For fresh eggs, separate the egg whites the day before, then sieve the egg whites through a fine sieve, cover and leave in the fridge to strengthen overnight.

2 *To beat by hand:* Beat the reconstituted albumen or fresh egg whites with ²/₃ of the sifted sugar for approximately 10 minutes until white and thick. Add the remaining sugar and a few drops of lemon juice or white vinegar if using fresh egg whites. Beat to off-peak consistency (see page 235).

3 *To beat by machine:* Place the reconstituted albumen or egg whites into the mixer bowl, stir in the sifted icing sugar then beat as slowly as possible until the icing is at off-peak consistency (between 10 and 20 minutes, depending on your mixer). For best results in a mixer, double the quantity in the recipe.

4 Keep the royal icing covered with a clean, damp cloth to prevent the icing from skinning over. If you have used dried albumen, leave the royal icing to stand overnight for best results.

Making a piping bag

If you are new to royal icing or you are short of time you can purchase piping bags ready-made from cake decorating shops. However if you would like to make your own, all you need is a large sheet of greaseproof paper and a large, sharp knife.

1 Measure a 76cm x 46cm (30" x 18") sheet of greaseproof paper. Fold the sheet over but do not make a crease. Using a large, sharp knife, cut the sheet in half. Fold the sheet in half again and cut to give the size required for a large piping bag (no. 3 nozzle or larger). To make a small bag (for a no. 2 nozzle or smaller), fold in half again and cut.

2 Fold the paper on the diagonal but not point-to-point: there should be a strip on either side of the triangle. This will make an overlap so that, when the bag is made, there are three layers of paper between your hand and the icing (on the fold) which gives the bag strength.

3 Bring one side of the bag round to create a point in the middle of the long side, approximately 4cm–5cm (1½"–2") below the point. Hold this in position then bring the other side round in the same way.

4 Fold in the corners of the bag then make two small tears or cuts and fold in to hold the bag in place. This will stop the bag from opening.

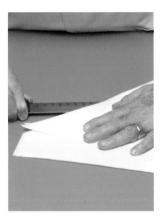   

Filling a piping bag

1 Always use rubbed-down icing for a smooth finish (see page 235). To add texture or definition to your work, use the icing fresh from the bowl or beaten to stiff-peak consistency. If you require the icing to be even stiffer and hold its shape, add a teaspoon of sifted icing sugar to every 90g (3oz) of icing.

2 Snip the tip off the bag and place the required nozzle into the bag.

Use fine nozzles such as a no. 0 or 00 for fine detail such as tiny dots and larger nozzles for flowers and figures so that you don't need to apply as much pressure. Use fine ribbon nozzles for details such as bows.

3 Half-fill the bag with icing then flatten the top and fold in the corners then fold over again to close the bag.

Pressure-piped Decorations

359

Pressure piping basic shapes and flowers

Basic shapes

All forms derive from these six shapes:

Circle

Oval

Pear

Crescent

Reverse S scroll

S scroll

Practise piping each of the shapes until you are confident at applying and releasing pressure on the bag.

Dot daisy

1   Pipe a small dot, making the take-off point to the side so that it disappears.

2   Pipe a dot on either side of the first one in the same way, then add two dots above and two dots below.

Pear-shaped daisy

1   Pipe a dot, stop piping and pull the nozzle down through the centre to leave a dimple. This forms a basic pear-shaped petal.

2   Pipe another petal in reverse underneath the first so that they meet in the centre.

3   Add two more petals on the horizontal, then four diagonally. Pipe a dot in the centre to finish.

Star-shaped blossom (daffodil)

1   Pipe a dot in the centre. Pipe another dot above this and pull through in an upward motion, making a point at the end. Repeat below in a downward motion.

2   Add two diagonal petals on each side to make a six-petal flower.

3   To turn the flower into a daffodil, prepare a piping bag of stiff royal icing for the trumpet. Pipe a circle around the central dot, then continue piping higher and higher around the circle.

Oval-shaped daisy

1   Pipe the top petal first, as for the round flower, but this time ease off the pressure as you come up through the petal to elongate it. Pipe another petal beneath the first.

2   Pipe two horizontal petals, making them slightly shorter than the first pair.

3   Pipe two petals on the diagonal in between each pair of petals.

4   To finish, pipe an oval dot in the centre of the flower.

Daisy in profile

1   Pipe the first two petals as for the oval-shaped flower.

2   Pipe one short horizontal petal, then add two petals above and two below on the diagonal to fill in the gaps.

3   Pipe four short petals on top to give the flower relief. Finish by adding a dot at the back for the seed box.

Heart-shaped flowers

1   To make a heart shape, pipe a dot and pull down slightly on the diagonal. Pipe another dot next to it and pull down onto the point of the first shape to make a heart.

2   To make a four-petal flower, add a horizontal heart on either side and one underneath, all joining at the central point.

3   To make a five-petal flower, pipe the first heart as before then work around the flower, keeping the petals close to each other.

4   For a three-petal flower resembling a clover, pipe the first heart as before then add a petal on either side on the diagonal.

5   Finish the flower by piping a dot in the centre.

Bell-shaped flowers (tulip, lily of the valley, bluebell)

1   Pressure pipe an S scroll in an upward motion for a tulip, or a downward motion for lily of the valley. Bluebells are piped in a downward motion and are more elongated.

2   Pipe a reverse S scroll next to the first one with the bases touching.

3   Pipe a dot between them and pull up through the centre.

4   Add a straight stalk for a tulip or long, curved stems for lily of the valley or bluebells.

tutor tip

To pipe a grapevine decoration, pipe the vines using long S scrolls and create the grapes using small round dots.

Pressure-piped Decorations

Pressure piping wedding motifs

Doves on branch

1 Pressure pipe a large dot and pull through to one side to make a teardrop shape for the body.

2 Pipe three pull-ups at the point of the teardrop for the tail feathers.

3 Pipe a dot for the head at the bulbous end of the teardrop.

4 Starting at the shoulder, squeeze a bulb and take the wing through between the tail and the body.

5 Add the eyes and beak and allow to dry under a desk lamp.

Bird in flight

1 Pipe two opposite wings onto greased cellophane, using a back-and-forth motion to make the feathers. Make sure both wings are solid and allow to dry.

2 Pressure pipe a large dot and pull through to one side to make the body and tail. Pipe down the tail again to make the second half.

3 Pipe a dot for the head at the top of the body and add the eye and beak.

4 Whilst the icing for the body is still wet, push both dried wings into the top of the body with the nearest one protruding outwards so that the bird appears to be flying.

Dove in flight

1 Pipe two wings onto greased cellophane following the instructions above and allow to dry.

2 To pipe the dove's tail, pipe a teardrop petal shape then add two horizontal teardrops and two more in the gaps so that they all finish at the same point.

3 Pipe a large bulb for the body then bring the piping bag up to make a teardrop that finishes at the base of the tail.

4 Whilst the icing is still wet, gently push the dry wings into the sides of the body and support until they are held firmly in place.

Pressure piping christening motifs

Swan

1 Pipe a dot for the head then bring the nozzle round in a circle, ease off the pressure as you pipe the neck, then increase the pressure again as you come down to form a reverse S scroll.

2 Squeeze a large dot in the centre of the lower part of the S scroll for the body, then taper off to the side to make the tail.

3 Using a smaller nozzle, start at the shoulder of the swan and pipe back and forth to create the wing.

4 Add a beak and eye to finish the swan.

5 To pipe a cygnet, pipe a small S scroll then a shorter teardrop and wing as before, making it around half the size of the swan.

Stork

1 Use the same techniques as for the swan but add a long beak and long legs. To make the knee joint, increase the pressure halfway along the legs to create a bulb before continuing down with an even pressure.

2 To make the blanket, pipe two small loops at the top and four teardrops underneath. Add a bulb for the baby's head and a little foot on the opposite side.

3 For added decoration, pipe a simple scroll design at the base.

Bootees

1 Using slightly rubbed-down royal icing (see page 235), pipe a large dot and, with the tip of the nozzle still in the icing, pull it up to make the dot rounded.

2 Pipe a second dot in the same way above the first. Pipe a wavy line in a circle on top of the second dot to form the ankle.

3 Pipe two small loops between the two dots for the bow.

Rattle

1 Pipe a large dot in the same way as for the first step of the bootees. Rather than pulling the nozzle out from the top, work to one side and continue to pipe a line in a slightly circular motion to form the handle.

2 Add a small loop at the end of the handle and a row of dots around the rattle.

Scratch piping

Scratch piping is where the tip of the nozzle is kept on the surface of the cake as the design is pressure piped. It is a useful technique to learn because it can be added to the top or sides of a cake to add extra decoration (see also the scratch-piped design in the Foundation chapter on page 247). Practise simple shapes and scrolls so that you can eventually pipe your own designs directly onto a cake. Follow the designs shown here or make up your own with the skills you have learnt.

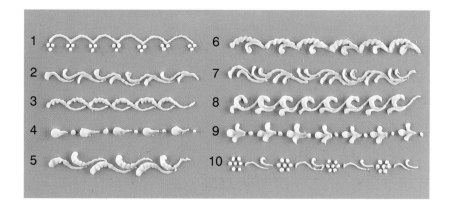

1 Scalloped line with picot dots

2 Series of interlinked S and reverse S scrolls

3 Interlinked S scrolls piped using a rope action (see page 353)

4 Teardrop and dot design

5 Series of interlinked S and reverse S scrolls piped using a rope action

6 Roped scallop with C scrolls underneath

7 Series of interlinked S scrolls with added S, reverse S and C scrolls

8 Series of C scrolls with small S scrolls underneath

9 Teardrop and dot design (see no. 4) and C and reverse C scrolls to make a fleur-de-lys

10 Dot daisy (see page 350) with an S and C scroll stem

Piping lettering and numerals

A great way to personalise a royal iced or sugarpasted cake is to add a piped inscription depicting the occasion, the recipient's name or initials, or their age. There are many styles of lettering that can be piped freehand onto cakes; as with the motifs you will need to practise them before piping onto a cake.

Piping and embellishing letters

You should always practise piping the basic, simple letter and number forms first, making sure that each of the letters or numbers is balanced and legible. Once you gain confidence you can experiment with different styles of embellishment to suit the style of cake and the occasion. The embellishments shown here on the letter 'A' demonstrate how you can add embellishments without overpowering the basic form.

1 Always start with the simple form, making sure it is large enough.

2 The basic form can be simply embellished with a straight serif at the top and bottom of each line.

3 Adding a double line down one side of a letter or number allows you to fill the space with simple patterns such as dots or basic scrolls.

4 A variation on the simple serif, small dots and S scrolls instead

of horizontal lines make the letter more ornate.

5 More ornate still, small C scrolls can be piped on the ends of the lines as serifs and a dot can replace a horizontal line.

6 The basic form of a letter or number can be extended at the top or bottom using scrolls with piped beads. Softening the horizontal lines makes the style less formal.

7 Add weight to the basic form by over-piping the lower half only with dots and lines.

8 Another way of adding weight to the lower half of a letter or number is to pipe a running bead over the lines.

9 For a romantic script style, make the lines more free-flowing and add embellishments such as a running bead and scrolls.

1 A 2 A 3 A 4 A 5 A 6 A 7 A 8 A 9 A

Anne *Anne* *Mother*

21 18 25 50 40th

Congratulations

50

Golden Years

Happy Birthday

With WK Love

Script lettering

('Congratulations 50 Golden Years')

This style of lettering can be piped using melted chocolate as well as royal icing, so is ideal for gateaux and chocolate cakes.

1 Holding the nozzle on the cake surface at an angle, pressure pipe clean up-strokes and running beads on the down-strokes on a right oblique angle.

2 If required, over-pipe the letters with your choice of embellishment, see page 364.

Monograms ('W K')

Monograms are ideal when you have a small space to fill, particularly on wedding cakes.

1 Pipe the first letter in your chosen style. Interlink the second letter with the first, positioning it beside and halfway down the first letter.

2 Add your choice of embellishment.

Over-piping using colour

('Happy Birthday' and 'With Love')

1 Pipe the inscription in your chosen style using the same colour royal icing as the cake covering.

2 Make up another bag of royal icing in a different colour using the same nozzle as in step 1. Over-pipe the inscription, taking care to keep on top of the initial lines.

Old English lettering

('To My Valentine')

1 Prepare a bag of rubbed-down icing suitable for drop-line work (see page 235). Drop-line the initial capital letter and embellish as required, following the ideas on page 364 as a guide.

2 Start the lower case letters just over halfway up the initial letter and continue to pipe your chosen inscription using squared-off lines.

Illuminated letters

('Tracy'; 'Happy Anniversary')

1 Choose the style of lettering you are going to use for the inscription. Pipe the initial capital letter with a double vertical line. Fill in the gap with your chosen decoration and add serifs to the top and bottom of the letter.

2 Pipe the rest of the inscription in a more basic form so as not to overpower the cake.

3 If you need to balance out the design, add motifs around the inscription, again taking care not to overpower the lettering or numerals.

tutor tip

When piping onto cakes, pipe in self-colour first, e.g. white piping on a white cake, then over-pipe in coloured icing.

Pressure-piped plaques

These plaques have all been decorated with pressure-piped motifs. The more proficient you become, the more complex the designs can be. Some of the more advanced designs include whole scenes with perspective and figures or animals which have fine detail piped in relief using stiffer icing.

Working on plaques is ideal because you can make them as off-pieces and attach them to the coated cake when dry.

Pressure-piped Decorations

Pressure-piped Mini Christening Cakes

The beauty of piped decoration is that it can be used on cakes, mini cakes, cupcakes and cookies, whether they are coated with royal icing or sugarpaste. These mini cakes are a contemporary alternative to a traditional christening cake and make perfect take-home treats for your guests.

EDIBLES

2 x round mini cakes covered with SK Bridal White Sugarpaste, see page 157

1 x square mini cake covered with SK Lullaby Blue Sugarpaste, see page 157

SK Instant Mix Royal Icing

SK Professional Liquid Food Colours: Bulrush, Rose

EQUIPMENT

Bootees

Piping nozzles: nos. 2, 43

Stork

Piping nozzles: nos. 1, 2, 43

Swan silhouette

Piping nozzle: no. 1.5

For essential royal icing edibles and equipment, see pages 230–231

Bootees

1 Using a no. 2 nozzle and slightly rubbed-down royal icing pipe two bootees in the centre of the cake following the instructions on page 363. You can pipe them either directly onto the cake or as off-pieces. Pipe on the bows with a little Rose-coloured icing (or Bluebell for a boy) once the bootees are in place.

2 Divide the cake into four, pipe two C scrolls at the front and at the back, then add a flounce on either side using a no. 43 nozzle. Pipe scallops along the top edge and shells around the base (see page 248).

3 Pipe dots down the cake sides with the no. 2 nozzle to finish.

Stork

1 Place some white royal icing into a piping bag with a no. 2 nozzle. Starting ¾ of the way up the top of the cake, pipe the stork following the instructions on page 363.

2 Use a no. 1 nozzle to pipe an S and C scroll underneath the stork then add a little daisy (see page 360).

3 Pipe around the top with a simple scallop design, then add a running bead with a no. 43 nozzle around the base to finish.

Swan silhouette

1 Start by piping around the side of the cake with a no. 1.5 nozzle and Bulrush-coloured royal icing. Pipe a repetitive C scroll with an S scroll underneath then pipe a repetitive C scroll of the same width underneath, almost at the bottom of the cake (see page 364).

2 Use the same icing to pipe the swans with a no. 1.5 nozzle (see page 363). Add in the water scene around the swans using the same nozzle.

Extension and Lace Work

TESSA WHITEHOUSE

Extension work is an advanced technique that gives an impressive, special touch to any celebration cake. It consists of a series of parallel piped lines which start on the side of the cake and finish on a piped bridge so that they extend away from the cake. This exquisite style of piping is sometimes known as bridge work and can be used on both royal iced and sugarpasted cakes.

EDIBLES

Cake covered with royal icing, see page 236, or cake covered with sugarpaste, see pages 139–140

SK Instant Mix Royal Icing

SK Instant Mix Extension Icing

EQUIPMENT

Piping nozzles: nos. 0, 1, 1.5, 2

Small, round cutter

For essential royal icing edibles and equipment, see pages 230–231

TECHNIQUES

- Marking up a cake for extension work
- Piping bridge work
- Piping extension lines
- Piping lace work

Extension work

Before you start piping, you must carefully measure and mark out the cake for the shape of the extension work. The lower edge of the extension work is usually scalloped or curved, with the top edge either shaped or straight. By mixing and matching the size and shape of the curves many different patterns can be created.

Making a template for bridge work

This template is for an extension pattern with a straight top edge and a scalloped bridge.

1 Cut a greaseproof paper template to the same circumference and depth as a round cake or the size of a side on a square cake and accurately fold it in half, then quarters and continue to fold until you have evenly sized sections that are between 2.5cm (1") and 5cm (2") wide.

2 Decide on the length of the extension lines and mark this distance from the base of the folded paper on the edges of the long sides. Join the two marks together with a straight line: this will be the top edge of the extension work. Typically, extension lines are piped approximately 3cm (1¼") from the top edge to the lowest part of the scallop. Please note that longer lines are harder to pipe.

3 To draw the lower scallop, measure 1cm–1.5cm (³⁄₈"–⁵⁄₈") up from the base of the template and mark on both edges. Place a small round cutter of the appropriate size between the marks and draw around it.

4 Cut the template along the pencil marks, unfold and wrap around the cake ensuring there is a gap between the lowest part of the scallop and the cake

board. Secure in place with masking tape, ensuring that the tape does not touch the cake.

Marking the cake

5 Mark the top edge of the template onto the side of the cake using a scriber.

6 Mark on the position of the scallops using the point of a scriber or a tiny dot of royal icing (in a piping bag without a nozzle) at the scallop peaks on the folds of the template.

See page 376 for an alternative method for marking a straight top edge on a royal iced cake.

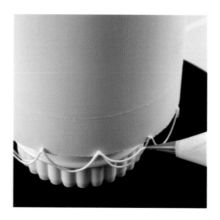

Piping bridge work

7 Place the cake on a tilting turntable and tilt the cake slightly away from you.

8 Fit a piping bag with a no. 1.5 nozzle, ½-fill with royal icing and pipe drop lines between the marks made for the scallops. Set aside to dry for 15 minutes.

9 Pipe another line exactly on top of the first, making sure there is contact along the whole length of each piped line. Repeat and set aside for another 10–15 minutes.

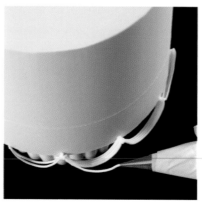

Extension and Lace Work

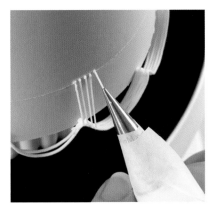

10 Continue piping more drop lines until the bridge is the appropriate depth: a bridge should be at least five lines deep. The more lines that are piped, the further the extension lines will stand away from the cake.

Piping extension lines

11 Make up the extension icing according to the instructions on the packet. Cover the bowl with a damp cloth or airtight lid to prevent it from crusting over.

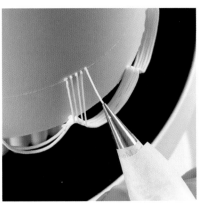

12 Fit a small piping bag with a no. 0 or 1 nozzle and ½-fill with extension icing. Tilt the turntable towards you slightly and attach the icing to the side of the cake above the scribed line marking the top edge of the extension work. While increasing the pressure on the bag, bring the piping nozzle forward slightly then bring it down and pipe to just beyond the bridge. Tuck the end of the line of icing underneath it but take care not to touch the bridge with the nozzle as this can cause it to break.

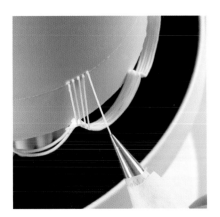

13 Gently tidy the end of the line with a barely damp paintbrush, then pipe the next line as closely as possible to the first without the lines touching. If you make a mistake, remove the line carefully with a barely damp paintbrush. Keep moving the turntable around so you are piping directly in front of you and make sure to keep the lines vertical.

14 Finish the edges of the extension work with drop lines, piped 'pearls' or lace work (see opposite).

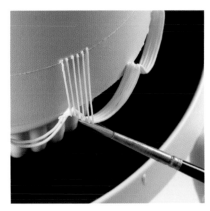

tutor tip

You can achieve a more delicate bridge by using a small nozzle, or by reducing the size of the nozzle with each subsequent pair of drop lines.

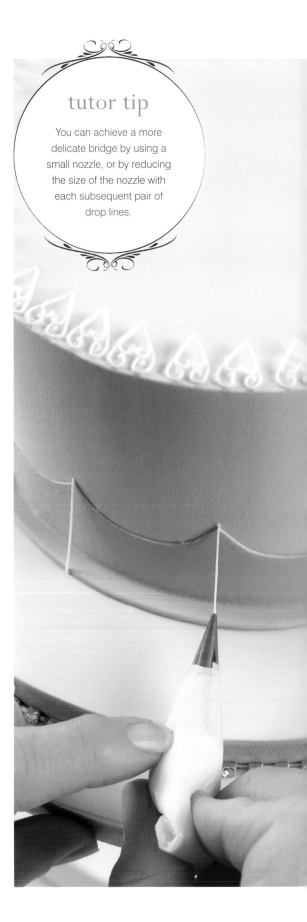

Lace pieces

1 Draw out a lace design or copy a lace template onto a sheet of paper. Place the template on a sturdy board or cake drum under a sheet of acetate that has been very lightly greased with white vegetable fat.

2 Very gently rub down a small amount of white icing and fit a small piping bag with a no. 0 nozzle. Half-fill the piping bag with the icing and pipe over the templates to create the lace pieces. Leave to dry; the drying time will depend on the size of the pieces but can be sped up by placing the icing under a desk lamp.

3 Once dry, attach the lace piece to the cake using small dots of royal icing. Use a paintbrush to adjust the position of the lace if necessary.

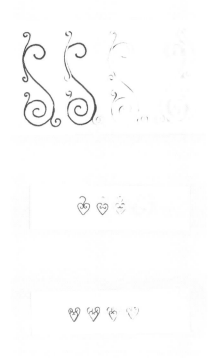

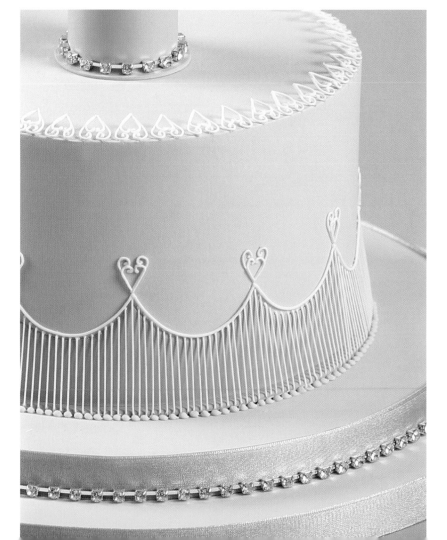

TUTOR TIPS

- It is easier to work if you have the cake at eye level when piping extension lines.

- Change the royal icing every 20 minutes when you are piping lace and extension work and quickly beat the icing each time before filling a new piping bag.

- When viewed from the side the extension work should appear to be the thickness of a piped line.

- Regularly check that the extension lines are straight. If they begin to slant, make sure to correct this when piping the next few lines.

- Pipe the lace pieces with freshly-made icing as they will be less likely to break.

- If you use coloured paper for the lace templates it makes it easier to see the piped lines.

Extension and Lace Work

PROJECT

'Something Blue' Engagement Cake

Any blushing bride-to-be will appreciate the sophistication and elegance that the extension and lace work lends to this design. This small tiered cake would make a great engagement gift and the diamanté trim adds that extra touch of sparkle.

EDIBLES

10cm x 7.5cm deep and 15cm x 9cm deep (4" x 3" and 6" x 3½") round fruit cakes

900g (2lb) SK Marzipan

1kg (2lb 3¼oz) SK Instant Mix Royal Icing

SK Professional Liquid Food Colours: Bluebell, Hyacinth

SK Quality Food Colour (QFC) Liquid: Black

SK Professional Dust Food Colour: Bluebell

250g (8¾oz) SK Instant Mix Extension Icing

SK Glycerine

5g (1tsp) SK Gum Tragacanth

65g (2¼oz) icing sugar

For essential royal icing edibles and equipment, see pages 230–231

EQUIPMENT

25.5cm and 30.5cm (10" and 12") round cake drums (boards)

10cm and 15cm (4" and 6") round cake cards

15cm and 20.5cm (6" and 8") round food-grade acrylic discs or cake boards

2m (6' 5") x 15mm (½") wide satin ribbon: soft blue

1m (3' 3") diamanté trim

2.5cm (1") diameter cylindrical former

4cm (1½") round cutter

Clear plastic cake dowel

Plastic side scraper

7.5cm (3") cookie cutter

Small food-grade plastic bottle

Templates, see page 510

Cake

1 Fix each cake to the corresponding size cake card and cover with marzipan following the instructions on page 95. Place the cakes on the acrylic discs or cake boards so that they can be moved easily and set aside to dry for up to 48 hours.

2 Mix 4 drops of Bluebell, 6 drops of Black and 2 drops of Hyacinth liquid food colours together in a small dropper bottle to make a soft blue colour.

3 Make up 1kg (2lb 3¼oz) of royal icing according to the packet instructions. Place 200g (7oz) of the icing into an airtight container and put aside for the lace pieces and bridge work.

4 Add drops of the soft blue liquid food colour to the remaining 800g (1lb 12oz) of icing until the required depth of colour is achieved. Place 200g (7oz) of soft blue icing in an airtight container: this will be used for coating the cake boards. Save a further 135g (4¾oz) of icing for making up the pastillage. Add 5ml (1tsp) of glycerine to the remainder of the icing and label the bowl 'glycerine'.

5 Coat the 15cm (6") cake with three coats of soft blue icing (see pages 236–238). Cover the top of the 10cm (4") cake with three coats and the sides with two coats of soft blue icing. Use

374

a craft knife to make a small notch on the long side of a plastic side scraper, approximately 2.5cm (1") up from the bottom. Cover the cake with a final coat of royal icing then immediately pull the side scraper around the cake once, with the notch side touching the icing. This will leave a line around the side of the cake which you can use as a guide for the extension work. Set aside to dry.

6 Make a scalloped side design template for the 15cm (6") cake, following the instructions on page 241 so that the peak of the scallop is 6cm (2³/₈") and the base is 7.5cm (3") from the top straight edge. Wrap the greaseproof paper tightly around the 15cm (6") cake and fix in place. Ensure the scalloped edge is wrapped tightly around the cake.

7 Colour some of the royal icing containing glycerine a darker shade of blue using the liquid food colour mixture. Place the 15cm (6") cake on a turntable and paddle the darker icing onto the exposed side of the cake. Use the side scraper to smooth the icing with one complete turn of the cake. Carefully remove the greaseproof paper and set the cake aside to dry.

Cake drums

8 Cover both cake drums with 200g (7oz) of glycerine-free soft blue icing and leave to dry (see page 238). Place a little well rubbed-down royal icing in the centre of the large drum and fix the smaller drum centrally on top. Trim both cake drums with soft blue ribbon and secure the diamanté trim around the base of the smaller board.

Pastillage plaque and pillar

9 Accurately measure the diameter of the larger cake and add 1.5cm–2cm (½"–¾") to this measurement. Cut a round template of this diameter from thin card.

10 To make the pastillage, add more of the blue food colouring to the 135g (4¾oz) of royal icing reserved earlier then turn it out onto a clean board and knead in 5g (1tsp) of gum tragacanth. Set aside in a sealed food-grade plastic bag for 30 minutes, then turn out onto a surface liberally sprinkled with icing sugar and knead in up to a further 65g (2¼oz) of icing sugar until the paste is soft and pliable but not sticky.

11 Dust a non-stick board with cornflour and roll out the pastillage to a thickness of 2mm (¹/₁₆"). Make sure the pastillage moves freely on the board and then cut out a round plaque using the template as a guide. Set aside to dry, carefully turning it over after a couple of hours to allow the underside to dry. Drying the pastillage plaque on a piece of smooth, food-grade foam sponge will speed up the drying time. Once dry, sand off any rough edges on the plaque away from the food preparation area. Brush off any dust with a pastry brush.

12 Roll out the remaining pastillage thinly and cut out a rectangle 7.5cm (3") high and wide enough to wrap around the cylindrical former. Make a cylinder following the instructions on page 224. Cut out two 4cm (1½") circles from the remaining pastillage and allow all the pieces to dry. When dry, use royal icing to stick the circles to each end of the cylinder, then secure diamanté trim around the base.

13 Fix the plaque centrally on the stacked cake drums with a little royal icing then secure the large cake centrally onto the plaque with a little royal

376

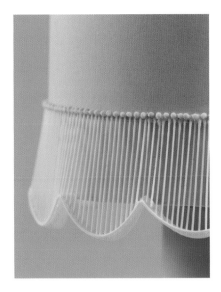

icing. If necessary, use a piping bag fitted with a no. 1 nozzle and dark blue icing to pipe a line of running beads around the edge.

First tier

14 Make a template and mark out the position of the drop lines following the instructions on page 371. The peaks of the scallops should be 5mm (¼") above the base of the cake. Fit a piping bag with a no. 1.5 nozzle, ½-fill with royal icing and pipe hanging bridges between the marks around the cake (see page 372). Pipe four further lines on top to build up the bridges.

15 Make up the extension icing then pipe extension lines from the marks around the cake down onto the top of the hanging bridges, keeping the lines straight (see page 372).

16 Use a no. 1 nozzle and off-peak royal icing to pipe a row of running beads around the top of the extension work, then pipe drop lines over the base of the lines to hide the joins.

Base tier

17 Place the pastillage pillar centrally on the large cake, mark the position of the dowel and dowel the cake (see page 143). Using extension icing, pipe extension lines from the top of the coloured scallops to the edge of the pastillage plaque. Make sure to keep the lines straight.

18 Use a no. 1 nozzle and some off-peak icing to pipe drop lines across the top of the extension lines, then pipe a running bead border around the base to hide the joins in the same way as for the first tier.

Lace pieces

19 Fit a piping bag with a no. 1 nozzle, ½-fill with rubbed-down icing and pipe approximately 100 lace pieces following the templates (see page 373), plus extras to allow for breakages. Allow to dry. Secure lace pieces around the top edge of each tier and at the peak of each scallop and dust the hanging pieces with Bluebell dust colour if desired.

Filigree top decoration

20 Place the filigree top decoration template on a drying board, lightly grease a piece of acetate and place over the template. Fit a small piping bag with a no. 1.5 nozzle, ½-fill with off-peak royal icing and pipe the small curls on the design. Pipe the larger curl with off-peak icing and a no. 2 nozzle. As these pieces are very fragile, it is a good idea to make extras in case of breakages. Set aside to dry.

21 Carefully release the filigree pieces from the acetate when dry and turn them over to pipe the same on the reverse side. Set aside to dry. Pipe a small dot of royal icing at the places indicated on the template to join the three filigree pieces together.

22 To fix the pastillage pillar in place apply a small amount of royal icing to the top of the pillar and place the second tier on top.

23 Attach the decorative topper centrally on the small cake with well rubbed-down royal icing after the cakes have been assembled. Hang a lace piece from the top curl of each section on the topper to finish.

'Something Blue' Engagement Cake

Susanna Righetto

BIOGRAPHY

M y biography on the Squires Kitchen International School's website reads, "Susanna Righetto is a talented sugar florist and creates flowers that are stylish and feminine with a romantic flair." This is very flattering, considering that all I'm trying to do is express my love for flowers through my work. My enthusiasm for flowers started during my childhood, and was initially fuelled by my mother, with whom I share this passion. Suffice to say, as a child my gifts of choice were potted plants rather than dolls.

I started out as a professional photographer before discovering that I could combine my passion for both photography and baking through the art of sugar floristry. It didn't take me long to

realise that although learning from books gives you a good start, to learn the secrets of any craft you need to study with an experienced tutor. This realisation led me to study under leading names in sugar floristry, such as Paddi Clark and Alan Dunn, and to obtain my Master Certificate from Squires Kitchen International School. More recently I had the honour of honing my hand-piping skills with Eddie Spence MBE, whose talents as a sugarcrafter and tutor are incomparable.

My first experiences of teaching sugarcraft were on my home turf, Italy. I was invited to teach and demonstrate several times at the two major sugarcraft exhibitions in Italy: The Cake Show and Cake Design Italian Festival. As a tutor with Squires Kitchen International School, I was given the chance to spread my love for sugar flowers further,

teaching at world-renowned events in both the UK and Spain.

You can find tutorials of my work on the pages of *Cakes & Sugarcraft*, *Squires Kitchen Bake School* and *Wedding Cakes – A Design Source* magazines, as well as several Italian magazines and on my personal blog, 'The Sugar Garden'. I also had the honour of being invited to star in two episodes of *Le Torte di Toni*, an Italian TV show hosted by Australian sugarcrafter Toni Brancatisano.

I try to keep my cakes as simple as possible to focus the attention on the floral decorations. My little secret? I keep several sprays of sugar flowers in vases around the house, they provide inspiration and I can't live without my flowers!

Tuberoses

SUSANNA RIGHETTO

The tuberose is a pretty perennial Mexican plant that has spikes of white, fragrant, lily-like flowers. This elegant yet unusual flower is ideal for those who are looking to make something a bit different. The flowers and buds are simple to make but still look impressive when presented on a cake.

EDIBLES

SK Sugar Florist Paste (SFP): Pale Green, White

SK Professional Dust Food Colours: Daffodil (yellow), Edelweiss (white), Leaf Green, Rose, Vine

EQUIPMENT

26-, 28-gauge floral wires: white

30-, 33-gauge floral wires: green

Small white seed-head stamens

Floral tape (¼-width): Nile green

Six-petal flower cutters: cutters 2, 3 and 4 from large set (OP)

Non-toxic craft glue

Non-stick mat (optional)

For essential floral edibles and equipment, see pages 254–255

TECHNIQUES

- Making wired tuberose flowers, leaves and buds

Flower centre

1 Cut six white stamens to approximately 2.5cm (1") long. Arrange the stamens next to each other so they are flat on the work surface and stick the stems together with non-toxic craft glue.

2 Cut several 26-gauge white wires into quarters. Once the glue is dry, wrap the stamens around a piece of 26-gauge wire and secure in place with craft glue. Dust the stamen heads with Daffodil dust food colour.

Petals

3 Knead some White SFP well and roll it out thinly on a lightly-greased, non-stick board. Cut out a six-petal blossom from the SFP using the smallest cutter from the set. Place the blossom on a foam pad and use a small ball tool to thin the edges of the petals whilst stretching the petals from the centre of the flower out towards the tips. Drag the ball tool from the tip of the petal in towards the centre to gently curl the petals inwards.

4 Dab a little edible glue over the base of the stamens and over the flower centre. Thread the wire through the

centre of the flower and push the flower up to sit behind the stamens. Pinch the base of the flower very lightly to secure.

5 Repeat steps 3 and 4 to make another set of petals using the next-largest six-petal cutter in the same way. Secure the second set of petals behind the first, positioning each petal between the gaps in the preceding petals.

6 Make a Mexican hat shape from a piece of well-kneaded White SFP (see page 266), then place the largest cutter over the paste so the bump is central and cut out the blossom. Place the blossom on the foam pad and work the petals with a ball tool as for the

previous layers. Use a cutting wheel to mark several shallow lines along each of the petals to represent the veins. As you have worked on this set of petals upside down, the petals should curl gently outwards. Alternatively, you can place the flower in a hole on a double foam pad and work as before but this method will make the blossom more closed.

7 Hollow out the centre of each set of petals with a CelStick. Apply a little edible glue in the centre then push the blossom up the wire and stick it to the previous set of petals. Position the petals between the gaps in the preceding petals, as before.

8 Smooth the back of the flower down around the wire until it is approximately 2cm (¾") long and narrows towards the end. Mark vein lines down the neck in the same way as for the petals.

Buds

9 Cut a 26-gauge white wire into quarters and make a small hook at the end of each wire. Roll a small ball of White SFP into a sausage shape, dab a little edible glue over the hooked end of the wire and insert into the sausage. Work the paste into a bud shape around the wire, making the top of the bud rounded then narrowing the paste as you work down the wire.

10 Use a cutting wheel to mark a few lines from the top to approximately a quarter of the way down the bud to represent closed petals. Add some shallow lines down the neck of the bud.

11 Blend some Leaf Green and Edelweiss dust food colours together in a small bowl or paint palette and brush a slight hint of colour over the neck of the bud. Lightly dust the top of the bud with the same colour, then finish with a touch of Rose dust food colour.

Leaves

12 Cut several short lengths of 33-gauge green wire, then lightly moisten one end of a wire with edible glue. Make a tiny ball of Pale Green SFP and insert the end of the wire into the paste. Model the paste into a teardrop shape (with the pointed end facing down the wire) and pinch the end to secure in position. Press a non-stick mat or other flat, non-stick surface (such as the flat side of a veiner or a piece of acetate) onto the paste to flatten it. Thin the edges of the paste with a small ball tool and repeat to make as many leaves as required in varying sizes.

13 Dust the leaves with a mixture of Leaf Green and Holly/Ivy dust food colours.

14 Take a 30-gauge green wire and attach the leaves with ¼-width green tape: fix a pair of the smallest leaves opposite each other at the tip of the wire and attach another pair a few millimetres below. Continue to attach more leaves down the wire, gradually increasing the size of the leaves and spacing them approximately 1cm (³/₈") apart. When you have completed the stem, brush the leaves with confectioners' glaze and allow to dry.

Scented Wedding Cake

Polianthes tuberosa has lovely, highly fragrant flowers that grow in elongated clusters. In traditional Hawaiian weddings, it is customary for the bride to wear a tuberose wreath, and during Indian wedding ceremonies the flowers are also used for decorative purposes. The Aztecs grew tuberoses because they were sacred to their goddess of art, beauty and love, so after the Spanish conquest in 1519 the flower found its way to Europe. Once introduced to Europe, it became part of the moon garden, a collection of white or pastel flowers which release an intense fragrance after dusk.

EDIBLES

15cm x 10cm deep (6" x 4") and 20.5cm x 10cm deep (8" x 4") round cakes, filled and crumb-coated (see page 92)

SK Sugarpaste: 600g (1lb 5¼oz) Bridal White, 1kg (2lb 3¼oz) Iced Mint

50 tuberose flowers, see pages 382–383

25–30 tuberose buds, see page 383

10–12 stems of leaves, see page 383

EQUIPMENT

2 x 15cm (6") and 1 x 20.5cm (8") round cake cards

3 or 4 cake dowels

Posy pick

Clear sticky tape

Organza ribbon: green

For essential floral edibles and equipment, see pages 254–255

This design was inspired by the 'Pearl' double-flower tuberose with its pretty, pink buds opening into white flowers. I chose single flowers and buds over clusters, adding just a touch of green with the tiny leaves for a pleasant counterpoint.

1 Place the cakes on their corresponding cake cards. Cover the 20.5cm (8") cake with 900g (2lb) of Iced Mint sugarpaste (see page 139). Mix 100g (3½oz) of the remaining Iced Mint sugarpaste with 600g (1lb 5¼oz) of Bridal White sugarpaste to achieve a very light shade of green and cover the 15cm (6") cake.

2 Dowel the larger cake (see page 143) and secure the organza ribbon around the base of the cake with a touch of royal icing or edible glue.

3 Arrange the flowers, buds and leaves in a circle around the edge of the spare 15cm (6") cake card and stick to the card with clear tape. Once you are happy with the arrangement, place the card centrally on the bottom tier and carefully position the smaller cake inside the flower arrangement.

4 Gather a few flowers, buds and leaves into a posy shape and secure with green floral tape (see page 261). Place a small amount of SFP in a posy pick and insert the pick into the cake towards the front of the top tier. Secure the posy into the pick and add a few more flowers to fill any gaps and hide the pick if necessary.

Important note: Remember to remove all inedible items from the cake before it is served, including the flowers, clear tape and cake dowels.

Paddi Clark

BIOGRAPHY

My love of cake decoration started when my three sons were very young and I used to enjoy making their birthday cakes. My passion for cake decorating grew from there really and sugar has become my passion ever since!

After discovering my enthusiasm for cake decorating, I decided to go to college and get my official City & Guilds qualifications in Bakery and Confectionery, Creative Studies in Sugarcraft and Creative Studies in Design & Decoration along with my ABC and NCFE qualifications. I just kept learning and gained different qualifications with different examination boards at all levels, as well as winning awards at national cake competitions.

Along the way I gained my teaching qualifications and began teaching sugarcraft skills at day and evening classes in six different colleges. I taught courses in Sugarcraft and Cake Decoration to beginners through to an advanced level; it was quite a marathon but hugely rewarding. A number of my students have gone on to be very successful in national competitions and have been awarded Best Cake in Show at the NEC. One student, whom I taught and mentored, even went on to win the prestigious UK Medal of Excellence in her final year. I was also pleased to be able to help a competitor in the World Skills Event at Earls Court to learn the art of sugar floristry as part of his competitive category. I went on to use my teaching experience to become an NCFE Inspector for Course Quality and Content where I visited colleges to check standards.

Throughout my career I have made and decorated cakes for several celebrities, as well as taking part in a TV programme called 'Icing on the Cake'. I was also one of the founder members of the Taste of Art group who exhibited sugar as an art form in art galleries in Guildford and The Bowes Museum in County Durham. These displays were the first of their kind, and proved both rewarding and successful.

As a member of the British Sugarcraft Guild, I have demonstrated sugarcraft techniques around the country. I have also taught classes in several countries around the world, including the USA, Sweden, Italy, Spain, Portugal, Germany and New Zealand.

I was originally offered a position by Squires Kitchen International School to join their team of tutors, but unfortunately had to turn it down at the time due to other commitments. However, fortunately two years later, I was able to accept a position as their Senior Tutor and I have held this position for approximately 15 years since. I designed and now teach the 6-day Professional Intensive Course at the school, which has proved extremely successful. More recently, I designed the 6-day Professional Extended Techniques Course which is growing in popularity with students who come from around the world to participate. Although I am well known for my sugar floristry, I also love teaching many other areas of sugarcraft, including royal icing and sugarpaste skills, which I have done throughout the years.

I am an established contributor to *Cakes & Sugarcraft* magazine and have a regular article in each issue called 'Floral Features'. I am also the author of two books on sugar floristry, *Sugar Flowers for Beginners* and the follow-up *More Sugar Flowers for Beginners* (B. Dutton Publishing). These introductory titles have proved to be very successful and the first title has been translated into Russian.

Most recently, one of my proudest achievements was being part of a team that decorated the Queen's Diamond Jubilee cake with Eddie Spence MBE and McVitie's Cake Company (United Biscuits). When I was asked to join Eddie on the team I was both honoured and delighted.

My journey through sugarcraft has been a joy and continues to be so.

Country Garden Flowers

PADDI CLARK

The simplicity of a white
and green colour scheme
gives a touch of elegance
and sophistication to a floral
arrangement. The greyish-
green eucalyptus leaves and
dark green rose leaves form
the perfect foundation for
large roses, flowing lisianthus
and frilly scabious as well
as delicate myrtle flowers
with their fluffy centres
and the arched stems of the
lily of the valley. This small
selection of country garden
flowers, with their different
shapes and textures, come
together to make an elegant
arrangement.

EDIBLES

Eustoma grandiflorum

SK Sugar Florist Paste (SFP): Holly/Ivy, Pale Green, Pale Yellow, White

SK Designer Pollen-Style Edible Dust Food Colour: Pale Yellow

SK Professional Dust Food Colour: Leaf Green

Scabious

SK Sugar Florist Paste (SFP): Holly/Ivy, Pale Green, White

Myrtle

SK Sugar Florist Paste (SFP): Holly/Ivy, White

SK Designer Pollen-Style Edible Dust Food Colour: Pale Yellow

Lily of the valley

SK Sugar Florist Paste (SFP): Holly/Ivy, White

Eucalyptus leaves

SK Sugar Florist Paste (SFP): Holly/Ivy

SK Professional Paste Food Colour: Edelweiss

EQUIPMENT

Eustoma grandiflorum

Small round-headed stamens: white

20-, 22-, 26-, 28-gauge floral wires: green

24-gauge floral wire: white

Strong craft glue

Petal veiner/friller tool: no. 12 (JEM)

Rose petal cutters: 3.5cm, 4.5cm (1³/₈", 1¾") (TT)

Floral tape: light green

Cupped former

Templates, see page 510

Scabious

6-petal cutter: 5cm (2") (OP)

8-petal daisy cutter: 3.5cm (1³/₈") (OP)

Petal veiner/friller tool: no. 12 (JEM)

24-gauge floral wires: green

Floral tape: light green

Fine round-headed stamens: white

Micro blossom cutter (Kit Box) (optional)

Template, see page 510

Myrtle

Stephanotis cutter: 12mm (TT)

Small blossom plunger cutter (FMM)

Small rose calyx cutter (FMM)

Fine cotton thread: white

30-gauge floral wire: white

Floral tape: light green

Lily of the valley

Blossom plunger cutters, set of 3 (FMM)

28-, 30-gauge floral wires: white

Floral tape: light green

Template, see page 510

Eucalyptus leaves

Round cutters: 1.5cm, 2cm, 2.3cm (1¼", ¾", ⁷/₈") (Kit Box)

30-gauge floral wires: white

Floral tape: white

For essential floral edibles and equipment, see pages 254–255

TECHNIQUES

- Making a Eustoma grandiflorum (lisianthus), scabious, myrtle, lily of the valley and eucalyptus leaves

Eustoma grandiflorum (Lisianthus)

A stylish, tall plant with large funnel-shaped flowers, lisianthus flowers grow in a selection of shades from pink to rose, mauve, blue and violet, as well as white, cream and two-toned colours.

Pistil

1 Cut a 24-gauge white floral wire into three equal lengths. Make a 'T' bar at the top of the wires as follows: bend a length of floral wire over on itself no more than 5mm (1/8") from the end of the wire. Bend the wire back again by another 5mm (1/8"). Hold this with the pliers then pull the long end back to the middle to form a long 'T' shape.

2 Take a 3mm (1/8") ball of Pale Yellow SFP, roll it into a tiny oval shape and place it on a non-stick board. Brush a little edible glue over the 'T' bar made previously and gently push it into the centre of the oval, covering the 'T' part completely with the paste.

3 Squeeze and flatten the ends of the paste, then use tweezers to pinch the centre, making a bow shape. Allow to dry.

4 Lightly brush the paste with edible glue and dip into Pale Yellow pollen dust colour. Allow to dry.

5 Roll a tiny piece of Pale Green SFP into a sausage. Brush edible glue over the base of the yellow pistil and roll the paste around the top of the wire. Thin the paste on the wire and remove any excess paste if necessary.

6 Take another small piece of Pale Green SFP and roll this into an oval shape. Brush edible glue over the wire under the base of the pistil, push the wire into the tiny oval and re-shape it. Allow to dry.

Stamens

7 Cut six stamens in half, lightly brush edible glue over the tips and then dip them into Pale Yellow pollen dust. Allow to dry.

8 Attach the stamens to the base of the prepared pistil with strong craft glue. Use 1/4-width light green floral tape to cover the stamens and wire. Once dry, separate the stamens and then gently curl them inwards with tweezers.

9 Cut a 22-gauge wire into thirds then tape a length underneath the centre with 1/4-width floral tape.

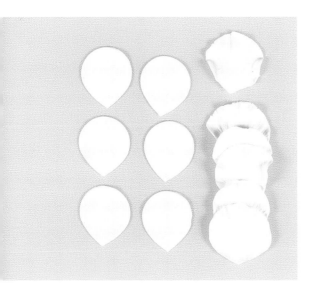

10 Roll a tiny piece of White SFP into a ball. Brush edible glue over the base of the pistil, push it through the paste and re-form into a small oval. Allow to dry.

Petals

11 Grease a non-stick board with white vegetable fat. Roll out the paste fairly thinly, turn it over onto a non-greased area of the board and cut out six petals using the larger cutter.

12 Use the veiner tool to add texture to the surface of the widest end of each petal and soften the edges with a ball tool on a foam pad. Elongate the pointed end of the petal with a ball tool.

13 Make a further set of petals for the double lisianthus using the same cutter.

14 Place the petals into a former or an apple tray so that the tips curl backwards and begin to hold their shape. The petals need to be assembled while they are still slightly soft but firm enough to hold their shape.

Assembling the flower

15 Brush the base of the petals with edible glue and stick them together in a fan shape.

16 Brush some edible glue onto the oval shape below the pistil/stamens and gently wrap the fanned petals around this, making sure they curl around evenly. The oval shape should not be visible if possible as it is only there to help with the attachment of the petals and for support. Squeeze the petals together gently at the base.

17 For a double lisianthus, brush some edible glue on the bottom of a petal and stick it over a join between the inner petals. Continue to add the second layer of petals, overlapping the petals around the flower. Squeeze the base together and curl the petals back. Place the flower into a former to firm.

Calyx

18 The calyx of this flower is very fine and wispy so I have made it with floral tape. Cut a 6cm (2½") length

of ½-width light green floral tape and cut it into pieces down the length. Make five for each flower. Cut one end of each piece into a point and twist it into a strand, leaving a wider base.

19 Place the wide end against the base of the petal and taped stem, press gently and twist it around the stem to hold it in place. Repeat this around the flower.

20 Tape over the calyx and around the base of the flower with ½-width floral tape and continue down the stem.

Country Garden Flowers

391

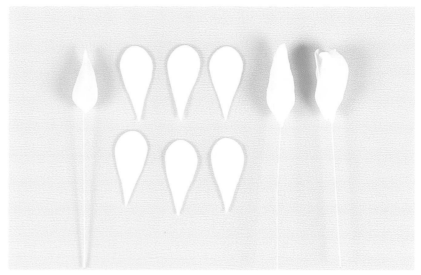

Buds

21 Form a small, pointed cone of White SFP measuring approximately 2.5cm (1") long. Insert a glued, hooked 26-gauge wire into the base and allow to dry. Cut out five petals using the template on page 510 from some White SFP. Shape each petal with a ball tool then brush them with edible glue. Wrap each petal around the cone and twist the petals to form the opening flower. Add a calyx to the base of the bud as before.

22 To make green buds, make a small cone from Pale Green SFP and insert a glued, hooked 24-gauge wire into the base. Use a craft knife to draw five lines from top to bottom around the bud. Twist the bud into a spiral then add a calyx as before.

23 Tape down the wire with ¼-width floral tape. The buds grow on long stems so do not trim the wire until later.

Leaves

24 Cut a 28-gauge green wire into three equal lengths.

25 Mix a small amount of Holly/ Ivy SFP with some White SFP to make a soft, grey-green colour.

26 Roll out the paste thinly and cut out the leaves either freehand or using the templates provided, then wire the leaves (see page 268).

27 Vein the leaves with a Dresden tool and soften the edges with a ball tool. Dust the leaves with a little Leaf Green dust food colour.

28 Repeat to make as many leaves as required: Eustoma plants usually have six to eight leaves per stem. Pass the leaves through the steam of a kettle to set the colour.

29 To make a stem, tape a green bud with one or two white buds together on a 20-gauge wire. Add a flower below these and a pair of leaves opposite each other. Continue taping down the stem then add another flower and a pair of leaves.

Scabious

Scabious flowers are showy, perennial sun worshippers, with their graceful, scented heads standing on finely-haired stems. They grow in many pretty colours and lighten a flower display with their frilly petals.

Calyx

1 Cut two 24-gauge green floral wires into four equal lengths.

2 Cut a small length of ½-width light green floral tape into three pieces.

3 Take the eight pieces of floral wire and tape them together with ¹/₃-width green floral tape, leaving 5mm (¼") at the top un-taped.

4 Open out the wires at the top and bend them down at right angles so they are equally spaced around the central wire.

5 Roll out some Pale Green SFP thinly and cut out two sets of petals with the 8-petal daisy cutter. Brush edible glue over the petals, then feed the first set up the wire. Adjust the angle of the wires at the top of the stem so they fit onto each petal.

6 Place the second set of petals over the top of the first petals so they fit together exactly and enclose the wires. Allow to dry flat.

Flower

7 Take a small piece of Pale Green SFP and roll approximately 30–35 very small balls of paste for the flower centre. To make the balls approximately equal in size, roll a thin sausage of paste, cut it into small, even pieces and then form each into a tiny ball. Allow these to dry.

8 Roll out some White SFP thinly, then cut out a set of petals with the 6-petal daisy cutter. Cut this set of petals in half and frill each petal with the frilling tool. Gently pleat each half of the petal and pinch the base together. Brush the base with edible glue and stick it over a section of the calyx.

9 Repeat to make seven more petals and attach to each section of the calyx. Gently bend the petals upwards as they are drying.

10 Roll a small ball of Pale Green SFP and flatten it into a disc. Soften some SFP with edible glue to make a tacky paste, then put some in the centre of the petals and over the calyx. Place the small green disc onto the softened paste over the edges of the petals and press down gently to neaten.

11 If you wish to make coloured flowers, you can dust the edges of the petals/sepals at this stage. I have left these white scabious flowers undusted.

12 Cover the disc with a small amount of softened SFP, use a pair of tweezers to pick up the balls individually and attach them to the disc until it is completely covered.

13 Roll out some White SFP very thinly then cut out several small blossoms with the micro blossom cutter. Use a scribing needle or a sterilised pin to place the blossoms between the balls and secure with edible glue. These small blossoms are the actual flowers of the scabious plant and when they are in full bloom they have many of these tiny blossoms; I prefer to just use a few in each flower centre to show how they will develop.

14 Cut a fine round-headed stamen in half and secure one in the centre of each small blossom.

Leaves

15 Mix some White SFP with some Holly/Ivy SFP to create a greyish-green colour and roll it out thinly. Cut a 28-gauge green wire into three lengths. Cut out the leaves using the template on page 510 and wire each of the leaves (see page 268). Make two or three leaves per flower.

16 To make a stem, cut a piece of ½-width light green floral tape into three lengths. Position a leaf under the flower and tape it to the stem, then attach another leaf on the opposite side. Continue down the stem attaching more leaves as required: a stem usually has three to five leaves, including the lead leaf.

Myrtle

Centre

1 Wind a length of fine, white cotton thread approximately 15 times around your forefinger and middle finger. Remove the cotton from your fingers then fold and twist to make a figure of '8' with the thread. Fold this over to make a loop.

2 Thread a 30-gauge white wire through the loop and fold it in half over the thread. Twist the wire tightly around the thread to secure, then continue to twist the rest of the wire below the cotton to keep it tightly in place.

3 Cut through the top of the cotton loop and separate the strands to make stamens. Wrap a piece of ¼-width green floral tape around the base of the cotton to cover the wire loop. Tape down the rest of the wire.

4 Spread out the cotton and trim the ends into a fan shape, so the stamens are approximately 1cm (³/₈") long. Lightly brush edible glue over the tips of the cotton and dip them in Pale Yellow edible pollen dust.

5 Take a piece of White SFP and make a Mexican hat shape (see page 266). Place the bump in the middle of the stephanotis cutter and cut out a small set of petals. Use a ball tool to gently cup and soften the edges of each petal. Brush edible glue over the centre, push the petals up the wire and secure behind the stamens. Allow to dry.

6 Mix some Holly/Ivy SFP with White SFP, roll it out thinly and cut out a calyx using a small rose calyx cutter. Brush edible glue over the base of the flower, push the calyx up behind the flower and secure.

Buds

7 Cut a 30-gauge wire into five pieces. Make a tiny ball of Holly/Ivy SFP and insert a lightly glued, hooked 30-gauge wire into the paste. Use a craft knife to mark four lines around the bud.

8 Cut out a tiny blossom from some White SFP. Cut off the tips of the petals and glue the blossom to the base of the bud.

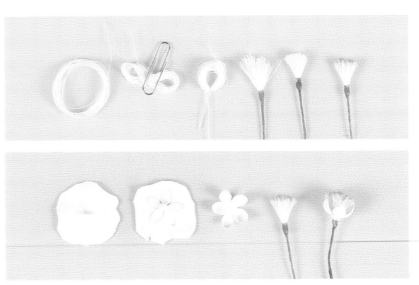

Lily of the valley

Flowers

1 Cut a 30-gauge white wire into four pieces, then make a tiny hook in the end of each piece.

2 Make a tiny ball of White SFP. Brush edible glue over the hooked end of a wire and push the ball onto the hook. If you stop at this point, you have a lily of the valley bud.

3 To make a flower, roll out some White SFP thinly and cut out a blossom with a small blossom cutter. Make blossoms in varying sizes to make the plant look more natural.

4 Brush the top of the ball with edible glue and gently press the flower onto the ball to secure it in place.

5 Cut the green ½-width floral tape in half again, so the tape is very thin. Start by taping the buds to the top of a 28-gauge white wire, graduating them down the wire and bending them outwards a little. As you move further down the wire, begin to tape the flowers to the stem. Do not attach any buds or flowers to the end of the stem as this will be taped into a spray.

Leaves

6 Mix some Pale Green SFP with a touch of Leaf Green paste food colour. Cut out several leaves using the template and wire each leaf with a 24-gauge green wire. Use a veining tool to mark on the central line, then mark long strokes down either side.

7 To make a stem, tape five to 11 lily of the valley flowers, five to 10 buds and one or two leaves together.

> ### tutor tip
> Leave the buds to dry for a short while before attaching the flower. This prevents the bud from becoming distorted.

Leaves

9 Roll a small sausage of Holly/Ivy SFP and insert a green 30-gauge wire into the end of the paste. Roll out the paste thinly around the wire and use a cutting wheel to cut out a long, pointed leaf shape that is approximately 3cm–4cm (1⅛"–1½") long. This should be the biggest leaf: make smaller leaves as well to make the stem look more natural.

10 Use a veining tool to mark a central vein down the leaf, then mark diagonal lines out from either side of the central line. Pass the leaves through the steam of a kettle to give them a slight sheen.

11 To make a stem, use ¼-width light green tape to tape one or two buds together. Secure one or two leaves beneath the buds, then tape a flower to the buds.

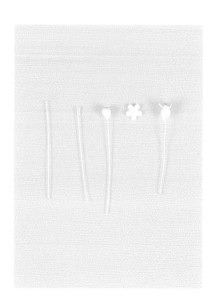

Eucalyptus leaves

1 Mix some Holly/Ivy SFP with a little Edelweiss paste food colour to make a lighter green. Use the round cutters to make leaves of varying sizes and wire them with a white 30-gauge floral wire (see page 268). Use a ball tool to shape the edge of each leaf and make a gentle point at the tip.

2 Tape six to 12 pairs of leaves down a 24-gauge white wire to the length required using white floral tape. Dust with a mixture of Holly/Ivy and Edelweiss dust food colours.

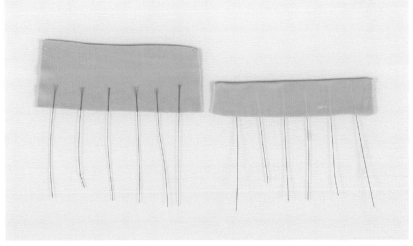

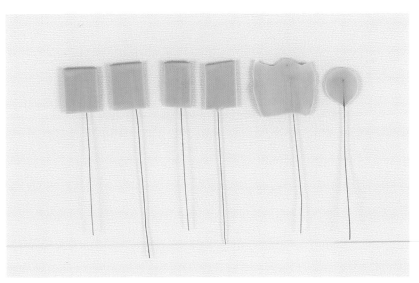

Country Garden Wedding Cake

The striking white flowers and green foliage on this impressive four-tier cake were inspired by flowers in a country cottage garden. The lavish abundance of flowers overflowing the tiers matched with the simplicity of the natural colour palette make this a striking centrepiece. The polystyrene separators between the tiers make the assembly of the display very simple.

EDIBLES

10cm, 15cm, 20.5cm and 25.5cm (4", 6", 8" and 10") round cakes (or dummies)

SK Sugarpaste: 3.8kg (8lb 6oz) Bridal White

EQUIPMENT

33cm (13") round cake drum (board)

20cm (8") round cake board

2 x 10cm (4") and 1 x 5cm (2") round polystyrene separators

2 x 10cm (4") and 1 x 5cm (2") round cake cards

Strip cutter no. 2: 5mm ($^1/_8$") (JEM)

For essential floral edibles and equipment, see pages 254–255

You will need the following sugar flowers for this cake:

	Roses (see pages 270–275)	Eustoma (see pages 390–392)	Scabious (see pages 393–394)	Myrtle (see pages 395–396)	Lily of the Valley (see page 396)	Eucalyptus leaves (see page 397)
Base tier	5 large roses 5 half-roses 5 buds 5 sets of leaves	9 flowers 7 opening buds 7 buds 13 leaves	5 flowers 7 leaves	9 flowers 11 buds 9 pairs of leaves	32 flowers 28 buds 5 leaves	3 stems
Second tier	5 roses 3 half-roses 3 buds 3 sets of leaves	7 flowers 7 opening buds 5 green buds	3 flowers 6 leaves	10 flowers 11 buds 9 pairs of leaves	24 flowers 21 buds 3 leaves	3 stems
Third tier	3 large roses 3 half-roses 3 buds 3 sets of leaves	6 flowers 5 buds 6 pairs of leaves	3 flowers 5 leaves	6 flowers 5 buds 4 pairs of leaves	17 flowers 15 buds 1 leaf	3 stems
Top tier	1 large rose 3 buds 1 set of leaves	4 flowers 4 open buds 3 green buds	2 flowers 2 leaves	5 flowers 7 buds 5 pairs of leaves	17 flowers 13 buds 1 leaf	2 stems

1 Cover all four cakes, the cake board, the cake drum and all three polystyrene separators with Bridal White sugarpaste (see page 139). Place each of the separators on a corresponding size cake card.

2 Dowel the first, second and third tiers to support the cakes above (see page 143).

3 Measure the circumference of each cake. Cut four strips of Bridal White sugarpaste that are long enough to fit around the base of each cake and are approximately 5cm (2") wide. Use a strip cutter to gently emboss lines along each length of paste and attach them around the base of the cakes with a little edible glue, positioning the join at the back of each cake. Place the cakes to one side.

4 Carefully lay out the prepared flowers on a soft surface such as kitchen roll, bubble wrap or tissue paper. Place the separators in front of you and sort out the flowers, leaves and buds that will be placed around each tier following the table above. It is a good idea to always make more flowers and leaves in case of breakages.

5 Tape the flowers and leaves together in stems following the instructions for each flower.

6 Secure the base tier in the centre of the covered cake drum with a little let-down sugarpaste or royal icing. Position a 10cm (4") separator centrally on top of the cake over the dowel rods. It is advisable to stick the separator down with royal icing to prevent any movement once the cakes are placed on top.

7 Insert a rose stem directly into the bottom of the first separator, using a scriber to help ease the wire in if necessary. Continue inserting the rose stems for this tier, so they are evenly spaced around the separator.

8 Fill in the areas between the roses with the other flowers and leaves, inserting them into the separator in the same way as the roses. Make sure that the flower sprays do not come up higher than the base of the tier above. To check this, place a spare cake board gently on top of the separator to make sure that the flowers are level.

9 Repeat steps 6–8 with the second and third tiers of the cake. Make sure that the attachment points in the separators are not visible: adjust the position of the leaves to cover them or cut out some extra leaves from White or Pale Green SFP and place these over the attachment points. Take care when assembling the other cakes on top of the separators.

10 Using a rose as the central flower, tape the remaining flowers into a small circular posy that will fit on top of the smallest cake (see page 276). Place the arrangement into a posy pick and insert the pick centrally into the top tier. Position the final tier on top of the cake and trim the cake board with a white satin ribbon to finish.

Important note: Remember that floral wires should never be inserted directly into a cake. Remove all inedible items before the cake is served.

Country Garden Wedding Cake

Exotic Bouquet

ALAN DUNN

Once your confidence in sugar floristry has grown, you can use your skills to create all kinds of wild and exotic flowers. Popular flowers such as orchids often have many different varieties which you can experiment with — you can even create your very own fantasy flowers and foliage to complement your work.

TECHNIQUES

- How to make Phalaenopsis orchids, bamboo orchids, Armenian beetroot leaves, Tropaeolum foliage, Ceropegia vines and pink berries

- How to create a bouquet

Phalaenopsis orchid (moth orchid)

There are about 60 species of Phalaenopsis orchid and many artificial hybrid forms, too. They are often known as moth orchids and are used extensively by florists for bridal work. The flower described here is based on a very bright, hybrid variety.

EDIBLES

SK Sugar Florist Paste (SFP): Daffodil (yellow), White

SK Professional Dust Food Colours: Edelweiss (white), Lilac, Sunflower, Vine

Clear alcohol, e.g. vodka or gin

EQUIPMENT

28-, 26-gauge floral wires: white

Floral tape (½-width): white

SK Designer Cutter Range by Alan Dunn: Phalaenopsis (Moth) Orchid Cutters

SK Great Impressions Phalaenopsis (Moth) Orchid Petal Veiners, set of 3

Non-toxic craft dust: plum

CelStick or smooth ceramic tool

Aluminium foil (optional)

Labellum (lip petal)

1 Knead some White SFP well and roll it out, leaving a central ridge thick enough to insert a 26-gauge wire. Use the pointed orchid lip cutter to cut out the labellum shape.

2 Moisten the end of a 26-gauge white wire and insert it carefully into the ridge in the paste. It is important that the wire is inserted through to the arrowhead section of the petal, as this can be a fragile part of the flower.

3 Narrow the neck section between your finger and thumb to make it much finer then trim away the excess length. Place the paste on a non-stick board or in the palm of your hand and use

For essential floral edibles and equipment, see pages 254–255

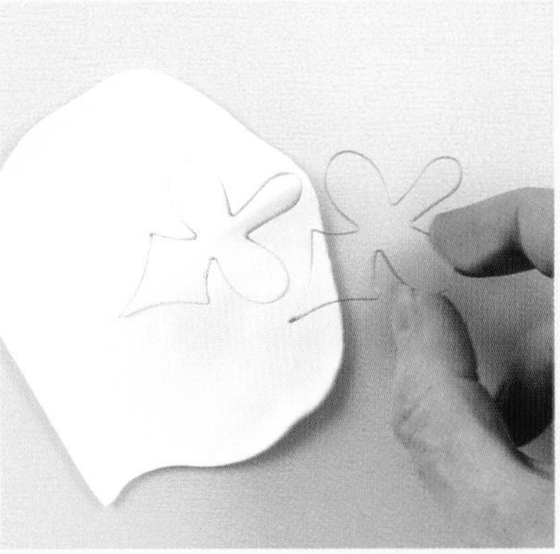
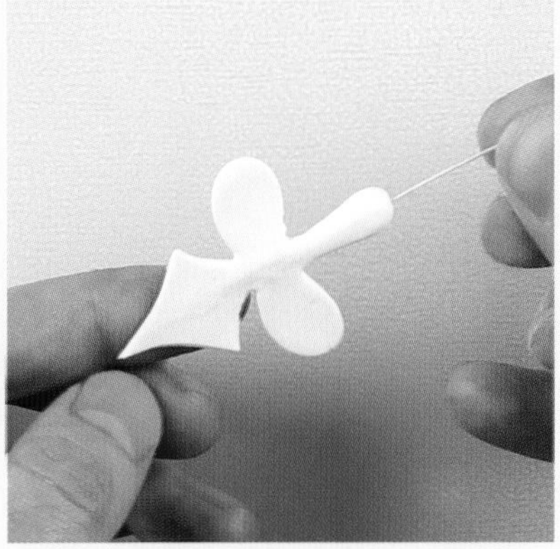
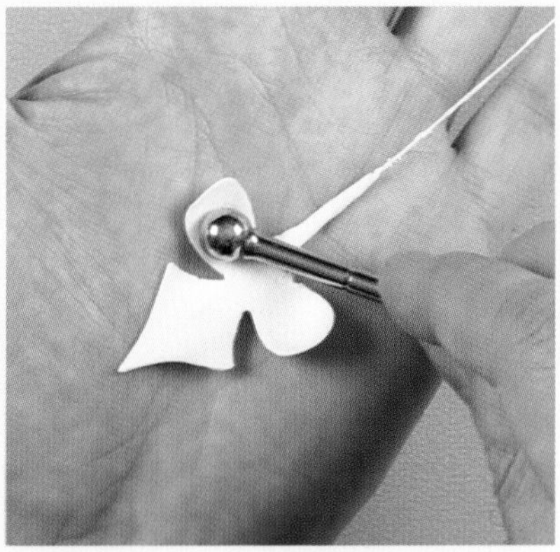
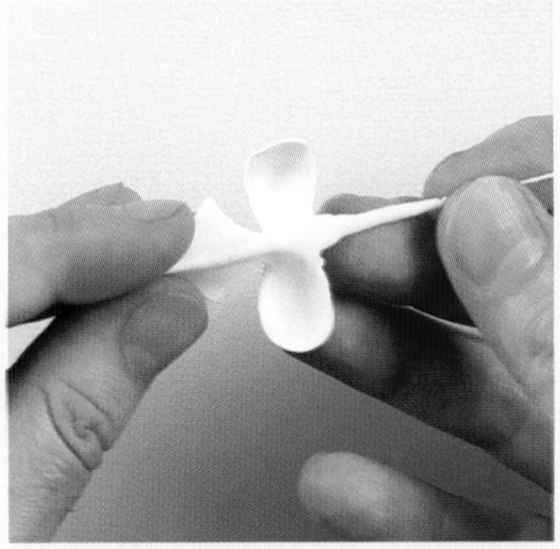
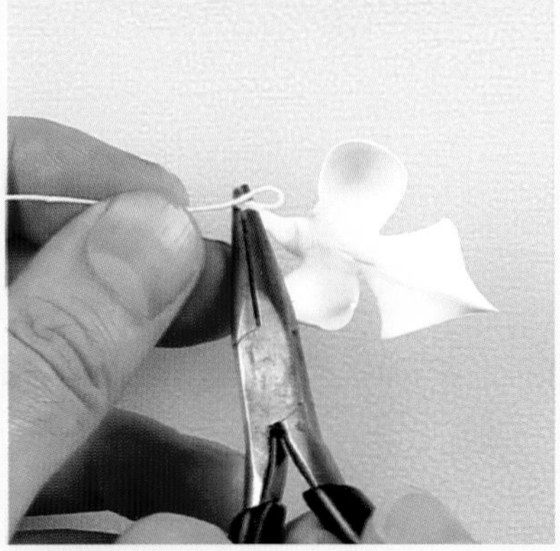
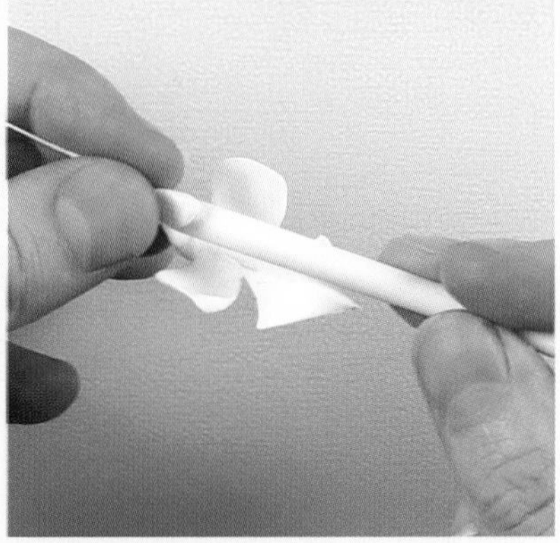
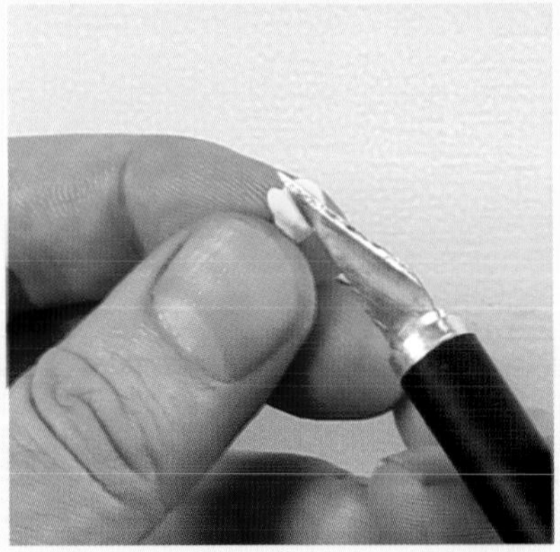
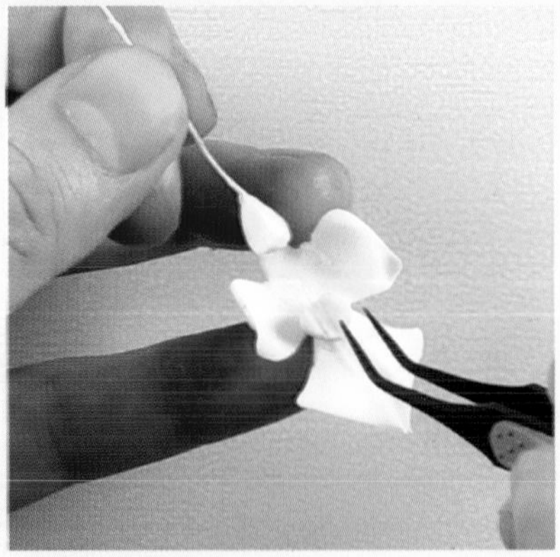
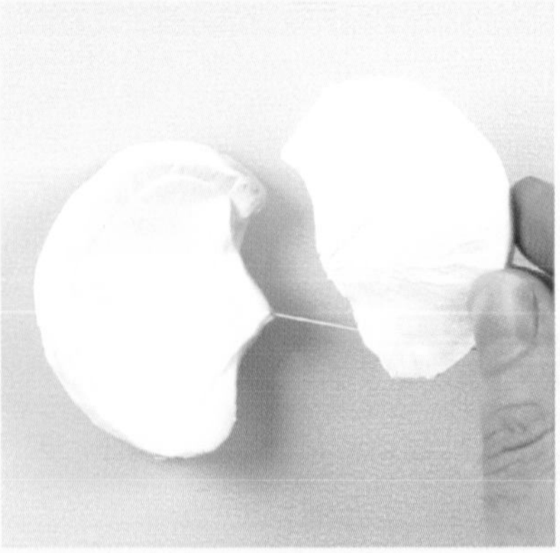
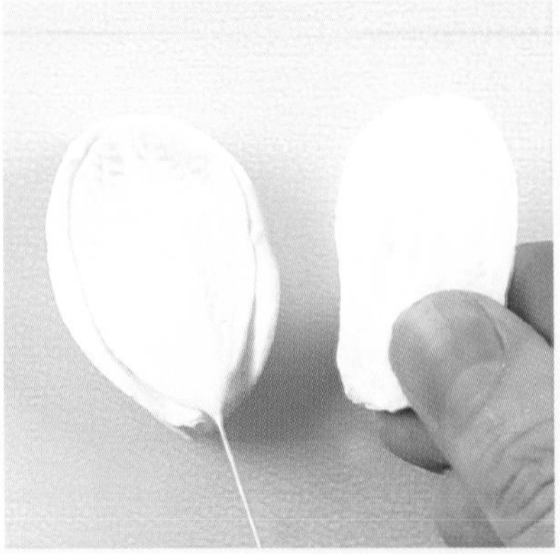
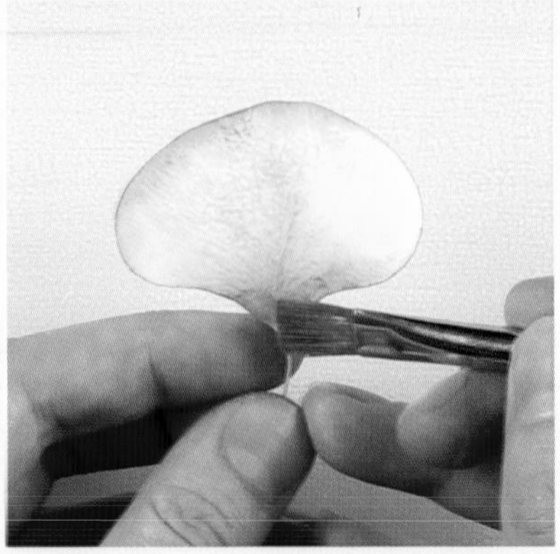
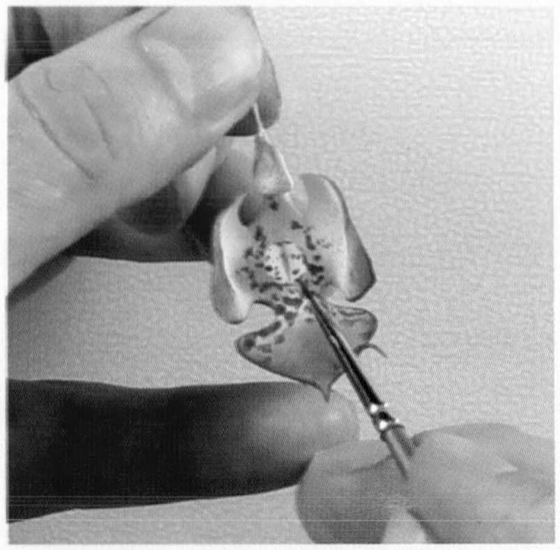

a CelStick or smooth ceramic tool to roll out and broaden the two rounded sections then use a ball tool to soften the edges around the lip. Thin the edges a little but do not frill them. Use a small ball tool or the rounded end of a CelStick to hollow out both of the rounded sections.

4 Use your finger and thumb to pinch a slight ridge down the length of the petal. You may need to trim the sharp point a little using fine scissors: this will depend upon the variety of Phalaenopsis orchid you are making as some have a very pointed labellum whereas other varieties are blunter.

5 Bend the fine neck part to create the characteristic curve of the labellum. Use fine pliers to bend a small hook in the wire at the base of the neck section. Curve back the edges of the side lobes gently with your fingers.

Column

6 Roll a small ball of White SFP into a teardrop shape and attach it to the small hook at the base of the labellum. Position the rounded end of the ceramic tool or CelStick at the underside of the column and press the paste into the tool to hollow out the underside.

7 Attach a very small ball of White SFP at the top edge of the column to represent the anther cap. Use a plain-edged cutting wheel or craft knife to draw a line down the centre of the anther cap. Allow to dry slightly before dusting (see step 16).

Raised platform

8 Form a small ball of Daffodil SFP into a cone shape and indent the wider end with a craft knife or cutting wheel. Pinch the edges of the wider end slightly between your finger and thumb then attach it to the centre of the labellum using edible glue. You may find it easier to use fine tweezers to help you lift and position the paste.

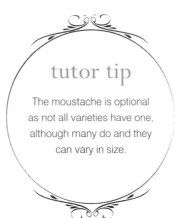

tutor tip

The moustache is optional as not all varieties have one, although many do and they can vary in size.

Moustache

9 Roll a very fine strand of White SFP, use edible glue to attach it at the tip of the labellum and curve the moustache slightly. Be aware that this part is very fragile and may need to be repaired later.

Lateral petals (wing petals)

10 Knead some White SFP well and roll it out, leaving a thick central ridge for the wire. Cut out the petal using the largest petal cutter in the set.

11 Insert a moistened 28-gauge white wire into $1/3$ of the thick ridge on the petal. Place it in your palm or on a foam pad and soften the edge very gently with a ball tool. Do not try to frill the petal.

12 Vein the petal with the lateral Phalaenopsis orchid petal veiner then gently pinch the petal from the base to the edge to create a very slight ridge down the centre. Repeat the process to make a second lateral petal. Rest the petals over some crumpled kitchen paper or aluminium foil and allow them to firm up a little.

Exotic Bouquet

Dorsal and lateral sepals (outer sepals)

13 Knead some White SFP well and roll it out, leaving a thick ridge for the wire (you may prefer to use a grooved board for this). Cut out the shape using the dorsal sepal cutter.

14 Insert a moistened 28-gauge wire into the thick ridge, 1/3 of the way up the sepal. Soften the edge of the sepal gently with a ball tool. Vein with the dorsal sepal moth orchid veiner and pinch gently from the base to the tip.

15 Repeat the process described for the dorsal sepal to create two lateral sepals. You will need to flip the cutter for the second petal to create a mirror image.

Colouring and assembly

16 Dust the lateral petals and outer sepals with a mixture of Sunflower, Edelweiss and a touch of Vine dust colours. Dust from the base out towards the edges, then from the edges towards the centre.

17 Dust the lip of the labellum with plum craft dust, gently catching the edges of the side lobes. Use slightly more plum craft dust on the arrowhead section of the petal and dust the raised platform with Sunflower dust.

18 Dilute some plum craft dust with clear alcohol and use a fine paintbrush to paint dots over the raised platform and the arrowhead shape.

19 Use ½-width white floral tape to attach the two large lateral petals either side of the labellum. Add the dorsal sepal in line with the column, then attach two lateral petals at the base of the flower.

20 Use plum craft dust and a flat brush to catch the edges of each of the petals and sepals. Drag the flat of the brush against the raised veins: this will highlight the veining and add more detail. Add a gentle touch of Lilac dust food colour to the back of the sepals. Allow to dry, then steam the flower to set the colour.

tutor tip

At the assembly stage, it helps if the paste is still pliable so that you can re-shape the petals or sepals a little to create a more natural display.

Bamboo orchid (Arundina graminifolia)

There are around eight species of Arundina orchids, but the Arundina graminifolia species are more commonly known as bamboo orchids because of their long, bamboo-like foliage. The flowers can be white, flesh-coloured, pink or magenta, often with very dark colouring to the lip petal. The size varies too, although the flower described here is one of the smaller varieties.

EDIBLES

SK Sugar Florist Paste (SFP): White

SK Professional Dust Food Colours: Edelweiss (white), Sunflower, Vine

EQUIPMENT

SK Designer Cutter Range by Alan Dunn: Bamboo Orchid Cutters

SK Great Impressions Wide Amaryllis Petal Veiner

SK Great Impressions Stargazer B Petal Veiner

Ceramic silk veining tool

Non-toxic craft dusts: African violet, plum

28-, 26-, 22-gauge floral wires: white

Floral tape (½-width): green

Curved former

For essential floral edibles and equipment, see pages 254–255

Column

1 Cut a length of 22-gauge wire into three using sharp floristry scissors or wire cutters. Knead a small ball of White SFP and insert a wire into it. Use your finger and thumb to work the paste down the wire to create a teardrop shape.

2 Using your finger and thumb, press the length of the wired teardrop firmly against the rounded end of the silk veining tool to hollow out the underside of the column. As you press against the tool, use your finger and thumb to create a very slight ridge down the upper surface of the column. Thin the edges at the top of the column by continuing to press the paste against the ceramic tool. Curve the tip of the column slightly and allow to dry for several hours.

3 Attach a tiny ball of White SFP to the top of the column to represent the anther cap. Use a plain-edged cutting wheel or sharp craft knife to indent a line down the centre of the ball.

Labellum (throat / lip petal)

4 Knead some White SFP well and roll out on a non-stick board, leaving a slightly thicker area down the centre of the paste: this thick area will give a little support to the petal shape. Cut out the petal using the large lip/labellum cutter.

5 Dust the petal lightly with cornflour then vein it with the amaryllis petal veiner. Use the wider end of a Dresden tool to thin the edges and create a series of lines that look almost frill-like along the edge of the petal. Keep the angle of the tool close to the work surface otherwise the tool will cut into the edge too much.

6 Use the silk veining tool to frill the edge of the petal. You can do this against the board or rest the petal over your index finger and use the tool to frill the paste in short sections. Keep the point of the tool pointed upwards so that it does not dig into the surface.

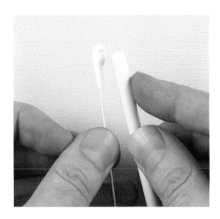
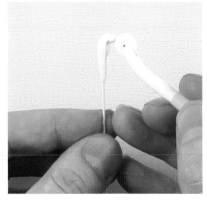

7 Use angled tweezers to pinch two long ridges close together down the centre of the petal: the thickness created in step 4 will help with this process. Place the petal in your palm or on a foam pad and hollow out the two side sections with a ball tool.

8 Moisten the edges towards the base of the petal with edible glue. Position the wired column, hollowed-side down, against the petal and carefully wrap the petal around it. Pinch the petal against the column to secure the two together. Carefully curl back the edges of the petal. Allow to dry a little before applying colour to the lip (see step 14).

Lateral petals (wing petals)

9 Knead some White SFP well and roll it out, leaving a thick ridge for the wire. Use the wide wing petal cutter to cut out the petal shape.

10 Cut a length of 28-gauge wire into three using floristry scissors or wire cutters. Moisten the end of a wire with edible glue and insert it ⅓ of the way into the thick ridge. Place the petal against your palm or on a firm foam pad and soften the edges using a ball tool, positioning the ball tool half on the edge of the petal and half on your hand or foam pad as you work the paste. Do not frill the edge, but only thin it a little to take away the blunt edge left by the cutter.

11 Vein the petal with the stargazer B petal veiner and frill the edges of the petal using the silk veining tool; this will also add a little extra textured veining. Use your finger and thumb to gently pinch the base and tip of the petal. Curve the petal gently and allow to dry over a curved former. Repeat to make a second wing petal.

Dorsal and lateral sepals (outer sepals)

12 Knead some White SFP well and roll it out, leaving a ridge for the wire (you might prefer to use a grooved board for this). Cut out a sepal shape using the narrow cutter from the bamboo orchid set. Insert a glued 28-gauge white wire halfway up the thick ridge of the sepal.

13 Soften the edge of the sepal using a metal ball tool. Vein the sepal with the stargazer B petal veiner then gently pinch from the base to the tip of the sepal. Repeat to make two more outer sepals. Curve one of the sepals forwards (the head) and two back (the legs).

Colouring and assembly

14 Use a small, flat paintbrush to apply Sunflower dust colour to the two pinched ridges down the centre of the labellum. Use a mixture of plum and African violet craft dusts and a slightly larger flat brush to colour around the edge of the petals. This may be pale or fairly intense in colour, as pictured.

15 Add some Edelweiss dust colour to the plum and African violet

craft dusts for the two wing petals and the three outer narrow sepals. Dust each of the petals/sepals from the base, fading towards the tips. The wing petals can be a little stronger in colour. Add a tinge of Vine mixed with Edelweiss dust colour to the very tips of the narrow outer sepals.

16 Use ½-width green floral tape to secure the two wing petals onto the base of the labellum. Tape the three outer petals behind the wing petals, positioning the head sepal so that it curves in towards the flower. Tuck the two leg sepals tight underneath the labellum to make it look at first glance as if this orchid only has three outer petals. (You might decide to use artistic licence and allow both petals to be seen clearly.)

17 Dust a little of the Vine and Edelweiss dust colour mixture at the base of the petals and sepals at the back of the flower. Allow the flower to dry then steam the petals to set the colour.

Important note: Inedible craft colourings and items have been used on these flowers, so they should never be placed directly onto a cake: always place them on a piece of clear acetate or a sugar plaque and ensure they are removed from the cake before it is served.

tutor tip

You may choose to allow all sections of the flower to dry completely before colouring and assembly: I prefer to apply the dust colours while the paste is still a little flexible as this creates a stronger colour in the finished flower. Taping the petals together while they are still flexible is also a better option as it will enable you to re-shape the petals slightly, creating a more realistic end result.

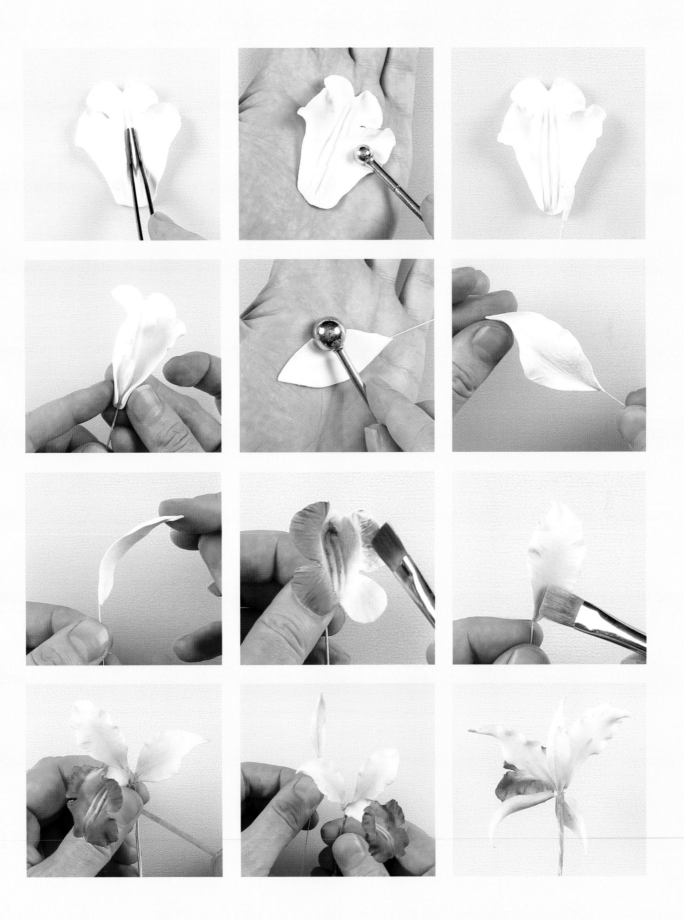

Armenian beetroot leaf

This is a fantasy leaf created using an Armenian poppy leaf cutter, a thistle leaf veiner and a touch of creative imagination.

EDIBLES

SK Sugar Florist Paste (SFP): Pale Green

SK Professional Dust Food Colours: Holly/Ivy, Lilac

SK Designer Dust Food Colour: Forest Green

SK Designer Bridal Satin Lustre Dust Food Colour: Myrtle

Edible glaze spray (PME)

EQUIPMENT

26-, 24-gauge floral wires: white

Floral tape: Nile green

Armenian poppy leaf cutter (AP)

SK Great Impressions Thistle Leaf Veiner: 11cm (4¼")

Non-toxic craft dusts: African violet, plum

For essential floral edibles and equipment, see pages 254–255

1 Knead some Pale Green SFP well and roll it out, leaving a long, thick ridge for the wire. Do not roll the paste too fine. Use the Armenian poppy leaf cutter to cut out the shape.

tutor tips

It will help if the paste sticks in the cutter so that you can pick it up and rub your thumb over the edge to create a cleaner cut.

The leaf can be used full-length or you can trim it to make a shorter leaf. It is good to have some variation in size.

2 Insert a moistened 24- or 26-gauge white wire about ²/₃ of the way up the thick ridge.

3 Place the leaf against the non-stick board with the ridge side uppermost. Use the wider end of a Dresden tool to thin the edges and create a slightly ragged, frilly edge. Keep the angle of the tool close to the work surface otherwise the tool will cut into the edge too much. If any of the sections become too large or ragged trim them away using the Dresden tool or sharp scissors.

4 Vein the leaf with the thistle leaf veiner and pinch from the base to the tip of the leaf to accentuate the central vein.

5 Mix Holly/Ivy dust with a touch of Forest Green dust to colour the upper surface, fading the colour slightly towards the edges. Use a lighter dusting of colour on the back of the leaf.

6 Use a mixture of Lilac, African violet and plum dusts to colour the edges of the leaf, then dust from the base and fade into the central vein. Use the same mixture to dust from the edges of the leaf on the reverse side. Dust over the leaf with Myrtle lustre dust and spray lightly with edible glaze spray.

7 Use the leaves individually or tape them into groups using Nile green floral tape.

Important note: Inedible craft colourings and items have been used on these flowers, so they should never be placed directly onto a cake: always place them on a piece of clear acetate or a sugar plaque and ensure they are removed from the cake before it is served.

Tropaeolum foliage

Otherwise known as nasturtium, this plant is native to Peru but has been cultivated extensively around the world. Nasturtiums are my favourite plants, not only for their cheerful flowers but for their wonderful plate-like foliage, which is a delight to use in floral displays.

EDIBLES

SK Sugar Florist Paste (SFP): Pale Green

SK Professional Dust Food Colours: Edelweiss (white), Holly/Ivy, Lilac, Poinsettia (Christmas red), Vine

SK Designer Dust Food Colour: Forest Green

Clear alcohol, e.g. vodka or gin

Edible glaze spray (PME) (optional)

EQUIPMENT

SK Great Impressions Nasturtium Leaf Veiners: 4cm, 6cm, 7.5cm (1½", 2¼", 2 ¾")

Tea light (optional)

26-, 24-, 22-gauge floral wires: white

Floral tape (½- or ¼-width): Nile green

For essential floral edibles and equipment, see pages 254–255

1 Use a 26-gauge wire with ¼-width or a 24-gauge wire with ½-width Nile green floral tape: the gauge of the wire and width of tape will depend upon the size of the leaf you are making. Use fine pliers to bend the end of your chosen wire into a 'ski stick' shape (see page 422).

2 Knead some Pale Green SFP well and roll it out into a small circle, leaving a raised pimple at the centre. Vein the leaf in a nasturtium leaf veiner with the pimple-side down against the back of the leaf. Use scissors or a plain-edged cutting wheel to trim away the excess paste to create a round leaf shape. Place the leaf on your palm or on a firm foam pad and soften the edges gently with a ball tool.

3 To attach the leaf to the wire, burn the end of the hook in the flame of a tea light until it is red hot. While the hook is still very hot, carefully press it into the pimple on the back of the leaf. The sugar will caramelise and harden, leaving a strong bond between the leaf and wire. Repeat to make leaves in varying sizes. Allow them to dry a little before applying dust food colour.

4 Mix together Poinsettia and Lilac dust food colours and use a flat dusting brush to catch the very edges with colour. Use a mixture of Holly/Ivy and Forest Green dusts to dust the leaf from the centre, fading out towards the edges of the upper surface. Dust over the whole leaf with Vine dust colour. The back of the leaves should be paler in colour.

5 Mix one part confectioners' glaze with three parts clear alcohol, then dip the leaves into the glaze mixture. Alternatively, spray the leaves very lightly with edible glaze spray.

6 Use the leaves individually in a spray or tape them onto a 22-gauge wire with ½-width Nile green floral tape to create trailing stems.

Ceropegia vine

Ceropegia woodii is an evergreen trailing succulent that is native to South Africa and Zimbabwe. The plant has many common names including 'hearts entangled' and 'sweetheart vine'. The heart-shaped foliage makes it a wonderful addition to bridal bouquets.

EDIBLES

SK Sugar Florist Paste (SFP): Pale Green

SK Professional Dust Food Colours: Edelweiss (white), Holly/Ivy, Lilac

SK Designer Dust Food Colour: Forest Green

SK Designer Bridal Satin Lustre Dust Food Colour: Myrtle

Clear alcohol, e.g. gin or vodka

Edible glaze spray (PME)

EQUIPMENT

Non-toxic craft dust: plum

35-, 33-, 30-, 28-gauge floral wires: white

Floral tape (¼-width): Nile green

For essential floral edibles and equipment, see pages 254–255

tutor tips

These leaves are best made using the freehand technique rather than with a cutter.

You might prefer to colour the leaves before you assemble them, or you can tape them into their long stems then carefully dust and paint them.

1 Cut several lengths of 35-, 33- or 30-gauge white wires into short lengths using wire cutters or sharp floristry scissors. The gauge will depend upon the size of the leaf you are making.

2 Knead some Pale Green SFP well and shape it into a small cone. Moisten the end of a short wire with edible glue and insert it into the wider end of the cone. Pinch the wider area of the cone with your fingers and thumbs to start to shape the leaf into a heart. Place the leaf onto your palm or onto a foam pad and thin the shape slightly using a metal ball tool. Remember the leaves of this plant are fairly fleshy in form.

3 Hollow out the underside of the leaf slightly using the ball tool. Pinch the back of the leaf to create a very subtle central vein. Repeat to make leaves in varying sizes, pairing them as you work.

4 Tape the leaves in pairs onto a length of 28-gauge wire using ¼-width Nile green floristry tape: start with the smallest leaves and gradually increase the size as you work. Add an extra 28-gauge wire if you need to give extra support to the stem.

5 Use a mixture of plum craft dust and Lilac dust food colour to add an intense colour to the back and edges of each leaf and the stem. Use a mixture of Holly/Ivy and Edelweiss dust colours to colour the upper surface of each leaf.

6 Dilute a mixture of Forest Green and Holly/Ivy dusts with clear alcohol and use a fine paintbrush to paint spots and markings over the upper surface of each leaf. Leave to dry then add more random spots using diluted Myrtle lustre dust. Allow to dry and then spray very lightly with edible glaze spray.

Important note: Inedible craft colourings and items have been used on these flowers, so they should never be placed directly onto a cake: always place them on a piece of clear acetate or a sugar plaque and ensure they are removed from the cake before it is served.

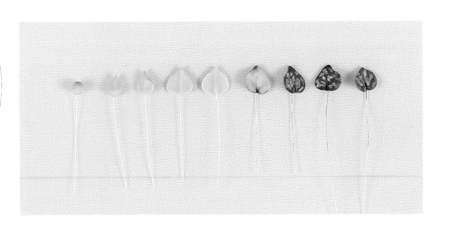

Pink berries

These pretty berries are a great, quick addition to a bouquet or arrangement.

EDIBLES

SK Sugar Florist Paste (SFP): White

SK Professional Dust Food Colours: Edelweiss (white), Lilac

Edible glaze spray (PME)

EQUIPMENT

28-, 22-gauge wires: white

Floral tape: white

Non-toxic craft dusts: African violet, aubergine, plum

For essential floral edibles and equipment, see pages 254–255

1 Cut several short lengths of 28-gauge white wire then bend a small hook in the end of each using fine pliers. Tape down each wire, excluding the hook, with ½-width white floral tape. Use the sides of a pair of scissors to smooth and polish the stems.

2 Knead some White SFP well and roll several small balls of paste for the berries. Moisten the hooked end of a wire with edible glue and insert into a ball of paste. Pinch the berry onto the wire to secure it in place.

3 Use a pair of fine, sharp scissors to make several small snips in the berry around the hooked wire area. Repeat for all the berries.

4 Secure the berries into sets of two and three using ½-width white floral tape. Tape these small groups onto a 22-gauge white wire to create a panicle (branched cluster) stem.

5 Dust the main stem with a mixture of plum and African violet craft dusts. Dust the berries with the same mixture but add a touch of Edelweiss dust colour to make it a little paler. Dust the snipped area of each berry with aubergine craft dust. Allow to dry then spray with edible spray glaze in a well-ventilated area.

Important note: Inedible craft colourings and items have been used on these flowers, so they should never be placed directly onto a cake: always place them on a piece of clear acetate or a sugar plaque and ensure they are removed from the cake before it is served.

Exotic Bouquet

414

Vibrant Orchid Bouquet

Bright bamboo and Phalaenopsis orchids form the focal flowers in this exotic bridal bouquet. Colourful berries and various decorative foliage add extra interest and assist the trailing shape of the display.

EDIBLES

3 Phalaenopsis orchids, see pages 402–406

3 bamboo orchids, see pages 407–409

7 Armenian beetroot leaves, see page 410

9 Tropaeolum leaves, see page 412

7 trails of Ceropegia vine, see page 413

5 clusters of pink berries, see opposite

EQUIPMENT

22-gauge floral wires: white

Floral tape (½-width): Nile green

Paper-covered craft wire: Bordeaux, green

For essential floral edibles and equipment, see pages 254–255

Important note: Inedible craft colourings and items have been used on these flowers, so they should never be placed directly onto a cake: always place them on a piece of clear acetate or a sugar plaque and ensure they are removed from the cake before it is served.

1 Use ½-width floral tape to attach a 22-gauge wire to any stems that need to be strengthened or lengthened. Use a tape shredder to prepare plenty of ½-width Nile green floral tape for the bouquet construction.

2 Choose the largest and most attractive Phalaenopsis orchid to use as the focal point of the bouquet. Bend the stems of the two remaining Phalaenopsis orchids using pliers and tape them either side of the focal flower with ½-width floral tape.

3 Tape in three bamboo orchids, alternating their positions and filling in the gaps between the three Phalaenopsis orchids.

4 Tape in the trailing stems of Tropoaeolum foliage to add length to the display and use single leaves throughout the bouquet. Use wire cutters or sharp floristry scissors to trim any excess wire as you work.

5 Add the Armenian beetroot leaves and the pink berries to fill in any further gaps in the bouquet.

6 To finish, add loops and trails of green- and Bordeaux-coloured wires. The trails of decorative wire will help to give the bouquet a more flowing design and can be used to support the trailing stems of the vine foliage.

Vase Arrangement

NAOMI YAMAMOTO

Roses, gerberas and carnations are some of the most popular flowers used in bouquets and sprays. I have put a twist on these classic flowers by using different techniques to those traditionally used in sugarcraft, and have made a cupped old rose which is quite distinctive from a modern rose. I also wanted to show that sugar flowers do not only have to be displayed on a cake but can make beautiful bouquets and arrangements for a table centrepiece.

Photography: Fumihiko Watanabe

TECHNIQUES

- How to make cupped old roses, gerberas, carnations, aspidistra leaves and stems of leaves and berries

- Arranging sugar flowers in a vase

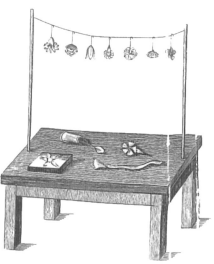

Illustration of a 19th-century sugar flower table from *The Italian Confectioner*

416

Cupped old rose

EDIBLES

Pink

SK Sugar Florist Paste (SFP): Pale Green, Pale Pink, White

SK Professional Paste Food Colours: Cyclamen, Rose

SK Professional Dust Food Colours: Cyclamen, Rose

SK Designer Pastel Dust Food Colour: Pale Lilac

SK Designer Bridal Lustre Dust Food Colour: White Satin

SK Pollen Style Edible Dust Food Colours: Pale Golden, Pale Green

White

SK Sugar Florist Paste (SFP): Cream, Pale Green

SK Professional Dust Food Colour: Vine

SK Designer Bridal Lustre Dust Food Colour: White Satin

EQUIPMENT

5-petal blossom cutters: F5, F6B (OP)

SK Designer Multi-Flower Petal Cutter: Set 1

Piping nozzle: no. 5

30-, 24- and 20-gauge floral wires: green

Floral tape: green

Pale yellow cotton thread

Round polystyrene formers: 3cm, 4cm, 5cm and 6cm (1¹⁄₈", 1½", 2" and 2³⁄₈")

For essential floral edibles and equipment,
see pages 254–255

Base

1 Roll out some White SFP very thinly and cut out a blossom with the largest five-petal blossom cutter. Make a hole in the centre of the blossom with a no. 5 piping nozzle. Lightly dust a round 5cm (2") polystyrene ball with icing sugar, then place the blossom over the former and fit it around the shape to cup the petals. Leave to firm up.

2 Before the paste is completely dry, remove the blossom from the polystyrene ball. Position the petals so that they slightly overlap and glue each petal to the next with edible glue. Leave the petals to dry completely.

Centre

3 Wind the yellow cotton thread approximately 50 times around three fingers to obtain the size of loop required. Cut the thread from the reel and remove it from your fingers. Twist the thread once in the middle to make a figure of eight then fold one ring over the other. Bend a 30-gauge green wire in half then twist the wire at the bend to make a small loop. Pass one end of the wire through the ring and twist the wires once or twice beneath the thread to fix it in place, leaving a small loop in the wire. Wind one end of the wire once or twice around the base of the cotton ring then twist the two lengths of wire together down the length to make them into one.

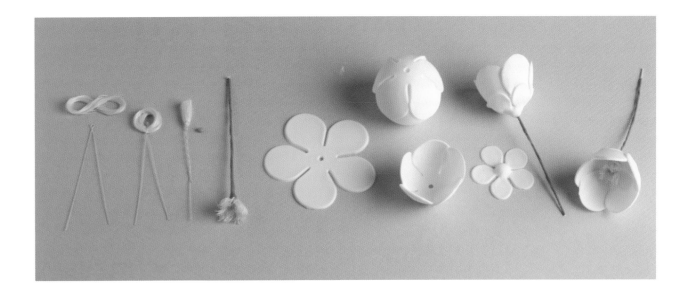

4 Cut through the ring to make strands of thread that are approximately 1.5cm–2cm (½"–¾") long. Cover the threads completely in edible glue and when they have dried slightly, pull each piece of thread with a cocktail stick to make it curl. Make a small hook in one end of a 20-gauge green wire then tape the hooked wire to the previous wire to make a stem.

5 Roll a small ball of Pale Green SFP and fix it onto the small loop of wire in the centre of the flower. Dab a little edible glue over the top of the ball and cover with Pale Green pollen-style dust. Brush Pale Golden pollen-style dust over the tips of the threads.

6 Make a small ball of White SFP into a Mexican hat shape then cut out a blossom with the smallest five-petal cutter (see page 266). Wrap a thin sausage of White SFP around the base of the flower centre. Brush a little edible glue over the hole in the centre of the first set of petals then push them up the wire and secure behind the centre. Secure the second, smaller set of petals behind the first set of petals in the same way. Hold the flower centre and the base petals together to secure, then leave to dry completely.

Inner petals

7 Mix together some White SFP and Pale Pink SFP to make a pale pink marbled paste. Thinly roll out the paste and cut out a petal using the 4.8cm (1⁷/₈") cutter. Vein the petal with a silk veining tool and shape the edge of the petal with a bone tool. Mix Lilac, Rose and Cyclamen dust colours together in a paint palette then brush as much colour over the petal as you desire. Dust any white parts in the marbled paste with White Satin lustre dust. Slice off the base of the 4cm (1½") polystyrene former so it does not roll, then place the petal over the former and pinch any excess paste at the centre of the base. Trim any excess paste and allow the petal to half-dry. Make four petals altogether for the first layer then attach these petals inside the white base.

8 Cut out a petal from the pale pink SFP with the 4.5cm (1¾") petal cutter. Dust the petal as before and frill the edge of the petal slightly with a bone tool. Gather the paste together at the base of the petal to make it narrower.

Make five more petals in the same way and attach them inside the first layer of pink petals, using a flower shaping tool to secure them in place.

9 Make five more petals in the same way using the 3.5cm (1³/₈") petal cutter and attach them in the gap between the second set of petals and the flower centre. You can adjust the number of the petals depending on the amount of space within the flower.

Vase Arrangement

419

Rose bud

1 Make a small hole in a 3cm (1¹⁄₈")
polystyrene ball former and fill the
hole with SFP. Insert a hooked 20-gauge
green floral wire into the hole and leave to
dry. You could make the centre from a ball
of flower paste if you prefer.

2 Cut out three petals from pale pink
SFP using the 3.5cm (1³⁄₈") rose
petal cutter. Turn the petals pointed-end
up and wrap each one around the flower
centre so they overlap at the top. If the
petals do not fit neatly around the centre,
pinch the bottom of the petal and trim
away any excess paste.

3 Cut out three more pink petals with
the 4.5cm (1¾") rose petal cutter
and cup them as for the flower petals
using a 4cm (1½") polystyrene ball former.
Leave them to half-dry, then wrap them
around the previous layer of petals.

4 Make three more pink petals
using the template and a 5cm (2")
polystyrene ball former. Attach around
the previous layer but open out the petals
slightly.

Outer petals

10 Make five petals in the same
way as described in step 8,
using the 4.5cm (1¾") rose petal cutter.
Allow the petals to firm on a 4cm (1½")
polystyrene ball former then attach the
them around the outside of the white
flower base.

11 Make a second layer of petals
as before using the 5.5cm
(2¹⁄₈") petal cutter and the 5cm (2")
polystyrene ball former. Attach around
the previous layer of outer petals.

12 Make a third layer of petals in
the same way as before using
the same cutter and the 6cm (2³⁄₈")
polystyrene ball former. Secure each
petal to the bottom of the white flower
base with edible glue.

Calyx

13 Cut five 7cm (2¾") long pieces of
green floral tape, then make cuts
down both sides of each piece to make
sharp points. Use your fingers to stretch
out the tape to make it sticky and attach a
piece to the outside of each petal. Wrap any
excess tape around bottom of the calyx and
secure with another piece of tape.

Old rose: white

To make a white rose, follow the
method above using Cream SFP
for the petals. Dust the whole
surface of each petal with White
Satin lustre dust.

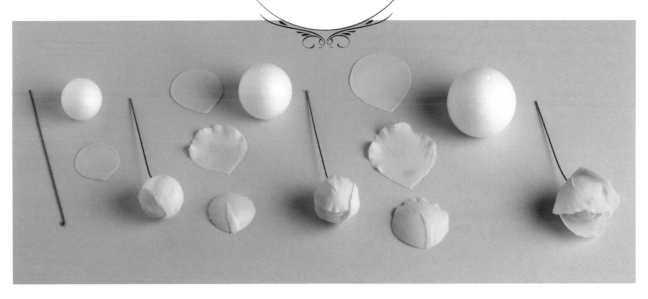

Gerbera

EDIBLES

SK Sugar Florist Paste (SFP): Holly/Ivy, Pale Green, Pale Pink, White

SK Professional Paste Food Colour: Cyclamen

SK Professional Dust Food Colours: Cyclamen, Lilac, Rose

SK Pollen-Style Edible Dust Food Colours: Pale Golden, Pale Green

EQUIPMENT

Daisy cutter collection, set of 5: 3cm–9cm (1¹⁄₈"–3½") (FMM)

Flower shaping tool

Leaf shaping tool

20-gauge floral wire: green

Floral tape: green

Fine-nosed pliers

Aluminium foil

For essential floral edibles and equipment, see pages 254–255

Centre

1 Add a touch of Cyclamen paste food colour to Pale Pink SFP and mix in well.

2 Make a 'ski stick' shape at the end of a green 20-gauge wire by holding 1.5cm (½") from the end of the wire with a pair of pliers, then wrapping the wire around the tip of the pliers to make a loop. Flatten the loop against the wire, then hold the straight length of wire at the central point of the loop and bend back 90° so that the loop sits horizontally on top of the wire.

3 Make a small ball of Pale Green SFP and attach this to the top of the wire so it covers the 'ski stick' shape. Brush the top of the ball with edible glue and dust with Pale Green pollen-style dust.

4 Roll out the dark pink SFP thinly and cut out two sets of petals with a 3cm (1¹⁄₈") daisy cutter, then roll out the paste even more thinly and cut out three more sets. Take the thinner sets of petals and draw a central line down each individual petal with a flower shaping tool. Turn the thinner blossoms veined-side up and push all three sets of petals up the wire, securing behind the flower centre with edible glue.

5 Place the thicker sets of petals onto a foam pad and run a ball tool over the petals in a circular motion to stretch out the flower. Draw central lines down the individual petals as before, then secure to the base of the flower centre behind the previous petals.

6 Roll out some more dark pink SFP and cut out another set of petals with a 4cm (1½") daisy cutter. Shape as before and attach behind the flower centre. Dust the tips of the petals with Cyclamen dust food colour and then brush Pale Golden pollen-style dust over the top.

Petals

7 Roll out some Pale Pink SFP very thinly and cut out one set of petals using a 5cm (2") daisy cutter. Stretch out the petals with a CelStick and cut each one in half lengthways. Draw a central line down each half-width petal with a leaf shaping tool, then turn the petals over so they are veined-side down. Attach the layer of petals behind the flower centre, then place the flower upside down and leave to dry.

8 Roll out some more pink SFP very thinly and cut out a 9cm (3½") daisy. Cut the flower into six equal sections, then stretch out each individual petal with a CelStick. Use a leaf shaping tool to add a central line and shape the edge of each petal with a flower shaping tool. Mix Lilac and Rose dust colours together, then brush the colour over the base of each petal. Arrange the petals so they overlap then pinch the edges together to merge them. Repeat to make six petal sections. Attach three petal sections evenly around the flower centre, then secure the remaining three sections between the first petals and turn the gerbera upside down.

9 Cut a square of aluminium foil that is slightly larger than the flower, then make a cut from one corner into the centre. Wrap the foil around the neck of the flower and turn it upright again. Adjust the position of the petals with your fingers while the paste is still soft. You can adjust the shape of the flower by changing the depth of the foil. Once you are happy with the shape, keep the aluminium foil in place and leave to dry. Once dry, remove the foil and tape down the wire with green floral tape.

Calyx

10 Mix together some Holly/Ivy SFP and White SFP and make a small ball of paste. Make a Mexican hat shape (see page 266) and cut out with the 5cm (2") daisy cutter. Place the bump in the biggest hole on the foam pad and stretch out each petal with a CelStick, then make dents in the bump with a ball tool. Push the calyx up the wire and secure it firmly to the neck of the gerbera with edible glue.

White carnation

EDIBLES

SK Sugar Florist Paste (SFP): Cream, Holly/Ivy, White

SK Professional Dust Food Colour: Vine

SK Designer Bridal Lustre Dust Food Colour: White Satin

EQUIPMENT

Garrett frill cutter: 7.5cm (3")

CelStick: 15.5cm (6") long

Flower shaping tool

Bamboo skewer

Corn husk

20-gauge floral wire: green

Floral tape: green

For essential floral edibles and equipment, see pages 254–255

Petals

1 Roll out some Cream SFP very thinly and cut out a Garrett frill shape. Make a 1cm (³/₈") cut between every two frills. Use a bamboo skewer to frill the edge of the paste and separate each section so they do not stick together. Lightly brush White Satin lustre dust over the edge of the paste and dust Vine towards the centre.

2 Turn the paste over so the dusted side is facing down, then fold the circle in half. At one end of the semicircle fold a third of the paste inwards, then on the opposite side fold a third outwards to create the shape of the flower. Brush a small amount of edible glue between the folds then roll the bottom of the paste into a sausage to create a bunch of petals. Make small cuts in the petals to make them look more natural, then push a hooked 20-gauge green wire down through the petals and leave to dry. These will make the central petals in the carnation.

3 Roll out some more Cream SFP and cut out two more sets of petals with the Garrett frill cutter. If you want to make a larger carnation, you can use three sets of petals at this stage. Cut, frill and dust in the same way as for the central petals, but cut the circle of paste in half before making bunches of petals. Brush some edible glue over the neck of the central petals then attach the bunches in pairs opposite each other. Leave the flower to dry completely then tape down the wire with green floral tape.

Calyx

4 Make a 2.5cm (1") long rugby ball shape from Holly/Ivy SFP. Make a hole in one end of the ball with the pointed end of a CelStick, then push the other rounded end into the hole nearly all the way through to the other end of the ball to hollow it out. With the paste on the end of the CelStick, roll it back and forth on a board to widen the hole, then press a corn husk into the paste to vein it.

Aspidistra

EDIBLES

SK Sugar Florist Paste (SFP): Holly/Ivy

SK Professional Dust Food Colour: Holly/Ivy (dark green)

EQUIPMENT

Flower shaping tool

CelStick: 15.5cm (6") long

Bamboo skewer

20-, 26-gauge floral wires: green

Floral tape: green

For essential floral edibles and equipment, see pages 254–255

5 Hold the CelStick upright then cut four shallow points into the base of the calyx. Remove the CelStick from the calyx and make 2mm ($^1/_8$") cuts into the opening to divide it into five equal parts. Use the CelStick to stretch the paste along cut edges, making more of a cone shape. Push the calyx up the wired petals and secure at the base of the carnation.

1 Cut a 26-gauge green floral wire to 25cm (10") long and brush the end of the wire with a little edible glue. Make a small rugby ball shape from some Holly/Ivy SFP and insert the lightly glued wire into one end. Push the ball down to the middle of the wire then use your hands to roll the paste along the wire to approximately 5cm–6cm (2"–2$^3/_8$") in length. Place the wire on a non-stick board and roll out the paste even further with your fingers to lengthen the paste to 10cm (4") long on the wire.

2 Roll out another piece of Holly/Ivy SFP to at least 5cm (2") wide and 10cm (4") long. Press a CelStick along the middle of the paste and dab a small amount of edible glue in the indent. Place the stick of paste into the dent, use a CelStick to secure then roll out the paste around the wire to merge the two pieces of paste together. Measure halfway down the wire, then make indents on either side of the paste that are approximately 2.5cm (1") from the central wire. Using a cutting wheel, cut from the marks in the paste out towards the ends of the wire to make a gentle curve. Smooth the edges of the leaf with a flower shaping tool.

3 Turn the leaf over and draw a central line down its length with a bamboo skewer. Hold both ends of the wires and bring them together, folding the leaf in half with the wired side on the inside. Tape both wires together with green floral tape. Shape the leaf with your fingers to make it look more natural then paint the whole leaf with confectioners' glaze.

Vase Arrangement

Berries and leaves

EDIBLES

SK Sugar Florist Paste (SFP): Holly/Ivy, Pale Green

EQUIPMENT

Flower shaping tool

Leaf shaping tool

24-, 26-, 30-, and 32-gauge floral wires: green

Floral tape: green

Rose petal cutters, set of 4: 1.5cm–4cm ($^5/_8$" –1½") (PME)

For essential floral edibles and equipment, see pages 254–255

Berries

1 Roll a small ball of Holly/Ivy SFP then use the tip of a CelStick to make small indents all over the surface of the ball. Insert a hooked 26-gauge green wire into the ball and leave to dry.

2 Make a thin sausage of Holly/Ivy SFP and cut it into several small pieces. Roll each piece into a very small ball and stick these over the indents in the first ball of paste. Paint with confectioners' glaze when the paste is dry. Tape down the wire with green floral tape.

Leaves

3 Roll out some Pale Green SFP leaving a mound in the centre to insert a wire, then roll the paste out even more thinly around the mound. Cut out with an inverted rose cutter then insert a lightly glued 30-gauge green wire into the mound. Draw three lines down the leaf with a leaf shaping tool and shape the edge of the leaf with a flower shaping tool. Tape down the wire with floral tape. Make three leaves with a 4cm (1½") rose cutter and three leaves with a 3.5cm (1$^3/_8$") rose cutter for one stem.

4 Use green floral tape to attach the leaves to a 24-gauge green wire, starting with the smallest first. Secure the berries in place with floral tape. Wind a 32-gauge green wire around a thin paintbrush to curl it, slide it off the brush and tape to the stem.

tutor tip

If you are using a leaf or petal cutter, place the paste over the cutter and roll over it with a rolling pin to cut out the shape neatly.

Vase Arrangement

'Pretty in Pink' Bouquet

This pretty, fresh-looking bouquet is made up of some of the most popular bridal flowers and would make the perfect centrepiece for a wedding table.

EDIBLES

6 pink and white cupped old roses, see pages 417–420

2 rose buds, see page 420

3 pink gerberas, see pages 422–423

7 white carnations, see page 424–425

7 aspidistra leaves, see page 425

3–4 stems of berries and leaves, see opposite

EQUIPMENT

13cm tall x 8cm wide (5¼" x 3⅛") glass vase

Small, glass marbles

20-gauge floral wire: green

Floral tape: green

For essential floral edibles and equipment, see pages 254–255

1 Make at least three stems of berries and leaves, four roses, seven carnations, one gerbera and three or four aspidistra leaves. Make two roses up to step 2 (see page 417) and make two gerberas up to step 5 (see page 422). Allow them all to dry before assembling the arrangement.

2 Fill the vase with small, glass marbles. The glass marbles are important as they will support the flowers and keep the arrangement stable, as well as looking pretty.

3 Tape a 20-gauge wire to each stem of berries and leaves then insert the wires into three or four points around the edge of the vase. Bend the wire at the join so it looks like the stem is hanging down the side of the vase.

4 Arrange the old roses, aspidistra leaves, carnations and the finished gerbera in the vase. Make two rose buds and arrange them between the roses while they are soft. Make the remaining petals for the unfinished gerbera then rest the finished flower in a piece of aluminium foil to shape. Arrange the gerbera naturally between the flowers before it dries out.

5 Check the overall balance of the arrangement and, if necessary, make a few more aspidistra leaves to fill in any gaps between the flowers. Insert the freshly made leaves into the arrangement and adjust the shape of the leaves to ensure they look natural amongst the other flowers.

tutor tip

When arranging a bouquet of sugar flowers, it is a good idea to leave some flowers unfinished as well as preparing some finished flowers in advance. You can complete the unfinished flowers as you make the bouquet: this allows you to assemble the flowers without damaging the petals and gives the arrangement a more natural look. Whilst the final petals or leaves are still soft, you can decide which direction the flower should face and fit it neatly within the bouquet.

MASTERCLASSES

Take your skill repertoire to the most advanced, professional level by learning from the very best experts in their respective subjects of modelling, royal icing and sugar flowers.

Carlos Lischetti

BIOGRAPHY

At the age of eleven, when most boys were out playing football, I was in my kitchen in Rosario, Argentina. I was dreaming of creating cakes like the ones I saw in the cookery books on our kitchen shelves. I grew up surrounded by my family baking and cooking and there were countless moments which influenced me in some way.

Always very self-motivated, I experimented with making cakes, biscuits and breads for my family. And then one day, my sister's birthday gave me the perfect excuse to put into practice all that I had been trying out on my own. I struggled to coat the cake with pale pink fondant and the result was a bit messy, but I finished it off with a bunch of marzipan roses. A passion was born.

I felt slightly embarrassed at my unusual interest and started sending my mother to buy all the ingredients, but this feeling soon passed. I was encouraged by my family and Omar who ran the sugarcraft shop; they all supported my newly found creativity. I looked at local artists on Argentinian TV who were demonstrating new techniques for decorating cakes with sugarpaste, sugar toppers and gum paste flowers. I knew where my future laid.

My career began with a period of working in a local bakery in Rosario, where they trained me to make French pastries, which gave me the tools to combine a good recipe with clean decoration. After a few years I felt confident enough to start making my own designs using as reference any object that inspired me, such as a piece of fabric. I went on to study and train in Buenos Aires, Paris and London where I learned from world-renowned sugar artists and pastry chefs and mastered the techniques of pastry and cake design.

I do what I do because I enjoy it and through baking and modelling with sugarpaste I found a way to express myself and my emotions through my work. I do not regret the experiences I have had of learning through my mistakes, of working through them and finally overcoming them.

When I was asked to write my first book by Beverley Dutton at Squires Kitchen, I felt the time was right to share my modelling techniques and ideas with other sugarcrafters and those new to the craft. I co-operated with my twin brother, Elio, whose career is in classical animation. I worked on transferring Elio's inspiring sketches into 3D and this collaboration formed the basis of my successful book, *Animation in Sugar* (B. Dutton Publishing). The challenge for me was to reproduce his characters in sugar, prompting me to explore new methods of modelling figures. I had to discover a system of making each figure in a way that was as easy as possible and, most importantly, achievable and enjoyable.

At present I spend most of my time teaching in several international culinary schools around the world, including Squires Kitchen International School. When I'm teaching I'm able to give people the tools to express themselves with a different medium or to generate an income for a living. I now focus on working on new projects in my studio in Argentina as well as regularly contributing to *Cakes & Sugarcraft* magazine.

Photograph: Toby Long

Mother and Baby

CARLOS LISCHETTI

As your modelling skills develop, you can become more creative with the figures you make. This masterclass is a great way to practise dressing a human character: it is important at this stage to be able to judge by eye the shape and size of the clothing to suit the model you are making. In this figurine, the mother's legs are slightly curved to give movement to the piece and I wanted to reflect the sense of tenderness between a mother and newborn child.

TECHNIQUES

- Covering a cake with sugarpaste, see pages 139–140

- Basic modelling techniques, see page 189

- Modelling animated characters, see pages 330–333

EDIBLES

15cm x 7cm deep (6" x 2¾") round cake, filled and crumb-coated (see page 92)

SK Sugarpaste: 2kg (4lb 6½oz) Bridal White

SK Mexican Modelling Paste (MMP): 250g (8¾oz) Cream Celebration, 250g (8¾oz) White coloured with Hydrangea paste food colour in three different shades, 50g (1¾oz) White coloured with Terracotta paste food colour

SK Sugar Florist Paste (SFP): 150g (5¼oz) White, 50g (1¾oz) White coloured with a touch of Poinsettia (Christmas red) paste food colour, 50g (1¾oz) White coloured with Olive paste food colour

SK Professional Paste Food Colours: Hydrangea, Poinsettia (Christmas red)

SK Designer Paste Food Colours: Olive, Terracotta

SK Professional Liquid Food Colours: Blackberry, Chestnut, Leaf Green, Poppy, Rose

SK Professional Dust Food Colour: Edelweiss (white)

SK Designer Pastel Dust Food Colour: Pastel Pink

EQUIPMENT

23cm (9") round cake drum (board)

15cm (6") round cake card

2 x 6cm diameter x 8cm deep (2³/₈" x 3¹/₈") polystyrene cylinders

Floral wire

SK Designer Great Impressions Range by Carlos Lischetti: Ballerina Head Mould

Paintbrushes: nos. 000, 3, 10

Food-grade, soft foam pieces

Hard-bristled vegetable cleaning brush (new)

Large blossom cutter (TT)

2cm (¾") teardrop cutter, from set of 3 (TT)

Round cutters: 1cm, 4cm, 10cm (³/₈", 1½", 4")

75cm (29") x 15mm (³/₈") wide satin ribbon: white

Closed scallop crimper

For essential modelling edibles and equipment, see pages 184–185

Mother

Legs

1 Roll a ball of Cream Celebration MMP into a sausage and narrow the paste halfway along to create the back of the knee. Roll one half into a long bowling pin shape to create the calf and ankle, leaving a small piece of paste at the end to make the foot. Hold the ankle gently and push the paste up towards the calf with your index finger to create the heel. Flatten down the remaining paste in the opposite direction to create the sole of the foot and trim the end at an angle. Make a second leg in the same way.

2 To bend the legs, press the back of a knife into the back of the knee and gently bend the paste to the required angle. Pinch the paste at each bend to make the angle more pointed and bring out the knees. Cut two pieces of food-grade foam into curved wedge shapes, place a piece underneath each calf and leave the legs to dry on a spare piece of polystyrene. Support with a cocktail stick, if necessary. In this figurine both calves are slightly curved in order to give movement and avoid stiffness in the final piece.

3 Once the legs are completely dry, position them on top of one of the polystyrene cylinders. Place the top of the thighs together, then position the figure's left leg so it is hanging down over the edge of the cylinder. Bring the right leg up and tuck the foot under the left thigh, then lift and support the right leg with a piece of foam. It is important to make sure that the legs are in a natural position. Insert a skewer through the join at the top of the legs, but do not glue them in place at this stage.

Torso

4 Roll a small piece of Cream Celebration MMP into a thick sausage. Narrow the sausage at one end to create the waist and hips. Model the other end of the paste into a bottleneck shape to bring out the neck and shoulders, then use a sharp knife to trim off the rounded end below the waist. Hold the sides of the torso and pinch the top end of the paste between your finger and thumb to sharpen the shoulder line.

5 Bend the back gently backwards and bring the neck slightly forwards in order to give a natural curved shape to the torso. Insert a cocktail stick down through the neck and into the top of the chest. Push the torso down onto the skewer in the legs so it sticks out of the hips and leave the body to firm up at the required angle. Do not glue the torso in place at this stage.

Arms

6 Roll some Cream Celebration MMP into a thin sausage. Stroke the paste gradually towards one end, making it into a long bottleneck shape for the forearm and wrist and leaving a tiny piece of paste for the hand. Flatten the paste for the hand, cut out a 'V' shape to bring out the thumb and trim the larger portion at an angle to give shape to the fingers. Make the other arm in the same way, ensuring the thumb is on the opposite side.

7 Narrow the middle of the sausage to separate the forearm from the upper arm, then mark the paste at the inner elbow with the back of a knife and bend to the required angle. Pinch at the bend to make the elbows pointed. Mark and bend the wrists into position so the palms are facing upwards. Arrange the arms on the body so that the forearms are resting on the thighs and the hands are in position to hold the baby. Push a piece of floral wire through both shoulders and across the chest to attach

them temporarily while they dry. Do not glue the arms to the torso yet as you will need to dress the pieces later.

8 Once all the pieces are dry, carefully take the parts of the body apart ready to be dressed. Discard the piece of floral wire.

Shorts

9 Colour some White SFP with a touch of Poinsettia paste food colour to make a pale pink. Roll out the paste and cut out two rectangles that are large enough to wrap around the thighs. Brush the pieces of paste with a little edible glue. Lay the top of the thigh in the middle of the rectangle of paste. Wrap both sides of the paste around the leg and bring the ends together underneath the thigh to hide the join. Trim away the excess paste with a pair of scissors and rub the paste gently with your finger to smooth the join.

10 For the hems, roll out more of the pale pink SFP and cut out two strips of paste. Attach the strips around the end of the shorts and press the back of a knife into the paste to make creases.

11 Place the legs back in position and stick them together with a piece of softened pale pink SFP. Position a piece of foam under the right thigh to support it until the leg is completely dry. Push a cocktail stick into the cylinder to support the left thigh and stop it from falling to the side.

T-shirt

12 Roll out a thin rectangle of White SFP that is large enough to fit around the torso. Using the pointed

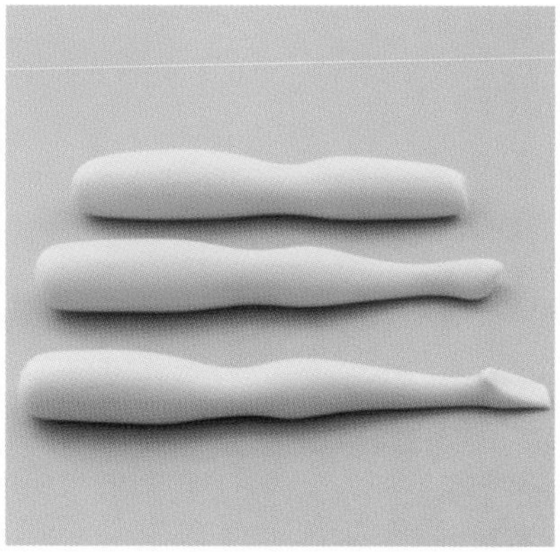
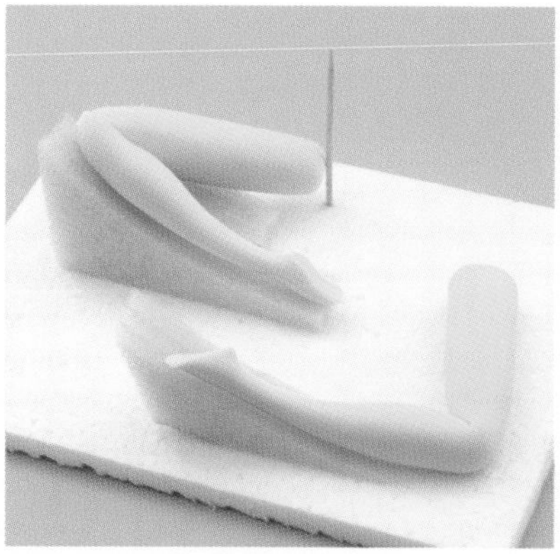
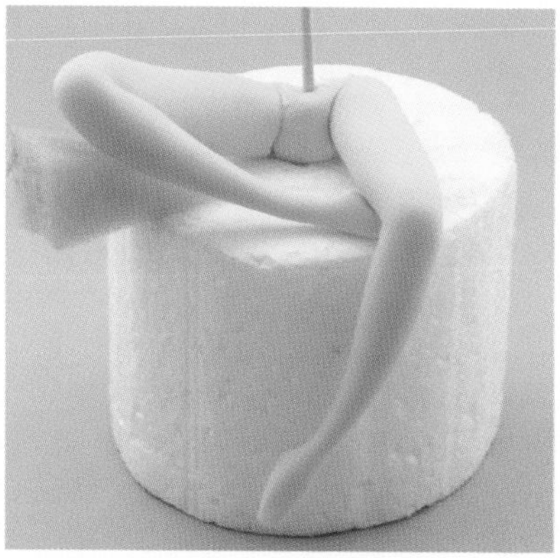
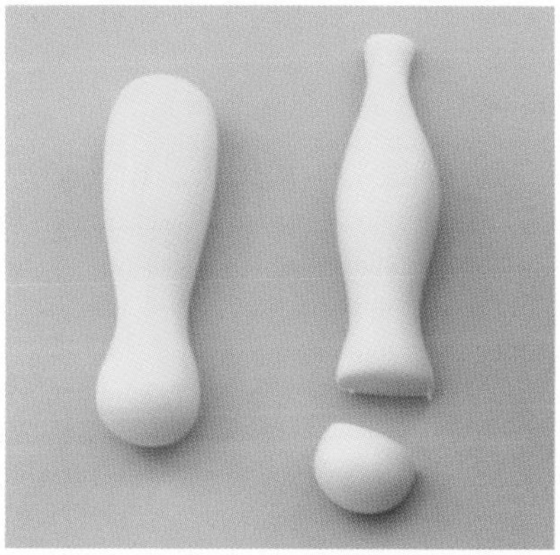
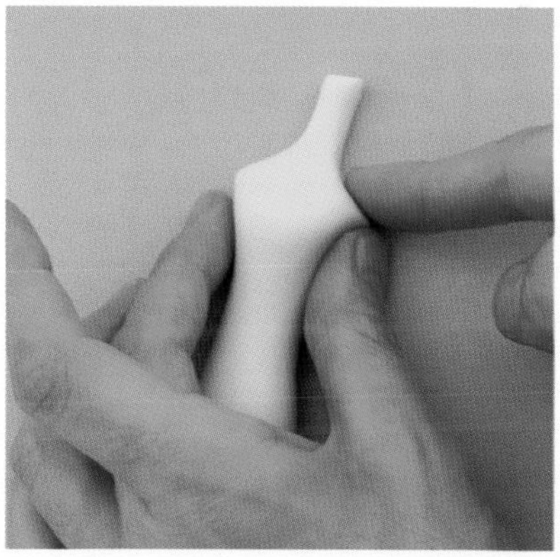
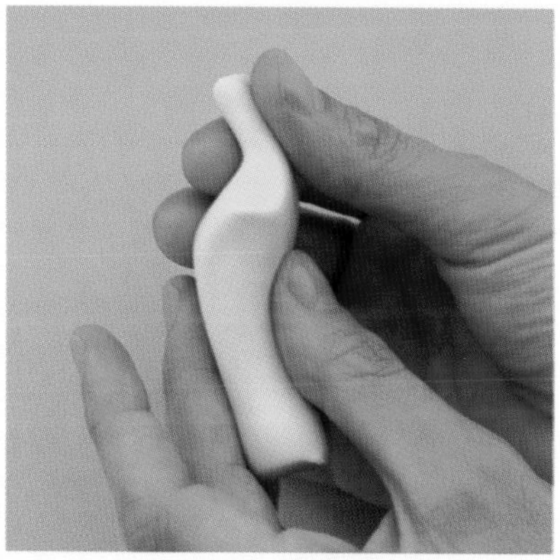
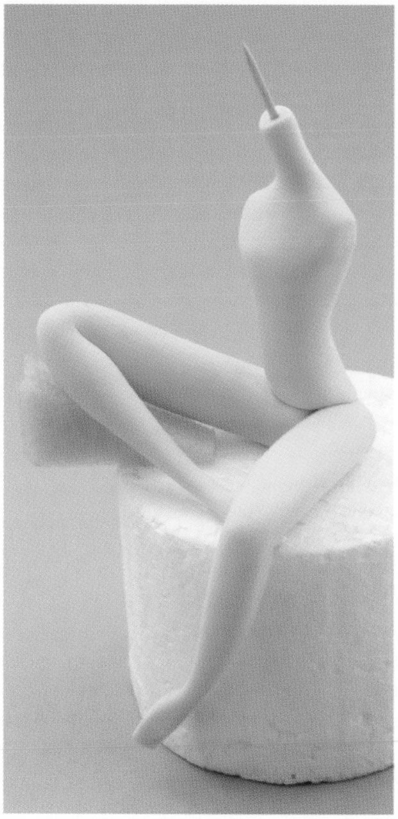
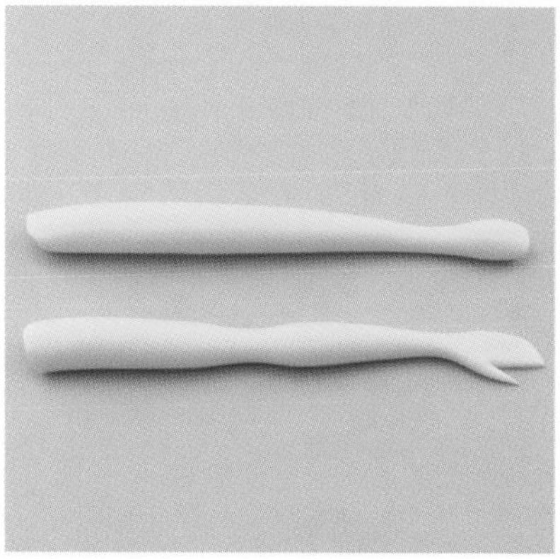
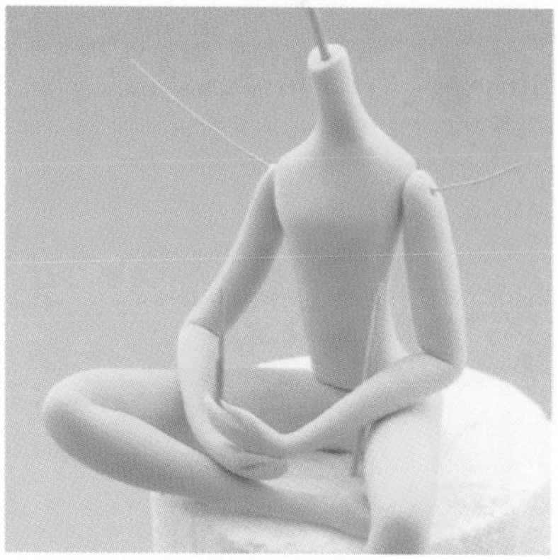
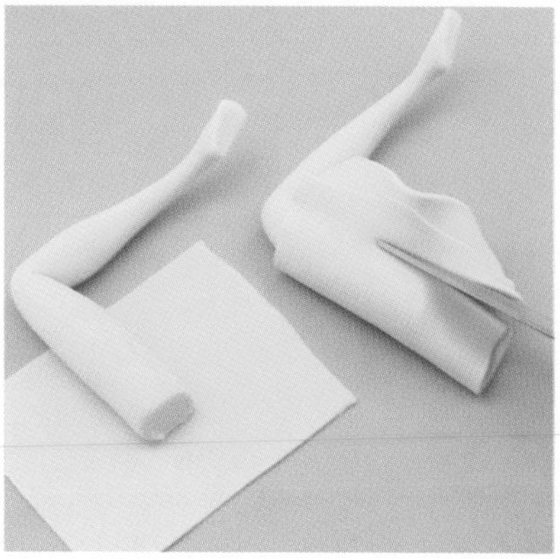
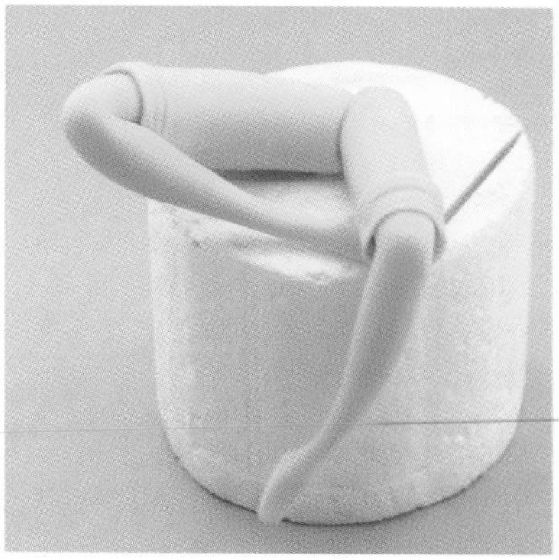

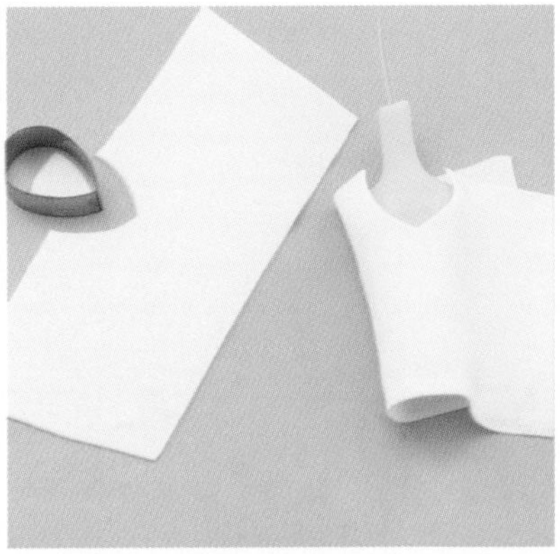
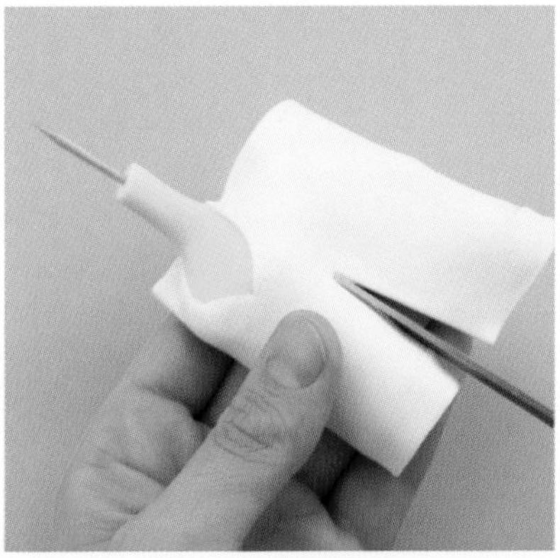
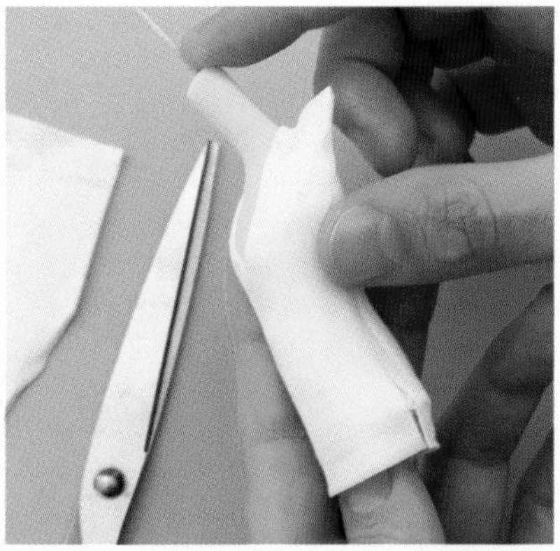
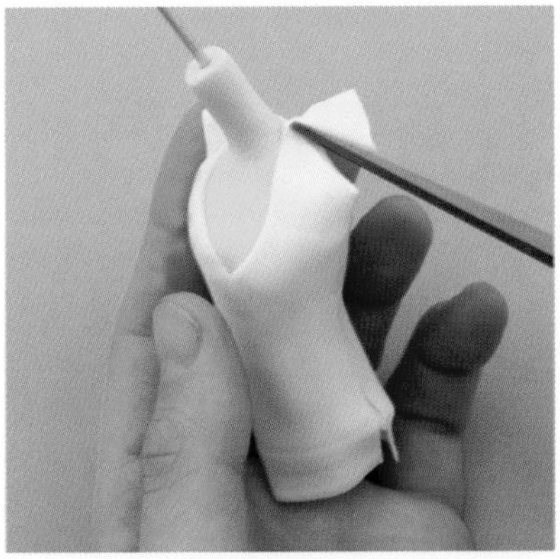
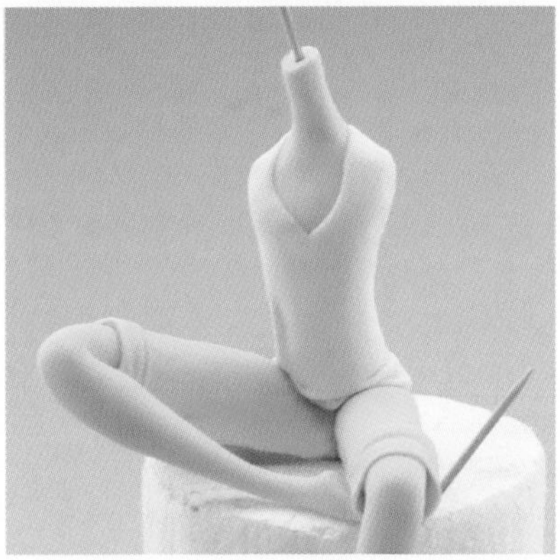
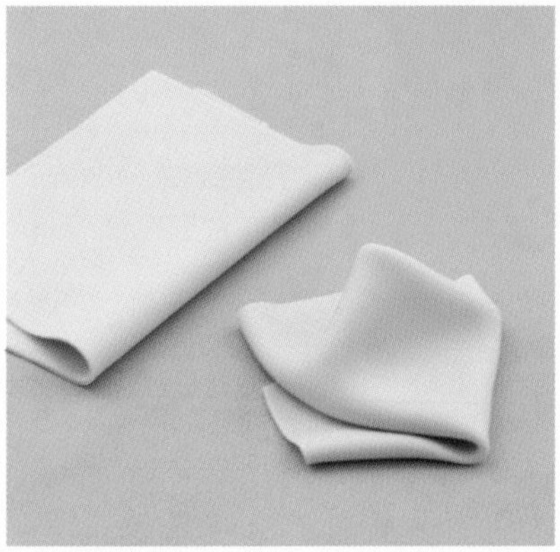
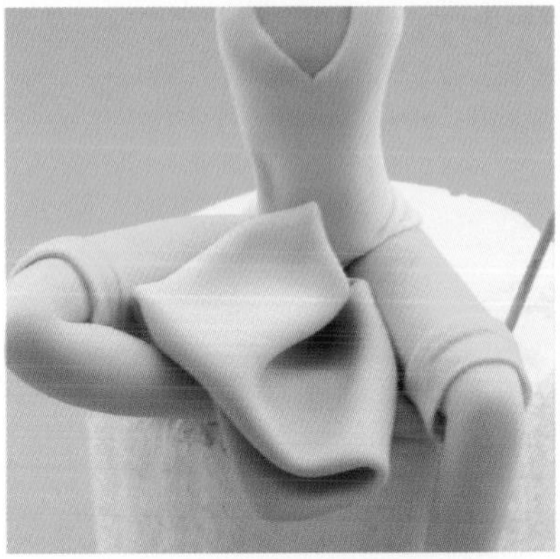
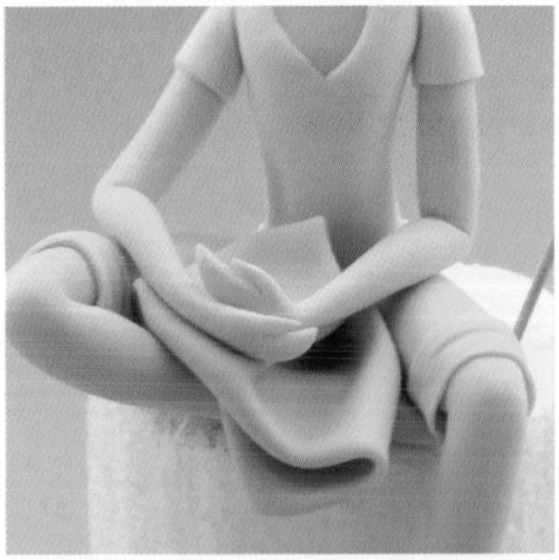
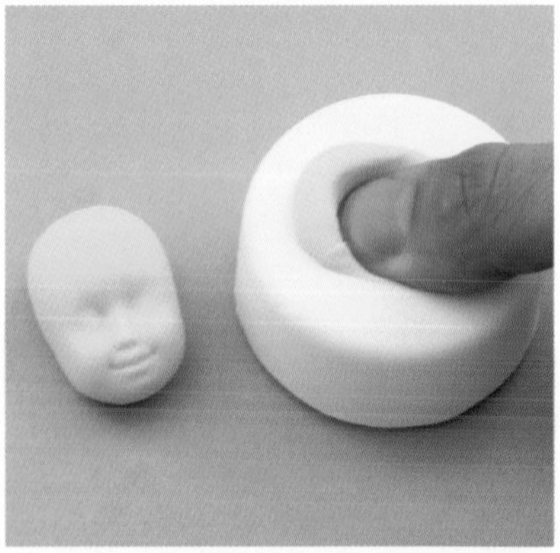
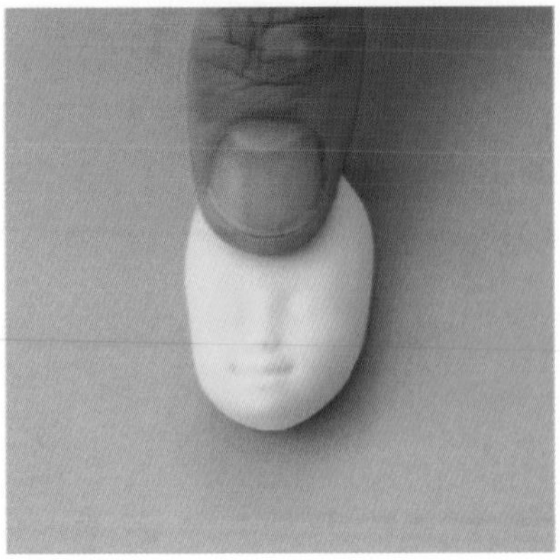
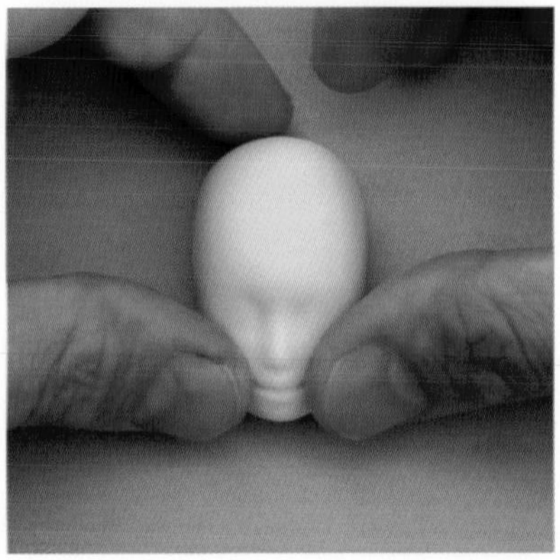
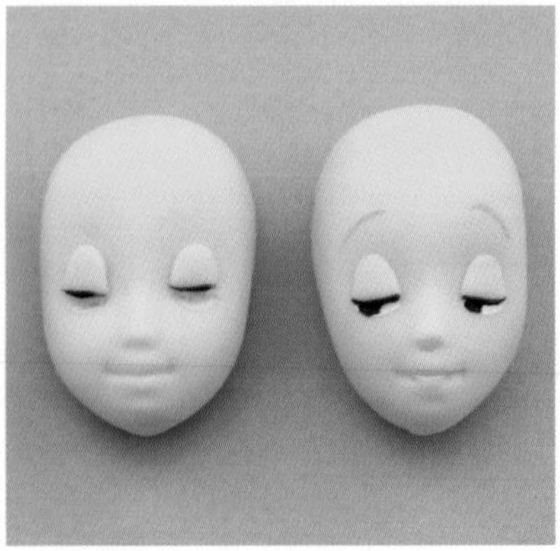

end of a small teardrop cutter, cut out the collar from the middle of one of the long sides of the rectangle. Brush edible glue over the paste then wrap it around the torso, bringing the ends together at one side of the body. Trim the excess paste from the side and from the shoulder line so the T-shirt fits snugly around the body, then smooth the joins with your finger. Gently push the torso back onto the skewer and attach to the legs with a softened piece of White SFP. Leave to dry. If you wish to personalise the T-shirt, you can paint a pattern over it using liquid food colours and a fine paintbrush, trim the collar and sleeves with thin sausages of paste or attach a sugar button with edible glue.

Blanket

13 Colour some SFP with Olive paste colour, roll out thinly and cut out a large rectangle. Loosely fold the paste in half and then fold it over again so the blanket looks naturally creased. Position the blanket over the bent right leg and over the join in the top of the legs and secure with a little edible glue.

Sleeves

14 For the sleeves, roll out a piece of White SFP to the same thickness as the T-shirt. Cut out a 4cm (1½") circle from the paste with a round cutter, then cut the circle in half to make two semicircles. Brush each semicircle with edible glue, wrap them around the upper arms with the rounded side facing down and tuck any excess paste under the arm, trimming if necessary. Glue the top of the arms to the shoulders with a little edible glue then allow the arms to dry in the required position.

Head

15 Roll some Cream Celebration MMP into an oval shape and press the paste firmly into the head mould using your thumb to fill the shape. Roll a little more Cream Celebration MMP into a ball and use it to fill the socket created by your thumb. If necessary, trim away the excess paste with a pair of scissors to shape the back of the head. Pull the head carefully out of the mould and cut away any excess paste from around the edge of the face if necessary.

16 Whilst the paste is still soft, press down evenly on the forehead to make it less prominent and slightly elongate the head. Gently press your thumbs into the cheeks and below the chin to make the face into more of a teardrop shape.

17 Roll a small piece of Cream Celebration MMP into a thin sausage, flatten it down with your fingers and cut the sausage in half. Stick each piece over the eye sockets to make the eyelids. Use a fine paintbrush and Blackberry liquid food colour to paint a fine line over the bottom of the eyelids.

18 Dilute a little Edelweiss dust food colour with a drop of cooled, boiled water and use the mixture to paint semicircles under the eyelids. Allow to dry, then draw on dots for the pupils with Blackberry liquid food colour or a Black food colour pen. If you are unsure where to position the pupils, you can paint them on after you have placed the head on the torso to ensure that the mother is looking down at the baby.

19 Add a very small amount of Poppy liquid food colour to the remaining Edelweiss dust mixture then paint semicircles over the upper and lower lip with a fine paintbrush. For the eyebrows, use a fine paintbrush and Chestnut liquid food colour to paint two curved lines above each eye. Mix Pastel Pink dust food colour with a little cornflour, brush the mixture over the cheeks and leave the head to dry.

20 Colour 50g (1¾oz) of White MMP with Terracotta paste food colour to make an auburn colour for the hair. Roll a piece of the Terracotta-coloured paste into an oval shape, flatten one side of the oval and stick it to the back of the head with edible glue. Make indentations in the paste with the back of a knife or a Dresden tool to represent the hair. Reserve the rest of the paste in a sealed bag to make the fringe later. Place the head onto the cocktail stick protruding from the neck, positioning the head to one side. If necessary, support the head in place with skewers to allow it to dry at the required angle

21 For the ears, roll two small pieces of Cream Celebration MMP into oval shapes and secure them to the side of the head following the eyeline. Press a small ball tool into each ear to shape.

22 Once the head is completely dry, roll thin sausages of Terracotta-coloured paste that taper to a point and attach them around the forehead with a little edible glue to create the fringe. Roll a thick, tapered sausage for the ponytail and add texture to the paste with the back of a knife. Stick the ponytail from the nape of the neck down over her right shoulder with edible glue. Roll more sausages of paste in the same way as for the fringe, then twist and glue them from behind the ears to the top of the ponytail.

Mother and Baby

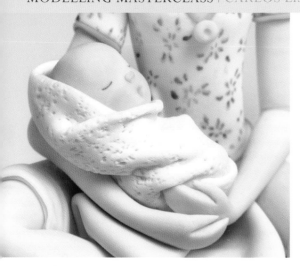

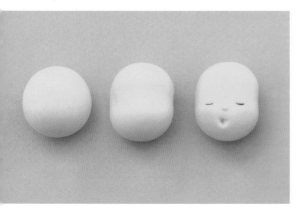

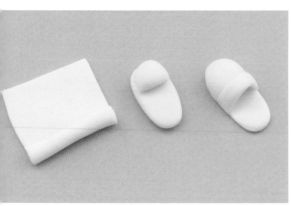

Baby

Body

23 Roll a piece of Cream Celebration MMP into a small, thick sausage and cut in half. Roll one piece into an oval for the body and the other into a ball for the head. In order to check the proportions of the baby in relation to the mother's body, position the pieces of paste in her arms to check the size and adjust if necessary. It is a good idea to make a 'raw' model first, then use this basic model to get the correct proportions for the final baby.

24 Once you are happy with the size of the head, pinch around the middle of the ball to separate the forehead from the cheeks. Use Chestnut liquid food colour and a fine paintbrush to paint two curved lines for the eyelashes following the imaginary middle line across the face (see page 332). Roll a tiny piece of Cream MMP into a very small oval shape for the nose and attach it centrally just below the eyes. Open up the mouth with the tip of a cocktail stick. Mix some Pastel Pink dust colour with a little cornflour, brush over the cheeks and leave the baby to firm up.

Swaddling blanket

25 Roll out some White SFP thinly on a lightly greased, non-stick board and cut out a rectangle that is big enough to fold in half and wrap around the baby's body. Texture the paste by pressing the hard bristles of a vegetable cleaning brush over the surface of the paste then loosely fold it in half. Place the baby's head and body on the blanket and wrap the paste neatly around the baby. Immediately position the baby in the mother's arms and stick in place with edible glue to allow the blanket to mould to the shape of the arms before it dries out.

Slippers

26 Roll some White SFP into two small ovals of equal size and flatten them down with your fingers to make the soles of the slippers. Attach one of the soles to the bottom of the mother's left foot with edible glue. For the other slipper, roll another small piece of White SFP into an oval and attach it to one end to give shape to the toe part.

27 Roll out some White SFP very thinly on a lightly-greased, non-stick board and cut out two small rectangles, then fold over one end of each rectangle. Place the folded end over the top of the left foot, fit the paste around the top of the foot and trim away any excess from around the sole. Attach the other rectangle over the piece of paste on the end of the second slipper and trim away any excess paste. For the final detail, roll two tiny balls of White SFP and stick one on top of each slipper.

Rug

28 Divide 150g (5¼oz) of White MMP into three equal parts and colour each piece with varying amounts of Hydrangea paste food colour to make three different shades of blue. Roll out a piece of the mid-blue MMP and cut out a 10cm (4") circle with a cutter.

29 To make the pattern on the rug, roll out the light blue paste and cut out three flowers with a blossom cutter. Use a 1cm (³/₈") round cutter to cut out three circles of dark blue paste. Place the smaller circles in the centre of the blossoms and arrange the blossoms on the larger circle. Press down on the paste with a hard-bristled vegetable cleaning brush to merge the blossoms into the circle of paste and give texture to the rug. Allow the rug to dry on a flat surface.

Cushions

30 To make the cushions around the pillar, roll the three shades of blue paste into balls and flatten them slightly with the palm of your hand. Press the centre of each one gently with your finger to give shape. Use the sharp edge of a Dresden tool to make marks from the centre of the cushion to the outer edges to create pleats. Mark a seam line around the edge of each cushion with the blade of a knife. To finish, roll a small ball of blue paste for each cushion and secure them in the middle with a little edible glue. Arrange the cushions around the pillar and on the rug so they are slightly folded and leave them to dry in the required position.

31 To make the cushion for the mother to sit on, roll a piece of light blue paste into a sausage with tapered ends and fit the paste around the back of the mother's hips. Add a few pleats around the cushion with the back of a knife and leave to dry.

Cake and board

32 Cover the 15cm (6") round cake, the cake board and the remaining polystyrene cylinder with Bridal White sugarpaste (see pages 139–141). Trim the edge of the board with white satin ribbon.

33 Once the figurine is completely dry, pull it carefully from the temporary polystyrene cylinder and trim the skewer level with the base of the body. Soften some White SFP and use it to stick the figurine on top of the covered cylinder.

34 Roll a long, white sausage of sugarpaste, attach it around the base of the cylinder and crimp along the length of the paste. Place the rug on top of

the cake and secure the cylinder onto the rug with a piece of softened SFP. Attach the whole piece to the top of the cake with another piece of softened SFP.

35 Secure the cushions and the second slipper on top of the rug with softened White SFP.

36 To finish the cake, roll out a thin strip of Bridal White sugarpaste that is long enough to fit around the circumference of the cake. Wrap the strip around the base of the cake and secure with edible glue. Paint the floral pattern over the strip of paste in the same way as for the T-shirt (see pages 434–437).

Important note: Where you have used inedible supports such as wooden barbecue skewers in models, make sure to inform the recipient that the models should be safely removed from the cake before it is served.

Eddie Spence MBE

BIOGRAPHY

I was born in Edinburgh on St Swithin's Day, 15th July 1932, and was brought up in a very close-knit family. Although we lived a very modest lifestyle, our parents were extremely loving and my siblings and I all enjoyed a very happy upbringing.

My career started as an apprentice at Mackie's bakery, J & W Mackie & Son Limited in Edinburgh, on my fourteenth birthday. That same year, I started going to night classes at bakery school four nights a week, where I learnt confectionery, bread making, cake decoration, and bakery science combined with bakery management and bacteriology.

I became Head Confectioner and I worked with the team at Mackie's to enter baking exhibitions up and down the country: we won the British Open Confectionery Trophy, the Fleming Trophy, the MacAdam Shield, and many other medals and accolades. My tutors at Mackie's were my manager and chairman of the Master Bakers Association, Bert Paterson, and my assistant manager, John Thompson. When you have tutors like John and Bert, their inspiration and encouragement helps your profession enormously. As a team, we produced four large window displays every year and typically made around fifteen to thirty wedding cakes a week, sometimes more.

At the age of 21, I met the love of my life, Betty, and it was love at first sight. We were married two years later and that same year I was asked to start teaching in the bakery school where I discovered I had a talent and passion for teaching. I was taken under the wing of William ('Willy') Tait, our head of department who was a brilliant technician and a wonderful friend. When one of the cake artistry teachers suffered from ill health, I was asked to take over the position and was very lucky to have a job that I loved to do. The Scottish equivalent to the London City & Guilds certification was still not recognised, so I took the exam and achieved

a first-class pass with distinction. Once qualified, I started teaching City & Guilds qualifications at the Castle Hill School of Baking, followed by Napier College.

After 23 years at Mackie's, unfortunately the business closed down so it was time for a change. Betty, our three children and I moved down to a bakery in Derby where I became Head Confectioner. I was awarded several medals and cups as well as the East Midlands trophy and also taught cake artistry on a part-time basis at Kedlestone Road College and Wilmorton College. We stayed in Derby for around nine years until a promotional opportunity came up as a Tutorial Manager at Mary Ford's prestigious sugarcraft school in Bournemouth. In 1981 I joined the British Sugarcraft Guild at its inauguration, demonstrating and judging for the members before being made president of the association from 1992 to 1995.

As a result of my close association with the Guild, I was asked by Beverley and Robert Dutton to be a judge at Squires Kitchen's annual cake decorating and sugarcraft exhibition in 1994, after which they asked me to become a regular tutor at the prestigious Squires Kitchen International School in Farnham. It was an honour and a privilege to do this for them; they were very welcoming to Betty and me and have been lovely friends ever since.

Over the course of my career I have worked on several cakes for the Royal family and other high-profile figures, including wedding cakes for Princess Margaret (my first royal wedding cake) and Sir Hugh Fraser at Mackie's, a wedding cake for Prince Charles and Lady Diana (one of twenty-three cakes, one of which was the official cake made by the Royal Navy), the Royal State Coach in icing to celebrate The Queen's Jubilee (which weighed a staggering 25kg/56lb) whilst at Mary Ford's, and Prince Andrew and Sarah Ferguson's cake and cake stand with Mark Bennett, and a

cake for the Queen's Golden Wedding Anniversary in 1997 with the Bournemouth Sugarcraft Guild.

Sadly, my beloved wife Betty died from a heart attack in October 1999. It was one of the saddest days of my life because without her, I wouldn't be in the position I am today. Just a few days later, I received a letter from Buckingham Palace to say that I had been nominated for the 2000 Honours List to receive an MBE for Services to The Sugarcraft Guild and Industry. Betty had known all about my friends in the trade who had put my name forward so I accepted the honour and went to Buckingham Palace for the ceremony in October 2000 with my son, Paul, and his wife, Jackie.

After working with Mary and Michael Ford for eight years, my next move was to teach full-time at Sparsholt College, after which I took a part-time position at Eastleigh College where I still teach today.

I also have regular classes at Squires Kitchen, am Chairman of Judges at Squires Kitchen's Annual Exhibition, and often judge and demonstrate for the British Sugarcraft Guild. I still live in Bournemouth and enjoy spending time with my son Paul, his wife Jackie, their two boys Christopher and Joshua, and my partner, Tracy.

2012 was a spectacular year for me – I was asked by McVitie's (United Biscuits) to put a team together to design and decorate a cake for The Queen's Diamond Jubilee. In July, I celebrated my 80th birthday and was lucky enough to have eight parties in total, one for each decade! In September 2012 I was honoured to accept a Lifetime Achievement Award at the annual Bakery Industry Awards in London, having been nominated by the British Sugarcraft Guild. It was a magical night and I was over the moon to win. I love teaching, demonstrating and judging and always say, if you love what you do, you never have to work.

Thistle and Bluebell Wedding Cake

EDDIE SPENCE MBE

Placing collars onto a wedding cake not only adds a beautiful, decorative touch but it also makes the design look bigger and grander. This design incorporates side panels which add width and pillars for extra height. The cake-top gazebo is made using all the same skills as the cake.

TECHNIQUES

- Covering a cake with royal icing, see pages 236–238
- Dowelling a cake, see page 143
- Run-outs and collars, see pages 340–342
- Scrolls, see page 360
- Piped flowers, see page 360

Sugar cones weighed from 5lbs–50lbs and were made in Europe for over 500 years.

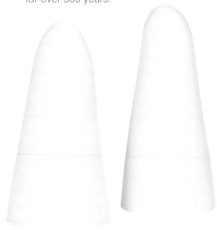

EDIBLES

15cm, 20.5cm and 25.5cm (6", 8" and 10") hexagonal cakes, measured point-to-point

2.78kg (6lb 2oz) SK Marzipan

2.78kg (6lb 2oz) royal icing for coating and decorating the cake, plus 500g (1lb 1¾oz) for gazebo

SK Professional Liquid Food Colours: Bluebell, Holly/Ivy, Violet (or colours of your choice)

SK Edible Metallic Paint: Silver

50:50 mixture of SK White Sugar Florist Paste (SFP) and SK Bridal White Sugarpaste, approximately 60g (2oz)

SK Sugar Florist Paste (SFP) in the colour of your choice

Small amount of pastillage (optional)

Small plunger blossoms and leaves (see page 164)

For essential royal icing edibles and equipment, see pages 230–231

EQUIPMENT

28cm, 33cm, 38cm (11", 13", 15") round or hexagonal cake drums (boards)*

Spare boards, at least 23cm, 30.5cm and 40.5cm (9", 12" and 16") square

8 cake dowels

Piping nozzles: nos. 0, 1, 1.5, 2

SK Paintbrushes: fine and large

8cm (3¼") round cutter

Rounded former (e.g. a teacup)

SK Barley Twist Plaster Pillars: 4 x 10cm (4"), 4 x 12cm (4¾")

3.2m (10' 6") x 15mm (½") wide satin ribbon: purple

Collar, panel, gazebo and flower stand templates, see pages 511–512

*If you are using hexagonal boards, measure them point-to-point; be aware that some boards are measured flat edge to flat edge. Always ensure the board is 13cm (5") larger than the cake, i.e. 6.5cm (2½") on either side when the cake is positioned centrally.

1 Marzipan all three cakes, starting with the top then covering each side one at a time (see page 95). When trimming the corners, the marzipan must be cut towards the opposite point so that the corners can be chamfered. Allow to firm.

2 Coat the top of the cake with royal icing and allow to dry (see page 236). Follow on with the first set of alternate sides (sides 1, 3 and 5), allow to dry, then complete the remaining alternate sides (2, 4 and 6). When applying the second coat, start with the top again, followed by the second set of alternate sides (2, 4, 6), then the first three (1, 3, 5) to keep the sides even. Repeat if a third coating is required.

3 Once the cakes are coated, cover the boards in the usual way (see page 238).

4 Dowel the middle and base tiers with four dowels each: position the dowels so that they are lined up with four corners of the cake (rather than four sides). Cut the dowelling rods to size according to the type of pillars you are using: if you are using plaster pillars with a shallow hole such as the Barley Twist design shown here, measure the depth of the hole using a spare dowel, then check that the holes in the pillars are all the same depth. Mark the dowels to the height of the cake then add on the depth of the pillar hole and cut all four to this height (the highest mark on all four dowels if they differ). Re-insert the dowels into the cake and place the pillars into position.

5 Draw the templates for the no. 1 (plain) collar on each cake: check that the internal framework is approximately 1.3cm (¼") inside the cake sides and the external framework 1.3cm (¼") outside the cake sides and adjust to fit if necessary. Repeat for the three large collars (no. 2), this time making sure that the internal framework is the same size as the cake and the external framework is approximately 1.3cm (¼") wider than the first collar on each side. Secure each

template to a spare board and cover with a sheet of greased cellophane.

6 Make the templates for the panels, again checking that they are the correct size for the coated cakes: each panel should be the same height as the cake sides and the same width as the outside edge of the first collar (this is what they will be attached to).

7 Outline collars 1 and 2 for each tier using a no. 1 or 1.5 piping nozzle (see pages 340–342 for further instructions on making collars). Cross over the internal lines on the larger collar to achieve sharp corners.

8 Make up a bowl of run-out icing (see page 235), place in a piping bag and cut a small hole in the end no bigger than a no. 1 nozzle. Flood in all six collars and leave under a desk lamp to dry.

9 Pipe in the scroll work on the no. 2 collars, ensuring that the scrolls touch the internal lines of the collar. Add some extra detail on the run-outs and scalloped pieces if required, making sure you do not overpower the design. For the picot dots around the edge of the collar, rub down some off-peak icing well: you may have to add a few drops of cold, pre-boiled water so that, when piping, the take-off comes away cleanly without a point. Place into a piping bag with a no. 1 nozzle and pipe two rows of dots (2 + 1) on the large radius curves and a single line of dots on the pointed scallops around the outside edge. Allow to dry.

10 Prepare the templates for the side panels under greased cellophane. Pipe in the filigree sections on the left and right with a no. 0 nozzle (see page 247), making sure it goes just over the lines of the template to strengthen the panel (this will prevent it from dropping out when the panel is dry). If the filigree doesn't look strong enough to hold in place, add in a few leaves touching the sides of the run-out to strengthen it.

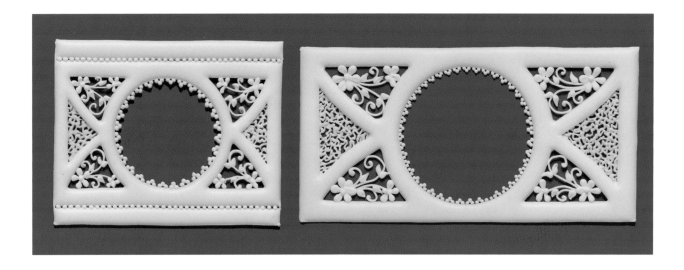

11 When the filigree is dry, pipe the outlines for each panel with a no. 1 nozzle. When complete, flood in with run-out icing and allow to dry under a desk lamp.

12 Pipe in the scrolls and flowers, making sure that the scrolls touch the edges of the panels so they stay firmly in place. If there are any slight gaps, pipe in a tiny spot of rubbed-down icing using a fine nozzle to ensure the scrolls adhere to the panel.

13 Using the centre of the panel templates, draw six circle templates for each tier and secure under greased cellophane. Pipe the outlines with a no. 1 nozzle then flood with run-out icing to make solid circular plaques (see page 240). Allow to dry then pressure pipe your chosen details to suit the occasion: this cake features a combination of thistle, bluebell and monogram motifs in blues and greens.

14 Using the panel templates as a guide, stick the circles to the sides of the cakes with rubbed-down icing, making sure they are central. Finish with a single row of picot dots around the outer edge of each circle.

15 Mark the central point of the middle and bottom tiers with a scriber. Pipe a scroll decoration onto the centre of the middle and bottom tiers to fit within the four dowels. To add some colour to the centre of the cakes I have piped a purple thistle in the middle of the scroll design using stiff royal icing. Allow to dry.

16 Stick the no. 1 collars in place on each tier with rubbed-down icing and allow to firm. Make up a bag of off-peak royal icing with a no. 1 or 1.5 nozzle and pipe a line along the top and bottom edges of one of the panels. Stick it in place so that the top edge touches the collar. Pipe down one side of this panel, then repeat with the second panel, ensuring it adheres to the first panel and the collar. Repeat all the way around the cake and then pipe running beads along the base and sides of the panels to neaten the joins.

17 Once the panels are in position you can pipe the decoration on the board to match the design on the no. 2 collar. To make a template for the board, copy the template of the top collar design for each tier and cut along the outside edge and one scallop. Make a tab on the top from tape so that you can lift it off without damaging the piping. Place on the board and pipe the outside edge with a no. 2 nozzle. Pipe the inner line with a no. 1 nozzle, either point-to-point or scalloped. Mark the centre of the daisy

through the template with a scriber so that the pressure-piped design balances with the top design and then remove the template and pipe in the same detail as on the no. 2 collar. Repeat around all six sides of the cake.

18 Use rubbed-down icing to stick the no. 2 collars in place on top of the first collars. Make sure they are lined up with the first collar on each cake and take extra care not to push down on them as they are very fragile.

19 Once all the collars are in place, pipe straight, built-up line work around the inside of the collars (see page 353). Add scratched scallops to the inside line to give it finer detail (see page 364).

20 Attach purple ribbon around the cake boards.

21 Paint the pillars with edible Silver paint and allow to dry. Place the four longest pillars in position on the bottom tier and carefully place the middle tier on top, ensuring that the collars line up. Position the shortest pillars on the middle tier and position the top tier in place.

22 Make the gazebo following the instructions overleaf and carefully place it on the top tier with the doors at the front.

Thistle and Bluebell Wedding Cake

Gazebo

1 If you are making your own icing, beat the egg white (fresh or pure dried albumen) a day before needed and leave in the refrigerator overnight to help strengthen the albumen (see page 358).

2 Make up the royal icing, including the strengthened egg white, to off-peak consistency (see page 235). This icing will be used to pipe the outlines of the run-out pieces.

3 To prepare the icing to flood the run-outs, use a palette knife to rub down a small amount of the freshly beaten icing on a clean work surface. Place the rubbed-down icing into a small bowl and stir in a teaspoon of very cold, pre-boiled water to thin down the icing to run-out consistency (see page 235).

4 Prepare the templates for the hexagonal solid run-out pieces on paper. Cut around the shape, leaving a tab at the side so that you can remove the template easily. Secure a piece of cellophane over the template using masking tape and grease the cellophane with a little white vegetable fat.

5 Place a no. 1.5 nozzle into a piping bag and half-fill the bag with off-peak royal icing. Pipe the outline of the solid hexagons: you will need two small hexagons, one medium and one large. When possible, pipe the lines from point-to-point to achieve sharp corners. If the corners are not sharp, they can be neatened using a damp paintbrush.

6 Use the run-out icing prepared earlier to flood in the run-outs. When flooding in, you may use a no. 1 piping nozzle, though I prefer to make a tight piping bag and cut a small aperture in the tip. The smaller the aperture, the better the run-out will be.

7 Flood in one large and one small hexagon for the base and the plinth of the gazebo respectively, plus one medium hexagon for the roof. Place the completed run-outs under a desk lamp to dry.

8 Prepare the templates for the side panels and doors: you will need five side pieces and two doors, plus spares to allow for breakages. Place under lightly greased cellophane. Make a bag of off-peak royal icing and pipe the internal lines

of the run-outs. Cross the lines over at the corners to give sharp corners and to form a dam for the icing when you flood the run-outs. Once the internal lines are complete, pipe the outer lines and allow to dry.

9 When all the outlines are complete, use run-out icing to flood the pieces. When flooding into corners, fill in towards the point. When flooding in-between narrow lines, squeeze the piping bag gently and use a back-and-forth motion, keeping a steady pressure on the piping bag. The weight of the icing will pull itself along and level itself out. Place under a desk lamp to dry.

10 Prepare six scroll templates for the roof under greased cellophane. Using rubbed-down icing and a no. 1 or 1.5 nozzle, pipe the roof pieces and the scroll work on the side pieces and doors. Make sure the scroll work touches the edge of the run-outs so it will stay in place when the pieces are removed from the cellophane. Allow to dry.

11 To make a domed top, cut out an 8cm (3¼") circle from a 50:50 mix of SFP and sugarpaste, dust the top and bottom surfaces with icing sugar and place into a rounded former such as a cup. Use a rolling pin to push the paste down into the cup to create a rounded finish. Make two in case one doesn't form correctly and allow to dry.

12 Using a no. 1 or 1.5 plain nozzle, decorate the top of the dome with a scroll pattern to match the central design on the middle and bottom tiers.

13 Allow all of the run-out pieces to dry thoroughly before assembly. Using rubbed-down royal icing, attach the small hexagon centrally on top of the large one for the base.

14 Use a bag of stiff icing to pipe a line along two adjacent sides of the hexagonal base (smaller hexagon). Pipe a line of icing along the right-hand side of a side panel, pick up a second panel and press the two side pieces against the base. Stick the two side pieces into position, sticking them together down the side. If you are worried about this stage, place a support behind each panel to hold them in situ. If the icing is stiff enough, however, this should not be necessary. Take a damp paintbrush and clean up the edges along the base and up the join between the panels.

15 Repeat around five sides of the hexagon, piping down the side of each panel individually before securing it to the base and the adjacent side piece. When dry, pipe running beads down the sides of the panels to neaten the joins. For added decoration you can pipe running beads on the inside of the joins (see page 242), but only on the back panels before the others are attached. You will not be able to reach the joins between the other panels so these are left plain.

16 Once you have attached the five side panels, you can attach the doors. Ease each door off the cellophane. Pipe a line down the side panels at the front then position the doors so that they are open.

17 To finish off the gazebo you can place a flower stand inside to suit the occasion. This should be done before the roof is attached. Mix equal quantities of White SFP and sugarpaste or mix up some SK Instant Mix Pastillage (see page 222). Roll out the paste thickly and cut out one large and two small hexagons using the templates. Indent one of the small hexagons to hold the flowers later. Roll a thick sausage of paste and cut to size for the upright piece. Allow to dry completely then secure the pieces together with royal icing.

18 Make some flowers in the colour of your choice from SFP using a mini blossom plunger cutter and cup using a ball tool (see page 164). Make several leaves from SFP, soften with a ball tool and allow to dry.

19 Make a small cone from the SFP/sugarpaste mix or pastillage and secure to the top of the flower stand. Attach leaves around the base of the cone, then secure flowers onto the cone itself by piping green leaves all over the cone (see page 250). Add tiny white dots to the flower centres.

20 To make the roof, attach the dome centrally on top of the medium hexagon. Hide the join by piping a series of dots around the dome. Allow to dry.

21 To attach the roof, pipe a line of stiff royal icing using a no. 2 nozzle around the top edge of the side panels and place the roof on top straight away.

22 Use a small, cranked palette knife to lift the scroll decorations for the roof off the cellophane. Pipe a line of stiff royal icing just inside the edge of the roof using a no. 2 nozzle, then place the pieces in place so that they stand vertically. Use a paintbrush to neaten the edge.

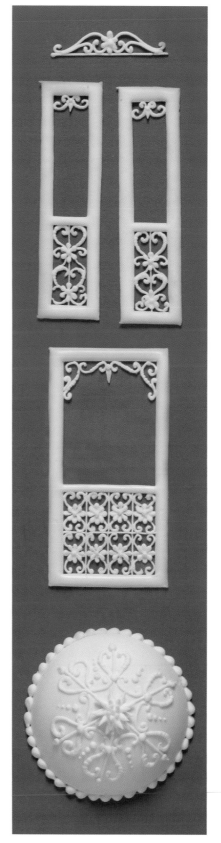

Thistle and Bluebell Wedding Cake

TUTOR TIPS

These panels are made for three different sizes of cake which are all 7.5cm (3") high. They can easily be enlarged or made smaller as required. If you need to increase the height of a panel but not the width you can add extra strips at the top and bottom, as shown on the template (see page 512).

When sticking down any collar, make sure the icing is well rubbed-down to expel the air (see page 235). If the icing is too stiff, the collar is more likely to break when you press it into place. Moreover, if the icing is stiff you will increase the height that the panels need to be in order to reach the collar.

The gazebo can be used on wedding cakes, christening cakes, and any other special-occasion cake. Although it looks complicated, once you know how to make run-outs and pressure pipe, it is a great project for all skill levels. The gazebo can be made in advance and the colour can be altered to suit the cake using liquid colourings.

When flooding a large area, pipe towards the outline, no more than 5cm (2") along to start, then flood in the area. Vibrate the tip of the bag/nozzle on the surface and give the work board a gentle knock on the table periodically to level out the icing and create an even run-out. The idea behind piping into the line is to always pipe onto wet icing to keep the finished result smooth.

To strengthen the gazebo the side pieces can be piped onto tulle pieces (see right); this looks delicate and has the added advantage of holding the scroll work in place. The pieces should be slightly smaller than the framework so that they can be attached to the run-out frame before the detail is piped on. Remember, however, that tulle is not edible so the gazebo must be removed before the cake is eaten.

tutor tip

To make a pointed roof top design, pipe each section separately then assemble the roof carefully using royal icing to join it together.

MARY FORD LTD
28 SOUTHBOURNE GROVE
BOURNEMOUTH
BH6 3RA

Silver separators and vase for the presentation wedding cake of Prince
Charles and Lady Diana Spencer by Mary Ford, 29th July 1981

Royal iced cake by F. Ogden, 1908

Brass piping tubes

Sugar cone illustration
by Peter Brears

19th-century
copper aspic mould
and cutters

Savoy cake, 1908

Coffee Sugar

TATE AND LYLE
Finest
CASTER
SUGAR
LONDON & LIVERPOOL

TATE AND LYLE
Finest
GRANULATED
SUGAR
LONDON & LIVERPOOL

TATE AND LYLE
FAIRRIE
SMALL CUBE
SUGAR
LONDON & LIVERPOOL

TATE AND LYLE
Finest
PRESERVING
CRYSTALS
LONDON & LIVERPOOL

Tate & Lyle
miniature sugar
boxes, 1953–1965

Sugar cone and Georgian sugar nips

19th- and 20th-century copper
jelly moulds and savoy cake mould

Alan Dunn

BIOGRAPHY

I started cake decorating at the age of 13 or 14, although I had been baking and using basic icing techniques for several years before that. I taught myself initially from cake decorating books I found in both the school and public libraries by authors such as Elaine MacGregor, Tombi Peck, Pat Ashby, Norma Dunn (no relation) and Jean Bowring. It was also during this period that I attended classes with Margaret Moreland (now Carter) – this was my first introduction to wired sugar flowers and also to The British Sugarcraft Guild.

At the age of 16 I left school and trained to be a baker and confectioner, studying a two-year full-time City and Guilds 120 and 121 at Newcastle Bakery School. Halfway through my course I started to teach and demonstrate to local groups and branches of The British Sugarcraft Guild.

Word spread quickly about my work and it was not long before I was demonstrating further afield.

In 1989 I attended my first class with Tombi Peck, who has been a huge inspiration to my approach to sugarcraft. We soon became great friends and gradually learned and shared ideas together, forming a mutual admiration for each other's work. In 1991 I was asked to demonstrate at the Squires Kitchen Annual Exhibition – one of the other demonstrators was ill and I was asked to fill in! As a result of this exhibition I was invited to teach as a guest tutor at Squires Kitchen International School and have been a regular guest tutor there for 23 years now. How time flies!

My first introduction to writing and working on books was also through Tombi. She was working on her second book, *Decorative Touches*, and I helped with many of the flowers and foliage

featured in the book. This led on to being commissioned to write my first book, *Wild Flowers* (1995). I have now written 16 titles about the art of sugar flowers, cold porcelain flowers and cake decorating techniques and have contributed many articles to magazines including *Cakes & Sugarcraft*.

As well as teaching and demonstrating for Squires Kitchen, I have also written two books for their publishing house, B. Dutton Publishing – the first with my friend Tombi, *Modelling in Cold Porcelain* (1998), and the second, *Flowers and Foliage for Wedding Cakes* (2006).

My work has enabled me to travel extensively, teaching and demonstrating around the UK and also in many other countries including Russia, South Korea, Italy, Spain, Portugal, Canada, USA, New Zealand, Australia, Brazil, South Africa, Japan, Holland, Sweden and France.

Oriental Trails

ALAN DUNN

A large Chinese peony combined with green Red ink berries and trailing stems of ipomoea foliage adorn this stunning two-tier cake that would be suitable for a small wedding reception or ruby wedding anniversary cake.

TECHNIQUES

- Covering a cake with sugarpaste, see pages 139–140

- Basic floral skills, see page 261

EDIBLES

Cake

15cm and 23cm (6" and 9") round fruit cakes

Apricot glaze

1.4kg (3lb 2oz) SK Marzipan

1.8kg (4lb) SK Sugarpaste: Bridal White

Clear alcohol, e.g. vodka or gin

Flowers

1 large Chinese peony plus 3 sets of foliage, see pages 458–463

5 stems of red ink plant berries, see page 264

3 trailing stems of ipomoea vine foliage, see page 465

For essential floral edibles and equipment, see pages 254–255

EQUIPMENT

15cm and 23cm (6" and 9") round thin cake cards

33cm (13") round cake drum

Fine braid/ribbon: pale aqua, pink

1.05m (3' 5") x 15mm (½") wide ribbon: aqua

Paper-covered craft wire: aqua, Bordeaux, green

Straight-edge and round-edge cake smoothers

Food-grade posy pick

Preparation

1 Cover the cakes and cake drum as described on pages 139–140. Place the small cake on top of the large cake and blend the join between them using the straight-edged cake smoother. Allow to dry overnight.

2 Attach a fine band of pale aqua/pink ribbon around the base of each cake using a tiny amount of royal icing or sugarpaste softened with clear alcohol to hold it in place at the back. Secure the broader aqua ribbon to the edge of the large cake drum using a non-toxic glue stick (see page 140).

Spray assembly

3 Use ½-width Nile green floral tape to secure the trailing stems of ipomoea foliage around the large peony. Use a long trail at the base of the spray and a shorter stem at the opposite side to create a relaxed, reversed S shape. Add a third short stem of the trailing foliage to the left-hand side to create a balanced effect. Tuck in and add the peony leaves to fill in the remaining gaps in the spray.

4 Add the stems of green red ink berries at intervals around the peony, trim off any excess bulk wire using wire cutters and tape together. Finally, add loops and trails of aqua, green and Bordeaux paper-covered wire, curling the wire at the tips of the trails and winding it gracefully around the trailing foliage. Use fine pliers to adjust any of the flowers, foliage or berries as necessary to create a balanced, natural shape.

5 Insert a large, food-grade posy pick into the top tier of the cake and then insert the handle of the spray into this. Ensure the spray and pick are removed from the cake before it is cut.

Oriental Trails

Chinese Peony (Paeonia lactiflora)

Originating in China and cultivated for over 1000 years, the peony has many different varieties. The Chinese peony created here is large and features many fine, fringed petals around the stamens, creating instant impact. As the flower is large you won't need to make many to create an eye-catching display.

EDIBLES

SK Sugar Florist Paste (SFP): Pale Green, Pale Pink

SK Professional Dust Food Colours: Holly/Ivy, Lilac, Sunflower, Vine

Clear alcohol, e.g. vodka or gin

Edible glaze spray (PME)

EQUIPMENT

SK Designer Cutter Range by Alan Dunn: Peony Petal Cutters

SK Designer Cutter Range by Alan Dunn: Peony Leaf Cutters

SK Great Impressions Peony Petal Veiner: 5cm (2")

35-, 33-, 26-, 24-gauge floral wires: white

Non-toxic craft dust: plum

Floral tape: Nile green

Ceramic silk veining tool

Small seed-head stamens: white or cream

Non-toxic craft glue

For essential floral edibles and equipment, see pages 254–255

Carpels

1 Cut a 26-gauge white wire into five short lengths and use fine pliers to bend a hook in the end of each wire. Roll a small ball of Pale Green SFP and insert a hooked wire into it. Use your finger and thumb to work the ball of paste into a slender teardrop shape.

2 Use your finger and thumb to pinch a ridge down the length of one side of the teardrop. Curl the tip of the teardrop over towards the ridged side. Repeat to make three, four or five carpels: the number varies between varieties of peony. Use ¼-width Nile green floral tape to tape the carpels together with the curled sides facing outwards. It is best to tape them while the paste is still pliable so they can mould around each other.

3 Dust the carpels with Vine dust food colour and catch the curled tips with a mixture of plum craft dust and Lilac dust food colour.

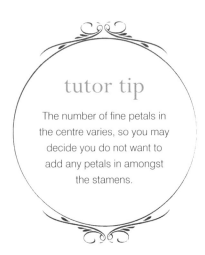

tutor tip

The number of fine petals in the centre varies, so you may decide you do not want to add any petals in amongst the stamens.

Fine inner petals

4 Cut 35- or 33-gauge white wires into several short lengths. Roll a tiny ball of Pale Pink SFP and insert a length of wire into the ball. Work the paste down the wire using your finger and thumb: the length of the inner petals can vary. Use the flat side of a veiner to press the wired paste firmly against a non-stick board to thin the petal a little and form the basic petal shape.

5 Use a ceramic silk veining tool to texture and thin the petal a little further, then pinch the petal from the base to the tip. You will need to make a few of these petals to tape tightly against the carpels, then many more to surround the stamens once they have been attached: the exact number of fine petals depends upon how full you would like the flower to be.

6 Use plum craft dust to colour each of the fine petals, then dilute some Lilac dust food colour with clear alcohol and paint dark veins at the base of each one with a fine paintbrush.

Stamens

7 Make two bunches of white or cream seed-head stamens for this flower. Divide the stamens into several smaller groups: the number in each group can vary. Line up the tips of the stamens and use non-toxic craft glue to bond each group together. Work the glue into the length of the stamens with your finger and thumb. Start the glue at the centre and work it towards either end of the stamens, leaving a short amount of the stamens unglued at either end. It is important the glue forms a fairly straight line.

8 Use sharp scissors to cut each group of stamens in half. Trim the length of the stamens from the glued end, making sure they are shorter than the carpels.

9 Use a little more craft glue to attach the groups of stamens around the base of the carpels. Hold the stamens firmly against the carpels until they are secured in place: they should hold firm after around 10 seconds. Repeat with the remaining groups until you have created a neat circle of stamens around the carpels. Allow to dry. Use tweezers to pull the stamens slightly and give a little movement.

10 Dust the tips of the stamens with Sunflower dust food colour and use plum craft dust to colour the length of the stamens.

Petals

11 Knead some Pale Pink SFP well and model it into a teardrop shape. Place the teardrop against a non-stick board and flatten it slightly with the side of your hand. Thin the paste, leaving a central thick ridge down the centre. (You might prefer to use a grooved board to create the ridge.)

12 Cut out the petal using the largest peony petal cutter. Insert a moistened 26- or 24-gauge white wire into the ridge 1/3 of the way up the petal. You can hook the end of the wire to give a little more support or insert two finer wires into the ridge if preferred. This will prevent the petals from spinning around on the wire.

13 Place the petal against a non-stick board and texture the surface using the ceramic silk veining tool. Use the tool at intervals across the petal in a fan pattern, then turn the petal over and repeat. Take care not to press the tool into the wired area.

14 Frill the edge of the petal using the ceramic silk veining tool and increase the pressure to create a more pronounced, frilled effect. You might prefer to rest the petal against your index finger as you frill it.

15 Cut a sheet of kitchen paper in half diagonally, then twist the triangle of paper back onto itself and tie into a loop too create a former. Make sure that it is large enough to support the petal as it dries. Make 20 large petals and 10 smaller petals altogether and allow to dry slightly in the formers before colouring.

Colouring and assembly

16 Use plum craft dust and a dry, flat dusting brush to colour both sides of the petals. Scrub the colour into the surface of the petal to create an intense colour. Dilute some Lilac dust colour with clear alcohol and use it to paint a series of markings at the base of each petal.

17 Using 1/4-width Nile green floral tape, tape the very fine petals to create a circle around the stamen centre: the exact number of fine petals depends upon the effect you wish to achieve. Trim away any excess wire as you work. Starting with the smaller petals, tape the outer petals around the flower centre.

Calyx

18 The calyx is made up of three rounded sepals and two longer, narrow sepals. For the rounded sepals, model a small ball of Pale Green SFP

tutor tip

Avoid using too much glue as it will take a long time to dry.

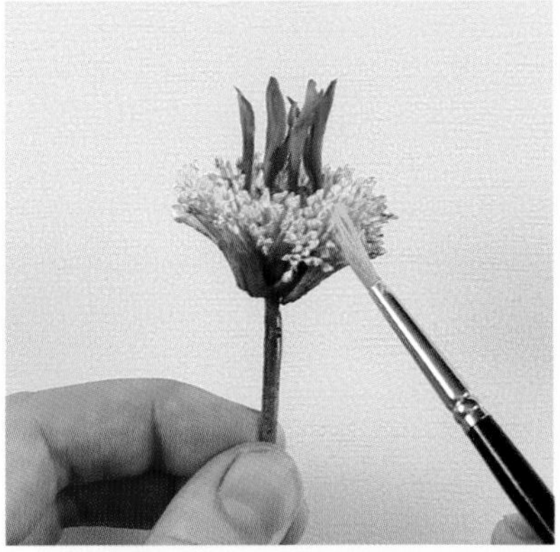
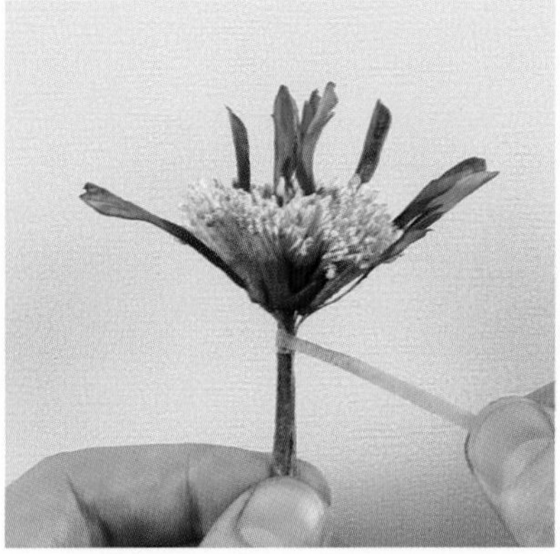
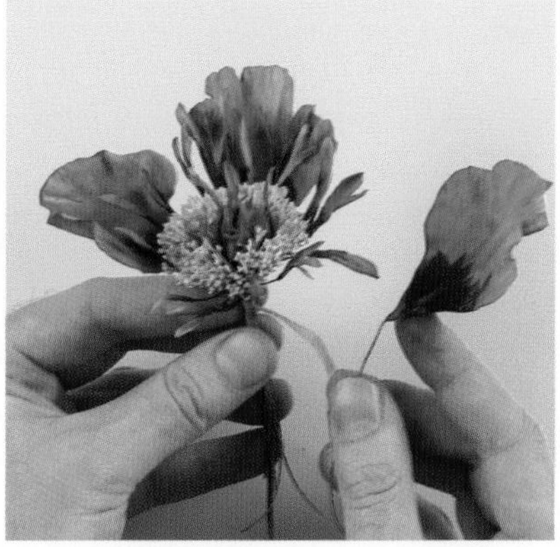
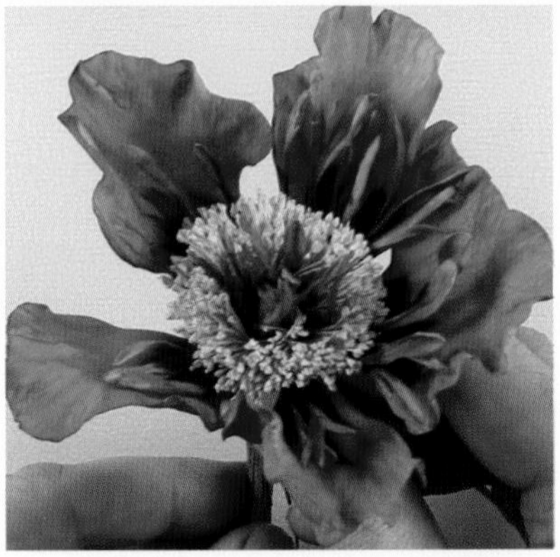
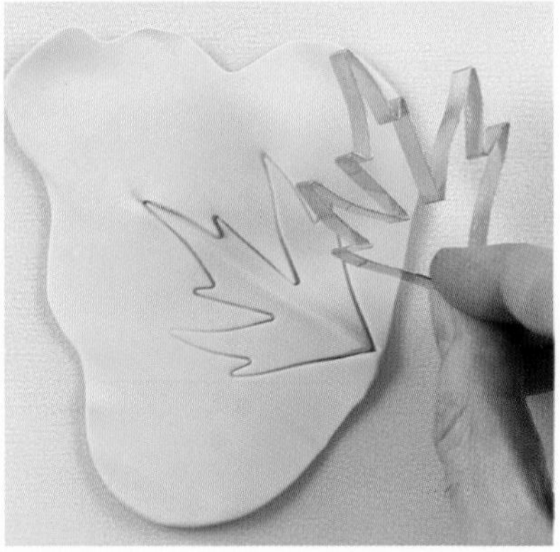
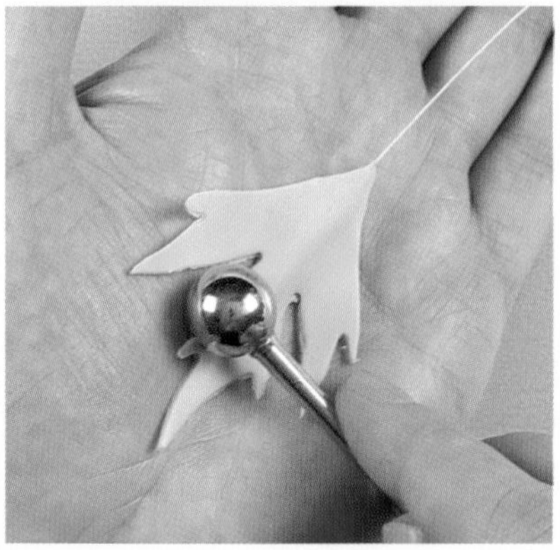
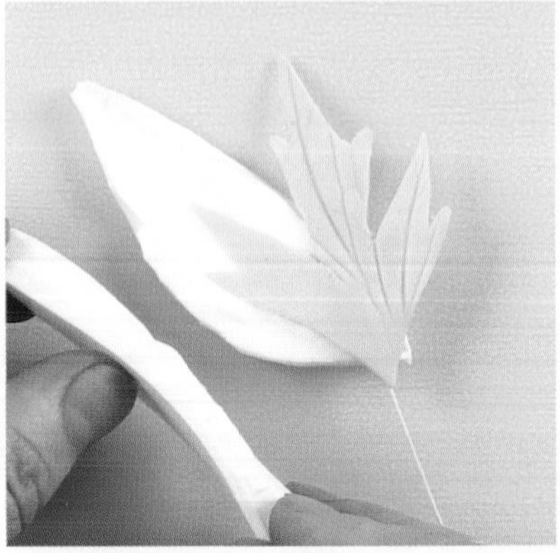
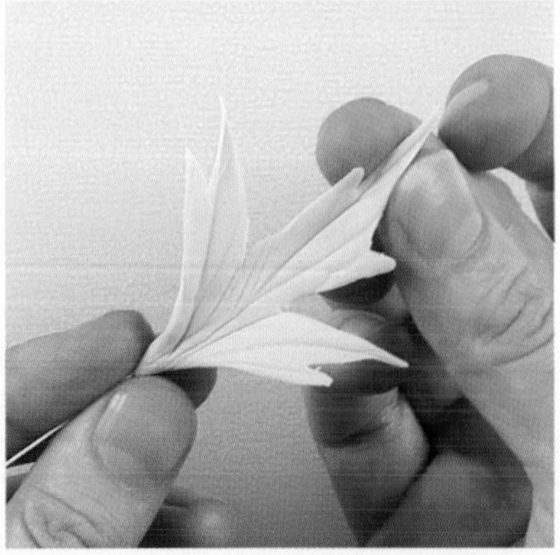
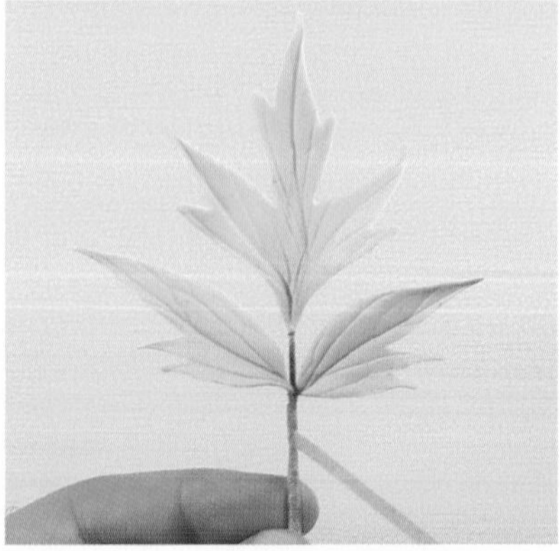
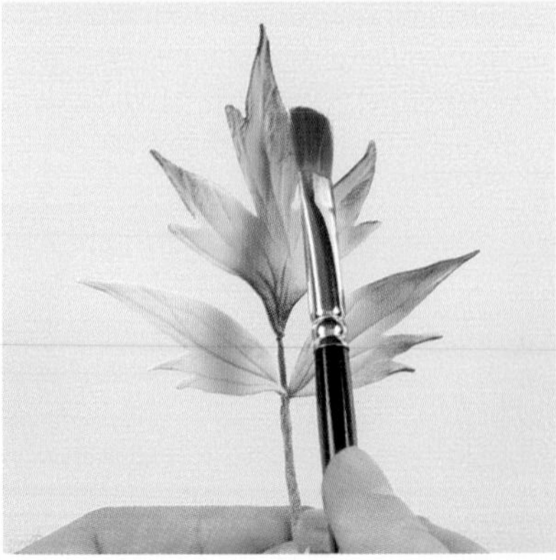
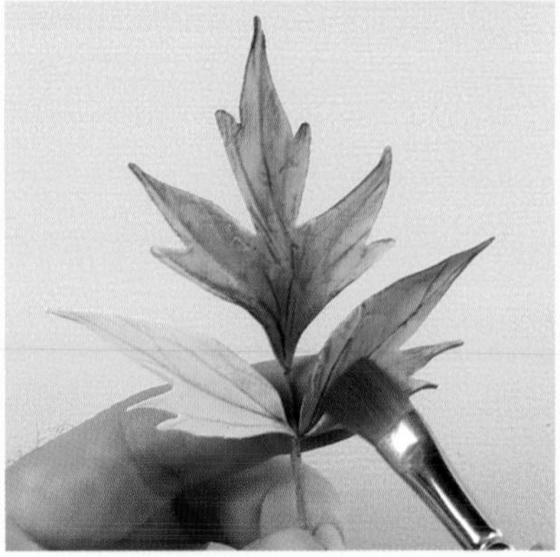
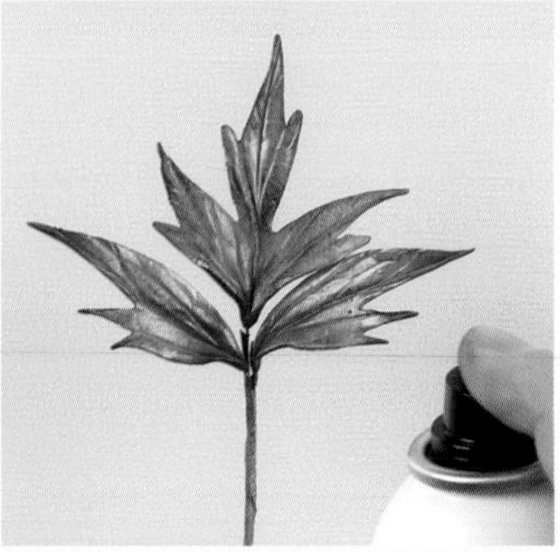

into a cone shape and insert a 28-gauge white wire into the tapered end of the cone. Flatten the cone against a non-stick board. Place the paste on your palm or onto a firm foam pad and use a ball tool to thin the edges and hollow out the centre. Repeat to make three sepals in graduating sizes. Pinch each sepal from the base into a point on the curved edge.

19 To make the narrow sepals, work a small ball of Pale Green SFP onto a 28-gauge white wire to form a tapered sepal shape. Place the shape against the non-stick board and flatten it using the flat side of a veiner. Pinch the sepal from the base through to the tip and curve. Repeat to make a second sepal.

20 Dust each of the sepals with Vine dust food colour and catch the edges with a mixture of Lilac dust colour and plum craft dust.

21 Tape three rounded sepals to the back of the flower, spacing them out evenly. Attach the two narrow sepals opposite each other at the front of the flower.

Leaves

22 Roll out some Pale Green SFP leaving a long, thick ridge for the wire. Cut out the leaf using the large tri-lobed peony leaf cutter: the ridge should extend into the middle section of the leaf. Moisten the end of a 24-gauge wire with edible glue and insert it into the thick ridge of the leaf. Insert the wire through to the long middle section to give maximum support to the fragile leaf.

23 Place the leaf on your palm or a firm foam pad and gently soften the edges using a large ball tool. Try not to frill the paste: you are aiming to remove the cut edge left by the leaf cutter.

24 Use the peony leaf veiner to texture the three sections of the leaf. Pick up the leaf and pinch from the base to the tip of the middle section to emphasise the central vein. Repeat for the two side sections. Make two side leaves in the same way, remembering to turn over the cutter for the second leaf. Tape down the wires with ½-width Nile green floral tape.

Colouring and assembly

25 Dust Lilac food colour in from the edges on either side of the leaf. Dust Holly/Ivy up from the base of each leaf and fade the colour towards the edges. The upper surface should be dusted with a deeper colour than the underside. Dust over the leaf with Vine dust food colour. Dip the leaves into a ½-strength glaze mixture (see page 275) or spray with edible glaze.

26 Allow to dry and then tape the two side leaves onto the larger tri-lobed leaf using ½-width Nile green floral tape.

Oriental Trails

Red ink plant (Phytolacca americana)

This wonderful plant has beautiful pink stems and jewel-like berries that ripen from a bright green to bright pink and eventually black. The plant Phytolacca americana was introduced from North America in 1768. In the past the berries were used to create a substitute for red ink and to colour food and wine, however, they are no longer used because the plant was found to be toxic in large amounts. Although the plant has small, pretty flowers and attractive foliage I have decided to use only the green berries with their beautiful bright pink, contrasting stems in the display.

EDIBLES

SK Sugar Florist Paste (SFP): Cyclamen, Holly/Ivy, Pale Green

SK Professional Dust Food Colours: Leaf Green, Vine

Edible glaze spray (PME)

EQUIPMENT

Non-toxic craft dust: plum

30- and 22-gauge floral wires: white

Floral tape: white or pale pink

Fine-nosed pliers

Frilling tool or small CelStick

Tiny 5-petal plunger blossom cutter (PME)

For essential floral edibles and equipment, see pages 254–255

Berries

1 Cut several very short lengths of 30-gauge wire using sharp floristry scissors or wire cutters. There are two ways to create the fairly short, fleshy stem effect: you could simply tape over each wire with ¼-width white or pale pink floral tape; or alternatively work a tiny amount of Cyclamen SFP onto each wire to create a fine coating. Squeeze the tape or paste firmly between your finger and thumb to create a smooth finish. Dust the stems with plum craft dust.

2 Roll a ball of well-kneaded Pale Green SFP. Flatten the ball slightly to make the berry shape. Moisten the tip of the coated wire with edible glue and insert into the berry.

3 Use a sharp craft knife or plain-edge cutting wheel to mark deep indents into the surface of the berry so that they radiate from the centre. Use the pointed end of a smooth frilling tool or CelStick to indent the centre of the berry where the indented lines join. Repeat to make numerous berries in graduating sizes.

4 Dust the berries with Vine and Leaf Green dust food colours.

Calyx

5 Roll out some well-kneaded, Cyclamen SFP thinly and cut out a calyx shape using the 5-petal plunger blossom cutter. Dust with plum craft dust and thread onto the back of a berry, securing with a tiny amount of edible glue.

Assembly

6 Use ¼-width white or pale pink floral tape to secure the berries onto a length of 22-gauge wire. Start with the smaller berries, gradually increasing in size as you work down the stem. Bear in mind that the number of berries used on each stem can vary.

7 Dust the tape with plum craft dust then spray the berries and stem with edible glaze.

Ipomoea vine

There are over 500 species of this plant which grows in subtropical and tropical parts of the world. The foliage can be a bright or dark green as well as the more interesting purple forms.

EDIBLES

SK Sugar Florist Paste (SFP): Pale Green

28-, 26- and 22-gauge floral wires: white

SK Professional Dust Food Colours: Holly/Ivy, Lilac

Edible glaze spray (PME)

EQUIPMENT

SK Designer Cutter Range by Alan Dunn: Ipomoea Vine Cutters

Non-toxic craft dusts: African violet, plum

Floral tape: Nile green

SK Great Impressions Large Cyclamen Leaf Veiner

For essential floral edibles and equipment, see pages 254–255

Leaves

1 Roll out some Pale Green SFP, leaving a thick ridge for the wire (you may prefer to use a grooved board for this). The paste needs to be quite fine for this foliage. Cut out the leaf using one of the ipomoea leaf cutters.

2 Insert a moistened 28- or 26-gauge wire into the thick ridge, approximately halfway up the leaf to support the paste. The gauge of wire will depend upon the size of the leaf. Place the leaf on your palm or on a firm foam pad and soften the edges gently with a ball tool.

3 Place the leaf into the cyclamen leaf veiner and press the two sides together firmly to texture the leaf. Remove from the veiner and pinch the leaf from the base through to the tips. Pinch the tips of the two side sections. Repeat to make leaves in varying sizes.

Colouring

4 Brush a little Holly/Ivy dust food colour in the centre of each leaf. Use a mixture of plum and African violet craft dusts to dust both the upper and lower surfaces to create a good depth of colour. Over-dust with lilac dust colour then spray with edible spray glaze or dip into a ½-strength glaze solution (see page 275).

5 Tape the leaves onto a 22-gauge wire using ½-width Nile green floral tape. Start with a small leaf and then continue adding leaves down the stem, alternating their position and increasing the size as you work. Add an extra 22-gauge wire if you need more support and length.

6 Dust the main stem and individual leaf stems with Lilac dust food colour to finish.

tutor tip

It is best to dust the leaves while the paste is still pliable so that the colour adheres to the surface, creating a stronger depth of colour. Moreover, the paste is not as fragile at this stage so is less likely to break.

Oriental Trails

Discover the steps you need to take to develop your hobby into a cake decorating business, ensuring you have all the advice and information you need to achieve success.

COMMERCIAL CAKES

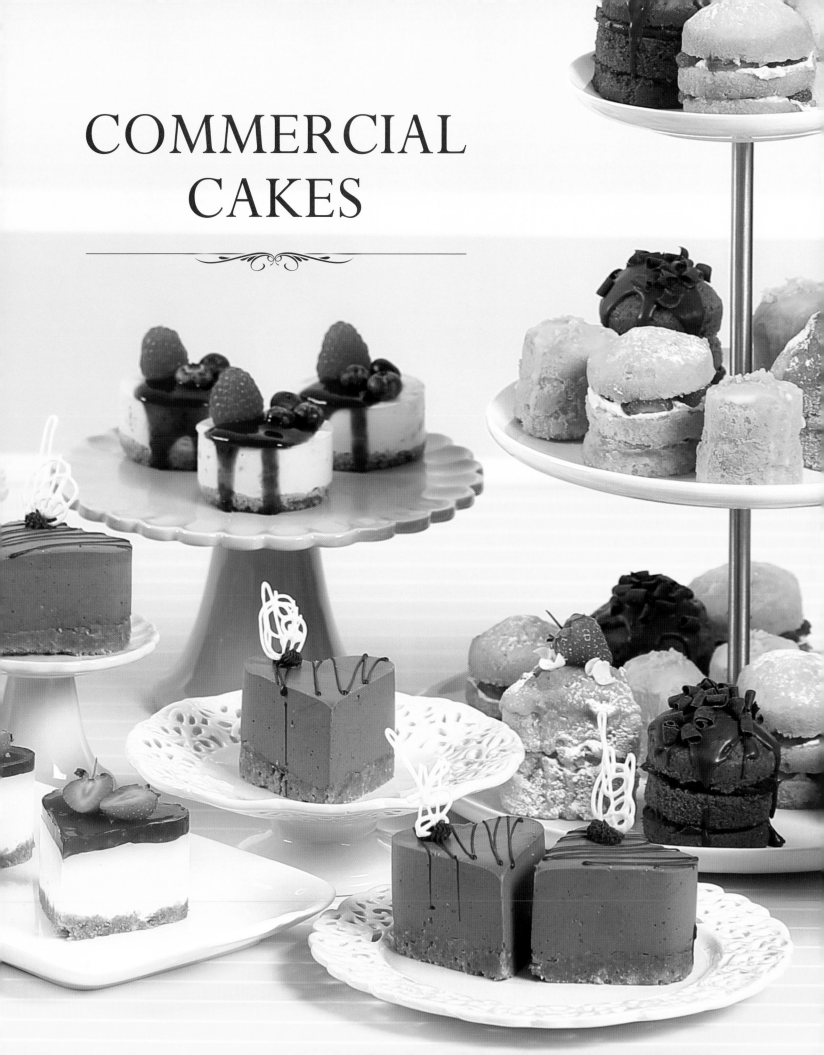

Kathy Moore

BIOGRAPHY

At a very early age I was spellbound by the cakes and biscuits my mum created from seemingly, to a five year old child, unrelated ingredients. Throughout my childhood our baking days were special and I was immersed in a world filled with the most enticing aromas of baked cakes and crisp, buttery biscuits.

As I grew older, under the watchful eye of a (very) patient, encouraging parent, I too learnt how to create those wonderfully light sponges, crisp little cookies and rich, tempting pastries that my mum made. I was captivated by all things cake and this passion has never been extinguished. My first entry into a cake decorating competition resulted in a very proud, and somewhat embarrassed, 11 year old taking first prize for a royal iced cake – a prize I still have!

In my quest to become a professional chef, I was fortunate to train and learn fron chefs at the prestigious Wordsworth Hotel and the Michelin-starred Michael's Nook Hotel in the Lake District where I focused on pâtisserie. I finally left catering college having qualified with distinctions in all three catering disciplines, including Cake Design and Decoration for which I was awarded the Goldex Trophy.

I subsequently established my own celebration cake business from home which developed rapidly and successfully, and gave me endless joy. I also gained my teacher training and external assessor qualifications which allowed me to teach and share my knowledge. Continuing to enter competitions, I won a medal in the pastillage category at the Salon Culinaire competition, as well as British Sugarcraft Guild awards in individual and group categories, and gained a much-cherished collection of trophies for sugarcraft and bakery work at both local and national levels.

When I took delivery of Squires Kitchen's very first issue of *Sugarcraft* magazine, little did I realise it would be the beginning of a long and happy relationship both as a magazine contributor and, for many years, as resident tutor at Squires Kitchen International School. I met many other tutors and have been inspired by their work, particularly Eddie Spence MBE who taught me the most amazing royal icing techniques. During my time as a resident tutor, I immensely enjoyed teaching sugar flowers, royal icing, pastillage (on one occasion to two delightful chefs from Buckingham Palace!), gold leaf and lace work, modelling and sugarpaste techniques.

Alongside the cake business and tutoring within the UK, I travelled across Europe and as far afield as Brazil to teach and demonstrate. I have also had much fun partaking in cake-related TV programmes and radio interviews, one of which was particularly memorable as a parrot escaped in the recording studio as I tried to decorate a cake!

In 2002, I wrote my first book *Cakes from Concept to Creation* (B. Dutton Publishing), which was designed to take the reader all the way through from the initial cake design to assembly and display ideas. I went on to write my second title *Starting a Cake Decorating Business from Home* (B. Dutton Publishing) in 2004, and there have been three updated editions printed since due to its immense popularity. I now also regularly teach the subject at Squires Kitchen International School, giving people the latest information on how to set up their own cake business from home. From its inception, I have been thrilled by the success stories of so many of our students worldwide.

My husband's early retirement meant a move back 'home' to Lytham St Annes in Lancashire. After the move, I began studying British Sign Language; I have since qualified as a British Sign Language Interpreter and additionally teach to those cake decorators who are Deaf or hard of hearing and whose first language is BSL.

My route to becoming a professional cake designer, tutor, demonstrator and author has brought me an enormous amount of joy, led to valued friendships, exciting projects and an appreciation of just how lucky we are to be able to do what we do.

Making Cakes, Thinking Commercially

KATHY MOORE

This is the first of two chapters featuring the commercial aspect of cake design and decoration for those considering starting a cake business from home. This chapter highlights the importance of viewing decisions from a commercial perspective and developing your business venture and cakes to meet the expectations and needs of your customers.

The information given here will help you to identify where and who your potential customers may be, and offer some ideas intended to extend and maximise business opportunities, including fabulous yet practical designs for cake pops, cupcakes, macaroons, wedding biscuits and individual table desserts, all with business in mind. Always remember the three key elements of commercial cakes: simple, quick and stunning.

Transition from leisure activity to commercial venture

Most people do not start cake decorating with the intention of turning it into a business. For many, their business evolves from a simple hobby stimulated by their love of baking, the appreciation of delicious home-baked flavours, the enjoyment of trying out new recipes and ideas, the pleasure in creating and designing, and the delight in seeing the finished product. This simple hobby can become a passion and the kindling for a new business venture upon which they would be reliant as a main source of income. However, passion alone is not sufficient for commercial success: the design choices when making cakes commercially differ widely to those taken when making cakes as a hobby, where time and cost elements may not necessarily be of prime consideration.

Your target market

As a commercial venture, cakes should be produced and marketed to the general public with the emphasis on saleability and on making a profit. To achieve this, commercial cake design and production will be geared to the needs and expectations of a target market. It is crucial for success in any business to identify that target market, i.e. the typical consumers who will be most likely to buy your product, and to have a clear understanding of their needs and expectations. This allows you to tailor your product/s to match more closely the demands of your known target market.

Research plays a large part in determining your target market and the subsequent

choices you make about the designs and service you offer. Look at the specific demographics within your trading area: population, age range, religion, ethnicity, professions, local business types and size, average income, percentage of residents that are internet users, and so on. All this will help you tailor your business to offer the right product to the right people in the right area at the right price. For example, if you live in an area dominated by industry, there could be an excellent opportunity in the corporate sector, including new product launches, staff incentives, retirement parties, baby showers, promotions, and team building away-days.

Design your business to attract, delight and excite your potential customers with fabulous designs, different ranges, a choice of colours and style and it will pay dividends.

Once you have researched the demographics in your target area you may identify several different markets for your skills. You may choose to offer high-end products alongside mid-priced cakes and those for lower budgets; offering a choice gives your business the possibility of reaching more than just one market.

Costing and pricing

To know your target market or markets is crucial but equally so is to know your costs. Having established your potential sources of business, it is then necessary to establish what price they will pay for your

products. This will vary across different regions within one country, depending on average income and disposable income. Knowing what customers are willing to pay helps in planning designs and establishing a price list which matches the expectations of your potential market and provides a satisfactory profit level. In order to establish a price list it is essential to know all your business costs and for them to be continually monitored thereafter.

Regulations

If you are making cakes commercially you will need to ensure that the products you make and your working environment comply with the latest food safety and hygiene regulations and that your business is registered as it should be. Anyone who owns, manages or runs a business in the European Union is bound by the Food Hygiene Regulations 2006, so contact the Environmental Health Service at least 28 days before you start trading. As a business owner you will also need to consider:

- Tax and National Insurance
- Trading Standards
- Insurance
- Your business accounts
- Copyright and legal protection
- Planning permission
- Labelling

Make sure you research all of these areas thoroughly before you start selling cakes to avoid problems further down the line.

Making Cakes, Thinking Commercially

Maximising business opportunities

Identifying your potential customers and setting prices are both crucial in any business; in the cake industry, having a broad range of baking and decorating skills means you can offer your customers more choice, thus extending your market share and opportunities. There are ever-increasing opportunities for the cake decorator to profit from new markets. Consider where your business can make a presence and remember that there are many occasions which might be celebrated with a cake, for example:

- Weddings, civil partnerships and anniversaries

- Stag parties, hen parties and engagements

- Baby showers, new babies, adoptions, baby namings and christenings

- Children's birthdays, adult birthdays, pets' birthdays

- Retirement, new home, graduation, emigration, coming-home parties

- Corporate events such as a new business launch, new product launch, anniversary, moving premises, in-house celebrations, leaving parties

- Christmas, Eid al-Fitr, Diwali, Easter, Hanukkah, Thanksgiving

- St David's Day, St Patrick's Day, St George's Day, St Andrew's Day

- Hogmanay, Burn's Night, New Year's Eve/Day, Valentine's Day, Mothering Sunday, Father's Day, Halloween, bonfire night

- Good Luck, Congratulations, Bar Mitzvah

- Election parties, street parties

Not all would warrant a traditional cake so consider cake pops, wedding biscuits,

cupcakes, macaroons and individual desserts. Each of these can also be offered in conjunction with a traditional cake as a way of upselling to your customers, or as a standalone product for favours, table gifts, party bags, and take-home treats.

If you are catering for a larger celebration, there may be opportunities to provide a range of cake styles. Celebration cakes, cupcakes, cake pops and cookies can be mixed and matched, combining traditional and contemporary if required. Whatever the size and scope of your business, a key element for success is to be time-efficient in all areas, in addition to ensuring that your finished product is of the highest standard possible.

Cake pops

Cake pops are particularly attractive to cake businesses as they can be economical to make yet offer a relatively high return. Most are made using cake crumbs but they can also be baked using most sponge recipes in specific baking moulds or made using no-cook recipes. Whether you choose a wickedly delicious chocolate and brandy truffle cake, an indulgent white chocolate and raspberry cake, or a light, summery

A selection of different designs for cake pops can be seen on pages 474–476.

sponge flavoured with fresh lavender or Limoncello, always use a trusted recipe with known good results.

Corporate cake pops have become increasingly popular because of their versatility. When making them with profit in mind, try to limit them to one or two colours linked to the company branding. Making a wide range of differently designed and coloured pops may not be practical, time effective or economical, particularly where larger quantities are required. Personalising can be achieved simply by incorporating branded ribbon or company logos into the presentation. (Remember to obtain copyright permission for the use of any logo or branding.) Consult your client about the use of alcohol in your recipe, particularly if the final product will be consumed on company premises.

Wedding biscuits

Decorated biscuits for weddings, civil partnerships, engagements parties, hen parties and so on can be made in many appealing designs. They can be very useful to cake businesses as they are simple to make and bake, easy to store,

have a relatively long shelf life and have excellent freezing qualities (remember to advise clients if products have been frozen). They are usually iced using royal icing, but can also be decorated exquisitely using sugarpaste or other roll-out pastes.

Cupcakes

A myriad of cupcake designs gives year-round selling opportunities. The main commercial consideration will be the viability of designs in relation to the labour involved and final costings. Gorgeous designs can be created with minimal effort and can be decorated to match a larger celebration cake, which can further maximise your selling opportunity.

If you are using fresh cream in the filling consider the availability of refrigerated storage both pre- and post-production and during delivery to ensure the products are kept at the required safe

temperature. Buttercream fillings, ganache and sugarpaste coverings have a longer shelf life and, where larger quantities are required, can often be a more practical and preferred option.

Macaroons

Macaroons are relatively easy to make and store and can be coloured to match any colour scheme. When making macaroons for commercial purposes, allow plenty of space and time for them to rest once piped before baking – on average between 30–50 minutes. It is useful, however, to know that macaroons freeze well and could be made in smaller batches. Use clear cellophane bags or pretty boxes for individual gifts and favours. If you have frozen your macaroons or cakes, remember to inform your client that they cannot be refrozen.

Individual dessert tables

Dessert tables laden with individual treats are fast becoming a popular alternative to a traditionally served dessert and cutting cake. Mouth-watering cheesecakes, light mousses, indulgent chocolate and mint truffles, fresh strawberry tarts, crisp meringues and wonderfully light individual

These cupcakes have been decorated to match the Antique Lace Wedding Cake on pages 493–495. Decorations include mini blossoms, ribbon roses, mini roses, lace pieces using cutters, dragées, textured paste using texture mats, embossed paste using quilt embossers, butterflies and flowers from moulds. Further piped details have been added in royal icing.

sponge cakes: the list is almost endless. However as a commercial venture three main issues need to be considered when making large quantities of individual desserts:

- Storage and transportation
- The use of fresh cream
- Practical issues: is the design feasible for large quantities? Do you need specialised containers? How well will they transport?

Advantages of mini desserts are that it is easy to regulate portion control and costs, presentation remains attractive (nothing is left part-cut), and it is easier to cater for different dietary requirements. Cheesecakes, mousses, individual tarts, mini cakes and jellied desserts are ideal: recipes for the desserts shown here are given on page 477–482.

Whatever range and design of cakes/desserts, cupcakes, cake pops and biscuits you decide to create, make sure you always think commercially: your work needs to be practical, viable and match your target market's expectations and needs. Try to maximise your business opportunities, stay ahead of trends, styles, design, and colour and focus your ideas for specific markets.

Remember to comply with the Food Hygiene Regulations 2006 (amended) and the Food Safety (Temperature Control) Regulations regarding transportation of foodstuffs in your vehicle.

Making Cakes, Thinking Commercially

White chocolate truffle cake pops

Made with a rich truffle filling and decorated with simple, clean and contemporary lines, this design is ideal where large quantities are required. For the covering you can use either a white 'choc' coating that doesn't need tempering (quicker and cheaper than real chocolate) or Belgian white chocolate (which is high quality for optimum flavour); your choice will depend on the time you have available and the price at which you are selling the cake pops.

EDIBLES

Cake pop truffle filling: mixture of SK Chocolate Ganache Mix, cake crumbs and orange liqueur or essence

SK Belgian White Chocolate or Easy Melt White Choc Coating (see note above)

SK Designer Edible Pollen Dust: Catkin or Pale Yellow

SK Professional Dust Food Colours: Leaf Green, Rose, Wisteria or colours of your choice

SK Professional Liquid Food Colours: Leaf Green, Rose, Wisteria or colours of your choice

SK Designer Metallic Lustre Dust Food Colour: Snowflake

SK Instant Mix Royal Icing

EQUIPMENT

Cake pop sticks

Bain marie or bowl for melting chocolate coating

Small pots or paint palette for colour mixing

Polystyrene block

For essential baking edibles and equipment, see pages 10–11

1 Make the cake pops in the usual way either using the truffle filling ingredients listed here, or your chosen recipe. Detailed instructions for making cake pops are given on pages 49–50.

2 Melt the white chocolate or coating and dip the cake pops. Push the sticks into a polystyrene block or similar and allow to dry.

3 Tip small amounts of Catkin or Pale Yellow edible pollen into separate pots and colour with the dust food colours plus Snowflake lustre dust.

4 Brush some of the cake pop tops with cooled, boiled water and sprinkle the coloured pollen over the top.

5 Colour some royal icing with liquid colours to make green, pink and blue, or your own choice of colours. Place into piping bags and spin over the cake pops. Allow to dry.

6 Dust the tops lightly with Snowflake lustre dust.

tutor tip

The same cake pop design can often be used for different celebrations simply by changing the colour scheme.

Strawberry chocolate cake pops

This pretty pink design could be used for a baby shower or baby naming, christening, birthday, welcome home party, hen party, or any other celebration where pink is in the colour scheme.

1 Make the cake pops in the usual way with your chosen recipe (see pages 49–50).

2 Melt the strawberry-flavoured coating and dip each cake pop. Push each stick into a polystyrene block to dry.

3 Roll out the SFP thinly and brush with Snowflake lustre dust. Cut out several small hearts and put aside to dry, then cut out several blossom shapes, frill with a veining tool and leave to dry in a curved former.

4 Attach a blossom to the top of each cake pop and secure three dragées to the centre with a tiny dab of royal icing. Attach the hearts with royal icing or melted chocolate.

5 Personalise the cake pops by adding a label to suit the occasion.

EDIBLES

SK Strawberry Choc Coating

SK Sugar Florist Paste (SFP): White

SK Metallic-effect Ball Dragées

SK Designer Metallic Lustre Dust: Snowflake

SK Instant Mix Royal Icing, small amount

EQUIPMENT

Cake pop sticks

Bain marie or bowl for melting chocolate coating

Polystyrene block

Blossom cutter, e.g. F6/7/8 (OP)

Small heart cutter

Veining tool

Curved former

For essential baking edibles and equipment, see pages 10–11

Commercial Cake Pops

White chocolate and raspberry wedding cake pops

These cake pops are made with sponge cake crumbs, freeze-dried raspberry pieces and white chocolate ganache mixed together. To decorate, the white chocolate is coloured with SK Cocol; the pink used here co-ordinates with the wedding cake featured on pages 493–495. Spin with melted chocolate and decorate with mini blossoms, dragées and coloured pollen (see page 474).

Place-name cake pops

A wonderfully simple dual-purpose cake pop: it is both a place name and take-home gift! The Squires Kitchen Great Impressions Rose Mould creates an impressively quick decoration once the pops have been dipped in white chocolate and brushed with edible lustre dust. (Instructions for making moulded roses can be found on page 163.)

PROJECTS: INDIVIDUAL DESSERTS

Basic cheesecake recipe

This cheesecake recipe uses gelatine to secure a set. The basic recipe results in a light and fluffy cheesecake but the addition of a small amount of gelatine offers more stability than recipes using only whipped cream and cheese. This can be particularly useful to commercial home bakers where transportation to a venue is a consideration. Remember, however, that gelatine is not suitable for vegetarians and some other special diets.

INGREDIENTS

175g (6oz) digestive biscuits

75g (2½oz) butter, melted

45ml (3tbsp) very hot, pre-boiled water

2 sheets gelatine softened in cold water

300g (10½oz) cream cheese

50g (1¾oz) caster sugar

150ml (5¼fl oz) double cream, softly whipped

150ml (5¼fl oz) natural Greek yoghurt

EQUIPMENT

12 cup mini sandwich tin with removable bases

1 Blitz the biscuits in a food processor until you have a fine crumb, then transfer to a mixing bowl. Add the butter and mix well. Place into the individual moulds, pressing down firmly and neatly. Leave to chill whilst making the filling.

2 Place the sheet gelatine in a small bowl and cover with cold water. Leave to soak for 5 minutes, then drain. Pour over the very hot, pre-boiled water and stir to dissolve.

3 Place the cream cheese and sugar in a mixing bowl and beat until smooth.

4 Add the yoghurt and softly whipped double cream and fold gently until combined. At this point you can add different flavourings following the variations given below or your own recipe. Stir in the dissolved gelatine quickly and mix gently until evenly incorporated.

5 Place into individual moulds and chill for several hours or overnight.

6 Decorate the cheesecakes to suit the flavour: use piped chocolate shapes and discs, cream/ganache rosettes, chocolate coffee beans, chopped nuts, edible flowers, or fresh fruits and berries.

For essential baking edibles and equipment, see pages 10–11

VARIATIONS

Lemon

Add the zest and juice of one large lemon. Just before serving, top with lemon zest.

Lemon and lime

Add the zest of one lemon and one lime. Just before serving, top with zest from both fruits.

Strawberry

Add 225g (8oz) strawberries to 30g (1oz) of sugar and cook until soft. Purée the mix in a blender and push through a sieve to remove any seeds.

Fruits of the forest

Make a sauce using 225g (8oz) of soft fruits (raspberries, blackberries, blackcurrants, strawberries, etc.) and 50g (1¾oz) of sugar. Cook until softened and sieve to remove any seeds or pips. Remove the cheesecakes from the sandwich tins and place on a serving dish. Pour over a little of the sauce and add fresh berries to decorate.

Crème de menthe

Add a little crème de menthe liqueur.

Irish cream

Add a tablespoon or two of Irish cream liqueur. Top with spun chocolate, crushed roasted hazelnuts and a chocolate coffee bean.

Amaretto

Add 3 tablespoons of Amaretto almond liqueur.

Passion fruit

Add the juice of three passion fruits. Use the seeds to decorate the top.

tutor tips

Please remember these are guidelines only. When trying out new recipes always test small amounts by chilling 100g (3½oz) of your mixture to check how firm it sets. Use more or less or let it down to achieve the optimum setting consistency.

You can generally substitute powdered gelatine with leaf or granulated gelatine in the following quantities: 1tbsp powdered gelatine = 1 x 8g (¼oz) envelope granulated gelatine = 3 sheets leaf gelatine.

Some foods affect the setting properties and strength of gelatine:

- Milk and dairy products strengthen the gelling process and support the structure of gelatine.

- Salt and acids (e.g. vinegar, red wine and citric fruit juices) lower the strength and can cause the collapse or prevent the setting of the gelatine; this can sometimes be counteracted by increasing the amount of gelatine used.

- Sugars increase the strength of gelatine (with the exception of fructose found in fruits).

- Raw kiwi fruit, pineapple, papaya and melon contain enzymes which slow down or halt the setting process.

20th-century Bakelite lemon squeezer

Individual Desserts

Triple-layer mousse

For a quick and easy dessert which is commercially viable, use Squires Kitchen Belgian Chocolate Mousse Mix. It is simple to make and can be frozen and decorated when required. If you are freezing desserts/cakes, remember to state clearly that the product has been frozen.

INGREDIENTS

Biscuit base

175g (6oz) digestive biscuits (or ginger/shortbread biscuits)

75g (2½oz) butter, melted

Triple layer mousse

500g (1lb 1¾oz) bag SK Belgian Chocolate Mousse Mix: Dark, Milk, White

White chocolate and raspberry mousse

500g (1lb 1¾oz) bag SK Belgian Chocolate Mousse Mix: White

225g (8oz) soft fruits

50g (1¾oz) sugar

1 sheet gelatine softened in cold water

EQUIPMENT

12 cup mini sandwich tin with removable bases

For essential baking edibles and equipment, see pages 10–11

Biscuit base

1 Blitz the biscuits in a liquidiser or blender until very fine and transfer to a mixing bowl. Add the butter and mix well.

2 Place a little of the mixture into each of the mini pans and press down firmly. Chill in the fridge whilst you prepare the filling.

Triple layer mousse

3 Use SK Dark, Milk and White Mousse Mix in equal quantities and fill the individual mini cake pans by piping the mixture on top of the base.

White chocolate and raspberry mousse

4 Make up a packet of SK White Chocolate Mousse mix and fill to within 5mm (¼") of the top of the cake pans.

5 Heat 225g (8oz) of soft fruits with 50g (1¾oz) of sugar in a saucepan and cook until soft. Pass through a sieve to remove the seeds. Add one sheet of pre-softened gelatine to the purée.

6 Leave the fruit mixture until it is just starting to set, then pour it on top of the mousse mix. Leave to chill for at least 3 hours.

Homemade chocolate mousse

If you prefer to make your own mousse from scratch, this chocolate mousse recipe is a family favourite which is easy to make and freezer stable. Using the individual, heart-shaped mini pans gives you perfectly sized portions each time.

INGREDIENTS

Biscuit base

175g (6oz) digestive biscuits

75g (2½oz) butter, melted

Filling

2 sachets of powdered gelatine

90ml (6tbsp) cooled, pre-boiled water

2 eggs, separated

150g (5¼oz) caster sugar

225ml (8fl oz) milk

200g (7oz) SK Belgian Chocolate: Dark, Milk or White, chopped into small pieces or grated

Natural vanilla extract to taste

275ml (9¾fl oz) double cream

EQUIPMENT

Squires Kitchen 16 Compartment Heart Mini Pan

For essential baking edibles and equipment, see pages 10–11

Biscuit base

1 Make the base following the instructions opposite. Chill in the fridge.

Filling

2 Sprinkle the gelatine over the cooled, pre-boiled water and leave until 'spongy'. Microwave on medium power in 10-second bursts until fully dissolved.

3 Whisk the egg yolks with 75g (2½oz) of sugar until the mixture forms ribbons. Bring the milk to boiling point and pour over the egg mixture, whisking all the time. Return to the saucepan and continue to heat until the mixture thickens. Do not allow it to boil otherwise it will curdle. Add the chocolate and vanilla to taste and stir until smooth. Leave until the mixture cools and just starts to show signs of setting.

4 Lightly whip the cream and fold it into the cooled mix.

5 Whisk the egg whites until stiff. Add the remaining sugar and whisk again to form soft peaks. Fold into the mix and then fill each of the hearts. Chill for at least 3 hours before decorating.

Individual Desserts

Raspberry and white chocolate champagne glasses

INGREDIENTS

500g (1lb 1¾oz) bag SK Belgian Chocolate Mousse: White

500g (1lb 1¾oz) frozen raspberries, defrosted

50ml (3tbsp) water

Sugar to taste

3 sheets (or one sachet) gelatine

EQUIPMENT

Approximately 10 champagne glasses

For essential baking edibles and equipment, see pages 10–11

1 Make up the white chocolate mousse mix following the instructions on the bag.

2 Arrange 10 (or more depending on size) champagne glasses to sit firmly at an angle, e.g. leaning against the sides of a square cake tin.

3 Carefully fill the champagne glasses down one side with the mousse mix, taking care not to mark the remaining glass. Leave to chill and set at an angle.

4 Heat the raspberries and water with the sugar to taste until soft, then pass through a sieve. Soften the leaf gelatine in water for a few minutes. Remove and squeeze out the excess water. Add to the hot raspberry mix and stir to ensure the gelatine is fully dissolved. Add more cooled, pre-boiled water to make it up to 500ml (17½fl oz). Leave to chill until the mix just starts to set.

5 Fill the remaining half of the glasses with the jelly. Leave to set until firm.

tutor tip

For an easier alternative use ready-made raspberry jelly with the white chocolate mousse.

Wedding Cake Design and Production

KATHY MOORE

Making wedding cakes as a commercial venture often requires very different choices to be made compared to those of a leisure activity. Whilst both require decisions to be made on the recipe, ingredients, materials, design and presentation, a commercial approach primarily would be influenced by cost, production time, profit and your potential customers. Making the right business choices, appealing to the right market with the right ideas, having a good-quality product and making the most of ingredients is crucial.

In this chapter you will find advice about how to create a wedding cake which is practical, commercially viable and stunning; why the choice of ingredients is key to a successful business; the importance of appropriate design selection; using design elements to your advantage; maximising your selling potential and choice for customers with a range of additional small cakes; and how to be economical with time using a work timeplan. Tips are included on skills such as how to dowel different tiered cake designs, achieve straight sides on cakes and make the most of presentation.

Choosing ingredients

Eating cake is a sensory experience! We see them, smell them and taste them. To attract our senses they need to be visually appealing with an excellent aroma, texture and taste. A common misconception for new business owners is to aim for the smallest financial outlay possible when choosing ingredients, without considering the quality or the resultant impact on new, future or repeat business. Using poor-quality, inferior ingredients can impact negatively on texture, taste, finish and overall production time. Good-quality ingredients result in a significantly superior flavour, texture, colour and aroma in both baked and non-baked goods. They offer greater reliability and consistency of product and in many cases are both time- and cost-effective.

Sugarpaste

It can often be false economy to use cheap sugarpaste as it can result in a poor standard of finish and inferior taste, and can be the least cost-effective should work have to be repeated and/or paste discarded. A good-quality sugarpaste should be malleable, allowing it to be shaped easily around corners without cracking or splitting; it should have excellent density of colour, good handling qualities, and a smooth finish. Look for sugarpaste with natural flavours.

Butter

This gives a rich taste to cakes and pastries which is absent when margarines are used. The choice of unsalted or salted butter is often down to personal preference. 'Light spreads' are unsuitable for cooking and baking as they may contain as little as 20%–25% fat compared with at least 80% in butter and margarine.

Dried vine fruits

Low-grade dried vine fruits can ruin a fruit cake with unwanted seeds, particularly in poor-quality currants. Raisins and sultanas which are plump and juicy and of a good size exude flavour as they have been allowed to develop fully and harvested at the right time to produce the most flavour. Currants need to be harvested when they are small to avoid unwanted seeds from developing.

Flours

High-grade flours help create a good crumb/texture and the lightest of sponges because of the quality and grade of wheat used for production. The fineness of the finished flour means that it rarely requires sieving, so saves time, too.

tutor tip

Dried vine fruits are sometimes coated with a preservative as a way of preventing the fruit from clumping together as it dries and to preserve their plumpness. This process often involves them being sprayed with a minimal amount of vegetable or mineral oil, which acts as a barrier so internal moisture is not lost. Equally, external moisture cannot penetrate so, for the best results, wash all dried vine fruits in lukewarm, pre-boiled water to remove the oil. Make sure the water is not too hot, otherwise it will dissolve the natural sugars too! Dry on kitchen paper before soaking the fruits in juices/spirits. Without the oil barrier they will soak up the juices and the flesh of the fruit will become noticeably plump and juicy and ooze flavour. It is time well spent and the perfect start to a deliciously moist cake!

Essences

Pure, natural essences and extracts are a good way to add different flavours to a standard recipe. Imitation essences often labelled 'flavour' or 'flavouring' are chemically created substances that aim to replicate the flavour of the original ingredient. These imitation essences do not usually have the delicacy of natural flavours and some may leave an unpleasant residual taste in both baked and unbaked goods. Extracts are made using the natural product and essences are often a more concentrated form of the extract.

Chocolate

Using good-quality chocolate in cakes and desserts infuses them with the most delightfully rich aroma and taste which cannot be attained with lower-grade counterparts or chocolate-flavoured products. Good chocolate will smell strongly of chocolate and will contain a high proportion of cocoa solids (a minimum of around 55% in dark chocolate and 35% in milk chocolate). Be aware of product descriptions such as 'choc' or 'chocolaty' as they only contain a low proportion of cocoa solids and are often flavoured to taste like chocolate. Whilst these can be a good value option for dipping cake pops (see page 460), it will not have the same flavour as good chocolate in cakes. Labels or descriptions of your own products must comply with The Cocoa and Chocolate Products (England) Regulations 2003 (see the Food Standards Agency website for more information).

Greaseproof paper

If poor-quality greaseproof paper is used to line a cake tin it can become soggy and is less likely to hold its shape during the baking process, which may result in misshapen cake sides. The paper may also stick to the baked cake once it has cooled.

Wedding Cake Design and Production

Lining cake tins – time well spent!

Whilst time is of the essence, lining a cake tin accurately is the secret to a well-shaped cake and a professional finish. (You will also benefit from using good-quality cake pans/tins: they conduct heat evenly which helps the cakes to bake evenly and do not warp when exposed to higher temperatures.) It takes less time to line a cake tin properly than to try, after baking, to reform a misshapen cake.

Lining square tins

1 Upturn the tin onto greaseproof paper or baking parchment and mark a line around the tin using a scriber or an edible food pen. Using a pencil or pen is not advised as ink and graphite are not edible. Remove the tin.

2 Using sharp scissors, cut 2mm (¹/₁₆") inside the scribed line. This allows for the thickness of the tin and the resulting greaseproof square to fit accurately to the base of the cake tin.

3 Cut a length of greaseproof paper 2cm (¾") deeper than the depth of the tin and 4cm (1½") longer than the total length of the four sides. You may need more than one strip if the sheet of paper isn't large enough. Fold a 2cm (¾") strip on one long edge and use sharp scissors to make cuts at an angle from the edge to the fold every 2cm (¾") or so.

4 Place the strip inside the tin and make a crease where the corners will be. Remove and fold along the crease lines firmly. Make a 45° cut at the base of each corner crease to allow the corners to fit snugly against the sides.

5 Lightly grease the tin (if necessary) by wiping a butter wrapper or piece of kitchen roll smeared with white vegetable fat around the sides: this should be just enough grease to help the paper stick. If your tin is non-stick you can omit this step.

6 Place the side strips inside the sides of the tin followed by the square in the base.

Lining round tins

1 Upturn the tin onto the greaseproof paper/baking parchment, mark a line around the tin and cut 2mm (¹/₁₆") inside the line in the same way as for the square tin.

2 Cut a length of greaseproof paper/baking parchment 2cm (¾") deeper than the depth of the tin and 4cm (1½") longer than the circumference. You may need more than one strip depending on the size of the cake tin.

3 Fold a 2cm (¾") strip on one long edge and make cuts at an angle from the edge to the fold as for the square tin.

4 Grease inside the cake sides if required then position the strip inside the cake tin followed by the disc in the base.

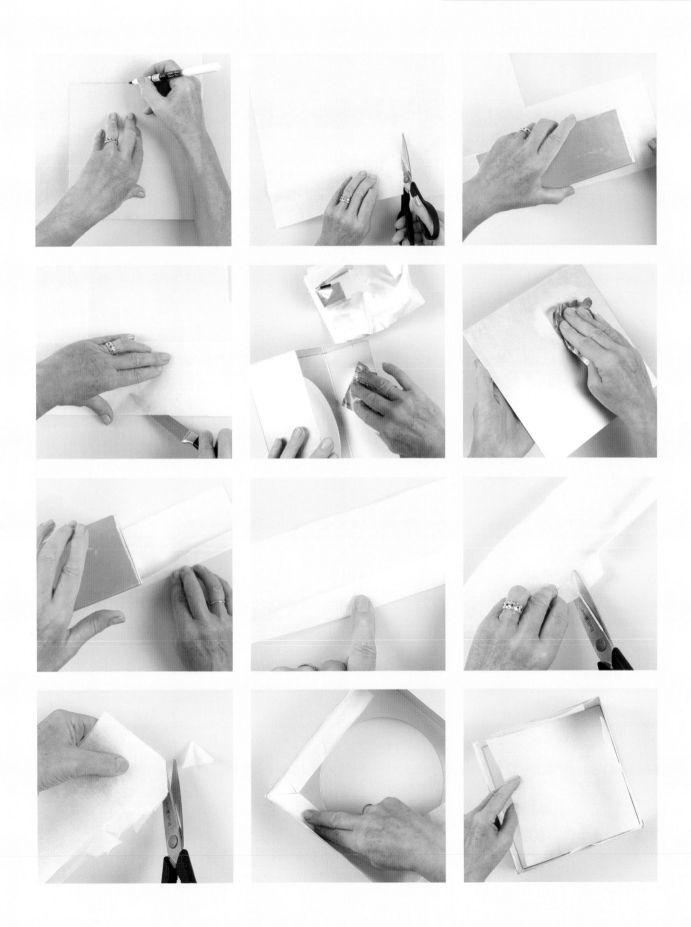

Dowelling cakes – more time well spent!

Nearly all stacked cakes or those using pillars or separators must be dowelled to avoid the upper tiers sinking into the ones below. Without the support of dowels the cakes can be unstable and, in the worst case scenario, topple over. Dowelling is particularly important for all tall cake structures, cakes being displayed in warm locations (especially marquees in summer), places where the floor is uneven or where there are large numbers of people close to the cake. For instructions on marking and cutting dowels to size, see page 143.

 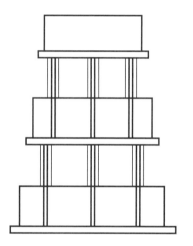 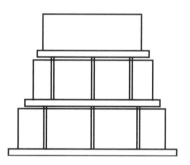

Positioning the dowels

The positioning and cutting of the dowels is crucial for safety and stability. The chart on page 504 can be used for both three and four pillars for a variety of sizes and shapes: once you know the central point on the cake, the positioning chart is straightforward to use. For larger cakes, simply extend the lines on the chart.

Stacked cakes

The dowels are not cut level with the cake but 1mm–2mm ($^1/_{16}$") higher. This is to be certain that they are clearly visible to the person cutting the cake. It is important to ensure that customers are advised, and

written acknowledgement gained, that all inedible items must be removed prior to cutting the cake.

Solid pillars

Cakes with solid separators or pillars can be dowelled following the same method as for stacked cakes, above. Remember that the position of the dowels will be particularly important because the pillars will be positioned on top.

Hollow pillars

Where hollow pillars are used the dowels should be cut to just above the height of

the top of the pillar. Position each dowel carefully, push it down through the cake to the base board, then place the pillars over the top. Mark, remove, then cut to size.

Solid pillars with dowel holes

Some plaster pillars have a pre-drilled dowel hole in the base to give them extra stability. Measure the depth of the hole, then add this measurement to the length of the dowel once you have inserted it into the cake. Adjust the length of the dowel if necessary so that the pillar only just touches the surface of the cake.

The importance of design

Making commercial decisions relies on good design choices which are relevant to your target market, viable to produce and meet your customers' expectations in all areas: quality, standard and price. In order to stay ahead of the competition you will need to keep up-to-date with trends, fashions, styles and colours. Copyright infringements bear a heavy penalty so select copyright-free designs or use your own (see the Intellectual Property Office website, www.ipo.gov.uk, for compliance requirements).

Factors to consider in design choice include the length of time the design takes to complete and the cost of producing the design. Practical design considerations are those of weight, height and size in respect of lifting and delivering. A carefully considered selection of designs offered to potential customers will allow choice for your market, known profit for your business and helps to regulate time management. Limiting design does not mean foregoing a stunning finish: far from it. A cake with a perfectly smooth finish, enhanced with designs which are well balanced and beautifully executed gives a stunning result and need not be wholly time consuming. Using design elements to your advantage – such as mixing simple with more detailed design elements – will allow you to balance the time factor in making the cake. Consider using moulds for fabulous lace work and enhance with lustre colour, sugar 'pearls' and piping.

An important consideration for weddings and other large celebrations is whether the design is still practical if large quantities of cake, decorated biscuits, or cake pops are required or where goods need to be refrigerated. If not, it may be worth considering ready-made decorations to save you time. Remember goods need to be kept at safe temperatures even during delivery to comply with the Food Hygiene Regulations 2006.

tutor tip

When making double-height tiers, place a thin card separator between the two cakes before covering to make for easier cutting: not everyone wants a piece of cake 15cm (6") deep.

Wedding Cake Design and Production

How much should my cake sell for?

As a rough guide, you can work out the cost of a cake using a simple calculation:

Cost of ingredients
+ Labour (hourly rate x number of hours)
+ Percentage of overheads (dependent upon how many cakes you make on average per week/month)
= Cost of cake

Cost of cake
+ Market value (see page 471)
= Selling price for cake

Please note this is only a very approximate guide. Only through research, planning and identification of your expected client base will an appropriate selling price be achieved.

Mix, match and maximise

With gorgeous designs and excellent flavours on offer, what more could we ask? Choice! Consider not just large cakes, but include small cakes, cake pops and macaroons and/or individual desserts to mix and match, as long as they are all cost effective. Take into account the age range at celebrations and how they can all be catered for. Offer some products as take-home gifts or table place names, or where celebrations continue well into the night maximise the opportunity by suggesting additional desserts, cakes or biscuits. Aim to increase market share through quality, reliability and product range. Most of all, aim for an excellent reputation with excellent products and excellent client service!

Antique Lace Wedding Cake

The guide to producing this wedding cake is accompanied by a timesheet to indicate the actual time spent in production. To maximise time efficiency in a commercial operation, prepare a number of cake orders simultaneously where possible. The same concept applies to any element of cake decoration, e.g. baking in batches, sugarpasting a number of cakes together and selecting and preparing similar decorative elements from several orders. The decoration is intended to illustrate how a simple design can be intermixed with more detailed design work, how moulds can be embellished to create greater detail, and how roses can be made quickly.

Timeplan

Three tier round cake: 15cm, 20.5cm and 25.5cm (6", 8" and 10"). Lemon madeira cakes, split and filled with lemon buttercream

Activity	Time (in minutes)	Time: cumulative
Lining cake tins x 3	12	12
Preparing, weighing and mixing ingredients ready to bake	35	47
Washing mixer bowl and paddle	3	50
Preparing filling: lemon buttercream	10	1 hour
Clearing and washing up	10	1 hour 10 minutes
Preparing cakes for filling and covering	35	1 hour 45 minutes
Filling and covering cakes (marzipan and sugarpaste) x 3	30, 35, 40	3 hours 30 minutes
Clearing up/washing down	15	3 hours 45 minutes
Dowelling cakes	10	3 hours 55 minutes
Decorating cakes: roses (8 commercial sugar roses + 10 minutes preparation, e.g. finding tools, kneading pastes, etc.); lace work (each panel 8 minutes x 6); other (piping, dusting, etc.)	60, 48, 30	6 hours 13 minutes
Leeway	30	6 hours 43 minutes
Assembly	30	7 hours 13 minutes
TOTAL TIME	433	7 hours 13 minutes

Edibles and equipment list

I have set out the edibles list as a table here so that the cost of each item can be added in. This should be updated regularly as prices are always subject to change.

Edibles	Cost
15cm, 20.5cm and 25.5cm (6", 8" and 10") round lemon Madeira cakes, at least 8cm (3¹/₈") deep*	
4kg (8lb 13oz) SK Sugarpaste: Antique Lace	
4kg (8lb 13oz) SK Marzipan (optional)	
Lemon buttercream	
SK Sugar Florist Paste (SFP): White	
8 sugar roses made on cocktail sticks, see page 496	
Small amount of royal icing	
Mini blossoms (pink or colour to match)	
SK Designer Metallic Lustre Dust Food Colour: Snowflake	
SK Professional Paste Food Colour: Rose	
Equipment	
10cm (4") round polystyrene dummy	
6 cake dowels	
Piping bags	
Piping nozzle: no. 1	
15cm, 20.5cm and 25.5cm (6", 8" and 10") round cake drums (boards)	
10cm (4") round cake card	
SK Great Impressions Lace Mould	
1.5m (59") x 50mm (2") wide satin ribbon for second tier: blush pink	
1m (39") x 3mm (¹/₈") wide satin ribbon for base tier: blush pink	
60cm (24") x 7mm (¹/₈") wide satin ribbon for top tier: blush pink	

*Minimum 8cm (3¹/₈") deep. This can be achieved by baking a deeper cake and/or placing an extra cake drum beneath each tier and covering as part of the cake.

For essential sugarpaste edibles and equipment, see pages 132–33

Preparation

For detailed instructions on preparing and covering cakes with sugarpaste, follow the instructions on pages 92 and 139–140.

1 Split and fill all three cakes with your chosen flavour of buttercream if desired. Place each on its respective cake board.

2 Cover the cake with marzipan (see page 96) or crumb-coat the surface with buttercream (see page 92).

3 Cover each tier with Antique Lace sugarpaste (see pages 139–140).

4 Attach the narrowest ribbon around the base tier and the 7mm (¼") wide ribbon around the top tier. Secure with a small dab of moistened sugarpaste.

Lace

5 Mix 200g (7oz) of White SFP with 100g (3½oz) Antique Lace sugarpaste. Add a touch of Rose paste colour to give a slight blush pink colour.

6 Roll out a piece of the blush pink paste quite thinly. Place onto the top of the lace mould and press firmly. Remove the paste and use a sharp craft knife or cutting wheel to cut carefully around the lace pieces, including the small segments within the pattern.

7 Dust each piece with Snowflake lustre before lightly brushing the back of the lace in places with cooled, boiled water. Starting at the back of the cake, attach the lace pieces to the cake side. Repeat as necessary until the sides are fully covered. You may need to trim the final section to fit.

8 Repeat for the top tier, using only one section of lace work and attaching it at an angle to go across the top and down the side of the cake.

9 Place the white royal icing into a piping bag with a no. 1 nozzle and pipe small dots around the perimeter of the lace and in between parts of the lace pattern. Attach the mini blossoms to enhance the overall design.

10 Make eight roses following the instructions on page 496.

Assembly

11 Dowel the cakes (see page 143) and assemble the base and middle tiers.

12 Tie the widest ribbon around the middle tier with a bow.

13 Place the polystyrene dummy centrally on top of the middle tier. Take one of the roses and partially push the cocktail stick into the dummy. Check that the dummy is the right depth: there should be a small gap between the roses and the top tier. Trim if necessary then secure the polystyrene dummy to the cake card with royal icing. Push the remaining roses into the dummy. For transporting the cake, do not attach the dummy to the middle tier.

14 On final assembly, attach the rose-covered dummy to the middle tier with royal icing or a small, flattened ball of moistened sugarpaste. Place the top tier carefully in position.

tutor tip

Use piping nozzles to remove small areas of paste and enhance the delicate lace pattern quickly and easily.

Antique Lace Wedding Cake

Quick commercial roses

These sugar roses are made on cocktail sticks, which enables them to be inserted into a polystyrene dummy securely (the rough surface of the stick does not twist round as would a smooth floral wire). The method shown here is a quick way of making roses in sugar so is ideal for commercial cakes and is exactly the same if you are making the roses on floral wires.

EDIBLES

SK Sugar Florist Paste (SFP): White

SK Professional Dust Food Colours: Edelweiss (white), Rose

EQUIPMENT

Blossom cutters: F6B and F6C (OP)

Cocktail stick (or floral wire)

Short piece of uncovered 18-gauge floral wire

Cupped flower former

For essential floral edibles and equipment, see pages 254–255

tutor tip

If you are making the roses with wires and you need to work on the cones straight away, make a hook on the end of a 24-gauge wire and use a cigarette lighter or tea light to heat the hook until it is white hot (take care when doing this). Insert the hook immediately into the base of the cone: this melts the sugar to the wire, holding it securely in place and allowing you to use the cone immediately.

1   Using the SFP, make a cone with a fine point to the required length and insert a cocktail stick into the base.

2   Roll out some White SFP thinly on a non-stick board lightly greased with white vegetable fat. Cut out a blossom shape using the smaller blossom cutter. Place on a foam pad and use a bone tool to smooth and spread each petal until the paste is very fine. Put to one side and leave to become slightly firm whilst cutting out the next two shapes.

3   Using the larger cutter, cut out two more blossom shapes. Use a bone tool on the first one to smooth and spread the petals as before. Turn the petals over and use a short piece of floral wire to create two curls along the top edge of each petal. Turn the petals to the front and cup each petal with the bone tool, creating a slightly concave shape. Place over a suitable former.

4   Take the second shape, cut off two adjacent petals and discard. Smooth, curl and soften the remaining three petals as before and place over a suitable former. Each of these layers will be used when part-dry.

5   Return to the first, smaller shape which should now be firmer to use. Lightly glue one third up the side edge of each petal. Remember that you can always add more glue but you cannot take it away.

6   Take the cone and thread the cocktail stick through the centre of the shape. Take one petal and place it just above the cone. Wrap it closely around the cone to form a tiny hole at the tip. Take the next but one petal and repeat, leaving a small gap between the first layer. Attach the remaining three petals closely to the base of the cone only and wrap each petal around the rose, making sure they overlap each other. By allowing the layer to become marginally drier, space can be created between the layers as the petals are firm enough to hold their shape and will not fall against the previous layers.

7   Glue the three-petal shape as for the first layer. Thread the centre through the cocktail stick and attach, making sure the petals overlap and there is a clear gap between the previous layer.

8   Take the final layer, thread the rose through the centre, upturn the flower and overlap each petal. Turn it the right way round and adjust as necessary. Place in a former to dry fully.

9   Dust the centres using Rose and Edelweiss dust food colours.

tutor tip

If you are using the roses around a dummy separator, you will not need to make a calyx as the back of the flower won't be seen. If you do need to add them, please refer to the instructions on page 275.

Colour Theory

TESSA WHITEHOUSE

The effective use of colour is key to good cake design. Colour is used freely in contemporary cake design and is less bound by convention or culturally-specific associations and perceptions than in the past. However, understanding the relationship between colours enables us to maximise the effect and impact of a cake design.

The colour wheel

The colour wheel shows the relationships between colours and can be used as a guide to combine colours. Whether the desired result is bright and zingy or soft and soothing, the colour wheel can help to make important design choices.

At the heart of the wheel are the three primary colours: red, yellow and blue. These colours cannot be created by mixing two or more colours and all other colours are made from these three. Mixing two primary colours 50/50 results in three secondary colours, represented by the medium-sized hearts: orange, green and purple. Mixing a primary colour with a secondary one results in one of six tertiary colours as represented by the smallest hearts: red-orange; red-purple; yellow-orange; yellow-green; blue-purple; blue-green.

A greater range of colours and subtlety can be realised by mixing these 12 colours into tints, tones and shades, as described opposite.

Tints, tones and shades

Tints, tones and shades are important for providing subtlety when combining colours in a scheme.

A tint is a paler version of the pure colour achieved by mixing in white. Varying the ratio of colour to white results in an almost infinite range of tints.

Tones are created by mixing the colour with grey and again, depending on the ratio of grey to colour, a wide range of effects can be achieved.

A shade is a colour mixed with black.

Tones   Pure colour   Tints

Colour combinations

The aim of combining colours is to achieve a harmonious, pleasing result that is balanced and interesting. Using the colour wheel and associated tints and tones can help achieve this. There are three key types of colour scheme based on the wheel:

- Monochromatic;
- Complementary;
- Adjacent or analogous.

A monochromatic colour scheme only uses one colour and its associated tints, tones and shades. Using only one colour means this scheme is simple to put together as the result will always be in harmony. Varying the balance between the main colour and its variants can change the mood from soothing to striking.

The complementary scheme uses two colours which are opposite each other on the colour wheel. These colours have a strong contrast to each other which results in a vibrant and energetic feel. Using both colours in equal amounts tends to generate an overpowering and dramatic effect so it is more usual for one colour to play a dominant role to the second.

The adjacent or analogous scheme uses two colours which are next to each other on the wheel, for example blue with green. These combinations are easy on the eye and tend to generate a calm and tranquil feel. Using the colours at full strength gives a very bold and perhaps gaudy impression, whereas using tints and tones of the colours results in a more relaxing and harmonious result.

The wheel can also help in selecting the bold and dynamic 'hot' colours versus the soothing and restful 'cool' colours. Hot colours are those which fall between the red-violet and yellow half of the wheel, the cool ones between the yellow-green and violet half of the wheel.

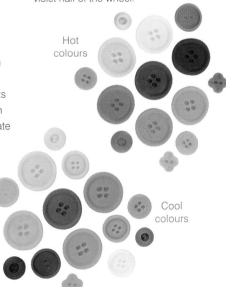

Hot colours

Cool colours

Pastel versus bright colours

A pastel colour is one which is soft in tone, such as baby pink, powder blue and lemon yellow. They are easy to combine and tend to have a soothing and gentle effect.

Bright colours are strong but not dark, resulting in a vivid impression that attracts attention. Use too many, however, and they can become a distraction to the overall scheme. Hot pink and royal blue are typical examples that can be used to striking effect.

Colour by occasion

Although traditionally white, wedding cakes can be virtually any colour to co-ordinate with the overall theme. New colours come into fashion with the result that wedding cakes now include not only the traditional white and pastels but also strong and dynamic combinations. One key influence on the choice of colour is season, as illustrated here:

Whatever your culture, certain occasions tend to be associated with a particular colour palette. In Western culture, cakes for christenings or naming ceremonies usually feature soft, pastel colours. Traditionally pink is used for girls and blue for boys with pastel lemon yellow or mint green as non-gender-specific colours. Teamed with white or ivory, these colours give a fresh and delicate impression suitable for a baby.

Key wedding anniversaries are measured out in precious metals and gemstones giving lots of exciting opportunities for cake makers: Silver (25), Pearl (30), Emerald (35), Ruby (40), Sapphire (45), Gold (50), Diamond (60) and Platinum (75).

• For a spring wedding the fresh, new colours of the season can be reflected with pastel shades of pink, lilac, blue and yellow teamed with cream and light gold.

Red, purple, dark green and gold have long been used to evoke the Christmas spirit; rich and warm colours for a festive season. But fresh, 'icy' colours, such as the very pale blue shown here, pick up on the snow and frost associated with the winter season and give a new twist to Christmas colour schemes.

• Create a fun and vibrant colour scheme for a summer wedding by using strong colours such as fuchsia pink, lime green, turquoise, orange and yellow in a complementary scheme, perhaps with a touch of silver.

• The rich tones of autumn suggest a sumptuous palette of russets, purples, deep blues, peach and copper.

• For a winter wedding consider strong and warm colours such as red, purple, green, rich gold and copper metallic, or opt for a lighter palette with white, ice blue and silver for a wintry effect.

Colour Theory

Mixing colours

The range of SK Professional Food Colours can be placed into a colour wheel, saving the effort of mixing colours from scratch. In the colour wheel they are:

- **Primary** = Poinsettia, Daffodil, Hyacinth

- **Secondary** = Berberis, Lilac, Mint

- **Tertiary** = Nasturtium (red-orange), Cyclamen (red-purple), Sunflower (yellow-orange), Vine (yellow-green), Violet (blue-purple), Hydrangea (blue-green)

The remainder of the Squires Kitchen range provides a further refinement of colours. All these can be further mixed and blended to achieve additional colour variations.

Using food colours in sugarcraft

Food colourings for sugarcraft are available in paste (gel), liquid and dust (powder) form. Each has its own uses according to the type of icing you are working with. Instructions for using colour can be found in each project throughout the book.

Paste colours are used to colour sugarpaste, modelling paste, flower paste (SFP) and marzipan. Knead the icing until it is soft and pliable, then add colour by dipping a cocktail stick into the food colour and wiping onto the sugarpaste. Knead well until the colour is evenly distributed through the paste. To test whether it is mixed fully, cut through the paste: if there are any streaks, continue kneading. Greater control in mixing a pale colour is achieved by colouring a small piece of paste to a deeper colour than required and then kneading small

pieces into the white paste. Glycerine- and glyceride-free paste colours can also be used to colour royal icing.

Liquid colours are most commonly used to colour royal icing as they contain no glycerides and so will not inhibit drying. Only pale to medium-strength colours can be achieved using liquid colours on their own, otherwise the consistency of the icing may alter if too much liquid is added. If a strong colour is required, use both liquid and dust food colours, ideally giving the colour 12 hours to develop fully. If a very pale tint is required, strongly colour a small amount of royal icing and mix it little-by-little into the remainder of the royal icing. It is possible to match colour batch to batch by weighing the amount of made-up royal icing and counting the number of drops used to colour it.

Dust colours are usually used to surface-colour paste once it is dry or semi-dry, particularly on sugar flowers and leaves. It can also be mixed with clear alcohol to make a quick-drying paint: the alcohol evaporates, leaving the colour on the surface of the cake. Lustre dust colours are a great way to add a metallic effect to cakes: brush onto dry/semi-dry paste using a large, flat brush or use Gildesol as a primer before brushing on the colour to give a more dramatic effect.

Other food colours which can be used to surface paint sugar work include edible paints (ideal for folk art painting), metallic paints and cocoa butter colours (e.g. SK Cocol). Turn to pages 172–175 to find out more about painting techniques.

Colour Theory

Templates

Peony templates for Croquembouche, page 72

Templates shown actual size

502

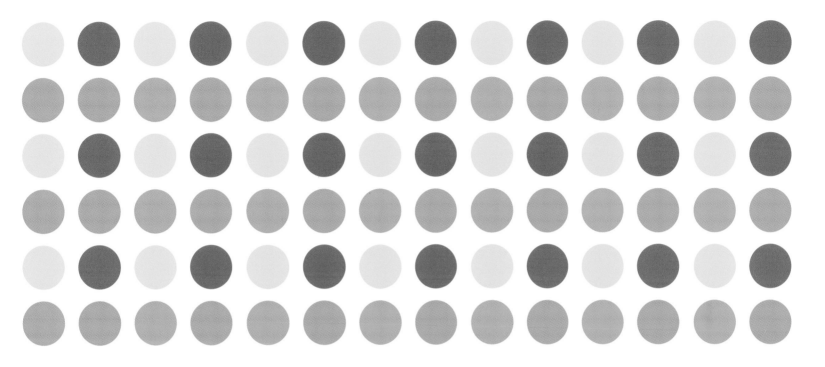

Sponge pattern templates for Pâte Décor, page 82

Templates shown at 71%
Enlarge to 141% (A4–A3) for actual size

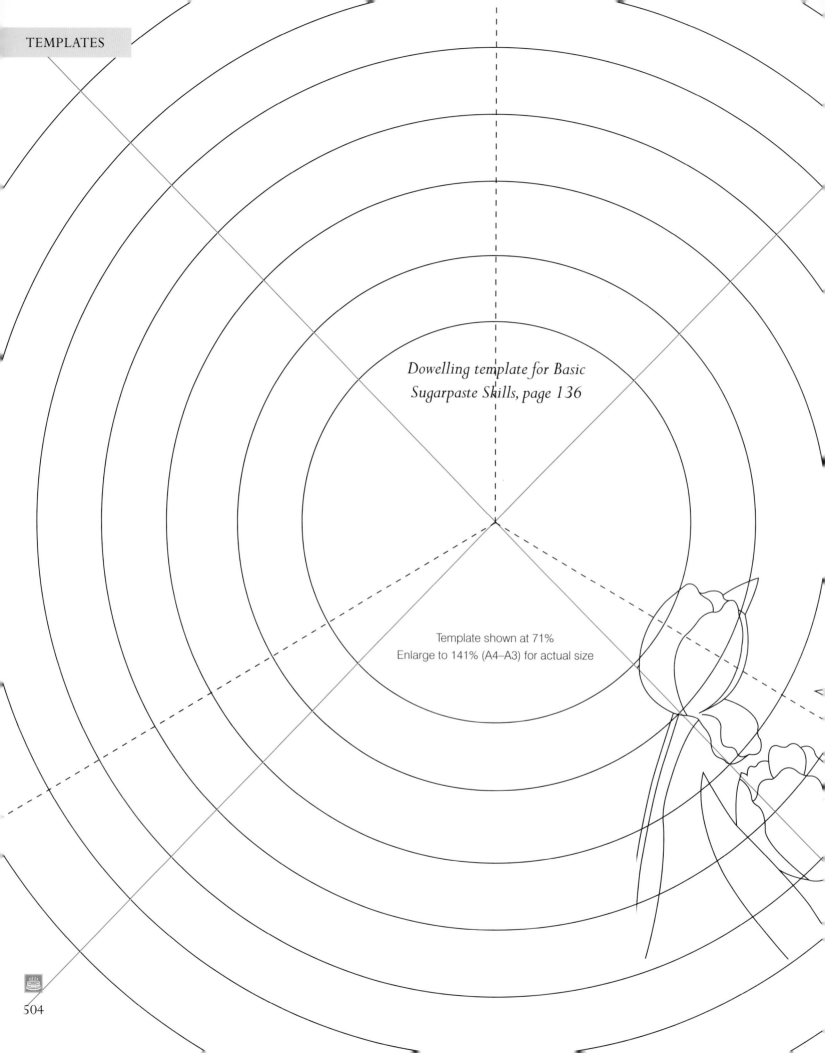

Dowelling template for Basic Sugarpaste Skills, page 136

Template shown at 71%
Enlarge to 141% (A4–A3) for actual size

Bow template for Foundation Mini Cakes, page 163

Templates shown actual size

Bird templates for Foundation Mini Cakes, page 159

Templates shown actual size

Side design for Springtime Tulips, page 177

Template shown at 71%, enlarge to 141% (A4–A3) for actual size

Run-out templates (no. 1, butterflies, plaque) for First Birthday Cake, page 234

Templates shown at 71%, enlarge to 141% (A4–A3) for actual size

Waistcoat and bandana templates for Caricature Figures, page 208

Templates shown actual size

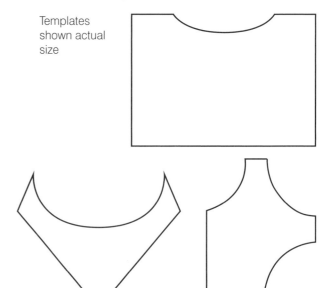

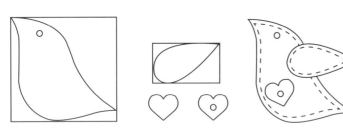

Run-out templates (flower pot, bow) for Mother's Day Cake, page 246

Templates shown at 71%, enlarge to 141% (A4–A3) for actual size

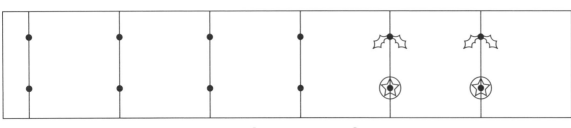

Bird and side designs for Christmas Gift Boxes, page 226

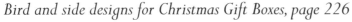

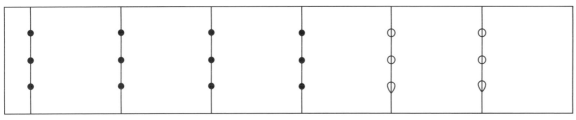

Templates shown at 71%, enlarge to 141% (A4–A3) for actual size

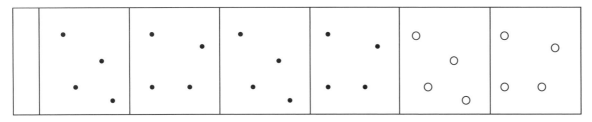

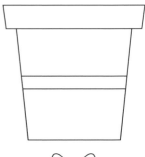

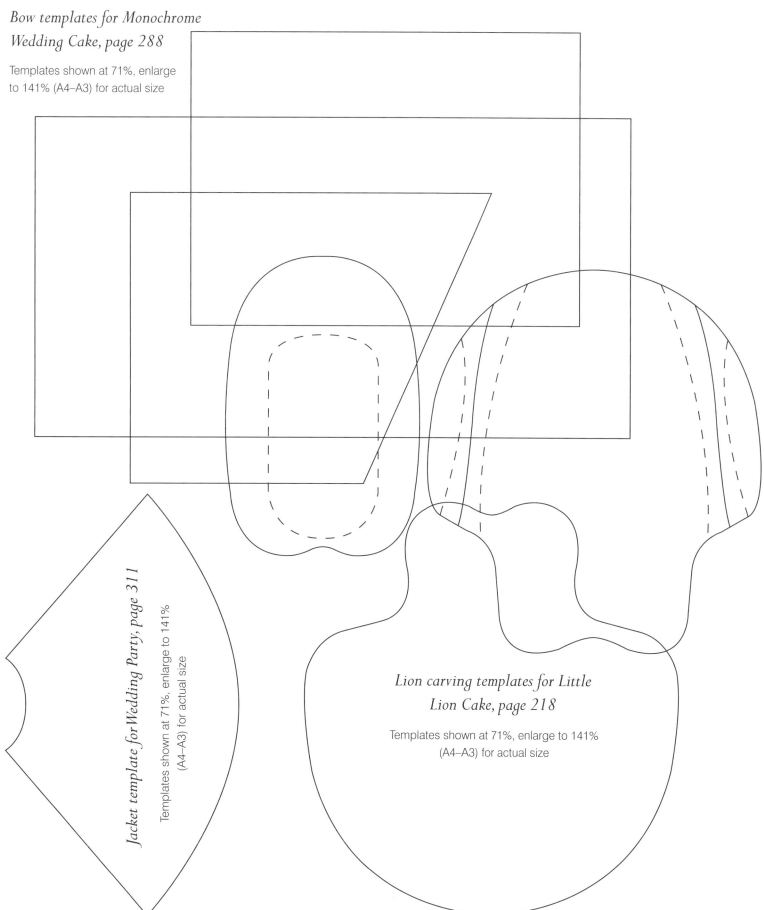

Bow templates for Monochrome Wedding Cake, page 288

Templates shown at 71%, enlarge to 141% (A4–A3) for actual size

Jacket template for Wedding Party, page 311

Templates shown at 71%, enlarge to 141% (A4–A3) for actual size

Lion carving templates for Little Lion Cake, page 218

Templates shown at 71%, enlarge to 141% (A4–A3) for actual size

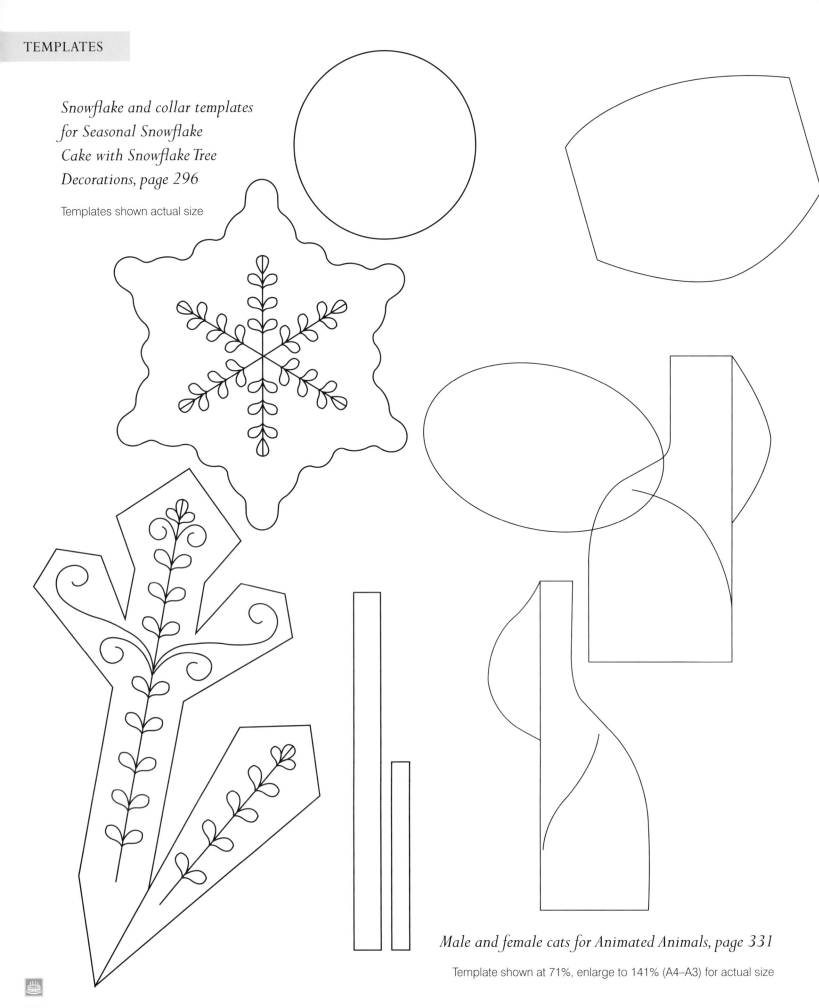

*Snowflake and collar templates
for Seasonal Snowflake
Cake with Snowflake Tree
Decorations, page 296*

Templates shown actual size

Male and female cats for Animated Animals, page 331

Template shown at 71%, enlarge to 141% (A4–A3) for actual size

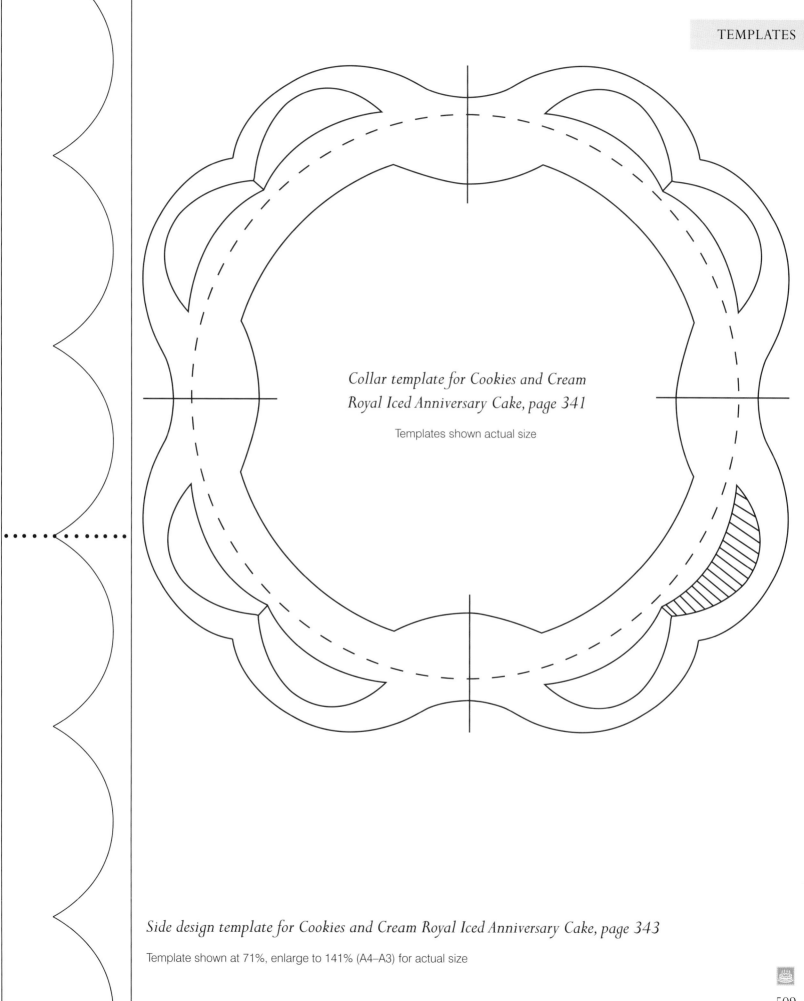

Collar template for Cookies and Cream Royal Iced Anniversary Cake, page 341

Templates shown actual size

Side design template for Cookies and Cream Royal Iced Anniversary Cake, page 343

Template shown at 71%, enlarge to 141% (A4–A3) for actual size

Lace and filigree templates for 'Something Blue' Engagement Cake, page 374

Templates shown actual size

Lily of the valley leaf, scabious leaf and Eustoma grandiflorum bud templates for Country Garden Wedding Cake, page 389

Templates shown actual size

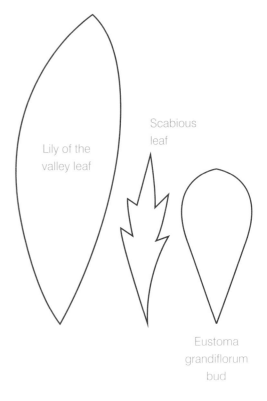

Lily of the valley leaf

Scabious leaf

Eustoma grandiflorum bud

Collar template for Thistle and Bluebell Wedding Cake, page 444

Templates shown actual size

To enlarge for lower tiers, ensure
the bold line is equal to the size
of the iced cake

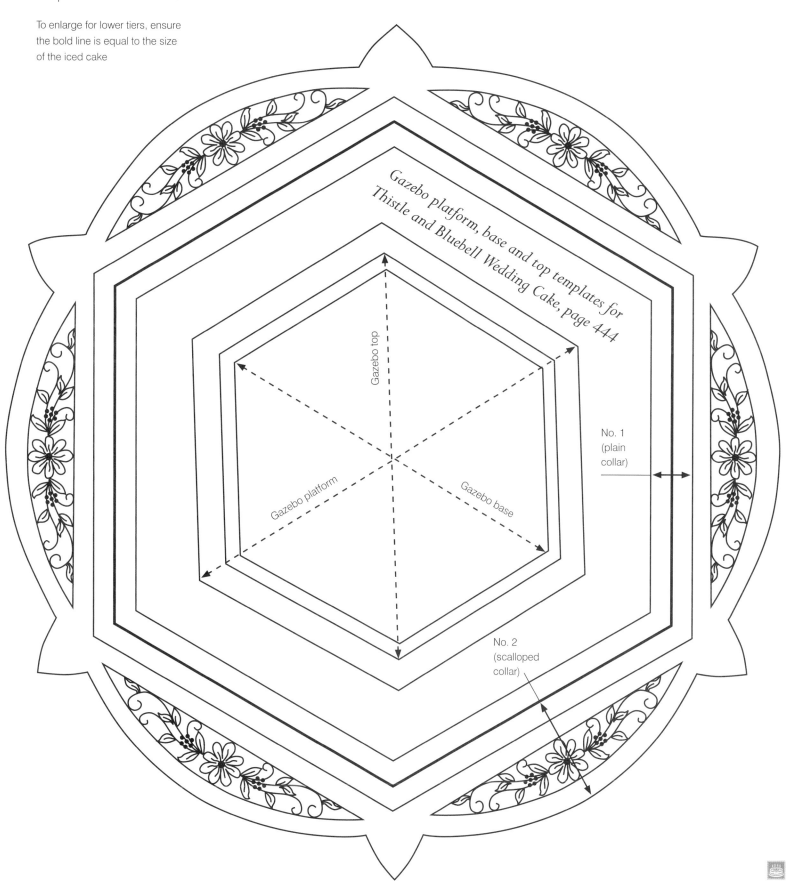

*Gazebo platform, base and top templates for
Thistle and Bluebell Wedding Cake, page 444*

Gazebo top

Gazebo platform

Gazebo base

No. 1
(plain
collar)

No. 2
(scalloped
collar)

Side panel: top tier x 6

Templates for Thistle and Bluebell Wedding Cake, page 444

Templates shown actual size

Upright scroll piece for gazebo roof x 6

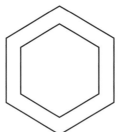

Flower stand:
1 x large (base),
2 x small

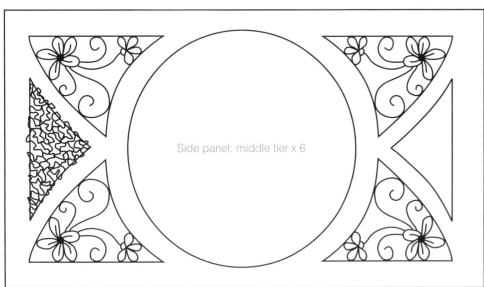

Side panel: middle tier x 6

Gazebo doors

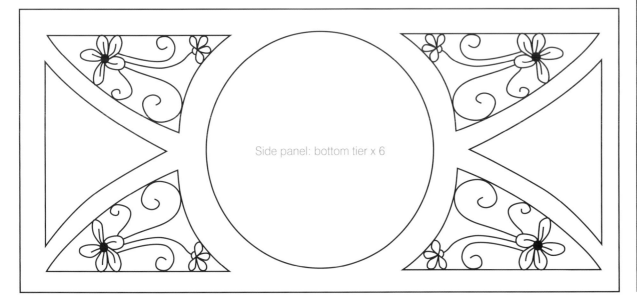

Side panel: bottom tier x 6

Gazebo side panel x 5

Conversion Chart

OVEN TEMPERATURES

Temperatures refer to conventional ovens. For fan-assisted ovens, reduce the temperature by 20°.

°C	°F	GAS MARK
100	200	low
110	225	¼
120	250	½
140	275	1
150	300	2
160	325	3
180	350	4
190	375	5
200	400	6
220	425	7
230	450	8
250	475	9

LIQUID MEASUREMENTS

METRIC	IMPERIAL	US CUPS
30ml	1fl oz	⅛ cup
60ml	2fl oz	¼ cup
90ml	3fl oz	⅜ cup
120ml	4fl oz	½ cup
140ml	5fl oz	⅔ cup
170ml	6fl oz	¾ cup
200ml	7fl oz	⅞ cup
230ml	8fl oz	1 cup
260ml	9fl oz	1⅛ cups
290ml	10fl oz (½ pint)	1¼ cups
500ml	17½fl oz	2 cups
600ml	20fl oz (1 pint)	2½ cups
1 litre	1¾ pints	4 cups

DRY MEASUREMENTS

METRIC	IMPERIAL
15g	½oz
30g	1oz
60g	2oz
90g	3oz
115g	4oz (¼lb)
140g	5oz
170g	6oz
200g	7oz
225g	8oz (½lb)
255g	9oz
285g	10oz
310g	11oz
340g	12oz (¾lb)
370g	13oz
400g	14oz
425g	15oz
450g	16oz (1lb)
680g	24oz (1½lb)
900g	32oz (2lb)

CAKE/CAKE BOARD SIZES

METRIC	IMPERIAL
10cm	4"
12.5cm	5"
15cm	6"
18cm	7"
20.5cm	8"
23cm	9"
25.5cm	10"
28cm	11"
30.5cm	12"
33cm	13"
35.5cm	14"

The conversions are approximate but the difference between an exact and an approximate conversion will not affect your cooking results. Try not to mix metric and imperial measures in one recipe; stick to one system or the other.

The Dutton Collection

AT SQUIRES KITCHEN

These items are just a small selection from my own personal collection of sugarcraft, baking and confectionery antiquities from the UK. Spanning a period of 300 years, they offer a glimpse of how sugar has been such an important part of our history. Many of these items are on display at Squires Kitchen in Farnham, Surrey where you can also see some of the most impressive works in sugar of our time.

My favourite pieces include a Tate & Lyle Sugar crate from 1929; a hand-carved wooden molinet dating from the late 1690s (I would love to think this came from one of the many London coffee and chocolate houses of this time); two wonderful copper chocolate pots dating from the 17th and 18th centuries; pewter ice cream moulds and Penny Lick glasses; fabulous 1920s sulphur moulds for marzipan work; bisqueware figurines from the early 20th century; and a rare miniature copper aspic mould found for me by my granddaughter, Flora.

Tala is one of the oldest icing brands still in existence (established 1899) and in the collection you can see piping nozzles and icing sets made in the 1920s. Today, Tala are still making the same dry measures and piping nozzles on the original 1920s machinery at their works in Liverpool – how brilliant to still have this manufacturing capability in the UK. It was a Tala piping set that was given to me by my mother at the age of seven that fired my passion for all things sugar and decorative.

More items include Tate & Lyle sugar cartons from the 1950s, and a collection of amazing confectionery books from the 1700s. I also have a rare Victorian ice cream maker designed by Mrs Marshall which, I understand (from the fascinating book, *Consider the Fork* by Bee Wilson), was one of only five known to be in existence in 1998. Three of these are owned by Britain's leading historian of ice cream, Robin Weir, and another by food historian Ivan Day. I am thrilled to have found another Mrs Marshall's Patent Freezer ice cream maker from 1885 which is in perfect condition and is possibly now the sixth!

The silver separators and vase for the presentation wedding cake of Prince Charles and Lady Diana Spencer by Mary Ford (see page 453) were given to me along with Mary's own personal collection of sugarcraft books. I can't thank Mary and her husband, Michael, enough for such a generous gesture. Having been passed to me for safekeeping, the vase and separators are now on display for you to see. Although now retired, Mary and Michael Ford built the famous Mary Ford brand and published books in the 1980s and '90s. Eddie Spence MBE was teaching with their company at the time and was involved with the decoration of the Royal wedding cake; you can also see photographs of this very special cake in Eddie's book, *The Art of Royal Icing* (B. Dutton Publishing).

The illustration shown here from W. A. Jarrin's book from 1820, *The Italian Confectioner*, shows

Illustration of a sugar flower table from *The Italian Confectioner*, 1820

Prospectus for Herr Willy's 'School of Piping and Ornamenting', 1891

Selection of 1920s Tala piping nozzles

sugar flowers hanging up to dry on a homemade 'washing line' just as we use today. Jarrin carved many of his own sugar moulds in pear wood or boxwood and although I do not have any of these to show you, some of Jarrin's original carved wooden moulds are kept safely in Ivan Day's 'Historic Foods' collection. Jarrin was a highly skilled confectioner who, in his own words, 'practised in the household of the Emperor Napoleon'. His book gives easy-to-follow lessons on how to make fine gum paste sugar flowers.

A particularly fascinating book in my collection is one by the German confectioner Herr Willy, published in 1891, which gives his school's prospectus as shown here: 'Herr Willy's School of Piping and Ornamenting.' Today at Squires Kitchen, 120 years later, we are not so tough on the dress code for gentlemen and jackets are optional!

So little is really new but it is fascinating to see fashions change and the uses for sugar reinvented and widened; to see how it is used for the most fantastical sugar creations in both medieval and modern day sugar work. It is an art form that has now become deservedly well recognised around the world and we are proud to be passing on this knowledge through our amazing teachers at Squires Kitchen.

BEVERLEY DUTTON
Founder, Squires Kitchen

19th-century metal sorbetière and pewter ice cream mould

'Penny Lick' ice cream glasses

Above: Mrs Marshall's Patented Freezer ice cream maker, 1885

Below: Drop machine for making boiled sweets, circa 1850

19th-century boxwood ice pick

Royal iced cake by W.E. Fortt, Bath, 1908

19th- and 20th-century brass pastry jiggers

Glossary

Albumen (fortified or pure): Pasteurised, dried egg white powder used to make royal icing and meringues. Pure albumen is stronger than fortified and is better suited to run-outs and intricate work.

Allergen: A substance that can cause an allergic reaction.

Allergy (food): A food allergy is caused when the immune system thinks certain foods are harmful to the body.

Appliqué: A decorative technique where a pattern is built up with pieces of sugarpaste, flower paste or modelling paste.

Apricot glaze: Apricot jam that has been boiled and sieved. This is spread over fruit cakes before covering with marzipan as it has a neutral flavour and colour and helps the marzipan stick to the cake.

Bain marie: A pan or bowl placed over a large, shallow pan of warm water to heat food gently, such as chocolate.

Ball tool: A rounded sugarcraft tool used for softening and shaping petals and leaves and for indenting sugar models and decorations.

Bone tool: A bone-shaped modelling tool used in the same way as a ball tool.

Brush embroidery: Using a paintbrush to emulate the effect of embroidery with royal icing, buttercream or chocolate.

Cake board: A generic term often used to refer to a board on which a cake is placed. A thin, hardboard cake board can be used between tiers when stacking cakes whilst a thicker, heavy-duty cake drum is commonly used as a base board (see *cake drum* below).

Cake card: A thin, foil-covered board that is suitable for supporting lightweight sponge cakes and small sugar models.

Cake drum: A heavy-duty cake board approximately 1.2cm (½") thick. They are used underneath cakes to give firm support and as base boards under decorated cakes.

Chocolate modelling paste: Also known as Cocoform and chocolate plastique. Made from couverture chocolate and glucose syrup, this can be moulded to make decorations or mixed 50/50 with marzipan or sugarpaste and used to cover a cake.

CMC Gum (Carboxymethylcellulose): A modified plant cellulose used as a gum in flower paste recipes or pastillage work to add strength.

Coeliac disease: An autoimmune disease. Gluten – which is found in wheat, rye and barley – triggers an immune reaction in people with coeliac disease.

Collar: A royal iced decoration that is placed on top of a cake and overhangs the sides to make a decorative border. Collars can also be made in pastillage for sugarpasted cakes.

Confectioners' glaze: An edible-when-dry varnish for use wherever a high gloss is required, such as leaves with a shiny surface, and which can be diluted with clear alcohol to reduce the strength of the glaze. Edible spray glaze can also be used for the same purpose and as a protective coating on sugar, chocolate or marzipan pieces for exhibition work.

Cooler spray: Mainly used in chocolate work to help melted chocolate set quickly.

Couverture: A high-quality chocolate that contains a high proportion of cocoa butter and should be tempered before use.

Crème pâtissière: Also known as pastry cream. A thick custard used for filling choux buns and éclairs.

Croquembouche: A conical tower of choux pastry buns traditionally stuck together with caramel and decorated with spun sugar.

Crumb-coating: Covering the outside of a cake with a thin layer of buttercream to seal the cake crumbs and help the sugarpaste coating to stick. Instructions for how to crumb-coat a cake are given on page 92.

Cutting wheel: A sugarcraft tool with two small, rotating wheels that is commonly used to cut out freehand, detailed shapes from roll-out sugar pastes.

Dowelling: Cakes with more than one tier must be supported with food-grade dowelling rods to prevent the upper tiers from sinking. The dowels are positioned in the cake within the shape and size of the tier above before being cut to size and re-inserted into the cake.

Dresden tool: Also known as a flower/leaf shaping tool. This sugarcraft tool is commonly used in sugar floristry to shape, soften and frill petals and leaves.

Drop-line work: A piping technique where royal icing is lifted up to extend it, then placed or 'dropped' onto the cake to create decoration such as lettering, scrolls and extension work.

Dummy cake: A polystyrene shape which can be iced and decorated if a cake is only needed for display purposes. Dummies are particularly useful for increasing the tiers on a wedding cake or if a display piece needs to be kept for a long time.

Dust food colour: Also known as powder colour and petal dust. Suitable for dusting dry sugar work and can enhance the colour of sugar flowers and leaves. Dusts can also be diluted with clear alcohol for surface painting and added to modelling paste, royal icing and sugarpaste if an intense colour is needed.

Edible food paints: An edible medium for surface painting on sugar and chocolate work to create a 'barge style' or 'poster paint' effect.

Edible glue: A tacky, gum-based glue suitable for all sugarcraft purposes.

Embossing: A quick and simple decorative technique for impressing patterns into sugar pastes.

Extension icing: Royal icing made from extra-fine icing sugar that contains a small amount of glucose, giving it the flexibility and stretch for piping very fine, straight lines in extension work.

Extension work: A form of drop-line work that consists of lines extended either down from the sides of a cake onto a board or onto a piped bridge.

Filigree: A random, wavy pattern which is piped with the nozzle resting on the surface of the cake. In some cases the lines must touch, e.g. in collar work, so the piping work sticks together and doesn't drop out when the collar is lifted.

Flooding (in/out): The process of filling in a piped outline with run-out icing. Also known as 'running in' and 'running out'.

Floral tape: Used for binding the wire stems of sugar flowers together, floral tape should be stretched before use to activate the glue on one side. Available in a variety of colours to match leaves and stems, floral tape can be cut to the width required using fine scissors or a tape shredder.

Floral wire: Wires that are available in different colours and widths (gauges) for use in sugar flower making. The lower the number the thicker the wire: 18-gauge being the thickest wire and 33-gauge the finest.

Flower (icing) nail: A nail-shaped tool with a wide, round head that is used for creating piped flowers with royal icing.

Flower paste: Also known as gum paste and Sugar Florist Paste™ (SFP™). A modelling paste which can be rolled paper thin, making it perfect for making sugar flowers and leaves and delicate models. Flower paste is firm and requires gentle kneading before use. Sugar Florist Paste was the first gelatine based flower paste created in the 1980s by Squires Kitchen and was awarded a British patent. Before this a form of simple gum paste/pastillage was used.

Fondant fancies: Small, shaped sponge cakes coated with a thin layer of marzipan then dipped in fondant icing.

Formers: Frequently used in sugar floristry and modelling to help pieces of paste hold their shape as they dry. Polystyrene formers are available from sugarcraft stockists or you can make cupped shapes for petals from tin foil or kitchen paper.

Ganache: A rich, smooth mix of cream and chocolate that can be piped or used as a filling for cakes, truffles and chocolate desserts.

Glaze cleaner (IPA): Used for cleaning brushes after painting and glazing. After cleaning, wash the brushes with warm water and washing-up liquid.

Glucose syrup: Derived from starch, glucose is used in sugar pastes to soften the texture and prevent the crystallisation of sugars.

Gluten free: A diet or product excluding foods containing gluten such as wheat, barley, rye and oats.

Glycerine: A sweet-tasting, syrupy liquid which can be used in royal icing for coating cakes. It is added to icing so that, when the icing is set, it does not become brittle or hard but remains soft enough to eat.

Gum tragacanth: A natural gum which is derived from plant extracts. It adds strength and stretch to sugar modelling paste so that it can be rolled out finely and dry firm enough to hold its shape.

Hidden design cakes: Cakes that have been baked with a pattern inside, so that once the cake is cut the design is revealed.

Lace work: Fine piping or moulding that emulates a lacy pattern.

Lactose or dairy free: A diet or food excluding all dairy products, i.e. products made from the milk of any animal.

Liquid food colour: Most often used to colour royal icing, fondant icing and buttercream, and can be painted directly onto sugar work to create a watercolour effect. When using with royal icing for run-out work, ensure that the product does not contain glucose or glycerides. Liquid colours can also be used in an airbrush.

Lustre dusts: Edible dust food colours that can be brushed directly onto sugar work to create a shimmer effect.

Marzipan: A pliable paste made from ground almonds and glucose syrup. It is used as a cake covering (particularly fruit cakes), as well as for making models and petits fours.

Modelling paste: Also known as Mexican paste and MMP. Not as strong as flower paste but stronger than sugarpaste, modelling paste is ideal for making models and material-effect cake decorations.

Off-pieces: Designs which are made off the cake and are allowed to dry before being positioned on the cake. This is necessary for run-out work and is also useful for pressure-piped motifs as it means you can practice piping away from the cake.

Oriental string work: Also known as string work. Delicate line work that is piped onto the side of the cake so that it is freestanding.

Palette knife: A blunt round-ended knife used in baking for spreading, filling and lifting cakes and biscuits. A small, cranked palette knife is useful in sugar modelling.

Paste food colour: Most often used for colouring modelling paste, sugarpaste and pastillage but can also be used to surface paint sugar pieces.

Pastillage: A paste made using icing sugar, cornflour, gums and gelatine (or vegetarian alternative) which dries very hard, making it ideal for plaques and structural pieces. Although it contains only edible ingredients, it is not recommended for eating because it dries extremely hard.

Pâte décor: A pâtisserie technique in which coloured sponge cake batter is piped to create a decorative pattern before baking.

Pollen-style dust: An edible dust that is used on stamens and the centres of flowers in sugar floristry to represent pollen.

Posy pick: These are inserted into cakes to hold wired sugar flowers. Place the flowers into the hollow end of the pick (filled with paste if needed to support the wires), then push the pointed end of the pick into the cake surface. Remove the pick and flowers before the cake is cut.

Pressure piping: Though all piped royal icing work is created using pressure, pressure piping is used when piping small and delicate figures, flowers, motifs and other decorations onto a cake or plaque.

Rope action: Rotating the nozzle when piping to create a scroll that resembles a rope.

Royal icing: An icing made using egg white and icing sugar which can be used to coat cakes, pipe decorations and create collars and run-outs. Royal icing dries to a firm finish and holds its shape.

Rubbing down (paddling): This is done to give royal icing more flow when piping. Take some royal icing on a palette knife and use a back-and-forth motion to rub it onto a clean work surface. To ensure the icing has enough flow after it has been rubbed down (paddled), scoop it up onto a palette knife and tap the knife on the edge of the table: if the icing appears shiny and wet, it is ready to use.

Running beads: A series of bulbs or 'pearls' which are piped in a line, either to hide a join, neaten an edge or add decoration.

Run-out icing: A thinner consistency of royal icing that is often used to decorate biscuits and create plaques and collars that are placed on a cake once dry.

Scratch piping: Pressure piping whilst keeping the tip of the nozzle on the cake.

Scriber: Also known as a scribing tool. A pointed, needle-like sugarcraft tool that is often used with a template to mark out a design onto a cake covering.

Scroll border: A decorative finish that is created by piping royal icing in repeated S or C shapes around a cake.

Shell border: A decorative finish that is piped around a cake with a star piping nozzle.

Smoother: A useful piece of equipment that is rubbed over sugarpaste-covered cakes and boards to give the paste a smooth and polished finish.

Spacers: Two lengths of metal or plastic which are placed either side of the paste on a work surface to create an even thickness when rolling out sugarpaste, marzipan and pastry.

Stippling: A decorative, mottled effect created by dipping a piece of food-grade sponge or kitchen paper, or a pastry brush, into food colouring or coloured icing, then blotting the colour over sugar work.

Straight edge: A long, metal rule that is pulled over the cake to create a neat finish when coating with royal icing.

Sugar Dough™: A Squires Kitchen product that is ideal for all modelled figures when you require the piece to hold its shape and dry quickly, but still remain soft enough to eat.

Sugarpaste: Also known as rolled fondant. A smooth, pliable, ready-to-roll paste which is used as a cake covering and to make basic modelled decorations.

Sugar syrup: A syrup of sugar and water, often flavoured, that can be brushed or drizzled over sponge cakes to keep them moist.

Tempering: The process of heating chocolate to a specific temperature before use to give it a shiny finish and a good snap once set.

Transfer sheet (for chocolate): A sheet of food-grade acetate with a cocoa butter design printed on one side. Melted chocolate is spread onto this side to transfer the design from the acetate to the chocolate.

Turntable: A useful piece of equipment which allows you to work around the sides of a cake without handling it. A tilting turntable makes it easier to paint or pipe directly onto the cake by angling the cake away from you as you work.

Veiner: Leaf and petal veiners are usually made from food-grade silicone rubber and are used in sugar floristry to impress a realistic vein pattern into flower paste.

Index

Squires Kitchen Contacts

The Grange, Hones Yard
Farnham, Surrey
GU9 8BB
0845 61 71 812
+44 1252 260262
school@squires-school.co.uk
www.squires-school.co.uk

At Squires Kitchen International School we have been teaching the art of sugarcraft since 1987. When you join us, you will learn all the skills and techniques you need to further your hobby, profession or passion.

Squires Kitchen, UK
Squires House
3 Waverley Lane
Farnham
Surrey
GU9 8BB
0845 61 71 810
+44 (0) 1252 260 260
www.squires-shop.com

Smeg UK Ltd.
www.smeguk.com
www.smeg50style.co.uk

Italian appliance manufacturer Smeg produces distinctive domestic appliances combining design, performance and quality.

For your nearest sugarcraft supplier, please contact customer@squires-shop.com.

B. Dutton Publishing is an award-winning publisher of cake decorating titles. To find out more about our books, follow us at **www.facebook.com/bduttonpublishing** and **www.twitter.com/bduttonbooks**.